Śakti's Revolution

Śakti's Revolution: Origins and Historiography of Indic Fierce Goddesses chronicles the historical evolution of Hindu and Buddhist fierce, Kālī-like goddesses and their devotees, from the Indus Valley civilization, *c.* third millennium BCE, to the present. The author documents and analyzes the undercurrents of misogyny, greed, and violence—the demonic forces against which Śakti wages warfare—that have formed the historiography of fierce goddesses in India.

Donna Jordan is an independent writer/researcher and organic gardener in Northern California. Despite her advanced academic degrees in religion, literature, and biomedical sciences [PhD, Philosophy and Religion, California Institute of Integral Studies, San Francisco; Masters (MA), English literature, University of California, Los Angeles; Masters (MPH), Public Health, University of California, Berkeley], she remains an open-minded free-thinker.

Śakti's Revolution

Origins and Historiography of Indic Fierce Goddesses

Donna Jordan

Munshiram Manoharlal
Publishers Pvt. Ltd.

ISBN 978-81-215-1192-6
First published 2012

PRINTED IN INDIA
Published by Vikram Jain *for*
Munshiram Manoharlal Publishers Pvt. Ltd.
PO Box 5715, 54 Rani Jhansi Road, New Delhi 110 055, INDIA

www.mrmlbooks.com

To Philip with Love

As is true of most divine figures, Kālī is a deity with a long, multi-layered history. Although worshipped throughout South Asia, she has traditionally been most popular in geographically peripheral areas of the subcontinent, such as Bengal, Assam, and Nepal in the northeast, Kashmir, Panjab, and Himachal Pradesh in the northwest, and Kerala, Tamilnadu, and Sri Lanka in the south. While individual myths, rituals, and iconographic traditions may differ somewhat in each of these areas, Kālī is commonly perceived as a goddess who encompasses and transcends the opposites of life. She is, for example, simultaneously understood as a bloodthirsty demon-slayer, an inflictor and curer of diseases, a deity of ritual possession, and an all-loving, compassionate Mother. That Kālī often delights in shocking her viewers into new modes of awareness and emotional intensity is obvious to anyone who has witnessed her Bengali iconographic representations, which often present her wearing fetuses for earrings, decapitating men, sticking out her tongue for all to see, wearing a garland of chopped-off heads and a miniskirt of human arms, and living in cremation grounds. To make matters even more complex, despite all of this, her devotees still insist upon affectionately addressing her as *Mā* or "Mother."*

* * *

A woman out of control is the very devil.

—D.H. LAWRENCE

*Rachel Fell McDermott and Jeffrey J. Kripal, "Introducing Kālī Studies," in *Encountering Kālī: In the Margins, at the Centre, in the West*, ed. Rachel Fell McDermott and Jeffrey J. Kripal (Berkeley, 2003), 4.

Contents

Part II

HISTORIOGRAPHY **141**

4

THE EARLY TAMILS: THE CAṄKAM AGE 143

5

THE EARLY ARYANS: VEDIC THROUGH EPICO-PURĀṆIC ERAS 177

Plates

Colored Plates

I. Folk painting representing the goddess Kālī straddled over the erect *liṅgaṁ* of the corpse-Śiva. Orissa, nineteenth century. Gouache on cloth 15 × 13 (38 × 33). [Ajit Mookerjee Collection.]

THE NAGAS

All the ancient Indian cities and temple sites were originally the sacred land of indigenous peoples such as the Naga tribes.

II. Paṅgmi village headman of the Naga Hills of Burma. He became a Christian in 1982 but still wears brass heads round his neck (symbolizing the seven skulls he took in his youth), 1985. (169)

III. Nagas on the Burmese side retain a way of life that is comparable with that of pre-state India, 1985. (174)

IV. The Indian Naga rebels (the NSCN) has its own gospel group who entertain the villagers on the Burmese side of the frontier. Christianity was introduced in the remotest parts of the Naga Hills of Burma by Indian Naga rebels, who established a base inside Burma for cross-border raids into India, from about the mid-1970s, 1985. (177)

V. Wife of the *Aṅg* of Chopnu village. Sketch, 1873–76. (180)

VI. Naga *Aṅg* or chief of Chopnu village. Sketch, 1873–76. (180)

VII. Colored drawing of Captain Butler surrounded by British officers and assembled Nagas, 1973–75.

VIII, X. Collection of head-taking trophies used as symbols of martial prowess and as a means of acquiring fertility for the head-taker and the entire village. (182–83)

Temples

Tamils have been among the world's greatest temple-builders, and classic Caṅkam literature is replete with historical scenarios that occur in or around the temples, dedicated to both devīs and male gods, built under the patronage of kings. Until AD 700, temples were constructed inside caves. The Pallava kings (up to AD 900) built temples in stone; the Coḷas (AD 900–1250) added many ornate *maṇḍapams* or halls to temples and constructed large *gopurams* or towers. The Pāṇḍyas (up to AD 1350) heightened the huge towers, adding high wall enclosures and enormous towered gateways. The Vijayanagar style (AD 1350–1560) is distinguished by the decorated monolithic pillars, and the Naik style (AD 1600–1750) added large *prakarams* (circumambulatory paths) and pillared halls.

Mahābalipuram (Mamallapuram) Temples: *c.* AD 630–88, Pallava period (sixth–ninth centuries AD), Mahābalipuram, Tamilnadu, was an ancient seaport of the warlike Pallava kings, situated along the Indian eastern coast thirty-two miles south of Chennai on the shores of the Bay of Bengal. The Mahābalipuram temples are among the earliest examples of monumental architecture in south India, and a center of pilgrimage for centuries. The Pallava sculptors carved images from a large granite hill 100 ft high, half-a-mile long, and a quarter-of-a-mile wide, with smaller protrusions. Mahābalipuram was one of the chief ports to south India, and emigrants carried strong Dravidian cultural influences to the Hindu colonies of Indonesia and Cambodia.

Tiruchirappalli: Tiruchirappalli, situated on the banks of the river Cauvery, was a citadel of the early Coḷas. Today it is the fourth largest city in Tamilnadu. The Rock Fort Temple complex in Tiruchirappalli is a collection of three temples (the Manikka Vinayakar temple at the foot of the hill, the Uchhi Pillayar Koyil at the top of the hill, and the Taayumaanavar Koyil Śiva temple on the hill) built on an 83 m high rock (charnokite) hillock that is the only outcrop in the otherwise flat inland of the city. A rock-cut temple, the Śiva temple is the most prominent landmark in Tiruchirappalli, reached by a flight of 420 steps on the way to the famous Ucchi Pillayar temple. The three hill Śiva temples in this area are Tiruchirappalli, Tiruverumbur, and Tiruveengoimalai, dedicated to Lord Śiva, constituting a sacred geography in which the *liṅgam* is the projection of the rock itself. There are two Pallava cave temples (about sixth–seventh centuries AD). A tank and a pavilion at the foot of the Rock Fort are used during the float festival of the temple.

XIII. *Durgā*: The goddess Durgā, standing on the head of Mahiṣa. Sculpted on a *maṇḍapam* (pillar) in front of the Trimūrti Cave Temple, dedicated to Durgā. Trimūrti Cave Temple, Mahābalipuram, Chengalpattu. Pallava (sixth–ninth centuries AD), Granite.

XIV-XV. *Mahiṣāsura-mardinī*: Riding astride a lion, Durgā slays the buffalo demon Mahiṣa on the quintessential cosmic war front. As his troupe of demons is defeated, Mahiṣa wields an impotent club against victorious Durgā. Mahiṣāsura-mardinī Cave Temple, Mahābalipuram, Chengalpattu. Pallava (sixth–ninth centuries AD), Granite.

XVI. *Yakṣī*: Flanked by lions, seated on a throne under the sacred pipal tree. The *yakṣī* is a female Earth spirit of fertility found in Hindu, Buddhist, and Jaina mythologies. Often referred to as Mother-goddess, she dwells in trees, lakes, and wells. She and her male counterpart, the *yakṣa*, are revered as protectors that must be propitiated to avert harm or induce fertility. A *yakṣī* is frequently depicted as a young, sensual woman often holding the branch of a tree while striking the well-known *tribhaṅga* (three-bend) pose (bending at neck, waist, and hip). Gurunātha Sastri Home, Pondicherry.

XVII. *Yakṣa*: Śrī Pārśvanātha, Jaina Temple, Hassan, Channarayapatna, Śravaṇabelgola (sixth–seventh centuries AD), Stone.

XVIII. *Yakṣa and Lion*: Śiva Temple, Śrī Mukteśvara, Bhuvaneśvara, *c.* AD 950 (fourth–fourteenth centuries AD), Gaṅga period.

XIX. *Ammaṉ*: Śri Māriyammaṉ Temple, Tiruchirappalli. Early Coḷa (ninth–tenth centuries AD). Granite cave temple. One of the most popular shrines in Tamilnadu, the temple is dedicated to Māriyammaṉ, a Tamil manifestation of the primeval energy Śakti, personified as the Mother-goddess. Māriyammaṉ is associated with prosperity and health; she is the cause and the cure of diseases such as smallpox and chickenpox. Every Sunday, Tuesday, and Friday, hundreds of devotees throng the temple and perform *pūjās*.

XX. *Kālī-Makālī*: Goddess Kālī Temple, Śrī Makālī Ammaṉ, Rayampuram, Tiruchchirappalli, Ariyalur. Early Coḷa (ninth–tenth centuries AD), Stone.

XXI. *Saptamātṛkās—Maheśvarī and Cāmuṇḍī*: Śiva Temple, Śrī Tarukavaneśvara Tirupparaitturai. Coḷa (ninth–twelfth centuries AD), Stone.

XXII. *Saptamātṛkā—Cāmuṇḍā*: Śrī Kundattu Kaliyamman Temple, Pariyur, Coimbatore, Gopichettipalaiyam, Coḷa (ninth–tenth centuries AD), Stone.

XXIII. *Saptamātṛkā—Cāmuṇḍā*: Śrī Kundattu Kaliyamman, Pariyur, Coimbatore, Gopichettipalaiyam, Coḷa (ninth–twelfth centuries AD), Stone.

XXIV. *Saptamātṛkās—Kaumārī, Vaiṣṇavī, Indrāṇī, Varāhī, Cāmuṇḍā, and Gaṇapati*: Śiva Cave Temple, Śrī Kokarṇeśvara, Tirukokarṇam. Pallava (sixth–ninth centuries AD), Stone.

(*between* pp. 272–73)

XXV. *Saptamātṛkā—Kaumārī*: Śrī Ponniyamman Temple, South Arcot, Ulundurpet, Iruveḷippaṭu. Coḷa (ninth–twelfth centuries AD), Stone.

XXVI. *Narthanā Kālī*: Śiva Temple, Śrī Mīnākṣī—Sundareśvara, Madurai, Pāṇḍya (twelfth century AD), Stone. The Śrī Mīnākṣī temple is dedicated to Lord Śiva and goddess Mīnākṣī, who were married in Madurai, according to legend. Between AD 600–1300, Madurai, the capital of the Pāṇḍya dynasty built on the banks of the Vaigai river, was the true center of Dravidian culture, and Pāṇḍya kings patronized not only literary *caṅkams*, or academies, but also the construction of great temples. Tamils in this era were prosperous maritime merchants who traded via the Arabian Sea with the Greeks and Romans. South India's oldest city, Madurai flourished under several dynasties until the early 1300s, when the Muslim rulers penetrated the barriers of the Vindhyas and Nilgiris to loot the prosperous towns in the south, including Madurai. Soon afterwards, Madurai was incorporated into the Delhi Sultanate.

XXVII. *Cāmuṇḍā*: Śrī Māriyammaṉ Temple, Madurai. Pāṇḍya (twelfth century AD), Stone.

XXVIII. *Devī Reṇukā*: Śiva Temple, Śrī Colīśvara, Kadakattur, Dharmapuri. Pallava (sixth–ninth centuries AD), Stone.

XXIX. *Durgā*: Śiva Cave Temple, Śrī Durgā Bhairava, Kottapalli, Prakasam, Kanigiri. Cola (ninth–twelfth centuries AD), Stone.

XXX. *Kālī and Musician*: Frenzied dance accompanied by drums and music is the prelude to spirit possession by Kālī. Śiva Temple, Śrī Mallikārjunasvāmī Temple West shrine. Basral, Māṇḍya, Karnataka (eighth–twelfth centuries AD), *c.* AD 1234, Soapstone.

Tanjavur (Tanjore): Under the reign of the great King Rājarāja, founder of the Coḷa empire which stretched overall of south India and its neighboring islands, the great Temple of Tanjavur, dedicated to Lord Śiva, was constructed between 1010 and 1003 BCE. Surrounded by two rectangular enclosures, the Bṛhadeśvara, built from blocks of granite and, in part, from bricks, is crowned with a pyramidal thirteen-storied tower, the *vimāna*, topped with a bulb-shaped monolith.

XXXI. *Ammaṉ—Māriyammaṉ*: Cholampettai, Tanjavur, Mayuram, Śiva Temple, Śrī Tantonrīśvara. Cola (ninth–twelfth centuries AD).

XXXII. *Vadabhadra Kālī*: Tanjavur Temple, Tanjavur—Kilvasal. Coḷa (ninth–twelfth centuries AD), Granite.

XXXIII. *Ammaṉ*: Śrī Māriyammaṉ Temple, Tiruchirappalli. Early Coḷa (ninth–tenth centuries AD), Granite.

XXXIV. *Kāmākhyā*: Icon of the fierce form of the goddess as she is known at Kāmākhyā, Assam, the sacred spot where the *yoni* of the goddess mythically fell to Earth. Rajasthan, nineteenth century AD. Watercolor on paper 13 x 10 (33 x 25). [Ajit Mookerjee Collection.]

(*between* pp. 320–21)

Photo Acknowledgments

The author gratefully acknowledges the following for permission to reproduce the illustrations indicated.

Colored plates: Edition Hansjorg Mayer, London: II, III, IV, V, VI, VII, VIII, IX, X, and XI. [Philip Rawson, *The Art of Tantra*, Ajit Mookerjee Collection. Thames & Hudson, London and New York: 1.]

Black and white plates: Edition Hansjorg Mayer, London: I, II, III, IV, V, VI, VII, VIII, IX, X, and XI. French Institute of Pondicherry: XIV, XV, XVI, XVII, XVIII, XIX, XX, XXI, XXII, XXIII, XXIV, XXV, XXVI, XXVII, XXVIII, XXIX, XXX, XXXI, XXXII, and XXXIII. [Philip Rawson, *The Art of Tantra*, Ajit Mookerjee Collection. Thames & Hudson, London and New York: 34.]

Preface

In the earliest times, humans everywhere were socially organized into hunter-gatherer tribes that survived by foraging, hunting, and horticulture. From the Mediterranean to the Ganges Valley, prehistoric material circumstances produced similar mythopoetic worldviews that became crystallized in the multicultural idiom of the Great Goddess of Life and Death, who gave birth to the gods, human beings, plants, animals, and minerals. This goddess cemplate originated among hunting tribes that rose to warrior status with the advent of warfare. Beginning with Paleolithic (*c.* 50,000–30,000 BCE) Magdalenian rock art in Europe, we find evidence of the Mistress of Wild Animals or Mountain Mother in the company of her intimate predator associates, the aurochs bull and the big cats.

When woman-centered horticulture (Latin: *hortus*, garden) was overtaken by male-dominated agriculture, including the plow, irrigation, and animal domestication, the Ice Age goddess of the hunt morphed into an agricultural deity, the spirit of Mother Earth, who surpassed the spirit of Father Sky. A Great Goddess was the Supreme Being in ancient Arabia, Persia, Sumeria, Babylonia, Akkadia, Phoenicia and Syria, Anatolia, pre-Hellenic Greece and Crete, Armenia, and Georgia long before the Abrahamic religions demonized and destroyed nearly all her manifold incarnations. Judaism, Christianity, and Islam are therefore relative newcomers in the ancient Near East (from the Iranian Plateau east to the Mediterranean, and from the Black and Caspian Seas south through the Arabian Peninsula), one of the oldest and most thoroughly excavated areas of the world. In the march of history, this goddess template was defeated and defamed throughout the Near East and eastern Mediterranean, remaining active only in South Asia (India and northeastern Sri Lanka), and in Tamil emigrant communities scattered around the world, especially Malaysia, Singapore, Fiji, Mauritius, South Africa, and in the Euro-North American Hindu diaspora.

Primal religions function to appease the forces of nature and to protect the people. The earliest myths and rituals represented an ethical ecological contract with Mother Earth: the goddess would cure illness or send fertility, sunshine, or rain as long as humans observed the rules and gratified her, and calamity may occur if she is not happy. She is thus the creator and the curer of disease and misfortune. In archaeological remains and surviving literature in the so-called cradle of civilization and South Asia, as well as among contemporary indigenous small-scale societies, all the incarnations of the Great Goddess possess the same essential qualities. This goddess represents the great womb and Creatrix of the universe, of the gods, and of all earthly life. She gives to her children not only life and good health, but also death and calamity. In a violent, testosterone-laden expression of the goddess's destructive potential, the ancient mythologies of warlike peoples deify the spirit of war; the Great Mother became the personification of the blood lust of warriors, a magnificent battle queen who is gratified by the human sacrifice inherent in warfare. In doling out destruction, she can be fierce and terrifying, but as giver of life, health, and renewal, she is nurturing, gentle, and inspiring. Kālī is a part of that ancient lineage and cosmological template; beyond the reach of the Hebrew prophets, she thrived in India prior to the third millennium BCE Indus Valley civilization.

In the first century of the Christian era, the fierce goddess all but vanished from the religio-cultural landscape of the Near East and the Mediterranean/Aegean region. When Christianity became the official religion of the Roman Empire under the second successor after Constantine, Theodosius II (AD 378–98), pagan trappings were revalorized as "Christian" traditions. Only one Near Eastern female deity of the Great Goddess lineage, the Virgin Mary (a composite of many versions of the Great Goddess in the ancient world), has survived the Abrahamic *coup* and remained central to a major religion in the twenty-first century AD. Unlike Mary, the Indic deity (and her *avatāras*) has retained to the present day her original identity as the fierce goddess whose domain subsumes fertility and war, birth, death, and rebirth, reflecting the archaic magico-religious stratum from which both Mary and Kālī emerged. Kālī has always been worshiped in India by women of all castes, elite and tribal warrior-priests, and the impoverished majority, who comprise today's "muted" or "subaltern" low-caste groups—śūdras, *ādivāsīs* (scheduled tribals), and dalits (*dalit* is the collective term for the "untouchable" castes of India).

In her most archaic Indic form, closest to the roots of the human genetic tree, Kālī manifests as non-Sanskritic village folk goddesses, often worshiped as trees, rocks, or rivers, representing a substratum of spirits of the Dravidians and autochthonous tribal peoples. The orgiastic nature of their worship reflects the religion of primal, or shamanic,[1] cultures. The original conception of Mother Earth represents a pre-state consciousness of the interdependency of humans and the environment. Goddesses were non-anthropomorphized energies present in the ecosystem of the forest. They probably first morphed into humanized deities as rock art, shamanic effigies, and statues depicting female figures. Although their human forms dominate in contemporary temples, they continue to be worshiped as the natural world to this day not only in India, but also among indigenous peoples throughout the world, who see land and nature as one with the rest of life.

> The spiritual, the social and the material are all entwined, and everything is believed to connect with everything else. . . . The environment is a sacred realm. God or gods are not generally believed to take a human form, as they do in say Christianity or Hinduism, but inhabit the natural world itself. God is thought to be all around, living in the landscape, and the earth is revered like a parent.[2]

In small-scale societies, the Great Mother is not anthropomorphized as a female form, but rather, she is the ecological system itself, the forest or jungle, the supernatural giver of life and death, as she is for contemporary Mbuti pygmies. The Mbuti's primary goddess figure is the forest, the Mother, the enormous ecological whole that is predominantly nurturing. The Mbuti devote their lives to keeping the forest happy so she will provide them with all their social, material, and spiritual needs. When calamity strikes, they know that the forest has been sleeping and not protecting her children, so they awaken her with joyous songs to reinstate ecological equilibrium. The diametrical opposite of the ancient warrior cultures, Mbuti pygmies are a sexually integrated, egalitarian, and basically unwarlike, non-hierarchical, cooperative, "immediate return" society[3] whose rituals and cosmology bring into high relief the channeling of sacred symbols of creative power into secular gender roles, social organization, and power distribution. Their forest Mother stands in stark contrast to the fierce Indian Mother-goddess, who causes calamity not because she is asleep, but as an expression of her rage (often directed against authoritarian injustices), and who is placated by blood sacrifice and warfare rather than by song.

As the mother protectress of the tribe, the Great Mother in male dominant tribes became the protectress in battle, personified as a valiant, triumphant warrior who could overcome any enemy. Because all soldiers morphed from hunters, the same Indian goddess, Ko<u>rr</u>avai, Kālī, or her more generic identity as Śakti, the active, hot, and self-perpetuating female energy of the cosmos, was worshiped by *ādivāsīs* as well as elite Aryan and Dravidian warriors. She promotes fertility by both hunter-gatherer tribes and their conquerors. In her role as elite battle queen, she transgresses the gender boundaries of the male-dominated state by wandering unveiled outside her home. This act, because it violates her duties to veil her face and body in public and to spend the majority of her time sequestered within her home tending to her domestic duties, has been historically prohibited (with the exception of the princesses of Rajasthan)[4] among elite Indian women. In an ironic role reversal, she assumes the most macho of male roles in a patriarchal society—the warrior.

The study of fierce goddesses evokes many historical and philosophical questions that are central to the lives of women, but goddesses are not entirely a female creation. The aspect of Kālī-like goddesses that is a patently male construct of the hunt and war has been backed up for over five millennia by myths teeming with battle and carnage and framed in the patriarchal structural binary of what Mark Jurgenmeyser terms "cosmic war,"[5] a battle between good and evil, to guarantee both abundant harvests and victory over specific historic enemies. The warrior cultures of the ancient Aryans, Iranians, Hebrews, and Tamils, as well as their modern descendants, are all underpinned by sacred warfare myths that govern their spiritual and political lives. Fierce goddesses as warriors *par excellence* represent the male attribution of sacrality to the slaughter of animals or enemies. Kālī-like goddesses demand blood sacrifice, particularly bulls or humans, and especially their heads. In myth and ritual, the buffalo is a symbol of power that is, through sacrifice, transferred to the goddess and the agricultural fields.

This work, an elaboration of my PhD dissertation in philosophy and religion, grew out of my graduate studies in Indo-Tibetan languages (Sanskrit and Tibetan) and culture, with an emphasis on religious history, literature, and art. Prior graduate work at University of California (Los Angeles and Berkeley), culminating in Master's degrees in both English literature and Public Health, gave me the vital tools of literary and intellectual criticism (research, historical context, and reasoning) that have helped me to decode and analyze religious symbols, ideas, and systems. I was initially drawn into the subject through my curiosity about ancient and medieval artistic and mythic motifs linking Kālī and her Tibetan counterparts (Vajrayoginī, Sipe Walmo) with sexual imagery, graveyards, warfare, and violent blood sacrifice while regarding her as a beneficent mother and a central inner yogic energy, Kula-kuṇḍalinī Śakti. I spent several years under the tutelage of a Tibetan Bönpo lāmā and began to practice yogic techniques to disengage the conceptual mind. I could hardly avoid noticing the contradiction in the worship of a goddess of high religious status by a caste society in which women and the Indian majority have low secular status and have been historically devalued and disempowered. I wanted to understand how the cosmology and iconography of Kālī and her *avatāras* correspond to evolve social realities.

In its original form, my dissertation did not include warfare, but only ritual violence. When I began my revisions, I was initially drawn into the study of fertility and war goddess Ko<u>rr</u>avai as the prototypical slayer of the buffalo demon, and the merging of Ko<u>rr</u>avai with Durgā–Kālī in brāhmaṇic texts. I found that

Caṅkam literature articulates the brutal nature of the Tamil warrior monarchies of the Caṅkam age, and noted the irony that their social realities—human organization based on the dominator hierarchy model, violence against widows and tribals, social stratification legitimated by conceptions of purity/pollution and high/low birth, the Spartan concentration on warrior's death and afterlife, and a population of laborers held in check by fear—were justified and mediated by cosmogonic warfare mythology, composed of bardic glorification and sacralization of war, that equates the battlefield with the agricultural field.

The Śākta classic *Devī-māhātmya* is a repetition of the central imagery of Ko<u>rr</u>avai's battlefield scenes of the third century BCE and much earlier. The source-myth for the ritual drama of buffalo sacrifice involving the goddess's defeat of the *asura* Mahiṣa who had assumed the form of a buffalo was a well-known tale by the author of the second century AD Tamil masterpiece, *Cilappatikāram* (The Ankle Bracelet), which contains an account of the episode. Because this ritual was cognate with what I knew of Near Eastern and eastern Mediterranean seasonal sacrificial ritual dramas, I fleshed out this aspect of the Neolithic Great Goddess, along with the common agricultural ritual of *hieros gamos* (sacred marriage) followed by bull or king sacrifice. The archaic idea underpinning *hieros gamos*, according to Mircea Eliade, is that " 'death'—ritual and therefore reversible—inevitably follows every act of creation or procreation."[6] This principle arises from observing the processes of the world of vegetative nature in which plants die back every year in order to return in spring. According to this perspective, death, manifested in ritual male sacrifice, produces life or rebirth and the continuity of the female principle. The similarities between the first civilizations of the Near East in Sumeria and the Dravidian culture do not stop at their common fierce fertility and martial goddesses astride a lion and the *hieros gamos* ritual between the goddess and the king, but also include the seasonal sacrifice of the bull/consort of the goddess (the enactment of the ritual drama of bloody death and resurrection of a god) and an institution of dancer-priestesses who are also sacred prostitutes of the goddess with high social status.

I discovered that these goddesses and their mytho-ritual motifs were replicated in pre-Islamic Arabian religion. Although the goddesses and myths disappeared during Muhammad's first *jihād* against his own tribe's polytheistic Ka'bah in AD 630, many external pagan traditions were co-opted to insure easy conversion to Islam, and continue today as magico-religious rituals that serve to unite the Muslim faithful.

The nineteenth century notion of the diffusion of cultural traits by a pan-human psychic unity or Jungian "collective unconscious" is no longer viewed as an acceptable explanation for the commonalities among the goddess religions of these regions. By land or sea, the archaic traditions of the Great Goddess were transmitted through the well-known trade routes connecting ancient Sumerian, Dravidian Indian, and Arabian cultures. By what means or conduit did the agrarian goddess template self-replicate in such geographically diverse locations? Contemporary anthropologists and historians usually attribute the viral-like spread of religious cults to demographic changes resulting from trade, war, and migration patterns, coupled with gender roles; the distribution of power, education, goods, and services; agriculture and animal domestication; and the introduction of bourgeois economic systems. Another intriguing explanation of self-replicating goddess templates is that of evolutionist and cognitive philosopher Daniel Dennett.[7] In his evolutionary scenario, religious traditions emerged on the human stage as cultural *memes*[8] that spread, like mystic viruses, through infection, natural selection, and socioeconomic forces.[9] Although we cannot know with certainty why religious motifs are replicated across cultures, it is a "known known" that religious cosmologies underlie, channel, and mediate social reality. However, the same cultural symbols and myths can have immensely different meanings over time and geography, and should never be viewed as immutable.

Barbara Ehrenreich's *Blood Rites*,[10] a fascinating psychobiological approach and a good introduction to the evolution of human violence and animal and human sacrifice, was my point of entry into the subject of blood sacrifice in religions. I had read convincing ideas about the motif of sacred "cosmic war" used as a blueprint for divinely sanctioned warrior behavior in Mark Juergensmeyer's *Terror in the Mind of God*,[11] Stan Harris's *The End of Faith: Religion, Terror, and the Future of Reason*,[12] and Jack Nelson-Pallmeyer's *Is Religion Killing Us?*[13] Fierce fertility and war goddess Ko<u>rr</u>avai seemed to be, on one level, the embodiment of what Nelson-Pallmeyer refers to as "violence-of-God" religions that legitimate and justify contemporary violence and wars, a phenomenon he explores in the Abrahamic religious scriptures. Because I was making an inquiry into the relationship between the sacred symbology and social realities of India, I decided to pursue the elephant in the barrel, the linkage between the Great Goddess and warfare.

In contemporary times, fierce Kālī-like goddesses play complex roles in the common arena of warfare and terrorism. My inclusion of some Muslim history and principles seemed to me to be a necessary element in the historiography of fierce goddesses. I do not discuss women under Islamic law. I confined my research on the Internet to primary Islamic texts, including three English translations of the *Qur'ān*[14] and *A Dictionary of Islam*,[15] Thomas Patrick Hughes' compilation from the *Qur'ān, Hadīth, Taurāt, Injīl*, and other sources (in which the *Comparative Index to Islam*[16] was particularly helpful). Among the secondary texts and histories I consulted, Samuel Noah Kramer's *Mythologies of the Ancient World*[17] was key in my understanding of the mythic undercurrent of Islam.

Authoritarianism and its organic emotional outcome, self-sacrifice or martyrdom, is a thread running through the history of fierce goddesses, one that conflates the spiritual and political planes of being. Reflected in bonds of dominance and submission, authoritarian ideologies underpin social injustice such as gender and caste oppression; androcentric mythologies of male god domination and female self-sacrifice that serve as social models; and the guru-disciple tradition, the most fundamental of Indian spiritual traditions of self-renunciation. John W. Dean's *Conservatives Without Conscience*[18] opened up a new perspective on the intertwining dynamics of individual, religious, and political authoritarianism, particularly in the twenty-first century, when the nature of transnational political discourse has become increasingly confrontational, religiously framed, and self-righteous.

The anthropology of religion held some explanations for me, and I familiarized myself with the conceptual framework of symbolic anthropology and the study of gender roles, since, as Fiona Bowie has pointed out, "[i]ntellectual trends in recent decades have made it increasingly difficult to ignore gender as a practical and interpretative issue."[19] One of the most salient, insightful, and critical aspects of contemporary symbolic anthropology is the study of the ways in which cosmologies underpin ecosystems, societies, and gender and power roles. Anthropologists Peggy Reeves Sanday,[20] Clifford Geertz,[21] Fiona Bowie, and Mary Douglas[22] relate the symbolic systems and governing cosmologies of small-scale indigenous societies to the relative power and equality of men and women on the ground. Clifford Geertz in *The Interpretation of Cultures*[23] argues that cultures set up symbolic templates or blueprints that define and guide behavior. Peggy Reeves Sanday uses the term *sex-role plan* to describe sacred symbols of creative power that help orient men and women as male and female to one another and the environment, and provide a commonly accepted mold that shapes worldviews. In her study of patterns of female power and male domination in over one hundred fifty tribal societies, ranging from the sixth century BCE to the present, Sanday discovered that secular power roles are channeled and mediated by sacred symbolism. Sanday's preliminary data analysis indicated that "sacred symbols are not, as I had originally supposed, an epiphenomena [*sic*] of secular power roles. In fact, it became clear that the reverse was more likely: Secular power roles are derived from ancient concepts of sacred power."[24]

The fierce Indian goddesses in their full mythic sense function as such a template in India, comprising the mythic domains of gender and caste oppression and institutionalized violence; their meaning has never remained static, but has evolved over time, accumulating layers of folk myth and elite didacticism, with the mode of production and dominant class ideology. This approach, which theoretically subsumes some of the ways that religions promote warfare and justify and implement violence against women and the underclass, addresses the nexus between sacred symbols, violence, healing, social structure and upheaval, gender roles, and divine and secular power.

Much of India's past survives in the present, and at all times in prehistory and history, fierce goddesses have steadfastly remained a bedazzling Indian idiom. As Kosambi has written, "the country has one tremendous advantage that was not utilized till recently by the historians: the survival within different social layers of many forms that allow the reconstruction of totally diverse earlier stages."[25] I have attempted to weave together the complex origins and the long evolution, historiography, and mythologies of fierce goddesses as they have interpenetrated the power structures and social realities on the ground. Because this book is based on library and Internet research, I cover material that has been elaborated by previous writers; however, I have deliberately transgressed traditional Western epistemological boundaries by attempting to flesh out ideas, interdisciplinary connections, and political equations that are crystallized in the origins and historiography of Indic fierce goddesses.

My research has been guided by my conviction that religion is a ubiquitous natural bio-cultural phenomenon commensurate with music, art, dance, poetry, and even disease and warfare; as such, religions should be the subject of comparative analysis and intellectual criticism. Religious traditions can be placed under a microscope and understood scientifically, through cultural studies in history, economics, anthropology, archaeology, and—especially given Dennett's hypothesis of the natural history of religions—biology. I agree with Danial Dennett:

> It is high time that we subject religion as a global phenomenon to the most intensive multidisciplinary research we can muster, calling on the best minds on the planet. Why? Because religion is too important for us to remain ignorant about. It affects not just our social, political, and economic conflicts, but the very meanings we find in our lives. For many people, probably a majority of the people on Earth, nothing matters more than religion. For this very reason, it is imperative that we learn as much as we can about it.[26]

Unfortunately, professional backbiting, low prestige, and dubious findings have made such a multidisciplinary approach to religions a thankless, at times even punitive, tasks. Even at esteemed American universities, intellectual criticism is often replaced by multiculturalism and cultural relativism, wrapped up in political correctness and a postmodern worldview that precludes historical and cultural analysis. Professors are often active participants in the religion about which they teach and write, academic gurus whose lectures functionally proselytize and result in student converts. Moreover, there exists a tacit taboo against serious non-biased investigations of religion, a subject considered by many to be a spiritual issue privately owned by the faithful, and any neutral inquiry is viewed as disrespectful, intrusive, and sacrilegious, if not impossible.

> It is just about impossible to be neutral in your approach to religion, because many people view neutrality in itself as hostile. If you're not for us, you're against us. And so, since religion so clearly matters so much to so many people, researchers have almost never even attempted to be neutral; they have tended to err on the side of deference, putting on the kid gloves. It is either that or

open hostility. For this reason, there has been an unfortunate pattern in the work that has been done. People who want to study religion usually have an ax to grind. They either want to defend their favorite religion from its critics or want to demonstrate the irrationality and futility of religion, and this tends to infect their methods with bias.[27]

No researcher can delve into the historical evolution of Indic fierce goddesses without stumbling upon the goddesses enthusiastically involved in horribly gruesome blood-and-guts rituals, including warfare, and various gory myths and narratives, that mimic and reflect the violent exploits of the cultures from which they emerged. In my efforts to present dominant symbolic themes, I have been obliged to include grisly human practices such as the head-taking motif that runs through Indian religions and history. Chronicling scenarios of macho violence and exploitation has been personally wrenching for me, a peace-loving vegetarian. However, I am well aware that keeping baser aspects of human behavior submerged below consciousness for the sake of political or religious correctness produces a distorted, even a delusional picture of the whole. (I believe Dr Freud had something to say about this.)

I have gained from writing this book the ability to face a hard truth. Although difficult, it is important to ever keep in mind that we humans, with the most evolved brains of all animals, have cleverly designed weapons that can kill anything, particularly one another, at a distance. Because the armed human has dramatically altered the environment and contributed to the extinction of a number of species, he has been described as the ultimate super-predator, or apex predator, on the planet. It follows, therefore, that many of our myths and rituals justify and legitimate predatory behavior. From Bronze age seasonal regicides, to medieval head offerings and *śmaśāna* rituals, to contemporary functions of Kālī in wartime, Indic fierce goddesses on one level are heroines of myths that justify, glorify, and mystify warfare and other human predatory rites, even as they defend us, slay our true enemies, and establish order. At the same time, we have the ability to transcend our base predatory nature, eschew violence, harvest the riches of the Earth, heal illness, and generate love and psychic resurrection. At once the antithesis and the cure of violence and warfare, the aspects of Kālī and her *avatāras* that incorporate the archaic healing tools of shamanic folk medicine have interpenetrated her divine warrior persona for over five thousand years.

References

1. I am using the minimal definition for simple shamanism, consisting of trance, direct contact with spiritual beings and guardian spirits, and ritual mediation. [Åke Hultkrantz, *Shamanic Healing and Ritual Drama: Health and Medicine in Native North American Religious Traditions* (New York, 1992), 10.]
2. Lotte Hughes, *The No-Nonsense Guide to Indigenous Peoples* (Oxford, 2003), 53.
3. "Immediate return" societies consume most food on the day it is gathered; because they receive an immediate return on their labor, they focus on the

present. In most agricultural and pastoralist systems, work with no immediate return can extend for long periods, constituting a "delayed return" on labor. [Hughes, 4.]

4. In Rajasthan, kṣatriya (high warrior caste) women have been given fairly thorough military training since the post-Vedic period or earlier, and Rajput princesses, as well as female guards of kings, are known to be quite adept at sword and spear. For contemporary Rajput women, the fierce goddess is a dual warrior symbol of their past glories on the battlefield, protecting male property and caste interests, and their modern role as house-bound family protectress. See, Lindsey Harlan, *Religion and Rajput Women: The Ethics of Protection in Contemporary Narratives* (Berkeley, 1992).
5. See Mark Juergensmeyer, *Terror in the Mind of God: The Global Rise of Religious Violence* (Berkeley, 2001).
6. Mircea Eliade, *A History of Religious Ideas*, vol. 1 (Chicago, 1978), 66.
7. Daniel C. Dennett, *Breaking the Spell: Religion as a Natural Phenomenon* (New York: Penguin, 2006).
8. British evolutionary biologist Richard Dawkins, in *The Selfish Gene* (Oxford, OUP, 1976, rev. edn., 1989), coined the term *meme* to describe a cultural replicator (an "information packet" that prescribes human behavior, such as religious symbols and traditions). Memes are the cultural equivalent of biological genes, since cultural transmission can mimic genetic transmission (Dennett, *Breaking the Spell*), 78.
9. Dennett propounds that "[r]eligions might turn out to be species of cultural symbionts that manage to thrive by leaping from human host to human host. . . . [I]t is not *our*fitness (as reproducing members of the species *Homo sapiens*) that is presumed to be enhanced by religion, but *its* fitness (as a reproducing—self-replicating—member of the symbiont genus *Cultus religious*). It may thrive as a mutualist because it benefits its hosts quite directly, or it may thrive as a parasite even though it oppresses its hosts with a virulent affliction that leaves them worse off but too weak to combat its spread." (Ibid., 84–85.)
10. Barbara Ehrenreich, *Blood Rites: Origins and History of the Passions of War* (New York, 1997).
11. Mark Juergensmeyer, *Terror in the Mind of God: The Global Rise of Religious Violence* (Berkeley, 2001).
12. Stan Harris, *The End of Faith: Religion, Terror, and the Future of Reason* (New York, 2004).
13. Jack Nelson-Pallmeyer, *Is Religion Killing Us? Violence in the Bible and the Qur'ān* (Harrisburg, PA, 2003).
14. http://www.oneummah.net/quran/quran.html; http://www.usc.edu/dept/MSA/quran/; and http://www.geocities.com/masad02/.
15. http://answering-islam.org.uk/Books/Hughes/index.htm.
16. http://answering-islam.org.uk/Index/index.html.
17. Samuel Noah Kramer, ed., *Mythologies of the Ancient World* (New York, 1961).
18. John W. Dean, *Conservatives Without Conscience* (New York, 2006).
19. Fiona Bowie, *The Anthropology of Religion: An Introduction* (Malden, MA, 2006), 101.
20. Peggy Reeves Sanday, *Female Power and Male Dominance: On the Origins of Sexual Inequality* (Cambridge, 1981).

21. Clifford Geertz, *The Interpretation of Cultures* (New York, 1973); Hildred Geertz and Clifford Geertz, *Kinship in Bali* (Chicago, 1975).
22. Mary Douglas, *Purity and Danger* (London, 1966); Douglas, *Natural Symbols* (New York, 1970); Douglas, *Implicit Meanings* (London, 1975).
23. Clifford Geertz, *The Interpretation of Cultures* (New York, 1973).
24. Sanday, *Female Power and Male Dominance*, xv–xvi.
25. D.D. Kosambi, *The Culture and Civilization of Ancient India in Historical Outline* (London, 1965).
26. Dennett, *Breaking the Spell*, 14–15.
27. Ibid., 32.

Acknowledgments

No book is the work of one person. This edition is the result of the combined research and study of hundred of authors in my Bibliography. Any mistakes or errors are mine alone. The formulation of my views was immensely influenced by the works of Narendra Nath Bhattacharyya, D.D. Kosambi, Tikva Frymer-Kensky, Romila Thapar, Mandakranta Bose, Fiona Bowie, Vandana Shiva, Arundhati Roy, Spengler, and others. I am indebted to Shri Ashok Jain of Munshiram Manoharlal Publishers, for their kindness and constant solicitude in the course of producing this book. I would like to thank James D. Ryan for his guidance as I wrote my PhD dissertation and his commentary on a draft of the Tamil material. I am grateful to Kathleen M. Erndl for her suggestions for my dissertation. I am particularly grateful to Hansjorg Mayer, London, for his encouragement and kind permission to reprint photo plates from *The Nagas*. I thank Dr N. Murugesan at the Institut Francais d'Indologie, Pondicherry, for his generous assistance and courtesy. I owe a special debt to my honored friend Philip C. Packard for his unwavering assistance and encyclopedic knowledge. I thank him for providing painstaking readings, wielding a clarifying editorial pen, and always being available to discuss ideas. Finally, I would like to thank the esteemed Cherokee medicine priest, David Winston, for generously giving his time to answer all my questions during our lengthy email correspondences; his encouragement infused me with strength of purpose, and his native lens continues to subtly clarify my "innerstanding" of human cultures, symbols, and religions.

DONNA JORDAN

Berkeley
December 2011

Abbreviations

Ain. — *Ainkurunūru*
AITMS — Ancient Indian Tradition and Mythology Series
ALS — Adyar Library Series
AN — *Akanāṉūṟu*
AOS — American Oriental Series, New Haven
ĀSS — Ānandāśrama Sanskrit Series
AV — *Atharvaveda*
Bṛhadd. — *Bṛhaddevatā*
Bṛhad. Up. — *Bṛhadāraṇyaka Upaniṣad*
BSOAS — *Bulletin of the School of Oriental and African Studies*, London
BSS — Bombay Sanskrit Series
BU — *Bṛhadāraṇyaka Upaniṣad*
Chānd. Up. — *Chāndogya Upaniṣad*
Cil. — *Cilappatikāram*
CRK — *Catakantaravanan Katai*
CSS — Calcutta Sanskrit Series
ERE — *Encyclopaedia of Religion and Ethics*, ed. James Hastings, 13 vols.
HOS — Harvard Oriental Series
JA — *Journal Asiatique*
JAOS — *Journal of the American Oriental Society*
JRAS — *Journal of the Royal Asiatic Society*
Kauś. — *Kauśikasūtra*
Mbh. — *Mahābhārata*

MS	*Manusmṛti*
Naṟṟ.	*Naṟṟiṇai*
Pat.	*Patiṟṟuppattu*
PN	*Puṟanāṉūṟu*
PP	*Paṭṭiṉappalai*
PTSS	Prakrit Text Society Series
RAS	Royal Asiatic Society, London
ṚV	*Ṛgveda*
SBAS	Sacred Books of the Aryan Series
SBB	Sacred Books of the Buddhist
SBE	Sacred Books of the East
SBH	Sacred Books of the Hindu
Ś. Br.	*Śatapatha Brāhmaṇa*
ŚGDOS	Śrī Gharīb Dāsa Oriental Series
Suś. Saṁ.	*Suśruta Saṁhitā*
SV	*Sāmaveda*
Tait. Br.	*Taittirīya Brāhmaṇa*
TK	*Tirukkuṟaḷ*
TMA	*Tirumurukāṟṟuppaṭai*
YV	*Yajurveda*

Part I
Origins

Introduction

THE QUESTION OF MATRIARCHIES

> The theory that there were full-fledged matriarchal societies or that such societies preceded everywhere the patriarchal ones cannot be proved historically. Though the concept of the Female Principle of creation can be associated with the relics of matriarchal cultural elements, no universal concomitance can be established between the two.[1]
>
> * * *
>
> Before the men could go to war, it was customary for the women to make the moccasins. If the women did not want war, they did not make moccasins.
>
> —Haudenosaunee teaching

Defining Female/Male Dominance

Nineteenth century evolutionary theorists such as Herbert Spencer, Edward Tylor,[2] and Sir James Frazer claimed that all the incarnations of the Great Goddess were underpinned by a unilinear evolutionary process, and that these goddesses constituted an essential unity. The early evolutionists, according to Fiona Bowie, shared three overarching articles of faith: (1) the notion of progress; (2) the theory of pan-human psychic unity; and (3) a belief in the unfailing efficacy of the comparative method.[3] A pan-human psychic archetype or model, along with the diffusion of cultural traits, accounted for the replication of the Great Goddess across cultures and time, according to evolutionary theorists. "If left alone, all human communities would pass through the same stages of social evolution. The supposition was that eventually all societies would reach the same peak of rational, civilized thought and behavior that characterized Victorian Britain."[4] Convinced that matriarchies preceded patriarchies as an evolutionary principle, evolutionary theorists presumed that the Great Goddess in her various archaeological images and mythological forms was an *a priori* signifier of matriarchal societies.

Contemporary feminists have revived the nineteenth century matriarchy theory, which until recently has been denigrated by anthropologists and historians. According to the argument initiated by German romantic idealist Johann Jakob Bachofen[5] and anthropologist Lewis Henry Morgan,[6] ancient cultures at the beginning of pan-human cultural evolution were ruled by women. In this Eurocentric, androcentric paradigm, savage and barbarian societies are viewed as the low point of origin of a unilinear evolutionary process. As humans progress, advance, and become civilized, they claimed, patriarchy, the pinnacle of creation, becomes the norm. Bachofen based his theory on the prevalence of powerful goddesses and queens in archaeological remains and mythology. Morgan's proposal was centered on his study of the Iroquois nation, in which the economic domination by women, the tradition of matrilineal descent, and the authoritative role of women in ritual and political activities provided evidence of a functioning matriarchy.

As explanatory devices, all of these theories failed: "they were based on armchair speculations and were heavily burdened with biases about human nature,"[7] writes James J. Preston. According to Carolyn Fleuhr-Lobban, there are three false assumptions in the evolutionists' argument for a matriarchate:

> First, there is the assumption that the presence of female deities and female figures in ancient myth and symbol is evidence for a historical epoch of mother-rule, or matriarchy. Bachofen originated the idea, and Engels utilized it in his formulations. Second, there is the assumption that matrilineal societies are survivals of a prior matriarchal era. Morgan arrived at this conclusion, and Engels did not take a different view. Third, there is the assumption of a natural and necessary relationship between matrilineality and matriarchy. All these assumptions are unwarranted.[8]

This evolutionary interpretation of prehistory came into disfavor among academics and scholars in the late twentieth century. Modern anthropologists reject the idea that civilization or history progresses in "stages" because the data now available from societies all around the world fails to support it. Joan Bamberger[9] reasons that myths of matriarchy, found in relative abundance in patriarchal societies, function as social charters that rationalize, justify, and legitimate male power. In societies in which woman is elevated to a deity in the pantheon but demoted to childlike chattel in law codes, Bamberger claims that matriarchal myths are a male tool to keep her "in her place." Sanday echoes Bamberger's thesis:

> Generally, myths of former female power are found in societies in which there is both male dominance and female power. . . . Myths of former female power provide men with a rationale for segregating themselves from women and a

> reason for dominating 'tyrannical' women. Wherever men perceive women in such terms, it is likely that women have considerable informal power. Thus, myths of former female power mirror the paradoxical relationship between the sexes that actually exists.[10]

Gerda Lerner[11] notes that most ethnographic evidence points not to a predominance in the ancient and Neolithic worlds of matriarchal societies, but rather to matrilineal and matrilocal social systems in which many or most of the economic and family decisions are made by male relatives, while women have participatory power. Christine Fielder and Chris King[12] have shown that Mitochondrial mtDNA and Y-chromosome DNA studies[13] provide genetic evidence that suggests that human emergence, like that of ape societies, is dominated by female exogamous migration amid a moderately polygynous system, an indication that matrilocal societies probably did not predominate on a population basis during the Paleolithic.

Because they have discovered no society in which women are the primary leaders, many anthropologists have concluded that male dominance is universal. However, as Sanday points out, "[t]here is a certain bias to this point of view, a bias that is understandable given the Western equation of dominance with public leadership. By defining dominance differently, one can show that in many societies male leadership is balanced by female authority."[14] Among Ashanti, Iroquois, and Dahomeans, for example, women are not foregrounded in public life, but they possess veto power against male actions, suggesting "a bipartite system of checks and balances in which neither sex dominated the other."[15] Iroquois women had the power to make political appointments or replacements and to veto warfare.

Many pre-contact North American Indian tribes such as the Cherokee were true matriarchies, both matrilocal and matrilineal, that functioned as societies ruled by women. According to to N.N. Bhattacharyya, D.D. Kosambi, and numerous other historians and anthropologists, many of the aboriginal peoples of India were similarly organized as full-fledged matriarchies.

Cherokee Matriarchy

> When the white man discovered this country, Indians were running it. No taxes, no debt, women did all the work. White man thought he could improve on a system like this.
>
> —Cherokee saying

Inheritance and descendants came through the matrilineal line in many Native American tribes, and the matriarch, as an integral part of tribal life, gave women power and control over the decision-making processes of their society.[16] The Cherokee nation (*Tsalagi*) was a full-fledged matriarchy (termed a "petticoat-government" by eighteenth century Scottish trader James Adair),[17] both matrilineal and matrilocal; women owned as their birthright the means of production (the land) and therefore controlled tribal economies.[18] Women and men had equal claim to clan privileges, but it was acknowledged by all that women were the source of the clan; the matriarch gave women power and control over the decision-making processes of their society.[19] Each town had a female judiciary that enforced regulations. Women "had more of a proprietary interest in men than men had in women,"[20] and married women, according to Adair, were adulteresses who "plant their brows with horns as often as they please;" unlike women of "all civilized or savage nations," Cherokee women did so "without fear of punishment."[21] Female infidelity rarely fazed men, but male infidelity ended in a bloody battle between the two women and the termination of the marriage.[22]

Perceiving the gender parity and sexual autonomy of the native people through their European lens, the early observers labeled women "slaves" because they did most of the labor, and "harlots" because of their sexual freedom.[23] "Perhaps," writes Theda Perdue, "women willingly performed most of the work in Cherokee society because they also controlled the fruits of their labor, the crops; the means of production, the land; and ultimately, the result of production, the children."[24] As Sarah Hill explains, the autonomy of Cherokee women was a product of their social and economic security, and the rights of women and children were protected and enhanced by marriage customs, residence patterns, and social structures.

> As long as women retained control of their resources and lived in female-centered households, they could support their descendants. When marriage partners separated, wrote Timberlake, 'the children go with, and are provided for, by the mother.' Women's ability to support their children and themselves emerged from a densely woven social fabric. Matrilineal ownership of land gave women access to foods, whether grown or gathered, served or sold. Matrilocal residence patterns facilitated sharing of responsibilities and resources. Nucleated settlements maintained and reinforced household connections. It is little wonder Alexander Longe thought 'the women Rules the Roost and weres the briches.' They appeared to be little dependent on their husbands.[25]

Indian Ādivāsī Matriarchy

One of the prominent strands of D.D. Kosambi's exegesis of Indian historiography is related to his belief that Indic tribal societies were originally matriarchal. This view echoes the ideas of S. B. Dasgupta and N.N. Bhattacharyya. Most of the aboriginal tribes the brāhmaṇas sought to assimilate, Kosambi maintained, had retained a mother-kin social organization since prehistoric times, and their religions likewise were dominated by a belief in and worship of the Supreme Being as Mother Earth.

There are many clues of matriarchal or matrilineal customs in ancient India. In ancient women-oriented societies, brother-sister marriages were common among both gods (Cronus and Rhea, Zeus and Hera, Baal and Anat, Osiris and Isis) and kings, who married their sisters "to insure their own title to the throne under a rule of female kinship which treated women and not men as the channel in which the blood royal flowed."[26] This matriarchal social custom survives in some parts of south India, cognate with brother-sister marriage referred to in the *Baudhāyana Dharmasūtra* and in the *Tantravārttika* of Kumārila, viz., the custom that a man marries the daughter of his maternal uncle. We learn in the *Mahābhārata* that among the Ārattas and Vāhikas, the nephews inherit the property rather than the sons. Brother-sister marriage was also practiced in India by the Śākyas, according to the Ambaṭṭhasutta[27] and the *Mahāvastu*;[28] by Sītā, who, in the *Daśaratha Jātaka*, is the sister as well as the wife of Rāma, and is described in Buddhist stories of sister marriage.

The *Mahābhārata* refers to the Madra country, a land governed by seemingly matriarchal laws: in the marriage of Pāṇḍu to a Madra princess, the dowry was taken by the kinsmen of the bride[29] as a brideprice. It was against the law to associate with the Madrakas,[30] who are described as outcastes who assembled in free sexual union that is reminiscent, as Bhattacharyya emphasizes, of agricultural rites.[31] We learn in a conversation between Pāṇḍu and Kuntī that formerly, women were unfaithful to their husbands, yet were not considered sinful according to the moral precepts of the time. Patrilocal marriage was introduced by Śvetaketu, son of Uddālaka.

Although there have been few field studies of Indian *ādīvāsīs*, evidence collected by A.A.D. Luiz, Edgar Thurston, Wilbur Theodore Elmore, and others highlights the prevalence of Kālī-like goddesses among tribal peoples in South Asia, and Luiz asserts that "very definitely mother right (*Marumakkathayam*, matrilineal) was the rule among primitive aborigines of Kerala."[32] Many scholars argue that most Indian tribes were primordial matriarchies and many remained matriarchal until the advent of Aryan hegemony. The present-day distribution of temples to the Sixty-four Yoginīs lies within the tribal belt of eastern Madhya Pradesh and Orissa.[33] Moreover, the names of local goddesses in these areas are often feminine inflections of tribal names: Mātaṅgī is the goddess of the Mātaṅga tribe, Cāṇḍālī of the Cāṇḍāla tribe, and so on. The principles of Sāṅkhya, magical fertility rites, and Śāktism are actively found today in the matriarchal tribes of the northeastern region, which, in the medieval period, encompassed the Brahmaputra valley, Kāmarūpa (which included, according to the Purāṇas, nearly all of the old province of Eastern Bengal, Assam, and Bhutan), and Prāgjyotiṣa.[34] When the process of brāhmaṇic hegemony brought the cult of the Hindu divinities to the many hill tribes of the northeast, the least influenced by the brāhmaṇic tradition were the Mizos, Nagas, and Khasis.[35] "Most tribals were greater recipients of the Śākta-Tantric ideas"[36] because vāmācāra and kaulācāra rites were grounded in primal magico-religious equations familiar to them.

The few wild hill tribes that escaped brāhmaṇization for nearly a millennium survive as resources of study for anthropologists and cultural historians. We learn from Bhattacharyya that their emphasis on blood sacrifice is parallel to that of left-hand Tantra, their goddesses are the creators and destroyers of the universe, and their priestesses deputize men to assist them in sacrifices to the goddesses:

> In all religious ceremonies sacrifices are essential. The spirits are to be propitiated with sacrifices. The sacrifice centers round the altar. Among the Garos, the victims are generally fowls or goats. In special sacrifices, the victim is a bull which is to be cut with a single stroke of blade. . . . In olden days the practice of human sacrifice was in vogue among the Dimasa-Kacharis. . . . [In] the rituals of Khasis, . . . [b]efore partaking of a meal one has to put something out of the dish as a libation to the gods uttering words of thanksgiving. In such ceremonies they appease the goddess and other deities by raising an altar on which they smear the blood of a sacrificial animal or some pieces of its entrails. The powers of sickness and death are all females. The protectors of the household are also goddesses. Priestesses assist at all sacrifices and the male officials are only their deputies.[37]

Baron Omar Rolf Ehrenfels'[38] mid-twentieth century research on the matriarchal tribes and castes of India provides specific evidence that goddesses are central to the lives of tribal groups whose agricultural economies are controlled by women. The massive efforts to break the resistance of matriarchy and establish male supremacy through child-marriage, hypergamy, and *satī*, which Ehrenfels characterizes as almost unparalleled aggression against women, did not succeed; matriarchal elements were eternally rooted in the lives of the low caste, *ādivāsīs*, and dalits. As Bhattacharyya stresses, "The special vigour to overthrow mother-right must have necessarily implied a corresponding special vigor which mother-right must have been enjoying in India since the pre-Vedic age."[39]

Debiprasad Chattopadhyaya argues that since a matriarchal social structure and worldview tend to dominate in undeveloped agricultural economies, and since the great majority of Indian muted groups remained primarily agricultural, it follows that to convert them to a subordinate existence in a patriarchal, authoritarian system would have required extreme measures. Matriarchal cultural elements, reasons Chattopadhyaya, would naturally survive in underclass groups that work the land.[40]

In 1940, Ehrenfels found more than one hundred such Indian tribes and castes, with the primary matriarchal zones located in Assam, parts of Baluchistan, parts of Andhra Pradesh and Madras, Mysore, and Kerala. These matriarchal social groups are allied with a Mother-goddess who is frequently depicted as their tribal ancestress. The religions of the Khasis of Assam and the Garos show markedly matriarchal traces, for example, and the matriarchal Pulayans or Cherumans worship Bhagavatī as a kind of caste goddess or ancestress.[41] The Kadirs of Kerala, also a matriarchal people, worship the goddess Kālī;[42] the matriarchal Nāyars, to whom the Great *Ucharal* feast is dedicated,[43] propitiate the Earth Goddess, Bhūmi Devī; the matriarchal Pārāyaṇas or Mālās of the far south worship their tribal mother Athal,[44] as well as three categories of Divine Mothers.[45] The mythology of the Gowri tribes of Madhya Pradesh depicts ancestors who were all husbands to the one great ancestress,[46] and the same region is home to matriarchal castes such as Bhunjias, Dumals, Gonds, Kamars, Kawars, Khangars, etc., all of which are ancestress-worshipers.[47]

While the aboriginal Kerala tribes were originally matriarchal[48] and matrilineal, only the Kurichchians, Kanikkars, Kundu Vadians, and Malayalars have preserved Marumakkathayam (matrilineal descent). All other tribal groups are now patrilineal. "The ancient rule made it imperative that the estate of the deceased devolved on the person who performed the obsequies and observed pollution," observes Luiz:

> Most of the tribes have no clear rule regarding succession because there is nothing to be inherited especially among those who are still in their hunting, food-picking, or nomadic stage of civilization. Some groups that have given up Marumakkathayam (matriarchal rule), divide the assets equally among sons and nephews. This is a mixture of matriarchy and patriarchy. The assets of the wife pass to the husband at marriage, and after his death to his heirs. If divorce takes place at the instance of the husband the assets of the wife have to be returned. Adoption is popular, and the adopted has a legal and social status. . . . Among most groups the woman has a status at par with man. They hunt, work and cultivate together. The wife and children are treated as assets, for the wife and sons contribute free labour, and the daughters can be sold.[49]

Because of a former deficiency of Western technology and economic development, India's economy has remained largely agricultural and rural, thus affording a strong survival of tribal elements and matriarchal traditions within the domain of the rural majority. A prominent theme of Kosambi's works is that much of India's past survives in the present. For him, this rich mine of prehistory made up for the absence of reliable historical records. Although many older matriarchal tribal groups have managed to survive, they are close to extinction today. After two thousand years of cultivation, almost all of the land is overgrazed and overfarmed, and "yield per acre is abysmally low because the methods are primitive and holdings too small to be economic."[50] Since agriculture remained undeveloped until the invasion by globalist corporatocracy and agribusiness, the mother-right elements that survived in India have been stronger in both degree and extent than anywhere else in the world, according to Kosambi.

Myths Reflect Patriarchal Coup

Consistent with the ideas of contemporary symbolic anthropologists and feminist theorists, Kosambi and Bhattacharyya perceive that the gradual shift from mother-right to father-right social structure is reflected in myths. As male domination, private property, and the caste system gradually encroached on tribal groups, many of their aboriginal goddesses were coupled with husbands in epico-Purāṇic mythology. Most of these goddesses were eventually assimilated along the fringe of the brāhmaṇical Śākta pantheon as the Kālī-like goddesses, the wild, terrifying, all-devouring, oral-aggressive, *ugra* (fierce) incarnations of Devī, whose rituals involved propitiation with blood sacrifice (preferably freshly decapitated human heads), meat, liquor, violence or self-mutilation, and frenzied spirit possession performance.

Hunter-gatherer societies at the base of our genetic tree are characterized by a balance between the major food resource brought in by gathering women, who also do most of the childrearing, and the animal foods, prized for sexual favors, provided by male hunters. In these societies, the relative status of men and women is separate but equal, as opposed to a dominant matriarchy. The Great Goddess is an ironic deity of Life and Death. Because they are forced to succumb to the pressures of more competitive patrilineal societies whose technologies and economic systems exploit women and the Earth, matriarchal, matrilineal, and matrilocal societies are a rapidly vanishing tiny minority in the contemporary world, as many cross-cultural studies have proven.

The Shift to Agriculture

> The way we look at the development of human culture is so familiar by now that many of us have forgotten that the whole scheme . . . was itself never more than a model and, like most models, tells us more about its own time than that which it claims to describe. Formulated in the nineteenth and early twentieth centuries, the view of prehistory as a progressive series of stages is indebted to Compte, to Darwin, and to what has been called the Whig Interpretation of History, the assumption that it was progress, upward development, which led to 'that pinnacle of achievement,' ourselves.[51]

Sophisticated technological advances such as carbon-14 and thermoluminescence dating have lent greater accuracy and reliability to late twentieth and early twenty-first centuries archaeological conclusions, propelling archaeology into the hard sciences and high technology. For this reason, recent finds are more highly valued than those using older methods or paradigms. Nevertheless, archaeology remains an interpretive field in which the standard is always in a state of flux. Like most fields of academic study, archaeology has obviously been dominated by Caucasian Christian men. Stylistic and philosophical shifts have occurred over the decades, and in some cases there is a return to older paradigms that had been discarded and later reconsidered. Archaeological hermeneutics generally echo the dominant paradigm of prehistory. Prehistorians have sought a new paradigm since the end of the twentieth century that would deliver them from the unilinear evolutionary notion of progress initiated by Childe, who also coined the phrase "Neolithic Revolution" to describe what many scholars characterize as the most important single event in human history: the shift from hunter-gatherer to agricultural mode of production. Childe's "oasis" theory, proven to be incorrect, was that drought forced humans into restricted territories at the end of the Ice Age, and they began of necessity to domesticate wild animals and grains that were indigenous to these oases. While the Near East did experience drought, it was after the earliest farming villages had already been established.[52]

The shift to agriculture, traditionally accepted as a Neolithic invention, probably began in Paleolithic times with the control of animals and plants, although the reason for the transition from nomadism to settled agricultural existence still remains an enigma. Modern archaeologists tend to avoid Childe's term "Neolithic Revolution," because they now view the changeover to plant and animal husbandry as more a gradual process of transition than a "revolution." In the last half of the eighth millennium BCE, Neolithic farming villages sprang up in Anatolia, Palestine, Syria, and the Zagros mountains of Iran. Early signs of metal work, domesticated animals and complex grains, a pottery tradition, and advanced architectural and interior design were all present, suggesting that these people were "experienced settlers whose techniques had been perfected elsewhere."[53] Archaeological records of known earlier sites give us no clue to their direct ancestors or original settlements.

After two thousand years without further innovation, a second major wave of farming settlements was developed by formerly nomadic or semi-nomadic peoples in the outskirts of Iran, the plains of Mesopotamia, and into the West as far as the Balkan countries in the last half of the sixth millennium BCE. Neither wave of farming settlements appears to have been stimulated by any economic advantage of agriculture over hunting and gathering; in fact, "the economic base of the pre-Neolithic forest dwellers of southeast Europe, who may well have controlled edible resources of their own (red deer, pig, fish, and forest plants), was actually equal or superior in terms of both nutrition and reliability to the grain-sheep-goat-cattle complex that replaced it."[54]

A so-called Epi-Paleolithic or Mesolithic age in the Near East was a transition period from around 10,000 BCE until the eighth millennium. In this period we find the first rock art glorifying war and battle scenes between archers in the Spanish Levant, Transcaucasia, Palestine, and Syria around the last half of the ninth millennium BCE.[55]

Between 9,000–6,000 BCE, the earliest permanent settlements arose, accompanied by the domestication of plants and animals. The sheep was domesticated by 9,000 BCE, and the dog had probably been domesticated in the Paleolithic. Goats, pigs, and cattle were all domesticated in the Near East by 5,500 BCE. Çatal Höyük remains strongly suggest the ancient origin of animal husbandry and the *hieros gamos* ritual. The first cities were built between 4,000–3,000 BCE, theoretically as an effect of population growth, more complex trade patterns, and the organizational requirements of irrigation and warfare. Between 9,000 BCE and the beginning of the Christian era, Western civilization came into being in Egypt and ancient Western Asia.

References

1. Bhattacharyya, *History of the Śākta Religion* (New Delhi, 1996), 27.
2. In *Primitive Culture* (1871), Sir Edward Burnett Tylor formulated the three stages of social evolution (animism–polytheism–monotheism) along with the notion of *diffusion,* the transmission of cultural traits across time and space. He termed instances where patterns coincide *adhesions.* Because the progress was ever upward, he assumed that "primitive" traits found in "advanced" societies

were *survivals* from an earlier evolutionary stage, closer to the root of the genetic tree.

3. Bowie, *Anthropology of Religion: An Introduction*, 221.
4. Ibid.
5. J.J. Bachofen, *Das Mutterrecht* (1861), abridged and translated by Ralph Mannheim, in *Myth, Religion, and Mother Right: Selected Writings of J.J. Bachofen* (Princeton, 1967).
6. Lewis Henry Morgan, *Ancient Society, or, Researches in the Lines of Human Progress from Savagery through Barbarism to Civilization* [1877], ed. Eleanor Burke Leacock, (Cleveland, 1963); *Houses and House-life of the American Aborigines* (Salt Lake City, 2003); Morgan, *League of the Iroquois* (Secaucus, N.J., 1972).
7. James J. Preston, ed., *Mother Worship: Theme and Variations* (Chapel Hill, 1982), 325.
8. Carolyn Fluehr-Lobban, "A Marxist Reappraisal of the Matriarchate," *Current Anthropology* 20 (June 1979), quoted by James J. Preston, ed., *Mother Worship* (Chapel Hill, 1982), 326.
9. Joan Bamberger, "The Myth of Matriarchy: Why Men Rule in Primitive Society," *Women, Culture and Society*, ed. M. Rosaldo and L. Lamphere (Cambridge, 1974), 171.
10. Sanday, *Female Power and Male Dominance*, 181.
11. Gerda Lerner, *The Creation of Patriarchy* (New York, 1986).
12. See Christine Fielder and Chris King, *Sexual Paradox: Complementarity, Reproductive Conflict and Human Emergence*, http://www.dhushara.com/paradoxhtm/3bl.jpg, accessed February 8, 2006.
13. M. Seielstad, E. Minch, and L. Cavalli-Sforza, "Genetic Evidence for a Higher Female Migration Rate in Humans," *Nature Genetics* 20/3 (1998): 278–80.
14. Sanday, *Female Power and Male Dominance*, 113.
15. Ibid., 114.
16. "Indigenous Women," Shannonthunderbird.com, http://www.shannon-thunderbird.com/indigenous_women_rights.htm (accessed March 12, 2005).
17. Theda Perdue, *Cherokee Women* (Lincoln, Nebraska, 1998), 56.
18. See histories about the matriarchal Cherokees such as Theda Perdue, *Cherokee Women* (Lincoln, University of Nebraska Press, 1998); Sarah H. Hill, *Weaving New Worlds: Southeastern Cherokee Women and Their Basketry* (Chapel Hill: University of North Carolina Press, 1997).
19. "Indigenous Women."
20. Perdue, *Cherokee Women*, 57.
21. Samuel Cole Williams, ed., *Adair's History of the American Indian* (1775) (New York, 1930), 133, 152–53, 174, quoted in Hill, *Weaving New Worlds*, 32.
22. Perdue, *Cherokee Women*, 57.
23. Ibid., 4.
24. Ibid., 24.
25. Hill, *Weaving New Worlds*, 33–34.
26. Frazer, *The News Golden Bough* (abridged), 384.
27. *Dīgha Nikāya*, 3.16, cited by N.N. Bhattacharya, "Śāktism and Mother-Right," in *The Śakti Cult and Tārā*, ed. D.C. Sircar, 66.
28. Karṇaparva, 45.13.
29. Ādiparva, 113.

30. Karṇaparva, 40.24–25, 27, 34, 41.
31. Bhattacharya, "Śāktism and Mother-Right," 68.
32. A.A.D. Luiz, *Tribes of Kerala* (New Delhi, 1962), 14.
33. R.S. Sharma, "Material Milieu of Tantrism," *Indian Society, Historical Probings*, ed. R.S. Sharma (New Delhi, 1974), 181.
34. Bhattacharyya, *Religious Culture of North-Eastern India* (New Delhi, 1995), 38.
35. Ibid., 65.
36. Ibid., 72.
37. Ibid., 25–26.
38. O.R. Ehrenfels, *Mother-Right in India* (London, 1941), 18–35.
39. Bhattacharyya, *History of Indian Erotic Literature* (New Delhi, 1975), 2.
40. Debiprasad Chattopadhyaya, *Lokāyata* (Delhi, 1985), 232ff.
41. L.K. Ananthakrishna Iyer, *The Cochin Tribes and Castes*, vol. 1 (Madras, 1909), 112.
42. Ibid., 11.
43. Ibid., 48.
44. Ibid., 8C–81.
45. E. Thurston and K. Rangachari, *Castes and Tribes of Southern India*, vol. 6 (Madras, 1909), 104–5, 123.
46. R.V. Russell and Hira Lal, *Tribes and Castes of the Central Provinces*, vol. 3 (Delhi, 1975), 161.
47. Ibid., vol. 2: 324, 428, 534; vol. 3: 89, 328, 391, 440.
48. Luiz, *Tribes of Kerala*, 14.
49. Ibid.
50. D.D. Kosambi, *Ancient India: A History of its Culture and Civilization* (New York, 1965), 13.
51. Mary Settegast, *Plato, Prehistorian: 10,000 to 5000 B.C. Myth, Religion, Archaeology* (Hudson, NY, 1990), 2–3.
52. Ibid., 3.
53. Ibid., 4.
54. Ibid.
55. Ibid., 59–61.

1

The Milieu of the Indus Culture: *c.* Third to First Millennia BCE

Tree Worship and the Holy Groves of the Goddess

> The Trees of Life and of Knowledge are at once suggested by the mysterious sacred tree which appears in the most ancient sculptures and paintings of Egypt and Assyria, and in those of the remoter East. It figures as a type of the universe, and represents the whole system of created things, but more frequently as a "tree of life," by whose fruit the votaries of the gods are nourished with divine strength, and one prepared for the joys of immortality. The most ancient types of this mystical tree of life are the date, the fig, and the pine or cedar.[1]

* * *

> [G]roves sacred to the mother goddess are mentioned in brahmin myth and legend. Such groves still exist in villages away from the road; but women are now generally forbidden entry excepting the few cases where the priesthood has remained in primitive hands not transferred to immigrant settled cultivators. Originally, the ban was on the entry of men. When society changed from matriarchal to patriarchal, the priesthood and ritual were correspondingly transformed.[2]

The original temples of goddess worship throughout the ancient world consisted of open space shrines under trees in sacred groves.[3] The tree cult is a universal phenomenon among Earth-based peoples, and the most archaic goddesses were originally identified with trees, the largest and most majestic of plants rooted in the Earth. Ancient magico-religious systems were means of communicating with, worshiping, and propitiating the divine spirit in all of

Earth's creations. Trees, plants, and animals were proto-fierce goddesses, perceived as powerful protectors and destroyers. Throughout Paleolithic and Neolithic cultures, the Earth Goddess and her creations were bonded by the idea that plants and animals were a manifestation of the Great Goddess herself. She was understood as the primordial origin of the fertility, creation, growth, nurturance, death, and regeneration of plants, animals, and humans. Before they were demonized, eliminated, or co-opted by patriarchal religions, archaic sylvan goddesses originally represented the quintessence of Earth's ecological cycles: the spirits of nature. Tree worship became supplanted by the worship of patriarchal male gods in temples and the conceptual split between spirit and nature, the sacred and the mundane.

The idea of Mother Earth remains a primary value of all indigenous peoples; every culture that maintains this attitude also has restrictions against any individual owning, mining, or selling land. Since contemporary technological societies do not see the Earth as alive, they are free of ethical and moral constraints on exploiting Earth's resources. The ancient Europeans worshiped trees; the Druids worshiped Oaks, and all of Old Europe maintained sacred groves. Plants were perceived as living and feeling beings of a higher evolution than humans, and they were personified and deified. "Even where no mention is made of wood-spirits," writes Frazer, "we may generally assume that when trees or groves are sacred and inviolable, it is because they are believed to be either inhabited or animated by sylvan deities."[4] The belief that the Earth is alive prevailed in Europe until the age of enlightenment and the scientific revolution in the 1700s.

Primal cultures not only recognize spirits in trees, but also in plants, rocks, waterfalls, rivers, crossroads, cemeteries, as well as in manmade ritual items such as drums, weapons, and other sacralized implements. For Earth-based cultures, spirits animate everything; the world is alive and moving. Ceremony stops this movement abruptly, placing the participants in a space out of time where there is no past, no present, and no future. Out of time, the world can begin anew again. One of the religious responsibilities of the shaman in ancient cultures was to work synergistically with nature spirits through ritual ceremony for the benefit of the whole ecosystem. For that reason, all indigenous peoples have a stringent tribal taboo on cutting down or harming sacred trees or groves. Old Austrian peasants still will not permit incisions to be made in trees without a special reason, and in Livonia if anyone cuts a tree in the sacred grove, he will die within a year.[5] A vestige of this ancient tradition is seen in the *Rāmāyaṇa*, when the unbeliever Rāvaṇa cries, "I have not cut down any fig tree, in the month of Vaiśākha, why then does the calamity [alluding to the defeats of his army in the war with Ramachandra, and the loss of his sons and brothers] befall me?" Clearly, there was a taboo against harming a sacred Indian fig tree. In the *Atharvaveda*, we are told that ancient Indian trees and medicinal plants appeared three ages earlier than the gods, thus trees and plants were considered elders and teachers. In south India, the most archaic form of fierce goddess worship was at the foot of a tree. The holy groves of the goddess are home to plants, trees, and animals, and cutting any tree or removing any plant is forbidden. In the Namakkal district of Tamilnadu, village goddess Kongayi Ammaṉ does not like the noise of tree-cutting, thus no tree can be disturbed in the area surrounding her forest abode.

In Indic epics, temples or shrines are referred to as *devagāra* (gods' houses) and *caitya*. *Caitya* (derived from the Sanskrit root *ci*) is something built or piled up, related to *citya*, the altar or fire-altar, hence their connection to funeral mounds built in honor of teachers, heroes, or prophets, such as Buddhist and Jaina *stūpas*. The word *caitya* applies equally, however, to sacred trees (*caitya-vṛkṣa*), and it is commonly used in the epics. A large number of seals and painted pottery unearthed at Harappa and Mohenjo-daro depict the acacia (probably the *śamī*) and pipal (*aśvattha*, or *Ficus religiosa*) trees more frequently than other poorly identified species. From times immemorial these two plants have been worshiped in India because they are believed to be inhabited by celestial deities.[6] *Caityas* are the resorts of *devas, mātṛkās, yakṣas* and *yakṣiṇīs, bhūtas*, and the like, according to the epics, and not even a leaf of a *caitya* should be disturbed. Jaina and Buddhist literature abound with stories of the Yakkhacetiya as the haunt or *bhavana* of certain *yakṣa*.

For the ancient Tamils, the spirits of sacred trees were sources of *aṇaṅku*, the contagious, potentially malevolent force that resides in certain individuals (especially women and kings), trees, animals, battlegrounds, death, and sexuality. The notion of *aṇaṅku* in one sense contradicts and negates the doctrine of *karma* and its definition of causality; rather than assigning responsibility for negative individual circumstances to their actions in a previous life, the ancient Tamils believed that an external fierce energy, *aṇaṅku*, unless properly channeled, caused calamity (and if properly channeled, caused prosperity). If a tree died and decayed, stone megaliths were set up in their stead as abodes for the tree spirits so that their *aṇaṅku* could be contained. As K.V. Zvelebil explains:

> According to G. Subrahmania Pillai, there was a direct connection between ancient tree worship and this *kantu*. Sacred trees were undoubtedly worshiped in the *maṉrams* (public places). When a tree which was held sacred and which was worshiped withered and perished, the worship would continue to the stump which would remain. It is possible that the worshipers took particular care in preserving the last vestige of the tree-spirit by constructing a platform around it, covering it with a roof, and in fact, building thus a primitive shrine. These remnants of sacred trees were compared to in our textual data to the post to which the elephants were usually tied; these posts were called *kantu*, "pillar." Ancient Tamils seem to have believed that to keep and/or propitiate the spirit or the sacred force (*aṇaṅku*) dwelling in a stump of a decayed tree it was necessary to carry on the usual offerings and worship. When war came, a town or village was invaded and destroyed, and the exodus of the inhabitants

took place, there was no one to offer worship to the *kantu*, and the deities were believed to desert such a place (cf. *Puṟ.*, 52 which speaks of *kaṭavuḷ*, "deity" leaving or abandoning the *kantu*). According to G. Subrahmania Pillai, when wooden stumps, subject to decay threatened to completely disappear, stone pillars were employed in their stead and the worship was carried on. This indeed agrees well with the fact that it was thought necessary for the deity to have some object where to persist to live: it was namely the place, the spot, the locus which was primarily sacred.[7]

Koṟṟavai, Kālī, Durgā, Nirṛti, Māriyammaṉ, as well as Nut, Isis, Hathor, Astarte, Asherah, Inanna, Ishtar, Artemis, and Aphrodite were all worshiped as tree goddesses. Both Hathor and Asherah, like all ancient Near Eastern and Mediterranean tree goddesses, were defamed and crushed in the violent overthrow of goddess-based religion; Egyptian male gods (Ra, Horus, and Osiris), like *Allāh*, Yahweh, and the Jewish prophets, were the instruments of the ideological shift to the male godhead.

Hathor

In ancient Egypt, the major Creatrix deity in Egypt for over 3000 years was Hathor, who, in the form of a Cow Goddess (a human goddess with cow ears), gave birth to the solar globe and held it between her horns while swimming through the cosmic ocean. As Lady of the Sycamore Fig Tree, Hathor was "the tree goddess par excellence."[8] She lived at the end of the Earth where the sun rose each morning from her branches. According to the Egyptian *Book of the Dead*, she also sat under her tree, where she kept company with the dead, offered them food and drink, and revealed to them her powers of regeneration. The dead then prided themselves in being members of Hathor's retinue. Hathor, like Indic fierce goddesses, was also depicted as "a martial goddess with a fiery temperament."[9] Nut, Isis, and Saosis were other Egyptian tree goddesses who were ultimately eclipsed by male gods Horus and Osiris.

Asherah

Asherah ("Lady Asherah of the Sea"), one of many Canaanite fertility goddesses who was frequently represented nude and voluptuous, was also worshiped as a sylvan deity or tree goddess who ruled not only regeneration, but also war, motherhood, and sex. The Canaanite goddess of fertility, growth and renewal in the cycle of life, Asherah was widely worshiped in ancient Israel. She was often portrayed with a lion or ibex on either side of her image, which was merged with a tree trunk. Asherah was typical of the ancient sylvan goddess traditions crushed by male gods, and it may therefore be instructive to review her fate under the stern patriarchal rule of Yahweh, for parallels can be drawn with the rise of Indian patriarchy.

The *Old Testament* is the record of the conquest and massacre of indigenous goddess-worshiping people by nomadic patriarchal Hebrew tribes, followers of Yahweh. In the *Old Testament* and the Ugaritic Canaanite myths from Ras Shamra, written *c.* 1350 BCE, Asherah was represented either by a living tree or, more often, by a tree-trunk with its branches removed, standing in a socket on a stone base beside the altar of Baal.[10] This upright wooden pole, called an *asherah*, symbol of tree goddess Asherah—life and death, generation and fertility—is cognate with the archaic trans-cultural Tree of Life that appears frequently in Canaanite art, and the prototype of the Hebrew *menorah*. These shrines were set in beautifully tended sacred groves, decorated with woven hangings made by female devotees.[11] Despite the fierce warnings of Yahweh, many Jews continued to worship Ashtaroth:

> [T]hey forsook the Lord, the God of their fathers, who had brought them out of the land of Egypt; they went after other gods, from among the gods of the peoples who were round about them, and bowed themselves unto them, and provoked the Lord to anger. And they forsook the Lord, and served Ba'al and Ashtaroth.[12]

When they invaded Palestine, the Israelites discovered the establishment of numerous *asherahs*. Gideon, on Yahweh's order, fearfully and surreptitiously took ten men to pull down his own father's altar of Baal and cut down both the *asherahs* standing beside it and the entire sacred grove of trees: "so it was, because he feared his father's household and the men of the city, that he could not do it by day, that he did it by night."[13] In Mizpeh, north of Jerusalem, temples of Yahweh and Asherah stood side by side in the ninth century BCE. The powerful Jezebel and her husband, King Ahab, were devotees of the Canaanite gods, maintaining 450 prophets of Baal and 400 prophets of Asherah. It was against these priests that Elijah fought his great ritual battle on Mount Carmel. He succeeded in calling down fire from heaven when they could not, but the reaction against him was so strong that he fled for his life.[14]

In the late seventh century BCE, the prophet Jeremiah records Yahweh complaining bitterly that "the children gather wood, and the fathers kindle fire, and the women knead their dough, to make cakes for the Queen of Heaven . . . that they may provoke me to anger."[15] When Jeremiah reproached the goddess worshipers for their wickedness, they replied that they would continue to burn incense and pour libations to the Queen of Heaven, as they and their fathers had done, because to do so ensured that they had "plenty of victuals, and were well, and saw no evil."[16] Yahweh's attempts to suppress her worship, they explained, had brought nothing but disaster: "But since we left off to burn incense to the Queen of Heaven, and to pour out drink offerings unto her, we have wanted all things, and have been consumed by the sword and by the famine."[17]

The Jewish prophets condemned the worship of Asherah not only because they believed that Yahweh was the one true god, but also because of the sexual rituals of the goddess, whose cult and temples were financed by the sacred prostitutes in her service. The sexuality involved in Asherah's worship was basically imitative magic, intended to sustain the fertility of the fields by recreating the universal agricultural myth of the goddess, Mother Earth, in union with her mortal lover, who plants seeds in her furrows. Asherah is mentioned frequently and with violent disapproval in the *Old Testament*, whose prophets, to decry the licentiousness of her rites, defamed the name of *asherah* by combining it with the Hebrew word for "shame," *bosheth*, forming the negative name Ashtoreth. (Not surprisingly, the Sanskrit word *lajjā*, "shame" has also been tacked on to Earth Mother Gaurī's name. Stone and terracotta images of "Lajjā Gaurī," a goddess with a female torso and a lotus flower head, posing with legs bent up at the knees and drawn up to each side, have been found in nearly all Indian states.[18] Ashtoreth was denounced in the *Old Testament* as an "abomination" and an enemy of God, and Jews and Christians later demoted her into a male demon with very bad breath. Many other deities who were rivals of Yahweh were similarly demonized. If Ashtoreth is summoned up by a magician, he appears in human form, half black and half white, and is said to know all events of the past, present, and future.[19] This denigration of the goddess in the Judeo-Christian tradition as a demon and a source of evil indicates the extreme misogyny of the jealous war god Yahweh. Although India has no equal to the oral-aggressive Yahweh, the *Laws of Manu* promoted misogyny in a similar manner. Eventually, Asherah became one of the fallen angels in Milton's *Paradise Lost*:

> . . . Astoreth, whom the Phoenicians called Astarte,
> Queen of Heaven, with crescent horns;
> to whose bright image nightly by the moon,
> Sidonian virgins paid their vows and songs.

The Tree Cult in India

The true banyan, *Ficus indica* (*bār*), and *Ficus religiosa* (the *aśvattha*, later *pippala* [Hindi: *pīpal*]) are sacred to this day in central India, a veneration that harks back to the Indus Valley civilization. Children are taught sayings like "it is better to die a leper than pluck a leaf of a *pīpal*," and "he who can wound a *bār* will kick his little sister."[20] The deity inhabiting the tree performs the same functions as fierce goddesses, viz., protection, fertility, and victory in war. *Phallic Tree Worship* identifies the *pīpal* as the male fig tree, and the *bār* as the female tree.[21] Barren women still worship and give offerings to the *pīpal*, since it is a male tree that will provide them offspring. An *Atharvaveda* incantation indicates that the *aśvattha* tree is male: "A male has sprung from a male, the *aśvattha* (*Ficus religiosa*) from the *khadira* (*Acacia catechu*). May this slay my enemies, those whom I hate and those who hate me!"[22] In this hymn, the *aśvattha* tree is depicted as a destroyer of enemies. Sacrifices made to the *aśvattha* tree were fortified with "thought, and also with my incantation," meaning concentration and repetition of the *mantra*.

These sacrificers were warris on the eve of battle, praying to the *aśvattha* deity for victory. In later Saṁhitās, female deities, *apsarās* (fairies), as well as male *gandharvas* were said to inhabit the *aśvattha* and the *nyagrodha* (banyan) trees, in which their lutes and cymbals resounded. The tree was extremely sacred in post-Vedic literature, representing the Tree of Life (Creation) and the Tree of Knowledge (*brahma-taru*),[23] parallel to the Bo tree, the Mesopotamian Tree of Life. The *aśvattha* would have been the abode of the highest Indus deity. As the *Atharvaveda* explains, this tree is the seat of the gods and associated with sacred medicine:

> The aśvattha-tree is the seat of the gods in the third heaven from here. There the gods procured the kushtha, the visible manifestation of amrita (ambrosia). A golden ship with golden tackle moved upon the heavens. There the gods procured the kushtha, the flower of amrita (ambrosia). The paths were golden, and golden were the oars; golden were the ships, upon which they carried forth the kushtha hither (to the mountain). This person here, O kushtha, restore for me, and cure him! Render him free from sickness for me![24]

Vessels made of *aśvattha* wood are mentioned in the *Ṛgveda* and references to it proliferate later. By planting its roots in the shoots of other trees, such as the *khadira*, it destroyed them. The tree was therefore known as *vaibādha*. According to the *Atharvaveda*,[25] the *aśvattha* tree was the apparent abode of Nirṛti, and the *Mahābhārata* specifically states that Nirṛti's "abode is the sacred fig tree, the *pippala*, where, every Saturday, Lakṣmī comes to visit her."[26] Nirṛti's talismanic protective energy generated fertility and victory in war. Nirṛti was propitiated by nonelites to promote fertility and avert misery, disease, and death, and by elite warriors to bring death, destruction, and bloody defeat to the enemy. As the goddess of destruction and death, Nirṛti would have been the war goddess beseeched for victory by Aryan warriors, who were led to battle by the great Aryan *soma*-swilling war god Indra. In the following passage, Nirṛti is beseeched to "bind in the toils of death that cannot be loosened," or cause the deaths of enemies, adding "may we conquer our rivals!"

> As thou didst break forth, O asvattha, into the great flood (of the air), thus do thou break up all those whom I hate and those who hate me! Thou that goest conquering as a conquering bull, with thee here, O asvattha, may we conquer our rivals! May Nirṛti (the goddess of destruction), O asvattha, bind in the toils of death that cannot be loosened those enemies of mine whom I hate and who hate me! As thou climbest up the trees, O asvattha, and renderest them subordinate, thus do thou split in two the head of my enemy, and overcome him! They (the enemies) shall float down like a ship cut loose from its moorings! There is no returning again for those that have been driven out by the "displacer." I drive them out with my mind, drive them out with my thought, and also with my incantation. We drive them out with a branch of the asvattha-tree.[27]

The *bār* or true banyan, the female fig tree, must be worshiped with offerings by those who desire boons. Stories told of and under the sacred fig tree proliferate in all Eastern literature. "Under its holy shade, gods, goddesses, men and animals disport themselves, and talk with each other on sacred and profane themes."[28] It was under this sacred tree, inhabited by a *yakṣiṇī*, that *Śākyamuni* became a Buddha, and "it is from the rubbing together of the wood of trees, notably of the three banyan trees—*pīpal, bār,* and *gūlar* (*Ficus sycamores*), the favorite woods for phallic images, that holy fire is drawn from heaven, and before all these species do women crave their desires from God."[29] The banyan tree is "perhaps the most beautiful and surprising production of nature in the vegetable kingdom."[30] Some banyans are enormous, and they appear to be always increasing in size. Each branch issuing from the trunk throws out its own roots, which shoot out new branches that in time bend downwards, take root again, and produce other branches.

The most extensive festival of tree worship in India is the Durgāpūjā, an ancient Indian tradition that continues to this day. The festival is a celebration of the promising crops growing in the fields, and can be traced to Uṣā, dawn worship, and the solar myth. This extremely archaic festival is evidence that Durgā originated as an Earth Mother, and may hark back to Atharvavedic lore. Her annual worship in her various aspects is in autumn, marking the beginning of the harvest season in Bengal. To Bengalese nonelites, the goddess Durgā is known as the autumnal goddess, symbolizing the fertile power of the Earth and a systematic, spiritual approach to ecology. The *Navapatrikā* or *Navarātra*, a significant aspect of Durgā worship and "the most popular expression of the mother-cult in our times,"[31] crystallizes the identity of Earth Mother Durgā with fertility and vegetation among agricultural communities. In the ritual, nine leaves or plants, *rambhā, kaccvi, haridrā, jayantī, bilva, dāḍima, aśoka, mānaka,* and *dhānya,* which correspond to the collective *Navadurgā,* represent the goddesses Brahmāṇī, Kālikā, Durgā, Kārttikī, Śivā, Raktadantikā, Śokarahitā, Cāmuṇḍā, and Lakṣmī, respectively, are tied up in a bundle with an *aparājitā* creeper, washed in the river or tank, anointed with various cosmetics and aromatic drugs and oils, and placed alongside the images of the goddesses. A *mantra* is chanted asking for boons, and then each plant goddess is individually worshiped. As Dasgupta observes, "In the autumnal worship of the goddess in the form of Lakṣmī, the goddess of harvest and fortune, the . . . Navapatrikā is taken in some parts of Bengal as the best representative of the goddess and, as a matter of fact, is worshiped as the goddess."[32]

In Indian art, the motif of "Woman and Tree" reached its zenith in the Graeco-Buddhist art of Gandhāra, in which *yakṣiṇīs* were often depicted in a three-bend pose with an arm and leg wrapped around a tree, seemingly one with it. Chanda observes that the later versions of the Rāmāyaṇic legends such as those found in the Purāṇas were specially invented to explain the transformation of Durgā from vegetation spirit to war goddess.[33] The legend in which the goddess is invoked by Rāma for bringing about the death of Rāvaṇa is therefore considered the later explanation of the metamorphosis, since this legend connecting the worship of Durgā in autumn with Rāma's slaying of Rāvaṇa is unknown to the *Rāmāyaṇa* of Vālmīki.

Astral Imagery

When humans began to cultivate the Earth, Neolithic astronomers discovered that the clockwork of the celestial bodies influenced the fertility of the Earth and predicted agricultural cycles. Goddess symbology in art, ritual, and scriptures thus became intertwined with agricultural production, fertility metaphors, and the nascent science of astronomy. The religious beliefs and practices of food-gatherers evolved along with new social ideas introduced by Neolithic changes, and agricultural rituals performed in conjunction with lunar phases, solstices, equinoxes, and eclipses began to supplement hunting magic to ensure the fruitfulness of the Earth. Hermes Trismegistus' immortal axiom, "As above, so below" was the metaphysical truth underlying the science of all ancient astronomers, whose study of celestial patterns became of paramount importance to merchants, who navigated oceans and deserts by the stars; to farmers, who sowed, planted, and harvested their crops according to the equinoxes; and, most importantly, to the priests of sacred time and space, whose religious calendars and intricately symbolic fertility rituals were designed to reflect, imitate, and perpetuate the divine order above. It is thus no surprise that astral symbolism entered into Neolithic mythology.

Ko<u>rr</u>avai, Durgā, Inanna, Ishtar, and Asherah are all buffalo-sacrificing goddesses with a lion mount, a description of the zodiacal constellation Virgo the Virgin, which is immediately preceded on the zodiac by Leo the Lion. In Neolithic times, the conjunction of Taurus the Bull with the Sun at the vernal equinox marked the beginning of the year during the Age of Taurus, *c.* 4000–2000 BCE.[34] It was probably in connection with the New-Year festival or sacrifices at both equinoxes that the bull sacrifice, widely practiced in the ancient Near East (at least since the seventh millennium BCE in Çatal Höyük) and Eastern Mediterranean, was performed. Neolithic bull-slaying goddesses in one sense constitute a star map of Virgo, Leo, and the spring equinox in Taurus; that is, the virgin goddess rides amount the lion Leo and slays the astral buffalo, the Age of Taurus, on the spring equinox, hence astral imagery is recreated in myth as the buffalo-slaying goddess, who fertilizes the field with blood before sowing. When the spring equinox was in Taurus, the summer solstice was in Leo.

The Great Goddess was identified as Virgo the Virgin by many ancient cultures, depicted holding an ear of wheat or corn, the Maiden of the Harvest. The stars of Virgo were worshiped as both Persephone and Demeter, as Kybele drawn by lions, as Egyptian Isis, and later, as the medieval Virgin Mary with the child Jesus, described by Shakespeare as "Good Boy in Virgo's lap" in *Titus Andronicus*. Virgo was worshiped by the Semites as Ishtar, "the Queen of the Stars," and as the Biblical enemy of Yahweh, Ashtart or Asherah, "the Queen of Heaven," by the Phoenicians and Canaanites.[35] All of these female deities, with the exception of Christian Mary, who was never eroticized in the *Bible*, were represented in their respective mythologies as simultaneously sacred virgins and goddesses of sexual love.

Several millennia later, Mithraic art (first through fourth centuries AD) was crystallized in the Mithraic tauroctony, the iconography of Roman god Mithras in the bull-slaying pose of Koṟṟavai-Durgā. Aside from the familiar supplanting of a female deity by a male god, the most notable difference between the earlier goddess-oriented tauroctonies and that of the Roman god is that Mithras is looking away from the bull, while the goddess gazes straight ahead. In Mithraism, the bull's blood was taken up and magically treated by the Moon, and the sacrificed bovine was consecrated to Anahita, the Persian Moon goddess whom the Greeks called Artemis Tauropolos, "Bull-Slayer." The Mithraic tauroctony has been identified as astral symbolism by nineteenth century German scholar K.B. Stark and numerous contemporary scholars, including Roger Beck, S. Insler, and David Ulansey.[36] The "spring equinox is important precisely because it marks the beginning of the yearly rebirth of vegetation and agriculture," writes David Ulansey. "Thus, if the bull does represent the spring equinox, it should not surprise us to find it associated with a symbol for agricultural fertility, such as sprouting ears of grain."[37]

Parpola believes that the sacrifices to the Bull of Heaven in Mesopotamia are historically related to both the water buffalo sacrifices and their evolutes, the royal rituals of the Aśvamedha—called the bull[38] and the king[39] of sacrifice—and Puruṣamedha in India.[40] Lal[41] has discovered at Kalibangan a sacrifical pit in which bull skeletons were found, and he reports that the horse was also present in late Harappan culture. Bull-slaughter in early Vedic India, according to Parpola, originated as human and water-buffalo sacrifices mythically related to astral Varuṇa, was revalorized in the brāhmaṇas of the late Vedic period as the royal rituals of the Aśvamedha, and evolved into human and buffalo sacrifices to Durgā and other *ugra* forms of Devī in medieval Vāmācāra Śāktism.[42] In addition, *bali* (human sacrifice) in both Vedic and Śāktic ritual is mystically linked to ritual copulation. Parpola believes that the Harappans sacrificed the water-buffalo to Varuṇa, citing as important evidence the title given to the chief queen, *Mahiṣī*, literally, "water-buffalo cow."

Parpola reasons that in the Indus culture, human sacrifice was a ritual synchronized with the equinoxes, solstices, and the new and full Moon.[43] In the *Śatapatha Brāhmaṇa*, reference is made to the spreading of a garment, an upper garment, and pieces of gold over the horse during the Aśvamedha. In his analysis of this garment symbolism in the Aśvamedha, Parpola points out that the same word, *nirṇīj*, is used to describe Varuṇa's garment in the *Ṛgveda*, particularly his "fatty garment" of rainclouds. "The dark rainy season is a veritable image of chaos,"[44] concludes Parpola. The themes of death, fertility, and rebirth echo down through the thick strata of homologizations, symbolically equating astral with earthly, semen with severed head, horse with king, queen with Mother Earth, garments with rainclouds, thus depicting a cosmos in which the material mirrors the celestial. In the Vedic cult, the head offering or the dying victim chosen for human sacrifice was the substitute for the sacrificing king, as well as his astral counterpart, king Varuṇa. According to Parpola, "Varuṇa was the primeval victim, the slaughtered cosmic man or the slaughtered sky-buffalo, the thundercloud. The victim at this death fertilizes the queen, the impersonator of Goddess Earth."[45] Apparently the victim, identified with god Varuṇa, or "proto-Śiva," was bound to the *yūpa* (sacrificial stake), where he was slaughtered as he impregnated the queen.

This mythic motif of fertilization through ritual killing is cognate with the ritual mythic template of *hieros gamos* in which the sexual union of god and goddess is followed by the death and agricultural rebirth of the male. The dying and resurrected male vegetation god is common to Tammuz, Osiris, Adonis, Attis, Śiva, and Dionysus, who from very early times were worshiped in rites of sympathetic magic designed to ensure fertility, health, and abundance. The ritual drama of their death and resurrection was the magico-religious catharsis for the decay and revival of the life and fertility of the whole society, as marked by the equinoxes, solstices, and full and new Moons. Cyclical regicidal ritual dramas, later transformed into bull sacrifices, reflect a shift from human to bull sacrifice mythically expressed in the frequent inversion of the consort and the bull in Tamil and Sanskritic texts, as well as in ritual dramas of the ancient Near East and the eastern Mediterranean.

Śiva was embodied in the white bull Nandi, and Yama, the Indic Lord of Death, had a bull's head and became the Underworld judge. Dionysus also took the form of a bull; one of his earlier incarnations was another version of the Minotaur, the Cretan bull-god Zagreus, "the Goodly Bull," a son and reincarnation of Zeus. The Cretan Moon-king Minos inhabited a succession of Minotaurs (Moon-bulls), who were sacrificed as the king's surrogates. The Persian Moon-goddess Anahita, identified with Greek Artemis Tauropolos, "Bull-slayer," played the original role later usurped by Mithra, whose cult was the major competitor to Christianity from the first to the end of the fourth centuries AD.[46] When the bull's blood was taken up and magically treated by the Moon in Anahita's ceremony, the blood of the Mithraic bull was invested with the female power to give birth and produce all creatures on Earth with no assistance from a female. In honor of Kybele/Attis and Mithra, the bull was slaughtered for a baptism of blood at the Roman Taurobolium. Apis-Osiris, the Egyptian savior god Osiris in bull form, was the Moon-bull of Egypt who was slain every year in atonement for the sins of the realm. In his ritual rebirth, he emerged as the Golden Calf, Horus, born of Isis, whose image was a golden cow. In Exodus 32:4, we learn that the identical Golden Calf was worshiped by the Israelites under Aaron.

The early appearance and predominance throughout Indian history of Mahiṣamardinī statues indicate that Mithra may have derived his formulaic stance from the Indian goddess (although the direction of his head and eyes was original). The Ellora caves feature a statue of Durgā/Kālī in the Mithraic posture, holding up the nose of the sacrificial bull and preparing to slaughter it.

The Great Goddess was not only accompanied by a sacred sacrificial consort/son often portrayed as a bull, but also sometimes a divine daughter, and, as in the Paleolithic period, she was associated with the big cats. Fierce goddesses of South Asia, the Near East, and the Mediterranean/Aegean regions are particularly associated, in something of a totemic sense, with the big cats: lions were sacred to Kybele and drew her chariot in Anatolia, Sekmet in Egypt is a lioness, Korravai-Durgā-Kālī in India rides a tiger or lion, and Asherah in Phonecia and Astarte in Canaan sit astride a lion. The Mistress of the Animals is seated between leopards at Çatal Höyük, Inanna (one of whose names was *Labbatu,* "lioness") is depicted standing on two lions in Sumerian frescoes and statuary, and Rhea is often portrayed flanked by lions in Greek statuary. Of Artemis, Homer wrote:

> Zeus has made you a lion
> Among women, and given you leave to kill any at your pleasure.[47]

Beyond the astronomical implications that the goddess riding a lion mount symbolizes the constellations of Virgo and Leo, early goddesses reflected "a predatory, even bestial, side,"[48] both as huntresses and as carnivorous deities affiliated with the big cats, with a special appetite for the blood and flesh of living humans and animals. According to an Egyptian document from about 2000 BCE, Sekmet endeavored to slaughter the entire human race, but was distracted from the job when she was given 7,000 jars of beer dyed the color of blood.[49] In Ehrenreich's construction, fierce goddesses are anthropomorphized versions of the large cats, the most ferocious predator beast of the forests, with whom the hunting peoples were well acquainted. The Naga belief in a tiger soul that migrates from human to tiger body, as well as their veneration of were-tigers and were-leopards, reinforce the hypothesis of the anthropomorphous big cat goddess. Spirit possession by a large cat soul, as opposed to possession by an anthropomorphic goddess or god, may underlie the big cat iconography of the Great Goddess. According to anthropologist Julian Jacobs,

> A unifying feature of Naga cosmology is the belief in a close connection between human beings and the large cats. Naga origin myths say that the spirit, man, and the tiger were the three sons of the same woman, and it is common to find that a *genna* period for the killing of a tiger would be the same as that for a man. The most developed beliefs about were-tigers appear to be those of the Sema and Konyak Nagas. This may be because this phenomenon is a kind of possession. . . . In 1947 one Sangtam were-leopard talked about this relationship to W.G. Archer. 'My soul does not live in my body. It lives in the leopard. It is not in me now. It visits me in sleep. I meet it in dreams. Then I know what it has been doing. . . . If anything happened to my leopard in the day, my soul would come and tell me. I would get the same wounds.'[50]

Sacred Prostitutes

Because woman's body was homologized with the Earth, her fertilization by different seeds year after year became a familiar dramatic motif in agricultural rituals of the ancient world. Agricultural fertility magic, therefore, also took the form of prostitution. In the mode of imitative magic, a temple harlot became the goddess, and her anonymous partners the serial consort God.[51] In the goddess temples of Western Asia, women were required to serve as sacred prostitutes before marriage. Women were venerated as divine receptacles of agricultural magic, and to have sexual intercourse with a sacred servant of the goddess was both an initiation and an economically imperative performance of homeopathic magic intended to increase agricultural yield as well as temple revenue.

Phoenician women prostituted themselves to propitiate the goddess and win her favor, and Amorite women were required by law to "sit in fornication seven days by the gate"[52] just before they married. Temple dancers were common in temples of Isis and Osiris in Egypt and in Venus temples at Corinth in Greece, where "thousands of women used to dedicate themselves to Venus and sell their bodies for the benefit of the the temple."[53] Religious prostitution survived in Greece until the second century AD, and there was no sin attached to women who could trace long ancestries of ancestress prostitutes.[54] In Syria, at Heliopolis or Baalbec, both matrons and maidens sexually serviced strangers at the temple of Astarte. In the sanctuary of Astarte in Cyprus, maidens copulated with strangers "not as an orgy of lust, but as a solemn religious duty performed in the service of [the] Mother Goddess."[55] Every woman, high and low, in Babylon was obliged once in her life to prostitute herself at the temple of Ishtar or Astarte, dedicating her earnings to the goddess. During the Old Babylonia period (the first half of the second millennium), women in great numbers participated in the Ishtar cult, and they served alongside men in the temples as priestesses, scribes, oracles, judges, prophets, diviners, and the like. Scholars are in agreement that "the designation of those women attached to the temples of Inanna and Ishtar who celebrated the specifically sexual aspects of the goddesses as temple harlots or sacred prostitutes."[56] Known as *Ishtaritu,* or sacred women of Ishtar, the hierodules correspond to the *viṟalis-cum-devadāsīs* of south India in many respects, and may be related through their common Tamil-Dravidian blood.

The Jewish prophets condemned the worship of Asherah in large part because they were threatened by the sexual rituals of the goddess, whose cult and temples were financed by the sacred prostitutes in her service. Patrilineal societies have always abhorred prostitutes, whose multiple sexual partners make it difficult for males to determine with certainty the paternity of offspring of unmarried women with multiple partners; thus prostitutes are a threat to the patriarchy. The Emperor Constantine abolished the practice and destroyed the temple, building a Christian church in its place.

In north India, the *veśyā* or *gaṇikā* were graceful sophisticates of culture, education, and high social status:

> Ancient India contained one class of women who were not bound by the rules and restrictions which limited the freedom of the high-caste wife. These were the prostitutes (*veśyā, gaṇikā*). There were certainly many poor and cheap prostitutes, who would end their days in beggary, or as menials and work-women; but the typical prostitute of literature was beautiful, accomplished, and wealthy, enjoying a position of fame and honor comparable to that of the Aspasias and Phrynes of classical Greece. As in Greece the higher class hetaira was an educated woman. The authorities on erotics demand that, as well as in the art immediately essential to her profession, she should be thoroughly trained in 'the sixty-four arts.' These were a stock list, which included not only music, dancing and singing, but also acting, the composition of poetry, impromptu and otherwise, flower-arrangement and garland-making, the preparation of perfumes and cosmetics, cooking, dress-making and embroidery, sorcery, conjuring and sleight of hand, the composition of riddles, tongue-twisters and other puzzles, fencing with sword and staff, archery, gymnastics, carpentry and architecture, logic, chemistry and mineralogy, gardening, training fighting cocks, partridges and rams, teaching parrots and mynahs to talk, writing in cipher, languages, making artificial flowers, and clay modelling.[57]

In ancient south India, the *viṟalis-cum-devadāsīs* were accomplished poets, dancers, singers, and temple prostitutes, who had ritual sexual union with the gods in the form of priests. Temple prostitution, according to Basham, was more common in the south, where it flourished until recent times as part of the fertility cults of the early Tamils.[58] Dubianski elaborates on the fertility rites engaged in by *viṟalis*:

> Bards in ancient India were known to take part in ritual intercourse during fertility rites. Although we do not know with certainty whether the other groups of Tamil bards took part in such practices, there is certain evidence concerning *viṟalis. Viṟalis* . . . took part in fertility rites as dancing girls and singers. One can assume, though, that their functions reached farther—as was the case with the *devadāsīs*, temple dance girls of a later period, whose duty was, apart from other things, to engage in ritual intercourse with the gods (that is, with the priests who represented them). The institution of *devadāsīs* is believed to have originated from the traditional function of a *viṟali*.[59]

The degradation of sacred prostitutes in medieval times occurred after the change in the mode of production and the encroachment of male domination, the class system, and patriarchal misogyny:

> In the Middle Ages the god in his temple was treated like an earthly king; he had his wives, his ministers, and attendants, and all the paraphernalia of a court—including his attendant prostitutes. These were often the children of mothers of the same profession, born and reared in the temple precincts, but they might be daughters of ordinary citizens, given in childhood to the god as pious offerings. They attended on the god's person, danced and sang before

him, and like the servants of an earthly king, bestowed their favors on the courtiers whom he favored, in this case the male worshippers who paid their fee to the temple.[60]

The Goddess and Her Cyclical Sacrificial Consort

Great Goddess, goddess Cybele, goddess lady of Dindymus,
May all your fury be far from my house.
Incite the others, go. Drive other men mad.[61]

* * *

During the festival, the God-King united with the queen to fructify the earth, to the accompaniment of rhythmic music, prayers, lamentations, orgiastic revelry, and a prescribed ritual system which culminated in the sacrifice and resurrection of the male and the triumph of the Mother Goddess.[62]

* * *

Rituals attempt to enact and deal with the most central and basic dilemmas of human existence—continuity and stability, growth and fertility, mortality and immortality or transcendence. It is the potential of rituals to transform people and situations that lends them their power. A ritual may create a docile wife or a fierce warrior, a loving servant or an imperious tyrant. The ambiguity of ritual symbols and the invocation of supernatural powers magnifies and disguises [sic] human needs and emotions. Because rituals are performed, sometimes in terrifying circumstances, the messages they carry act at a psychobiological level that includes but exceeds the rational mind. Symbols and sacred objects are manipulated within ritual to enhance performance and to communicate ideological messages concerning the nature of the individual, society, and cosmos. Far from being an epiphenomenon of religious behavior, rituals are fundamental to human culture. They can be used to control, to subvert, to stabilize, to enhance, and to terrorize individuals and groups. The study of ritual can indeed provide a key to an understanding and interpretation of culture.[63]

Neolithic Great Goddesses of Life and Death at one time were the supreme overseers of sexuality and war; the sea, mountains, and desert; the land of the dead and the land of the heavens. In the societies they reflected, female power was derived from women's ritual orientation to plants, the Earth, and fertility, and male power was associated with hunting and warfare, the subjective masculine counterpoint of the creation of blood by female menstruation and childbirth. The personification of the processes of nature, the Neolithic planter goddesses ruled the cycles of birth, death, and resurrection of the agricultural seasons, and their sons, kings, and consorts were cyclically sacrificed to ensure the productivity of the fields.

What was the mystical rationale for these bloody rituals? Sir James Frazer observed that "in rude society human beings have been commonly killed as an agricultural ceremony to promote the fertility of the fields."[64] Frazer's evidence of the sacrifice for the crops motif is thematically replicated in a meme found worldwide, that of the slain and resurrected divinity, or creation by a violent death, termed the "immolation myth" by the Danish scholar Gudmund Hatt.[65] It is based on the radical notion that life can only be born out of another life that is sacrificed.

We know that the earliest religious texts are expressions of Neolithic beliefs, and that agricultural fertility magic to promote the crops was the basis of Neolithic and Bronze age religious rituals; therefore, because agricultural cycles were deified and sacralized, there is an inherent religious justification for blood sacrifice, including warfare, in ancient sacred texts, commensurate with Frazer's principle of sacrifice for the crops. The ruling metaphor is derived from the processes of the world of vegetative nature, in which plants die back every year in order to return in spring, and rituals simulating this ecological process are believed to stimulate fertility via homeopathic magic. In this magico-religious paradigm, death appears to bring forth life. The mythic motif of the dying male vegetation god is common to Tammuz, Osiris, Adonis, Attis, and Dionysus, who from very early times were worshiped in rites of sympathetic fertility magic designed to ensure fertility and abundance; the ritual drama of their death and resurrection was the magico-religious catharsis for the decay and revival of the life and fertility of the whole society.

The region and mythology of all these cultures represent an oral tradition linking the primal symbology of the Great Mother, the sacrifice of the male principle (the goddess's consort or the Primordial Bull), and the big cats. Kybele, Inanna, Ishtar, and Anath, like India's Koṟṟavi and Kālī, were mythically associated with the big cats, blood sacrifice (particularly buffalo and human heads), war, and victory. These associations are echoed in archaeological digs at such sites as Çatal Höyük, where a female figure interpreted as the Mistress of Wild Animals is depicted in a statuette flanked by leopards, and depictions of the now extinct aurochs bull, as well as actual bull skulls plastered over, fill the walls of densely symbolic shrines.[66]

When fierce love and war goddesses were given male consorts, the divine pair projected a Neolithic principle of agricultural fertility magic that is expressed in the ancient ritual drama that historians and anthropologists have termed *hieros gamos*, a celebration of complementarity and the union of opposites, fertility and the continuity of the female principle via the male sacrifice. In the Neolithic Near East, the *hieros gamos* fertility drama performed throughout Mesopotamia for two thousand years "focused on how to assure fertility to the land and its people."[67] As plants germinate, sprout, bloom, bear fruit, and die back to arise anew, either from seed or after dormancy, so death was judged to be a crucial element not only for the continuity of the female principle, but also as a necessary precondition for rebirth. In return for donating her fertility, therefore, the ancient cosmic Creatrix demands bloody sacrifices, primarily animals and male humans. The bull is considered a more recent substitute for the husband of the goddess incarnate, the tribal queen. In every Neolithic culture, the goddess had many lovers. When the consort's period of office expired, the priestesses sacrificed him and fertilized the agricultural fields with his blood. The *Epic of Gilgamesh* suggests that there was a religiously motivated struggle between the gods and goddesses during the second millennium BCE based on the male fear of becoming the goddess's sacrificial victim.

In sacred marriage texts covering a span of two thousand years, the venue for sexual union between Inanna and Dumazi, represented by an elite woman and the king, is the sacred storehouse.[68] The polyvalent symbolic message of the sacred marriage includes the cosmogonic union of humans (through their creation of agriculture, canal irrigation, and surplus storehouses) and gods (through their control over the Earth and her elements), a union that creates and maintains the fertility of the world. As Assyriologist/Sumerologist Tikva Frymer-Kensky asserts,

> the union takes place at the sacred storehouse, and Inanna, the goddess-partner, is not only the goddess of sexuality but also deity of the storehouse. Dumazi, her divine partner, with whom the king is identified, probably represents the living spirit within vegetation and animals. Through their union, civilized endeavor is mated to this natural regenerative ability, and their combination enables the true surplus abundance upon which urban civilization depends.[69]

The *hieros gamos* of the Great Goddess with dying and resurrected vegetation gods constitutes a trans-cultural mythic motif that permeates agricultural ceremonies of warrior societies. Kings became stewards of the state through the ritual of *hieros gamos* or sexual union with the goddess/queen, thus the sacred marriage was the goal of many kings. First enacted by Kybele and Attis in seventh millennium BCE Anatolia, *hieros gamos* ritual dramas continued through the third millennium BCE and later, performed by Inanna and Dumazi in Sumeria, Ishtar and Tammuz in Assyria, Astoreth/Anath and Baal in Canaan, and Korṟavai/Kālī and Murukaṉ/Śiva in India. Gods and the king were one, and both were subject to women's magic. Alain Daniélou[70] postulates that Śaivism emerged from an archaic religious stratum characterized by myths of *hieros gamos* featuring the Great Goddess and her sacred son/consort, the Lord of the Animals, an anthropomorphic male deity who was seasonally sacrificed and resurrected. The close archaeological and mythological correlation among these Neolithic goddesses led Narendra Nath Bhattacharyya to conclude that Śiva and Umā, originally Dravidian deities, are Indian versions of the Great Mother and her consort.[71] Likewise, Mircea Eliade suggests that the principal Near Eastern erotic mythic motifs of the sacrifice of the male were transported to the Hindu Kush:

> Toward 1500 BC the creative period of Mesopotamian thought seems definitely to have ended. During the ten following centuries, intellectual activity appears to spend itself in erudition and compilation. But the influence of Mesopotamian

culture, documented from the most ancient times, continues and increases. Ideas, beliefs, and techniques of Mesopotamian origin circulate from the western Mediterranean to the Hindu Kush. It is significant that the Babylonian discoveries that were destined to become popular imply, whether more or less directly, correspondences between heaven and earth, or macrocosm-microcosm.[72]

The original meaning of "holy matrimony" (*hieros gamos*) referred to the essential link between the position of kingship and marriage with the earthly representative of the goddess, in the form of the queen. Once every four or more years, the king was ritually sacrificed and replaced by a new consort for the goddess, the assumption being that the goddess needed a periodic and refreshing change of lovers. A surrogate victim (a condemned criminal or a divine animal) was sometimes used. The death and rebirth of the god was the magical enactment of an ecological process whose performance, through sympathetic magic, became the catharsis for the decay and revival of fertility upon which the welfare of whole societies depended for sustenance.

Since the fertility of the land was determined by the queen's sexual acceptance of the candidate king, it followed that abundant crops resulted from the queen's happiness with the king's sexual skills. If he no longer pleased her, the king could be killed, often by his successor, called a "son" though he was no blood relative. A bad crop season or a declining birth rate could be blamed on the impotency of the king, thus engendering an unscheduled regicide. The metaphysics of this conception is recorded in Proverbs: "In a multitude of people is the king's honor; but in the lack of people is the downfall of a prince."[73]

The goddess is not only divinely sexual, but she is also bloodthirsty, since blood was regarded as the fertilizer *par excellence* for the agricultural fields. In terms at once violent and romantic, Sumerian, Assyrian, Ugaritic, and Tamil myths all describe the insatiable lust of their respective war goddesses for blood and killing. Fierce goddesses routinely demanded blood sacrifices, preferably human heads and buffalo, as their payment for abundant crops and prosperity. These memes are in part a forceful reminder to humans that ecological balance (a gratified Mother Earth) is dependent on human reciprocity with the spirits of the natural world.

Archaic magico-religious ritual dramas, the progenitors of all drama, were seasonal performances of the same universal mythic themes of the challenge, trial, marriage, sacrifice, and resurrection of the sacred king, hero, or savior. A journey to the Underworld, the battlefield, or, in India and Tibet, the cremation ground, the land of Death, was a common motif of ancient and Neolithic mythology, a mythopoetic representation of at once a shamanic journey and the dormant period of the fields. The most famous of the myths of Inanna/Ishtar depict the descent of the goddess to the Underworld to reclaim the slain divine son/consort, Dumuzi/Tammuz. The sorrowing and wandering mother searching for her abducted daughter, who is condemned to pass part of the year in the Underworld, was the central mythic theme of the Demeter-Persephone legend, suggesting that the earliest form of the agricultural myth may have been an esoteric women-only ritual drama. The descent to Hell was a necessary peril in the sacred drama, lasting three days and climaxing in the Day of Joy, when the god was resurrected. After penitential atonement and sacrifice, this inaugurated a new year. In a secret chamber of the temple stands the nuptial bed of the goddess, where Ishtar and Tammuz enjoy divine sexual union on New Year's Day, when the king reenacts this mythic ritual drama with a hierodule who embodies the goddess on Earth. The consummation took place in an extravagant public ceremony and was followed by a great feast. In its innumerable enactments, the sacred marriage between a high priestess of Inanna and a "king," representing king Dumazi, who was later deified, was ritually performed as sexual intercourse between the king and the Great Goddess.[74] The practice of *satī* (suttee) is an Indian cultural idiom that is a violent patriarchal inversion of both ritual king killing and the shamanic descent of the Great Goddess to the Underworld. The myth became woven into that of Śiva's wife Satī, who immolates herself for her spouse, and her voluntary act of suicide—which parallels in cruelty the Christian witch burnings of Europe—became the mythically sanctioned fate of widows.

According to Judith Ochshorn, the primary element common to all sacred-marriage literature is "the dominance of the goddess, who selects the ruler privileged to cohabit with her, and actively and explicitly enjoys him sexually."[75] The union produces not children, but rather, fertility of the tilled soil and a bountiful harvest; the goddess's validation of the king's authority; and the goddess's pledge to lead the king's army to either victory in battle or victory in maintaining state order and the stability of the throne. Since the *hieros gamos* brings together the goddess and the king, the rite relates that goddesses mediated between the human and divine domains. Like the Old Tamil kings, the Mesopotamian and Old Babylonian kings were regarded as intermediaries or conduits between the sacred and the mundane, and their special union with the goddess was their assurance that she would satisfy their most basic needs. "Indeed, not only is Inanna/Ishtar the source of the king's power, but the personal intervention of the goddess to guarantee his success, especially in war, also guarantees the continued welfare of the community."[76]

> Thus the sacred-marriage texts rapturously portray the active sexuality of the goddess as purely good, as yielding blessings for the king and the whole community. At least with reference to divine female sexuality, it held no connotations of evil or danger to the pursuit of righteousness by men. The goddesses' sexuality was reproductive capacity. The heart of the sacred-marriage rite resided in Inanna/Ishtar's great power over fertility, war, and the destiny of peoples and cultures; in her energizing and beneficent nature of her sexuality in her aspect as goddess of love and fertility, and in the consequent good fortune for the human community which it, in turn, fervently commemorated.[77]

Later, when human sacrifice went out of vogue, surrogate-consorts in the form of animals, particularly bulls, were substituted for the king. The underlying reasoning was that blood, being the concentrated essence of life, was needed to fertilize the Earth and sustain the community. On a realistic level, the bull sacrifice was a sacralization of ritual animal slaughter and community feasts of roasted beef. On a metaphorical level, it enacted the process of agricultural renewal that permeates sympathetic magic among hunter-gatherers. In its earliest articulation, this motif originated as the goddess giving birth to a theriomorphic god in bull form.

The most evocative representation of ancient Near Eastern, eastern Mediterranean, and South Asian Neolithic religion is the so-called tauroctony, or bull-slaying scene, in which the slayer is the Great Goddess. The goddess-oriented tauroctony preceded the later masculinized Mithraic version by several millennia, and may have been a mythic motif in eighth millennium BCE Anatolian Çatal Höyük and Stone Age Magdalenian rock art. Kybele and Attis as a divine pair are one of the earliest manifestations of the long lineage of the Great Goddess, her *hieros gamos* with her serial sacrificial king, and the ritual slaying of the bull. The Great Goddess in all her manifestations became the archetypal slayer of the Primordial Bull in his various guises as the "Bull of Heaven," the "Buffalo Demon," and "the Great Ox" in the original tauroctony ritual dramas that guaranteed fertility and abundance of crops, humans, and animals. This pre-Indo-European bovine motif is expressed in the Minotaur legend attributed to Crete as well as in the mainland art and artifacts of the horse-charioteering Mycenaean aristocracy.

The annual festival of Kybele and Attis culminated with bull slaughter and baptism in the bull's blood by Kybele's male devotees, the *galli*, eunuchs who castrated themselves, emulating Attis's act of self-mutilation after going mad, just following Kybele's amorous advances. (Some theorists postulate that Attis was not interested in heterosexual activity and when it was forced on him, it drove him insane enough to castrate himself.) Human or animal sacrifice and self-mutilation have historically been an integral part of fierce goddess worship in India. These ancient agricultural theatre rituals are premised on the logic that death and destruction cause creation and life; rebirth without first dying is not possible; thus blood sacrifice (including warfare) as an offering to Earth Mother is reborn as a bountiful agricultural harvest. Sacrifice and warfare therefore are sanctified and sacralized, the precious gift to the goddess.

Among a plethora of ancient Dravidian traditions in India were twin ritual myths involving sexual union, blood sacrifice, and resurrection: in the earliest version, male/female, spirit/matter complementarity was symbolized by *hieros gamos* between Dravidian Murukaṉ and Vaḷḷi, culminating in the cyclical sacrifice of the Buffalo Demon, whose identity is conflated with Koṟṟavai's consort or a surrogate male. The myth of the fierce goddess slaying the Primordial Bull originated as a south Indian Tamil tradition with analogues everywhere in the ancient Near East and the eastern Mediterranean region, an area that may comprise the original homeland of Tamil Palaeo-Mediterranean Dravidian progenitors.

Like the *hieros gamos* and cyclical sacrifice of the Near East, Indian fertility rites of both tribal and class societies centered on ritual coitus often accompanied by head offerings or human or animal sacrifice. The *Ṛgveda*[78] emphasizes that seasonal sacrificial slaughter is to be done with a knife, which corresponds with the bloody sacrifices to the *ugra* forms of Devī, in which the victims are decapitated with a sword or axe. In Vedic seasonal *hieros gamos* sacrifices, the queen often took the role of Earth Mother, and copulated with one of the priests, who was killed afterwards. Vedic *bali* (animal and human sacrifices) frequently included ritual copulation, real or simulated, between the queen or the sacrificer's wife, enacting the archaic role of the Earth Mother Goddess, and the sacrificial victim. The *Śatapatha Brāhmaṇa*[79] contains numerous passages that identify sexual union with sacrifice, and a hymn in the *White Yajurveda* (*Vājasaneyi Saṁhitā*)[80] clearly depicts the promotion of agricultural production through ritual copulation and human sacrifice. The legend details a primitive agricultural rite revalorized into a royal drama in which the queen (*vāvātā*) had sexual union with the priest (*udgātā*), who was killed after he ejaculated. A number of observers participated in the rite. In all the verses, Bhattacharyya emphasizes,

> sexual union is brought in relation to agricultural operations. Originally this ritual was a part of the Aśvamedha sacrifice in which the priest had to die after his ceremonial intercourse with the queen. Later on, beasts like the horses were supplied as substitutes for men in such rituals, and the sexual scene used to be mimed.[81]

The motif of Ko<u>rr</u>avai's ritual slaying of the buffalo demon is probably first represented on seals of the Indus Civilization, symbolizing the quintessence of the pan-Indian, particularly the Dravidian cult of the goddess known as Ko<u>rr</u>avai, Devī, Kālī, Durgā, Māriyamma<u>n</u>, Bhagavatī, and Yellammā. When Ko<u>rr</u>avai and Kālī-Durgā coalesced in the pan-Indian pantheon, they were linked with Śiva, and hence they acquired Śaivite attributes. The Indic fierce buffalo-demon slaying goddess, Mahiṣa-mardinī, makes her literary debut as an amalgamation of Dravidian Ko<u>rr</u>avai and brāhmaṇical Durgā-Caṇḍī-Kālī in the *Mārkaṇḍeya Purāṇa*, written down by brāhmaṇical authors between the third and sixth centuries AD. The buffalo figure was probably the goddess's male consort who was cyclically sacrificed in a fertility ritual. In the Purāṇas, the brāhmaṇas transformed the buffalo into their own enemy by identifying him as a demon (*asura*).

THE DEMISE OF SHAMANISM, THE RISE OF THE MILITARY, THE WAR GODDESS, AND THE LAW

> Proud Queen of the Earth Gods, Supreme among the Heaven gods,
> Loud Thundering Storm, you pour your rain over all the lands and all the people.

You make the heavens tremble and the earth quake.
Great Priestess, who can soothe your troubled heart?
You flash like lightning over the highlands; you throw your firebrands across the earth.
Your deafening command, whistling like the South Wind, splits apart great mountains.
You trample the disobedient like a wild bull; heaven and earth tremble.
Holy Priestess, who can soothe your troubled heart?
Your frightful cry descending from the heavens devours its victims.
Your quivering hand causes the midday heat to hover over the sea.
Your night time stalking of the heavens chills the land with its dark breeze.
Holy Inanna, the riverbanks overflow with the flood-waves of your heart. . . .[82]

* * *

She binds the heads to her back, fastens the hands in her girdle, she plunges knee-deep in knights' blood, hip-deep in the gore of heroes. . . . Now Anath goes to her house, the goddess proceeds to her palace. Not sated with battling in the plain, with her fighting between the two towns, she pictures the chairs as heroes, pretending a table is warriors, and that the footstools are troops. Much battle she does and beholds, her fighting Anath contemplates: Her liver swells with laughter, her heart fills up with joy, Anath's liver exults; for she plunges knee-deep in knights' blood, hip-deep in the gore of heroes. Then, sated with battling in the house, fighting between the two tables. . . . She washes her hands of knights' blood, her fingers of the gore of heroes. [Chairs turn back] to chairs, table also to table; footstools turn back into footstools.[83]

* * *

[T]hey forsook the Lord, the God of their fathers, who had brought them out of the land of Egypt; they went after other gods, from among the gods of the peoples who were round about them, and bowed themselves unto them, and provoked the Lord to anger. And they forsook the Lord, and served Baal and Ashtaroth.[84]

* * *

If a woman speaks out against her man,
her mouth shall be crushed with a hot brick.[85]

—First Mesopotamian written law code, *c.* 2350 BCE

Before any of the organized religions developed, folk religions and their culture of shamanic healing were the earliest forms of medicine—and the only recourse if one fell ill. Folk religions, as Daniel Dennett observes, "provided the cultural environment from which organized religions could emerge."[86] As shamanism began to die out, the folk templates of shamanic trance, divine possession, and magic passed from shaman to priest. Shamans and folk religions deified and interpenetrated the forces of nature, while priests and organized religions abstracted the sacred from nature and separated the spiritual from everyday life.

The erosion of the fierce goddess link with shamanism and its medical healing aspect was caused in part by the invention of written language, which led to the formalization in doctrinal texts and sacred myths of two of the central traits of shamanism: spirit possession by a tutelary deity and the journey to the Land of the Dead—located in the sky, the cremation ground, the Underworld, or on the battlefield. As we have seen, a prominent motif in many early Neolithic myths, and echoed in rock art and statues, is the archetypal shamanic descent of the Great Goddess, the supreme arbiter of Life and Death, to the Land of the Dead (Ereshkigal in Sumerian mythology was the Mother-goddess of the Underworld; Greek Demeter seeks her daughter in the Underworld; both Ishtar and Inanna command earthly armies and make subterranean journeys in pursuit of their lover/son; Kālī and her *avatāras* trek to cemeteries and battlegrounds).

Spirit possession, once institutionalized in formal religion, morphed into an internal process in which elite or Sanskritic gods and goddesses are localized in the guru or in the subtle anatomy of the individual worshiper. (Fierce non-Sanskritic goddesses continued to possess worthy vehicles in subaltern rituals.) The soul journey of the "shamanic religious virtuoso who goes through the experience of death, journeys to the land of the dead, survives physical destruction of body, and returns to life triumphant over death and with special powers"[87] is evoked through recitation and visualization in an institutional religious context. Ceremonies that were once shamanistic began to be expressed in text-based religious contexts not related to curing.

In third and second millennia BCE Mesopotamia, men herded horses and drove horse-drawn chariots of wood and bronze for transport as well as for warfare. The chariot, symbolic of the culture of the first early river civilizations in the ancient Near East, connotes an expansive, exuberant phase of virility, machoism, and predatory violence. In the second millennium BCE, the widespread migrations of charioteering peoples may have played a role in the fall of the Indus civilization. Aryans had the advantage over aboriginals in war because of their horse-drawn chariots, which were flanked by an equal number of foot soldiers. During King Solomon's reign over Israel (970–931 BCE), chariots and horses were imported from Egypt and exported to Asia Minor.

Males with weapons shifted from the hunt to war as livelihoods; their weapons became more deadly. As both predator and protector, the Mistress of the Animals of the hunter was militarized with the rise of military states (although she had always carried weapons), morphing into the soldiers' guardian goddess, a goddess of war. The shift from hunting to war was depicted, in both religious iconography and epico-Purāṇic texts composed by brāhmaṇa, as an overlay of soldier imagery over huntress imagery: wild animals, especially the bull and big cat, are found in texts and art depicted alongside a heavily armed goddess in a victory pose. At the same time, brāhmaṇas domesticated and demoted fertility goddesses into subordinate wives, creating mythic modeling of the incipient degradation of women on the ground. In north India, the brāhmaṇas' monopoly over sacrifices and communication with the gods enabled them to control the common people and women, thus serving the property interests of male elites, the tiny minority who would subjugate the Indian majority and all Indian women.

When Neolithic god-kings ruled lands, female deities continued to be homologized with wild animals, as in the Paleolithic period; thus goddesses remained shamanic at their core. With the advent of irrigated farming in what historians call ancient Western Asia (modern-day Cyprus, Syria, Lebanon, Israel, Jordan, Turkey, South-Western Russia, Iraq, and Iran), the shamanic goddess was not only the mother of wild game, but also of agriculture. Female social and ritual authority shifted from the communal hunt to plant domestication. Human maternity was equated with fertility of the soil, and the female principle (the reproductive and productive functions of women) became deified as the origin of plant, animal, and human life. The Great Planter Goddess retained her immemorial hunter traits, which were "altered, revalorized, camouflaged"[88] versions of her archaic roles as the huntress of the mountains and valleys, the spirit of the fig tree and the vine, the Gaian earth-snake, and the cow goddess of grassy steppes, attended by demonesses, nymphs, and fairies. She also retained her totemic association with her bull and big cat forms when she morphed into the seasonal fertility goddess.

Hunter-gatherer societies depend on woman not only for pragmatic reasons of safety and survival, but also because woman as Creatrix is enshrined as a cultural idiom that is not so much an infinite mother as she is an ironic deity of birth, death, and regeneration. During the Neolithic, the veneration of the goddess begins with women's horticulture as the economic basis of egalitarian societies, and usually ends with the ox-drawn patriarchal plow, advanced agriculture, slaves or serfs, and private property. As societies became more agrarian and agricultural labor ceased to be the exclusive domain of women, their social prominence declined, and women came to be viewed as cumbersome chattel whose value rested solely on their procreative functions as the perpetuators of the patriliny.

In this and all other contexts in which patriarchal religious traditions have supplanted indigenous magico-religious traditions, the common denominator is always language, with all its nuances, denotations, and connotations. A competitive, male-supremacist worldview is constructed by framing sacred texts in violent binary opposites that amount to mythic demonizations of the Other. The ethical tenets of a highly polarized warrior society are justified, channeled, and mediated by their mythology and dominant ideology. The slave/war/agricultural economies ruled by kings and warriors were mirrored in the archaic Manichaean cosmologies of the dominant religions, such as India's *Ṛgveda* and Persia's Pahlavi *Bundahisn.* As Sumer's *Epic of Gilgamesh* makes manifest:

> It was the competitive drive for superiority and preeminence, for victory, prestige, and glory, that provided the psychological motivation sparking the material and cultural advances for which the Sumerians are justifiably noted: large-scale irrigation, technological invention, monumental architecture, writing, education, and literature.[89]

The rise of Sumer, however, contained the seed of its own destruction. Aggressive, competitive, war-driven Sumer gradually became a "sick society" of perpetual warfare that was filled with deep psychological contradictions: "It yearned for peace and was constantly at war; it professed such ideals as justice, equity, and compassion, but abounded in injustice, inequality, and oppression; materialistic and short-sighted, it unbalanced the ecology essential to its economy; it was afflicted by a generation gap between parents and children, and between teachers and students."[90] The social order and family structure broke down completely; cities, residences, stalls and sheepfolds were destroyed; the once magnificent and fertile land became a lawless, desolate, ravaged desert where only weeds and "wailing plants" would grow; and its people died of famine or slaughter. The "mystery religions" that originated in Babylon were subsequently transported to Pergamos under the Persians and later to Rome, where they formed the basis of pagan religion.

In Hammurabi's Babylonia, slavery was a legal institution, and the "temples, palaces, and rich estates owned slaves and exploited them for their own benefit."[91] The majority of slaves were prisoners of war. A man could enslave his entire family to a creditor to pay off his debt (but for no more than three years), or he could sell his children as slaves. Slavery was sometimes the punishment doled out to freemen for legal offenses.

> The slave was the property of his master. He could be branded and flogged, and was severely punished if he attempted to escape. He did have certain legal rights, however: he could engage in business, borrow money, and buy his freedom. If a slave, male or female, married a free person, the children were free. The sale price of slaves varied with the market and the quality of the individual for sale. The average price for a grown man was ten shekels, which at times was less than the price of an ass.[92]

Later, in Manu's India, the situation was worse, because slaves could not purchase their bond and the slavemaster had no obligation to house, feed, or clothe his slaves; on the contrary, elites kept low-caste people out of sight and rural in order to avoid contact with their innate pollution. The conditions of low caste and untouchability were biologically inherited, irrevocable economic states caused by one's *karma*, whereas Sumerian slaves were either war booty or the last resort of a debtor. Slaves can be freed, but sacred texts ordain that low castes are condemned to ironclad hereditary poverty from which they and their offspring are freed by death alone. The promise of a higher birth in the next incarnation is of course contingent upon one's adherence to caste laws (*dharma*).

Militarism in the Indian state accompanied the expansion of the brāhmaṇas and kings as they consolidated land and elite hierarchical power, thus strengthening the patriarchy. The rise of the military state was underpinned by a competitive, male supremacist worldview that manifested in a dominator hierarchy and harsh legal oppression of women and the dispossessed. In the emerging urban militaristic societies of ancient Asia, repressive legal codes such as the Code of Hammurabi, the Assyrian Code, the Talmud, and the later *Manusmṛti* lowered women's status and made them and their children male chattel. The attitude of male supremacy was reflected and articulated in the Hindu pantheon: gods supplanted goddesses, most of whom they domesticated and demoted to wife-goddesses and consorts. The Great Goddess, the ambivalent giver of life and death, however, remained fierce, autonomous, unwed—and became militarized. With the disappearance of the gender parity and egalitarianism of small-scale indigenous peoples, the more sexually egalitarian symbols associated with goddess fertility ultimately were overburdened by symbols that sacralized the male hierarchy and warfare. Goddesses of Life and Death such as Inanna (Mesopotamia), Ishtar (Babylonia), Asherah (Canaan), Anath (the Levant), and Ko<u>rr</u>avai (south India) became fierce goddesses of victory in Neolithic warrior societies.

In addition to their common function as catalysts of agricultural fertility magic in *hieros gamos* rituals, all cultural incarnations of fierce goddesses are mythically located well outside the sequestered domestic sphere to which women were bound in the stringent patriarchies of the ancient Near East and South Asia: Kybele wanders in the mountains with her wild devotees, Ko<u>rr</u>avai/Kālī and Inanna/Ishtar are battle queens presiding over male warfare, and Kaṇṇaki has unjustly been made a widow, the most accursed role of the Indian woman. These goddesses, like their male followers, transgress patriarchal roles and structures: Kybele enrages her father by begetting a child out of wedlock, while Ishtar and Ko<u>rr</u>avai/Kālī are notoriously promiscuous and never marry, and Kaṇṇaki retaliates against the patriarchal system by burning down the city of Madurai. The Kaṇṇaki cult was eventually absorbed by the Kālī or Bhagavatī cult. Often more destructive than beneficent, such goddesses are sophisticated ironic deities that function as both the secret weapon of male warriors and the revolutionary mirror image of the patriarchal state.

Inanna

The Sumerians, a militarized urban society, revered the female principle embodied in their fertility and war goddesses, Inanna and Ishtar, while women on the ground became disempowered and subordinated to men. Inanna, the Great Goddess of the ancient Sumerian civilization beginning in the fifth millennium BCE, is the marginalized model of an "undomesticated woman," an undesirable social role that women were not encouraged to emulate. Although married to Dumuzi, Inanna, contrary to normal Sumerian wives, is attached to neither children nor household economic functions. She is, above all, independent, and as such, "she has no true niche in society," which "makes her, despite her prominence, an essentially marginal figure,"[93] according to Tikva Frymer-Kensky. Exemplifying "all the fear and attraction that such a woman elicits," Inanna is "the exception to the rule, the woman who does not behave in societally approved ways, the goddess who models the crossing of gender lines and the danger that this presents."[94]

Glorified for her bloodthirstiness and militarism, Inanna makes Heaven and Earth tremble with fear. As the goddess of war and strife, she held the title Nin-kur-ra-igi-ga, "the queen who eyes the highland," meaning that other lands feared her warlike nature. The symbol of Inanna was a double axe (*labrys*), "probably representing the ax with which sacrificial animals were killed."[95] The "dance of Inanna" was the epithet for battle, and, as the star of war, she could whip up warlike feuds between the most loving of brothers, making them fight to the death. Inanna is known for causing the fall of the city of Agade (Akkad):

> The gates of Agade, how they lay prostrate; . . . the holy
> Inanna leaves untouched their gifts;
> The Ulmas (Inanna's temple) is fear ridden (since) she has
> gone from the city, left it;
> Like a maid who forsakes her chamber, the holy Inanna has
> forsaken her Agade shrine;
> Like a warrior with raised weapons she attacked the city in
> fierce battle, made it turn its breast to the enemy.[96]

Ishtar

Since the Indus script has not yet been deciphered, we have no literary evidence from the Indus Valley civilization that would explicate protohistoric Indian female deities or the shift from hunting to warfare as the most "masculine" male vocation. We can look for clues to the cataclysmic event that ushered in patriarchalism, however, in the *Epic of Gilgamesh*, which dates from the beginning of 2000 BCE, coeval with the Indus culture.

One of the oldest and most widely known literary works of ancient Mesopotamia, the epic documents the events that led to the decline and fall of Sumer within the larger story of the death of goddess worship in that era. The epic comes down to us in the Akkadian language of Sumeria's Babylonian conquerors, a testament to the significance of the earliest vilification of Indo-European goddesses to subsequent cultures and eras. The epic suggests a conflict during the Old Babylonian Empire (*c*. 1760 BCE) between elite male warriors of Sumeria and the Great Goddess Ishtar, the most powerful goddess of Mesopotamia, patroness of sexuality and war, who also rode a lion. Gilgamesh's demonization of Ishtar and his refusal of her advances point to his fear of becoming yet another of her cyclical sacrificial kings. This "ongoing eclipse and the marginalization of the goddesses" was underway when the first epics were put to writing. War is the consistent theme of the first written human records; in the ancient Near East and South Asia, Earth Mother, militarized, assumes her role as the giver of death on the battlefield. "This process did not suddenly begin in the Old Babylonian period, nor should it be attributed to the influx of new peoples. On the contrary, this process seems already under way as soon as a written record becomes available,"[97] according to Tikva Frymer-Kensky.

> Goddesses are present and active in Sumerian mythology. Later during the second millennium, information about the goddesses is much harder to glean from the texts. The myths record the exploits and relationship of male gods, and the goddesses have been marginalized. The religion of Israel's contemporaries was not one in which gods and goddesses had equal roles and import. There was no longer possible a choice between monotheism and the goddesses, but rather one between monotheism and a male-dominated polytheism.[98]

Gilgamesh, king of Uruk, two-thirds god (he was born of a goddess) and one-third man, was known as the Wild Ox. As the epic goes, Gilgamesh, "who knew the way things were before the Flood, the secret things, the mystery"[99] went on a journey to the end of the Earth, returned, and wrote the story on a stone tablet. He built Uruk and the shrine of Anu and Ishtar, a magnificent sanctuary whose "outer wall shines in the sun like brightest copper; the inner wall is beyond the imagining of kings."[100] Each of the city-states of Sumer was dominated by a many-storied temple, or *ziggurat,* constructed "to house a tutelary deity under whose auspices the city was thought to live out its destiny and to prosper."[101]

It is clear from the epic that the Sumerian people invoked goddesses in the second millennium BCE for aid in times of civic strife. When the people of Uruk, whom Gilgamesh has been terrorizing, ask the goddess Aruru to create Gilgamesh's *doppelgänger* to occupy him, Aruru compassionately complies with the peoples' request and creates Enkidu out of "earth clay and divine spittle" to tame and subdue Gilgamesh. Half-human, half-beast, Enkidu is a primordial hunter, "the hairy-bodied wild man of the grasslands, powerful as Ninurta the god of war,"[102] who feeds with gazelles and visits the watering places of wild beasts. Enkidu is the wild obverse of civilized Gilgamesh, builder of cities.

This epic depicts Ishtar as a fierce goddess who is intimately connected to temple prostitutes, revealing her archaic role as fertility goddess. The character of the temple prostitute is an interesting study of second millennium attitudes about sacred harlots. Today the words "harlot" and "prostitute" are negatively charged, but during their time, these ancient prostitutes were viewed as a positive cultural force of fertility and prosperity. Yahweh, it must be remembered, equated the worst of all sins with female sexuality.[103] After the harlot sexually initiates Enkidu, the wild animals now flee from him because he has cast off his innocence. In the company of the prostitute, Enkidu goes to Uruk, where they are met with processions, music, and dancing outside Gilgamesh's palace hall. Enkidu was made wise and fully human by the harlot, his gentle teacher who instructs him in human behavior and dress, and makes him long for human companionship. Like the active sexuality of Inanna/ Ishtar in the sacred-marriage rites, the sexuality of the harlot results in good luck for the community and the king. This theme is echoed in Naga agricultural rituals and in Tantric rituals and cosmology.

Gilgamesh is contemptuous of the Great Goddess Ishtar in the epic, making her appear "sexually promiscuous and predatory."[104] Ishtar propositions Gilgamesh and offers to him, in exchange for sexual favors, "riches beyond the telling: a chariot of lapis lazuli and brass and ivory, with golden wheels, and pulled, instead of mules, by storm beasts harnessed," a house with cedar floors and doorpost, the "best of the yield of orchard, garden, and field,"[105] as well as goats, ewes, chariot steeds, and oxen beyond compare. Gilgamesh rebuffs and insults Ishtar ("You are the fire that goes out. You are the pitch/ that sticks to the hands of the one who carries the bucket"), recounting her male "lovers and bridegrooms" whom Ishtar, with her Circe-like[106] power, metamorphoses into a bird, lion, and goatherd. When her father's gardener rejected her, "Some say the goddess turned him into a frog/among the reeds, with haunted frog voice chanting,/beseeching what he no longer knows he longs for;/some say into a mole whose blind foot pushes/over and over again against the loam/in the dark of the tunnel, baffled and silent, forever," said Gilgamesh to Ishtar, "and you would do with me as you did with them."[107]

Ishtar, enraged, went to her father Anu in heaven and demanded a predator beast, "the Bull of Heaven,"[108] the vehicle of Śiva and always the victim of choice for blood sacrifice, with which to kill Gilgamesh and destroy his city, Uruk. She demonstrates her vast power when she threatens to release the dead from the Netherworld if she does not get her way, so that "the hungry dead will come out to eat the living."[109] She emphasizes her role as fertility goddess by stocking up grain for the people: "I have garnered grasses and grain to help sustain the people/during the time of seven years of husks."[110] However, Gilgamesh and Enkidu wrestle and kill the bull instead. In response, Ishtar went to her temple and ritually mourned over the haunch of the Bull with the temple prostitutes and her votaries.

Ishtar takes moral responsibility for the flood, which she caused equally with Enlil. When Utnapishtim, the Sumerian Noah, offers sacrifices to the deities when the flood is over, Ishtar laments the dire effects on "all my children," the humans, plants, and animals of Earth, and forbids Enlil, due to his destructiveness, from partaking of the sacrifice.[111] This is a clear statement of Ishtar's role as Earth Mother. Gilgamesh's judgmental refusal of Ishtar's offer of marriage, and his fear of becoming another of her ill-fated lovers, is literary evidence of the decline of the Great Goddess and the rise of male dominion over women and nature.

Anath

In the myths that are preserved from Canaan from around 1350 BCE, we see the interplay of economics and religion at work in the precarious environment of the Fertile Crescent, where survival of the people depended on their ability to preserve and enhance the agricultural fertility of the land. This religion controlled and eroticized their deities in the economic interests of humans, mirroring the agricultural, warfare, and hunting interests of the elites of the high civilizations of the third and second millennia.

Anath, the daughter of Asherah and the sister and wife of Baal, was one of the Great Goddesses of the ancient Levant (present-day Israel, Jordan, and Syria), as well as a Canaanite, Amorite, Egyptian, and Cyprian war goddess. Invoked as the "Queen of Heaven," Anath was long worshiped by the Israelites, who burnt incense for her.[112] According to Cyprian inscriptions, Anath was identified with war goddess Athene in Greece, and with Inanna (Sumeria), Ishtar (Babylonia-Assyria), Astoreth (Cyprus), and Anahita (Persia). Her extreme antiquity is reflected in her bloodthirsty enjoyment of not only warfare, but also its historical antecedent, hunting. When she asked a young prince to give her his bow, he insulted her by saying, "Bows are for men! Do women ever hunt?"[113] Naturally, Anath had him exterminated for his impertinence.

The role of Anath as Mistress of the Animals exists side by side with her sexual and reproductive functions, rendering her the archetype of the aggressive, bloodthirsty, victorious warrior, on the one hand, and the symbol of love, sex, and fertility, on the other. In her role as Mistress of the Animals, the goddess provided game for the all-male hunting band prior to their becoming full-fledged warriors, thus when she dons the accouterments of a soldier, she continues to be the guardian of male hunter-protectors. Eliade has pointed out that the magico-religious experience of the shaman, who collects guardian spirits from their dwelling places in wild animals, rocks, plants, and water, extends to the realm of warriors, who have guardian spirits in their armor, their drums, and wild beasts (the "Bull of Heaven").[114] Heesterman has pointed out that ancient shamanic priests doubled as warriors. Hence we find warrior-priests dominating the entire history, and a good part of prehistory, of the world's great civilizations.

Anath, like other classic fierce goddesses, is associated in an intimate way with the buffalo. Although she is often called "virgin" Anath, a fragmentary Ugaritic text relates that she gave birth to a bull calf that is the son of Baal,[115] and her bovine identification seems to fortify her control of the animal world. Anath's primitive sacrificial rites were described in raw, gory detail in the Ras Shamra texts, where we learn that she is fertilized not by men's semen, but rather, by their blood. Anath's image was reddened with "rouge and henna"[116] on the occasions when hecatombs of men appeared to have been sacrificed to her; according to myth, she castrated her enemies and hung their shorn penises on her goatskin apron, or aegis.[117] When Baal was beset by his enemies, Anath came to his aid; however, rather than limiting her slaughter to demons, she went on a drunken rampage against mankind, from the rising of the sun to the shore of the sea. In the end, Baal was forced to intervene in order to stop the goddess from annihilating the human race.

Her role as a war goddess is depicted in the myth as follows: "She locked the gates of her [Anath's] house and met the picked fighter in [. . .]. Now Anath doth battle in the plain fighting between the two towns; smiting the Westland's peoples, smashing the folk of the Sunrise. Under her are heads like sheaves; over her, hands like locusts."[118] J.B. Lloyd[119] interprets Anath's violence as the depiction of the ritual execution in ancient warrior cults of prisoners-of-war.

Law Codes

The high status of Inanna, Ishtar, and Anath in the pantheon was inverted in repressive, misogynistic law codes that demeaned and disempowered the muted majority. Like Indian women, ancient Mesopotamian women hardly enjoyed the prominence of their goddess in secular reality. "The existence and power of a goddess, particularly of Ishtar," according to Tikva Frymer-Kensky, "is no indication or guarantee of a high status for human women."[120] The overt discrimination against women is evident in the earliest Mesopotamian law code (2350 BCE) attributed to King Urokagina of Lagash, which begins with a prohibition against polyandry. "The women of the former days used to take two husbands, but the women of today (if they attempt to do this) must be stoned."[121] The later Mesopotamian Code of Hammurabi (eighteenth century BCE) dedicated the majority of its laws to marriage and family. Mesopotamia was a patriarchal society in which women possessed far fewer privileges and rights in marriage than their husbands. "The woman in Sumer had certain important legal rights: she could hold property, engage in business, and qualify as a witness," according to Samuel N. Kraemer, "But the husband could divorce her on relatively light grounds; and if she had borne him no children, he could take a second wife."[122]

The family was the basic unit of Sumerian society, and the family's wealth was administered by the husband/father. A woman's sexuality was the exclusive possession of her husband, and any interference had to be punished like any other serious theft. A wife caught in the act of adultery was tied to her lover and both of them were thrown into the water and drowned. A husband was allowed to save his wife, but if he did, he had to also save her lover. (129)

Marriage, at least in theory, was arranged by the fathers or brothers of the bride, and the preeminent item negotiated was the size of the bride price. In preliterate societies, bride price compensated the bride's family for the loss of her labor. The bride price almost always became part of the dowry in Babylonia. While a husband had to repay the dowry if he divorced his wife because she was not able to bear children, he did not have to repay the dowry if he divorced her because she tried to leave the home to engage in business. The bride price from a family of high social status could represent a considerable transfer of property and wealth (a house and several acres of land), while a few kitchen utensils might constitute the bride price from a family low on the economic ladder. Since it was designed for the support of the wife and her children, the bride price had to be kept separate, but it became part of the new household's assets.(151–52)

Since woman's place was in the home, failure to fulfill her duties was grounds for her husband to divorce her. However, a husband could drown his wife if she was a "gadabout" who humiliated him and neglected her home. A wife caught committing adultery was summarily pitched into the river. If someone other than her husband accused a woman of adultery, she was forced to swear her innocence before the gods and then jump into the river. If she was guilty, she drowned; if the river spirits verified her virtue, she survived. (131–32) Survival was not common, however, since few women in Babylonia knew how to swim.

Fathers ruled their children as well as their wives, and absolute obedience was expected from both. A son who struck his father was punished by cutting off his hand. The daughter might be dedicated by her father to the service of some god as a vestal or a hierodule, or given as a concubine. Such matters were often decided in her childhood, and she had no choice but to obey. However, if she wished to become a votary, perhaps to escape an unwanted marriage, her father had to agree. Only sons normally inherited the father's property; daughters did not usually inherit anything from their father's estate. Instead, they received a dowry intended to give the bride as much economic security as her family could afford. A man could divorce his wife without stipulating a reason, but if she had borne him children, she got the dowry and the children, as well as the use of a field or property so she could raise her children. She received a portion of her ex-husband's estate when he died that was equal to that given to each of her sons, and she was free to marry someone else. (137) If a wife had borne no children, she could be divorced by merely refunding her dowry along with a sum equal to the purchase price, or one mina of gold (a sum that would take a shepherd about six years to earn). (137–40)

If the woman rather than the man wanted the divorce, or if the husband wanted to avoid returning the dowry, the matter had to be taken to the courts. If the wife could prove her innocence and her husband's neglect, she could take her dowry and children and return to her father's house. "If it were established, however, that she was to blame and had neglected her house and husband, then he sent her away without dowry or children; if he wished, he could opt to keep her as a servant. In serious cases the court might rule that she should be thrown in the water and drowned."[123] (141–43)

A barren wife could give her maidservant to her husband, and if the maidservant produced a baby it was regarded as the wife's child. If neither wife nor maidservant bore a child, a man could marry a second wife, who was not permitted to be equal in status to the first wife. If sons by a slave or concubine were acknowledged by the father during his life, they shared equally in his estate. If he had not acknowledged them they had no right to inherit, but the slave or concubine and her children were freed on his death. (170–71) He was required to look after his first wife for as long as she lives, but if she acquired a long-term illness he could take a second wife. (144–49)

Women in ancient Assyria, according to the Middle Assyrian laws of ancient Israel, fared no better than Sumerian women, and their goddess Ishtar, "the female with the fundamental attributes of manhood, does not enable women to transcend their femaleness."[124] Married women had no rights to their husband's property (even to movable goods), they could be struck or mutilated by their husbands, and they were required to wear veils. Frymer-Kensky observes that Ishtar,

> in her being and her cult (where she changes men into women and women into men), . . . provides an outlet for strong feelings about gender, but in the final analysis, she is the supporter and maintainer of the gender order. The world by the end of the second millennium was a male's world, above and below; and the ancient goddesses have all but disappeared.[125]

Parents in ancient Israel arranged their daughters' marriages, and the groom's family gave an appropriate gift in exchange for the bride. The woman moved to her husband's home, but still retained a kinship relationship with her birth family. Although the husband was obligated to support his wife, she could keep her own property. However, since a married couple was an economic partnership, the wife would be sold into slavery along with him if the man became bankrupt and unable to pay his debts. As in Babylon, a childless wife in a well-to-do family with slaves could give her personal slave to her husband. Any child that resulted would give the wife as much status as actually giving birth herself.

The Indus Valley Civilization

The über-narrative of Kālī and her *avatāras* may begin millennia before the emergence of the Indus Valley civilization, in the ruins of a Neolithic culture submerged off the coast of Gujarat province such as legendary Dvāraka in the coastal waters of Dwaraka in Gujarat,[126] or in the ruins discovered forty metres deep in the seabed of the Gulf of Cambay (also known as the Gulf of Khambat).[127] Many of the finds recovered from the area have been radiocarbon dated to 7500 BCE. Under excavation now, the sunken cities remain mysterious, although they are a rich source of speculation. Until these marine archaeology sites are excavated and understood, the Indus Valley civilization bears the first recorded imprint of Indic fierce goddesses in the Chalcolithic age.

In the late fourth and third millennia BCE, three resplendent centers of high civilization and urban cultured life arose around the large alluvial systems of the Tigris-Euphrates, Nile, and Indus rivers: Mesopotamia (including Elam), Egypt, and the Indus Valley civilization. Sumer in Mesopotamia, constituting present-day Iraq, is the earliest known civilization on Earth. By 4,000 BCE, the Sumerian culture was established on the Tigris and Euphrates and began to expand northward into Elam, located in present-day Iran or Persia. Each center developed a unique form of writing; only the Indus script remains undeciphered. We know a great deal about Western Asian cultures because of the proliferation of clay tablets and their modern translations, including *The Epic* of *Gilgamesh, The Cycle of Inanna,* and *Hammurabi's Code.* Texts and archaeological artifacts from Mesopotamia and Egypt clearly indicate that wars occurred in the region. The culture known as the Indus Valley or Harappan civilization, however, remains enigmatic, only revealing itself through its material culture, architectural form, and artistic themes. Evidence of war is absent in the excavated areas of the Indus Valley. Since only a small percentage (about five) of the total has been excavated, very little can be said about the culture without veering into speculation. Many archaeologists and historians have attempted to link archaeological remains with descriptions in the Vedas, epics, and Purāṇas, which are privileged over Tamil Caṅkam literature (300 BCE–AD 300) as archaeological touchstones. Most but not all theorists find evidence of the Indian Mother-goddess inscribed on copper, stone, and terracotta seals.

Ancient Elam, the closest western neighbor of the Indus culture, was situated in the far west and southwest of present-day Iran (in the Ilam province and the lowlands of Khuzestan). Elam flourished after the Proto-Elamite period, which began around 3200 BCE when the later capital of the Elamites, Susa, began to mix with the cultures to the east on the Iranian plateau. According to Genesis 14:1, the original Semitic patriarch Abraham (*c.* 2000 BCE) was a contemporary of King Chedorlaomer of Elam. Many scholars maintain that Egyptian, Sumerian, Elamite, and Tamil peoples belong to the same Mediterranean race that created all the great ancient civilizations.[128] Scholars only partly understand the Elamite language, which does not relate to Sumerian, Semitic, or Indo-European languages, but may be related to Tamil. After 3000 BCE, the Elamites developed a semi-pictographic writing system known as Proto-Elamite, and later the cuneiform script was introduced. Elamite was an official language of the Persian Empire from the sixth to fourth centuries BCE. The last written records in Elamite appear about the time of the conquest of the Persian Empire by Alexander the Great.

Elam was distinguished for its matrilineal system of succession; a newly appointed ruler was always referred to as the "son of a sister," perhaps connoting seasonal regicide. Elam was not as culturally gifted as its neighbor countries, and much was imported from them. Most of Elam's architecture came from Babylonia, and writing came from the Sumerians. Art historian Ananda K. Coomaraswamy emphasizes that many Indus seals resemble those found in Mesopotamia, especially Susa and Kish, dating from the fifth to third millennia BCE.[129] The last written records in Elamite appear about the time of the conquest of the Persian Empire by Alexander the Great.

Elam was known as the land of witches and demons in Mesopotamia.[130] Elamites were superstitious and like the Indus people, strongly inclined to magic and sorcery; their religious system apparently centered on a reverence for the female element in magic, the powers of the Underworld, and snake worship. The Elamite Great Goddess Pinikir was at the peak of a goddess-ruled pantheon until around the second millennium BCE. Like Ishtar, Pinikir and the other Elamite goddesses suffered disempowerment by male gods, but they remained the favored divinities of the people. Pinikir was called "Mother of the Gods," but when she married Humban, he usurped her place as chief deity in the Elamite pantheon. After he had supplanted her, Humban left Pinikir and married another goddess, Kiririsha. Although Pinikir lost much of her importance after being divorced from Humban, she was always known as the Protectress of Susa. Throughout the archaeology of Elam are innumerable clay images of the so-called "naked goddesses" holding their breasts in both hands, believed to represent Pinikir or Kiririsha.[131]

Late Neolithic cultures emerged in the Indus Valley region between 6000 and 2000 BCE, and in southern India between 2800 and 1200 BCE. There is both literary and archaeological evidence of mutual influence and trade between the Indus civilization and Greater Iran and Mesopotamia. Distinct Indus seals have been found in ancient sites in Israel, Iraq, and the Persian Gulf, and a "Persian Gulf" type of seal was discovered at Lothal (otherwise found in the Persian Gulf ports of Bahrain and Failaka, and in Mesopotamia) sometime between the Sargon of Akkad and Ur III to the Isin-Larsa periods (*c.* 2370–1900 BCE). Ancient Mesopotamian texts refer to trade with at least two seafaring civilizations, Makkan and Meluhha (the latter corresponding most closely with Indus products), in the neighborhood of India in the third millennium BCE. This trade was a wealthy exchange that probably involved tons of copper. Meluhha is described by Mesopotamians as an aquatic culture, where water and bathing played a central role, an apt characterization of the Great Bath at Mohenjo-daro and the ancient Tamil society.

Little can be known with certainty about the religions or the goddesses of the Indus Valley civilization because no one yet has successfully deciphered the Indus script; therefore, any absolutist, broad-brush assertions about the culture are premature. As Romila Thapar argues, Indian archaeologists who claim that their major project is constituted by matching archaeological remains with the touchstone of sacred Hindu texts are hardly practicing an exact science:

> In the absence of contemporary written records or deciphered scripts, any attempt to co-relate archaeological material with traditional accounts of the past becomes a venture into speculation. This is particularly so as the literary sources represent accretions over a period of many centuries and the archaeological evidence is partial, supported more by exploration than excavation and ultimately based on vertical rather than horizontal excavation.[132]

Claims have been made that the Indus people were Dravidians, countered by assurances that they were Ṛgvedic Aryans. The recent discoveries of ruins older than the Indus culture off the coast of Gujarat are interpreted by many scholars as *prima facie* evidence of the continuity of either Vedic Aryan or Dravidian culture from 5,000 BCE or earlier, while others question whether the ruins represent a culture at all.

The Indus civilization grew from the first agricultural communities in South Asia, which emerged by 6500 BCE in the hills of Balochistan, west of the Indus Valley. Wheat, cattle, and other animals were domesticated, and pottery developed by 5500 BCE. By 4000 BCE, the so-called pre-Harappan culture arose in the area. A self-contained agricultural society, the pre-Harappans were connected to distant raw materials such as lapis lazuli by a trade network of regional cultures. Cotton, dates, peas, and sesame seeds were domesticated, as well as a wide range of domestic animals, principally the water buffalo, the animal that remains the *sine qua non* of intensive agricultural production throughout Asia today. Earlier scholars doubted that this rural agricultural society suddenly transformed into a sophisticated urban civilization that originated city planning, preferring to attribute its high culture to foreign conquerors or migration. However, archaeologists have demonstrated that the Indus culture arose from the pre-Harappan society. Moreover, since Mesopotamian and Egyptian streets meandered like village roads, archaeologists claim that nearby civilizations could not have served as prototypes of the Indus civilization. Uniform imperial town planning on perfect rectangular grids was strictly an Indus invention, a manifestation of the people's intellectual gifts and physical labor.

Indus Culture

A recent discovery places indigenous early writing at Harappa at 3500 BCE,[133] approximately the same time that Egyptian, Mesopotamian, and Proto-Elamite writing developed. The Indus script of over five hundred pictographic characters, many scholars now suggest, may not have been a form of writing like ideograms or phonograms, but simply a set of signs. It is not similar to Sumer's cuneiform or Egypt's hieroglyphics; the Harappans had their own distinctive style, so cryptic that it has evaded deciphering for three-quarters of a century. Indus symbols appear on a large percentage of ritual objects that were mass-produced in molds, inferring an organized production system of talismanic art unknown in any other early civilization. Two bodies of ancient elite Indian literature, Vedic and Tamil, are considered by scholars to be possible chronicles of Indus life and religion. Both Vedic and Tamil literary traditions are influenced by Kālī-like fierce goddesses who originated as tree goddesses in hunter-gatherer tribes. The foundations for modern Indian civilization were laid down in Bronze Age civilizations in the Indian subcontinent, including the development of Vedic ideology, fierce goddesses, and urban settlements, which constitute core traditions of Hinduism.

The Indus Valley civilization flourished from *c.* 2800 BCE to *c.* 1500 BCE in present-day Pakistan and parts of present-day India and Afghanistan, and at its height, covered a geographical area twice the size of Egypt and Mesopotamia combined. Its settlements were scattered from the Himalayas to Mumbai (Bombay) and from Delhi to the Iranian border. Mohenjo-daro in northwest Sind and Harappa in central Punjab (near the Ravi river) were once the principal urban centers of the Indus civilization, each measuring more than three miles in circumference. Dholavīra, Ganweriwala, Lothal, and Rakhigarhi were other important cities discovered among over 1,400 settlements found thus far, mainly located in the general region of the Indus river in Pakistan. Sutkagen Dor in Baluchistan, situated next to Iran, was the westernmost known Indus site. Believed to have once been on a navigable inlet of the Arabian Sea, it would have been on the trade route from Lothal to Mesopotamia. The formulaic Indus citadel and town are present in Sutkagen Dor, along with defensive walls thirty feet wide. By around 2500 BCE, the Indus (also known as the Harappan) civilization was well established. At its peak, the Indus civilization may have had a population exceeding five million. Archaeologists posit that by 2600 BCE, warehouses for grain, irrigation, public streets, and brick-lined drainage systems for sanitation had developed, evidence of a state level society with hierarchical rule and large-scale public works.

The culture was clearly class-divided by wealth: the "rows of mud-brick tenements contrast visibly with the spacious two-storeyed houses comprising courtyards, bathrooms, private wells, etc., which accommodated what may be termed as the Harappan bourgeoisie."[134] All the major settlements are paragons of city planning structured into three hierarchical areas. The innermost building is a citadel that most scholars agree was the elite abode of the ruler. The massive citadels in each Indus city, larger and more complex than most Mesopotamian ziggerats, housed palaces, granaries, and baths, the latter probably used for sacred ablutions. The Great Bath at Mohenjo-daro, about forty feet long and twenty-three feet wide, could not have been designed for purposes of hygiene, since all the private houses of the *haut monde* were furnished with excellent bathrooms.

The middle town had spacious houses, frequently two-storied, equipped with the world's first urban sanitation systems in which household wastewater drained into brick-lined sewers. The lower town had densely packed, less well-developed houses. Each settlement traces a parallelogram, encircled by a five meter-thick stone-and-brick wall. Inside, the wall of the citadel is 18.5 meters thick. The middle town, probably home to wealthy traders, has its own fortification. Dholavīra stands apart from the other settlements found thus far in its burial custom: while in earlier digs the heads of corpses always point northward, many of Dholavīra's graves face east, or northeast. Except for some pottery, all the graves in Dholavīra are empty. The common explanation is that the graves were memorials for citizens buried or cremated elsewhere. Dholavīra had an intricate system of reservoirs, hewn out of rock, that captured rainwater and a provided a year-round supply of water. The Dholavīra dig reveals evidence that it was continuously inhabited from about 2900 to 1500 BCE. Around 2100 BCE, the citadel was abandoned and the settlement fell into decay.

An organized agricultural economy was supplemented by a flourishing maritime trade with the ancient Mesopotamians, probably in ivory, etched beads, and pearls, and later in timber and grain. In addition to the Indus river, there is evidence of a dried-up river that ran parallel to and east of the Indus, which some scholars and Hindu nationalists interpret as the Vedic Sarasvatī river of the *Ṛgveda.* Other archaeologists argue that the old river had dried up in the Mesolithic Age at the latest and had been a seasonal stream thousands of years before the Vedic period.

The Indus civilization produced the sciences of mathematics, astronomy, and metallurgy. Indus metrology laid the foundation of science and technology. The engineering skill of the Indus people, especially in building docks after a careful study of tides, waves, and currents, is remarkable for the age. They not only followed modern principles in building docks, warehouses, drains, and baths, but also achieved advanced standards of construction. They observed and even fixed the position of stars for navigational purposes with the help of an instrument similar to the sextant.[135]

Slaves and War

As we have seen, *Hammurabi's Code,* written shortly after the decline of the Indus civilization, around 1800 BCE, provided that in Babylonia slavery was a legitimate form of property ownership, and that slaves, whose labor was necessary to build royal palaces and monuments, were the legitimate loot of war; debtors could be enslaved, and a man could put out his daughters or wife as a slave. Although Megasthenes wrote that there was no slavery in India, the "literary evidences right from the Vedas, testifying to slavery, are overwhelming, and cannot be brushed aside on account of Megasthenes' testimony."[136] According to Banerji and Chakraborty, slavery was in vogue during the Ṛgvedic period. Prisoners of war were used as slaves by the old Tamils, and "captured women" were put to work as temple prostitutes. We have no textual or archaeological evidence that the Indus people had slaves, forced labor, or a standing army. Museum curator David Kamansky proffers that the social structure of the Indus civilization was more egalitarian than contemporaneous high civilizations: "For seven hundred years this sophisticated, orderly and stable civilization dominated the region and traded with the rest of the ancient world. Unlike the Egyptian and Mesopotamian cultures, the Indus civilization gave primacy to its ordinary citizens."[137] However, if it was a Dravidian culture, the social organization would have been strictly feudal and slave-owning.

Evidence of slaves and wars may have eroded over time or may be discovered in the future, when more Indus sites have been excavated. Some theorists claim that no civilization as advanced as the Indus could have existed without irrigation, which could only be accomplished by a tyrannical warrior ruler who enslaved prisoners of war and his own people to perform the labor. Slaves or menial workers (Dravidian serfs or Vedic śūdras or untouchables in the nascent caste system) lived in mud and bamboo huts that would have long ago disintegrated. Furthermore, most scholars agree that the giant walls backing the citadels of all Indus cities were defense fortifications against military attack (as well as flood barriers). Although there is little evidence of organized armies, Indus people were well fortified against attack. Furthermore, we know that Vedic priests drank *soma*, chanted battle charms, and propitiated Nirṛti, goddess of death and destruction, before warriors led by Indra charged in their chariots to the battlefield, and that Tamil kings and warriors high on toddy were accompanied into battle by war goddess Ko<u>r</u>ravai and her ghouls, who ecstatically danced on corpses and scarfed down bodies and blood of fallen soldiers. The primary opponents of both Vedic and ancient Tamil warriors were indigenous hunter-gatherer societies, whose land was desirable to kings. Thus we probably should not be lulled into accepting an idealistic conception of a peaceful, egalitarian Indus Valley civilization.

The Goddess and the Bull

Based on its material culture, the Indus civilization has been perceived by scholars as deeply religious, immersed in a metaphysical system of offerings and sacrifices to countless deities and genii in an animistic or shamanistic pantheon. The Indus people, or at least its upper crust, were patrons of the arts, and a host of exquisite objects of copper, bronze, and pottery, many of them female figurines usually interpreted as goddesses and sacred dancers, have been uncovered. In Harappa and Mohenjo-daro, annular pieces have been unearthed that may have been symbols of the *yoni* (female genitalia, the female principle), and *liṅgaṁ* (phallus, the male principle), both linked to primal religions. A large number of terracotta nude female figurines identified by many writers as "Mother-goddesses" in fantastical headdresses have also been found. The predominance of female figurines, which outnumber male images by seven to one at one site, is open to wide interpretation. In the third millennium BCE, idol worship was not yet in vogue. Goddesses and gods resided in astronomical bodies and in the ecosystem, and their images appeared not as votive objects of worship, but as shamanic magic. The Paleolithic Venuses found from France to Mongolia are, like the Siberian shamans' *dzuli*, images of women's set of guardian spirits associated with motherhood, and offerings were made to the images as symbolic rituals of homeopathic magic. Since terracotta is the art medium of the common people, we might presume that these female images of the Indus Valley corresponded to either Atharvavedic or Tamil ritual magic and were used as effigies in magic rites, as protective talismans, or as spirit helpers.

No temples per se have been found in the Indus civilization, although elite rituals were probably conducted in the citadel complex. For the Indian majority, Indus temples were sacred groves. If it was a Vedic culture, the *Śatapatha*

Brāhmaṇa describes temples made of post and thatch, with mat walls. Vedic and post-Vedic temples were not elaborate architectural constructions as they would later become. Detailed instructions are given in the *Śulvasūtras* for the construction of fire-altars, and it appears that individual Indus houses were centered round a domestic fire-altar. By the second century BCE or earlier, there are references everywhere—the Gṛhyasūtras, the epics, Manu, and so forth—to temples and images of gods and goddesses. Although both temples and divine images were established by the second century BCE, according to art historian Ananda K. Coomaraswamy, there were no stone images of deities produced before the first century BCE; earlier figures represented either humans or *yakṣiṇīs-yakṣas.* Steatite female figurines in the Indus Valley may have represented *yakṣiṇīs* (*mātṛkās*), while terracotta images were probably especially created for homeopathic magic such as effigies and spirit helpers.

The most mysterious and important objects discovered at all the sites are the more than three thousand steatite (stone) seals and seal impressions of terracotta and copper. Indus seals have been found in Mesopotamia, Oman, and Bahrain (Ur, Kish, and Tall-al-Asmar), with whom the Indus people traded. The motifs on these seals are found in all agricultural societies, reflecting their paramount social and religious values, which evolve out of their conception of a primordial Mother-goddess, who is also Mother Earth or Gaia; astronomical symbols of the movement of the stars and planets for the creation of calendars and cultivation cycles; the Primordial Bull; sowing, tilling, reaping, and other agricultural activities homologized with human sexuality in fertility rituals; and the necessity for the crops of blood sacrifice offered to the goddess.

The steatite seals are engraved with animal and human figures and often a line of pictographic script. They have a perforation on the back for a cord that passed through the center of the handle (or boss), and were usually used to authenticate or identify commercial goods in both internal and external trade. The copper and terracotta seals were probably amulets, talismans, and charms against black magic, enemies, wild animals, and disease, reflecting a worldview of superstition and animism. The amulets were worn around the neck or wrist, or used as personal identification. The talismanic copper tablets with legends and wild animals "were undoubtedly intended to be worn as amulets or charms for propitiating those animals."[138]

Cognate with the Çatal settlement, the most frequent image found in the Indus Valley was the bull. Proto-Mahiṣa, the so-called "unicorn," is a stylized white water buffalo with only one horn, or depicted from an artistic perspective that reveals only one horn. The single "unicorn" horn may in fact be an artistic representation of the dagger or sword used in the tauroctony. The unicorn probably had a religious connotation in the Indus Valley, like the Golden Calf of the Near East, as the sacrificial animal/consort of the Great Goddess. The Indus version of the buffalo-slaying goddess, a remnant of the archaic goddess/bull totem, may have been the Dravidian Koṟṟavai, the original slayer of the buffalo-demon/lover, and her myth could well be the source-myth connoted by the Indus seals.

It is possible that the seals were astronomical in nature; after all, the Indus people were agriculturists who calculated the heliacal movement of stars, the solstices, and equinoxes, and created religious calendars that scheduled sacrifices. According to George Hart, "the astrological system used by the north Indians came originally from Babylon and . . . that system was so superior to any used by people of the ancient world that it spread all over Europe and the Middle East as well as India."[139] Moreover, the city engineers could not have aligned their city plans in perfect grids along cardinal directions if they did not have a rudimentary knowledge of the cardinal points. They must have divided their year into twelve lunar months. In this construction, the seals represent zodiacal symbols or myths of celestial events. The Indus animals depicted on seals—the humped bull, the small bull, tiger, elephant, ram, buffalo, rhinoceros, hooded python, alligator, onager or wild ass (no horse), rabbit, scorpian, stag, and frog—may be zodiacal symbols, and the seals with the seven figures may refer to myths of the Vedic *nakṣatras* or constellations such as the Pleiades. S.R. Rao[140] and Asko Parpola,[141] discussed below, have explored some aspects of the astronomical theme of Indus seals in their work.

The Fall

Could the fall of the Indus Valley civilization have been caused by nuclear technology? Is the *coup de grâce* of Mohenjo-daro described in cosmic warfare scenarios in Indian sacred writings? Amid fighting sky chariots and final weapons, the sound of an atomic blast such as experienced in Hiroshima and Nagasaki is described in the Droṇaparva of the *Mahābhārata*. In this ancient battle, explosions of final weapons decimate entire armies; warriors, elephants, steeds, and weapons are swept away like dry leaves; giant parasols of billowing smoke clouds open consecutively in the sky; food is contaminated and hair falls out. In the upper layers of Mohenjo-daro, excavators find six groups of skeletons in postures of flight, suggesting sudden and violent death. Nearby, in three square miles in present-day Rajasthan, a heavy layer of radioactive ash covers the ground, the remnant of nuclear technology operating eight to ten millennia ago.

The Aryan Invasion Theory (AIT)

> Myths continue to thrive and to exert their power over contemporary societies. . . . [T]he distinctions between myth and history are not always clear-cut, and feminist scholars in particular have taken an interest in the power of myth to shape our ideas and to legitimate social structure. The Imperial Emperors of Japan justified their absolute power through appeal to divine kingship, claiming descent from the sun-goddess, Amaterasu. In nineteenth-century Germany science and mythology became entangled in the myth of Aryan supremacy,

reaching its apogee in the rise of Nazism and the Holocaust. The links between myth and power are sometimes more subtle than in these two examples, but real nonetheless.[142]

The Aryan invasion theory of German romantic idealist Friedrich Max Müller, devised before the Indus civilization was discovered, originated as an attempt to relate the languages of the Middle East and Europe. In the nineteenth century, needless to say, Europeans were united by an imperialistic worldview. Max Müller was writing when India was a British colony and the idea that indigenous people (particularly those under European rule) might have built an advanced culture on their own was probably unimaginable to him. On the contrary, a crucial facet of imperialism was to subdue and control by any means necessary the local population. In order to provide a historical explanation for the existence of Indo-European languages in India, Max Müller and others in the mid-nineteenth century first proposed the Aryan Invasion Theory (AIT), which asserted that the Aryans originated in south Russia and eastern Ukraine, from where they invaded or migrated to Iran, India, Central Asia, and Europe. Max Müller, who never journeyed to India, viewed Dravidians and other non-Aryans through an imperialistic lens: they were perceived as barbarians who were easily displaced southward by the superior Aryans. Later writers proposed that the Aryans were pale-skinned people who conquered the dark-skinned aboriginals, a historico-racial hypothesis that modeled and validated rampant nineteenth century European hegemony, white supremacy, colonialism, and Eurocentrism.

Since the Aryans were the authors of all the triumphs of Indian civilization, reasoned European colonials, it followed that a return to Aryan rule was necessary for India's renaissance. Upper-caste Hindus with legitimate grievances against the Muslim nobility were naturally quite receptive to the theory. Too emasculated to fight for their rights and too alienated from the low castes to join popular rebellions against feudal inequalities, high caste males acquiesced to colonial rule in exchange for small privileges doled out by the British rulers. If the Aryans originated in remote northern Europe, upper-caste Hindus could rationalize that they had no common heritage or cause with the Indian low-caste majority; hence the Aryan invasion theory provided the rationale for both caste and colonial oppression of the masses.

Vedic texts neither describe a homeland outside of India nor an invasion or migration into India; thus the original theory was a purely linguistic construct based on the discovery that Sanskrit was related to the Indo-European language group (the principal languages of Europe). Opponents of the AIT point out, however, that invasion and migration are not the only sources of linguistic groups; the extensive trade and commercial ties of the Indus culture with Babylon and civilizations further west could also account for the structural commonality of the Indo-European group of languages.

Until the discovery of the Indus Valley sites in 1920, the culture of India was attributed solely to the Aryan invaders. It is unfortunate that Max Müller did not live long enough to learn that the Indus culture was an advanced civilization with scientifically engineered cities complete with elaborate sewers, one of the first systems of standardized weights and measures, and highly evolved fine arts, including dancing, painting, and sculpture.

Most histories of India begin with the Aryan invasion and the Aryan-Dravidian conflict, which many Indologists such as Wheeler,[143] "dean of subcontinent archaeology in the 1940s and 1950s,"[144] claim culminated in the wholesale massacre and destruction of the Indus civilization. Initially, historians validated the invasion theory, but after the Indus Valley civilization was discovered in 1920, the invasion theory has been gradually supplanted by combinations of migration and linguistic theories that hypothesize various models of the first emergence of Indo-Aryan peoples and language on the subcontinent.

The Indigenous Aryan Argument

The sunken cities off the coast of Gujarat province are often cited as evidence that Indic civilization is a continuous stream of Vedic Aryan handiwork that precludes an Aryan invasion. The submerged Gujarat sites and the Indus culture probably reflect a remarkable continuity of Indic civilization, hence the relatively paltry contribution of any invading or migrating peoples. If the Gujarati and the Indus cities were all Dravidian, we then have an explanation for the astonishing cultural achievements of India long before the supposed arrival of the Aryans. If these prehistoric cities were all Vedic, we must discard forever the idea of an Aryan invasion.

Even if there was an Aryan invasion, the religion of the invaders was never accepted by the Indian majority, and it had a very short lifespan. Aryan gods described in the *Ṛgveda* did not linger long in public consciousness; a few centuries after their possible introduction in India, they ceased to be worshiped. Some brāhmaṇas originated among animistic, totemistic tribals who, prior to their assimilation into the caste system, worshiped fertility symbols such as the *yoni* and the *liṅga* and propitiated fierce goddesses of destruction and death who lived in trees, rocks, caves, waterfalls, cemeteries, and crossroads. Most tribes and villages have retained these elements of their primordial forms of worship for over five millennia. For example, Kālī and Śiva are totally unrelated to an Aryan invasion, and their prototypes may in fact reside in the Indus Valley civilization and the tribal groups in the environs. Neither the philosophy of Indic high culture nor the popular religions of villages and tribes owe much of note to the greatly overworked Aryan invasion.

The word *ārya* as it is used in the *Ṛgveda* and other texts, according to critics of the invasion theory, does not connote nationality, race, or even linguistic group. The preferred translation is "one of noble character, noble deed, or noble background." Thus the European use of the term "Aryan" to depict the national or racial characteristics of an invading clan is not valid. Even if invading warriors identified themselves as Aryans, they were not trumpeting their national or racial origin, but rather their claim to noble status. In other words, they were superior to the conquered not because of their white race or European origin, but because they were self-recognized nobility.

Because no weapons or other evidence of an invasion have yet been found at Harappa, Mohenjo-daro, or Dholavīra, many Indologists now substitute the term "migration" for the Aryan "invasion." In interviews with Indian scholars, Edwin Bryant found that those who supported the indigenous Aryan camp far outnumbered scholars who argue in favor of the external origin of the Aryans.[145] Proponents of the indigenous Aryan school emphasize that the urban culture of the *Ṛgveda*, which makes numerous references to bodies of water unknown to Central Asian nomads, is indigenous to the subcontinent and coeval with, if not identical to, the Indus civilization.

Many prominent archaeologists like R.S. Bisht and B.B. Lal believe that the Indus civilization is the Vedic culture. According to Lal, it has been proven by skeletal examination that there was a basic biological continuity in the Indus culture from 5400 BCE to the second millennium BCE, and that the Indus people were Aryans.[146] Rather than succumbing to the Aryan hordes, the Indus civilization, according to archaeologists, came to an end because of earthquakes, the unruly fluctuations of the Indus river, heavy floods, and gradual devolution due to climate changes, the wearing out of the soil, and agricultural and economic decline.[147]

The historical paradigm of indigenous Aryan theorists is borrowed from B.B. Lal,[148] and corresponds to contemporary archaeological and archaeo-astronomical research. This school holds that the flowering of the Indus age was 2600–1900 BCE,[149] coeval with the Ṛgvedic age, which is dated by this school from the fifth to the third millennia BCE, when neighboring civilizations were the Egyptian Third and Fourth Dynasties and later Sumeria, Mesopotamia (Ur), Oman (Kish), and Bahrain (Tall-al-Asmar). From 1800 BCE until possibly *c.* 900 BCE, an age of chaos forced the migration of Indian elites to West Asia and Mesopotamia, and the Kassite, Hittite, and Mittani Empires were founded.

References

1. *Phallic Tree Worship: Cultus Arborum* (Varanasi, 1971), 4.
2. Kosambi, *Ancient India*, 47.
3. Sir James Frazer, *The New Golden Bough*, ed. Theodor H. Gaster (New York, 1959), 106.
4. Ibid., 112.
5. Ibid., 113.
6. K.N. Sastri, *New Light on the Indus Civilization*, vol. 1 (Delhi, 1957), 25.
7. S.C. Kersenboom-Story, "Viṟali," *Journal of Tamil Studies* 19 (June 1981), 37, n. 21.

8. C. J. Bleeker, "Isis and Hathor: Two Ancient Egyptian Goddesses," *The Book of the Goddess Past and Present*, ed. Carl Olson (New York, 1983), 43.
9. Ibid., 44.
10. It is also possible that the stone base represented the *yoni* of Asherah, and the pole was the *liṅgaṁ* of Baal. Phallic worship has ever been a complementary part of goddess worship. The symbolic significance of the wooden pole can be seen as parallel to the megaliths of the pre-Christian Nagas.
11. 2 Kings 23.7.
12. Judg. 2.12–13.
13. Judg., 6.27–28.
14. 2 Kings 18.
15. Jer. 7.18.
16. Jer. 44.17.
17. Jer. 44.18. Cf., the lament of the Nagas when the British outlawed head-taking, *infra*, chap. 3, "The Nagas: A Modern Fertility and Skull Cult," pp. 112–13ff.
18. See Carol Radcliffe Bolon, *Forms of the Goddess Lajjā Gaurī in Indian Art* (University Park, PA, 1992).
19. Richard Cavendish, ed., *Man, Myth and Magic: An Illustrated Encyclopedia of the Supernatural*, vol. 1 (New York, 1970), 144.
20. Frazer, *The New Golden Bough* (abridged), ed. Gaster (New York, 1959), 113.
21. *Phallic Tree Worship*, 7.
22. *AV*, III.6.1.
23. Sastri, *New Light on the Indus Civilization*, vol. 2 (Delhi, 1957), 143.
24. *AV*, V.4.3–6.
25. III. 6.3–8.
26. 1.67.52.
27. *AV*, III.6.3–8.
28. *Phallic Tree Worship*, 7.
29. Ibid. [Italics in original.]
30. Ibid., 13.
31. Bhattacharyya, *The Indian Mother Goddess*, New Delhi, 1977, 44.
32. Dasgupta, *Aspects of Indian Religious Thought*, Calcutta, 1957, 51.
33. Ibid.
34. The equinoxes move along the ecliptic in a direction opposite that of the Sun's annual course, shifting from Virgo the Virgin (12,000–10,000 BCE) to Leo the Lion (10,000–8000 BCE) to Cancer the Crab (8000–6000 BCE) to Gemini the Twins (6000–4000 BCE) to Taurus the Bull (4000–2000 BCE) to Aries the Ram (*c.* 2000–0 BCE) to Pisces the Fish (AD 0–2000). The next equinoctial constellation will be Aquarius, the sign of the Water Bearer. [Georg Feuerstein et al., *In Search of the Cradle of Civilization: New Light on Ancient India* (Wheaton, IL, 1995), 239–40.]
35. Richard Hinckley Allen, *Star-Names and Their Meanings* (New York, 1936), 460ff.
36. David Ulansey theorizes that the Mithraic tauroctony represents the mystery of the precession of the equinoxes, and that Mithras was regarded as a god capable of moving the universe. According to Ulansey, Mithras ended the Age of the Bull by moving the spring equinox out of the constellation Taurus the Bull. The bull-slaying symbolizes the precession because the previous constellation of the spring equinox had been Taurus. As a star map, the constellation Perseus

lay directly above Taurus, projecting the image of the hero slaying the bull directly below him. Ulansey asserts that "there is good evidence that Mithras represents the constellation Perseus, and that the other tauroctony figures represent the constellations which lay on the celestial equator when the spring equinox was in Taurus." [David Ulansey, *The Origins of the Mithraic Mysteries: Cosmology and Salvation in the Ancient World* (New York, 1989), 67.]

37. Ibid., 55.
38. *Ś.Br.*, 8.1.2.2.
39. Ibid., 2.2.1.
40. Asko Parpola, "The Sky Garment: A Study of the Harappan Religion and its Relation to the Mesopotamian and Later Indian Religions," in *Studia Orientalia* 57 (1985): 90.
41. Lal, "India Adds New Dimensions to the Indus Civilization," in *Revisting Indus-Sarasvati Age and Ancient India*, ed. Bhu Dev Sharma and Nabarun Ghose (Atlanta, 1998), 11.
42. Ibid.
43. Ibid, 120.
44. Parpola, "The Sky Garment," 99.
45. Ibid., 152.
46. Ulansey, *The Origins of the Mithraic Mysteries* (New York, Oxford, 1989), 4.
47. Quoted in Ehrenreich, *Blood Rite* (New York, 1997).
48. Ibid., 100.
49. Anne Baring and Jules Cashford, *The Myth of the Goddess: Evolution of an Image* (London, 1991), 217.
50. Julian Jacobs, *The Nagas: Society, Culture and the Colonial Encounter* (London, 1990), 85–86.
51. Frazer, *The New Golden Bough*, 357–58.
52. Ibid., 357.
53. Altekar, *The Position of Women in Hindu Civilization. From Prehistoric Times to the Present Day*, 1938; repr. (Delhi, 1956), 184–85.
54. Ibid.
55. Frazer, *The New Golden Bongh*, 357–58.
56. Judith Ochshorn, "Ishtar and Her Cult," in *The Book of the Goddess Past and Present*, ed. Carl Olson (New York, 1983), 24.
57. A. L. Basham, *The Wonder That was India: A Survey of the Culture of the Indian Sub-Continent Before the Coming of the Muslims* (New York, 1959), 183.
58. Ibid., 185.
59. Alexander Dubianski, *Ritual and Mythological Sources of the Early Tamil Poetry* (Groninger, the Netherlands, 2000), 69.
60. Basham, *The Wonder*, 183.
61. Catullus, Poem 63, quoted in Marvin W. Meyer, *The Ancient Mysteries: A Sourcebook* (New York, 1987), 128.
62. Carmel Berkson, *The Divine and the Demoniac* (Delhi, 1995), 153.
63. Bowie, *The Anthropology of Religion*, 168.
64. Frazer, *The New Golden Bough*, 506.
65. G. Hatt, "The Corn Mother in American and in Indonesia," *Anthropos* 46 (1951): 853–914.
66. This reflects James Mellaart's interpretation, which has recently been challenged by Ian Hodder, "Contextual Archaeology: An Interpretation of Çatal Höyük

and a Discussion of the Origins of Agriculture," in *London University Institute of Archaeology Bulletin* 24 (1987): 43–56; Hodder, *Reading the Past: Current Approaches to Interpretation in Archaeology* (Cambridge, UK) 2003; Hodder, "Women and Men at in Çatalhöyük," *Scientific American* (January 2004): 76–81. Hodder and his Cambridge cohorts coined the terms "pre-processualist," "processualist" (old, passé archaeology), and "post-processualist" (the "new archaeology"), the latter identified with cognitive or contextual archaeology. During the re-excavation of Çatal Höyük, Hodder found figurines that depicted men as well as women, many of an indeterminate sex, and he found that animals were depicted more often that women. This led to a suspicion of Mellaart's universalist goddess theory. Hodder's approach has been one of "contextualizing" the evidence; hence he attaches great significance to the fact that the enthroned, headless Mistress of the Animals flanked by leopards was found in a grain bin. Hodder's reasoning, ostensibly based on the culture-bound notion that a female religious icon would have been placed only in a formal public temple, is that the Mistress of the Animals statue is not necessarily a religious icon. Another probable explanation for the presence of the goddess in the catal Höyük grain bin can be found later in third and second millennia Sumerian religion, which itself may be a transformation of the earlier Çatal mythology. As noted earlier, in sacred marriage texts covering a span of two thousand years, the venue for sexual union between Inanna and Dumazi, represented by an elite woman and the king, was the sacred storehouse. (Frymer-Kensky, *In the Wake of the Goddess*, 56.)

67. Ochshorn, "Ishtar and Her Cult," 22.
68. Frymer-Kensky, *In the Wake of the Goddess,* 56.
69. Ibid.
70. Alain Daniélou, *Shiva and Dionysos* (London, 1982).
71. Bhattacharyya, *History of the Śākta Religion*, 22–28.
72. Eliade, *A History of Religious Ideas*, vol. 1, 83–84.
73. Proverbs 14:28.
74. Ochshorn, "Ishtar and Her Cult," 22.
75. Ibid.
76. Ibid.
77. Ibid., 23.
78. 1.162.9.
79. 1.9.2.7; 4.3.7; 6.2.8, 3.1.28; 11 et seq.
80. *Vājasaneyi Saṁhitā*, 23.22–31.
81. Bhattacharyya, *History of the Śākta Religion*, 33.
82. Quoted in Diane Wolkstein and Samuel N. Kraemer, *Inanna, Queen of Heaven and Earth: Her Stories and Hymns from Sumer* (New York, 1983), 95.
83. Quoted in Steve Davies, "The Canaanite-Hebrew Goddess," in *The Book of the Goddess Past and Present*, ed. Carl Olson (New York, 1983), 70.
84. Judges 2.12–13.
85. Quoted in Gerda Lerner, *The Creation of Patriarchy* (New York, 1986), 63.
86. Dennett, *Breaking the Spell*, 140.
87. Robert Paul, "Some Observations on Sherpa Shamanism," in *Spirit Possession in the Nepal Himalayas*, ed. John T. Hitchcock and Rex L. Jones (Warminster, 1976), 143. Paul is referring to a Tibetan Buddhist concept of the reincarnate lāmā, or the Bodhisattva who reincarnates endlessly to fulfill his earthly mission.

88. Eliade, *History of Religious Ideas*, vol. 1, 5.
89. Wolkstein and Kraemer, *Inanna, Queen of Heaven and Earth*, 126.
90. Ibid.
91. Ibid., 120.
92. Ibid., 142.
93. Frymer-Kensky, *In the Wake of the Goddess*, 27.
94. Ibid., 25.
95. Ehrenreich, *Gilgamesh*, 101.
96. Quoted by Samuel N. Kramer, *The Sumerians: Their History, Culture, and Character* (Chicago, 1963), 63.
97. Frymer-Kensky, *In the Wake of the Goddess*, 70.
98. Ibid., 5–6.
99. David Ferry, *Gilgamesh: A New Rendering in English Verse* (New York, 1997), 3.
100. Ibid.
101. Ochshorn, "Ishtar and His Cult," 19.
102. Ferry, *Gilgamesh*, 4.
103. See Ezekiel 16:1–49, 23 and Revelation 17:15; 18:2–8, 21; 19:3.
104. Ochshorn, *Gilgamesh*, 21.
105. Ferry, *Gilgamesh*, 29–30.
106. *Gilgamesh* is referring to the reputed magical ability of goddesses like Circe to change men into animals.
107. Ferry, *Gilgamesh*, 31–32.
108. The Sumerian Bull of Heaven is cognate with Durgā's arch-enemy, the Buffalo demon Mahiṣa.
109. Ferry, *Gilgamesh*, 32.
110. Ibid., 33.
111. Ibid., 73.
112. Jeremiah 7:18; 44:17–25.
113. Michael D. Coogan, trans., *Stories from Ancient Canaan* (Louisville, KY, 1978), 37.
114. Eliade, *Shamanism: Archaic Techniques of Ecstasy* (Princeton, 1964), 104.
115. Davies, "The Canaanite Hebrews Goddess," 69.
116. S.H. Hooke, *Middle Eastern Mythology* (Harmondsworth, 1963), 83.
117. Theodore Gastor, *Myth, Legend, and Custom in the Old Testament* (New York, 1969), 416.
118. Quoted by Davies, "The Canaanite Hebrews Goddess," 70.
119. J.B. Lloyd, "Anat and the 'Double' Massacre of KTU 1.3.ii," in *Ugarit, Religion and Culture: Essays Presented in the Honour of Professor John C.L. Gibson*, ed. N. Wyatt, W.G.E. Watson, and J.B. Lloyd (Münster, Germany, 1996).
120. Frymer-Kensky, *In the Wake of the Goddess*, 80.
121. Ibid., 79.
122. Wolkstein and Kraemer, *Inanna, Queen of Heaven and Earth*, 121.
123. James C. Thompson, "Women in the Ancient World," June 2005, http://www.womenintheancientworld.com/hammurabilawcode.htm (accessed August 1, 2005).
124. Frymer-Kensky, *In the Wake of the Goddess*, 80.
125. Ibid.

126. See S.R. Rao, "Further Excavations of the Submerged City of Dwaraka," *Proceedings of Second Indian Conference of Marine Archaeology of Indian Ocean Countries, Jan 1990.* Published for the Society for Marine Archaeology National Institute of Oceanography of India, 1991.
127. "The Gulf of Khambat Debate" (interview with Asko Parpola and Iravatham Mahadevan), *Frontline* 18, issue 7 (March 30–April 12, 2002), http://www.frontlineonnet.com/fl1907/19070940.htm (accessed October 26, 2006).
128. See, for example, H.S. David, "The Original Home of the Dravidians: Their Wanderings in Prehistoric Times BC 4,500 to 1,500," *Tamil Culture,* III, 2 (April, 1954): 77–81; J.T. Cornelius, "The Dravidian Question," *Tamil Culture,* III, 2 (April 1954): 92–102.
129. Coomaraswamy, *History of Indian and Indonesian Art,* 4.
130. Walter Hinz, "Elam," in *Cambridge Ancient History* 1, 2 (1971), 662–64.
131. Ibid.
132. Romila Thapar, "Puranic Lineages and Archeological Cultures," in *Purātattva* 8 (1978): 86.
133. Edwin Bryant, *The Quest for the Origins of Vedic Culture: The Indo-Aryan Migration Debate* (New York, 2001), 301.
134. Bhattacharyya, *History of the Śākta Religion,* 13.
135. Venugopala Rao, "Astronomy in Ancient India: Observations and Speculations," in *Revisiting Indus-Sarasvati Age and Ancient India,* ed. Bhu Dev Sharma and Nabarun Ghose (Atlanta, 1998), 306.
136. Suresh Chandra Banerji and Chanda Chakraborty, *Folklore in Ancient and Medieval India* (Calcutta, 1991), 66.
137. "Digging Dholavīra," *Hinduism Today,* January–February 2001: 44.
138. Sastri, *New Light on the Indus Civilization,* vol. 1, 123.
139. George L. Hart, *The Poems of Ancient Tamil: Their Milieu and Their Sanskrit Counterparts* (Berkeley, 1975), 77–78.
140. S.R. Rao, "Deciphering the Indus Valley Script," *Indian and Foreign Review* 17, no. 3 (Delhi, 1979), 13–18; Rao, *Decipherment of the Indus Script* (Bombay, 1982).
141. Asko Parpola, *Deciphering the Indus Script,* 2nd edn. (Cambridge, 2003); Parpola, "The Sky Garment: A Study of the Harappan Religion and its Relation to the Mesopotamian and Later Indian Religions," *Studia Orientalia* 57 (1985): 8–210.
142. Bowie, *The Anthropology of Religion,* 276.
143. Mortimer Wheeler, *Civilizations of the Indus Valley and Beyond* (London, 1966), 78.
144. "Indus: Clues to an Ancient Civilization," in *National Geographic* 197, 6 (June 2000): 127.
145. Bryant, "The Quest for the Origins," 294.
146. B.B. Lal, "India: New Dimensions of Indus Civilization," *Keynote Address,* International Conference on Indus–Sarasvatī Age and Ancient India, 5 October 1996, Atlanta, GA.
147. Ibid.
148. The Harappan civilization, according to Lal, falls into three periods of evolution, maturity, and decline, which are tentatively dated as follows: (1) the early Harappan civilization, which coincides with the Ṛgvedic age, commenced before 3700 BCE, ended with the Battle of Ten Kings, 3730 BCE, and was coeval with the First Dynasty of Egypt and Proto-Assyria (Lal finds a Pre-Harappan

period exclusively in Kalibangan from 4500 BCE through the fourth–third millennium BCE, to which he assigns the indigenous development of the civilization); (2) the middle Harappan civilization, 3700–3000 BCE, corresponded to the Mahābhārata war, 3100 BCE, and the closing of the Vedic age, and was contemporaneous with the First and Second dynasties of Egypt, the Proto-Sumerians, and Proto-Assyrians; and (3) the late Harappan civilization, 3000–1800 BCE, coeval with the Egyptian Third and Fourth dynasties and later Sumerians, when the brāhmaṇas wrote the Sūtras and Brāhmaṇas. [Ibid.]

149. Ibid., 38.

2
Warfare and Male Supremacy

> Sports hunting, contests of courage, ritual killings, and human sacrifices came into being because of men's need to replace the excitement of the hunt. Eventually, war-to-the-death superseded the hunt as the principal means of periodically lancing the boil of the men's innate combativeness. Nevertheless, farming progressively reined in the male's predatory impulses by yoking his killer instinct to the plow.[1]

* * *

> Originally the two figures, priest and warrior, were not mutually exclusive. They seem, on the contrary, to be intimately related. Thus, the Celtic druid "is not only priest but also a warrior." Conversely, the *fianna*, the warrior bands, did not admit an aspirant "unless he was a poet and had studied the twelve books of poetry." As often is the case, there is a striking suggestive resemblance with the archaic conditions that have left copious traces in the Vedic texts.[2]

* * *

> Doubting the authority of "sacred texts" that legitimate violence is an essential act of faithfulness.[3]

The advent of warfare, dated in the Mesolithic age, may be the fulcrum of the fall of the goddess, woman's loss of status, and the rise of the male god. When the patriarchal revolution and advanced agriculture erupted, elites created city-states and nation-states that were sanctified and ruled by the gods of patriarchal pantheons. In our ancient Indo-European literary heritage, the

Sumerian heroes Gilgamesh and Enkidu were, like all the heroes of Greek myths and legends, both hunters of big predatory animals and warriors. Unfortunately for such heroes, when the game and wild predator population began to diminish, so did their opportunities for heroism. Possibly wishing to escape the unglamorous grind of growing crops, which women could do with no assistance, males with weapons were otherwise desperate for employment.

According to Marvin Harris, male supremacist institutions arise as a "by-product of warfare, of the male monopoly over weapons, and of the use of sex for the nurturance of aggressive male personalities." Warfare "is not the expression of human nature, but a response to reproductive and ecological pressures. Therefore, male supremacy is no more natural than warfare."[4] Peggy Reeves Sanday, drawing from the work of Margaret Mead and Mary Douglas, regards male supremacist behavior as a people's reaction to stress, such as migration, disease, or depletion of the food supply. In such stressful conditions when

> people sense that their universe is out of order, that they are victims of circumstances beyond their control, they look among themselves for the oppressor, or they examine their behavior for wrongdoing, or they do both. . . . A major disorder in one part is presumed to disturb the relations that exist among all the parts. People respond to the disorder by fixing blame and establishing punishments in order to restore balance. Who or what is blamed, and how and why, affects the relationship between the sexes.[5]

There is no evidence for the practice of war before the late Paleolithic Age (35,000 to 12,000 BCE).[6] Many historians situate the origin of war in the later Neolithic, when surplus agricultural products were stored, became objects of desire worthy of risking death to possess, and raided. In response, the theory goes, a defensive apparatus was set in motion by the community being raided which eventually became the army *sui generis*, poised ever on the offensive and ever on the march. However, there is archeological evidence of numerous and deadly wars in the Mesolithic period,[7] when the stock of game and predators was diminishing. War became a prestigious alternative for male hunters to hunting and defending the community against wild beasts. Another problem with locating the origin of war in the Neolithic is that serious conflicts were not always fought over critical material resources. Human male hunters had a tendency to "overkill" big game, and the actual loot and spoils of war often

> serve little function except as badges of prestige and warrior prowess: scalps and skulls; severed heads, hands, penises, and other portable body parts; captives for rituals of human sacrifice. Just as prehistoric humans probably killed animals for reasons other than hunger, they no doubt killed one another for purposes other than gain—such as the accumulation of a particularly imposing collection of severed heads.[8]

Eliade[9] and Keeley[10] provide ample evidence from numerous sites of prehistoric headhunting cults such as the one in Jericho, bolstering the idea that early wars may have been motivated in some cases by factors other than hunger and thirst. The Nubian cemetery at Djebel Sahaba, dated between 12,000–9000 BCE, which contains the first collection of traumatic deaths known in Africa and perhaps the Mediterranean area, is often cited as evidence of early warfare. Of some 59 burials, nearly half had died a violent death; crude flints were found embedded in the bones of the dead, in the lower abdomen, chest, and vertebrae.[11] Other warriors of the Mesolithic era are evidenced in Ukrainian cemeteries on the Dnieper river above the Black Sea, which also show flint points lodged in the bones of men, women, and children, as well as all-male burials signifying a common grave for warriors who died in battle.[12]

Man's aggressive "killer instincts," both as hunter of animals and a killer of other men, are prodigiously illustrated in archaeological finds such as fortifications, weapons, cave paintings, and skeletal remains. (The controversy continues over whether these "instincts" are biological or cultural.) Men by the end of prehistoric times were fighters capable of waging organized warfare. Along the Nile and in the Mesopotamian valley, the earliest civilizations depended on warfare to increase the power of the new states. When alphabets were devised and humans learned to write, their first recorded epics were about wars.[13] Thus ancient history is for the most part military history, and modern history replicates the pattern. Ninety percent of contemporary hunter-gatherer societies are known to engage in warfare, and 64 percent of these tribes wage war at least once every two years, according to Carol Ember.[14] In an investigation of 99 groups of hunter-gatherers from 37 cultures, W.T. Divale found that 68 were at war at the time, 20 had been at war five to twenty-five years before, and all the others reported warfare in the more distant past. It is reasonable to conclude, therefore, that human universals include conflict, rape, revenge, jealousy, dominance, and male coalitional violence.[15] In traditional societies, most attacks are ambush attacks that are won based on superior numbers and advance planning to take advantage of the element of surprise.

MASTERS OF WAR

> [I]n the cosmologies of the powerful . . . there is no place for chaos. For, if the contingent and chaotic nature of the world were acknowledged in these, it would have the potential to dismantle the structures of legitimacy through which suffering is imposed upon the powerless. Clothed in the language of responsibility, the discourse of power ends up with the equation that pain is equal to punishment and that the injustice of life, testified to by suffering, can only be redeemed by further suffering.[16]

* * *

> The soldier of Christ kills safely; he dies the more safely. He serves his own interests in dying, and Christ's interest in killing! Not without cause does he bear the sword!
>
> —Saint Bernard

* * *

> Indeed, intolerance is essential only to monotheism; an only God is by nature a jealous God who will not allow another to live. On the other hand, polytheistic gods are naturally tolerant; they live and let live. In the first place, they gladly tolerate their colleagues, the gods of the same religion, and this tolerance is afterwards extended even to foreign gods who are, accordingly, hospitably received and later admitted, in some cases, even to an equality of rights. . . . Thus it is only the monotheistic religions that furnish us with the spectacle of religious wars, religious persecutions, courts for trying heretics, and also with that of iconoclasm, the destruction of the images of foreign gods, the demolition of Indian temples and Egyptian colossi that had looked at the sun for three thousand years; all just because their jealous God had said "Thou shalt make no graven image," and so on.[17]

The idea of "perpetual war for perpetual peace," to use Gore Vidal's ironic book title, is not new. Judging from classic epics and religious myths, the history of humankind can be described as a repetitive narrative of conquering males who have justified their militant co-optation of land, goods, and power by invoking heavenly sanctions and proclaiming their moral, intellectual, racial, and spiritual superiority to their enemies. The primary source of both human sacrificial victims and slaves for most warrior cultures, from fifteenth century Aztecs to Canaanite Anath worshipers to Indian Nagas to medieval Muslims, were prisoners-of-war taken during ceremonial battles; in fact, the divine purpose of war was often considered its provision of sacrificial victims.

The warrior economies of early civilizations were mirrored in the Manichean worldview of the dominant religions. Probably more powerful than law codes and politics, religious myths communicate values and expectations. While they can be cathartic, even ennobling, religious myths have an equally destructive potential to vilify women, class/caste, or race by stimulating reflex reactions such as fear, bigotry, and violence. Highly polarized warrior societies usually invent sacred myths of cosmic war in which an authoritarian male or female deity demands the death of enemies, thus creating ethical tenets that are sacralized by their mythology and dominant ideology. Sumerian, Assyrian, Ugaritic, and Tamil myths romanticize and deify warrior violence by attributing men's war lust to the Great Mother. Arising from the first urban militaristic high cultures, the ancient Near Eastern fierce polytheistic goddesses Inanna, Ishtar, Asherah, and Anath, like South Asian Ko<u>rr</u>avai and Kālī, were all associated with blood sacrifice, war, and victory, the favored sports of armies.

Why should violence and war be themes of elite religious texts? As pure philosophical abstraction, the struggle between the classic polarities of good and evil, life and death, can be viewed as the natural interaction of the great forces of the universe. On the religious level of symbology, warfare is human sacrifice on a grand scale. We have seen that Frazer's principle of "human sacrifice for the crops among primitives" is one explication of the Neolithic religious justification for human sacrifice; viz., because agricultural cycles were deified and sacralized as Mother Earth, the notion that human death must precede and fertilize agricultural life was enacted as a cathartic tribal ritual drama. Given this arcane agricultural logic, there is an inherent religious justification for blood sacrifice, including warfare, in ancient sacred texts.

French literary scholar René Girard proposes that ritual sacrifice is "society seeking to deflect upon a relatively indifferent victim, a 'sacrificeable' victim, the violence that would otherwise be vented on its own members, the people it most desires to protect."[18] The surrogate victim is linked to the original object of violence (for example, the king), and represents the community itself, according to Girard, making a violent offering to protect itself from its killer predator nature. The sacred realm of goddesses and gods, spirits and genii, being external to mundane reality, is a numinous screen onto which is projected human violence. Girard observes that "although men cannot live in the midst of violence, neither can they survive very long by ignoring its existence or by deluding themselves into the belief that violence, despite the ritual prohibitions attendant on it, can somehow be put to work as the mere tool or servant of mankind."[19] The community, he explains, must separate itself from the sacred violence inherent in human nature, or "it risks being devoured by it;" at the same time, it must not drift too far away for fear that it will be "out of the range of the sacred's therapeutic threats and warnings,"[20] thus losing the "fecund presence" of the blood sacrifice.

Gerard shares with many modern theorists the conviction that the psychoanalytic conception of *displacement* underpins ritual violence. Fiona Bowie likens ritual violence to sexual violence, noting that anthropologists and other scholars have viewed the nexus between sex and violence as a form of displacement: "The perpetrator of violence is frustrated by his (or her) lack of ability to control others, particularly their sexual behavior, which jeopardizes a carefully constructed identity dependent on a self-image of power and authority." She extends this argument to societies "in which a dominant discourse of masculinity includes the superiority of men over women, children, and 'nature' (as in most if not all human cultures)"[21] and concludes that masculine values are reasserted by deflecting violence onto the weaker victim.

Maurice Bloch argues that myths of cosmic war and violence enacted in rituals function to maintain the hierarchical status quo of a society via the phenomenon of "rebounding violence" or "conquest." As an integral part of patriarchal rites of passage, ritual violence is projected or displaced onto a deity or supernatural figure. Bloch observes that in the middle stage of a rite of passage, the *vitality* (life force, *śakti*, power, energy) is transformed from a mundane individual or group level to a level of heightened transcendent vitality, constituting "a conquered vitality obtained from outside beings, usually animals, sometime plants, other peoples or women."[22] Rituals are based on faith in the existence of a transcendental world of causation that is beyond earthly life and thus beyond death. The "irreducible structures of religious phenomena" are mythic representations of human relations with one another and the environment. "In fact," writes Bloch, "this ritual representation is simple transformation of the material processes of life in plants and animals as well as humans."[23] The normal ecological processes of life (birth-maturation-death) are reversed in ritual, "an idiom which has two distinguishing features: first, it is accomplished through a classic three-stage dialectical process, and secondly, it involves a marked element of violence . . . or of conquest."[24]

On the secular level of power relations, cosmic religious wars in mythic imagery assert the "primacy of order over chaos" entailing the establishment of a bourgeois socioeconomic system defined and delimited by a tiny minority of male elites. Veena Das has pointed out that chaos cannot be accepted in the cosmologies and discourse of the powerful because the system of "order" imposed by elites might be revealed in its true meaning: the unjust legitimization of the marginalization, pauperization, and suffering of the majority, "[c]lothed in the language of [religious] responsibility."[25] Thus the cosmological triumph of order over chaos, the religious rationale for warfare, is a means of perpetuating the suffering of the powerless:

> When religious cultures portray warfare as something that is acknowledged and ultimately controlled, . . . they are presenting an almost cosmological reenactment of the primacy of order over chaos. In the stained glass windows of the great European cathedrals portraying Christ as king, emerging from his grace like a general victorious in battle, the designers were stating something fundamental about Christianity and every other religious tradition: religion reaffirms the primacy of order, which requires that violence and other forms of disorder be conquered.[26]

Just as mythic cosmic war, hegemony, and oppression of the muted majority go hand in hand, so the Goddess, ecology, and the women's movement are interrelated.

> There is a close relationship between myths, rituals, the environment, and gender roles. We are not talking about simple causal links—a myth, for instance, does not give rise to a particular social structure. Myths and rituals can be seen both as a partial reflection of ecological and social realities and as a justification for them.[27]

In imperialist designs, psychoanalyst Frantz Fanon has observed that the colonial or conqueror tends to demonize the native population as a rationale for attacking, dominating, and reeducating them.

> The colonial world is a Manichean world. It is not enough for the settler to delimit physically, that is to say with the help of the army and the police force, the place of the native. As if to show the totalitarian character of colonial exploitation the settler paints the native as a sort of quintessence of evil. Native society is not simply described as a society lacking in values, It is not enough for the colonist to affirm that those values have disappeared from, or still better

> never existed in, the colonial world. The native is declared insensible to ethics; he represents not only the absence of values, but also the negation of values. He is, let us dare to admit, the enemy of values, and in this sense he is the absolute evil.[28]

Brāhmaṇic Religion

I am not the first to observe that the primary Hindu sacred texts representing the religion of the Aryan brāhmaṇas are structured around a central metaphor of cosmic war against the demonized Other—indigenous tribals and the Dravidian population. Clearly, male compositions such as the Vedas, epics, and Purāṇas reflect elite male interests and exist for their benefit, hence it should be no surprise that the Sanskritic religious texts of India are variations on the theme of elite males, armed to the teeth, performing blood sacrifices and marching to war, where they will establish order over chaos.

The *Ṛgveda* describes a battle between the *devas* (gods) and demons, variously identified as *daityas, dāsas, dasyus, paṇis, rākṣasas,* and in later Vedic literature, *asuras.* In the universal language of light symbology, the gods represent the forces of light and the demons are the forces of darkness. The unfortunate "demons" were stripped of their land and then consigned to the lowest rung of the caste system, the śūdras, or condemned into posterity as dalits, and there they have remained to this day. References to warfare abound in the Vedas and related texts. The *Rāmāyaṇa* and the *Mahābhārata,* textual versions of an oral tradition of unwritten bardic recitation, are based on conflicts and wars, and make allusions to theories of warfare, military formations, and sacred symbolic weaponry. The *Rāmāyaṇa* describes the Aryans, their conquest of the indigenous Indian peoples and Dravidians, and the penetration of the Aryan culture. Ayodhyā is depicted in the *Rāmāyaṇa* as a city whose military is defensive rather than aggressive (a deep moat and strong fortification surrounded the city), and whose warriors were undefeated in battle, fearless, skillful, resembling lions guarding their mountain caves. The *Mahābhārata,* which attempts to integrate the various tribes into the Vedic fold, is a sacred war epic recording the conflict between the two claimants to the throne, a tale that is said to symbolize the eternal struggle between good and evil.[29] The *Bhagavadgītā,* a part of the *Mahābhārata* written about the second century BCE, depicts a supremely binomial world of active struggle between good and evil forces, one in which God becomes an active participant.

Finally, the *Devī-māhātmya,* the Śākta classic written by brāhmaṇas, recounts another sacred cosmic war in which the Great Goddess Caṇḍī defeats the buffalo-demon to save the pantheon of male gods from annihilation. The Mahiṣāsura-mardinī myth, although a narrative about the goddess, is a male myth about war, establishing order over chaos, and the instrumentality of the Great Goddess. Since this goddess is the composite energies of the male gods, she is neither self-creating nor autonomous; her mission is to serve the pantheon of male gods. There is a great profusion of demon blood on the battleground, consumed with relish by fierce goddess Kālī's lolling tongue. This gory battleground scene echoes heroic Tamil descriptions of Ko͟r͟ravai and her troupe of goblins ecstatically devouring blood on the battleground. Tantric practitioners construe the demons and their seed as negative emotions that the savior goddess destroys. Eschatologists interpret the *Devī-māhātmya* in light of cataclysm and divine intercession at the close of the Kaliyuga. Cosmologists see in the *Devī-māhātmya* the battle between gods and fallen angels, who were cast down to Earth and lived among humans. In its most abstract philosophical dimension, the *Devī-māhātmya* depicts a metaphysical conception of order over chaos and, ultimately, death. If the theme is the transmutation of chaos into order, the counter-theme is the inability of ruling elites and warriors to continue their domination of the majority without an enemy, real or imagined, who constitutes a threat. Throughout prehistory and history, kings and tyrants have maintained their rule by observing these principles.

Tamil Religion

Unlike jealous monotheistic gods, the gods and goddesses of the Old Tamil kings were beneficently tolerant of many organized religions, thus kings never raided or pillaged Buddhist or Jaina temples. Their religious tolerance was tempered, however, by their warrior mentality, which justified frequent raids on hunter-gathere, indigenes whose land they coveted. In Tamil Caṅkam society, warfare was the highly propagandized central individual and group concern of both men and women. Like the Vedic Aryans, the ancient Tamils were dominated by a warrior-priest culture based on a dominator hierarchy and male supremacy.

The ancient Tamil warrior worldview not only articulates the principle of blood sacrifice for crops, but also expresses the symbolic equivalence of blood sacrifice in war and blood sacrifice in ritual that marks the psychology of the male hunter. During the Indian Caṅkam age, the glorification of war is the subject of elaborate, haunting war poetry written by the bards of the Old Tamil kings. War, like ritual sacrifice, is sacralized by the bards as the physical manifestation of the meeting point of the divine and the human; the ancient Tamils in battle were therefore performing a religious ritual. On the battlefield, Ko͟r͟ravai's devotees included women dancers who, drumming, dancing, and singing, accompanied male soldiers to war. Ko͟r͟ravai and a multitude of ghosts and demonesses feasted on the flesh of the enemy slain on the battlefield, the prototype (*avec* cannibalism) of the Caṇḍī-Durgā-Kālī myth in the *Devī-māhātmya.* Mythic cosmic war becomes the mental reality of the warrior or sacrificer at the killing moment. Thus in contemporary Kerala, ritual performers perceive the blood sacrifice (*guruti*) in ritual performances as analogous to ancient sacrifices in mythic battles.[30]

The most common metaphor found in Caṅkam *aham* poetry describes a macabre battlefield of corpses in flowery poetics as a glorious agricultural harvest, a bardic conceit grounded in the homeopathic magical rite of sowing blood into the agricultural fields. Such imagery reveals an equation in the minds of warriors between blood and decapitated heads on the battlefield and a bountiful harvest, which we have related to the primal conception of blood sacrifice for the crops. This correlation is also found among the Naga warrior tribes' equation of head-taking with agricultural yield. The corpses were regarded as forms of human sacrifice, and the slain enemies became a cannibalistic sacrament.

The Tamil paradigm is undergirded by the notion of *āṇaṅku* and other philosophical remnants of an archanic shamanic substratum. The deities of the ancient Tamils were "frightful beings"[31] whose activities are reflected in their etymologies. The root words to denote *deity* include *aṇaṅku*, "to afflict," *cūr*, "to fear," and *kaṭavul*, "debt" or "sacrifice." There was believed to be a god living in anything that causes fear, pain, or suffering. In another cosmic war, the primary god, Murukaṉ, is reputed to have killed the *cūr* (demon) and his tribe with his famous long spear (*neṭuvel*), described by bards in flowing, polyvalent images that equate carnage with agricultural produce by homologizing blood and flowers. The Murukaṉ-Cūr conflict is interpreted by Dubianski as a variant of the basic Tamil myth of the demon slayed by his consort, with "a functional replacement of the goddess by her son."[32] It is the quintessential male creation tale, wrought in blood, death, and destruction.

> as he kills
> so the field grows red
> and his anklets whirl.
> This is his hill
> and it is thick
> with blood bunches
> of your *kāntaḷ*.[33]

Mazdean Religion

Zoroastrianism was apparently the religion of the Persian people by the sixth century BCE; when Cyrus the Great founded the Medo-Persian Empire, he ruled as a Zoroastrian from 558 to 530 BCE, as did Darius (522–486 BCE). For two centuries, Persia conquered and controlled the Near East. In 538 BCE, when Cyrus conquered Babylon and the Jews came under Persian control, many Jews who lived in captivity were allowed by Cyrus to return to Jerusalem.[34] The majority of Jews, however, remained in Mesopotamia and blended into the culture. The king of Persia, according to the book of Esther, took a Jewish woman as his wife. The arch-enemies of the Zoroastrian communities of north Iran were the nomadic horsemen, whose religion was animistic polytheism. Zoroaster consistently pits these two peoples against one another as the People of Righteousness (*asha*) and the People of the Lie (*druj*). The religion focused on increasing the harvest and protecting the domestic animals that labored to produce food. Exemplifying the common archaic foundation of the ancient

Indo-European religious traditions (the separation of the Indo-Iranian tribes is dated about 2500 BCE),[35] Zoroaster's polarizing theology may have existed coeval with the *Ṛgveda*, around the sixth millennium BCE[36] or later, and underpins all later Iranian spirituality, including the *Qur'ān*. (Zoroastrians are regarded as *gabars*, or "infidels," in Iran, and have suffered much persecution since the Islamic rule of Ayatollah Ruhollah Khomeini in 1979.[37]) Iran's heroic age of remote antiquity is described in the Yashts of the *Avesta*, where Kayanian kings offer sacrifice to the gods in order to earn their support and gain strength in the perpetual struggle against their enemies, the Turanians. As the major concern of the Kayanians, this eternal bitter feud with the Turanians constitutes the main theme of the Iranian epic. Zoroastrianism adopted these legends of the past to create a male binomial world of perpetual warfare.

According to Zoroaster, Ahura Mazda is the supreme male god who, without the womb of a Mother-goddess, creates Good and Evil, the holy one and the destroying demon, Ahriman (Angra Mainyu). In the Pahlavi *Bundahisn*, Ahriman is a free agent who created evil spirits and demons to wage cosmic war between Heaven and Earth. His six commanders are Aka Manah, Indra, Sauru, Nāoṅhaithya, Taurvi, and Zoicha. Zoroaster proclaimed that Ahriman and Ahura Mazda, respectively, shall be in constant war until the final millennial cycle of the world, a time when righteousness (*aśa*) will finally triumph over the power of evil (*druj*). Zoroaster converted abstract concepts into demons such as *taromaiti* (arrogance), *methaxta* (false speech), *āzi* (greed), *būsyātā* (inordinate sleep or sloth), *asto-vidātu* (divider of bones at death), *apāośa* (drought), *zemaka* (winter), and so forth.

The religion teaches that the entire history of the universe, past, present, and future, is divided into four 3,000-year periods: in the first period, there was no matter; the second period preceded Zoroaster; in the third period, his faith is propagated. The first nine millennia constitute the struggle between good and evil—good humans help Ahura Mazda and evil humans help Ahriman. Each person after death crosses the Chinvato Peretav, or bridge of the separator, which spans the fires of hell. If the individual helped Ahriman, the bridge narrows and he falls to hell, but if he supported Ahura Mazda, he is worthy of salvation and he finds a wide road to the realm of light. In the fourth and final period of the universe, Saoshyant, a savior, will appear, the human dead will all rise for their final reward or punishment, and the reign of eternal good begins.

The premises of Zoroaster's preaching are that (1) the ultimate God is Ahura Mazda, (2) by choosing Ahura Mazda, the Mazdean chooses good over evil, the *true religion* over that of the demons (*devas*), (3) therefore, the fight against the *devas* is required of all Mazdeans. By demanding that his disciples no longer worship the Mazdean *devas* and that they cease sacrificing bovines, Zoroaster was rejecting a part of the Aryan religious tradition.[38] He did not require stringent adherence to his laws, apparently: the *haoma* ritual, the cult of Mithra, and the animal sacrifices continued.

"Zoroastrianism is the oldest of the revealed world-religions," writes Mary Boyce, "and it has probably had more influence on mankind, directly and indirectly, than any other single faith."[39] One of the earliest eschatologists, Zoroaster warned his disciples that Ahura Mazda has decided to cause "the imminent and irrevocable *eschaton.*"[40] Zoroaster provided the prototype not only for the Abrahamic eschatologies, but also for the Satan figure and his demons,[41] Heaven and Hell, the doctrines of the future resurrection of the body, the Last Judgment, and everlasting life for the reunited soul and body.[42]

Judeo-Christian Religion

Chrisitianity's Satan was, like the Vedic *asuras* and the Mazdean Ahriman, originally part of a host of divine spirits, a "son of God" who revolted and became evil. As Bhattacharyya points out,

> Hebrew mythology has preserved the memory of a heavenly court of spirits and kept alive the tradition of how some of these spirits were commissioned in olden times to find out roots of evil leading mankind to destruction, and from this cycle of ideas there was born a belief in an arch-enemy of God, namely, Satan. Christianity inherited the demonological tradition from Mesopotamian, Greek, and Hebrew mythology but it was in the New Testament that the company of evil spirits was synthesized into a single Satanic figure, leader of the demonic troops of the fallen angels.[43]

When, according to the early Christian tradition, Satan was sent on a mission to investigate human virtue, he transgressed his own limits and became a permanent skeptic. Satan as a popular concept was related to Egyptian sources, since the Coptic Christians have given him, among others, the name of Zet, a vestige of the Egyptian Typhonic god Set, who impersonated evil and killed Osiris. The Islamic Satan, known as Shaitān, and his retinue are the beings behind the images of false gods. The name, which occurs fifty-two times in the *Qur'ān,* is derived from *shaṭn,* "opposition."

Gods whose worshipers were opposed to Israel or the prophets were denounced in the *Old Testament* and reduced to the rank of demons. Hebrew demons such as Bel, Leviathan, and many others had Mesopotamian or Canaanite origins. In Babylonia, Tiamat (cf. Taimāta of the *Atharvaveda*), the Deep, was a dragon known in post-exile Hebrew literature as Rahad, a female demon who revolted against Yahweh but was defeated by him. In this myth, Yahweh clearly performs the function of Babylonian Marduk in annihilating a guilty female.[44] In an obvious reference to the Babylonian creation epic, Leviathan in the *Old Testament* was a many-headed mythical dragon slayed by Yahweh, who "broke the heads of Leviathan in pieces, and gave him as food to the people inhabiting the wilderness."[45] According to Bhattacharyya, there is no counterpart of Satan in the Indian tradition. "The Buddhist concept of Māra is [Satan's] nearest approximation so far as the external similarities are concerned," he writes. "The Vedic counterpart of the Avestan *druj* is *Nirṛti* and that of *aśa* is *ṛta*."[46]

Jack Nelson-Pallmeyer points to the "never-ending spiral of violence"[47] at the heart of the Abrahamic violence-of-God tradition, in which

> God becomes an instrument of human revenge. Compassion and salvation are militarized, that is, understood as the crushing defeat of enemies within or at the end of history. In the apocalyptic view, God is the ultimate avenger of wrongs at the end of history rather than within it because the imperial situation makes it difficult for humans to carry out the desired punishments. The violence-of-God traditions at the center of the exodus, exile, and apocalyptic story lines in the Hebrew Bible are, contrary to the views of many Christians, at the heart of the New Testament as well.[48]

Violence performed in the name of Yahweh, a jealous deity who blesses one particular group and required his followers to destroy the shrines of other gods and goddesses and their worshipers, is the subject of many biblical passages. Not only are his followers coached to commit acts of violence, but God Himself will "repay those who hate Him to their face to destroy them."

> When the Lord your God brings you into the land which you go to possess, and has cast out many nations before you, the Hittites and the Girgashites and the Amorites and the Canaanites and the Perizzites and the Hivites and the Jeusites, seven nations greater and mightier than you, and when the Lord your God delivers them over to you, you shall conquer them and then you must utterly destroy them. You shall make no covenant with them nor show mercy to them. . . . But thus you shall deal with them: you shall destroy their altars, and break down their sacred pillars, and cut down their wooden images, and burn their carved images with fire. For you are a holy people to the Lord your God; the Lord your God has chosen you to be a people for Himself, a special treasure above all the peoples on the face of the earth. . . . He repays those who hate Him to their face, to destroy them. He will not be slack with him who hates Him; He will repay him to his face.[49]

Nelson-Pallmeyer and Richard Hoseley agree that the hostile rhetoric of such sacred passages is guided by the self-interest of priests and their effort to justify and legitimize the reconstituted Jewish socio-political order.[50] In the Hebrew scriptures, priests were empowered by their special understanding of what pleased or displeased Yahweh, and rival priestly groups had competing descriptions of God and His sites of worship. As Jack Nelson-Pallmeyer points out, some priest claimed that they must sacrifice directly to El, while their rivals swore that making offerings to El would invoke Yahweh's wrath; some believed Elohim (a plural name changed to singular Yahweh) was merciless, while others asserted that Yahweh was merciful. "These conflicts, which led to violence and fed the pathology of God as adversaries, claimed divine approval."[51] Yahweh's demand that proselytizers of foreign religions be stoned to death, even if they are one's own family, places into perspective the Indian fierce goddesses on the battlefield. Deuteronomy warns the ancient Hebrews that

> you shall not listen to the words of that prophet or that dreamer of dreams, for the Lord your God is testing you to know whether you love the Lord your God with all your heart and with all your soul. . . . But that prophet or that dreamer of dreams shall be put to death, because he has spoken in order to turn you away from the Lord your God. . . . If your brother, the son of your mother, your son or your daughter, the wife of your bosom, or your friend who is as your own soul, secretly entices you, saying, "Let us go and serve other gods," which you have not known, neither you nor your fathers . . . you shall not consent to him or listen to him, nor shall your eye pity him, nor shall you spare him or conceal him; but you shall surely kill him; your hand shall be first against him to put to death, and afterward the hand of all the people. And you shall stone him with stones until he dies, because he sought to entice you away from the Lord your God. . . . So all Israel shall hear and fear, and not again do such wickedness as this among you.[52]

Islam

The sacred scriptures of Abrahamic religions are as filled with chapters that morally legitimate war and violence as the holy writ of Zoroaster or the sacred epics of India, and it may be tempting to the historian to bracket them all together as classic male predatory behavior. This conclusion is incorrect on two counts. First, a distinction should be drawn between the relative religious tolerance inherent in polytheism, where gods and goddesses of various sects generally tolerate one another as parts of a whole or cogs in a wheel, versus the rigid authoritarianism implicit in the jealous monotheistic God. Second, a serious study of Islamic texts and the history of Muslim world conquests will convince any researcher that Islam in not your garden-variety religion.

The militant spread of Islam is driven by a unique warrior ideology of world conquest, led in spirit by the unparalleled warrior, Muhammad. *Allāh* himself declares, "I will instill terror into hearts of the Infidels," commanding the faithful, "Strike off their head, then, and strike off from them every fingertip."[53] Of all major religions, only Muslims are given a *standing order* by God (*Allāh*) to commit violence against the rest of the world until the ultimate triumph of Islam. One of the common elements to all Islamic schools of thought is *jihād,* the Holy War, a divine institution whose ultimate aim is to conquer the entire world and require all people to either submit to the rule of the one true religion and *sharī'ah* law or be reduced to the status of *ẓimmīs,* the protectees or wards of the Muslims. In exchange, *ẓimmīs* pay a *jizyah,* the tax that will protect them from the resumption of *jihād* against them. Refusal to pay the tax is punished by death. All Muslims have a sacred duty, established in the *Qur'ān* and the Traditions, to proselytize Islam *specifically through jihād.*[54]

> Fight those who believe not in Allāh nor the Last Day, nor hold that forbidden which hath been forbidden by Allāh and His Messenger, nor acknowledge the religion of Truth, (even if they are) of the People of the Book, until they pay the *jizyah* with willing submission, and feel themselves subdued.[55]

The *Qur'ān* spells out the Muslim's proper attitude and behavior regarding unbelievers:

> As for the unbelievers for them garments of fire shall be cut and there shall be poured over their heads boiling water whereby whatever is in their bowels and skins shall be dissolved and they will be punished with hooked iron rods.[56]
>
> Believers, when you meet the unbelievers preparing for battle do not turn your backs to them. Anyone who does—shall incur the wrath of God and Hell shall be his home: an evil dwelling indeed.[57]
>
> And when the sacred months are passed, kill those who join other gods with God wherever ye shall find them; and seize them, besiege them, and lay wait for them with every kind of ambush: but if they shall convert, and observe prayer and pay the obligatory alms, then let them go their way, for God is Gracious, Merciful. If any one of those who join gods with God ask an asylum of thee, grant him an asylum, that he may hear the Word of God, and then let him reach his place of safety. This, for that they are people devoid of knowledge.[58]
>
> Say to the infidels: If they desist *from their unbelief,* what is now past shall be forgiven them; but if they return *to it,* they have already before them the doom of the ancients! Fight then against them till strife be at an end, and the religion be all of it God's. If they desist, verily God beholdeth what they do: but if they turn their back, know ye that God is your protector: Excellent protector! excellent helper! And know ye, that when ye have taken any booty, a fifth part belongeth to God and to the Apostle, and to the near of kin, and to orphans, and to the poor, and to the wayfarer.[59]

Divine Feminine Violence

Why is a female deity given a role typically filled by males, that of the victorious warrior? Ancient fertility and war goddesses Inanna, Ishtar, Anath, Ko<u>rr</u>avai, Kālī, and Durgā are all Great Mother-goddesses and protectresses representing the heroic martial spirit that began to dominate and shape world history in the third millennium BCE. Logically, their motherhood may be linked to their assuming the role of valiant warriors and protectresses in battle, able to fight for their subjects and to overcome any enemy. The female Rajputni (woman warriors) attest to the fact that women have been deemed capable of armed warfare in the recent past in Rajasthan.

While it is true that brāhmaṇas co-opted native and Dravidian goddesses for their own purposes, Indic tribals and Dravidians have worshiped for millennia fierce goddesses who morphed from the Mistress of Wild Animals into patently militaristic and violent wargoddesses such as Tamil Ko<u>rr</u>avai, the latter necessary to combat Vedic warriors led by Aryan male war-god Indra, to defeat tribals and confiscate their territories, and to oversee internecine conflicts of succession and inheritance.[60] In epico-Purāṇic myths, the brāhmaṇic authors, either by design or resignation, marginally assimilated indigenous and Dravidian war goddesses into the persona of brāhmaṇic Durgā, an erstwhile fertility goddess not associated with victory or war. Ko<u>rr</u>avai lay submerged in Durgā, but was resurrected as the dalit goddess Māriyamma<u>n</u> after the caste Hindu appropriation of south India.

As in elite literature, the folkloric domain is dominated by Indian women and goddesses linked with killing and violence. In the Pandav Lila (*pāṇḍava līlā*), a traditional folk ritual and dramatization of the *Mahābhārata* found only in Garhwal, a formerly princely state in the Himalayan districts of Uttar Pradesh, martial valour and violence are glorified in the characters of the Pāṇḍava warriors, who are violence specialists. Fully equal to the warriors' brutality is the Pāṇḍavas' wife Draupadī, who is identified as Kālī, and foregrounded as one of the most violent characters in the folk ritual drama. She is the warrior's wife *par excellence* who aids her husband by directing her divine rage to his enemies. The ritual includes animal sacrifice, dancing, competitive recitation of folk versions of the *Mahābhārata*, and an aspect of tree worship following military victory in which an uprooted tree is worshipfully converted to a pole-like pivot, similar to the Canaanite *asherahs*, around which characters dance.[61] The war violence is depicted as specific to the kṣatriya *varṇa* (warrior caste).

According to local mythology around Draupadī, "Draupadī is Kālī";[62] the two goddesses are explicitly equated in the cult of Draupadī in Tamilnadu.[63] She is both goddess and the supreme paragon of the loyal Rajput wife and proponent of military authority. "That both Draupadi and Kali should be strongly associated with Rajput women should come as no surprise," writes Sax, "since Pandav Lila is clearly a Rajput tradition."[64] In Rajput society, the expression of male violence is linked to warfare, while female violence is manifested in ritual, myth, and sacrifice.[65] Warriors' wives are encouraged to internalize violence in the self-sacrifice of *satī*, modeled by Satī, who set herself ablaze for the sake of her husband, and by the deification of women who incinerated themselves on the funeral pyre of their husbands.

The Tamil Draupadī cult enacted scenes from the *Mahābhārata* in the first century AD, and the cult coexisted with the composition of the Sanskrit *Mahābhārata* (between 500 BCE and AD 400), yet the critical edition of the *Mahābhārata* privileges the Sanskrit manuscripts over the contemporary Tamil versions. The reason for this may lie in the fact that the brāhmaṇas do not dominate the Draupadī cult; rather, it is the cult of a major peasant caste such as the Velalars. Spirit possession séances are crucial for itinerant professionals, while possession is abhorred in brāhmaṇical ideology. "The attempt to produce a critical edition of these traditions is almost against their very nature."[66]

A Tamil chapbook, the *Catakaṇṭarāvaṇaṉ Katai* (*CRK*), springs from a similar inversion of a classic Sanskritic epic, the *Rāmāyaṇa*. Sītā's battle against the demon Śatakaṇṭharāvaṇa, unknown to the *Vālmīki Rāmāyaṇa*, is a women's inversion of the classic Sanskrit tale. Sītā is the diametrical opposite of the brāhmaṇic didactic model of the modest, self-sacrificing wife of Rāma, the paragon of wifely virtue. In this epic she is a fierce militant goddess, "very close to the powerful and aggressive Tamil village goddesses. . . . Like them, she takes violent action against a male enemy; and she insists upon acting alone while her cohorts simply sit and watch."[67] In this account, Rāma is faced with a powerful *rākṣasa* named Catakaṇṭarāvaṇaṉ whom no one can conquer. Sītā convinces Rāma that she can destroy the demon: "Then Rāmamūrti knew, by the eye of wisdom that Sītā would conquer the Rākṣasa Rāvaṇa; she knew what she was saying. And he thought hard about it."[68]

Most of the *CRK* text is lurid description of Sītā's glorious nine-day battle, which Shulman, like many scholars, finds tediously gory:

> We may, I think, spare ourselves a detailed recital of these reports from the battlefield—the repeated, indeed formulaic descriptions of the superbly equipped *senāpatis* and their hosts of warriors, the endless array of symbolically matched *astras*. . ., the ritualized roaring and thundering, the hackneyed *pralaya* imagery, the conventional dismemberings and disembowelments, the dances of the headless corpses, the gruesome feasts of the demons—all, in short, that must constitute for the Tamil audience of this text its main interest and beauty.[69]

When Sītā defeats Śatakaṇṭha, the world is free of evil and the rule of Rāma (*rāma-rājya*) is secure, but only temporarily. Threats to order will arise again, and other battles will be necessary to maintain order. "Order," of course, is defined by the conquerors, who are historically both revolutionaries (during the freedom movement against the British) and elite predators. In all cases, the beneficiaries of the order established by the goddess have been high-caste warriors and brāhmaṇas, never women or the low caste majority. As David Shulman analyzes this theme of the battle against chaos as the necessary prelude to order:

> Indeed, one feels that such a threat is somehow necessary to the reality of order: the text involves the audience in a process, in the course of which the always latent sense of fear and potential evil is released, externalized, and conquered. On a more abstract level, we might say that the ideal social and cultural order symbolized by Rāma's kingship has neither life nor meaning until it is brought into relation with a much more ambiguous and dynamic reality.[70]

In Rajasthan, kṣatriya women have been given fairly thorough military training since the post-Vedic period or earlier, and Rajput princesses, as well as female guards of kings, are known to be quite adept at sword and spear.[71] There is evidence that female Rajputani served in standing armies when they were needed. Daughters of elite rulers also received military and administrative training. "If such were not the case," according to A.S. Altekar,

> dowager queens like Nayanikā of the Sātavāhana dynasty (second century BC), Prabhāvatī Gupta of the Vākāṭṭārikā family (fourth century AD), Vijayabhaṭṭārikā of the Chālukya house family (seventh century AD), and Sugandhā and Diddā of Kashmir (tenth century AD) could not have successfully administered extensive kingdoms during the minority of their sons. . . . [I]n the Chālukya administration (*c.* 980–1160 AD), queen governors and officers were quite common. The due discharge of these administrative duties presupposed a good training on proper lines.[72]

By contrast, Lindsey Harlan has studied contemporary Rajput women's conceptualization of their local warrior *kuladevī*, the unmarried and fierce virgin who protects the *kula*. Rather than being polarized against the benign, maternal *kuladevī*, as we find in Sanskrit literature, the fierce *kuladevī* was equated with the maternal or protectress *kuladevī*. Rajput women identify with their *kuladevī*, who, sword in one hand and spear in the other, represents the ancestor female Rajputani and their loyal performance of military service in a time of historical necessity.[73] The fierce goddess is a dual symbol for Rajput women of their past glories on the battlefield, protecting male property and caste interests, and their modern role as house-bound family protectress. "The *kuladevī*," says Harlan, " has one job, that of protection, but two arenas of activity, the battlefield and the household."[74] Both arenas of the *kuladevī*'s sphere of influence protect elite male property interests and the caste system. As Harlan writes,

> The goddess on the battlefield represents the discrete political identity of her *kul* or *shakh*. This *kuldevi* is wholly martial and her form is a lone beast. She has no husband to serve, only power to wield. Moreover, though benign from the *kul's* (or *shakh's*) point of view, she is a consumer of husbands, a protector sustained by family blood. *For the sake of their group she sacrifices them as warrior-protégés and in doing so enables them to fulfill their caste duty and attain the ultimate goal of a Rajput protector, warrior heaven.*[75]

The warrior aspect of the goddess came to serves elite male interests and their idea of cosmic order, which is crystallized in the caste system. The domestic *kuladevī* plays the female role rejected by ancient Amazons: she is totally restricted to her home (*parda*), where she is the protectress of the household. Here, rather than sacrificing men on the battlefield, she sacrifices herself as a *pativratā* (one who has vowed to protect her husband). Her failure to protect her husband, before the prohibition on self-immolation, was punished by her self-sacrifice as a *satī* in the cremation fires of her husband. The practice became popular again in the late twentieth century.

Satī

> What links *kuldevi* images is the conception of the complementary and symmetrical protective services she performs in each jurisdiction. When any warrior dies in battle, however, all conceptual symmetry crumbles. Sacrificing a warrior, the *kuldevi* takes the life of a husband, whose death suggests a failure of her domestic protection and that of her *pativrata protégé*, his wife. Symmetry is reestablished only through a further sacrifice that of the wife on behalf of her husband.[76]

* * *

> The wife is usually the dearest relation of a man, and the visitations of a chief's ghost were popularly attributed to his desire to be united with his quondam queen. Why not lessen these dreaded visitations by burning or burying her along with his remains? This custom also made the life of the patriarch very safe; it practically eliminated all possibility of any one among his numerous

mutually envious wives intriguing against his life. They all knew that even if successful, they had no chance of surviving him. They were therefore all care and attention to see that no preventable accident intervened to shorten the husband's life.[77]

The custom of *satī*, or the burning of wives on the funeral pyres of their husbands, is the inversion of the male sacrifice of seasonal regicide practiced in ancient Neolithic societies. *Satī* is not unique to India, but was widely prevalent in primitive tribes in ancient times, practiced among the Norwegians, Gauls, Celts, Goths, Slavs, Chinese, Thracians, the Aryans in the Indo-European period, and probably also common among the Scythians. The premise that the deceased will enjoy the same goods and services in the afterlife as he had on earth underlies a variety of forms of funerary ceremonial involving the suicide or self-sacrifice of particular classes of survivors.[78] In patriarchal cultures, the ruler, master, or husband will require in the afterlife his horse and his weapons, fine garments and accessories, and food, as well as his human servants, counselors, and wives. In ancient China and Scythia, for example, kings or great warlords were buried with their warriors, counselors, horses, offerings, artifacts, and wives. If a Chinese widow sacrificed her life in order to follow her husband to heaven, a great procession was held to carry out her corpse with much civic fanfare, cognate with Indian processions held for *satīs*.

It is assumed that the custom went out of vogue among the Aryans by 1500 BCE, since it is neither mentioned in the *Avesta*, nor referred to in the funeral hymns of the *Ṛgveda*, nor mentioned in the Buddhist literature; thus *satī* was probably not practiced in 500 BCE. From about 300 BCE, references to the custom of *satī* appear in the *Mahābhārata*,[79] which records only a few cases, compared with numerous instances of widows surviving their husbands. Manu does not prescribe *satī*. By about AD 400, when the Purāṇas were written in their present form, the custom of *satī* gradually came into general vogue,[80] becoming one of a wide range of religious rituals signifying self-mutilation and self-sacrifice that both Indian men and women observe.

Most theorists surmise that *satī* was primarily a kṣatriya tradition among the women of kings, warriors, and men who had died a heroic death. Through the process of Sanskritization, according to a theory developed by anthropologist M.N. Srinivas in the 1950s, the lower castes gradually assimilated elite religions and customs such as *satī*. The warrior ethic glorified the *satī* as the pinnacle of self-sacrifice; as the reward for their self-sacrifice, she and her husband were guaranteed eternal conjugal bliss in heaven. The patriarchal widow-burning tradition instrumentalized the template of fierce war goddesses, especially in Rajasthan, the kṣatriyan stronghold. *Kuladevīs* in Rajasthan function as Earth Mothers, the warrior-protectresses of land, male property, and family, and faithful wives are programed to emulate their deified ancestresses—whose iconic temple figures are depicted surrounded by flames—and become *satīs*. From the seventh century onward, *satī* became a common practice among the

Rajputs, the prototypical "warrior caste" of modern India; hence widow-burning became associated with the kṣatriyas. However, there is no conclusive evidence that *satī* was originally the exclusive custom of the martial caste, and numerous early textual and epigraphical accounts point to a whole range of other castes, from brāhmaṇas to impure castes groups, who practiced widow-burning.

The psychological coercion and shakedown inherent in the *satī* tradition left the widow little chance to escape her fate. She would not only live in heaven with her husband for eternity, but she would also redeem the sins of seven generations in the lineages of her father, mother, and in-laws, and, as the ultimate blessing, she would never be born again into the "impure" female sex. Myths, hagiographies, literature, *satī* temples in which *satīs* are deified icons, and the political equation of communalist violence and propaganda, have conspired against women in castes where *satī* was homologized with the ideal faithful, dutiful wife, which itself was the sole measure of a woman's worth. Futhermore, the widow was bombarded with guidance from family, brāhmaṇas, and bards to take the solemn vow to become a *satī*.

During the period AD 700–1100, *satīs* became more frequent in northern India and quite common in Kashmir, possibly because of its proximity to Central Asia, home of the Scythians. There is some evidence that the custom of *satī* was practiced outside Kashmir and became gradually more popular in northern India. Harṣa's mother, queen Yaśomatī, upon hearing that her husband's medical case was hopeless, gave away her ornaments, took a sacred bath, put on all the marks of a wife living with her husband, and was taken to the funeral pyre.[81] In her final grand procession to the burning pyre, the *satī* was honored by great pageantry and reverence:

> The *Satī* was an object of the highest veneration, and so was taken out to the accompaniment of music in a grand procession through the town to the cremation grounds. She was given a bath, and then she put on her person all the insignia of *saubhāgya* or married bliss. She used to carry with her *kumkum*, mirror, comb and betel leaves which were the insignia of *saubhāgya*. Very often she used to give away her ornaments and belongings to her friends and relations, who used to keep them as sacred mementos. Then she used to take final leave of her relations. Some travellers have narrated that people used to entrust to her messages to their dead relations in heaven; whether such was really the case may well be doubted. Ascending the funeral pyre, she used to place her husband's head on her lap. Then the pyre was lighted.[82]

Usually the *satī* ascended the same pyre that was prepared for her husband, except in cases of multiple wives, where the favored wife would be honored in the same pyre, or they might all burn together if jealousies were reconciled. If the husband died in battle, the *satī* mounted a pyre with her husband's turban or shoes in place of his body. Special funeral arrangements were made in case the *satī* lost her nerve at the last minute: the funeral pyre was piled in a deep pit in many regions, particularly the Deccan and western India, which made the widow's escape impossible. In Gujarat and northern Uttar Pradesh, the widow was tied to one of the pillars of a specially constructed wooden house, about twelve feet square; in Bengal, the feet of the widow were tied to posts driven into the ground, she was asked three times if she really wished to go to heaven, and, if she assented, the pyre awaited her.

Although we have evidence that *satī* was a Dravidian custom in south India during the Caṅkam age, in the extreme south the custom was more an exception than a rule down to *c.* AD 1000, according to Altekar.

> The queen of only king Bhūta Pāṇḍya of the Saṅgam age is know to have followed the custom (*Puram*, 246–47). Her historicity is, however, a matter of uncertainty. Among the members of the Pallava, the Chola and the Pāṇḍya ruling families, . . . we do not come across any cases of Satī down to *c.* 900 AD. It is therefore clear that the custom was yet to obtain a footing in South India.[83]

In the Tamil *Puṟanaṉūru*, the chief wife of King Pūtapāṇṭiyaṉ preferred a fiery death to the slow torture of widowhood, instructing:

> Go ahead, spurn the pyre of black wood
> heaped on the burning ground.
> To me,
> since my great-armed husband is dead,
> that fire
> and a large pond of lotuses
> that have loosed from buds rich petals
> are the same.[84]

It is clear that by the twelfth and fourteenth centuries, the custom had spread to south India and penetrated into the brāhmaṇa community, which prided itself on its asceticism and self-sacrifice, and did not want to appear outdone by kṣatriyas in the custom of *satī*.[85] The custom was transported by Hindu emigrants to the islands of Java, Sumatra, and Bali, and medieval writers enthusiastically promoted *satī*.

Between the period AD 1200 and 1600, about twenty cases of *satīs* are referred to by records in Rajputana, most the widows of royal or kṣatriya families. The custom became firmly established by this period among the ruling Rajput families of northern India. Rajput princesses became psychologically programed to welcome the opportunity to become a *satī*, refusing to allow their husbands to be cremated alone. Therefore, generally at the funeral of almost every Rajput king or nobleman, his widows who were not pregnant or required to direct the government as regents would ascend the funeral pyre. According to Altekar,

> Their number was sometimes appallingly large. When Raja Ajitsingh of Marwar died in 1724, 64 women mounted his funeral pyre. When Raja Budhsingh of Bundi was drowned, 84 women became Satīs. The example of Rajputs was emulated by the Nāyakas of Madura. When two rulers of this family died in

1611 and 1620, we are told that as many as 400 and 700 women ascended the funeral pyres. These numbers are probably exaggerated by missionary reporters; it is, however, clear that a large number of women used to become Satīs at the death of each member of the Nāyaka family.[86]

Although Amaradas, the third Sikh Guru (AD 1552–74) condemned *satī*, when the Sikhs developed into a fighting community, the custom became common in Sikh aristocracy in spite of its prohibition by the Gurus, because they did not wish to be outdone by the Rajputs in the matter of time-honored martial traditions, including *satī*.[87]

In the seventeenth and eighteenth centuries, *satī* stones found in almost all of India indicate that the *satī* custom was practiced by the nonelite, as well. For example, there are fifty-one *satī* stones in the Saugar district ranging in dates from *c.* AD 1450 to 1624 that proclaim that women of all classes, including barbers, weavers, and masons, became *satīs*. It is estimated that about two percent of widows sacrificed themselves during this period.

Muslim rulers were generally opposed to the custom. Humayun wanted to prohibit it in the case of the widows past child-bearing age, but he only succeeded in appointing inspectors to insure that widows were not forced to burn themselves against their will. As a consequence, in the territories contiguous to Agra, widow sacrifice became rare. Many Muslim administrators established a rule that no widow should be allowed to mount the funeral pyre without the permission of the local Government officer. This provision proved ineffectual, since the prescribed permission was usually easily obtained.

The *satī* custom reached the height of its popularity in the first quarter of the nineteenth century, particularly in Bengal in districts under British control.

> A lengthy debate took place over how *Satī* was to be understood. Consensus emerged among colonial authorities and some Hindu reformists that Satī was not an integral part of Hinduism but a medieval perversion of its core values. The principal beneficiaries of these religiously glossed murders of women were Brahman priests who collected fees for performing the rituals and family members who stood to benefit from inheritances that otherwise might have come to the surviving widow.[88]

In December 1829, Lord William Bentick issued his famous regulation making the custom illegal in British India. Despite its prohibition, it continued until the late 1880s. The moral outrage of European at this custom, however, occurred only a decade or two after European "witches" were burned alive at the stake. Like Indian *satīs*, witches were often widows—unwanted, anomalous, or in some sense outsiders—who threatened the patriarchal rule of order.

By the end of the century, because the law against *satī* was rigorously imposed, the custom appeared to vanish; after the independence of India in 1947, the abolition of *satī* was reiterated, and the issue was considered a barbaric practice of the past. The concept of *satī* continued to pervade the lives of Rajput women, since the *satī* had been redefined: "A *satī* can now live, so long as she lives as if dead."[89] Since 1943, there has been a revival of *satī* in four north Indian states: Bihar, Uttar Pradesh, Madhya Pradesh, and particularly Rajasthan, a former *satī* stronghold. In September 1987, the highly publicized "Deorala affair"—the burning of a young Rajput widow named Roop Kanwar in Rajasthan "by 'modern,' 'educated' Maruti-driving Rajput men and women"[90]—caused nationwide shock and trauma. Kanwar, a well-educated woman from a semiurban, well-to-do family from Jaipur (the state capital of Rajasthan), was the last of a series of widows who immolated themselves in a rural region of Rajasthan, Shekhavati, one of the most underdeveloped and conservative Indian states. The federal government took legal action against *satī* by issuing the Sati Commission (Prevention) Act a year later.

Secular humanists and feminists interpret Kanwar's fate as the manipulation of ignorant rural folk by high-caste agents (particularly the Rajputs and Marwaris) whose socio-economic interests would be furthered by the revival of *satī*. In the analysis of Ashis Nandy,[91] the Westernized and English-speaking elite were threatened by Kanwar's sacrifice because her social background and level of education made her a symbol of an economically rising social group that they could not conveniently conflate with ignorance, rural life, and backwardness. As Mandakranta Bose sees it, the *satī* is an instrument of ideology:

> [T]he burning of Roop Kanwar and several other women in the past few years has shocked the Indian nation into a reexamination of its present and past. Why this resurgence of *Satī*? And why particularly now? Why and how has Roop Kanwar taken on an iconic status?. . . Because Roop Kanwar is known to have been a devout worshiper at a *Satī* temple, let us grant that she was neither drugged nor held down to the pyre but voluntarily chose to die with her husband. Yet, how autonomous is a woman whose entire life is appropriated by an ideal?
>
> My thesis is that the phenomenon of *Satī* shows an ideological manipulation of women—and, in many cases, of men as well—and this ideology has now been seized on as an effective propaganda tool for achieving political ends. Even in a populous and politically volatile country such as India, enormous organizational skills and resources are needed to mobilize hundreds of thousands of supporters. Like the Ayodhyā mosque issue, *Satī* is the key to turn on that mobilization, and it cannot be mere coincidence that the same political groups have taken leadership on both issues. The purpose behind *Satī* is no longer only the subjugation of women but the subjugation of an entire nation.[92]

The recent accounts of *satī* emerge "as an important part of the discourse of feminist criticism of Hindu culture's patriarchal structure," writes Courtright.

> From this perspective *Satī* is the most egregious example of an attempt to simultaneously repress women and celebrate to the point of deification their self-annihilation in the name of religion. In both the early colonial period and the contemporary moment Hindu traditionalists have argued that *Satī*, when properly understood and undertaken, is a sacred religious act that only the most extraordinary women who have a highly evolved moral vision and discipline

are capable of performing. In those rare cases, it is argued, such women should not be impeded by the state from carrying out their religious destinies. For both critics and admirers of *Satī* there is a shared sense that it fits into the total system of Hinduism as an emblem of its moral bankruptcy or its noble heritage. In the contemporary debate between religious and secular visions of Indian society, *Satī* has taken on renewed meaning as a contested symbol that contains contradictory interpretations.[93]

The "Myth" of Women Warriors

Although it is clear that women are naturally fierce, and that they have been successfully trained in India as warriors, classical reports of Amazons and women warriors written by Homer, Herodotus, Diodorus, and Justinus from the eighth to the first centuries BCE have been interpreted until recently by many male scholars as fantasy material. From these ancient accounts, we learn that the Amazons worshiped a warrior goddess. As Carmel Berkson writes,

> Some legends described the goddess as a powerful, courageous warrior, a leader in battle. The worship of the goddess as valiant warrior seems to have been responsible for numerous reports of female soldiers, later referred to by the classical Greeks as the Amazons. More thoroughly examining the accounts of the esteem the Amazons paid to the female deity, it became evident that women who worshiped a warrior goddess hunted and fought in the lands of Libya, Anatolia, Bulgaria, Greece, Armenia, and Russia and were far from the mythical fantasy so many writers of today would have us believe.[94]

In Homer's *Iliad*, Priam, King of Troy, remembers an encounter with Amazons when he was young:

> I went to Phrygia once, the land of vines and galloping horses,
> and learnt how numerous the Phrygians are
> when I saw the armies of Otreus and King Mygdon
> encamped by the River Sangarios.
> I was their ally and I bivouacked with them
> that time the Amazons, who fight like men, came up to attack.
> But even they were not as many as these Achaeans with their
> flashing eyes.[95]

The great Greek historian Herodotus, named the "father of historic writing" by Cicero, journeyed in 450 BCE to Scythian lands north of the Black Sea, where he heard tales of armed women riding on horseback out of the eastern steppes. He learned from Scythian tribes in the region and reported in *The Origin of the Sauromatae People* that Amazon virgins could not marry until they had slain a male enemy, and that some women remained unmarried all their lives because they were unable to fulfill this duty.[96] Herodotus relates that when the Scythians saw the fierceness of the Amazons in battle, they wanted their men to breed with these women. They therefore sent their youngest soldiers to woe them rather than fight them, and the young men successfully completed this assignment. However, the Amazons would not become Scythian wives. In a revealing passage, Amazons explain to Scythian soldiers why the women warriors could not settle down in a traditional domestic arrangement with them in Scythia. Conspicuously absent from their list is the Scythian tradition of widow burning on the pyres of their dead husbands.

> Now the men could not learn the women's language, but the women mastered the speech of the men; and when they understood each other, the men said to the Amazons, "We have parents and possessions; now therefore let us no longer live as we do, but return to our people and consort with them; and we will still have you, and no others, for our wives." To this the women replied: "Nay, we could not dwell with your women; for we and they have not the same customs. We shoot with the bow and throw the javelin and ride, but the crafts of women we have never learned; and your women do none of the things whereof we speak, but abide in their waggons working at women's crafts, and never go abroad a-hunting or for aught else. We and they therefore could never agree. Nay, if you desire to keep us for wives and to have the name of just men, go to your parents and let them give you the allotted share of their possessions, and after that let us go and dwell by ourselves." The young men agreed and did this.[97]

Diodorus Siculus (Diodorus of Sicily) wrote in the first century BCE that women in Ethiopia carried arms, and in parts of Libya, women warriors formed all-female armies that invaded other lands. According to Diodorus, the women warriors worshiped the goddess (identified by Merlin Stone[98] as Neith, the Libyan and Egyptian war goddess) and established temples in her honor. One nation in Libya, wrote Diodorus, was completely controlled by women, while men were responsible for the household and child-rearing. Children were immediately after birth given to male caretakers. To prevent men from organizing and revolting against the domination by women, men were not allowed to serve in the military or in any government office.

Archaeologist Jeannine Davis-Kimball's recent groundbreaking expedition in Russia has resulted in the first archaeological evidence of the Amazons yet discovered. From the sixth to the second centuries BCE, the homeland of nomadic tribes known as Sarmatians stretched from Russia's Don and Volga rivers east to the Ural mountain foothills. Centuries later, the women warriors spread westward and attacked many Greek cities beyond the Black Sea. By the fourth century AD, evidence shows that they were occupying outposts of the Roman empire in the Balkans. Davis-Kimball and her team have opened nearly 100 sixth century BCE graves in the grasslands of the steppes near the Russian town of Pokrovka near the border of Kazakhstan and found fifty female skeletons buried with martial grave goods such as bronze arrowheads, iron swords or daggers, whetstones for sharpening weapons, and fossilized seashells probably used in rituals. Some female skeletons had been placed with their legs bowed as if they were to be mounted on horseback, and the bowed leg bones of a 13- or 14-years-old girl are testimony of a life on horseback. Reinforcing Diodorus' discovery of role reversal, Davis-Kimball also reported that some men's graves held clay cooking pots and skulls of young children.

"The Pokrovka women cannot have been the Amazons of Greek myth—who were said to have lived far to the west," writes Davis-Kimbell, "but they may have been one of many similar nomadic tribes who occupied the Eurasian steppes in the Early Iron Age."[99]

References

1. Leonard Shlain, *The Alphabet Versus the Goddess: The Conflict Between Word and Image* (New York, 1998), 34.
2. J.C. Heesterman, *The Broken World of Sacrifice: An Essay in Ancient Indian Ritual* (Chicago, 1993), 2.
3. Nelson-Pallmeyer, *Is Religion Killing Us?*, 54.
4. Marvin Harris, *Cannibals and Kings* (New York, 1977), 81.
5. Sanday, *Female Power and Male Dominance*, 185.
6. Arther Ferrill, "Neolithic Warfare," http://www.witiger.com/centennialcollege/GNED117/neolithicwar.htm (accessed July 21, 2005). This essay, widely available in several locations on the Internet, is a revision of some ideas of Arther Ferrill expressed in *The Origins of War: From the Stone Age to Alexander the Great* (London and New York, 1985).
7. See Lawrence H. Keeley, *War Before Civilization: The Myth of the Peaceful Savage* (New York, 1996).
8. Ehrenreich, *Blood Rites*, 122.
9. Eliade, *Shamanism*, 434-36.
10. Keeley, *War Before Civilization*, 100.
11. F. Wendorf, "Site 117: A Nubian Final Paleolithic Graveyard Near Djebel Sahaba, Sudan," *The Prehistory of Nubia* II, F. Wendorf (Dallas, 1968): 954–95.
12. Settegast, *Plato, Prehistorian*, 39–40.
13. Ferrill, "Neolithic Warfare."
14. See Carol Ember, "Myths about Hunter-Gatherers," in *Ethnology* 17 (1978): 438–48; Ember, "A Cross-Cultural Perspective on Sex Differences," in *Handbook of Cross-Cultural Human Development*, ed. Monroe and Whiting, 531–80 (New York, 1981).
15. Donald E. Brown, *Human Universals* (New York, 1991).
16. Veena Das, personal communication with Janet Chawla (August 1983), cited by Janet Chawla, "Negotiating Narak and Writing Destiny: 'The Theology of Bemata in Dais' Handling of Birth," in *Invoking Goddesses: Gender Politics in Indian Religion*, ed. Nilima Chitgopekar (New Delhi, 2002), 180, n. 22. Chawla emphasizes that Das has not taken into account the significance of an autochthonous bipolar goddess/demoness and related systems of causality, radically different from the brāhmaṇic, that "signify in the realm of female physiology" and women's ethno-medicine.
17. Arthur Schopenhauer, *Parerga and Paralipomena*, vol. 2 (New York, 2001), 358–59.
18. René Girard, *Violence and the Sacred* (Baltimore, 1992), 4.
19. Ibid., 268.
20. Ibid.
21. Bowie, *The Anthropology of Religion*, 164.

22. Maurice Bloch, *Prey into Hunter: The Politics of Religious Experience* (Cambridge, 1992), 5.
23. Ibid., 4.
24. Ibid.
25. Das, cited by Chawla in "Negotiating Narak and Writing Destiny," 180, n. 22.
26. Juergensmeyer, *Terror in the Mind of God*, 159.
27. Bowie, *The Anthropology of Religion*, 117.
28. Frantz Fanon, *The Wretched of the Earth* (New York, 1963), p. 41.
29. Sarvepalli Radhakrishnan and Charles A. Moore, eds., *A Sourcebook in Indian Philosophy* (Princeton, NJ, 1957), 99.
30. Sarah Caldwell, "Margins at the Center: Tracing Kālī through Time, Space, and Culture," in *Encountering Kālī: In the Margins, at the Center, in the West*, ed. Rachel Fell McDermott and Jeffrey J. Kripal (Berkeley, 2003), 255.
31. Hart, *The Poems of Ancient Tamil*, 21.
32. Dubianski, *Ritual and Mythological Sources*, 35.
33. Kuṟuntokai [Kuṟ] 1, quoted in Hart, 22.
34. Lewis M. Hopfe, *Religions of the World* (New York, 1991), 287.
35. Coomaraswamy, *History of Indian and Indonesian Art* (New York, 1985), 7.
36. Eliade suggests a range from 6,000 BCE to 551 BCE. [Eliade, *A History of Religious Ideas*, vol. 1, 304.]
37. Hopfe, *Religions of the World*, 5th edn. (New York, 1991), 289.
38. Eliade, *History of Religious Ideas*, vol. 1, 311.
39. Mary Boyce, *Zoroastrians: Their Religious Beliefs and Practices* (London, 1979), 1.
40. Eliade, *History of Religious Ideas*, vol. 1, 313.
41. Hopfe, *Religions of the World*, 287.
42. Boyce, *Zoroastrians: Their Religious Beliefs*, 29.
43. N.N. Bhattacharyya, *Indian Demonology: The Inverted Pantheon* (Delhi, 2000), 20.
44. Ibid., 21.
45. Psalms 74.14.
46. Bhattacharyya, *Indian Demonology*, 20–21.
47. Nelson-Pallmeyer, *Is Religion Killing Us?*, 54.
48. Ibid., 54–55.
49. Ibid., 76.
50. Deut, 7:1–2, 5–6, 10.
51. Richard Horsley, *Jesus and the Spiral of Violence: Popular Jewish Resistance in Roman Palestine* (Minneapolis, 1993), 14, quoted in Nelson-Pallmeyer's *Is Religion Killing Us?*, 40.
52. Deut, 13:3, 5–11.
53. *Qur'ān*, 8:12.
54. See Thomas Patrick Hughes, "Jihād," *A Dictionary of Islam*, http://answering-islam.org.uk/Books/Hughes/index.htm (accessed February 24, 2008); Bernard Lewis, *Islam and the West* (New York, 1993), 9–10.
55. *Qur'ān*, 9:29.
56. Ibid., 22:19–21.
57. Ibid., 8:15–16
58. Ibid., 9:5–6.
59. Ibid., 8:39–42.

60. S.C. Kersenboom-Story, "Virali," in *Journal of Tamil Studies* 19 (June 1981), 23.
61. William S. Sax, "Gender and the Representation of Violence in Pāṇḍava Līlā," in *Inverted Identities: The Interplay of Gender, Religion and Politics in India*, ed. Julia Leslie and Mary McGee (New Delhi, 2000), 255.
62. Ibid.
63. See Alf Hiltebeitel, *The Cult of Draupadi*, vol. 1: *Mythologies: From Gingee to Kurukṣetra* (Chicago, 1988); ibid., vol. 2: *On Hindu Ritual and the Goddess* (Chicago, 1991).
64. Sax, "Gender and the Representation of Violence," 262.
65. Ibid., 263.
66. Peter van der Veer, *Imperial Encounters: Religion and Modernity in India and Britain* (Princeton, 2001), 121.
67. David Dean Shulman, "Battle as Metaphor in Tamil Folk and Classical Tradition," in *Another Harmony: New Essays on the Folklore of India*, ed. Stuart H. Blackburn and A.K. Ramanujan (Berkeley, 1986), 116–17.
68. CRK, 11, cited by Shulman, "Battle as Metaphor in Tamil Folk and Classical Traditions," in *Another Harmony: New Essays on the Folklore of India*, ed. Stuart H. Blackburn and A.K. Ramanujan (Berkeley, 1986), 109.
69. Shulman, "Battle as Metaphor in Tamil Folk and Classical Tradition," 111–12.
70. Ibid., 114–15.
71. Altekar, *Position of Women in Hindu Civilization*, 21–22.
72. Ibid., 21.
73. Lindsey Harlan, *Religion and Rajput Women: The Ethics of Protection in Contemporary Narratives* (Berkeley, 1992), 71.
74. Ibid., 223.
75. Ibid. [Italics added.]
76. Ibid., 224.
77. Altekar, *Position of Women in Hindu Civilization*, 116–17.
78. See Émile Durkheim, *Suicide: A Study in Sociology* (Glencoe, NY, 1951).
79. *Mbh.*, XVI.7–18; 73–74.
80. Altekar, *Position of Women in Hindu Civilization*, 121.
81. Ibid., 127.
82. Ibid., 133–34.
83. Ibid., 128.
84. *PN* 246. Quoted by Hart, 103.
85. Altekar, *Position of Women in Hindu Civilization*, 129.
86. Ibid., 131.
87. Ibid., 131–32.
88. Paul B. Courtright, "*Satī*, Sacrifice, and Marriage: The Modernity of Tradition," in *From the Margins of Hindu Marriage: Essays on Gender, Religion, and Culture*, ed. Lindsey Harlan and Paul B. Courtright (New York, 1995), 185.
89. Harlan, 226.
90. Kamia Bhasin, Ritu Menon, and Nighat Sa'id Khan, "Introductory Note," in *Against All Odds: Essays on Women, Religion and Development from India and Pakistan*, ed. Kamia Bhasin, Ritu Menon, and Nighat Sa'id Khan (New Delhi, 1994), iv.
91. Ashis Nandy, "Sati as Profit versus Sati as a Spectacle: The Public Debate on Roop Kanwar's Death," *Sati: The Blessing and the Curse*, ed. J.S. Hawley (New York, 1994).

92. Mandakranta Bose, "Satī," in *Faces of the Feminine in Ancient, Medieval, and Modern India*, ed. Mandakranta Bose (New York, 2000), 28–30.
93. Courtright, "*Satī*, Sacrifice, and Marriage," 186.
94. Merlin Stone, *When God was A Woman* (New York, 1976), 3–4.
95. Iliad, III, 184–90.
96. IV, 117.
97. IV, 114.
98. Stone, 35.
99. Jeannine Davis-Kimball, "Warrior Women of Eurasia," *Archaeology* 50, no. 1 (January/February 1997), http://www.archaeology.org/9701/abstracts/sarmatians.html (abstract) (accessed October 30, 2005).

3
Tribes

> The careful study of primitive societies is important today . . . because they provide case material for the study of cultural forms and processes. They help us to differentiate between those responses that are specific to local cultural types and those that are general to mankind. Beyond this, they help us to gauge and understand the immensely important role of culturally conditioned behavior. Culture, with its processes and functions, is a subject upon which we need add the enlightenment we can achieve, and there is no direction in which we can seek with greater reward than in the facts of preliterate societies.[1]

India has twenty-two million tribes that comprise over eight percent of the Indian population. What constitutes a *tribal*? Tribal peoples in India should not be defined merely by physiological type; nor by their isolation, usually in forests and mountains, far from advanced civilization and educational institutions; nor their practice of polygamy, polyandry (both fraternal, in which husbands are brothers or cousins, and matriarchal, in which husbands are not related), and other marriage traditions (by capture, service, purchase, or exchange) that, being essentially matriarchal, run counter to the orthodox brāhmaṇic credo; nor by their animistic, totemistic, shamanistic religion and crude polytheism; nor by their communalistic spirit. Although these elements are all important, there is another crucial feature necessary to define a tribe:

> Prior to declaring a group as a tribe, it is necessary to investigate the social discriminations they have been, and still continue to be subjected to, the exploitations and victimizations they endure, past and present customs, and the extent to which all these are non-acceptable to modern society. . . . The

existence of discrimination, culture, and customs combined with the fact that they are nomadic, primitive, and still observe taboos and conventions likely to be described by modern society as derogatory and anti-social is proof to confirm a group as tribe.[2]

Tribal peoples have been marginalized and victimized by elites throughout recorded history. Tribals are survivors of genocide, geographically isolated by greedy kings and landowners who have squeezed them from their rich, valuable land into mountains and forests, the outskirts of the kingdom or estate. Indic tribes live in huts of bamboo thatched with grass, leaves, or straw, or in caves, in the hollows of large trees, in pits, or under overhanging rocks. They are horticulturalists, and hunting is not usually a principal occupation. Before capitalism, a "pure" form of subsistence economy in India revolved around male hunting and female gathering, supplemented by slash-and-burn cultivation. There is no conception of private property in these indigenous societies; rather, the emphasis is on the communal territory. Poverty, orphans, destitute women, and overpopulation are completely absent in a tribal milieu. Social asymmetry is nonexistent, even though there is sexual division of labor: "women enjoy both more freedom and power than Hindu women and a higher rate of participation in the productive process."[3] The societies are egalitarian, with little vertical stratification, and they lack puritanical Hindu cultural prohibitions on drinking, dancing, meat consumption, and sexuality. They also lack the work ethic of the dominant society, and only work as much as they need for subsistence.[4] The majority of *ādivāsīs* have been dispossessed of their land by moneylenders, rural agriculturalists, and more recently, the imperial forces of globalism—multinational corporations and the World Bank's mega-projects. Some work as farm laborers, and women earn extra money by collecting and selling firewood, begging, and concubinage. Such marginalization, according to Sanders and Mead, accounts for their shift from matriarchy to patriarchy.

Due to deforestation, the perennial encroachment of elites, and short food supply, most tribals are malnourished. "Their day starts and ends with the battle for food, and they seldom find time to earn for other essential purchases. Often a couple has to wander in the forests and dig for the whole day to get enough roots for one good meal. Very often the hungry man refuses to share his find with his wife and children."[5] Women hunters who wander and stalk with men are regarded as "unclean," and prohibited from participation in tribal religious ceremonies. For *ādivāsīs*, the soul lives in blood, and blood is life.[6] They are thus overwhelmed by menstrual blood and menstruating women, who are isolated in huts during menses. "They firmly believe that the touch of a woman in menses blights crops, kills livestock, brings on attack by wild life and other misfortunes. A milder form of taboo is the restraint on a husband from conjugal pleasures with his wife once she has entered her seventh month of pregnancy, and until six months after childbirth."[7]

Young girls in Kerala tribes live in a separate dormitory supervised by an old spinster or widow. *Ādivāsīs* believe that marriage is an organic requirement for the perpetuation of the tribe, self-defense, and "the discharge of the obsequies at death by a son born of the alliance."[8] Methods of acquiring a bride are archaic and include capture, service, purchase, and exchange. Most tribals are exogamous, meaning men select wives outside the connected clans; both pre- and post-puberty marriages occur among Allars, Mala Malassars, and Malassars. Marriage ceremonies are attended by celebrants in brightly colored clothing, who sing and dance to music of flutes and drums. Marriages are prohibited when the bride or her mother are "in pollution connected with menses or death."[9] Both monogamy and polygamy are practiced, the latter being a sign of wealth; however, most males divorce one wife before marrying another, and the divorced woman is returned to her parents. In groups with an excess of females, polygamy is encouraged and is permissible. "It cannot, however, be totally overlooked that a man is not unaware of the material comforts and the increase of wealth possible through the free labor of wives."[10]

The dead are usually buried, although some tribes practice cremation or exposure. Solemn burial ceremonies are believed to be necessary to placate the spirits, who might torment the living. "Respect for the dead seems to have been an outstanding characteristic of the aborigines,"[11] according to Luiz. Memorial stones and megaliths found all over Kerala are intended to perpetuate the memories of ancestors. "Though the present generation ignores these structures their ancestors considered them sacred and dangerous to desecrate."[12] Stone structures are no longer erected in Kerala; it was an archaic tradition that has died there.

For thousands of years, Indian tribes generally lived in their sylvan setting totally out of contact with the population of the outside world and untouched by civilization. Their backwardness, born of isolation, made tribal people and their ecological contract with Mother Earth living anachronisms. Throughout the dynastic rule of the Śatavāhanas, Cālukyas, Rāṣṭrakūṭas, Kakatiyas, Qutbshahis and Āsifjāhī in Andhra, the *ādivāsīs* were pushed back from their homelands to the woods and hilly regions, which remained the forests of the nomadic hunter-gatherers and horticulturalists. Until the nineteenth and twentieth centuries, tribals and Hindu caste society tensely coexisted.

Resistive Dimensions of Tribal Religion

> Interestingly in the case of both Ellaiyamman and Mariyamman, even though one component of their constitutive nature is rooted in being the spouse of a Brahmin rishi, once they come into being as deities they claim independence from their past relationships. Both these goddesses cease to be obliged to the hierarchy of Hindu gods. This buttresses the resistive dimensions of the Paraiyars deities.[13]

In many ways the diametrical opposite of elite religions, the religion of Indian tribals and *dalits* is based on a healthy respect for the web of life and the ecosystem's critical balance of components, including human intent and action. This ecological dimension of underclass religion has merged with their urgent need to protect their boundaries from the encroachment of human predators. The religion of *dalits* and tribals is not a shadowy replication of caste Hinduism, but rather, it represents both resistance to and refiguring of the dominant dharma to serve its own ends.

"Popular religion is crassly materialistic," propounded Antonio Gramsci, who pointed to the "many beliefs and prejudices" of "almost all popular institutions (witchcraft, spirits, etc.)" that reveal its "materialist conception."[14] The object of fasting, sacrifice, feasting, and dancing for tribal peoples has always been the attainment of a material end, either in the form of secret knowledge of plants and their proper uses attained by shamans in hallucinatory trance; community concerns such as fertility, abundant harvest, rains, and continued prosperity; or protection from enemies, both internal (disease, possession), and external (invaders, drought, floods, etc.). Like the religions of the ancient Near East, *ādivāsī* religious rituals are intended to avert misfortune by propitiating the fierce Goddess of Life and Death with blood sacrifice. Among autochthonous Indic peoples, evil events, ill will, and the disdain and armed attacks of civil authorities constitute tribal social reality. Tribal people stripped of their land are today the primary prey of globalists, moneylenders, landlords, and liquor merchants who perpetuate the brāhmaṇic, Muslim, and British colonial model of tribal disenfranchisement and exploitation.

Since Indian *ādivāsīs* are accustomed to living in hostile territory, their primary goddess guards their boundaries and "protect[s] the harijans from the torture of the high caste."[15] A.A.D. Luiz emphasizes that Kerala tribal society treats the supernatural with more fear of its power than reverence, and fierce goddesses are usually not beseeched in prayer for benefits, but rather propitiated to avert evil, illness, or misfortune. Oracles in shamanic trance become possessed by the goddess, communicate the reasons for her displeasure with the people, and specify rituals or festivals to appease her. In her myths and folktales, motifs of suffering, self-sacrifice, death, and rebirth are intertwined with metaphors of symbolic revolution against inhumane caste and gender roles. The sacrificial paradigm in south Indian folklore evolves around an ordinary woman who is sacrificed for violating unjust laws levied by men against women and the dispossessed low-caste majority. Because her suffering elevates her to the rank of a goddess, the polyvalent message includes the psychology of female rage and women's self-sacrifice within an exploitive social system.

All tribal groups have a *pujārī* or *purohit* (priest), a *kaniyān* (astrologer), and a *mantravādī* (magician or sorcerer). Totemism, a religion *sui generis* that links families and clans to the other (nonhuman) inhabitants of the Earth—animals, plants, and rocks—is the basis of tribal ecological ideology and practices.[16] Kerala tribes practice magic, which "appears to originate from the belief that some kind of power should intervene to manipulate the natural order of events."[17] Mantravādīs practice white and black magic in both homeopathic and contagious forms of sympathetic magic. Luiz asserts that

> [t]here are references in the *Atharva Veda* to the numerous types of black magic practiced by ancient society. Words like "Hrim," "Hrom," "Om" are used while performing black magic, which often involves the use of corpse and human bones, etc. There is [*sic*] also the positive and negative applications of magic. The former is to make a phenomenon to pass away, and relates to harmless devices to control wealth, crops, etc., and one form of it is taboo. The latter is to prevent happenings and consists of devices to obtain by unlawful means a mastery over others.[18]

Fierce tribal goddesses are the prototypes of elite war goddesses. Because tribal deities are linked historically and metaphorically to the elite war goddesses who relish warfare, we cannot conclude that the fierceness of tribal goddesses is simply a dramatization of the angry response of tribals to the injustices of gender and caste oppression. According to psychoanalyst Frantz Fanon, the terrifying deities and spirits of tribals living under colonial control are symbolic means by which the tribals take the sting out of their oppressors and their taxes, prohibitions, and laws, which seem less devastating and threatening than the fierce goddess persona. As Fanon has observed, the native draws on terrifying myths of

> maleficent spirits which intervene every time a step is taken in the wrong direction, leopard-men, serpent-men, six-legged dogs, zombies—a whole series of tiny animals or giants which create around the native a world of prohibitions, of barriers and of inhibitions far more terrifying than the world of the settler.[19]

In Fanon's view, the fantasy of a fierce tribal goddess is a powerful psychological surrogate for political revolution against the elite oppressor-settlers:

> The supernatural, magical powers reveal themselves as essentially personal; the settler's powers are infinitely shrunken, stamped with their alien origin. We no longer really need to fight against them since what counts is the frightening enemy created by myths. We perceive that all is settled by a permanent confrontation on the phantasmic plane.[20]

The terrifying goddesses, from the point of view of *ādivāsīs*, may also function to counter-terrorize the elites. The highest religious aspiration of Kerala *ādivāsīs* is to control the evil spirits, and, if possible, the deities as well. Although animistic religions normally do not worship deities,[21] Ammaṉ is the village mother, the protecting deity of all Tamil villages. Kerala tribals worship protector deities such as Māriyammaṉ, Kālī, Kuruppuswāmī, Śasta, Śiva, Viṣṇu, Subramania, Ayyappan, sylvan deities, and spirits of ancestors. (Many consider their domestic gods to be spirits of ancestors.) Among the most popular *grāma-devatās*, who normally represent specific localities, are Māriyammaṉ and Kālī (Durgā). Kerala tribals believe that the soul lives after death, and good people are reborn as humans, and others as animals.[22] Caves, trees, rocks, rivers, and other natural phenomena are filled with pantheistic supernatural power and are objects of worship.

Māriyamman̲

Māriyamman̲ (Mother Māri) is an ancient Goddess of Life and Death who probably originated in Dravidian tribal religion as proto-Kor̲r̲avai/Aiyai-Kumārī before the arrival of the Aryans and the brāhmaṇic religion. In very early times, the Dravidian mountain tribes such as those in Coorg in southern Karnataka offered human sacrifices to Māriyamman̲, which were replaced with animal victims (particularly bulls, sheep, and chickens), or in some brāhmaṇa-influenced villages, vegetarian sacrifices. Māriyamman̲, an integrative force among south Indian agricultural folk since prehistory, was originally a low-caste goddess who protects villagers and their lands.

Māriyamman̲ is one of the most popular goddesses in south India, Sri Lanka, and in the Southeast Asian region (especially among speakers of Tamil, Telugu, Kannada, Malayalam, and Tulu). The Māriyamman̲ Temple in Singapore, established early in the nineteenth century, is the country's oldest, largest, and most revered Hindu temple. Māriyamman̲ is worshiped by millions of villagers across south India in almost every village, particularly in Tamilnadu and Karnataka. She is a polyvalent village goddess (*grāma-devatā*), a deity often worshiped as a head sitting upon the land, since she is identified with the village and rooted in the land; she is the Earth under the village as well as the Creatrix of the village. Each village can have several *grāma-devatās*, each with its own function. Māriyamman̲ (also known as Māri, Māriamma, and in the Purāṇas, Mārika) is worshiped throughout south India. Māri can mean *śakti*, female power, and *amman̲*, is mother; thus she is the mother-power of the village.

In the worldview of Māriyamman̲'s devotees, the land of the village belongs to Māriamman̲, and they live upon or inside the body of the goddess; thus all of life is sacred space. The goddess is the guardian of the boundaries of the village and the village protector. She is the central divine energy of the village, which is conceived as an entire cosmos unto itself. Outside the village, Māriyamman̲ cannot protect people. Consistent with the ancient template of the Goddess of Life and Death, she is not an all-benevolent mother; if angered, she is capable of causing destruction, disease (she is the smallpox, cholera, and chickenpox goddess), and calamity.

Māriyamman̲ emerged from the agricultural cultural system shared with the majority of Indians. Myths of Māriyamman̲, whose sacred abode is the neem tree (*vīpurmaram*), are enacted in festivals, spirit possession rituals, dance, and animal sacrifice. A.K. Ramanujan reports that the fierce village goddesses are seen as *avatāras* of Kālī or Śiva's relative.[23] Urban and rural areas, high and low castes form her core devotees today. "Some high-caste

Hindus, however—influenced both by the British Raj and by indigenous forces of elite reform—denounce Māriyamman̠ and her ilk as pre-enlightened, irrational superstition."[24] When Elaine Craddock visited a great number of Māriyamman̠ temples in south India, she learned that the devotees of Māriyamman̠ were far from the cruel and barbarous worshipers depicted in European missionaries' accounts. The missionaries failed to emphasize that Māriyamman̠ "was not just a fearful deity but the object of intense love."[25] Cognate with northern Śītalā, she is the traditional smallpox goddess who can both cause and cure the disease. In her myriad myths, she either murders her husband or remains unmarried.[26] Although Māriyamman̠ and Śītalā are probably more familiar throughout India than many local fierce goddesses, they all embody "*the inimitable and immediate power of violent death transformed that characterizes the most sought after local deities.*"[27] The cause of smallpox is understood to be her anger over neglect of ritual duties or some other infraction, and its presence is a reminder to be devoutly ever mindful of her.

> In the past, whenever an outbreak of smallpox would occur—usually once a year—a clay image of Māriyamman̠ would be made, or a clay pot would be used to call her down. Blood offerings would be made to her, she would be taken around the boundary of the village, and then her image would be thrown into the river. If she were satisfied with the devotions, she would take the pox away from the village. Since the eradication of smallpox Māriyamman̠ continues to function as both a destructive and healing force, a mother whose children are her devotees, whom she punishes and rewards as she sees fit. She is often pictured as a fierce, angry goddess with a voracious appetite for blood sacrifice and a capricious character, a vivid manifestation of ambivalent power.[28]

A.K. Rāmānujan points out that many of the Māriyamman̠ goddesses are identified with Pārvatī and Śiva in legends, and there is

> a continuity between the Sanskritic elements and the village ones, and between the village sacrifices and the Vedic ones. The buffalo-sacrifice (buffalo = bull; buffalo fat smeared on the buffalo's head = omentum smeared in the Vedic sacrifice; the lamp on the head of the buffalo—the sacrificial fire; the post representing Poturāju or Buffalo-king = the *yūpa* post of Vedic sacrifices made of *sami* wood). Also, the village goddess, or the Amman̠ killing the buffalo is seen as no other than the Devī (in the Purāṇas) killing the Mahiṣāsura, the Buffalo-demon, in cosmic battle.[29]

Although *amman̠* means "mother," Māriyamman̠ is often depicted as a woman without children. In most myths of Māriyamman̠, she is either a widow, a little girl, or a woman cast out of her home by her husband—in all cases, she is the sacrificial victim of male arrogance and cruelty involving brāhmaṇic laws concerning caste and gender. Māriyamman̠ is a fallen form of Pārvatī; her fall to the *dalit* caste was caused by her forbidden lustful thought. Whether Devī or Māriyamman̠, the goddess "stands clearly contrasted with consort goddesses like Lakṣmī or Pārvatī, who are married and auspicious; their shrines are a part of the larger temples devoted to their husbands."[30] However, like Māriyamman̠, neither Lakṣmī nor Pārvatī has borne children, since Pārvatī's offsprings are "extrauterine miracles."[31]

Bavāniyammaṉ, whose stories are used interchangeably with those of Māriyammaṉ in a village near Madras, Periyapāḷaiyam, is regarded by her devotees as one of the Seven Sisters, probably descendants of the ancient Sanskritic Saptamātṛkās. "Many of the village temples in Tamilnadu have seven stones that are frequently interpreted as the Seven Sisters or the Seven Mothers," [32] according to Craddock. The inevitable blood sacrifice and concentration on suffering, self-sacrifice, and death motifs constitute archaic ritual forms involving rebirth. Māriyammaṉ is a fiercely protective mother who is also

> a bloodthirsty deity who traditionally requires blood sacrifices from her devotees. Both explicit and implicit themes of sacrifice, suffering, and death pervade the myths, songs, and ritual activities associated with Bavāniyammaṉ/Māriyammaṉ. These themes are closely tied to the Goddess's nature as Śakti, power. As Śakti, the Goddess embodies the power of life and death that pervades and sustains the created world (*saṃsāra*). Such power is associated also with the act of sacrifice, especially blood sacrifice, along with the act of killing that it entails and the physical suffering that comes with sacrificial death. It is especially the transformative nature of this power that is emphasized in myths and rituals associated with the Goddess in this context.[33]

Festivals are held in Māriyammaṉ's honor, and in some villages she renews the soil in cyclical rituals involving the goddess's requirement of animal sacrifice, storytelling, singing, magic dance, and spirit possession. Blood sacrifice is sometimes substituted by vegetarian offerings to Māriyammaṉ, but the original principle of sowing blood into the agricultural fields remains active among small-scale Indic farmers. Sacrifices to Māriyammaṉ are usually propitiatory; some are thank-offerings—for example, if a personal enemy suffers misfortune, "an animal is at once sacrificed as a thank-offering!"[34] Mystically linked with the Great Goddess in archaeology and mythology since earliest antiquity, the buffalo is "traditionally the favored sacrifice to the goddess, with a special role reserved for the head," according to Craddock, who interprets the buffalo as a symbol of power that is "transferred to the Goddess through sacrifice."[35] Through sacrifice, the bull's blood is transmitted to the goddess as a fertilizing agent for the crops. The blood of the buffalo is sometimes drunk during the ritual to capture internally the animal's power. In buffalo sacrifices to village goddesses, the male buffalo to be sacrificed is called *Devara-potu*, "devoted to the goddess." The head of the *Devara-potu* is cut off before the image of the goddess, and the *bali haranan* (presentation of the offering) begins:

> The blood is caught in a vessel and sprinkled over some boiled rice, and then the head, with the right foreleg in the mouth, is placed before the shrine on a flat wicker basket, with the rice and blood on another basket just below it. A lighted lamp is placed on the head, and then another Mādigā carries it on his

> own head round the village, with anew cloth dipped in the blood of the victim tied round his neck. This is regarded here and elsewhere as a very inauspicious and dangerous office; and the headman of the village has to offer considerable inducement to persuade a Mādigā to undertake it. Ropes are tied round his body and arms and held fast by men walking behind him, as he goes round, to prevent his being carried off by evil spirits, and limes are cut in half and thrown into the air, so that the demons may catch at them instead of at the man. It is believed that gigantic demons sit on the tops of tall trees ready to swoop down and carry him away, in order to get the rice and the buffalo's head. The idea of carrying the head and rice round a village, so the people said, is to draw a kind of cordon on every side of it and prevent the entrance of the evil spirits.[36]

At festivals without animal sacrifice, offerings of boiled rice, fruit, flowers, cakes, and sugar are prepared, and incense and camphor are burnt. In the Abishegam ritual, the image of Māriyammaṉ is ceremonially bathed twice a day with water, oil, milk, coconut milk, turmeric, rose water, sandalwood, honey, sugar, limes, and a solution of the bark of certain trees. Twice a day, the image of the goddess is carried on the shoulders of devotees around the village, sometimes including a car procession. At many festivals the Mātaṅgī, an unmarried low-caste woman who retains the role for life, is the centerpiece of the event. As a living manifestation of the goddess, she becomes possessed by the goddess, performs a wild, frenzied dance, shouts obscene language, spits at devotees, and shoves people around with her buttocks. Since the festival reverses social norms, the Mātaṅgī's behavior, which would ordinarily be highly polluting, is purifying, and people seek out her spit and insults.

In the mid-twentieth century, as her *dalit* worshipers became integrated into the larger social order, Māriyammaṉ entered the "great tradition," drawing devotees from both urban and rural areas and across caste lines.[37] Brāhmaṇas and Muslims participate in her festival, and, in an inversion of the everyday social order, there is a free mixture of different castes during Māriyammaṉ festivals. Pilgrims usually wear yellow, the color of the goddess. Men sometimes dress as tigers and other animals. Their intentions may include asking the goddess to free them of debt or disease, or thanking her for curing them of disease. Before the festival, pilgrims fast, and they often bring money offerings. Vows pilgrims make to Māriyammaṉ in exchange for material relief include performing hookswinging, fire-walking, or carrying burning pots on their heads.

The name Māri is associated with pestilence and disease, thus a possible meaning of Māriyammaṉ is "the disease mother." Since *māri* can also means "to change" in Tamil, some scholars associate the name Māri with her unpredictability, her ability to suddenly morph, and her dangerous capacity for anger, violence, and heat. She likes to be cooled with water and rain during the peak of the hot season, when infectious diseases pose the greatest threat to the people; thus her worshipers request cooling rain.

Ellaiyammaṉ

In Tamilnadu, dalits represent three *jātis*: 59 percent are Paraiyars, 21 percent are Pallans, and 16 percent are Chakkilis. The Paraiyars are considered exemplars of untouchability in Tamilnadu.[38] "Even though the Paraiyars are an ancient and distinct people, they have had to endure a long and systematic process of economic oppression and cultural marginalization, primarily because their particular heritage was not in conformity with traditions of the caste Hindu communities."[39] Elite Hindus have forced them into dry, nonproductive lowlands, and they are forced to work as landless laborers completely in thrall to the landlords. Living on the outskirts of the caste village community, the Paraiyars are cut off from social intercourse with caste Hindus and because of their geographically location, they are endangered by natural forces.

"It is within this historical situation," writes Clarke, "that one must comprehend the characteristic of Ellaiyamman as a deity that protects the boundaries of and for the Paraiyars. She shields and polices the geographic, social, and cultural space of the Paraiyars from the continued colonizing of the caste peoples."[40] Ellaiyamman, the inverse of Māriyamman̲, is the Paraiyar hamlet or colony goddess with the head of the Paraiyar and the body of a caste Hindu woman. She has remained a distinctly revolutionary *dalit* goddess who subverts gender and caste oppression, and who has not been co-opted by caste Hindu mythology or iconography. Ellaiyamman̲ represents what Sathianathan Clarke terms an "iconic symbol of collective resistance" and "emancipatory re-mythologization," a process that

> reimagines the accepted social configurations of South Indian polity by reversing the position of the Paraiyars and the brahmans. The head that symbolizes power/knowledge of the Brahman (erudition in the Vedas and schooling in the proper practice rituals: wisdom of orthodoxy and orthopraxis) is replaced with the head that signifies the power of the Paraiyars (brute mundane power in the realm of the material/physical: tangible power to protect and to punish). This is in many senses a symbolic act of subversion: an inversion of the status quo as propagated by Hindu myth and practice.[41].

The Mother-goddess and guardian of the boundaries, Ellaiyamman̲ (*ellai* is the Tamil word for "boundary") protects the Paraiyars' boundaries as the caste Hindus encroach on them. The *uur* (the hamlet of the "higher castes" in Tamil villages, excluding *dalits*) does not have discreet boundaries, but is more a fluid area that invades and usurps the *ceri* (colony). The *ceri* is the counterpart of the *uur* and the space of the Paraiyars. A song praising Ellaiyamman̲ alludes to the primordial buffalo sacrifice offered to the goddess, reminiscent of the Eyinar tribe's ritual bull sacrifice to Aiyai during the Caṅkam age, and relates that Ellaiyamman̲ resides in neem leaves and heals women's afflictions:

> You are the deity who expels our troubles; come rid us of evil.
> You are present in the neem leaves used for drying out women's afflictions.
> You are present in the fire, in the head of our religion.
> You have lived with fame in our village, Malaipallaiyam.
> In Padavethi a buffalo was sacrificed to You, even in Poothhukaadu;

A sacrifice to inspire You, our goddess, to destroy evil.
You are the goddess who guards our boundaries:
You protect with your spear;
You will protect us from 4408 diseases;
You will protect the harijans from the torture of the high caste.[42]

Māriyammaṉ and her *avatāra* Ellaiyammaṉ represent female sacrificial victims to the caste system who are deified much like *satīs* because of their suffering and self-sacrifice. The only distinctive difference between Ellaiyammaṉ and Māriyammaṉ is that Ellaiyammaṉ has the head of the *dalit* and the body of the brāhmaṇa woman, while Māriyammaṉ has the head of the brāhmaṇa and the body of the *dalit*. In some versions, the untouchable body is Mātaṅgī. In some of Ellaiyammaṉ's iconography, she is depicted with the decapitated head of the brāhmaṇa woman in her hand. Māriyammaṉ is thus understood to have a brāhmaṇa head and an untouchable body, which reinforces her ambivalent nature and her role as a village goddess exemplifying the social status quo in which brāhmaṇas are at the "head" of the social system, as both authoritarian leaders and intellectual paradigm-builders. In Elliyammaṉ, on the other hand, the head that symbolizes the power and knowledge of the Brāhmaṇa (erudition in the Vedas and knowledge of the proper practice of ritual) is replaced with the head that signifies the power of the untouchables. This head reversal is an act of subversion against the caste Hindu system, a symbolic inversion of the status quo as propagated by brāhmaṇic myth and practice. Sathianathan Clarke maintains that "the Paraiyars' resistance to the expansionist and overpowering nature of caste Hindu hegemonic forces" is embodied in Ellaiyammaṉ, "an iconic representation of the resistance of Paraiyars to the conquering tendencies of the caste Hindu world."[43]

Deification of Suffering and Violent Death

Dalits and *ādivāsīs* situate their goddess within the caste Hindu mythological framework in order to re-create their own history and identity, hence Māriyammaṉ's folk myth is an ironic inversion of the Vedic myth of Reṇukā in the *Mahābhārata*,[44] the latter a didactic tale of filial piety. Māriyammaṉ's myth of origin begins with the Sanskrit account of Reṇukā's loss of her chastity because of an impure thought, and a portrait of the ideal son, who obeys his father's order to murder his mother Reṇukā for her capital offense of unchastity. Richard Brubaker[45] found in seven village goddess versions the motif of the transposition of *dalit* and brāhmaṇa heads, which pollutes the originally pure brāhmaṇa wife, Reṇukā. Because of caste laws, she must leave her husband and become a village goddess.

Reṇukā's suffering and untimely death is the cause of her worship; suffering and violent death are the twin forces that transform an ordinary woman into a goddess[46] —a dynamic that is also crucial to the Christian savior, Jesus Christ. "A person who has suffered and died a violent and unnatural death," writes Craddock, "has too much power and must be transferred to an acceptable category—a deity people can propitiate—rather than left to wander around tormenting people on Earth. By worshiping this deity, people can safely make contact with this force, and that power is made accessible."[47]

In addition to their suffering and martyrdom, many of the south Indian village goddesses embody mystical, transformative rage. The folk myth of Māriyammaṉ's origin unfolds as follows:

Once Śiva took the form of the great [brāhmaṇa] Ṛṣi Nilakandar, and Pārvatī took the form of his wife Reṇukā. They had four sons. Every morning Reṇukā would go to a river, swirl her fingers in the water, and a mud pot full of water and flowers would emerge from the river. This she would carry to Nilakandar for his morning *pūjā*. One morning Reṇukā is collecting water for her husband's *pūjā* and, spying in the river the reflection of a *gandharva* (male fairy) flying overhead, she admires his robust physique. Nilakandar flies into a jealous rage when Reṇukā admits her lustful thought, accusing her of losing her "chastity." Nilakandar called his four sons to him and asked, "Which one of you will behead your mother?" Three refused, but the fourth, Paraśurāma, agreed to do so, exclaiming, "You are my father, and there is nothing above a father's word." Her husband orders their son, Paraśurāma, to murder his mother. Paraśurāma asks his father for a boon, and Nilakandar agrees. Paraśurāma finds his mother hiding in a washerwoman's house, so he cuts off both their heads. When he returns to his father, he asks his father to bring his mother back to life, so Nilakandar gives him a vessel of water, explaining that he must attach Reṇukā's head to her body, sprinkle her with water, and wait until she returns to life. In his haste to finish, Paraśurāma transposes the heads, giving Jamadagni's wife the body of an untouchable. Thus Reṇukā was transformed into Bavāṉiyammaṉ,[48] and the washerwoman morphed into Mātaṅkiyammaṉ.[49]

Nancy Auer Falk points to the caste and gender roles articulated in this mythic structure:

> It would be hard to find a more appropriate symbol for a South Indian Hindu village community—a being relying on Brahman brains and directions but dependent on low-caste groups to carry out its vital functions. Like Hindu society as a whole in classic *dharmashastra* constructions, a village community is a body whose various members must work together in harmony if maximum benefit is to be accomplished. The major difference in this case is that the body is female. . . .[50]

In the version of the Reṇukā myth in the *Mahābhārata*, the didactic message to sons is that nothing, not even love for one's mother, supersedes the word of the Vedic father; wives are warned in the myth that lascivious thoughts, even those evoked by the mere reflection of a male fairy in the river, can result in a death sentence. The Periyapāḷaiyam version, on the other hand, contains a rich combination of mythic motifs that underlies the study of Māriyammaṉ and her devotees. The primary message is the glorification of woman's self-sacrifice: through suffering and violent death, Reṇukā is transformed from a woman into a powerful goddess, created from the *dalit* woman who protects Reṇukā when her son chases her with an ax. "Suffering is an experiential link between goddess and devotee,"[51] not only because her devotees suffer from smallpox and other infectious diseases, but also because they, like their goddess, must sacrifice their lives to the patriarchal caste system. In Egnor's interpretation, the Tamil women she studied did not see themselves as victims, but rather, women with *śakti*: "None of these women saw a contradiction between her possession of *śakti* and her subordinate role as female. . . . On the contrary, for each woman the possession of extraordinary *śakti* came as a consequence of her subordinate status, or more accurately, as a consequence of the suffering that that subordination entailed."[52]

The metaphor underlying Reṇukā's individual dismemberment and reconstruction is an effective sociological vehicle for increasing community integration through the social catharsis and transformative effect of violent death and head-swapping.[53]

> Her grisly murder echoes the crucial element in the deification of local beings: the innocence of the victim is not what matters, it is suffering and violence that transforms a person into a deity. . . . A person who has suffered and died a violent and unnatural death has too much power and must be transferred to an acceptable category—a deity people can propitiate—rather than left to wander around tormenting people on Earth. By worshiping this deity, people can safely make contact with this force, and that power is made accessible.[54]

In another version of the Māriyammaṉ myth reported by Whitehead, we learn that the rationale for bull slaughter lies in caste laws and notions of pollution:

> Once upon a time there lived a Ṛishi who had a fair daughter. A Caṇḍāla, *i.e.*, an Outcaste, desired to marry her. He went to Kāsī (Benares) in the disguise of a Brāhmaṇa, where, under the tuition of a learned Brāhmaṇa, he became well versed in the *śāstras* . . . and learnt the Brāhmaṇa modes of life. On his return he passed himself off for a Brāhmaṇa, and after some time made offers to the ṛishi lady, and somehow succeeded in prevailing upon her to marry him. She did so, her father also consenting to the match. They lived a married life for some time, and had children. One day it so happened that one of the children noticed the father stitch an old shoe previous to going out for a bath. This seemed curious, and the child drew the mother's attention to it. The mother, by virtue of her *tapas*, . . . came to know the base trick that had been played upon her by her husband, and cursed him and herself. The curse on herself was that she should be born a Mari, to be worshiped only by low-caste men. The curse on him was that her children should be born as sheep and chickens. Therefore, during the periodical Mari festivals, buffaloes, sheep and chickens are used as victims, and the right leg of the male buffalo is cut off and stuck in his mouth, in memory of his having stitched the shoes in his disguise as a Brāhmaṇa.[55]

This story, like the Reṇukā tale, depicts an ordinary housewife in the domestic (*akam*) sphere who is transformed, via her desecration by her husband, into a goddess in the public (*puṟam*) sphere. The subject of the mixing of castes, especially brāhmaṇa and *dalits*, is "an ever-present and ever-explosive theme in Tamil folklore."[56] Because she learns that her husband's untouchability has defiled her and her children, the brāhmaṇa wife curses her entire family, including herself, "to reenact the blood sacrifice to the goddess again and again."[57]

A more elaborate Kannada version of the Māriyammaṉ myth collected by A.K. Ramanujan explicates the same cause of the goddess's rage: her discovery of her husband's deception and subversion of caste laws by his knowledge of shoe repair (the vocation of an untouchable). In the Kannada version, the brāhmaṇa girl is also alerted to caste anomalies by her mother-in-law's yearning for mutton. The latter myth is told as follows:

> A long time ago, elders arranged marriages for girls before they came of age. That was the custom. If a girl menstruated before she was married, they would blindfold the girl and leave her in a forest. This practice was chiefly among Brahmins. Once, a Brahmin girl did get her period before she could get married. Her father blindfolded her and left her in a jungle. A Liṅgāyat man watched him abandon his daughter in the jungle, and felt compassion. He said, "*Ayyo pāpa*, poor thing!" and rescued the girl; he untied the cloth round her eyes, brought her home, and treated her as his own daughter.
>
> A *mādiga* [Untouchable] saw her one day, and fell in love with her. He vowed to himself, "I must marry this girl, I must." He told his mother, "Avva, you'd better learn to dress like a Brahmin woman. Help me get this girl for your daughter-in-law." He persuaded her against her will, dressed himself in Brahmin-style clothes, went to the Liṅgāyat's house, and asked for his foster-daughter's hand. The Liṅgāyat agreed, because he too wanted to get this Brahmin girl married to a Brahmin. He arranged the marriage, and sent the girl to her mother-in-law's place. There she did all the housework and cooked for her husband and mother-in-law. The mother-in-law liked the young woman's Brahmin cuisine, but would grumble now and then, "What good is this tasteless stuff? Is this food? How nice it would be to have a leg of mutton!" The Brahmin daughter-in-law overheard this a few times and was puzzled by it. But she was afraid to tell her husband about it. Some years passed, and she bore two sons. The children—after all, they were boys—were curious to find out what their father did all day. "What does Appa do, why does he go to the foot of the hills?" they wondered. One day, they followed him without his knowledge. They observed him as he sat at the foot of the hill, as he measured people's feet, and sewed sandals for them. They came home and gathered broad banyan leaves and leaves of the milkhedge. And they placed their own feet on the leaves, took measurements, and cut outlines along the curves of their feet. Their mother saw what they were doing; she was disgusted. She scolded them: "Don't do such things, children!" But can boys keep quiet? They said proudly, "We are doing exactly what Daddy does. He does just this all day under that hill."

She knew now what her husband was up to. She realized what "caste" of man she had gone and married. She also understood in a flash why her mother-in-law grumbled, and craved for sheep's flesh every day.

As she thought of it, anger rose in her. It rose and rose in her body, and became a terrible rage that was all over her. She grew bigger and bigger, standing tall, joining earth and heaven in one body, and became a Māri [terrifying goddess]. She put out her tongue and went in search of her husband. He saw her, and knew he had to flee. As he fled, she said, "I'll finish off these children who were born to that man. Then I'll get him." The children were terrified by the Māri, their mother, and hid themselves in a couple of goats that were around. The Māri broke off the goats' heads, drank her children's blood, and went again in search of her husband. The Mādriga man saw that the Māri was coming after him. So he entered a he-buffalo that was grazing in the field nearby. Māri saw him hide himself in the animal, and moved toward him, making angry noises, taking dancing steps. And she slit open the he-buffalo, drank her husband's blood, and took a vow standing right there. "I'll cut you down every year, and get lamps lit from the fat of your body." Saying that, she came leaping forward. Saying, "I've taken my husband as my *āhuti* [sacrifice], taken my children as *āhuti*. Where shall I settle down?" she moved forward. As she came, midway she met a Dāsayya (a religious mendicant).

This Dāsayya was from Alsandi. He would roam the town all day and sleep in the village chieftain's [*gauḍa*'s] cattle shed. He had a piece of coconut frond with him. The village chieftain's daughter-in-law would watch over it in his absence. But one day, when he was asleep, she moved it somewhere. The Dāsayya woke up next morning, looked for his coconut frond all over and couldn't find it anywhere. "Whoever has taken it, they'd better return it," he screamed. "Please," he begged. But nobody came forward to return it to him. He got exasperated, and shouted, "I'll go get Māri. She'll get it back for me." And he went in search of her.

On the way, he saw an old, old woman picking dry cow-dung patties and putting them in her basket. She was looking for someone to lift the basket to her head. When she saw the Dāsayya walking that way in a hurry, she called him and asked him, "Come here, my man. Please help me get this basket on my head."

"I've no time to help you with your baskets and things. I'm looking urgently for Māri. I've got to get to her soon. Don't interrupt me." The old woman replied, "I'm the village Māri. Come here." The Dāsayya didn't believe her. He scolded her: "Hey, old woman! Don't tell lies. I'll let it pass, and help you this time with your basket. Then I'll go my way." But when he went near her and tried to place the basket on her head, he shuddered with fear—becaue she had a coiled seven-headed serpent on her head for her basket-rest [*simbi*]. He knew this was Māri, and stood there in terror, not knowing which direction he was facing. Then the Māri comforted him and told him: "You walk in front of me. I'll walk behind you. You'll hear the jingle of my anklets. You must never turn around and look at me. If you do, you'll be my third *āhuti*."

The Dāsayya agreed to do as he was told, and walked ahead. Behind him, the old woman changed into Māri, stood tall, joining earth and sky, put out her lolling tongue, and started walking. When they came near Alsandi, the Dāsayya felt he couldn't hear the anklet sound any more. So he turned around and looked. He saw the incarnation of Māri, was dumb struck, stood there shivering. Māri was furious. She lashed out with her tongue at him, slapped him to the ground, killed him, drank his blood, and came to Alsandi. There she wasted [*nāśa māḍḍu*] the village chieftain, all the people of the village, destroyed the whole place, and she left untouched only the lane where calves are tethered. Then she came to Begūru, drank the blood of the people there, and finished all the fodder and water the Begūru chieftain had stored for thousands of cows. Her thirst was still not quenched. At the boulder [*nerigekallu*], she shook the borders [*nerige*] of her sari, took it off and threw it at Zmailigehalli ["the village of dirty clothes"]. She struck the rock with her fist. As Māri's hand struck the stone, water sprang from it—the Earth Goddess below made it spring from rock. Māri drank from the spring, she went to Antaragaṭṭe ["a bund with intervals"] and stayed there, showing her long lolling tongue. This Māri hopped and hopped [*antarisi*] from place to place, and arrived at Antaragaṭṭe. That's why she is called Antaragaṭṭamma. This story also tells you why goats, sheep, and a buffalo are sacrificed to her when she is angry.[58]

The Sanskritic myth of *Devī-māhātmya* that the folk myth ironically inverts is summarized by David Shulman:

> When Mahiṣa the buffalo-demon was lord of the demons and Indra lord of the gods, the gods were cast out from heaven by the demon host. From the energy [*śakti*] born from the anger of the gods, Devī became incarnate. The gods bestowed their divine weapons upon her and sent her to do battle with Mahiṣāsura. Riding on a lion, she fought with the demon and finally placed her foot upon his neck and pierced him with a spear; he half came forth from his own mouth, and the goddess cut off his head and killed him.[59]

The contrasts between the village story and that of the *Mārkaṇḍeya Purāṇa* are telling. Significantly, the folk myth is not a narrative about elite cosmic war led by a soldier-goddess defending the gods; rather, it refers to a village housewife whose miscegenation and rage transform her into a Māri (a fierce goddess). Because she has been ruined by her outcaste husband, she is forbidden by caste law to participate in domestic or community life. Thus, in an act subverting the idealized model of the wife in brāhmaṇic myths, she destroys her home, setting it ablaze in some versions, murders all her relatives, and lays waste the village; "violated, she violates in turn."[60] There is a distinct parallel between Kaṇṇaki in the Tamil epic *Cilappatikāram* and the folk goddess Māriyammaṉ, both of whom "have pent-up fires of self-control and a tendency to start conflagrations," representing "the power of an ordinary woman to explode into a goddess when she is given a sufficient charge of anger. . . . It is as much a theory of emotion as a theology,"[61] writes Rāmānujan. Also prominent in the gory tragedies of fifth century BCE Greece, the theme of the destructive powers of self-liberated women in male supremacist societies is usually construed as a classic patriarchal gynophobic nightmare. Kaṇṇaki also became identified with Kālī or Bhagavatī, although how and when the cults merged is unknown.[62]

A common trope of Indian folklore, the mythic motif of the transposed heads symbolically exposes the arbitrary nature of caste distinctions while explaining metaphorically the origin of the Māri. Clarke recounts another version of the Māriyammaṉ myth of origin that refers to the woman who was restored with the head of Reṇukā and the body of the Paraiyar woman. In this Paraiyar myth of retaliation against oppressors, Māriyammaṉ, the goddess of the Paraiyars, thwarts all the major caste Hindu deities, usurps arenas of their powers, and punishes them all with disease and her dreaded curse. Her realm becomes the universe, including the Underworld, which she controls without male intervention. Māriyammaṉ's legend is recorded as follows:

> Reṇukā who now has the body of the Paraiyar woman returns home. The rishi is not willing to accept her in her changed form and curses her. She becomes the bearer of the "Pearl," which is the name given to smallpox. Reṇukā has authority over this agonizing disease. She brings this disease upon the rishi who begs for healing. She offers him healing if she be permitted to go the four worlds of Shiva, Vishnu, Brahma, and Yama. He enables her to visit the four worlds. She goes to Shiva and causes a disease on him. In exchange for healing she receives his Shoolam (a forked weapon) and his cow. She inflicts Vishnu and gets from him his Conch shell and wheel. From Brahmā she gets consent for converting her name. She is no longer Reṇukā but assumes the name Mariyamman (the changed Mother). She then inflicts Yama with a disease. She requires that Yama's wife arrange for a huge festival for her. She agrees to this and asks her to remove the "pearl-like" disease in return.[63]

Māriyammaṉ's Koṅku festival, studied by Brenda Beck,[64] unfolds not as a dramatization of the Reṇukā tale, but as a didactic ritual drama of the dire consequences of the mixing of castes. In this myth, Māriyammaṉ was originally a brāhmaṇa's adopted daughter who was tricked into marrying a low-caste drummer disguised as a brāhmaṇa. When Māriyammaṉ learned of the deceit, she flew into a state of incandescent rage and cursed him, causing him to burn to ashes. Although freed from his pollution, she has become a widow. In the last phase of the festival, Māriyammaṉ has substituted her white widow clothing for "married woman" clothing, assumed the identity of Pārvatī, and taken a new husband, Śiva. "The message cautions that caste violation is dangerous,"[65] writes Nancy Auer Falk, and thus it does not challenge the status quo of gender and caste oppression. The power of Māriyammaṉ's rage is directed against the violator of caste law, not against the caste system. A crucial element of Indian festivals is "the ecstatic catharsis" experienced simultaneously by the community participants. Like the Aristotelian notion that a tragic drama, through the evocation of pity and fear, is a cathartic experience that purifies the emotions of the audience, Indian village goddess festivals "generated an experience of extreme collective tension and then dispersed it, locating the cause of village crisis in one or more threatening 'demons' and then killing these or driving them beyond the village borders back into the 'wilderness' from which they supposedly came."[66] The highly charged symbology weaves together the cathartic effect of village goddess festivals on participants both as individuals and as a collective.

> As the goddess-presence intensifies at her temple, reflected in both her images and in her heaps of food and flowers, so the community's awareness of its own collective *shakti* becomes intensified as it gathers and waits for her manifestation, crystallized by its king's appearance at the appropriate hour. The message is clear: once again, coming together, they have the power to dispel demonic threat.[67]

Spirit Possession

> Oracular possession is adaptive to complex societies where status positions are hereditary and rigidly defined. In this sense, this type of spirit possession in Hindu [societies] bears a close relationship to the oracles of the classical slave societies of Greece and Rome where women and slaves were denied traditional positions of authority and power in the society at large but could achieve them through the oracle.[68]

Fierce goddess worship among south Indian nonelites is almost always accompanied by archaic practices consistently denigrated by the Indian elite minority: animal sacrifice, liquor, violence or self-mutilation as part of shamanic ordeals (firewalking, hookswinging), and oracular spirit possession performance acted out in frenzied dances of possession. Sanskritic goddesses do not possess their devotees.

Possession by a deity is referred to in Tamil as *iṅaṅku*, to "descend" on a person, who then becomes a *cāmyāti* or "god-dancer."[69] Indic tribal/dalit goddesses Kālī and Māriyammaṉ interact with their devotees via the oracles, whom the goddess "comes down" and possesses. "Diviners run into a trance (frenzy) and disclose causes for the displeasure of the gods, and suggest methods for appeasing them," writes Luiz. "While in a trance they are believed to have divine inspiration. Oracles are popular and held in esteem."[70] Michael Moffatt studied the goddess Periyapalaiyattar, a form of Māriyammaṉ who represents the low, impure, possessed, inauspicious form of the goddess. Twice a week, Periyapalaiyattar came down and possessed one of her male devotees, a landless Pannaikkar in his mid-thirties named Mugan. While possessed, he sits on a platform and becomes an oracle, making prophecies and conducting exorcisms of *pēys* for all who come to the goddess. People like Mugan who are regularly possessed are called "god-dancers" (*saamiyaaDis*) or "god-people" (*saamiyaaLs*), and possession séances with god-dancers are regular features of dalit goddess worship.[71] It is understood that once possessed, Mugan is the goddess, and he has complete amnesia about what transpires when he is possessed.

> Mugan's possession is relatively mild; his limbs go stiff, his eyes close, and his breathing becomes heavy and spasmodic. He does not really lose control in the manner of many other *saamiyaaDis*, which is just as well, since the inner

shrine of Periyapalaiyattar's temple is tiny and crowded with ritual paraphernalia. The *pucari* drummer signals the possession with a rapid, heavy beat, and the onlookers shout "Govinda! Govinda!" Mugan-as-the-goddess then rushes out of the temple, his eyes now open and staring, his hair loose and long, and circumambulates the temple three times, at a run, inspecting its preparations. He carries with him some of the weapons which "are" the goddess's power or *shakti*—a whip in his right hand, and a heavy rod in his left. When the goddess is satisfied, he reenters the temple and sits in the outer shrine, in the area called *kuṛi meedai* ("foretelling platform") and faces the goddess's petitioners from behind a small stone to her low guardian god, a male being called *Munadiyan* ("he who comes before"). The goddess is now ready to hear the "problems" and "grievances" (*kastams* and *abitus*) that have been brought to her.[72]

Most of the petitioners are women who come from both the Colony and *uur* castes, and sometimes from outside the village, with problems including lost items, infertility, domestic difficulties, and possession by demons. The exchange between the spirit medium and the petitioner is characterized by Moffatt as a negotiation or "bargaining" session in which the goddess tests the petitioner's faith in her and "the petitioner's potential as a regular worshiper and devotee to the goddess," while the petitioner "evaluates the possible accuracy and usefulness of the goddess's words, and the possible effectiveness of her *shakti*."[73] The spirit medium's message is that belief in and devotion to the goddess will cure the problem or disease.

Fanon stresses the importance of understanding the phenomena of spirit possession and the dance of possession when studying the colonial world. The rituals are means of transforming and conjuring away violence. As Fanon writes,

> we see the native's emotional sensibility exhausting itself in dances which are more or less ecstatic. This is why any study of the colonial world should take into consideration the phenomena of the dance and of possession. The native's relaxation takes precisely the form of a muscular orgy in which the most acute aggressivity and the most impelling violence are canalized, transformed, and conjured away. The circle of the dance is a permissive circle: it protects and permits. At certain times, on certain days, men and women come together at a given pace, and there, under the solemn eye of the tribe, fling themselves into a seemingly unorganized pantomime, which is in reality extremely systematic, in which by various means—shakes of the head, bending of the spinal column, throwing of the whole body backward—may be deciphered as in an open book the huge effort of a community to exorcise itself, to liberate itself, to explain itself.[74]

While Fanon emphasizes the instrumentality of the spirit possession sèance for tribals who have been disenfranchised by the colonial world, Fiona Bowie points out that spirit possession is also used by women as an instrument of temporary power in societies in which women are powerless and denied authority because of their sex. "Claims to religious experience, be it spirit possession, visions, or locutions," according to Bowie, are a common means by which women in gender repressive societies gain access to political power. With spiritual impunity, women possessed by the goddess can wield great power and defy the authority of both their husbands and political authorities. "The corollary of this is that without a myth that authorizes such female power, it is much harder for women to legitimate their claims to any form of equality with men."[75] In India, the plethora of both orthodox and folk myths of fierce goddesses authorizes the female power claimed by women possessed by Māriyamman̲ or her *avatāras*. Folk myths depict the goddess as a strong, courageous woman who has been victimized, abused, and disempowered by males. In folk myths, the superior cosmic power of the goddess is maximized. She is parthenogenetic rather than born of the conglomerate energy of male gods, as depicted in myths written by male priests. In both elite and folk myths, the goddess's anger is a sign of her great destructive power.

Spirit possession is an archaic worldwide phenomenon that has not been historically restricted to tribal rituals. In "complex societies where status positions are hereditary and rigidly defined"[76] and gender roles are stringently polarized, spirit possession is an institutional means for powerless individuals (women and the underclass) to have a voice and to rise to a position of prominence and respect. In the patriarchal hierarchy of the monastery, the reincarnate Tibetan Buddhist lāmā (*tulku*) is a medium of spirit possession; he is considered holy because he is possessed by an "emanation body" (a deity or a deceased lāmā) that enters a series of rebirths into predestined individuals, usually young boys.[77] Spirit possession as a descent of a goddess or god into worthy human receptacles became institutionalized in the ancient Mediterranean/Aegean world, where, as we have seen, male devotees of Kybele became possessed by the goddess and castrated themselves as a sacrifice of the male principle to the goddess, and kingdoms would go to war if the Pythia[78] (the priestess) at Delphi had visions of successful battle. Fifth century BCE Greece was a hotbed of spirit possession: the state oracle at Delphi became possessed by the god Apollo (who supplanted earlier goddess Aphrodite) and issued written prophecies to kings, commanders, and commoners alike, while shamanic Dionysus-possessed women followers (*maenads*) reverted to communal hunting behavior, dancing wildly in ecstatic trance and ripping live animals or humans apart with their bare hands in frenzied states of divine, non-prophetic possession. Like most ancient gods, Dionysus was represented as a bull in Greek myths. The perfect social order in fifth century BCE Greece, as in earlier Mesopotamia and India, was considered to be "a warrior-society of obedient, disciplined male citizens in hoplite ranks who protect the enclosed, walled space of the city in which the women are safely secluded and secured," according to Charles Segal. "Inevitably symbols sacralizing the male hierarchy competed with and finally overshadowed the more sexually egalitarian symbols associated with fertility."[79]

In contemporary Christianity, spirit possession is practiced by the Pentecostal and Assemblies of God Protestant denominations, as well as by other charismatic groups. Not surprisingly, the Pentecostal sect has made great inroads among Indic tribes since the late twentieth century, in part because of the sanctity of Pentecostal spirit possession, a favored tribal practice that Baptist and Welsh Presbyterian reformers forbade. The Pentecostals have also exploited the primacy of the communitarian spirit among Indian tribal peoples. Pentecostals connect their practices to the happenings on the First Day of Pentecost, when flames or tongues of fire appeared on the heads of each of the apostles and "they were all filled with the Holy Spirit and began to speak in other tongues, as the Spirit gave them utterance."[80] Christians believe that Jesus's apostles were possessed by the Holy Spirit, and that the practice still exists within Christianity, characterized by lay people speaking in strange tongues or languages and entering an alpha or trance state of consciousness. In 1935, the Welsh Presbyterian Church issued a fiat: "listening to the Voice [of the Holy Spirit during possession], prophesying, speaking an unknown tongue, and all other signs of revival should be discouraged."[81]

Like Dionysus, Apollo, and the Holy Spirit, Indic folk goddesses "come down" into and possess those worshipers who are worthy vehicles. The shaman or lay person is able to go into trance, spurred on by frenzied ecstatic dancing and drumming, and, with the aid of the tutelary goddess in trance, diagnose and treat illness, or explain why a village goddess is angry, and what can be done to pacify the goddess and rectify the situation. The ability of fierce goddesses to talk to the people about their lives, diagnose and medicate, and exorcise demons is a highly charged vestige of an ancient magico-religious tradition that came to be exploited and manipulated by British imperialists, Gandhian social workers intent on puritanical, authoritarian reforms, and Hindu and Muslim landlords and moneylenders.

Spirit possession practices today serve as approved methods of social protest for powerless peoples such as tribals and women. Rex L. Jones explains that "the system of spirit possession not only functions as a system of explanation for misfortune and disaster, but it also functions as a means by which individuals are capable of achieving social positions and respect otherwise denied them."[82] Spirit possession is usually interpreted in the caste context as a means of understanding and giving meaning to the hardships of oppressed people's lives without their having to accept personal blame for their condition. In one sense, it is an alternative to the "blame the victim" orientation of *karma*.

THE NAGAS:
A MODERN FERTILITY AND SKULL CULT

The Tibeto-Burman speakers, probably the Kirātas of Indian literature, settled in the northern, north-eastern, and eastern borders of India. These people of the Mongoloid stock inhabited the Himalayan region by the middle of the first millennium BC. There were apparently wave after wave of migrations of the

Pl. I. Folk painting representing the goddess Kālī straddled over the erect *liṅgaṁ* of the corpse-Śiva. Orissa, nineteenth century. Gouache on cloth 15 × 13 (38 × 33). [Ajit Mookerjee Collection.]

Pl. II. Paṅgmi village headman of the Naga Hills of Burma. He became a Christian in 1982 but still wears brass heads round his neck (symbolizing the seven skulls he took in his youth), 1985. (169)

Pl. III. Nagas on the Burmese side retain a way of life that is comparable with that of pre-state India, 1985. (174)

Pl. IV. The Indian Naga rebels (the NSCN) has its own gospel group who entertain the villagers on the Burmese side of the frontier. Christianity was introduced in the remotest parts of the Naga Hills of Burma by Indian Naga rebels, who established a base inside Burma for cross-border raids into India, from about the mid-1970s, 1985. (177)

Pl. V. Wife of the *Aṅg* of Chopnu village. Sketch, 1873–76. (180)

Pl. VI. Naga *Aṅg* or chief of Chopnu village. Sketch, 1873–76. (180)

Pl. VII. Colored drawing of Captain Butler surrounded by British officers and assembled Nagas, 1973–75.

VIII
(*Caption-detail with Pl. X*)

Pl. IX. Carved female figure. Probably Konyak. (213)

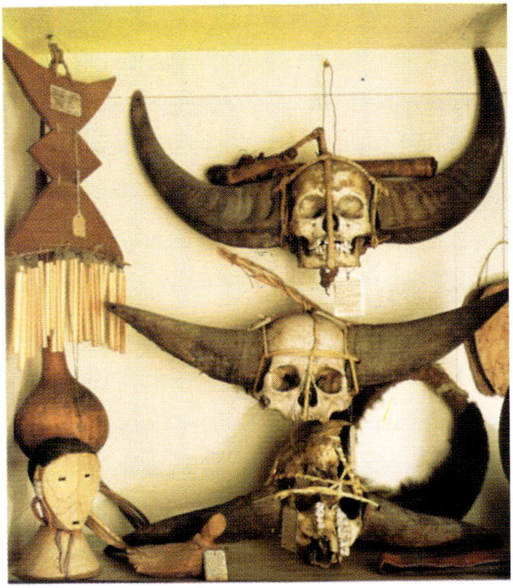

X

Pls. VIII, X. Collection of head-taking trophies used as symbols of martial prowess and as a means of acquiring fertility for the head-taker and the entire village. (182–83)

Pl. XI. Chief's cane helmet with a plume of red dyed goat's hair and sections of boar, tiger, and leopard jaws. The atypical basketry straps suggest it may be Burmese Naga. (219)

> Tibeto-Burman speakers to North-Eastern India even down to the early medieval period. These people, because of their late arrival, could not penetrate far into the interior plains and were not in a position to leaven the whole of it, so to say, in the way the Austrics, the Dravidians, and the Aryans did. . . . Matriarchal survivals among the Himalayan tribes and also countless Mother Goddess shrines in the lower Himalayan region, stretching from west to east give us some idea about their female-oriented religion and it is likely that these Kirāta people contributed something to the esoteric side of the Tantric rituals which is indicated by the story of Vasiṣṭha's initiation into the secrets of the Tārā cult.[83]

Because the transition from food gathering to food production in India did not occur in a uniform sequence, Neolithic cultures are extremely difficult to define and fix chronologically as economic entities. However, anthropological gradations can be "traced, identified and documented from the life of the surviving tribes and also from the literary records of the advanced peoples."[84] We may thus use anthropological studies of surviving tribes to clarify the analogical correspondences of sexual intercourse, agricultural fertility, sexual union, death, warfare, and head-taking among the pre-Aryan tribes. Twentieth century pre-Christian Nagas provide us with living specimens of almost unadulterated prehistoric warlike tribal lifestyle and religion, a fact recorded by Kosambi. Numerous texts are cited that refer to areas where prehistoric primitive practices survived despite the zeal of brāhmaṇa and Buddhist missionaries. To these isolated hunting tribes, the Mother-goddess was conceived as a shamanic Mistress of the Animals figure, a fierce Śabara or Kirāta woman who relished wine, meat, and animal and human sacrifice.[85]

Contemporary Nagas live in a state they call Nagalim, or Nagaland, at the conjunction of China, India, and Burma; some are refugees today. Both Bhattacharyya and Julian Jacobs have written that the Kirātas were ancestors of the Nagas, a notion verified by numerous references in epico-Purāṇic texts. They were classified as niṣādas, the fifth class of men, in Sanskritic literature. The epico-Purāṇic term Kirāta denoted a wide generalization of tribes that inhabited a large area of India, including parts of south India until they were driven north by Tamil warriors in the first century BCE. In the Purāṇic lists of *janapadas*, Kirāta tribes are depicted as dwelling in the Udīcya or Uttarāpatha region, as well as in the Himalayan or the Parvatāśraya region. In the *Vājasaneyī Saṃhitā*[86] they are presented as Himalayan mountain dwellers. In *The Periplus of the Erythraean Sea*, dated the latter half of the first century AD, the anonymous author observes that the Kirātas (Cirrhadae) are one of many "barbarous tribes"[87] that live to the north of Dosarene ("the Sanskrit Daśārṇa, the modern Orissa, 'the Holy Land of India'").[88] *The Periplus* depicts them as "a race of men with flattened noses, very savage,"[89] who are distinguished from the "Horse-faces and the Long-faces, who are said to be cannibals."[90] Bhattacharyya concludes that

> the ancient hunting tribes of India were scattered in different regions and . . . the terms Śabara, Pulinda, Kirāta, etc., originally denoted the hunting tribes in general. It was among these peoples that the cult of the Mother Goddess had

a prominent position. Their descendants also, who survive to this day in different parts of the country, follow the same religious tradition. Many tribes again have become completely Hinduized and having lost their original tribal character now belong to lower strata of Hindu society. With the development of agriculture and cattle-rearing, numerous tribes that previously subsisted on hunting and food-gathering came under the new system of production and became settled in villages as agriculturists or followers of other occupations. Most of the village deities were thus originally tribal deities.[91]

The pre-Christian Nagas were a patrilineal, patrilocal, warlike people with a culture of institutionalized violence, organized into cross-cutting group ties of lineages, clans, age-groups, classes, *morungs* (young men/women's dormitories), and villages. Children were born into both a household and a clan, and often took their name from a deceased ancestor on their father's side. Two days after birth, an infant's ear was pierced and a tuft of hair was cut off by the father, signifying the child's membership in the patrilineal clan. Even if it was known that the husband was not the father, the legal paternity of a child was more important than the biological paternity, and the child was claimed by the clan of the husband. If the mother was unmarried, the father was the man who paid a brass plate to the mother's father as a token of his paternity. If the parents of a child divorced, the child was raised by the father's clan, after giving the mother a "milk price." Since women did the bulk of agricultural work, they were the providers of the food for feasts, and their highest status derived from giving Feasts of Merit with their husbands. (Unfortunately, male ethnologists who have done field studies on the Nagas, like most anthropologists, have not explored Naga women's rituals and initiations.) As in most patriarchal societies, male exploits dominate culture and religion, but women provide the food and the offspring.

Naga chiefs, or Great *Aṅgs*, held a tenuous grasp on their chiefdoms contingent upon the prosperity of the village and the abundance of the crops. If villages did not prosper or crops failed, the *Aṅg* might be blamed. If there were no crops, he would be unable to give a Feast of Merit, which was one of the reasons he became chief. Some Naga villages such as the Thenkoh and Konyak are egalitarian, while living side-by-side with autocratic Thendu villages.

When the brāhmaṇas introduced the cult of the Hindu divinities to the many hill tribes of the northeast, the least influenced by their hegemony (and the most remote and agriculturally self-sufficient, due to plentiful jungle land) were the Mizos, Nagas, and Khasis. As a result, these tribes retained their original worldview and pantheons, unfettered by brāhmaṇic ideology, until most of them were converted to Christianity by British imperialists and American Baptist, Roman Catholic, and Welsh-Calvinistic Presbyterian missionaries.[92]

Ritual Specialists and Sacrifices

Most pre-Baptist Naga communities had both a shaman (*ratsen*) and priests (*puthi*). The *ratsen* tended to be a non-hereditary position that was determined by an individual being "called" by a god or spirit to be a shaman by frenzied spirit possession, a common aspect of fierce goddess worship in India, and also an aspect of Christian Pentacostal sects. The shaman did not conduct rituals, but served as a god- or goddess-possessed healer (remedies are given by the god to the shaman in a dream), counselor, dream interpreter, and fortuneteller. The *puthi* was usually a hereditary post held by a respected leader who had performed many Feasts of Merit, commensurate with the potlatch ceremonies of North American Indians. The *tevo* was the Aṅgāmis ritual specialist who played a central role in uniting their community. He wore a special white kilt and head-taker's ornaments, although he ceased raiding when he was installed. He was a privileged leader who lived on the housesite of the original village founder, and only he could found new villages. He ate first at Feasts of Merit and blessed the feast-giver. For seven harvests after taking office, he and his wife observed severe dietary and sexual prohibitions. It was his association with the descent of the tribe and the founding ancestor that accounted for his sacred character. He acted as intermediary between the village and the supernatural world of magical forces that pervade the Earth and individuals.[93] The egalitarian Aṅgāmis had the only Naga female supreme being and Creatrix goddess, Kepenopfu, but their sacrifices were offered to lower Earth spirits or *terhoma*, the spirits of evil, game, fertility, the household, and so forth. By contrast, the hierarchical Konyak gave most power to the high god Gawang, who directly affects earthly life.[94] The Zemo foregrounded malign deities, while the Lhota gave primary importance to sky spirits or *potsos*, who are only one of several spirit worlds that extend from the Earth upwards. These spirits visited the village shaman, bringing him symbols and omens of the future.

The central Naga ritual was the sacrifice—*genna* combination, a dramatization of their theory of fertility as a divine contagious energy. The sacrifice at the great Feast of Merit festivals is a buffalo (*mithan*), while at less splendid ceremonies, an egg, a leaf, or rice may be offered to the deity, Creator God, Creatrix Goddess, or jungle spirit. Following the sacrifice, the *genna* took place, which fixed the boundary of the social group and channeled fertility energy directly to the social unit making the sacrifice.

> In the *genna* period everything that is normally active becomes inactive: there is a prohibition on sex, work, certain foods, and travel. This period of *genna* may be up to several days, and transgressions are dealt with severely. What is the purpose of this restraint?. . . Obviously, it is a dramatic way of indicating that something special is occurring, and the unit observing the *genna* (a man and wife at the time of childbirth or sowing; the whole village in the case of a major Feast of Merit) is brought into clear focus. But we can go beyond this by noticing that a key part of the *genna* is the prohibition on people crossing the

boundary of the unit concerned: people may not, for instance, enter or leave the village. The purpose of the sacrifice-*genna* is to facilitate the proper flow of fertility in the relevant social group, but not outside it. The inactivity is a period of calm in which the group makes itself receptive to fertility, to act as its vehicle, but only for the particular social group concerned.[95]

Fertility and Megaliths

Predominantly Mongoloid, the pre-Baptist Nagas exhibited the megalithic culture and stone axe-heads (anthropological criteria for determining origin of peoples) of the Austroasiatic and the Austronesian (Malayo-Polynesian) language groups. The latter influence, thought to be the more recent, around the middle of the second millennium BCE, originated either in the islands of southeast Asia or China, according to Jacobs.[96] Megalithic culture, found throughout the islands of Southeast Asia (the Indonesian culture area), the north Indian Nagas, and south Indian Dravids, is characterized by the erection of large stone monuments and wooden posts as religious, fertility, and tribal status symbols are associated with "a set of beliefs about ritual prohibition or taboo and about a powerful soul-substance or virtue—known to the Nagas as 'fertility'—residing in the human head."[97,98] The shamanic religion of the Nagas subsumed a mystico-physiological belief that the head is the seat of the soul, a credo found in head-hunting societies, or those that perform ritual beheading.

To the Nagas, all natural and social phenomena are linked by the dangerous energy of fertility, conceptualized as a primal contagious force; if it is channeled and handled properly, good fortune and crops will result, but "misfortune is explained not as mere accident, but as the result of the presence of the negative aspect of fertility."[99] This conception bears a marked resemblance to the capricious, ambivalent, earthy nature of the ancient Tamil *aṇaṅku* energy. Both the Naga fertility meme and Tamil *aṇaṅku* are specifically related to warfare, blood sacrifice, sexuality, agriculture, and death, and both societies devised complex ritual forms to store, manipulate, and channel the energy for the benefit of the whole community.

According to Heine Geldern, notions about life and death as well as fertility are associated with megaliths.[100] They are believed to contain a link between the living and the dead, as well as the power engendered through sympathetic magic to increase the fertility of both nature and humans. Stones, like the plant kingdom, arise from the body of Mother Earth. For the Khasis and Nagas, monoliths and dolmens provide "phallic memorials through which the soul-matter of the living or of the dead assist the fertilization of nature, the upright stone representing the male and the flat one the female principle."[101] This analogical conception is explicated by Jacobs as follows:

> Others have used terms such as potency, life force . . . a quality inherent in the world which can be channelled and increased, and which is in a sense "contagious." The individual who has it is able to spread it around his family and his village, where it is manifested in wealth (that is, the fertility of his crops). The belief in

> fertility is a central element in the cosmology which unites the diverse Naga communities. Agriculture, sex, death, feasting, and martial prowess are all united by the underlying concept of fertility, which is both gained by these activities and manifested in them.[102]

The stones are often phallic in shape, or they are erected as a male and female pair. First dragged around the village ceremoniously, they are then implanted in the Earth, where the stone acts as a vehicle for fertility, channeling accumulated fertility into the Earth and then out to the rice fields. Heads of Naga enemies taken in a successful raid were brought back to the village and placed on a stone that has been set up in front of the *morung* (the youth's dormitory and the dominant building of the village). The fertility dynamic is that the stones conduct the fertility of the heads to the *morung* unit.[103]

Sexuality was considered a positive force that brought the individual in contact with fertility.[104] The stones were not only vehicles of fertility, but also sexual symbols of male and female genitals, precursors to the *yoni* and *liṅgaṁ* images. In many Naga communities, the *morungs* and dormitories were decorated with erotic carvings of couples in sexual embrace, the artistic precursor to the Indic articulation of the *hieros gamos* template, the *mithuna* and Umā-Maheśvara groups of later art. The cult of fertility based on a male and female principle associated with the phallic menhirs and dolmens is found from both the ancient remains and present practices of nearly all the tribes, particularly the Nagas. According to P.C. Choudhury,

> the megalithic culture of all the tribes has been part and parcel of their whole social existence, bound up with their life here and hereafter. The use of stone for graves and other purposes is no doubt primitive and ancient; so also is the belief in magic and fetishism or animism, which can be traced back to the lithic stage of culture. Both the grave and the phallic stones serve the same idea of fertility and are, therefore, functionally indistinguishable. The elaborate rituals connected with them may have been worked out differently by different tribes, but all are basically the same.[105]

Head-taking

Head-taking as a male activity was central to the fertility complex. In the nineteenth century, British writers observed that in order to be a fully eligible marriage candidate, each young man was required to take a head. As Jacobs writes,

> Raiding by Naga warriors with a view to obtaining slaves who could be brought back to the village, and whose heads could later be taken, remained an intractable problem for Government officers in the eastern areas of the Hills, up to Independence. . . . Different communities treated captured heads differently, but in all cases heads (or their substitutes or representative motifs) were a focal point of village life.[106]

Before the British imperialists outlawed it, head-taking was "a classic three-stage ritual." First, the *agjucho* ritual was performed to inaugurate hostilities; then an offering was made to the spirit-endowed stones lying near the chief's house; and the warriors then observed a *genna*, or a period of abstinence and the observation of taboos, "which takes them out of normal time and space and lifts them onto a ritually distinct level."[107] The head-taking attack was then carried out, and if the hunters were successful, they returned in "a dangerous and holy state."[108] After their heads had been buried at the *hazoa* stone, the head-takers were re-incorporated into normal society by the *aghupfu* ritual, a purification process involving their retreat in temporary huts where "they wore only white cloths, with no black thread, ate food cooked only by men, and remained chaste for a period of time."[109]

Purification before re-entry into the community was a requirement after Vedic animal sacrifices, as well:

> After he has performed that animal offering, he must not sleep upon (a couch), nor eat flesh, nor hold carnal intercourse; for that animal sacrifice is the first Dīkṣā, and improper surely it would be, were the initiated to sleep upon (a couch), or were he to eat flesh, or hold carnal intercourse.[110]

The heads taken were used as the cult object, the ceremonial *sine qua non* in all varieties of Naga rituals, and in some cases, the need for a ritual head was so urgent that "[i]f a stranger happens to pass by the village he is immediately beheaded."[111] Jacobs explains the mystical rationale underlying head-taking: "Taking a head is the ultimate transformative action. By killing another person, a man transforms life into death, and the accompanying rituals transform the biological (natural) fact of death into a social (cultural) object, that is, a skull."[112] In the Chang village of Hakchang, women whose blood relations on the male side have taken a head may cook the head, with chillis, to get the flesh off, after which they are ornamentally honored with the male tattoo, the double ostrich-feather tattoo worn by head-takers.[113]

For the Lhota, the "head-tree," which stood at the center of the village, was the symbol of village unity. Heads that had been taken in raids were hung on the tree, and sacred stones were arranged at its roots. The Zemi placed at the ritual center of the village the *hazoa*, a tilted block of stone standing over buried trophy heads, where foundation ceremonies of the village were held. Young men used the stone as a take-off point for a ritualized long-jump.

Warfare

Warfare was conceived by the Nagas as a sacred art that brought them into contact with fertility. The Naga's view of war and fertility is cognate with the ancient Tamil warrior philosophy of the sacred complex of the battlefield and the contagious *aṇaṅku*. The battlefield in a warrior's mind is conceptualized as a form of sacrifice; "the earth cries for blood to activate fertility," writes Carmel Berkson. "Moreover, as Hart has observed, for the Tamils, the battlefield symbolized the chaos which precedes creation. The sacred power inherent in the chaos is dangerous, and its eruptive forces can be brought under control only by the total annihilation of the enemy."[114] Such destruction brings the warrior and his village into contact with fertility. As Jacobs relates, "Although this would help explain the interest in taking heads, it would be wrong to suppose that this is the only reason why Naga society was traditionally characterized by institutionalized violence."[115]

Naga villages were organized as discrete political fighting units that perpetuated warfare by regarding peaceful restraint as "at best ill-advised and [possibly] catastrophic."[116] Violence was regarded as a positive cultural force, and warfare was a favored and exciting "sport, game, or way of life,"[117] as it has been among most warlike societies throughout human history. Young men eager to compete for heads and therefore "more alert to any possible insult or slight from a neighboring village"[118] caused an increase in raiding and head-taking. Pitched battles in which one village challenged another through an intermediary were prearranged at a set date and time, when warriors turned up in full ceremonial dress.

> Fatalities were low, in comparison with the typical stealthy raid, in which one party had the advantage of surprise. The women of the village (whose own heads, ironically enough, were the most highly-prized trophies, because they were held to be harder to obtain) might in this sort of battle bring up the rear, carrying and throwing stones.[119]

The Konyaks and Aos practiced forms of aggressive warrior magic prior to raids: they would blow on an egg, wish misfortune upon an enemy village, and then place the egg in the enemy village, or they would make wooden effigies of enemies that they would decapitate. If disease struck a village, other villages were suspected of practicing this kind of magic. The rationale for warfare was not so much the desire to inflict harm on an enemy village as it was to use the victory to enhance individual and village prestige, status, and macho reputation. "This resulted in a phenomenon noted by various observers, that Naga feud killings were conspicuously impersonal, even without malice," writes Jacobs. "Rather, it is as if the emotion were channeled into celebrating the return of the head to the village, and hence the political status of the successful warriors."[120] In some cases, feud-based warfare resulted in high levels of casualties; between 1902 and 1905, along a stretch of border country about 30 miles long, an average of 90 heads a year were taken. On a single day in 1936, 96 heads were taken in the unadministered area, and in 1939, one village was exterminated and 400 lives were lost.

> [T]hese levels of fatalities were the response to particular, identifiable, historical conditions. One changed circumstance, for instance, concerns guns. Despite attempts at licensing guns, it is clear that these examples of raids with high casualties were all raids which involved large numbers of guns; it is at least arguable that warfare with spears and *daos*, between roughly equal villages, could not result in such levels of death. By the turn of the century it was clear that attempts to control access to guns through licenses were failing. . . . [V]iolence of this kind is . . . symptomatic of a system which is in some sense breaking down, and there is a reasonable explanation for this: it was an unintended consequence of the British colonial policy toward the practice of head-taking.[121]

Fertility, Agriculture, and Death

Ritual practices marked the agricultural year among the Nagas, ranging from small-scale ceremonies to village-wide festivals that went on for several days of dances, feasting, drinking, and sacrifices. The importance of the magic dance is seen in the special dancing platforms constructed outside the house of the chiefly clan. In the Konyak villages, the Spring Festival marked the beginning of the agricultural year. Individuals painted their faces and wore their most prized ornaments, often clan heirloom objects or emblems of military prowess. The village priest prayed to the Konyak high god, Gawang, for fertility in the crops and among the people. "Other voices chant that the village will achieve victories over its neighbors, and at this point in the year the captured enemy skulls stored in the *morung* are ritually fed with rice beer."[122] The ritual symbols of feeding the skulls and fertilizing the fields express the conception that death produces life, as life produces death.

Like head-taking, agricultural activities were organized into three stages of ritual: the initial clearance of the jungle and the burning of the felled trees (mostly male labor), followed by the sowing (mostly female labor) and reaping (both male and female labor). These rituals included an offering of sacrificial animals, the observance of a *genna* period of general abstinence from work, sex, and other everyday activities, and feasting and dances. Most significantly, the rituals were grounded in the homologization of human sexuality and the fertility of the fields. Women did the majority of agricultural labor, based on slash-and-burn and terraced wet-rice cultivation. The following Naga sowing ritual is a fertility rite based on imitative magic:

> [T]he Lhota Nagas require an old woman to act as a ritual First Sower. Before the actual sowing by the man and his wife begins, the First Sower goes down to the fields and leaves a small offering of leaves and rice. . . . [T]he old woman is the same old woman who played an important part in the marriage ceremony of the couple, placing a leaf on the ears of the bride and groom: a link is being symbolized between marriage (as the basis of human fertility) and sowing (the basis of agricultural fertility), and both require the mediation of an old woman, the *ponyiratsen*, who is distinguished by being no longer fertile. The interplay between fertility and non-fertility is further seen in the fact that the Lhota couple abstain [*sic*] from sex the night before the fields are sown.[123]

The relation between death and agricultural fertility was explicated by Naga rituals. In the funeral rituals of the village of Laruri, the corpse was smoked in the house to dry it, and then hung in a canoe-like coffin under the house eaves until the first day of the new year's sowing *genna*. In the meantime, little houses were built on stilts for the souls of the dead to inhabit. On the first day of the sowing *genna*, all the coffins were brought down from the eaves, and the skull and bones were separated, placed in a covered pot, and taken to rest in the family's granary. The flesh remains and wrappings were returned to the coffin, which was then tipped over the side of a cliff. The little house was of little concern between sowing and harvest. When the harvest was reaped, a small amount was given to the little house as a final recognition of the deceased. Afterwards the house and the deceased were no longer considerations to the living. Thus for the Nagas, the fertility-enhancing soul-substance in the skull and bones was released to fertilize the land when the bones were placed in the pot, demonstrating the primal belief underlying imitative magic that human death is symbolically linked to agricultural fertility and regeneration.[124]

There is evidence, therefore, that many elements of Neolithic Indian fertility rituals—including the ancient male skull cult, warfare, sexo-religious agricultural magic associated with death, totemic big cats, proto-*liṅgaṁs* and *yonis*, and a full explication of a tribal conception of fertility as a primal contagious force—survive in the worldview, art forms, myths, legends, and rituals of contemporary tribes of the northeast that were, like the Nagas, least affected by brāhmaṇical hegemony. As Bhattacharyya has observed, "these Kirāta people contributed something to the esoteric side of the Tantric rituals."[125] The Naga skull cult, traces of which are evident in Indus seals, was in turn translated and revalorized into the medieval Kāpālika and Yoginī cult rites of head offerings so cherished by the fierce forms of the goddess.

Christian Reforms

The first S. Baptist missionaries were invited into the Naga Hills by early British explorers in the 1830s, and significant missionary activity developed in the 1870s. The Baptist prohibitions were destroying Naga culture by the 1920s, but the British Government regarded the conversion to Christianity as an appropriate colonial concern. As Jacobs reports,

> The Baptists prohibited the drinking of rice beer, condemned sexual freedom and forbade young men to sleep in the morung. They destroyed house carvings, forbade songs and dances, expected converts to renounce and despise their "heathen" neighbors, and banned Feasts of Merit (because of their apparently reckless celebration of conspicuous consumption). All of this implied not merely giving up "customs" but also "opting out" of the obligations normally attendant on every villager. . . . All the traditional rituals and festivals have given way to the Christian celebrations. Rituals concerning sowing, transplanting and harvesting of the rice crop have lost their importance.[126]

According to Reverend Mar Imsong, a Naga Baptist pastor at First Baptist Church in Bedford, Massachusetts, mass conversions by Nagas to Christianity was due to their deep spiritual link with their ancestors and clans; only when the whole community become Christians, keeping alive the communitarian tribal spirit, did salvation becomes relevant:

> When India forced foreign missionaries to leave the area in 1956, Naga became orphans spiritually. But because the missionaries had built up the native leaders, Naga Baptists took up the responsibility to be self-governing, self-perpetuating, self-supporting and self-theologizing. A distinctive Naga Baptist so much different from American Baptist evolved in Nagaland. And what we are today is because

of what our missionaries have done. It is because of these reasons Naga Christians still consider American Baptists as their "Spiritual Parents." Sin for Naga Christians was living a life of fear and inter-tribal warfare. People lived in fear, separated from one another, contesting and attacking one another. Self-righteousness was their spirituality and religion. Exclusion was a way of life for the Nagas. But when the Naga people become Christians, the Naga concept of community life was expressed and realized in a much wider concept. Not only sin, but also salvation for Naga Christians, was communitarian. You can be saved only in relationships.

American Baptist Missionaries came and taught from the *Bible* and said to our forefathers, "If you do not believe in Jesus Christ, you are sinners and you will go to Hell! But if you believe in Jesus and get baptized, you will go to heaven of eternal joy and you will be saved." Theologically sound! Very much of a Baptist faith! But do you know what response those villagers in Nagaland gave to the missionaries? "We would rather go to hell because all of our people and loved one are there in Hell." Heaven will be a better place when both liberal and conservative Baptists are there together, singing at the top of our voices! A community of faith is important. The Naga concept of community life fitted very well with the biblical view of KOINONIA or Communion, Sharing. Salvation becomes relevant only when the whole community become Christians. That is one of the reasons why there was mass conversion among the Nagas. When Naga Christians celebrate communion, whether one is a liberal or conservatives, politician or a businessman, freedom fighters or a Christian minister, rich or poor, we all come together as one Body in Jesus Christ. Communion is the time when we are incorporated to the Body of Christ and we are also incorporated to one another.[127]

The Nagas themselves attributed their slim harvests to the British outlawing of their head-taking ritual:

Since head-taking was stopped, Wanching (harvest) has got smaller. Formerly when illness swept through the village, we took a head, offered it and the sickness stopped. Nowadays we cannot offer heads and the sickness goes on and on. Man after man falls ill and dies, and there is nothing we can do. The fields too have gone off and we do not get the crops we did. . . .[128]

The Naga territories were part of the regional kingdom of Assam when British took over in 1826. Nagas fought alongside the British in both world wars. When the British left India in 1947, they turned Naga territories over to Indian rule. At the same time, rebels in the Naga territories sought their own independence from India, since they claimed that they were not Indian. Influenced by Baptist ideology, they formed the Naga National Council and adopted the slogan "Nagaland for Christ." They created a flag with a rainbow intersecting a blue sky, an allusion to God's covenant with Noah in the Book of Genesis, revalorized as God's covenant with the Nagas. In 1963, Nagaland was the first of several states carved out of the larger territory of Assam. Today Nagaland is nearly ninety percent Baptist, ripped apart by a guerrilla war fought to establish a free Christian nation. An estimated 200,000 Nagas have died in the struggle for freedom from Indian rule, a cause supported by leadership of the American Baptist Churches, USA.

Since their independence, many villages of the Ao Naga area have been influenced by Christian revivalism, by-products of Christianity such as "the Suffering Party," a blend of traditional animistic Naga religion and Christianity organized by Rev. Shihoto of the Sema tribe in the mid-twentieth century, and the Revival Movement of the Dehra Dun Pentecostal Center, which has emphasized healing through prayer, dreams, and salt-taking.[129] The convergence of Christian and animistic belief systems in these revivalist groups explain and treat illness through the familiar medium of spirit possession.

Fierce Tribal Goddesses in Sanskritic Literature

The ancient tribes speaking the Austro-Asiatic dialects belonging to the Austric language family survive in the Kol or Munda, the Nicobarese, and the Mon-Khmer Indian speeches, but in archaic times the speakers were spread over almost all of northern India. "Very probably," writes Bhattacharyya, "the Austric speakers with their dark skin and snub nose were known to the Vedic peoples as niṣādas, and they gradually became Aryan-speaking roughly between *c.*1500 and 600 BC."[130] They were horticulturalists whose digging sticks doubled as cult objects, the phallus or *liṅga*. They worshiped a goddess called Mātṛkā who sometimes signified the Pleiades, and the term "Mātṛkā" has become the common term for the Indic Divine Mothers.[131] Their tribal mother, Ka-mei-kha (derived from the Khasi speech, *ka*, mother, and *mei-kha*, mother-born),[132] was Sanskritized as Kāmākhyā, who is worshiped in the form of a *yoni* or female organ of generation at her shrine in Guwahati in Assam. Kāmākhyā is now accepted as a form of the Supreme Being of the Śāktas. Gait describes the ceremonies conducted at the opening of the restored temple of Kāmākhyā in Assam:

> When the new temple of Kāmākhyā was opened, the occasion was celebrated by the immolation of no less than a hundred and forty men, whose heads were offered to the goddess on salvers made of copper. According to the *Haft Iqlīm*, there was in Kāmarūpa a class of persons called *bhogīs* who were voluntarily victims. From the time when they announced that the goddess had called them, they were treated as privileged persons; they were allowed to do whatever they liked, and every woman was at their command; but when the annual festival came round, they were killed.[133]

The cult of the fierce goddess was particularly developed among the aboriginal tribes such as the Nagas, niṣādas, and other the so-called fifth class of men.[134] As we know, the earliest peoples were hunters and food-gatherers, living in a social order in which there was no class division due to the very low level of production. Many references to such peoples can be found in Vedic texts, and their cults and beliefs are described in post-Vedic literature. The niṣādas are the most primitive non-Aryan ethnic elements of the Indian goddesses, whose "extraordinary names lead one to suspect connection with some diminutive tribal group now defunct or absorbed (without any other trace) into the general rustic population."[135] There is a clear link between the fierce Devī and the niṣādas as dramatized in Indian secular and sacred literature, and it was only after definitive modifications that fierce goddesses became acceptable to male elites. The Āryāstava contains a graphic portrait of the Devī's association with the wild Śavaras, Barbaras, and Pulindas tribes:

> O Mahādevī your dwelling is on the frightful mountain-peaks, in caves, rivers, forests and also in the wind. Crowded by cocks, goats, sheep, lions and tigers, and accompanied by the dingling of bells, you are well worshiped by the Śavaras, Barbaras, and Pulindas. O you, having peacock-tail as a mark, so renowned as Vindhyavāsinī, walk among all people in all places.[136]

Not only do these verses declare that the wild hill tribes were worshipers of the goddess Mahādevī, but they also point to the fact that the goddess Vindhyavāsinī mingled among "all people in all places." Bhattacharya asserts that this is the same goddess referred to in the Durgā-stotras, proved by her common association with forests, mountains, and beasts, and by similar epithets applied to her (e.g., *Śikhipicchadhvajadharā* in the Durgā-stotras and *Mayūrapicchadhvajinī* in the Āryāstava), as well as from the reference to the Devī's fondness for wine and meat in both the texts.[137] This tribal goddess was accepted in the Purāṇas as a member of the Śākta pantheon. Kālī in the Kalanjar mountain, Caṇḍikā in Makarandaka, and Vindhyavāsinī in the Vindhya mountain are mentioned as the different manifestation of the Devī,[138] and her particular predilection for wine and meat is emphasized.[139]

The association of the sanguinary *ugra* aspect of the Devī with tribal headhunting peoples is corroborated by evidence in secular literature. According to Bāṇabhaṭṭa in his description of the nature of the Śavaras in the *Kādambarī*,[140] the wild Śavaras regularly appeased their goddess by animal sacrifices (*paśurudhireṇa devatārcanaṁ*), and regarded human sacrifices to their goddess as an act of merit (*puruṣapiśitopahāra-dharmabuddhi*).[141] In the *Harṣacarita*,[142] as well, Bāṇa refers to the destructive character of the Devī and to the animal sacrifices to her. King Lāṅgā of Mewar, according to the popular tradition of Rajasthan, sacrificed his nine sons to Cāmuṇḍā, but the goddess was not appeased, and ultimately, she received the head of the old king himself.[143]

It is the *Gauḍavaha*, a Prākṛta *kāvya* composed by Vākpati in the first half of the eighth century AD, however, that contains the most illuminating details about the goddess of the Śavaras. The *Gauḍavaha* identifies Vindhyavāsinī with Kālī or Pārvatī,[144] associates her with the Kols and Śabaras, and refers to human sacrifices offered to propitiate her. In the historical poem, the hero, king Yaśovarman, arrives at the valley of the river Śoṇa (Red) and then proceeds to the Vindhya mountain, where he offers a hymn of fifty-two couplets to the celebrated tribal goddess Vindhyavāsinī Devī, or "the Goddess residing in the Vindhyas."[145] The hymn evokes the macabre atmosphere of the temple of Vindhyavāsinī and its surroundings, and details the *ugra* roles of the goddess, including her slaying of the buffalo-demon, her familiar association with peacocks, her bloodthirsty nature, and, most significantly, the daily human sacrifice before the goddess of the Śavaras who lived in a cave of the Vindhya.[146]

Subandhu's *Vāsavadattā* makes reference to the bloodthirsty goddess Bhagavatī or Kātyāyanī of Kusumapura. Bhavabhūti's *Mālatīmādhava*, discussed above, dramatizes the ritual of human sacrifice before the goddess. The *Devī Bhāgavata Purāṇa* describes the cosmic form of Śakti as her *Virāṭa-Swarūpa*, the fierce, cosmic aspect of the goddess:

> The gods began to behold her cosmic (*Virāṭa*) appearance with eyes wide awake with wonder. Thousands of fiery rays emitted from her form; she began to lick the all-horrible sounds; fires came out from her eyes, various weapons were seen in her hands, the brāhmaṇas and the kṣatriyas became the food of that awful deity. Thousands of heads, eyes, and feet were seen in that form. It was so terrific that all the gods fainted having looked on that form. Afterwards, coming to their senses, they requested the Devī to withhold her fearful cosmic form and to show the very beautiful form. Then her body became soft and gentle; in one hand she held the noose, and in another the goad. The other two hands made signs to dispel all their fears and ready to grant the boons. Her eyes were emitting rays of kindness and her face was adorned with beautiful smiles.[147]

The following Purāṇic passage on the religious life of the Chutiyas of Assam is significant:

> The religion of the Chutiyas was a curious one. They worshiped various forms of Kālī with the aid not of the brāhmaṇas but of their tribal priests or Deoris. The favorite form in which they worshiped this deity was that of Kesai Khati, "the eater of raw flesh," to whom human sacrifices were offered. After their subjugation by the Ahomms, the Deoris were permitted to continue their ghastly rites; but they were usually given, for the purpose, criminals who had been sentenced to capital punishment. If none were available, victims were taken from a particular clan, which in return was accorded certain privileges. The person selected was fed sumptuously, until he was plump to suit the supposed taste of the goddess, and then he was decapitated at the copper temple at Sadia or at some other shrine of the tribe. Human sacrifices were also formerly offered by the Tipperas, Kacharis, Koches, Jaintias, and other Assam tribes.[148]

The Bolāī or Bolhāī, the most famous archaic goddess cult site near Poona, a mile from the village Vadem-Ghoḍeṁ, not far from Koregão, is described by Kosambi:

> With her, we come to the full-blown primitive stage, for in spite of a temple built in the time of the Peshwās, and endowed by the Gaekwārs, she has not been brāhmaṇized beyond being labelled a "sister" of the Pāṇḍavas. At least one goat is sacrificed to her every Sunday (her special day), with additional blood-sacrifice which some devotee might consider necessary on any other occasion. She is still a huntress who sets out on a two-month hunting tour in winter, symbolized by a palanquin procession at the beginning and the end.[149]

Banerjea[150] and Hazra[151] emphasize the tribal strands in the character of the fierce Devī on the basis of two Durgā-stotras of the *Mahābhārata*[152] and the

Harivaṁśa.[153] In the *Mahābhārata,*[154] she is described as fond of spirituous liquor and flesh and residing in the Vindhyas. The descriptions of the Devī in the two Durgā-stotras highlight her role as fierce warrior, destructive and victorious, manifested as Kālī, Karālī, Mahākālī, Kapālī, Kapilā, Kṛṣṇapiṅgalā, Aṣṭaśūlapraharaṇā, Khaḍgakheṭakadhāriṇī, Vijayā, Jayā, Mahiṣasṛkpriyā, Aṭṭahāsa, Kākamukhī, Raṇapriyā, etc.

Furthermore, in the Durgā-stotra of the Bhīṣmaparvan in *Mahābhārata,* she is characterized as "she who dwells in great forests, frightful places, and unapproachable countries," and in the second *stotra* of the Virāṭaparvan, her habitat is clearly the Vindhya mountain. The *Harivaṁśa*[155] also places her in the Vindhya mountain, where she is described as a maiden who is annointed by ghosts, worshiped by bands of robbers, and honored with jars filled with wine and meat. Living in dense forests, associating with wild animals, she kills two mountain-roaming demons, Śumbha and Niśumbha. As the goddess Vindhyavāsinī, Devī as a tribal goddess is well-known from the lines of the Āryāstava, previously cited, which specify that the Śavara, Barbara, and Pulinda tribes were Devī-worshipers, and emphasize her universal appeal to "all people in all places." Like the goddess in the Durgā-stotras, this one is identified with forests, mountains, and beasts, and she is characterized in both texts as being partial to wine and meat. In addition, similar epithets are applied to her in both texts, e.g., *Śikhipicchadhvajadharā* in the Durgā-stotras and *Mayūra-picchadhvajinī* in the Āryāstava.

This tribal goddess, with her great fondness for the brāhmaṇical taboos of wine and meat,[156] has been appropriated in the Purāṇas as a part of the brāhmaṇical Śākta pantheon of the Purāṇic worshipers: Kālī in the Kalanjar mountain, Caṇḍikā in Makarandaka, and Vindhyavāsinī in the Vindhya mountain are identified as different manifestations of the Devī.[157] In the *Varāha Purāṇa*[158] she is addressed as Kirātinī or Kirāta (Naga) woman. In the *Gauḍavaha*[159] she is addressed as Śabarī, i.e., a Śabara woman. One of her rituals is called *Śābarotsava,* meaning "the festival of the Śabaras."

The Kirātas (Nagas), Bhramaras, Nāhalakas, Pulindas, Bhillas, and other tribes are described as descendants of the niṣādas in the *Padma Purāṇa.*[160] In medieval Sanskrit literature, the Śabaras, Pulindas, and Kirātas refer to tribes of the Vindhya hills that belong to the niṣāda stock. In the *Aitareya Brāhmaṇa,*[161] the Śabaras are classed with the Pulindas, Puṇḍras, Andhras, and Mutibas as Dasyus, characterized as wild tribes that depend on hunting for their livelihood. According to Jayakar,

> The Śavaras were reputed to be great magicians with a knowledge of witchcraft, astrology, and palmistry. They practiced medicine and had archaic knowledge of herbs and of mantras to induce healing. The Śavaras give no anthropomorphic forms to their gods. Their *sonum,* ancient ancestor-spirits, appear in the form of sacred pots smeared with turmeric and filled with rice, chillies, garlic, and salt. These pots are hung from the roof.[162]

According to the Purāṇic lists of Janapadas, the territory inhabited by the Śabaras is located to the south of the Vindhyas. In the Jaina lists of the Janapadas, the land of the Śabaras—described as *mleccha* peoples—is mentioned along with those of the Kirātas, Pulindas, Draviḍas, and others. The Śabaras worship various forms of the Mother-goddess. In Madhya Pradesh, they worship her as Bhavānī.[163] In Purāṇic literature, the Śabaras are called the *Vindhya Maulikas*, "the wanderers in the Vindhyas," an ancient tribe mentioned in the *Rāmāyaṇa* and the *Mahābhārata*. The epics depict them as a primitive people who live in thick forests and wear garments made of leaves. As they rose to historical power, they became rulers of immense tracts of the heartlands of India. In the seventh and eighth centuries, they were found in Mirzapur (Uttar Pradesh), Andhra and Ganjam, Keonjhar, and Puri in Orissa. The archaic Śabara cults are closely associated with the cult of Jagannātha. After the eighth century, "the fortunes of the Śavaras declined, they were defeated in battle, lost their kingdoms and disappeared again into the forests to continue life as primitive hunters and wandering cultivators. For many centuries after their defeat, the Śavaras continued to influence the life and art of the peoples of central and eastern India."[164]

The Pulindas, like the Śabaras, were hunting tribes of Deccan.[165] Ptolemy refers to these *Poulindai* as *Agriophagoi* (tribe subsisting on raw flesh, roots, and wild fruits).[166] The Purāṇas depict them as foresters,[167] and the *Bṛhat Saṁhitā*[168] refers to them as a particular tribe (Pulinda-gaṇa). According to the *Kathāsaritsāgara*,[169] the land of the Pulindas was in the Vindhyas on the route from Kosambi to Ujjayini. Epigraphic and literary evidence suggest that there were several branches of the Pulindas, i.e., a southern branch, a western branch, and a Himalayan branch related to the Kirātas and Taṅganas. According to Bhattacharyya, the term *pulinda* was later used to describe any "hunting people,"[170] a statement supported by Buddhist literature in which even the Veddas and other wild tribes of Ceylon were identified with the Pulindas.[171] The Indian tribes described by Herodotus include the Padaeans, whom he characterized as nomads living on raw flesh.[172] Ptolemy writes of the Poulindai Agriophagoi or the Pulindas, "who lived on raw flesh, roots and fruits, and may be identified with the Pulindas among the *Vindhyāśrayinas* (or the Proto-Australoids), living on the Vindhya mountain."[173]

We have ample evidence from Sanskritic texts that fierce, autonomous, unwed tribal fierce goddesses of protection and destruction originated in tribal societies. Vindhyavāsinī, Kauśikī, Kālī, Śabarī, Karālī, Mahākālī, Kapālī, Kauśikī, and Caṇḍikā were originally goddesses of the Kuśika tribes. Kātyāyanī was the goddess of the Kātya tribe, Kālī of Kalañjara mountain, Vindhyavāsinī of the Vindhyas. These goddesses were later to become the Mātṛkās and Yoginīs.

Archaic Tribal Festivals

The power of local goddesses is most evident during their festivals. In contrast to the rather quiet and contemplative festivals of the brāhmaṇical, orthodox goddesses, those of the local goddesses are vibrant and dynamic. The nature of local festival rituals is an important factor in establishing the Sanskritic and non-Sanskritic nature of a goddess. For instance, a brāhmaṇical goddess would not accept a blood sacrifice, nor would she possess her devotees. The devotees of an orthodox goddess might sing devotional songs or read the sacred texts defining her exploits rather than testing their faith by walking across a pit of hot coals or venturing into the cremation ground late at night.[174]

Hookswinging (Covadi)

In shamanistic cults, the initiatory ordeal is a rite of passage that dramatizes the ritual death and resurrection of a shaman, medicine-man, or medium-diviner. As Eliade emphasizes, the ritual death can be suggested by "extreme fatigue, tortures, fasting, blows, and so on,"[175] which serve as evidence that the individual has been possessed by a spirit or deity; "in fact, the sufferings, intoxications, and blows that have brought on his loss of consciousness are in a manner assimilated to a ritual death."[176] In the tribal setting, the ordeal is undertaken in order to authenticate a journey to the land of the dead, followed by spiritual transformation or rebirth in which the profane human condition is transcended. In Indian theistic cults, ordeals are forms of self-torture that enable the penitent to ecstatically communicate with his or her tutelary deity and gain divine favors. In both tribal and theistic spheres, the ordeal manifests an individual's capacity to bear ritual torture in a state of ecstasy, representing an initiation into union with the divine. As Eliade points out, ecstatic self-torture is a magical means of self-hypnosis:

> We find . . . extremely ancient "magical" practices, which yogins use to influence the gods and even to terrorize them. The phenomenology of this magical asceticism is archaic: silence (*mauna*), extreme torture (*ātivatapas*), "desiccation of the body," are means employed not only by yogins but also by kings. To move Indra (*ārirādhayiṣur devam*), Pāṇḍu stands on one foot for a day and thus obtains *samādhi*. But this trance exhibits no yogic content; rather, it is a hypnosis provoked by physical means, and the relations between the man and the god remain on the level of magic.[177]

The archaic practice among Kerala *ādivāsīs* of "hookswinging" of human corpses has been replaced by swinging dolls rather than corpses. Hookswinging has taken another form in contemporary south Indian villages since antiquity: low-caste or dalit males hookswing as an initiatory ordeal while possessed by Māriyammaṉ. In most of Māriyammaṉ's temples, animal sacrifice and hookswinging are performed, although a few Māriyammaṉ temples only allow "bloodless oblations." The origin of hookswinging remains an enigma, but, as Elaine Craddock recognizes, the practice "has explicit connections to blood sacrifice."[178] In the following excerpt of a lullaby to Māriyammaṉ, the goddess is addressed as "the queen of all women":

> O lady who appeared, swinging on the hook,
> People don't know you are the supreme guru,
> You who swing here and there on the heavy hook with side ropes.

You sit as Śakti;
You received the sacrifice of a single sheep.
You sat on the village boundary and received the sacrifice of a
male buffalo.[179]

The first record of the hookswinging performance, a sixteenth-century European account, describes a devotee of Māriyamman̲ who makes a vow to the goddess to perform this ritual. He is "suspended in the air by means of hooks inserted into the flesh of his back; the hooks are tied to a rope, which in turn connected to a horizontal beam balanced on a vertical pole."[180] The vow was made not to achieve enlightenment or to win wars, but "in response to illness, danger, childlessness, or other personal distress."[181] The swingers are usually low-caste or *dalit* males, whose status is enhanced by their self-sacrifice. Significantly, they dedicate their performance to the health and well being of the whole village. The practice began to decline in the nineteenth century, during the Madras Presidency. Attempts to abolish hookswinging increased after 1853 due to pressure from missionaries, government officials, and some educated Indians. By 1893, sheep were substituted for humans in Periyapāḷaiyam hookswinging performances. Hookswinging apparatus remained outside the Periyapāḷaiyam temple in 1906.[182]

Hookswinging is emblematic of self-sacrifice to Māriyamman̲, much as the self-flagellation of devotees of Kybele represented surrender to her. It is "a self-sacrifice that the entire community can participate in and derive benefit from,"[183] according to Craddock. "The fact that Māriyamman̲ is praised as 'swinging on a hook' points to the notion that she herself models the kind of self-sacrifice that characterizes profound devotion. When a true devotee enacts the sacrifice by swinging on the hook, Māriyamman̲ herself appears, drawn by the devotion of her worshiper."[184] Hookswinging is a metaphor and ritual dramatization of the painful contraction of smallpox, and, like the disease, is emblematic of the goddess's grace; only "the chosen" are afflicted with pox. "The goddess directs attention to herself through the disease: devotees need Māriyamman̲, but she also needs to be fed, to be sustained by her devotees. Her concern that she get enough food is one of the reasons she gives people pox."[185] Like hookswinging, firewalking is an ordeal of self-torture involving possession by and propitiation of Māriyamman̲ or one of her sisters. In contemporary eastern Sri Lanka, ordeal vows of body piercing and firewalking are made to Kāḷī by Tamil devotees trapped in a civil war zone (discussed *infra*, chap. 13).

Navarātri/Daśaharā Festival

At the end of the rainy period in India, the rebirth into the new year coincides with the celebration of Durgā's victory over the buffalo demon Mahiṣa in the Navarātri/Daśaharā festival, at which, until 1799, buffaloes and human beings were traditionally sacrificed to the goddess.[186] Like the Indus seal depicting an animal with a buffalo body and human face, Mahiṣāsura has a human face and buffalo body.[187] In the *Mārkaṇḍeya* and *Vāmana* Purāṇas, and also in the later Devī-oriented Purāṇas, the sacrificed buffalo-god is Mahiṣa *asura*, with a buffalo body a human face, who woos the warrior goddess Durgā (Caṇḍī) and is vanquished by her. On the day after the Dusserah, which concludes the Navarātri festival commemorating Durgā's victory over the buffalo demon, all the beacon lights were lit and burned all night, signaling the warriors to start from home for the military camps. They were away from home for the whole fair season. The main event at the great festival was the offering of *nara-bali*, "human sacrifice," a ritual that echoes the archaic Indic motif of the transposed heads, a dark signature of the caste system. Three human beings were always sacrificed on this day; they were decapitated on the stone, and the heads were removed from the bodies, picked up and arranged in the form of a hearth.

> Food was cooked on this hearth. Later the heads were picked up again and reunited with the bodies to which they belonged, while an oblation (*arthī*) was made. This oblation and offering was of the food that had been cooked over the three heads. It seems that on one occasion the men were unable to rejoin two of the heads to their respective bodies.[188]

Such practices, including the *meriah* sacrifice, are the continuation of a long tradition that was fully alive until 1799. Parpola traces the interchange of heads (signifying transformation and rebirth) to the *vrātyas*, who also ceremonially interchanged trunks and heads[189] of decapitated victims chosen for head offerings and human sacrifice to the fierce goddess Bhairava and her consort, Rudra-Śiva, and who had "intimate dealings with Prajāpati,"[190] the Sun-god. Their practices and ceremonials suggest the head-taking ceremonies of the Nagas, as well as the later Śākta-Tantric ritual use of taboos such as intoxicating drink, flesh, and grain.

For socioeconomic reasons discussed below, the trend toward *ahiṁsā* developed in the sixth century BCE in the śramaṇic and brāhmaṇic *dharmas*, and offerings of metal and clay images began to be substituted for human and animal sacrifices, but the ancient rites of fertility survived in subaltern consciousness and religion. Memories of human and animal sacrifices to the Earth materialize each year during Navarātri, the nine nights of the bright half of the Moon that are sacred to the goddess. The ancient agricultural symbols of death and resurrection resound in the imagery of Navarātri:

> During Navarātri, women plant corn in baskets or pots, symbolic of the body of the goddess. The corn sprouts in darkness and the pale golden shoots are worshiped for nine nights and then consigned to the waters. These rituals are found in peasant, tribal and urban societies. Amongst the tribals of central India, the corn-seed is sown by the daughters of the headman, in sandy soil mixed with a quantity of turmeric. When the blades sprout and unfold, they are pale yellow. In autumn, the sprouted corn is taken up by the roots and carried in baskets to the open meeting place of the village. A karma tree is worshiped and the sprouted blades distributed amongst young unmarried boys and girls.[191]

Rites to Awaken Earth Mother

Ancient sacrifices to the Earth were performed at the main solstitial rites to awaken the Mahāvrata, Earth Mother, in autumn after the rains and in the spring after the harvest. Several well-known Indian religious observances can be traced back into prehistory, including the Holi (spring) festival, "an obscene and nowadays rather depraved saturnalia"[192] that features participants dancing around a great bonfire, fire-walking on the embers, followed the next day by a dramatization of the reversal of social standards, exemplified by "a great deal of vociferous public obscenity,"[193] such as the practice of the Mātaṅgī at Māriyammaṉ festivals, and sexual license and promiscuity in remote areas. Clearly, sexual freedom on planting, harvest, or other auspicious days in agricultural societies is believed to stimulate the fecundity of Mother Earth through homeopathic or imitative fertility magic. Especially during harvest celebrations, low-caste, *dalit*, and *ādivāsī* women are encouraged to engage in wanton promiscuity:

> Among the Hos of Chotanagpur, during the harvest festival, complete sexual liberty is given to the girls. The Kotas of Nilgiri hills have a similar festival of sexual freedom. In Orissa, among the Bhuiyas, sexual freedom is given to the girls during their harvest festival called *māgh porāi*. In Assam, women are allowed during spring festivals complete freedom without any stain, blemish, or loss of reputation. The Zemi villagers (Kacha Nagas) at their sowing season make a model of the sexual organs in coitus. The female organ is exactly modeled in clay, with dry grass representing the pubic hairs, while a wooden stake serves for the male organ. Young men and girls surround this model, and one of them work the stake in the appropriate way, to the great amusement of the rest of the party. In some cases their original purposes have been forgotten. The *Holi* festival was a celebration of this type in which even persons of great responsibility were not ashamed to take part in orgies which mark the season of the year. Today men run about the street dousing each other with red powder or water, the significance of which is entirely forgotten.[194]

Another common imitative practice requires a man (called the *kolina*) to wear woman's clothing and join the dancers ringing the Holi fire. At the great annual Karagā festival at Bangalore, the primary male participant, as well as the priest of the quail-snaring, must dress as a woman before officiating. These practices, according to Kosambi, hark back to a prehistoric matriarchal stage:

> These rites and festivals have been taken over by men though originally a women's monopoly. Similarly, groves sacred to the mother goddess are mentioned in brahmin myth and legend. Such groves still exist in villages away from the road; but women are now generally forbidden entry excepting the few cases where the priesthood has remained in primitive hands not transferred to immigrant settled cultivators. Originally, the ban was on the entry of men. When society changed from matriarchal to patriarchal, the priesthood and ritual were correspondingly transformed.[195]

Tantrism

Primitive Tantrism was a set of practical techniques to stimulate the generative powers in nature; as such, "it was closely related to the Mother Goddess, the puissant and eternally active Śakti, representing the force of life in nature."[196] The survival of Neolithic fertility magic and the planter goddess in the literary themes, iconographic motifs, and collective practices of heterodox Śāktism is clearly evident in the ritual traditions of head and blood offerings (*bali*), and the sacramental use of wine and meat. As Bhattacharyya writes,

> Magical fertility rites, originally performed by women to ensure the process of nature, were invariably associated with . . . a conception of a material Earth Mother. These rites, surviving through the ages in popular beliefs and customs, were conserved and crystallized in the later Tantras, while the more rational speculations centering round the conception of a material Earth Mother (*prakṛti*) developed subsequently into a distinct metaphysical form, the Sāṅkhya system.[197]

Motifs in Tantric art related to Neolithic fertility magic and *bali* reveal the ancient ritual origin of Vāmācāra practices within both Buddhist and Hindu Tantrism. In the later brāhmaṇic tradition, the demon is rationalized as a symbol of the animal-man stage of human consciousness whose slaying, rather than benefiting the crops and community, is characterized as a conceptual tool of the individual yogī in his quest for salvation. As Kumar writes of the demon: "He has the unregulated, wild emotions of the animal, and these have now to be controlled by the discriminative faculty of the mind. He is half man and half animal, [which] is, so to speak, the buffalo stage in human evolution."[198] A similar rationalization or revalorization of the taboo icongraphy of ritual coitus and *bali* occurs in Tibetan Buddhist philosophy.[199] This is an important esoteric subtext of the Mahiṣamardinī symbology: the conquest of violence in the form of the inner predator-warrior, the unthinking aggressor, must precede spiritual enlightenment.

Chanda has noted the parallel between the sacred prostitution of the Mediterrannean goddess cults and the promiscuous ritual coitus practiced by Kaulācāra-Vāmācāra Śāktas in India.[200] Primal fertility magic underlies the Tantric *pañca makāras* or *pañca tattva*, which includes the use of *madya* (wine), *māṁsa* (meat), *matsya* (fish), *mudrā* (intertwining of the fingers), and *maithuna* (sexual intercourse). The fish is also closely associated with matriarchal beliefs as a fertility symbol,[201] and the relation between fish and the Mother-goddess is a common feature of primal religion.[202] Another connection may exist in images of Neolithic Western Asian and Aegean goddesses like Artemis, Hera, Demeter, and the Chaldean Nana, which were inscribed with geometrical patterns reminiscent of Tantric *yantras* and *maṇḍalas* representing the female genitalia, and suggestive of fecundity symbols.[203] As Bhattacharyya emphasizes:

> In Tantricism special importance is attached to the rituals centering round the female genital organ and these rituals are called *bhagayāga* or *latā-sādhana*.

The word Tantra is derived from the root *tan*, the most simple meaning of which is "to spread," "to multiply." The Tantric Śrīcakra is nothing but the representation of the female generative organ. In the Durgā worship, a Tantric diagram showing the picture of female generative organ called *Sarvatobhadramaṇḍala*, is drawn upon the ground and a *pūrṇakumbha* or *pūrṇaghaṭa*, i.e., an earthen vessel filled with water, a symbol of the female womb, is placed on it. The figure of a baby, called *sinduraputtalī*, is drawn on the surface of the vessel. The open mouth of the *pūrṇaghaṭa* is covered with five kinds of leaves, and a coconut, smeared with vermilion, is placed on it. The *Kathāsaritsāgara* (70.122) identified *kumbha* or *ghaṭa* explicitly with uterus. What is stated above is simply a fertility rite by which the plants are brought into contact with female reproductive organ to insure multiplication.[204]

The medieval Śākta-Tantric cults that participated in Vāmācāra[205] rituals worshiped both the *Ugra* Devī (Caṇḍikā, Kauśikī, Cāmuṇḍā, Durgā, Kālī, Kāmākhyā, and others) and her consort, Bhairava [or his Buddhist counterparts, Śambara, Vajradāka, Heruka, Hevajra, Caṇḍamahāroṣaṇa (Fierce and Greatly Wrathful), Cakrasaṁvara, Mahākāla, etc.], the *ugra* form of Śiva. Whether as yogi or yoginī, these subaltern Tāntrikas were considered unrespectable, crazy, and frightening by orthodox Hindus and Buddhists[206] because they perpetuated many tribal practices of fertility magic, such as head-hunting (the specialty of the goddess-worshiping Kāpālikas and Kālāmukhās), head-offerings, and *bali*, as well as the fertility rites inherent in the *pañca makāra* (the Five Ms), including feasting, drinking liquor, and ritual coitus. The left-hand rites of both Buddhist and Hindu Tantrism featured sexual intercourse with women of the lowest caste (the *ḍombī*) as the highest road to enlightenment. Tribal megalithic fertility symbols lived on in the Śāktic unhewn stone as symbols of the Devī, and in the sculpted *yoni* and *liṅgaṁ*, emblems of the female and male principle that together, through sexual union (*hieros gamos* or *maithuna*), give birth to the material world of the senses. Most tribals-cum-*jātis* or śūdras were eventually receptive to Śākta-Tantric ideology and ritual,[207] and became the most desirable participants in the medieval *cakrapūjā*.

References

1. Ruth Benedict, *Patterns of Culture* (New York, 1934), 32.
2. Luiz, *Tribes of Kerala*, 1.
3. Maria Mies, Veronika Bennholdt-Thomsen, and Claudia von Werlhof, *Women: The Last Colony* (London, 1988), 37.
4. Ibid.
5. Luiz, *Tribes of Kerala*, 10.
6. Ibid., 16.
7. Ibid., 16–17.
8. Ibid., 18.
9. Ibid., 23.
10. Ibid., 21.
11. Ibid., 24.

12. Ibid.
13. Sathianathan Clarke, "Reviewing the Religion of the Paraiyars: Ellaiyamman as an Iconic Symbol of Collective Resistance and Emancipatory Mythography," in *Religions of the Marginalised: Towards a Phenomenology and the Methodology of Study*, ed. Gnana Robinson (Delhi, 1998), 44.
14. Antonio Gramsci, *Selections from the Prison Notebooks*, trans. Quintin Hoare and Geoffrey Nowell Smith (New York, 1971), 396.
15. This is a portion of an opening prayer of adoration sung by a local Paraiyar Pucari, K. Pallaiyam and accompanied by drums. [Clarke, "Reviewing the Religion of the Paraiya," 43, n. 18.]
16. Luiz, *Tribes of Kerala*, 12.
17. Ibid.
18. Ibid.
19. Fanon, *The Wretched of the Earth* (New York, 1963), 55.
20. Ibid., 56.
21. Luiz, *Tribes of Kerala*, 11.
22. Ibid., 10.
23. A.K. Ramanujan, "Two Realms of Kannada Folklore," in Stuart H.Blackburn and A.K. Ramangan, eds., *Another Harmony: New Essays on the Folklore of India* (Berkeley, 1986), 61.
24. Elaine Craddock, "Reconstructing the Split Goddess as Śakti in a Tamil Village," in *Seeking Mahādevī: Constructing the Identities of he Hindu Great Goddess*, ed. Tracy Pintchman (Albany, NY, 2001), 147.
25. Ibid., 146.
26. Harald Tambs-Lyche, "Introduction," in *The Feminine Sacred in South Asia* (New Delhi, 1999), 24.
27. Craddock, "Reconstructing the Split Goddess as Śakti," 149–50. [Italics added.]
28. Ibid., 147.
29. Ramanujan, "Two Realms of Kannada Folklore," 56.
30. Ibid., 57.
31. Ibid.
32. Craddock, "Reconstructing the Split Goddess as Śakti," 147.
33. Ibid., 147–48.
34. Whitehead, *The Village Gods of South India*, 85.
35. Craddock, "Reconstructing the Split Goddess as Śakti," 153.
36. Whitehead, *The Village Gods of South India*, 62–63.
37. Craddock, "Reconstructing the Split Goddess as Śakti," 147.
38. Clarke, "Reviewing the Religion of the Paraiyars," 37.
39. Ibid., 41.
40. Ibid.
41. Ibid., 51.
42. This is a portion of an opening prayer of adoration sung by a local Paraiyar Pucari and accompanied by drums. Ibid., 43, n. 18.
43. Ibid.
44. 3.116.1–18.
45. Richard L. Brubaker, "The Ambivalent Mistress: A Study of South Indian Village Goddesses and Their Religious Meaning," University of Chicago PhD dissertation (September 1978).

46. See Margaret Egnor, "On the Meaning of Sakti to Women in Tamil Nadu," in *The Powers of Tamil Women*, ed. Susan S. Wadley, 1–34 (Syracuse, 1980).
47. Craddock, "Reconstructing the Split Goddess as Śakti," 149–50.
48. Bavāṉiyammaṉ, whose stories are used interchangeably with those of Māriyammaṉ in a village near Madras, Periyapāḷaiyam, is regarded by her devotees as one of the Seven Sisters, probably descendants of the ancient Sanskritic *saptamātṛkās*. In Tamilnadu, many of the village temples have seven stones that are frequently interpreted as the Seven Sisters or the Seven Mothers. (Ibid., 147.)
49. Summary of version of Reṇukā myth collected by Elaine Craddock from numerous devotees between April and August 1990. (Ibid., 148–49).
50. Falk, "Mata, Land, and Line," 149 .
51. Craddock, "Reconstructing the Split Goddess as Śakti," 167.
52. Margaret Egnor, "On the Meaning of Sakti to Women in Tamil Nadu," in *The Powers of Tamil Women*, ed. Susan S. Wadley (Syracuse, 1980), 14.
53. Ibid., 149.
54. Ibid., 149–50.
55. Whitehead, *The Village Gods of South India*, 84–85.
56. Craddock, "Reconstructing the Split Goddess as Śaktī," 154.
57. Ibid.
58. This version of the myth was told by Ms Sarvamaṅgalā, after her grandmother's version, Mysore, 1977. Quoted in Ramanujan, "Two Realms of Kannada Folklore," 58–61.
59. Shulman, "The Murderous Bride," 178–79.
60. Ramanujan, "Two Realms of Kannada Folklore," 62.
61. Ibid., 64.
62. Bhattacharyya, *History of the Śākta Religion*, 79.
63. Clarke, "Reviewing the Religion of the Paraiyar," 52, n. 31.
64. See Brenda E.F. Beck, "Color and Heat in South Indian Ritual," in *Man* 4 (1969); Beck, *Peasant Society in Koṅku: A Study of Right and Left Subcastes in South India* (Vancouver, 1972); Beck, "The Goddess and the Demon: A Local South Indian Festival and its Wider Context," *Puruṣārtha* 3 (1981).
65. Falk, "Mata, Land and Line," 149, 156.
66. Ibid., 150.
67. Ibid., 162.
68. Rex L. Jones, "Spirit Possession in Society in Nepal," in *Spirit Possession in the Nepal Himalayas*, ed. John T. Hitchcock and Rex L. Jones (England, Warminster), 1976, 5.
69. Lynn Foulston, *At the Feet of the Goddess: The Divine Feminine in Local Hindu Religion*, Brighton, 2002, 141.
70. Luiz, 11.
71. Michael Moffatt, *An Untouchable Community in South India* (Princeton, 1979), 235.
72. Ibid., 237.
73. Ibid., 238.
74. Fanon, *The Wretched of the Earth*, 57.
75. Bowie, *The Anthropology of Religion*, 278.

76. Rex L. Jones, "Spirit Possession in Society in Nepal," 5.
77. Barbara Aziz, "Reincarnation Reconsidered: or the Reincarnate Lama as Shaman," in *Spirit Possession in the Nepal Himalayas*, ed. John T. Hitchcock and Rex L. Jones, 343–60 (Warminster, 1976).
78. Delphi was a venerable prehistoric oracular site where "the sacrality and the powers of Mother Earth were manifested" long before the reign of Apollo. The Greeks linked the name with *delphys*, "womb," since the sacred place contained a mysterious cavity that was likened to the mouth, vagina, navel of the Earth, or more generally, to the "center of the world." The Pythia's oracular tripod was positioned over a cleft in the Earth, or *chasma*, from which "vapors with supernatural virtues rose." Some investigators have suggested that intoxicating gases may have escaped from a deep subterranean fissure that would explain the shamanic trance of the Pythia. Under the new religious orientation of Apollo, the Pythia, chosen from the peasant women of Delphi, prophesied on specifically scheduled dates. "In the beginning, consultations took place once a year (on the god's anniversary), then once a month, and, finally, several times a month, except during the winter, when Apollo was away. The operation included the preliminary sacrifice of a goat. Usually the consultants put their questions in an alternative form: that is, was it better to do one thing or another. The Pythia gave the answer by drawing lots in the form of white or black beans." (Eliade, *A History of Religious Ideas*, vol. 1, 271.)
79. Charles Segal, "The Menace of Dionysus: Sex Roles and Reversals in Euripides' *Bacchae*," in *Women in the Ancient World: The Arethusa Papers*, ed. John Peradotta and J.P. Sullivan (Albany, 1984).
80. Acts 2:4.
81. Bhupinder Singh and J. S. Bhandari, eds., *The Tribal World and Its Transformation* (New Delhi, 1980), 124.
82. Rex L. Jones, "Spirit Possession in Society in Nepal," 5.
83. Bhattacharyya, *History of the Śākta Religion*, 19–20.
84. Bhattacharyya, *The Indian Mother Goddess*, 4.
85. *Mahābhārata*, 4.6; *Harivaṁśa*, 58; *Gauḍavaha*, 305ff.; *Varāha*, 28, 34.
86. 30.16.
87. Schoff, trans., *The Periplus of the Erythraean Sea* (hereinafter cited as *The Periplus*), cited by Sudhakar Chattopadhyaya, p. 134.
88. Orissa also appears as *Daśārṇa*, "a populous and powerful country," in the *Viṣṇu Purāṇa* and the *Rāmāyaṇa*. [Schoff, trans., *The Periplus*, cited by Chattopadhyaya, 134.]
89. *The Periplus*, cited by Sudhakar Chattopadhyaya, 134.
90. Ibid.
91. Bhattacharyya, *The Indian Mother Goddess*, 70.
92. Bhattacharyya, *Religious Culture of North-Eastern India*, 65.
93. Julian Jacobs, *The Nagas: Society, Culture and the Colonial Encounter* (London, 1990), 96.
94. Ibid., 83–84.
95. Ibid., 84–85.
96. Ibid., 10–11.
97. Ibid., 11.

98. According to Fürer-Haimendorf, "The megalithic complex found in Assam and in many other parts of Southeastern Asia appeared thus not as an accidental aggregation of various culture elements, but as a well-coordinated system of customs and beliefs, a philosophy of life and nature." [Christoph von Fürer-Haimendorf, "The Problem of Megalithic Cultures in Middle India," in *Man in India* 25 (1945): 74.]
99. Jacobs, *Nagas*, 128.
100. Heine Geldern, "Prehistoric Researches in the Netherland Indies," in *Science and Scientist in the Netherland Indies*, 1945, 149, cited by Bhattacharyya, in *Religious Culture of North-Eastern India*, 12–13.
101. Mills and Hutton, *Journal and Proceedings of the Asiatic Society of Bengal* 25: 285–86, cited by Bhattacharyya, in *Religious Culture of North-Eastern India*, 13.
102. Jacobs, *Nagas*, 117.
103. Ibid., 118.
104. Men wear particular ornaments that communicate how many lovers they have had, and one communitiy erects small stones indicating the number of lovers the deceased had alongside the large megalithic gravestone honoring the dead.
105. P.C. Choudhury, *History of Civilization of the People of Assam to the Twelfth Century*, Gauhati, 1966, 73.
106. Jacobs, *Nagas*, 119.
107. Ibid.
108. Ibid., 120.
109. Ibid.
110. *Ś. Br.*, 6.2.2.39.
111. W.G. Archer, *Papers of W.G. Archer*, private collection of Mrs Mildred Archer, cited by Jacobs, *Nagas*, 120.
112. Jacobs, *Nagas*, 121.
113. J.H. Hutton, "Diaries of Two Tours in the Unadministered Area East of the Naga Hills," *Memoirs of the Asiatic Society of Bengal* 12 (1929): 51.
114. Carmel Berkson, *The Amazon and the Goddess: Cognates of Artistic Form*, Bombay, 1987, 13.
115. Jacobs, *Nagas*, 135.
116. Ibid., 136.
117. Ibid.
118. Ibid.
119. Ibid., 138.
120. Ibid., 142.
121. Ibid., 143–44.
122. Ibid., 86.
123. Ibid., 38.
124. Ibid., 126.
125. Bhattacharyya, *History of the Śākta Religion*, 20.
126. Ibid., 153, 176.
127. Rev. Mar Imsong, "God's Community: Communion in the Suffering and Rejoicing," in *Minister*: A Journal of the American Baptist Ministers Council Speaking to the Practice of Ministry, vol. XXVIII, no. 1 (Summer, 2005) Valley Forge, PA http://www.ministerscouncil.com/Periodicals/documents/Summer 05.pdf. (accessed August 12, 2006).
128. W.G. Archer, *Papers of W.G. Archer*, private collection of Mrs Mildred Archer, cited by Jacobs, *Nagas*, 121.

129. Singh and Bhandari, eds., *Tribal World*, 129.
130. Bhattacharyya, *History of the Śākta Religion*, 19.
131. Ibid., 18–19.
132. Bhattacharyya, *The Indian Mother Goddess*, 74.
133. Edward Gait, *A History of Assam* (Calcutta, 1963), 56.
134. Bhattacharyya, *The Indian Mother Goddess*, 68.
135. Kosambi, "At the Crossroads: A Study of Mother-Goddess Cult Sites," in *Myth and Reality*, 89.
136. *Harivaṁśa*, 2.3.6–8.
137. A.K. Bhattacharya, "A Non-aryan Aspect of the Devī," in *The Shakti Cult and Tārā*, ed. D.C. Sircar (Calutta, 1967), 57–58.
138. *Matsya P*, 13.32, 39, 43.
139. *Viṣṇu P*, 5.2.84.
140. Pūrvabhāga/Kathāmukha.
141. Bāṇa, *Kādambarī*, Pūrvabhāga, chap. 8.
142. Chap. 8.
143. R.L. Mitra, *Indo-Aryans: Contributions Towards the Elucidation of Their Ancient and Medieval History*, vol. 1 (Delhi, 1971), 61.
144. *Gauḍavaha* 285–347.
145. Ibid., 285–338.
146. Ibid.
147. *Devī Bhāgavata P*, 7.33.53–56.
148. Ibid., 42.
149. Ibid., 89–90.
150. Jitendra N. Banerjea, *The Development of Hindu Iconography* (Calcutta, 1956), 491.
151. R.C. Hazra, *Studies in the Upa-purāṇas*, vol. 2 (Calcutta, 1963), 16–22.
152. 4.6 and 6.22.
153. 3.3.
154. 4.6.
155. 2.22.52–56.
156. *Viṣṇu P*, 5.2.84.
157. *Matsya P*, 13.32.39.43.
158. 28.34.
159. 305.
160. 2.27.42–43.
161. 7.18.
162. Pupul Jayakar, *The Earth Mother* (New Delhi, 1989), 142–43.
163. R.V. Russell, *Tribes and Castes of the Central Provinces of India*, vol. 4 (London, 1916), 506ff.
164. Jayakar, *The Earth Mother*, 142.
165. *Mbh.*, 13.207.42; *Matsya P*, CXIV.46–48; *Vāyu P*, 142–43.
166. Cited by Bhattacharyya, *The Indian Mother Goddess*, 69.
167. Cf. *Mārkaṇḍeya Purāṇa*, 57.47.
168. 4.22; 5.39.77–8; 9.17.29.40; 16.2.33.
169. 4.22.
170. Bhattacharyya, *The Indian Mother Goddess*, 69.
171. G.P. Malalasekera, *Dictionary of Pali Proper Names*, vol. 2 (London, 1938), 241.
172. Cited by Bhattacharyya, *The Indian Mother Goddess*, 69.
173. *The Periplus*, cited by Sudhakar Chattopadhyaya, 1980, 113.

174. Lynn Foulston, *At the Feet of the Goddess: The Divine Feminine in Local Hindu Religion* (Brighton, 2002), 124.
175. Eliade, *Shamanism*, 84.
176. Ibid., 84–85.
177. Eliade, *Yoga*, 150.
178. Craddock, "Reconstructing the Split Goddess as Śakti," 154.
179. Portions of Craddock's 1990 translations of two songs to Māriyamman̠, D-306: "Māriyamman̠ Kaliveṇpā" and D-171: "Māriyamman̠ Tālāṭtu." [Ibid., 168, n. 6.]
180. Ibid., 155.
181. Ibid.
182. Ibid.
183. Ibid.
184. Ibid., 155–56.
185. Ibid., 156.
186. Parpola, *The Sky Garment*, 68–69.
187. Om Prakash Misra, *Mother Goddess in Central India* (Delhi, 1985), 110.
188. Parpola, *The Sky Garment*, 90–91.
189. Ibid., 91.
190. George Weston Briggs, *Gorakhanātha and the Kānphaṭā Yogīs* (Delhi, 1973), 212.
191. Jayakar, *The Earth Mother*, 69.
192. Kosambi, *Ancient India*, 47.
193. Ibid.
194. Bhattacharyya, *History of Indian Erotic Literature*, 10.
195. Kosambi, *Ancient India*, 47.
196. Bhattacharyya, *The Indian Mother Goddess*, 1977, 224.
197. Bhattacharyya, *History of the Śākta Religion*, 17–18.
198. Pushpendra Kumar, *Śakti and Her Episodes* (Delhi, 1981), 36.
199. The iconography of Tibetan Buddhist Tantric art, with its proliferation of sexual and graveyard imagery, especially skulls, is regarded as metaphor only, representing a symbology of the mind. Such images in art are used by lāmās to instruct the student on the nature of impermanence, the necessity to tame the mind, and the nature of yogic and intuitive processes. The original agricultural metaphors inherent in such imagery are lost in Buddhism.
200. R.P. Chanda, *Indian Antiquary Review* (1916), 148–49, cited by Bhattacharyya, in *History of the Śākta Religion*, 6.
201. S.K. Dikshit, *Mother Goddess* (Poona, 1943), 30–36.
202. N.N. Bhattacharyya, *The Indian Mother Goddess*, 224.
203. Ibid.
204. Bhattacharyya, *History of Indian Erotic Literature*, 12.
205. While the dominant dharma accepted the principles of Dakṣiṇācāra or Right-hand Tantrism, which, among other differences, prioritizes Śiva over Śakti, they were somewhat suspicious of Vāmācāra, or Left-hand Tantrism, the subaltern majority and heterodox variety during the medieval period, in which Śakti prevails over all gods as supreme Goddess of fertility and war. The conception of Vāmācāra historically precedes that of Dakṣiṇācāra, and it is possible that the first word in the expression *vāmācāra* is not the pejorative *vāma*, left, but rather *vāmā*, a woman.
206. Edward Conze, *Buddhism: Its Essence and Development* (New York, 1951), 196.
207. Bhattacharyya, *Religious Culture of North-Eastern India*, 72.

Part II
Historiography

4
The Early Tamils: The Caṅkam Age

THE TAMIL COUNTRY

Southern India is comprised of four states: Tamil nadu, Kerala (to the west), Karnataka (to the northwest), and Andhra Pradesh (to the north). In India's approximately one billion people, sixty million are Tamils.[1] Dravidian roots in India date back several thousand years before the Common Era. The Dravidians had from their inception their own unique culture expressed by scriptures, scholars, deities, temples, priests, and holy sages. Some scholars assert that the Tamils (Dravidians) or Tamilar were foreigners to India who settled there at different times, and others claim they are "of direct Neolithic descent on Indian soil."[2] There are several theories of their foreign origin, including Sumeria and Elam. Other possible Tamil homelands include Ilam in Ceylon, the Tibetan plateau,[3] the Eastern Mediterranean, and Africa. The argument for a Sumerian origin, which posits a migration of Tamil culture from Sumeria and possibly the Indus cities, is bolstered by the existence of the Brahui tribe in Baluchistan (west of the Indus), who speak a Dravidian language like south Indian Tamil. The Brahui people are believed by many scholars to be a remnant of an extremely widespread Dravidian tract extending from Baluchistan and Sind through Rajasthan and Malwa into Maharashtra, Mysore, Andhra, Tamilnadu, and Kerala.[4] "The assumption that the Harappans spoke a primitive Dravidian speech is favored by many a historian," reports Bhattacharyya, "but there is no definite evidence to support the Dravidian authorship of the Harappa civilization."[5] In pre-Aryan times, the Dravidians either occupied the whole territory of India or Dravidian tribes migrated to the north from their original territory; for this reason, perhaps, despite the powerful Aryan influence, scholars widely agree that Hinduism today is more Dravidian than Vedic. There is an alternative theory that Tamilnadu is the north section of a much larger continent that existed long before the Aryans arrived; the southern part now lies under the Indian Ocean.

An adventurous maritime people, the Dravidians settled in north and south India. They welcomed guests with pleasure and great hospitality, sharing what they had. They avoided "crushing even a crab under their chariot wheels," meaning that "their lifetime and wealth were for service to others."[6] Because Tamils were famous seafarers from earliest times, Singapore and Malaysia today have large Tamil populations for whom Mahiṣāsura-mardinī statues are the perennial temple icon. Cities along the east coast of Tamilnadu were known as international trading sites, attracting ancient Greeks, Romans, and Chinese alike. Merchants traveled far north on the Ganges, and, since earliest antiquity, there was extensive trade between the people of the Mediterranean and the Deccan; spices, precious woods, pearls, and cotton were imported from south India to the Mediterranean countries. Salt merchants exchanged their salt for paddy, and fishermen traded their salt for toddy.[7] Two Greek works, *The Periplus of the Erythraean Sea* (first century AD) and Ptolemy's *Geography* (second century AD), mention the flourishing Roman trade with southern India that was encouraged by the Tamil kings. There is evidence of maritime trade among all the lands on the shores of the Indian Ocean from Indonesia to South Africa, confirmed by similar stone beads and glass discovered at prehistoric levels in south India and the Philippines. South India exported rice, sandalwood, and peacocks to Babylon before the fifth century BCE, and their Tamil names were retained in Western Asian languages.[8]

Radha Kumud Mookerji has attempted to prove that ancient marine trade was controlled by Dravidians, who may have been the ancestors of the present-day Mohanas and Machhi tribes of Sind,[9] an idea that seems to be corroborated by the fact that boats depicted on seals discovered from Mohenjo-daro resemble the ones used today by the Mohanas in River Indus. Both types of boats have an upturned prow and stern, and one terracotta amulet found at Mohenjo-daro depicts two birds symmetrically on the boat. The Mohanas still keep pelicans and cormorants on their boats, according to Shaikh Khurshid Hasan, to swoop down from great heights and capture fish when they cannot be netted easily. The birds are prevented from swallowing the fish by a string around their necks.[10]

The Vedas depict Dravidians as "noseless" (a commentary on their racial type), and refers to their towns, or *purs.* Many theorist identify the Dravidians as the *dāsas* or *dasyus* against whom the hegemonic Aryans waged warfare. In what Coomaraswamy characterizes as "the final victory of the conquered over the conquerors," the Dravidians contributed more to Indian life and religion than the Aryans.

> Amongst the elements of Dravidian origin are probably the cults of the phallus and of mother-goddesses, Nagas, Yakṣas and other nature spirits; and many of the arts. Indeed, if we recognize in the Dravidians a southern race, and in the

> Aryans a northern, it may well be argued that the victory of kingly over tribal organizations, the gradual reception into orthodox religion of the phallus cult and mother-goddesses, and the shift from abstract symbolism to anthropomorphic iconography in the period of theistic and *bhakti* development, mark a final victory of the conquered over the conquerors. In particular, the popular, Dravidian element, must have played the major part in all that concerns the development and office of image-worship, that is, of *pūjā* as distinct from *yajña.*[11]

In the third and second millennia BCE, brāhmaṇas spoke Sanskrit, had holy oral texts called Vedas that only the twice-born castes were allowed to recite, and only they could officiate as Vedic priests. In the north of India, the tribals and Dravidians were overwhelmed by Aryans militarily, politically, culturally, and linguistically (although they continued to constitute the great majority of the population), and the northern Tamil branch became extinct a few centuries after the Great War.

From the fourth century BCE, the Pāṇḍya, Coḷa, and Kerala (Cera) dynasties ruled south India. While the religions from the north, Brāhmaṇism, Buddhism, and Jainism, were also influential at that time, Dravidian beliefs comprised the most popular religion. Employing the same mythological template as the ancient Near Eastern cultures (subsuming *hieros gamos,* seasonal regicide/ bull sacrifice symbolizing dying and resurrected gods, fertility and martial goddess astride a big cat, and temple dancer-priestesses who functioned as institutionalized sacred prostitutes of the goddess), the Pāṇḍya kingdom and its dynasty were chosen by the Great Goddess-cum-queen. This fact is verified in fifth century BCE Sanskrit texts, third century BCE accounts by Megasthenes, the second century AD Tamil classic *Cilappatikāram* (The Ankle Bracelet), and Marco Polo in the thirteenth century. The Caṅkam texts, written down about the last three centuries BCE to the first three centuries AD or earlier, were based on a much earlier oral tradition.[12] In the commentaries of *Cilappatikāram,* there are some vague historical memories about three literary academies (*caṅkam*) that existed in prehistory, with corollaries in Sumeria, where the royal palaces held libraries and an academy of poets. Although sharing academies and an advanced literary tradition does not necessarily involve migration, some scholars postulate a migration of Dravidians from Sumeria to south India. However, George Hart points out that there is "no reference to this legend in all of early Tamil literature, in spite of the fact that if any of the academies had existed it would have been of great importance,"[13] and suggests instead that the invented Caṅkam legend was modeled on a permanent Jaina assembly in Maturai about AD 604. We also find in *Cilappatikāram* several passages about Tamil fertility/war goddess Ko<u>rr</u>avai (identified with Durgā and Kālī in *Cilappatikāram* due to their common slaying of the buffalo demon) that bear a distinct similarity to Near Eastern descriptions of fertility/war goddesses Inanna/Ishtar/Astoreth/Anath.

Caṅkam literature paints vivid pictures of the Pāṇḍya, Coḷa, and Kerala kings of these three prosperous kingdoms conquering and raiding towns of rival kings and the villages of autochthonous tribes. Poetry, dance, and religion were intermingled and considered the ideal expression of love, the transcendental, redeeming emotion that defined Tamil religion. According to Pillai, "the rationalistic Tamilar preferred mountain-homes, were monotheists, and worshiped god with flowers and incense symbolic of the heart and its melting."[14]

While ancient Tamils loved life, they worshiped death. They regarded violence as a natural manifestation of high emotion, and violent death on the battlefield was the most auspicious death possible, one that guaranteed everlasting bliss in warrior heaven. In each city-state, the god-king luxuriated in a magnificent palace citadel, entertained by *koṇti makaḷi* (temple harlots) and dancing *viṟalis* (female bards who also functioned in fertility rituals as sacred prostitutes). Tamil *viṟalis* were low-born Dravidians or prisoners-of-war, thus a repository of *aṇaṅku* from which the king drew his power; they served the same *hieros gamos* function as the sacred harlots of Inanna and Ishtar at Ur in Mesopotamia. *Viṟalis* were required to carry begging bowls that may have been skull cups. Outside the palace walls, the landless agricultural laborers and tribals under the fiefdom lived in small huts with open yards and "live fences" of forest along the roadside. Both elites and serfs worshiped Koṟṟavai/ Aiyai and Murukaṉ. Bhattacharyya sums up the material culture and social institutions of the pre-Vedic Dravidians as follows:

> From the evidence of the words in use among the early Tamils, we can derive the following of the material culture and social institutions of the pre-Vedic Dravidians. They were agricultural peoples (*ér*, plough, *velānmai*, agriculture) living in villages (*paḷḷī*) and towns (*ūr*, *peṭṭai*) which formed parts of districts (*nāṭu*) of a country ruled by kings (*ko*, *véntaṉ*, *mannaṉ*) who lived in palaces (*koṭṭai*, *araṇ*) and maintained the laws and customs (*kaṭṭalai*, *pazakkam*). The soldiers were armed with bows (*vil*), arrows (*ampu*), spears (*vel*), and swords (*vāḷ*) which testify the use of metals. Canoes, boats and even ships (*toṇī*, *otam*, *vallam*, *kappal*, *patava*) were known to them. They also knew the art of writing on palmyra leaves (*olai*) and bundles of such leaves were known as books (*eṭu*). The title *ko* denoting the king was also attributed to god to whose honor they used to dedicate temples (*koil*, *koyil*, *kovil*).[15]

To Bhattacharyya's summary should also be added that daughters and wives of defeated enemies, kidnapped as Tamil men's favored form of booty, were impressed as palace slave-harlots or so-called "captive women." According to Pillai,

> Women captured in war were reduced to slavery and employed in places of public worship, where they were expected to bathe every evening and light the lamps, besides sweeping the threshold and adorning it with flowers. In a righteous war, women were spared along with cows, Brahmins and the sick.[16]

If both Vedic and Dravidian texts are examined for evidence of king-sized baths, only the *Cilappatikāram* contains historic references to a fresh "water tank" that fits the description of the Great Bath at Mohenjo-daro, which may be the antecedent to the later construction of artificial lotus ponds used during historic times for purification ceremonies. It seems reasonable to infer from the architecture that sexo-religious fertility rituals were performed following purifying baths in the small ante-chambers adjoining the Great Bath. Passages in Caṅkam texts such as *Nedunalvādai* and *Cilappatikāram* relate that the king's palace had a luxurious interior featuring sumptuous women's apartments and bedrooms.

After bathing in the fresh water tank (where the king also took a ritual bath before battles), the captive women were responsible for kindling a lamp at the public hall in the evening as a symbol of the divine presence immanent in the world. In *Paṭ.*, 246–49, an archaic Tamil "temple" is intricately described as

> the public hall with the *pillar,* where the wayfarers [used to] rest, and where captive girls, after plunging into the fresh-water tank, would kindle the 'perpetual' lamp at twilight, and where many [people] would cross over the ground prepared with cowdung, and beautified with flowers would worship.[17]

"Captive woman" rather than "prostitute" is the translation of *koṇṭi makaḷi.* The public hall was probably a proto-temple, according to Hardy, who parses the passage as follows:

> The meaning of "prostitute" would seem to reflect the value-system or institution of a later age. . . . [I]t may nevertheless be legitimate to infer that a somewhat institutionalized form of worship existed in the old period, involving a special building, the *potiyil,* "public hall" (at the same time used for "secular" purposes, such as accommodating travelers) and a symbolic representation of the divine, the *kantu;* moreover that "captive girls" were in charge of kindling a lamp at the *kantu* in the evening. Thus we may well be dealing here with a prototype of the later "temple" which can be related without difficulty to other forms of "divine presence" and to the general conception of the divine being present in this world.[18]

The king and his bards, dancers, drummers, and musicians were led to the battlefield by fertility/war goddess Ko<u>rr</u>avai and her band of cannibalistic *pēys*[19] (demonesses), who feasted on the corpses of fallen soldiers. The entire battlefield scene was a blood offering made to the Great-goddess, who in turn would grant them agricultural abundance and community prosperity, commensurate with the Neolithic mythic motif of "sacrifice for the crops" first recorded by Frazer. These battles, complete with horse-drawn chariots, amounted to land and cattle grabs, the loot of Tamil kings in their wars against indigenous hunter-gatherer peoples. Like Inanna and Ishtar, Ko<u>rr</u>avai was also associated with ritual bull sacrifice, which had became the animal substitute for the cyclical sacrifice of the goddess's consort in ancient Near Eastern ritual dramas. Ko<u>rr</u>avai in her Vaḷḷi (tribal girl) incarnation and Muruka<u>n</u>, the

Dionysian god of love, fertility, and spirit possession, formed a mythic *hieros gamos*, the king and his earthly goddess in passionate embrace.

The dynasties of north India conquered most of the Deccan after the fall of the Mauryan Empire, although they were unsuccessful in attempts to invade the three Dravidian kingdoms. Inscriptions on copperplates in the south were all in Sanskrit, most often registering gifts of land to brāhmaṇas. The northern elites brought with them their theocratic accouterments, Sanskrit and brāhmaṇas, and soon dissolved Murukan̠ into Śiva (he became Śiva's son) and Kor̠r̠avai (Murukan̠'s mother, wife of Śiva) into Durgā–Kālī, and rescripted and Sanskritized Tamil myths of wars with demons and the battlefield exploits of fertility and martial goddess Kor̠r̠avai.

In the south, the Dravidians successfully resisted and maintained dominance until the end of the Gupta age. Except for a brief Muslim interlude (AD 1324–70) in Madurai, Tamilnadu remained relatively isolated and free from the invasions that plagued the rest of the country throughout its history. South India had been subjected to Aryanization since the first millennium BCE, but Tamilnadu and Kerala were separate from the rest of India until the British period.

In a Dravidian (Tamil) Indus construction, the Aryans seized by force, chicanery, and/or hypnotism the Indus culture of the ancient Tamils and condemned them and their progeny to a life of extreme poverty and caste slavery involving hard labor. Although the ancient Tamils were of eight classes (*arivar*, ascetics who lives outside the towns; *ulavar*, farmers, including the *vellalar* and *karalar*, lords who formed the landed aristocracy; *ayar*, shepherds; *vedduvar*, hunters; smiths of all kinds; *padaiadchier*, armed men who formed the military class; fishermen; and scavengers),

> [t]he iron-bound caste system was purely Aryan, and the Aryans ruthlessly foisted it on the Tamilar. . . . [T]he Aryans soon after their commingling with the Tamilar, first in the Panjab and then in the Gangetic basin, set to destroy the original class system but could not consistently redistribute the classes into their fourfold caste.[20]

The most ancient stratum of Tamil literature reveals the influence of the growing religions of the north. Brāhmaṇical, Buddhist, and Jaina religions began their penetration into the south in the last three centuries BCE. Jaina caverns of this date exist in the Tamil country. There is literary evidence of Buddhist migration to the south and Ceylon, and Kauṭilya's *Arthaśāstra* and Megasthenes' *Indika* describe the trade of south India.[21] As M.S. Pūrṇaliṅgam Pillai elaborates, in Caṅkam literature we come across

> Buddhist monasteries and Jain abbeys in the land of Chola, which shows not only the prevalence of the religions but the religious toleration of the kings of old in south India. The descriptions of the city, its forts and ramparts, parks and bowers, alms-houses and ascetic homes, streets and palaces, beach and customs-houses are really charming. It is truly delightful to look over in imagination

the bales of goods in the customs-house bearing the tiger-mark and the immense variety of natural products imported from different shores, *viz.*, horses, victuals, gold, pearls, corals, pepper, sandal and scents. Muruga worship, devil dances, toddy-drinking and cock-and-ram fighting indulged in by the hardy Kurumbas find emphatic expression in it.[22]

The Religious Landscape

Since earliest times, the Great Goddess of the south Indian conquerors has also been worshiped by the defeated rural people of the settled villages and countryside as a tree or rock spirit, due to the assimilation by ancient Dravidians of the religions of the earliest primal cultures of India. For the ancient Tamils, mountains and hills are the abode of the son of Ko<u>rr</u>avai and the highest god, Muruka<u>n</u>: he is "the god on the mountain slopes where black pepper grows,"[23] and "the god high up on the hills."[24] Muruka<u>n</u> remains the highest god of the mountain tribes today: "All the hill tribes of the Madurai district pay homage to 'Poomporai-nathan,' an image of Muruka<u>n</u>, installed in the temple at Poomporai or Poomkunru, ten miles to the west of Kodaikanal."[25] Muruka<u>n</u> lives in trees, particularly the *kaṭampu* tree ("he in the *kaṭampu*,"[26] and "the lord residing in the *kaṭampu*")[27] and the *marā* tree, or seaside Indian oak tree. The threshing-ground and meeting place of an ancient Tamil village, the *kaḷam* (or *ma<u>nr</u>am*), is surrounded by such trees, or has one in its center, and is viewed by Tamils as a locus of divine presence. Thus we read of "the broad *kaḷam* where offerings are found under the lofty branches of the *marutu* tree in which snakes live. . . ."[28]

> [T]he forest [was] exalted [because of] the god in the *marā* tree of fine stem, in which the names [of heroes]—for people to know—had been written in stones that had been "sculptured". . . .[29]

Oracular spirit possession performance, liquor, ecstatic dancing, and shamanic drumming were important elements of the Muruka<u>n</u> cult. Muruka<u>n</u>, like Dionysus, is associated with wild shamanic spirit possession dances. Dionysus was believed to possess young women (*maenads*) and Śiva had a similar association with his *gaṇas*; likewise, Muruka<u>n</u> possessed young love-smitten maidens and drove them to frenzied dances of possession. Both the Indian and Greek gods were associated with violent dances of possession and human or animal (especially buffalo) sacrifice.[30]

Among the early south Indian Tamils, the religious impulse was articulated and channeled via human communication with nature, often through an intermediary spirit medium. Muruka<u>n</u> was believed to come down and take possession of people, causing illness that requires the intercession of a *vela<u>n</u>* ("one with a spear") shaman or priest, who became possessed by Muruka<u>n</u> and performed healing rites. Among the mountain tribes, according to Caṅkam literature, maidens who are stricken by "love-sickness," suspected of being possessed by Muruka<u>n</u>, are taken by their mothers to the *vela<u>n</u>*, whose vocation is to appease Murukan̲ and to perform rituals to cure the girls of their illness. Brandishing a *vel* or spear, which functions as a proto-trident, the *velan̲* performs an energized dance (the *ver̲iyāṭu*, "dance of wild frenzy") that infuses him with Murukan̲'s spirit, and, in a state of divine possession, he utters prophecies of the maiden's future happiness. The *ver̲iyāṭu*, according to Hardy,

> is not the privilege of the *velan̲* alone; while he dances it under special circumstances, anybody may dance it in worship. Thus in *Paṭ*. (154–8) we hear of "the large marketplace where festivals never cease, which is crowded with girls (dancing) the *ver̲iyāṭu* of Cevvel̤." In *Kur̲i*: 174–7, that "garlands were put round the thick stem of the firmly rooted *kaṭampu* as decorations." Thus religious customs connected with Murukan̲ involve music and items like flower-garland.[31]

The *velan̲*'s healing rituals, like those of the Vedic priest, involved the use of an effigy of the afflicted person that the priest "lifts up and scrutinizes,"[32] empowering him to divine the cause and cure for the affliction. Such prehistoric effigies still exist as archaeological relics in the myriad female figurines discovered in archaeological digs in the Indus Valley civilization. Since women were considered more prone to affliction and possession than men due to women's intimacy with *aṇaṅku*, we find a far greater proportion of female effigies than male effigies in Indus digs. Similarly, the sacrificial procession of Bhairava among the Newars is accompanied by the frenzied possession that must have been a central feature of the ancient Murukan̲ cult before the cult, like Śiva, became vegetarianized.

In folk goddess Aiyai (Earth Mother) worship in the third century BCE and earlier among Tamil primal cultures, the same customs of spirit possession and prophecy were expressed by a priestess of the goddess, as opposed to Murukan̲'s male *velan̲*. The priestess became possessed by Aiyai and, speaking as the goddess, revealed future events to the community or acted as divinely inspired medicine-woman and healer.

Dances pervaded every level of Tamil society, from the high court dances, to war dances, to fertility dances, to the ecstatic spirit possession dance, a standard feature of Tamil worship. The literature contains references to drunken men dancing in a frenzy; a dancing bull who frolics like a low-caste woman possessed by Murukan̲; and frenetic dances ("devil dance") as goats are sacrificed. In south Indian primal religion, this "Lord of the Dance" is immortalized in the Śiva *Naṭarāja* pose of innumerable sculptures, carvings, and paintings—an image supplanted in north India by Śiva dancing in the cremation grounds, or the corpse-Śiva in sexual union with Kālī. (The latter image is cognate with the regicide of Near Eastern versions of *hieros gamos*, in which the male principle is sacrificed to the goddess for the crops.) "The custom of ecstasy in worship survived in Tamilnadu to produce the Nāyanmārs and Alvārs, who went about Tamilnadu singing ecstatic songs about Śiva and Viṣṇu, and were largely responsible in later times for the position of preeminence those gods attained as well as for the Bhakti movement, which produced the *Bhāgavata Purāṇa* and spread all over India."[33] This extremely archaic cultural system is rapidly changing in the age of globalism.

Feudalism, Divine Martial Law, and the Glories of War

> For about two thousand years the social formation in Tamilnad has been feudal. The main classes standing opposed to each other with contradictory interest have been the feudal land lord, the Brahman executives of the land owning temples, the religious heads of feudal mathas and other non-productive exploiting sections. The poor peasant and the agricultural laborer produced the food that all sections of the society consumed. The auxiliary exploiting class was the individual merchant and the merchant guilds who bought and sold the product of labor of the handicraftsmen, weaver, and artisans. The history of class society goes back to 2000 to 2500 years. Clashes and open struggles had occurred between the exploiters and the exploited many a time. The stratification of society underwent certain changes but thanks to the self sufficient village community organization and the rigidity of the caste system the society remained in a stage of stagnation till the 18th century AD.[34]

The Tamil heroic age of the Caṅkam period is a transient time marking the shift from tribalism to feudalism and individual monarchic states. Supplanting earlier tribal agricultural peoples whose hunter-gatherer economy was based on egalitarianism, gender parity, and the importance of group participation in community affairs, the Tamil warriors and rulers, like their Aryan counterparts, turned the autochthonous social organization on its head and claimed all social and economic goods as the property of the elites.

> Society consisted of a fairly gay crew of kings, chieftains and nobles at the top, befriended by Brahmins and entertained by Poets, musicians, and dancers, and indulging in war, the chase, and the company of women. The life of the masses was simple but by no means devoid of joy and amusement. There was an abundance of the necessities of life and a reasonably brisk inland and maritime trade.[35]

The early history of Dravidians in the Deccan and south India is elusive, but there is abundant evidence that elite Dravidian culture in the centuries preceding the Christian era had reached great heights in art, economics, and the art of war. The powerful Andhra empire covered the Deccan from east to west, and the luxurious Pāṇḍyan kingdom with its capital at Korkai flourished before the beginning of the Christian era. The earlier indigenous agricultural communities were violently supplanted by the three kings of the Cera, Coḷa, and Pāṇḍya lines that dominated the history of south India during the Caṅkam age, when poetry, painting, sculpture, architecture, music, drama, and cosmopolitanism developed to a lofty, almost effete level in the aristocratic high culture of court life. It may have been a cultural system similar to the Indus Valley civilization two millennia earlier.

Feudalism cannot develop without first annihilating hunting tribes; thus, juxtaposed against the elite refinements and effetism of the Caṅkam high culture, a confederation of patriarchal kingdoms and advanced agricultural communities assaulted and largely destroyed tribal organization. References to tribes that unsuccessfully attempted to defend themselves against the onslaught of agricultural expansion fill the pages of Caṅkam classics, illustrating the emergence of agricultural communities and kingdoms on the land of the fallen primal cultures. In the south, the Dravidians subdued the aboriginal Naga tribes of Maravar, Eyinor (Vedar), Oliyar, Oviyar, Aruvalar, and Parathavar and settled in the southern region as lords of the land. Three tribes, the Marar (Minavar), Thirayar, and Vanavar, founded respectively the Pāṇḍya, Coḷa, and Cera kingdoms, whose kings (tribal chiefs-cum-feudal lords and military leaders) ruled the land of the ancient Tamils. The henchmen of the crowned heads were the military caste, made up of the kings' chieftains, who reaped "psychological and material benefits and rewards for loyalty in times of war."[36]

Poets were employed by the king to glorify his exploits and to encourage submission to him. Similar in function to contemporary corporate media, the poetry of the Caṅkam period reflects the high culture of an elite caste of military warriors, chieftains, and rulers, as distinct from the conquered majority over whom they ruled. The enforcement of elite authority with harsh threats and punishments for disobedience is reflected in the poetry of the king's bards. Tamil poets programed people to believe that war was a natural, organic part of life and that the king had a sacred duty to wage war. The poets juxtaposed sadistic violence and carnage with scenes of life-enhancing beauty, placing a romantic, necrophiliac veneer over warfare. Caṅkam literature is divided into *akam* (poems involving subjective experience, especially love and family life) and *puṟam* (objective experience from the male elite point of view, including poems about warfare, blandishments to the king, and so on). Warriors and kings "alone were deemed to have the proper virtue, refinement, abilities, and education required for participation in the higher attainments of life: love and war, *akam* and *puṟam*."[37] For ancient Tamils, the divine was not transcendent, as it was for the Vedic Aryans; rather, "the 'divine' was conceived of as something that could be met with in this world."[38] Not only nature, but also the gory battleground, manifests the "divine" or "supernatural," cognate with the sacred battles of the Nagas.

The king was the absolute authority. The Tamil "king" was less a great sovereign than he was a sacred *poligar,* landlord, on whom the fertility of his agricultural fields and the well-being of his subjects depended.

> Rice is not Life,
> water is not Life.
> The king endows with Life
> the world of fertile surface.
> Therefore, to say,
> "I am Life,"
> is the duty of the king,
> his army stocked with axes and spears.[39]

The king was "the central embodiment of the sacred powers that had to be present and under control for the proper functioning of society."[40] Like the Naga Great Ang and the kings of the ancient Near East and eastern Mediterranean, the Tamil king was held responsible for water scarcity, lack of rainfall, and other atypical situations. As J.M. Somasundaram Pillai summarizes: "Good rule was said to be synonymous with the cosmic order; the rain obeys the call of a righteous king, and his subjects blame his government if the rain does not fall in time or water grows scarce or if any unnatural occurrences take place, and the agriculture which depends so much on the king's righteousness is at once the basis of the state and its martial strength."[41] We may assume, therefore, that the fate of the ancient Near Eastern kings when they disappointed the community and the Great Goddess also awaited the nonproductive Tamil king. The equation of the king's persona with the sacrificial buffalo demon in women-oriented south Indian folk materials intimates the substitution of the bull sacrifice for the archaic male sacrifice of regicide.

"The acceptance of the ideal of a king bent on aggrandizement was its bane," according to Pillai. "It made lasting peace an utter impossibility,"[42] resulting in perpetual wars. As the central embodiment of sacred power, the divine king was the absolute Tamil authority; total subservience to him was required as both a religious and a civic duty, and disobedience never went unpunished by bullying henchmen:

When they failed to pay
In due form and mode, their tribute to the
 Pāṇḍya,
Lord of murderous war-elephants and of
resounding war drum
Their godly land was step by step bereft of cattle
And of lovely women, and of manly men,
Until alas—it has now become a secure home
For goblin mother and child.[43]

The punishment for disobedience to the king was the theft of a farmer's cattle, the kidnapping of girls and women, and the "disappearance" of "manly men." In another poem, "The Owl Sings a Lullaby," those who refuse to bow to the king are threatened with the same barren, punishing landscape, their land stripped of cattle, women, and warriors, corresponding to a level of hell inhabited by owls and goblins:

In those lofty mansions
Where victorious kings
Wearing gay chaplets
Of fragrant sirissa flowers
Once sat enthroned in regal state
And where joy reigned supreme

The horrid owl
Now hoots his doleful lullaby
To horrible goblins
On the land of those
Who do not bow
To the Command of the Southern King.[44]

The Vallals, the seven ancient Tamil chieftains, were portrayed by their bards as self-sacrificing and sensitive to plant, animal, and human life. The general purpose of female and male bards was "to render support to the king's vital breath of life or, in other words, to cool or to channel the king's sacred force."[45] This age produced notions of unambiguous territorial settlements and land ownership, and their wars destroyed the means of tribal subsistence. Bards were depicted as the fortunate few who were able to live in an imaginative realm of idealized beauty while practicing subliminal psychological coercion and bullying through poetics.

> The jasmine creeper with its pure and fragrant pearl-like flowers is so beautiful to the eye of the chieftain Pari that he leaves his own chariot for that propless creeper to spread and flourish on. Another chieftain, Pekan, charmed by the beauty of the dancing peacock, rushes with his own costly covering to protect that beauty from the rains and biting cold. From the plant world through the animal world, one passes on to the world of human art, where another chieftain, Atikamān, gives away a precious *neli* fruit, said to prolong one's life to the poetess Avvai instead of enjoying it himself, thus proclaiming that a poet's life of ideal beauty is worth more than a king's life.[46]

In north India, the king was outranked by brāhmaṇas, but in south India before the arrival of the brāhmaṇas, the king was unsurpassed in power and the caste system *per se* did not exist. The Tamil belief in high and low status at birth, however, determined certain vocations; in particular, "those members of society who dealt closely with sacred powers were of low status."[47] The king and his bards were interdependent: the king supported the bards, and the bards functioned to stimulate bravery on the eve of battle and on the battlefield, to glorify mothers and wives who loved war, and to praise the glorious accomplishments of the king, thus promoting his fame during times of peace.[48] As the *Puṟanāṉūṟu* illustrates,

> the Tamil bards [possessed] a high sense of self-respect though poverty stricken. They were faithful and fearless advisors and confidants of kings, they averted war and ruin to the rulers by telling plain truths. They were broad-minded, generous, firm and impartial, perfectly honest and sincere, even in their extreme distress.[49]

Parallel and possibly historically linked to the sacred prostitutes of Inanna and Ishtar in ancient Sumeria, the female bards attached to the queens were known as *viṟalis*, and "the Tamil king is called a fool if he fails to pay proper attention towards the *viṟalis*."[50] *Viṟalis* played several musical instruments, a *yāḻ* (stringed instrument), a trumpet, and various drums (*ākuḷi, patalai, muḻava*) at royal courts and at the beginning of a military campaign. As we have noted, they were also dancers who performed fertility rites: "Let the rain fall upon the field in the village where the *viṟalis* are dancing!" (*Naṟṟ*, 328, 12). Their dancing and singing were believed to have the power to bring rain and conquer adversaries. Addressing the enemies of prince Pāri, Kapilar claims that the domain of Pāri will only fall as a result of the enchantment of the *viṟalis*:

I know but of one way to conquer it
Playing a small *yāḻ* with woven strings
Follow your *viṟalis*, whose hair is fragrant,
Dance and sing—
Then he will be sure to give away both his hill and his country.[51]

The male counterpart of the *viṟali* was the low-caste bard,[52] known as the *pāṇaṉ*, the male poet-performer-musician attached to the king and the households of noble warriors. The venue of the *pāṇan* was either in the court of a king or chieftain, where he played a *yāḻ* to glorify the warrior and warfare, or the battlefield, where the *pāṇaṉ*, in a frenzied state with "tiger looks," sang war songs, beat the *taṇṇumai* drum, and rallied the soldiers. The *pāṇaṉ* was also an intermediary between traumatized wives at home and their soldier husbands in military camp.

As an agent of the sacred, the Tamil king possessed many accouterments and symbols of authority that explicate Dravidian notions of kingship. The king's staff served the function of the World Tree or Axis Mundi, uniting the profane and the sacred worlds, and the king was the guardian of that union. Anyone who had a connection with the sacred—the priest of Murukaṉ, bards, village elders at marriage ceremonies—held a staff. Similarly, Hebrew Moses and Egyptians Osirus and Horus wielded magical staffs.

The king also possessed a royal drum, a *muracu*, made of the skin of a bull that had defeated his rival in a bull-fight and of the wood of an enemy's tutelary tree. Like the Vedic war drum, the "fearful drum" of the Tamil king was personified by the poets: the drum "thirsts for blood, / its black sides lined by leather straps / and adorned with a sapphirelike garland / of the bright eyes of long peacock feathers."[53] The *muracu*, as Hart points out, bears a resemblance to the magic drums of the Siberian shamans, which were the vehicles of their ecstatic flight to the center of the Earth, or their ascent or descent along the axis of the Cosmic Tree.[54] "It seems certain that when the *muracu* was beaten in the morning to awaken the king and bring him back from the other world and when it was beaten during battle, its function, like the drum of the Siberian shaman, was to create sacred space and time."[55] Immediately after a victory in war, a triumphant king would take his enemy's drum, which gave him the property rights to his kingdom. When a king won a battle, he cut down his enemy's tutelary tree, which was sacred to the king, evidence of ancient Dravidian tree worship. The wood was sometimes used to make a *muracu*.

After victory in battle, a war sacrifice was memorialized in the original *poṅgala* by cooking the flesh of the slain enemies in order to create a close bond between the triumphant king and the slain kings.[56] *Aṇaṅku* energy, like Naga fertility, was unleashed when the soldiers were slain, and the king's responsibility for their deaths made him especially vulnerable to danger. Hence the rite functions to protect the king from the power released from the death of his enemies. "This rite is homologized to the marriage ceremony in one description, marriage also being a rite in which a bond is created between two people. Moreover, in marriage, the woman protects her husband with her power, just as in the war sacrifice the dead king is supposed to lend his power to the victor."[57] The capricious, ambivalent, earthy nature of *aṇaṅku* energy, its fluctuations and ability to shift-shape, and its capacity to build up or to be wasted were regarded by early Tamils as principles of a sacred science of energy, much like the primal Naga conception of fertility, and a complex of ritual forms was devised to store, manipulate, and channel the energy for the benefit of the whole community. *Aṇaṅku* energy, which "can be viewed as a product of the mythopoetical mind,"[58] was stored primarily in ancient Tamil kings and women.

In the Caṅkam age, warfare was practiced as an art; Tamil warriors were specialists in the methods of fortification (defending and assaulting mountain fortresses and sea-forts). Caṅkam literature offers a portrait of the well-fortified Pāṇḍyan capital Madurai, with its tall mansions, wide streets, and colorful bazaars protected by moat, fortress walls, and towered gates. Some fortresses were reinforced with an additional wall of dense forest. The traditional four-fold army subsumed infantry, cavalry, chariots, and elephants, with an emphasis on the crucial importance of the horse and elephant. Warriors wore body armor of tiger skin and a leather forearm cover and carried sword and shield for close combat. A missile or slingshot (*tomaram*) was a projectile directed at the enemy from a distance. Warfare commenced with the capture of the enemy's cattle. On the battlefield, drums and conchs were sounded as soldiers drank toddy and donned garlands of flowers. As Pillai expresses the Tamil war scene, "It was a language of flowers in War as in Love."[59]

In the Dravidian warrior tradition, dying in war guaranteed that soldiers would go to a Valhalla (*vīrasvarga*) at death similar to that of ancient Norse and Iranian men, and warriors who died ignobly in their beds were, in a macabre dramatization of a hero's battle death, hacked to pieces with swords and spears in order to ensure an afterlife in *vīrasvarga*. (Brāhmaṇas were often given the task of immolating warriors who died in bed rather than the battlefield.) Heroes were honored by the erection of memorial stones (*nadukal*) with inscriptions detailing their battle prowess.

The ancient Tamils promoted the ritual pageantry of pre-war activities as means of building up and sustaining the emotion of warriors and community. An enormous war drum, the *taṇṇumai*, is beaten by a *pāṇa<u>n</u>* to assemble the soldiers. The drummer rides an elephant around the city, beating the drum, and a flower girl sells flowers to the soldiers, who wear garlands when they go to battle. A spear is plunged in water up to the shaft, while the king bathes in a tank in preparation for battle. The best warrior is given a cup of liquor by the king before battle. The *taṉṉumai* drums reverberate, hypnotically leading the men into battle, followed by the beating of the royal *muracu* and the invocation of the spirit within the drum.

Puṟam poems contain many references to various dances, the most important of which is the Tunaṅkai, an exemplar of the heroic age. The poem *Patirruppattu*, which extolls the military exploits of the early Cera kings, describes the Tunaṅkai dancers as striking their sides with arms bent at the elbows, a dance "that is executed, with the movement of the shoulders, in the battlefield which is heaped with corpses."[60] The poem depicts the entire victorious army of warriors performing the dance, with the leader in the most prominent position.

> The headless trunks, holding hands, rise up and dance to the rhythm of the *tunaṅkai* dance that resounds with the clamor of the crowds of demon girls who drip fat from their mouths.[61]

The origin of the Tunaṅkai lies in an ancient Tamilnadu myth of a battleground scene in which female devils consumed the fallen soldiers' corpses, dancing ecstatically over the dead and bending their arms, striking against their sides, and thanking the brave soldiers who killed the men. The Tunaṅkai ritually mimes the dance of the female devils, and was performed to appease the demonesses, who were beseeched to bring the warriors further victories. Cannibalism is suggested in the dance,[62] and it is known that cannibalistic rites followed battles.[63] In an advanced form of this dance called the Munterkkuravai, the leader performs the dance on the seat plank of the chariot after defeating other kings; the Pinterkkuravai, performed after drinking the gruel of corpses, is known as the dance of the Goddess Koṟṟavai,[64] who led the band of female devils. Tunaṅkai, which "started as a cannibalistic ritual, must have emerged as the ritual dance of the warrior hero performed to maintain the solidarity of the group,"[65] in the view of K. Ṣivathamby.

When the Aryans psychologically infiltrated the south, their *modus operandi* was not overt physical conquest as it had been in the north. Rather, they co-opted the Tamil gods and goddesses, melded them with their Aryan counterparts, and identified them by their new Aryan names, viz., Murugaṉ became Subramania (Śiva) and his vehicle changed from elephant to peacock; Kaṇṇan became Kṛṣṇa and his consort Nappinnai became Rādhā and Bāmā; Veṇḍan became Indra, and Koṟṟavai became Durgā and Kālī. "With great ease, the Aryans metamorphosed Murugaṉ and his mother Koṟṟavai into Subramania and Uma and included them in their pantheon. . . . [T]he worshippers of Muruga propitiated him with animal sacrifices, hypnotic or devil dances, and Kurinchi songs."[66] Vedic rites and rituals were introduced to Tamilnadu by brāhmaṇas, who were held in high esteem by the kings and the people. The Tamil kings were persuaded to perform *yajñas*. Buddhism and Jainism also entered Tamilnadu, "but the total impression one gains from Caṅkam classics is that Vedic religion got mixed up with the local religion and held sway over the whole of Tamil Nadu."[67] When Vedic myths arrived in south India, the Tunaṅkai ritual began to be used not to glorify the mighty warriors and divine king, but rather, the deeds of an Aryan god. By the post-Caṅkam period, the brāhmaṇas had succeeded in assimilating the elite Tamil literature into the Vedic idiom; in *Tirumurukārrupatai*, the Tunaṅkai was performed by the female devils in praise of Lord Subramania, when he defeated the Avunar.[68] The dance was thus transposed from the real world of the cannibalistic battlefield to the abstract realm of brāhmaṇic myth, disappearing slowly as a popular dance form. When this assimilation occurred, around the sixth and fifth centuries BCE, the *akam* and *puṟam* tradition also vanished. Only during the time of the Imperial Coḷas, and only in literature, was the martial Tamil mythology resurrected.

Women and the Warrior Ethic

Where is your son? you ask,
Leaning against the pillar of my house.
I don't really know where he is.
This womb, that bore him, is now a desolate cave
a tiger once prowled about.
Go, look for him on the battlefield.

—*Puṟanāṉūṟu*, 86

During the Tamil Caṅkam age in Tamil Nadu, the status of women was equivalent to that of Vedic women in north India. Women were a lively part of society who participated openly in everyday life. They attended temples and public dances and could freely choose their husbands. Women of the high culture of the Caṅkam age were not excluded from the best education, evidenced by the number of women poets during the period. The *Naṟṟinai* anthology relates that elite women wore costly dresses "as white and soft as of heron's feathers."[69] Elite Tamil women of the landowning or merchant families were dependent economically on their husbands or fathers, the economic supporters of the family. Women were thus "but the shadow of the menfolk," according to Vanamamalai, with "no right to freedom of action"[70] at any time in their lives. As the Tamil proverb depicts elite woman's lot: "The woman is the shadow of her father when she is a maid, share of her husband in married life, and the servant of her sons after her husband's death." Women of the artisan and craftsmen families differed very little from elite women. They were not allowed to ply their husbands' trade, serving only as "housewives like their counterparts in the landowning and merchant families."[71] Among agricultural laborers and weavers, women contributed to their family's economic support, although they received lower wages than men for the same work, and certain labor such as weeding and transplanting was restricted to woman's domain. "Though these castes are patrilocal, the women enjoy comparative freedom and can fight injustice with comparative ease."[72]

The treatment of Tamil widows—particularly dead warriors' wives—was cruel and inhumane. Because her mere presence was regarded as inauspicious, the widow was not welcome at weddings, births, infant-naming ceremonies, or other happy events, and her attendance at religious festivals was forbidden. A widow's folk song expresses her desolate and lonely condition:

> If I carry a plantain leaf and go to my son's house
> They refuse to feed me because it is a happy event.
> If I take a measure of rice and go to Palani mountain to worship,
> The priest tells me that prayer will do me no good.
> If I take two measures of rice to Chruli mountain to worship God
> The priest tells me, prayer will do me no good.[73]

Among the high martial classes, a soldier's death on the battlefield was the masculine ideal, assuring ascent to warrior heaven, and *satī* was the feminine ideal for the wives of warriors: "the ideal wife was held to be one who mounted the funeral pyre of her husband with no more concern than if she was entering a tank of cool water for a bath."[74] Because she had failed in her duty to protect her husband's longevity, the Tamil widow was expected to be miserable, and her duties were all self-punishing austerities, including beating her breast in mourning for her deceased husband, shaving her head, removing and discarding her bangles and all ornaments, abstinence from good food, and leading an austere and impoverished life. Judging from references to widowhood in Caṅkam poems, there is "no doubt that sensitive women must have seen very good reason to follow their husbands in death as in life, rather than face the hardships and social contempt which was the widow's fate."[75] Even queens preferred death to such austerities; in the *Puṟanāṉūṟu*, the chief wife of King Pūtapāṇṭiyaṉ chides men dependent on her husband who urged her not to commit *satī* so that she could ascend to the throne as queen, and thus continue to subsidize them:

> Listen, all of you good men
> with your wicked schemes,
> who would hinder me with words of restraint
> and not urge me to go.
> Listen, you good men!
> I am no woman to suffer austerities,
> eating for food
> *veḷai* leaves
> boiled with tamarind
> with white sesame paste

and a squeezed ball of rice
untouched by fragrant ghee
whose light color
resembles the seeds of a curved cucumber
with chipmunk lines
split with a sword,
and to sleep on a bed
covered with stones
without even a mat.
Go ahead, spurn the pyre of black wood
heaped on the burning ground.
To me,
since my great-armed husband is dead,
that fire
and a large pond of lotuses
that have loosed from buds rich petals
are the same.[76]

Tamil poems written by women[77] in the Caṅkam period reflect the indoctrination of the warrior ethic in women, or, perhaps more realistically, their fear of the repercussions if they did not support war and coach their sons to be brave warriors. Cognate with the Purāṇic didactic system, the poems set up psychological models for women in a warrior culture. Women were to think of themselves as having two chief functions: to rear fierce warrior sons and to push their husbands and sons to the battlefield.

As Mandakranta Bose points out, "These poems are written in the heroic mode and tell us little about women except that their ideals of self-worth conformed wholly to the demands warfare made on their menfolk."[78] For example, an old woman's greatest joy is learning that her son died a brave warrior:

When she learned her son had died killing an elephant,
The joy of the old woman,
Her hair pure grey like the feathers of a fish-eating heron,
Was greater than the day she bore him.[79]

When a first-born son was born to a Tamil family, a ceremony was performed for the first meeting of father and baby son a few days after birth. The father would don a war dress and, surrounded by warriors, visit the son "to imprint on the heart of the child a warlike mentality and spirit when he first saw his father."[80] Women were required to conquer fear, to support war, and "to abandon maternal tenderness in exchange for heroic pride."[81] The Tamil warrior mother persona was clearly "fully imbued with the psychology of the heroic,"[82] as is elucidated in another poem:

Her purpose is frightening, her spirit cruel
That she comes from an ancient house is fitting surely.

In the battle, the day before yesterday
Her father attacked an elephant and died,
there on the field.
In the battle yesterday, her husband faced a
row of troops and fell
And today, she hears the battle drum, and
eager beyond reason
Gives her son a spear in his hand
Wraps a white garment around him
Smears his dry tuft with oil
And having nothing but her one son
"Go!" she says, sending him to battle.[83]

One of the old songs in the *Pattuppāṭṭu* entitled "Neṭunalvātai" (The Long Strong Northwind) written by the poet Nakkīraṉār, relates a tale of the wife of a warrior out on a mission who is distraught with worry about her husband and prays to a goddess to grant him victory. In ll. 167f. appears the prayer: "That my bitter, unbearable pain be removed, grant him victory and let him complete his task now, please, O Mother!" According to Hardy, "the 'mother' prayed to here is in all likelihood the ancient Tamil goddess of victory, Koṟṟavai."[84] Although women were programed and threatened by the Tamil warrior ethic, the profound pain they experienced when their husbands and sons are on the battlefield or are killed is only allowed to overtly surface when they are in the presence of Koṟṟavai.

The Decline and Fall of the Heroic Bardic Mode

Around the last three centuries before Christ, brāhmaṇical, Buddhist, and Jaina religions penetrated into the south and received royal patronage, halting the bardic tradition and reducing the *viṟali* to the Indo-Aryan status of courtesan (*gaṇikā*), lady-in-waiting to the queen, or prostitute (*parattai*). Hinduism as we understand it emerged from the mixture of Dravidian and Aryan culture. In the third century BCE, when Tamil kingdoms entered into diplomatic relations with the Mauryan Emperor Aśoka, the Aryo-Dravidian civilization had more or less fully formed itself.[85] During this time, the Mauryan Empire expanded to include all of north India and a large part of the Deccan, growing along the merchant routes already established between the north and the southern kingdoms. Since he is credited in one inscription with being the first king of Kanchipuram, Emperor Aśoka probably traveled as far south as Kanchipuram, which would account for how the city became one of the thriving Buddhist centers until the seventh century AD.

Bhakti, or devotional religiosity, represents a fusion between "the bardic universe of the complementary *akam* and *puṟam*,"[86] brāhmaṇic, and Indo-Aryan religion. During the Bhakti period, the *viṟali* reemerged as a *devadāsī*.[87] Both *gaṇikā* and *parattai* are Indo-Aryan terms, appearing first in the post-bardic period. As Kersenboom-Story asserts,

> Where formerly the king had to be interpreted as a divine power, the divine is to be understood now as a king, and, in particular, a king who understands the modes of *akam* and *puṟam* and responds to the devotee's love (*bhakti*). Eros and fervent devotion are translated in religious song, music, dance, and mystical poetry. Whereas on the one hand the cosmic equation is performed by Brahmin priests employing Sanskrit, the old Tamil milieu on the other hand has re-asserted itself in the form of female bards who sing and dance, as well as new bards who approach God by mystical poetry. . . . [I]n contrast to the Vedic hymns, these Tamil hymns are not ritual at all in nature. The intimate side of worship is very highly developed and indeed, like in a number of early bardic poems of the *puṟam* genre, the most important feature is the relation between the subject who praises and asks, and the object who listens and gives.[88]

The high artistic level of the heroic bardic tradition was altered in both character and function, and the social status of the artist declined. In the new society, artists performed for the pleasure of an audience. The *viṟalis,* once great dance artists and female bards, became concubines and *hetaerae,* with the male member of that caste group, the *pāṇaṉ,* acting as their procurer. The artistic forms that originated in collective rituals were now confined to only one caste of people to perform them. In post-Caṅkam literature all the dances were performed by this caste, and Vedic myths displaced the indigenous myths.

Following the Caṅkam age, the Dravidians were oppressed for three centuries under the rule of the Kalabhra dynasty. Buddhism and Jainism arose as the dominant dharma, suppressing the *joi de vivre* of the early Tamils. In the sixth century AD, the warlike Pallavas began their reign over the region subsuming Kanchipuram and Madras. By the eighth century, Buddhism and Jainism nearly vanished. The Pallavas were eliminated and the Coḷas reasserted their sovereignty from the ninth to the twelfth centuries. Each kingdom competed with the others for the highest cultural achievement, attempting to produce the most opulent temple architecture, the most aesthetic religious art, and the most eloquently dogmatic literary discourses on Hinduism. Temple building, land development, and internecine warfare dominated the activities of the dynasties of the Deccan.

Muslims began invading north India and attacking Hindu culture in the eighth century, and the Sultan of Delhi invaded Deccan in the early thirteenth century. A coalition to drive the Muslims out of south India was formed and successfully executed, except for the north of the Deccan and the Sultanate of Madurai, by the Hindu kings of the south in the early fourteenth century. Two Hindu princes, who were forced to convert to Islam but reverted to Hinduism, subsequently created the empire of Vijayanagar. This empire integrated all the small southern Hindu kingdoms and forged a robust state that protected the south until the seventeenth century. Hindu kings, Muslims, and Europeans (Portuguese, French, and the dominant British) competed for control of India via warfare or imperialist alliances after the seventeenth century. The Hindu kings were transformed into Maharajah landlords. The French retained five settlements, the Portuguese kept Goa, and the British controlled India until 1947.

ANCIENT TAMIL SYLVAN GODDESSES

Before you the gods humbly bow.
Your arm has never known defeat.
You are the wisdom of the Book of Books.
How came you to appear,
robed in a tiger skin,
standing on the black head of a wild buffalo?. . .[89]

Ancient Tamil tribals and landless laborers believed that they must fulfill an ethical ecological contract with goddesses or gods, the ultimate spiritual authorities who often resided in a tree. If the people broke the compact of reciprocity by neglecting the deity, atonement was required. The oldest mode of Bhagavatī worship, according to C.A. Menon, is "at the foot of the tree without any form of idol or icon."[90] The objective of tree worship, which is still practiced by the autochthonous forest dwellers of both north and south India, is "to request protection and avert harm from the Goddess, who is believed to be dangerous and capricious by nature."[91] This tradition was described in the *Cilappatikāram,* where we find that

> the forms of worship of the rural folk offered to the folk deities are in the nature of appeasement or thanksgiving. When they suffer, they believe that it is due to the anger of a particular god or goddess. When the whole community suffers they seek to appease the presiding deity of the community by offering communal worship to it. In tribal communities, this is always accompanied by dance and song.[92]

Although ancient Tamils did not have the large panoply of transcendent deities of the Aryans, the great number of goddesses worshiped in the Caṅkam classics is evidence of the "currency of the cult of the Female Principle in south India in the early centuries of the Christian era,"[93] according to Bhattacharyya. Kumārī, Gaurī, Durgā (Mother Goddess of the hunters), Āpya, Bhāratī, Āmarī, Sāmarī, Vaiyai (Umai), Māyaval, Āryāni (the Tamil version of Indrāṇī), Sayyavaḷ, Nallāl, Śaṅkarī, Kaṇṇī, and Śūlī were active in south India from the third century BCE to the third century AD. Cāmuṇḍā or Pitari is one of the seven Lokamātās (mothers of the world). The *Cilappatikāram,* XI–XII refers to Kālī worship at a temple where Kaṇṇaki and Kovalaṉ stopped on the road to Madurai. There they witnessed a Kālī-attired priestess who performed a frenzied dance of spirit possession and announced that Kālī was angry because the Maṛavar had failed to offer her a sacrifice for too long.

In addition to Kālī and Durgā, who merged with Ko<u>rr</u>avai, there were three significant fierce goddesses in Caṅkam literature: Ko<u>rr</u>avai, Aiyai-Kumārī, and Kaṇṇaki. Ko<u>rr</u>avai and Aiyai were of the same divine essence, equated with Vaiyai (Earth Mother), Ammaṉ, and Śakti, while Kaṇṇaki was a human being who became deified as Pattanikaḍuvul, the goddess of chastity and vengeance.

Korr̲avai

The ancient Tamils of the Caṅkam age worshiped fertility and war goddess Kor̲r̲avai or Koṭṭavai (Koṭṭavai-ai-paravu-val), Goddess of Victory, the original slayer of the Primordial Bull. The *Tolakappiyam*, the earliest Tamil grammatical text, describes Kor̲r̲avai as the goddess of the region of Pālai,[94] where the Eyinor worshiped her and sacrificed buffaloes at her temple. In the *Cilappatikāram*, Kor̲r̲avai is beseeched by a hymn of the Eyinor:

> Accept the blood that flows from our severed young heads,
> the price of a victory you granted
> to the powerful and valiant Eiyannars.
> Accept the blood and flesh we offer you,
> in thanks for the great victories
> you showered on the Eiyannars
> when they adventured out on raids
> to seize vast herds of cattle.[95]

Kor̲r̲avai's role as war goddess is clearly delineated in Caṅkam literature, but her role as loving Mother-goddess must be inferred from references to Tamil women going to Kor̲r̲avai's temple for solace. Like Kālī, she infused dread and awe in her worshipers:

> Her hair was matted. She was clad in skins of tiger and cobra while a stag was her vehicle. She was so much dreaded that when once the doors of her shrine could not be opened, the Pāṇḍya king felt that it was due to the divine displeasure and sought her mercy by the grant of the revenue of two villages for her worship.[96]

Tamil Caṅkam *pur̲am* poetry, teeming with male warrior heroes against a backdrop of jungle tigers, elephants, bull sacrifice, and poetic allusions to the Mistress of Wild Animals and her predator jungle associates, is imagistic evidence of the primordial shamanic origin of Kālī and her *avatāras*. The ancient Tamil forest-dwelling war goddess Kor̲r̲avai carries within her the fertility goddess/buffalo/lion totem, the blood-and-guts passions of the warrior, and the loving influence of a mother who can incite women to violence against the state (in the myth of Kovalan̲ and Kaṇṇaki, Kaṇṇaki retreats to Kor̲r̲avai's temple and emerges a violent revolutionary).

Her name, which means "Goddess of Victory," derives from *korram*, victory, but the *Tamil Lexicon* links her name with the root *kol*, to kill. In Caṅkam literature, Kor̲r̲avai is the primary deity of male warriors who attribute their success in raiding local cattle herds to the "blood and flesh" offerings they have made to her, including the ultimate sacrifice, self-immolation. According to George Hart, "Kor̲r̲avai must have been an indigenous (Dravidian) goddess, at least in her character as a goddess of war and victory who lives in a forest and dances the tunankai."[97] She was intimately associated with wild animals, and she is the original Indic slayer of the buffalo demon in a Neolithic meme commensurate with Ishtar and Inanna.

In Caṅkam literature, both hunting tribes and elite warriors propitiated Koṟṟavai. The *raison d'être* of elite warriors and war chariots was to confiscate the land and cattle of indigenous peoples such as the Eyinors, a Vaḍuvar (hunting) tribe that also offered buffalo sacrifice to Koṟṟavai in return for profitable cattle raids. Both Koṟṟavai and Aiyai rode buffaloes and exchanged bountiful harvests for bull sacrifices. Koṟṟavai is equated with Malaimagal, daughter of the mountain, or Pārvatī.[98] As the Dravidian victory goddess of war who danced soldiers to the battlefield with her legion of bloodthirsty goblins, Koṟṟavai is the prototype of Cāṇḍi (Durgā) in the *Devī-māhātmya*—an example of the central brāhmaṇic strategy of co-opting the goddesses of the conquered peoples and shifting their allegiances to the gods of the conquerors. Invoked by warriors before battle, Koṟṟavai influenced the outcome for good or evil; human heads and other blood sacrifices were offered for fear that she "withhold her servant Victory." Riding a tiger, sporting a tiger teeth necklace, and carrying a skull bowl filled with a magical brew of blood, intestines, and flesh mixed with grain,[99] she shouts her mighty victory cry as she escorts the forces of the king to the battlefield, backed up by her army of female goblins. By feasting on the corpses of dead soldiers, they entered the divine realm. Koṟṟavai was the female counterpart of Aryan war god Indra. Aryan brāhmaṇas known as *purohitas* accompanied Indra and his warriors, high on *soma*, to the battlefield comparable to the Tamil tradition in which *viṟalis* and male bards accompanied the warriors led by Koṟṟavai and her retinue, who sang and danced their warriors, fortified with toddy, to battle.

Great Goddess Koṟṟavai was worshiped in several aspects: as the Tamil war goddess Koṟṟavai, for whom the sacred ritual of war is performed, and mother of fertility and war-god Murukaṉ; as tribal Vaḷḷi (Koṟṟavai's "benign aspect," according to Dubianski),[100] Murukaṉ's consort; and as tribal Aiyai-Kumārī, propitiated with bull sacrifices by tribal hunter-gatherers and highway robbers. Koṟṟavai and Murukaṉ represent the same ancient template of the mother/son/consort divine pair found in the Near East. Murukaṉ is represented variously in the Caṅkam anthologies and poems as a local guardian-spirit, a rustic Tamil fertility deity cognate with Dionysus, and also as Skanda (Kārttikeya, Kumāra), commander of the heavenly army, a son of Śiva, who battles the demons in a typical patriarchal cosmic war scenario that parallels the Aryan and Zoroastrian cosmic battles between the gods and demons. Koṟṟavai, as Śiva's wife, shares most of her symbolic motifs with her husband: the trident, the frenzied possession dance, the kingship, the third eye, the bull, the cobras, and sometimes the ability to swallow poison.

The brāhmaṇas corralled Koṟṟavai into the fringes of the elite pantheon as Durgā-Kālī and her *avatāras*, who have retained continuously the intermingling motifs of *hieros gamos* and blood sacrifice that form the whole complex template of the Great Goddess. In her Tantric complementarity with Śiva, the goddess creates the universe; the *tattvas* arise as a product of their sacred marriage of opposites, much as Inanna receives the Sumerian *mes* (principles of civilization) through sexual union with her consort An.[101] In south India, the possession dance and erotic love of Śiva and Śakti have dominated the Great Goddess folk tradition for five millennia. The complementarity of female reproductive functions and male activities is essential to social survival.

The Tamil tradition of cyclical sacrifices constituted Indian versions of the *hieros gamos* of the ancient Near East, an area that some theorists claim comprises the original homeland of Tamil Palaeo-Mediterranean Dravidian progenitors. This construction, based on trade and migration patterns, is favored by Narendra Nath Bhattacharyya,[102] who emphasized the importance of the Dravidian tradition in Indian culture and religion. Bhattacharyya traces the Dravidian origin of Śiva and Umā/Ammā, the Indic divine couple who were, according to Bhattacharyya, Indian versions of the Great Mother of the ancient Near East and her consort/son. Such a fierce goddess template is reminiscent of the ancient cult of Kybele, whose vehicle was a lion, and for whom bull sacrifices, ecstatic dancing, and ritual blood self-sacrifice were performed at festivals, which "formed undoubtedly one of the bases on which the Śiva-Umā cult of Hindu India grew up."[103] There is probably a Dravidian link, by trade and migration, according to this perspective, between Western Asian goddesses Kybele, Inanna, Ishtar, and Anath; Tamil Koṟṟavai, Māriyammaṉ, Ellaiyammaṉ, and other dalit village goddesses worshiped today in south India. These Indic folk goddesses are the Great Goddesses and village Earth Mothers bearing the epithet *ammaṉ* or *amma*[104] (mother), who cause and cure disease, and, unless brāhmaṇized, are always worshiped with animal sacrifice, oracular spirit possession performances, liquor, and frenzied dances. When a woman becomes possessed by an evil spirit, the goddess, with the assistance of a priest or priestess, exorcises her through lengthy rituals. The goddess then occupies the empty space left by the evil spirit and the "cured" woman becomes benevolently possessed. Thus the goddess is a potentiality in all women, her divinity shining through them without male intervention.

A mythical figure closely related to Koṟṟavai is the *pēy*, a demon, or, more frequently, a demoness who roams around after dusk scarfing down sacrificial offerings to the gods or devouring enemy warriors on the battlefield, and thus directly entering the realm of the divine. The word *pēy* may derive etymologically from the root *pe*, "rage, madness," as well as from the Sanskrit *preta*, the spirit of a dead person, an evil spirit, *bhūta*. In the Tamil *Tirumurukāṟṟuppaṭai* [*TMA*], we find gruesome battlefield poems describing *pēys* performing the *tunaṅkai* dance.[105] "Similar episodes, frequently recurring in the Tamil heroic poetry represent battle as offering to goddess Koṟṟavai and, possibly, describe, allegorically, the earliest military rituals, with a tinge of cannibalism, aimed at obtaining the life-force from the defeated enemy,"[106] according to Alexander Dubianski. In *Akanāṉūṟu* [*AN*], savage hunters living in the wasteland slay a young bull, roast it over a fire, and devour its flesh[107] in the manner of *pēys*, who are defined as "grotesque representations of performers of ancient traditional sacrifices (human or animal), most frequently the slaying of a bull or a buffalo."[108] In *AN*, "*pēy*-demonesses [are] known for their rare *aṇaṅku*,"[109] which they display not only on battlefields, but also on the hellish lands that have been devastated by war raids, "inspiring horror, fiery-mouthed jackals are howling; and owl is hooting, cadaver-eating *pēys*, their hair in loose strands, are crowding with dwarfish creatures."[110] These erstwhile flourishing lands were mythically reframed by early Tamil bards as the *pālai* region, "a mytho-poetical disaster zone, symbolizing danger, suffering, blood, dryness, fire, and death."[111] The hell-like quality of the imagery parallels the Underworld journeys of Ishtar and Inanna, conveying the idea of heat and the Tamil *aṇaṅku* energy. In general, Ko<u>rr</u>avai, *pēy*, and *aṇaṅku* are all connected with overheating, manifested in blood, death, danger, and impurity.[112]

Long before the Caṅkam age, legends homologized Durgā with the southern Ko<u>rr</u>avai or other local goddesses, and linked the goddess with the buffalo. This harked back to a protohistoric goddess/buffalo totem and sacrificial rituals involving bull sacrifice, as well as the archaic roots of the myth of Mahiṣāsura-mardinī. The motif of Devī's ritual slaying of the buffalo demon is first represented on seals of the Indus Civilization, representing the quintessence of the pan-Indian, particularly the Dravidian cult of the goddess known as Ko<u>rr</u>avai, Devī, Kālī, Durgā, Māriyamma<u>n</u>, and Bhagavatī. When Ko<u>rr</u>avai and Kālī-Durgā coalesced, in the pan-Indian pantheon, they acquired Śaivite attributes. According to Dubianski, the source-myth for the ritual drama of buffalo sacrifice is "the story of her defeat of the *asura* (demon) Mahiṣa who had taken the shape of a buffalo," a well-known tale by the author of *Cilappatikāram*, which contains an account of the episode. According to the myth, Mahiṣa had the ability to shift-shape into various forms, and when the goddess wrestled the buffalo's head to the ground, Mahiṣa in his human form as the goddess's consort emerged from the carcass of the buffalo,[113] cognate with Tamil myths explored by David Dean Shulman that implicitly attribute the murder of Śiva to Devī.[114]

> The aim of the rites reproducing the ritual of buffalo sacrifice is to propitiate the goddess, to "cool" her wrath and, having thus reduced the excess of the sacred force to a "safe" level, to be granted certain boons: rainfall, good crops, relief from epidemics, etc. The shedding of blood is one of the ritual's central points. It is perceived as the nourishing of the goddess and therefore has a cooling effect, which can be compared to the cooling effect of sexual intercourse. This parallel is not incidental: erotic motifs are intrinsic to the ritual. *In numerous instances . . ., the goddess's "marriage" with the demon is enacted. Then the goddess slays her consort.* Although the demon (Mahiṣa, Potu-rāsu in the villages of Andhra and Mhasobā in Maharashtra) has come to be represented as a tree trunk or a stone, the links between the ritual events and the slaying of the demon, that were so apparent in the past, are still explicit. They vividly represent the dangerous side of the goddess's sexuality and—in a more generalized way—the power of *aṇaṅku*.[115]

After the fall of the Gupta empire in the north, incursions of northern Aryan kings and brāhmaṇas overpowered the south Indian Dravidian Tamils militarily, economically, politically, and linguistically. The Tamil goddess Koṟṟavai was consolidated with Durgā and Kālī in the Sanskritic tradition, since they all distinguished themselves as slayers of the buffalo demon Mahiṣa in mythic cosmic war scenarios. Hart maintains that "the northern goddess Durgā is not associated with victory, and none of her names has that meaning."[116] However, Bhattacharyya regards the coalescence of Koṟṟavai and Durgā as part of the strategy of the brāhmaṇic expansion to the south.[117]

Another mythic motif characteristic of the Neolithic Great Goddess in the Near East and India is her perpetual virginity. The significance of this motif lies in the ancient Tamil conception of virginity as "a state characterized by the utmost concentration of the power, a great potency for both creation and destruction."[118] Notably, Koṟṟavai's Aiyai incarnation is also known as Kumārī, "Virgin," and one of Koṟṟavai's names in *Cilappatikāram* is Kumārī.[119]

Tiger iconography associated with fierce goddesses may connote symbolically their totemic relation to the big cats. We have seen evidence of the Naga tiger totem, their belief in shamanic were-tigers and were-leopards, including the notion that tiger souls reside in all humans and communicate with them in dreams. Koṟṟavai wears a tiger teeth necklace and she rides a tiger into the battlefield. The lion in Purāṇic literature (though not in the epics) is identified as Durgā's *vāhana* or vehicle.

Murukaṉ and Vaḷḷī are the divine couple worshiped by peaceful mountain hunter-gatherers. The most complete and authoritative version of the Murukaṉ-Vaḷḷī myth appears in the fourteenth century AD *Skanda Purāṇa*, or the *Kantapurāṇam*, while the folklore version of the myth is represented in an anonymous modern poem published by Brenda Beck.[120] Murukaṉ's complex nature includes his role as fertility deity worshiped by the tribal *kuṟavars*, mountain hunter-gatherers who practiced slash-and-burn agriculture, raised millet crops, and collected wild honey, the fruit of the jack-tree (*palā maram*), tubers of the *vaḷḷi* plant, and manifold classes of flowers. According to the myth, when an ascetic, Śivamuṉi, was interrupted from his austerities by the sight of a lovely gazelle prancing by, his lascivious thoughts impregnated the gazelle, who gave birth to a human child, Vaḷḷi, the personification of a plant with edible tubers (*vaḷḷi*). Murukaṉ's sexual union with Vaḷḷi, who "symbolizes the vegetable, the earthly, or, in more generalized terms, the feminine in nature"[121] and the productivity of shifting agriculture, cools and fertilizes the region and the earth, ensuring bountiful harvests and hunts and many offspring.

"Vaḷḷi can be viewed as the hypostasis of the Tamil goddess in which she represents the benign side of the female power," according to Dubianski. "In this aspect she is contrasted with Koṟṟavai, although they are of one essence."[122] Vaḷḷi's association with the cultivated tuber and the gazelle represents the hunter-gatherer's sense of interconnection with the plant and animal life of their ecosystem. The marriage of Murukaṉ and Vaḷḷi solidified the bond between the local ethos of the hunter-gatherers and the elite Tamil deities, while Murukaṉ's marriage to Indra's daughter Devasenā signifies the influence of the "high" Sanskrit tradition.[123]

The images and cults of Murukaṉ and Māl-Kṛṣṇa share many common features, including their manifestation of fertility and sexual prowess; the importance of singing and women's ring-dancing (*kuravai*); and their mutual association with the peacock and with mountains. Ko<u>rr</u>avai is depicted as both the daughter and the sister of Māl. According to Dubianski, the earliest Tamil characters in the myth of the Murukaṉ-Cūr conflict were brother and sister, the goddess Ko<u>rr</u>avai and her brother Māl, who personified the light and dark half of the year. The Murukaṉ-Cūr conflict is interpreted by Dubianski as a variant of the basic Tamil myth of the demon slayed by his consort, with "a functional replacement of the goddess by her son."[124] In the symbolical context of the Mahiṣa myth depicting the slaying of the buffalo by his consort, the goddess, the equation of the archaic Māl with Mahiṣa "would represent a hypothetical basic Dravidian myth of the incest of the ancient goddess with her demon brother whom she eventually slays retaining her virginity."[125] Furthermore, since Ko<u>rr</u>avai and Māl are brother and sister, Murukaṉ's marriage to his uncle's daughter (Vaḷḷi) legitimates and sanctifies the tradition of cross-cousin marriage.[126]

Aiyai-Kumārī

In the *Cilappatikāram* epic, we learn that the Eyinors, a hunting tribe (Vaḍuvar) of Palai, were highway robbers who did not particularly prosper in their profession and "had become as gentle as Jains or Brahmins."[127] When their wives and children were starving, Śālinī, their chief priestess, explained to them that they had failed to be thankful to the grace of the goddess Aiyai. To make amends with the goddess, they were told to hold a festival in Śālinī's honor and appease her with rituals.

> But the poet throws light upon the existence of such a society in his days in his description of the Eyinars. Hence the folk motif here is only a realistic description of a tribal society whose contact with the civilized world around them was through murderous assaults and highway robbery. We find societies in just such [a] stage of development except that they do not indulge in pillage, in the interior mountain fastnesses of the western ghats. The Eyinars do not think any harm to their guests even today. Tribals do not attack any stranger without provocation. The poet excites the sympathy of the reader to these outcastes of society who had taken recourse to banditry to earn their livelihood.[128]

In order to prepare for the tribal rituals and celebration, an Eyinor maiden was selected to impersonate Aiyai-Kumārī in the manner of the pan-Indian Kumārī tradition of worship. Her hair was swept into a bob, a rope of grass in the shape of a snake wound around her head, and a long boar's tooth in the shape of a crescent moon placed in her hair. Encircling her neck were tiger's teeth set in a chain, and her waist was girded with a lion's hide. The tribals gave her a bow and "set her upon (a lion)."[129] Offerings of cooked rice, spices, and meat were placed before her as young mountain women offered burning incense, flower garland, and the fertility symbol of wet seeds, laying them at her feet. Behind them, male musicians filed in with their drums, flutes, and other musical instruments. The drama reached a climax when the priestess-oracle came forward, bowed to the Aiyai maiden, and told a prophecy.

Praises of Aiyai during the ritual echo the symbolism, narratives, and imagery of Śiva and Viṣṇu,[130] a manifestation of the early correspondences with the brāhmaṇic pantheon during the Caṅkam age. As the tribe of highway robbers praised Aiyai:

> One with an eye in the forehead,
> The eyelids never more
> Pearl lipped smiler,
> One with dark neck, because she swallowed poison
> The one who churned the ocean with a mountain bound by a snake
> One who holds a trident and wears the hide of an elephant
> Amari, Kumari, Samari,
> Sooli, Neeli, the younger sister of Mal
> you hold the chakra and caṅkam in both your hands
> Red eyed Mal riding on the bullock
> Wear river Ganga on your hair
> And occupy a part of the brow eyed one
> Take the shape of a woman praised by the Vedas.[131]

The Eyinors' offerings to Aiyai are forest produce, forest animals, and flowers, her favorite offering. They also offer beans, salt, oil, seeds of grains, cottonseed, black gram, and other available staples. Liquor, sheep, cocks, tobacco, and mountain produce are offered by the tribal folk on the western ghats.[132] Contemporary folk goddesses such as Māriyammaṉ, whose abode is the neem tree, correspond to this tribal goddess, and long folk songs praising Māriyammaṉ on her lion mount contain the thematic elements of archaic songs glorifying the heroic exploits of Aiyai.[133]

Kaṇṇaki

The tale of Kovalaṉ and Kaṇṇaki in the *Cilappatikāram* is an ancient south Indian myth of great popularity in the Caṅkam age. The myth depicts women's lot in Tamil life, the male idealized model of wifely "chastity" (self-sacrifice and self-mortification), the contrast between high and low cultures, and the revolutionary potentiality of women's rage. After Kovalaṉ has squandered his wealth on the prostitute Mātavi in the Coḷa capital Pukār, he and his wife Kaṇṇaki set out to make a fresh start in Madurai. Kovalaṉ, after selling an ankle bracelet of Kaṇṇaki's in town, is falsely accused of stealing it from the queen and executed without investigation or a trial. A suffering, chaste wife-heroine, Kaṇṇaki prays to the goddess Koṟṟavai in her temple.

Kaṇṇaki vowed:
"Till I have seen the husband
My heart has known, I will neither sit nor stand."
Her golden bracelets she then broke in the temple
Of Korravai, and wept:
"With my husband
I entered this city through the East Gate:
I now leave by the West Gate, alone."[134]

According to ancient tradition, an Indian woman's life is traditionally over with the death of her husband. She has been infected by her husband's *aṇaṅku*-laden death, making her dangerous and inauspicious. Further, she had failed in her duty to keep her husband alive. By law, as a widow she must remove her ornaments, refrain from putting the *tilaka* on her forehead, and shave her head to indicate her inauspicious status as a widow. This is the degraded condition of Kaṇṇaki when she goes to the temple of Ko<u>rr</u>avai and vows that she will not rest until she can see her husband, intimating that she will take action against the Pāṇḍya empire. She ceremoniously breaks her golden bracelets, a symbol of female power which elite males order women to discard when their husbands die. Kaṇṇaki is so grief-stricken over her husband and enraged at the king's injustice that she rips off one of her breasts and sets Madurai on fire, the only act that sates the fiery truth of her anger. Her objective was not only revenge, but also to end the unjust rule by ignorant kings and elites, burning down the seat of their power.

> [B]esides the familiar theme of grief and thoughts of the sufferings of widowhood we have Kaṇṇaki, fixing the responsibility for the death of her husband on the king. While the unjust king lived and ruled without punishment for his misdeed, why should she suffer for his wrongs? This thought rouses her indignation. She seeks justice and destruction of the rule that brought this grievous wrong on her. This thought transforms her into a heroine fighting for justice against the might of the Pāṇḍya rule. Again, this transformation produces the revolutionary heroine of the epic for the first and the last time in Tamil literature.[135]

Walking toward the Western ghats, she ascends the hill Tiruchengunru and stands under a Veṅkai tree, where the gods respond to her wish and come to her. When local tribals ask her who she is, she tells them of her destruction of Madurai. Kovala<u>n</u> then meets Kaṇṇaki and swoops her up to heaven with him. When the tribal folk witness this, they take it as a miracle of divine ascension, and Kaṇṇaki is deified as the goddess of the hill, for whom the hill tribes sing and dance Kunrakkravai as forms of worship.[136] She may have been a heroic folk goddess of revolution against social injustice, tyranny, and institutionalized misogeny. Significantly, Kaṇṇaki's apotheosis is immediately preceded by her connection with the Veṅkai tree.

Kaṇṇaki is the only female insurgent in classic Indian literature. Her story is a mythic explanation of fierce goddesses as well as a psychological study of women living in a repressive patriarchy. She is the antithesis of paragons like Lakṣmī: proud and unsubmissive, she does not bear her widowhood in self-abnegation. Her incandescent rage at the patriarchal warrior state is expressed in a single act of violent subversion. This myth in one sense represents a classic motif based on a common terror among repressive patriarchs: the gynophobic fear of women unrestrained by men, reminiscent of Euripedes' *The Bacchae* and many other Greek tragedies in which women such as Clytemnestra, driven by passion and rage, rebelliously murder their children and husbands. Women in ancient Greece were viewed as "caged tigers waiting for a chance to break out of their confinement and take revenge on the male world."[137] In a masculinist interpretation, the Kaṇṇaki myth is a morality tale suggesting that men must hold their *aṇaṅku*-laden women in check to prevent the ultimate male nightmare of women rising against them and destroying the social order they have built. As Gabrielle Dietrich observes, "The south Indian concept of *karpu* (chastity) is founded on the very real anxiety in men that if women's sexuality is not controlled, actual identities will change in unimaginable ways."[138] As such, the myth is a dramatization of the Tamil notions of *karpu* and *aṇaṅku*. As Hart explains,

> As a chaste, young woman, Kaṇṇaki is filled with aṇaṅku even while her husband is alive; but her power is in control. When he is killed, it goes out of control and is able to cause the city to be consumed because the city has been deprived of the protection of the king and of his power, which left at the moment he realized he had committed an injustice. It is notable that her power is concentrated in her breast. It is strengthened by her wildly flying hair and ornaments: it is because these things rendered a widow dangerous that she was supposed to shave her head and break her ornaments.[139]

References

1. B.K. Gururaja Rao, "Racial background of south Indian history," in *South Asian Studies*, ed. H.M. Nayak and B.R. Gopal (Mysore, 1990), 31.
2. Coomaraswamy, *History of Indian and Indonesian Art*, 5.
3. M.S. Purnalingam Pillai, *A Primer of Tamil Literature* (Madras, 1904), 3.
4. Bhattacharyya, *History of the Śākta Religion*, 21.
5. Ibid.
6. *Naṟṟ.*,135.11, 186, 236, cited in Pillai, *A Primer of Tamil Literature*, 127.
7. Ibid., 189.293, cited in ibid., 128.
8. M.S. Purnalingam Pillai, *A Primer of Tamil Literature* (Madras, 1904), 321.
9. Radha Kumuda Mookerji, *History of Indian Shipping and Their Own Ships from Earlier Times in the Persian Gulf* (Bombay, 1960), 62. Cited in Shaikh Khurshid Hasan, "Ethnoarchaeology as an Aid to Interpret Indus Civilization," *Pakistan Archaeology* XXVI (1991): 112.
10. Hasan, "Ethnoarchaeology as an Aid," 112.
11. Coomaraswamy, *History of Indian and Indonesian Art*, 5.
12. Berkson, *The Amazon and the Goddess*, 9.
13. Hart, *The Poems of Ancient Tamil*, 9.

14. Pillai, *A Primer of Tamil Literature,* 3–4.
15. Bhattacharyya, *History of the Śākta Religion,* 21–22.
16. Pillai, *A Primer of Tamil Literature,* 312.
17. *Paṭ.*, 246–49.
18. Friedhelm Hardy, *Viraha-Bhakti: The Early History of Kṛṣṇa Devotion in South India* (Oxford, 1983), 137–38.
19. The Dravidian counterpart to the northern demons or ghosts such as the *piśācas* and *rākṣasas* who inhabited the domains of death, the battlefield, and the cremation ground were the *pēy, kaḻutu,* and *paḻu.* They were not the same as the malevolent deities, the *avuṇar* and *cūr,* killed by Murukaṉ and equated, with the northern *asuras* (Hart, *The Poems of Ancient Tamil,* 24).
20. Pillai, *A Primer of Tamil Literature,* 4.
21. Ibid., 329.
22. Ibid., 31–32.
23. *Aiṅ.*, 243.1, cited in Hardy, *Viraha-bhakti,* 136.
24. *Kuṟi.*, 207, cited in Hardy, *Viraha-bhakti,* 136.
25. Vanamamalai, *Studies in Tamil Folk Literature* (Madras, 1969), 35–36.
26. *Perump.*, 7, cited in Hardy, *Viraha-bhakti,* 136.
27. *Pari.*, VIII. 126, cited in Hardy, *Viraha-bhakti,* 136.
28. *Perump.*, 232f., cited in Hardy, *Viraha-bhakti,* 136.
29. *Mal.*, 394–96, cited in Hardy, *Viraha-bhakti,* 135.
30. Numerous Greek myths reported by Plutarch suggest that human sacrifices were offered at one time to Dionysus.
31. Hardy, *Viraha-bhakti,* 139.
32. Ibid.
33. Hart, *The Poems of Ancient Tamil,* 29.
34. Vanamamalai, *Studies in Tamil Folk Literature,* 125–26.
35. *A Comprehensive History of India,* vol. 2, 569, cited in ibid., 298.
36. Berkson, *The Amazon and the Goddess,* 9.
37. Ibid.
38. Hardy, *Viraha-bhakti,* 136.
39. *PN,* 186, quoted in Kersenboom-Story, "Viṟali," 23.
40. Hart, *The Poems of Ancient Tamil,* 13.
41. Pillai, *A Primer of Tamil Literature,* 303.
42. Ibid., 306.
43. Hart, *The Poems of Ancient Tamil,* 5.
44. *Muttollayiram,* trans. P.N. Appuswami (Calcutta, 1977), quoted in Berkson, *The Amazon and the Goddess,* 10.
45. Dubianski, *Ritual and Mythological Sources,* 61.
46. Pillai, *A Primer of Tamil Literature,* 305.
47. Hart, *The Poems of Ancient Tamil,* 13.
48. Kersenboom-Story, "Viṟali," 24.
49. Pillai, *A Primer of Tamil Literature,* 179.
50. Kersenboom-Story, "Viṟali," 33.
51. *PN,* 109.15–18.
52. Both drummers and bards were of lowly birth in ancient Tamil culture (Hart, *The Poems of Ancient Tamil,* 119).
53. Quoted by Hart, in *The Poems of Ancient Tamil,* 15.

54. Eliade, *Shamanism,* 170–76.
55. Hart, *The Poems of Ancient Tamil,* 16.
56. Ibid., 88.
57. Ibid.
58. Dubianski, *Ritual and Mythological Sources,* 37.
59. Pillai, *A Primer of Tamil Literature,* 310.
60. *Paṭ.*, 45, cited by K. Sivathamby, "The Ritualistic Origins of Tamil Drama," paper presented at First International Tamil Conference-Seminar, Kuala Lumpur, Malaysia, April 1966.
61. *Mat.*, 25–27, cited by Hardy, in *Viraha-bhakti,* 136.
62. K. Sivathamby "Ritualistic Origins."
63. Hart, *The Poems of Ancient Tamil,* 88.
64. *Tolkappiyam. sūtra* 76, cited by K. Sivathamby in "Ritualistic Origins."
65. Ibid.
66. Pillai, *A Primer of Tamil Literature* (Madras, 1904).
67. E.S. Muthuswami, *Tamil Culture as Revealed in Tirukkural* (Madras, 1994), 128.
68. *TMA*, 46–51, cited by Sivathamby in "Ritualistic Origins."
69. *Naṟṟ.*, 70, cited by Pillai, in *A Primer of Tamil Literature,* 127.
70. Vanamamalai, *Studies in Tamil Folk Literature,* 126.
71. Ibid.
72. Ibid., 127.
73. Ibid., 147.
74. Pillai, *A Primer of Tamil Literature,* 317.
75. Ibid., 318.
76. *PN,* 246, quoted by Hart, in *The Poems of Ancient Tamil,* 103.
77. "Never voluminous, women's writing became scarcer as society became more rigid, pushing women into the margin of a male-dominated society and making education less accessible to them." [Mandakranta Bose, "Preface," in *Faces of the Feminine,* ix.]
78. Ibid
79. *PN,* 277, quoted by Hart, in *The Poems of Ancient Tamil,* 162.
80. Hart, *The Poems of Ancient Tamil,* 95.
81. Berkson, *The Amazon and the Goddess,* 10.
82. Ibid., 11.
83. Hart, *The Poems of Ancient Tamil,* 200.
84. Cited by Hardy, in *Viraha-bhakti,* 162–63.
85. K.A. Nilakanta Sastri, *The Hindu,* quoted by Pillai, in *A Primer of Tamil Literature,* 14.
86. Kersenboom-Story, "Viṟali," 34.
87. Ibid., 32.
88. Ibid., 34.
89. *The Cilappatikāram of Iḷanko Aṭikaḷ: An Epic of South India,* trans. R. Parthasarathy (New York, 1993).
90. C.A. Menon, *Kālī Worship in Kerala,* sec. edn. (Madras, 1943), 59, cited by Sarah Caldwell, "Waves of Beauty, Rivers of Blood: Constructing the Goddess in Kerala," in *Seeking Mahādevī: Constructing the Identities of the Hindu Great Goddess,* ed. Tracy Pintchman (Albany, 2001), 95.

91. Caldwell, "Waves of Beauty...," 95.
92. Vanamamalai, *Studies in Tamil Folk Literature,* 21–22.
93. Bhattacharyya, *History of the Śākta Religion,* 78.
94. Ibid.
95. *Cil.,* 20: 34–35.
96. Bhattacharyya, *History of the Śākta Religion,* 79.
97. Hart, *The Poems of Ancient Tamil,* 23–24.
98. Bhattacharyya, *History of the Śākta Religion,* 78.
99. R. Nagaswamy, *Tantric Cult of South India* (New Delhi, 1982), 6–7, cited in Berkson, *The Amazon and the Goddess,* 12.
100. Dubianski, *Ritual and Mythological Souress,* 21.
101. See Wolkstein and Kraemer, *Inanna Queen of Heaven and Earth,* 16–18.
102. Bhattacharyya, *History of the Śākta Religion,* 22–28.
103. Ibid., 22.
104. The mother-syllable *Ma,* one of the most fundamental of sounds, is cognate with the first woman in Sumer, Matu, the mother of gods. Pygmies also worship Matu, whose name means both "womb" and "underworld." She was known as Mater Matuta in Rome; as Mat, the mother of the people, by the Hittites; as Ambā, Umā, Jaganmātā, and Mā in India. Among the European Celts, Ma became Danu or Anu, the Mother whose waters were the Danube. Later she became the Mother-goddess in Ireland.
105. *TMA,* 47–56.
106. Dubianski, *Ritual and Mythological Sources,* 15.
107. *AN,* 265.
108. Dubianski, *Ritual and Mythological Sources* 15, n. 23.
109. *AN,* 265.
110. *PP,* 257, 260.
111. Dubianski, *Ritual and Mythological Sources,* 16.
112. Ibid.
113. Ibid., 17, n. 27.
114. Shulman, *Tamil Temple Myths: Sacrifice and Divine Marriage in the South Indian Śaiva Tradition* (Princeton, 1980), 182.
115. Dubianski, *Ritual and Mythological Sources,* 17. [Italics added.]
116. Hart, *The Poems of Ancient Tamil,* 23–24.
117. Bhattacharyya, *History of the Śākta Religion,* 111.
118. Ibid.
119. *Cil.,* XII.67.
120. Brenda E.F.Beck, "A Praise-Poem for Murugan," *Journal of South Asian Literature* 11 (1–2).
121. Dubianski, *Ritual and Mythologica Sources,* 21.
122. Ibid.
123. Ibid., 22, n. 37.
124. Ibid., 35.
125. Ibid., 32–33.
126. Ibid., 35, n. 59.
127. Vanamamalai, *Studies in Tamil Folk Literature,* 22.
128. Ibid., 24–25.
129. Ibid., 22.

130. Ibid., 23.
131. Ibid.
132. Ibid.
133. Ibid.
134. *Cil.*, 23:185–90.
135. Vanamamalai, *Studies in Tamil Folk Literature*, 32.
136. Ibid., 34.
137. Eva C. Keuls, *The Reign of the Phallus: Sexual Politics in Ancient Athens* (New York, 1985), 4.
138. Gabriele Dietrich, "Women and Religious Identities in India after Ayodhya," in *Against All Odds: Essays on Women, Religion and Development from India and Pakistan*, ed. Kamia Bhasin, Ritu Menon, and Nighat Sa'id Khan (New Delhi, 1994), 44.
139. Hart, *The Poems of Ancient Tamil*, 106.

5

The Early Aryans: Vedic through Epico-Purāṇic Eras

The "Civilizing Mission" of Brāhmaṇic Hegemony

Came as nomads and raiders!
Searching for survival and life,
Food fodder females fortunes!
Being deadly dangerous devils,
Turned against the sons of soil,
Dravidians and other *ādivāsīs*!
As nomadic raiders and looters
Always on the move and run—
Valued the Gems and glittering
Materials like Diamond Gold
As also the Sapphires and Silks
Which can be pilfered plundered
Stolen from others rather easily
Stealthily hidden hoarded quickly
Safely taken away with them—
Wherever and whenever they go!
Worn with out any wear or tear,
Shown off exhibited for others!
Continuing with these evil traits
Keep exploiting SC and ST dalits
Working classes of all Shudras
To acquire add and accumulate
Gold, Silk, Diamonds, Sapphires!
And an easy way of good life—

With all the comforts of World
With out having to ever work!
—A Dravidian[1]

The Ṛgvedic tribes loathed agriculture and refused to cultivate the soil themselves, regarding it as the occupation of the *ādivāsīs* and Dravidians. This was later reinforced by the *Laws of Manu*, which forbade members of brāhmaṇa and kṣatriya castes to engage in agricultural work, but ordained it for the vaiśya caste.[2] Although there were some female deities in the pantheon of the Ṛgvedic tribes, the conception of the female principle ran against the grain of their patriarchal worldview. The Vedic religion is characterized by a predominance of gods, while goddesses "may be said to be almost conspicuous by their absence or unimportance."[3] Since cultivation was not the dominant mode of food production of the Ṛgvedic tribes, Pṛthivī or Earth Mother was an anachronism and is invoked only twice in the *Ṛgveda*.[4] The purely pastoral economy of the Vedic Aryans ultimately declined after the introduction of the ox-drawn plow, but their heirs retained their highly patriarchal bourgeois social organization and patrilineal inheritance. The misogyny of Ṛgvedic males may have been sharpened by the fact that they had never experienced domination by women in the fields.

Bourgeois Ideology

My use of the term *bourgeois* refers to a specific ideological system incorporating the caste/class patriarchal social structure, property ownership, and male domination. The bourgeois system annihilated the more egalitarian, often matriarchal tribal system, and is its antithesis. It is an exploitive system that glorifies and promotes the individual, greed, and monopoly. To Kosambi, bourgeois greed for property was the true purpose of the brāhmaṇical process of adoption and assimilation of non-brāhmaṇical tribal and village deities and rites. In pre-class egalitarian tribes and villages, neither the patriarchal institutions of land ownership, surplus agricultural production, monopoly of the means of production, nor the caste/class system had previously existed to any significant degree. The term *bourgeois* connotes the historical developments in the means and relations of production, the primacy of male property holding, and the caste/class system in which the impoverished masses labor for the tiny privileged nonproductive class. The term acknowledges the cultural universe of the subordinate classes, particularly women, and provides a framework that facilitates the recovery of suppressed folk history.

The bourgeois system is not different in intent from later feudalism, when land was traded for cash; the system was transformed in India into capitalism with British domination, when feudal lords became bourgeois landowners. In feudalism, property holding was also paramount, and former tribal lands were controlled by the elites: Tamil kings in the south and Vedic Aryans in the north appropriated the land of indigenes and made serfs of the tribals. The serfs who worked the land were sharecroppers who received a portion of what was produced, even under usufruct rights. Wealthy landlords were made aware that they could have higher returns from their lands by paying wages to serfs who were now "workers," thus allowing them to buy their own commodities. In turn, this enabled landlords to manipulate the difference between prices and wages and squeeze the laborers. The elites' interest became selling and profiting, as it remains today.

The term "civilizing mission," although coined by nineteenth century British imperialists along with the theory of "the white man's burden" to rationalize their conversion of indigenes into marginalized Christians, is applicable to the brāhmaṇic aggression against both indigenous peoples and high-caste women. The brāhmaṇas' justification for the imposition of strict marital laws was the innate promiscuity of women, which required restraint by early marriage and constant supervision by male kinsmen. Their imposition of harsh, inhumane, and segregating caste laws on the indigenes was ostensibly based on the purity of the high born, which at all costs had to be protected from the pollution of the low-born. While Tamils had an ironic sense of pollution, and assigned to the low-born the most sensitive spiritual tasks (as did the later Tantrics), the brāhmaṇas' notion of pollution would not permit any association with the lowly for fear of contamination or miscegenation. Thus the landless laborers were bracketed with high-caste women, and their common subjugation by the civilizing/brāhmaṇizing mission of male elites was the backdrop against which Ko<u>rr</u>avai/Kālī played out her part. The objectives of the brāhmaṇas—to institute the patriarchal bourgeois mode, to increase the property and power of male elites, to convert tribals to indentured agricultural labor, and to control the reproductive functions of high-caste women—were realized in a two-layered strategy of conquest in which high-caste women and the subjugated domain of tribals and villagers would slowly be disempowered, tamed, and forced into servitude.

The Caste System

Historians and social theorists have often failed to grasp that social organization by caste divisions is not unique to India. The unequal distribution of wealth, political power, and access to goods, education, and services in all non-egalitarian societies often means inborn privileges for the elite at the expense of legally and/or socially sanctioned persecution of those viewed as socially and spiritually inferior. The notion of private property caused class/caste stratification in ancient and medieval patriarchal agriculture societies, in which an elite class was formed by landowners and warrior-priests, and social privileges varied according to social rank, with landless laborers and slaves constituting the bottom of the hierarchy. The corollary to this premise is that primal cultures that are not predicated on private land ownership, but rather jointly work ancestral land, deified as Mother Earth, are sexually integrated, egalitarian, and basically unwarlike, non-hierarchical, cooperative, "immediate return" societies such as Mbuti pygmies. Such village communities may have once thrived throughout India, and some still survive, especially in the hills.

Most contemporary civilizations, including the United States, Mexico, Europe, Africa, the Near East, and Asia, have caste-like divisions in their histories based on land ownership. The Samurais (warrior nobles) and priests of medieval Japan justified caste oppression by doctrines of purity and defilement; members of society who carried out "unclean" tasks were treated as pariahs, as they are in India. Of all the ancient civilizations, the Roman civilization was one of the most stratified and oppressive; encoded into law were a multitude of caste-like inequities, in addition to legalized slavery. European knights and landed barons in the Christian era were born with a plethora of privileges under feudalism, including their own law courts, while artisans were discriminated against and female aristocrats were treated as the property of their male kinsmen, who arranged daughters' marriages and dowries.

As Kosambi maintained, an important clue to understanding India's past lies in the socioeconomic transition from tribe to caste, and from small local groups to a generalized society.[5] Because of the muscle-power labor needed for the multiple oxen-drawn plough, agriculture shifted from the ken of women and digging sticks to the domain of men, ploughs, domesticated animals, irrigation, and the bourgeois caste/class system of land ownership elitism. The first food production on a large scale in India (present-day Pakistan) was introduced by the Indus culture in the valley of the Indus river in West Panjab and Sind from *c.* 3700 BCE–1800 BCE (the flowering of the Indus Valley age, according to Kak, was 2600–1900 BCE),[6] followed by the ambitious hegemonic expansion 1,800 kilometers to the east into the Gangetic basin, which was completed by *c.* 700 BCE. The great expansion "required totally different techniques of food production, accompanied by a new social organization—caste," explains Kosambi, "Such a diffusion would not have been feasible under primitive conditions without an early stage of the caste system under which the fruits of labor could be expropriated without slavery."[7] The twice-born upper castes, who were demarcated from the others by the early brāhmaṇas, had to observe the precepts of Śruti (the Vedas) and of Smṛti (the auxiliary texts to the Vedas, particularly the Dharmaśāstras). *Dharma* lay in conforming to the individual social observances and ritual functions of each caste. The nature of belief in any particular deity was ambiguous, and theism was not required; rather, the focus of brāhmaṇic worship was the *yajña* or sacrificial ritual.

Caste, "the spinal cord of Hinduism, . . . the anchor of the Hindu ship,"[8] is basically a system of apartheid developed by the brāhmaṇas to support and perpetuate their economic and religious monopoly. The system was first presented metaphorically in the form of Cosmic Man in the Puruṣasūkta of the *Ṛgveda*,[9] a classic male creation tale intended to create a sense of the unity of all brāhmaṇic social constructs, in which humankind was, due to past *karma*, divided into four separate but dependent categories at birth. The four caste groups that form Puruṣa are brāhmaṇas, effete intellectuals and privileged scholars who impose their system of knowledge on the next generation, issuing from the mouth of Puruṣa; kṣatriyas, warriors and kings, from his arms; vaiśyas, merchants, bankers, and traders, who keep society running, from his thighs; and śūdras, the serfs who work the land and produce India's food, from his feet. At the bottom of the śūdra caste are the untouchables, whose only occupations are to haul human sewage, mend shoes, cremate the dead, and other lowly, "polluting" tasks. These people exist below Puruṣa's feet, shameful exiles from Cosmic Man and humanity. The untouchables are classified thus because even their shadow crossing one's path mandates that one remove and discard her clothes, and if an individual accidentally touches an untouchable, she must perform drastic ablutions to purify herself.

Caste is a hereditary system from which there is no escape in Hindu India, and which "ensures no revolution from within or without."[10] After centuries of transformation, each caste has developed many sub-castes; at least two thousand castes exist today in India. Approximately 20 to 25 percent of the total Hindu population is comprised of untouchables, and about 85 per cent of the total Hindu population is of the śūdra caste, constituting a system that separates the races and privileges Aryans.[11] The only antidote for untouchability and bonded servitude is conversion to a religion that promotes human equality.

The method used to determine caste or subcaste position is murky; scholars propound various theories of caste determination, including religious, social, tribal, occupational, and division of labor arguments. *Varṇa*, or color, is the word for caste, and the untouchables are "[c]ollectively . . . the black people of India."[12] Many scholars maintain that the notion of *varṇa* is embedded in the Aryan conquest of Dravidians.

> [Aryans] found [India] occupied by *Adi-Dravidians* and *Dravidians*, a dark-skinned people. . . . Their descendants are the oppressed "low caste" Untouchables of today's India. The Aryans quickly subjugated the natives. . . . and built up another civilization known as . . . Hindu Civilization. To perpetuate (their) enslavement . . . Hindu intruders created the diabolical caste system, which excluded the dark-skinned Dravidians from their society and made them serfs. . . . Caste originally was a color bar in India. . . . Gradually over the centuries it became the foundation of a religiously ordained social fabric for the Hindu people. The four original divisions had multiplied like cancer cells into almost 5,000 sub-castes, 1,836 for the Brahmins alone. Every occupation had its caste, splitting society into a myriad of closed guilds in which a man was condemned by his birth to live, work, marry and die.[13]

The highly developed northern society and its newly acquired knowledge of metals sponsored the next major offensive, into the peninsula proper.

Because the new territory was more varied, it could not be settled in the same way as the northern region, and caste developed new functions. As they pursued their course of clearing the forests in the Ganges Valley for large-scale agriculture, the brāhmaṇas and warriors confiscated tribal and village lands in the name of local rulers and converted communally owned tribal land into private holdings.[14] Almost every extant copperplate (discovered throughout the country by the ton) is a charter that records land-grants to brāhmaṇas that were not linked to any temple.[15] The brāhmaṇas, as legitimizers of political authority, thus became major landowners beginning in the first century AD, and "the institutions that emerged out of these grants such as the *agrahāras* became centres of control over rural resources as well as of brāhmaṇical learning and practice."[16] *Matsyanyāya,* a political doctrine in which "the big fish swallowed the little fish in a condition of anarchy,"[17] became the competitive credo of the Aryan patriarchs:

> [T]he tribal peoples . . ., unable to maintain themselves by their traditional mode of production, had to come in contact with the advanced peoples and were put in different social grades on the basis of the quality of services they offered to the existing class society. Thus the tribes subsisting on war and plunder could easily become kṣatriyas by offering their war-services to the king while those depending on lower occupations (*hīnaśilpas*) formed sub-castes among the śūdras. Such a process, of tribes coming into the fold of the caste system, had always been an important characteristic of Indian society, and its religious reflex was also of great historical consequence.[18]

Conversion or Marginalization/Pauperization of Tribals

Brāhmaṇa missionaries became pioneers in undeveloped localities, first bringing plough agriculture to replace slash-and-burn cultivation, or hunter-gatherer economies, and then offering their knowledge about new crops, distant markets, village organization, and trade. As a result, kings or kings-to-be invited brāhmaṇas, generally from the Gangetic basin, to settle in and develop vast unopened expanses of tribal lands. In feudalism, caste was transformed into an administrative function that ensured the labor of the primary producer without overt coercion. Plough agriculture and the introduction of iron technology into the Ganges valley, as well as irrigation systems, a change in crop patterns with a dependence on rice agriculture, and the use of labor in these new technologies,[19] led ultimately to the growth of urban centers and a non-productive elite that was supported by the labor of landless peoples.

A few brāhmaṇas of a different persuasion progressed into the dense forest to the east in fairly small groups with their own cattle; some even managed the trek alone, with no property and no arms for defense or hunting. They were obviously innocuous, and their very gentleness was instrumental in their coming to terms with the food-gathering Naga[20] natives of the forest, whom they often joined or with whom they lived on friendly terms. The tribals' highly developed knowledge about the medicinal uses of native plants was written and systematized by these brāhmaṇas as *Āyurveda.* In contrast, traders were transported by armed kṣatriyas to protect them against the aboriginal niṣādas. These kṣatriyas grew into mercenary groups willing to fight indiscriminately for hire.[21]

In the egalitarian tribes and villages targeted by the brāhmaṇas, neither the patriarchal institutions of surplus agricultural production, land ownership, monopoly of the means of production, nor the caste/class system had previously existed. It is understandable that such tribes hold out against servitude in the feudal system as long as they can, since primitive subsistence agriculture controlled by women is superior to a male-dominated agrarian system in many ways.[22] Most of the indigenous tribals who survived genocidal onslaughts were branded as peasants who cultivated the land, or śūdras,[23] the lowest caste in the brāhmaṇic system, who "still regarded land as territory deriving from kinship rights."[24] These people were regarded very much like tribal cattle; they were not, as were the three higher castes, recognized as Aryan with full membership in the tribe. The three respectable (bourgeois) castes, the brāhmaṇas (brahmin priests), kṣatriyas (warriors and rulers), and vaiśyas (the settlers who produced all the food surplus by agriculture and cattle-breeding), had a common need for chattel slaves to labor as complements to means of production such as plows, oxen, and appropriated land. The creation of the śūdra caste eliminated this need, since śūdras could always produce the expropriable surplus. The fact that subjugated indigenes were toiling in the fields to support the nonproductive elites was justified by dharma, the moral code instituted to preserve the relative spiritual and physical purity of high-caste males. As Bandyopadhyaya explicates:

> From the later Vedic age, the abstract ethical conception of Dharma came to play a prominent part in the social ideal of the Indian thinkers. Dharma in their eyes upheld the universe and comprised the natural duties of mankind or its sections taken separately in relation to the social whole. It was regarded as the basic principle in the evolution of the various aspects of the phenomenal world. Applied to mankind or to different sections, Dharma comprised that body of rules and precepts of life which, if obeyed, conduced to man's happiness (both mundane and spiritual) and prosperity. Dharma, as such, was the basic element in the maintenance of the moral order of the rāṣṭra and the head of the state was under an obligation to maintain it.[25]

Brāhmaṇism was supported by rent from land and fees for religious services which were inheritable and given in perpetuity. The position of the brāhmaṇa in the body-politic, thanks to his divine link with moral imperatives and human destinies, was really quite remarkable. He held coordinate authority with the king, he was exempt from taxation, he was given immunity from all corporeal punishments for crimes and sins, and he was the monopolistic caretaker of the spiritual life of the people. The brāhmaṇa and the king are expressly declared the upholders of the *rāṣṭra* in the *Gautama Dharmasūtra.* Vaśiṣṭha, who supported this view, attributed the brāhmaṇa's exemption from taxation to his spiritual services of protecting and blessing the people. Therefore, he and the king enjoyed similar immunities and, since the brāhmaṇa was "the protector of moral life, the expounder of the mysteries of Dharma, and his tapas brought peace to society,"[26] the privileges of the brāhmaṇa outstripped those of the kings, who were merely the physical protector of dharma. When brāhmaṇas committed crimes and sins, corporeal punishment was substituted with "horrible penances of self-mortification.... The karma theory contributed to its elaboration. For, since there was no redemption except through actual suffering, the absolution from regal chastisement could not ease the sufferings of the soul in lives yet to come. Hence penance was necessary, inasmuch as it freed men from sufferings which were the necessary consequences of violation of Dharma."[27]

The prosperity and safety of the kingdom depended on "the closest possible cooperation"[28] between brāhmaṇa and king. The "Rājādharma"[29] depicts the interdependence of the brāhmaṇa and the kṣatriya castes, and proposes a compromise between the extreme claims of the rival elements, viz., the political aspirations of the ruling elites are synthesized with dharma idealism. This text equates the high virtue, status, and privilege of brāhmaṇas, as well as their role as divinely inspired protectors and proprietors of the universe, with their intimate relation with dharma: "*brāhmaṇo jāyamāno hi pṛthivyāmadhijāyate / īśvarāḥ sarvabhūtānāṃ dharmakośasya guptaye //*" As Bandyopadhyaya insists, such

> constant extolling of the position and the privilege of the Brāhmaṇas and their description as mundane gods was not the only sequel to the elaboration of the Brāhmaṇical Dharma ideal. This later gave rise also to an abnormal conception as to the possibility of governance with a moral ideal and without any coercive authority. The rule of Dharma came to be the ideal condition of human excellence and consequently, the highest stage of man's moral self-realization. The influence of this idea is apparent not only in the conception of the primeval state of nature characterized by the absence of coercive authority but also in the dream of an ideal social existence in which individuals were to be freed from coercion or punishment and the object of the latter is to be attained by penance and moral regeneration.[30]

At the bottom of the caste system were marginal tribals, some still extant, who propitiated fierce goddesses:

> When there are forests close by one may still see people like the Kāthkaris of the Western Ghāṭs, or the Mundas and Orāons of Bihār who are barely out of the food-gathering stage. Such marginal tribesmen are dying out because of disease, drunkenness, the disappearance of forests, the advance of civilization and of moneylenders. If these people practice cultivation, it is often mere slash-and-burn on shifting plots. If they provide irregular labor at harvest-time along with the poorest of the peasants who have regular landholdings, they are paid less and generally in kind. As a rule they have also the right of gleaning

after the harvest whether they have helped in the work or not. Some hunting, eating insects, rats and mice, snakes, and even monkeys . . ., the chaff and leavings of peasant cultivation supplement their diet. They still practice witchcraft on a deadlier level than the peasant; at least Indian newspapers announce every few years the arrest and trial of tribal men and women in a group, on suspicion of ritual murder (human sacrifice). Their primitive tribal gods have something in common with the lower village gods. Often they pay worship to the gods of a village and the village recognizes their deities, too. The country festivals that draw many villagers from a distance can often be traced back to a primitive tribal origin, though the actual tribe may have vanished. The names of local village cults also prove such primitive beginning. Often a peasant caste bears the same name as some aboriginal tribe in the same region. The two groups no longer intermarry, for the peasant has become a superior being; in fact the difference in food supply, ampler and more regular diet, changes the physique and even facial index in a few generations. Nevertheless, some traces of common origin remain and are admitted; sometimes by a common annual worship, particularly of mother goddesses with peculiar names not known in other villages.[31]

The aboriginal fertility rites of head-hunting and head-offering (human sacrifice) pervaded most of the marginalized tribes. As historian Basham writes,

> The Gonds of the Eastern Deccan offered human sacrifices at their fertility ceremonies until well into the last century, the victims often being unfortunate villagers kidnapped from the more civilized settlements, while head-hunting among the Nagas of Assam is even now not completely stamped out. At one time, of course, practically the whole of India was inhabited by such peoples, and in ancient and medieval times they were more numerous and occupied a wider area than at present. . . . Many primitive peoples were exterminated and many more lost their identity in the course of the growth of Hindu civilization; but some accepted the suzerainty of their civilized overlords, and retained their ancestral lands. The *Arthaśāstra* mentions such people as useful in times of war. Many of these tribes came more and more under the influence of Aryan ways, and their tribal cults were roughly assimilated to Hinduism by wandering brāhmaṇas. Such tribes were undoubtedly the ancestors of many lower Hindu castes of later times. Some primitive tribes may well have learnt enough to become powerful, and it has been reasonably suggested that more than one important medieval dynasty originated in such a way.[32]

Settled villagers lived in continuous fear of the wild tribesmen, who, according to Sanskrit and Dravidian medieval literature, continued to live freely in the outlying districts, pillaging crops, herds, and houses, as well as kidnapping victims for human sacrifice. The brāhmaṇas gradually squeezed tribals off their ancestral lands, and tribes became less dangerous as greater and greater numbers were assimilated into the brāhmaṇical fold. Eventually, most of the tribes that resisted the oppression of plough agriculture and the patriarchal caste/class system through violent struggle and battles were either exterminated in massive genocide or pushed off their territory by population pressure, thus forced to survive either by theft, work on the feudal farms, or begging (the latter being the primary occupation of *yogīs* and *yoginīs*). As land became more scarce in relation to population, tribal food-gathering groups were relegated to the servile *jāti*[33] or śūdra castes. Kosambi analyzes the system as follows:

> This theoretical system is roughly that of classes, whereas the observed castes and sub-castes derive clearly from tribal groups of different ethnic origin. Their very names show this. The relative status of the small local castes depends always upon the extent of, and the caste's economic position in, the common market. . . . The lower one goes in the economic scale, the lower the caste in the social scale on the whole. At the lowest end we still have purely tribal groups many of whom are in a food-gathering stage. The surrounding general society is now food-producing. So food-gathering for these very low castes generally turns into begging and stealing. Such nethermost groups were accurately labelled the "criminal tribes" by the British in India because they refused as a rule to acknowledge law and order outside the tribe.[34]

Mythic Legitimization of Tribal Oppression

The judicious utilization of religious symbology and beliefs enabled the brāhmaṇas to convert the system of production to the patriarchal feudal or bourgeois mode, to dismantle the archaic egalitarian and usually matriarchal tribal structure, and to establish caste as the mandatory new system of social organization in which the brāhmaṇas were preeminent. Plough agriculture and the brāhmaṇas who introduced it became the major agencies of social control in caste society, and local folk cults were "Sanskritized"[35] or co-opted by such means as interjecting officiating brāhmaṇa priests and rituals into aboriginal religious rites, identifying tribal spirits and deities with epic heroes and heroines, and embroidering legends about tribal cults and deities into Sanskrit mythology. Kosambi, who traced this process in part by the evolution of clan totems into clan names and then into caste names, parses the stages of the assimilation:

> It can easily be shown that many castes owe their lower social and economic status to their present or former refusal to take to food production and plough agriculture. The lowest castes often preserve tribal rites, usages, and myths. A little higher up we see these religious observances and legends in transition, often by assimilation to other parallel traditions. Another step above, they have been rewritten by brāhmiṇs to suit themselves, and to give the brāhmiṇ caste predominance in the priesthood, which in the lower castes is generally not in the hands of brāhmiṇs. Still higher we come to what is called "Hindu" culture, the literate traditions that often go back to much older times. But even these stories of gods and demons are basically much the same in the lower groups. The main work of brāhmiṇism has been to gather the myths together to display them as unified cycles of stories, and to set them in a better-developed social framework. Either many originally different gods and cults are identifed (syncretism) or several deities made into a family or into a royal court of the gods. At the very top come the philosophical developments formulated by the great religious leaders of Indian history.[36]

Pl. I. Group of young women and men planting rice in a flooded terraced field. Aṅgami, Yorobami village, 1936.

Pl. II. Circular stone sitting platform, *tehuba*, situated in front of the house of the descendant of the village founder, *kemovao*. Both irrigated and dry terraces can be seen in the background. Aṅgami, Khonoma village, 1918–45.

Pl. III. Girls winnowing. Konyak, Longhai village, 1937.

Pl. IV. Sagazumi village. The horns on the houses show status gained through Feasting. Aṅgami, 1936.

Pl. V. Soul effigies and grave goods are placed under a pipal tree in which corpse platforms are placed for exposure. Konyak, Totok village, 1918–45.

Pl. VI. Head-tree. Chang, Tuensang village, 1947. For the Lhota, the "head-tree," which stood at the center of the village, was the symbol of village unity. Heads taken in raids were hung on the tree, and sacred stones arranged at its roots.

Pl. VII. Men in full dress dancing at the annual ceremony after sowing, the Moatsu. Ao, Uṅgma village, 1918–45.

Pl. VIII. Bull mithun. Saṅgtam, Changtorr village, 1947.

Pl. IX. Girls dancing at the Spring festival. Konyak, Chingphoi village, 1937.

Pl. X. Simulated attack with guns and daos.

Pl. XI. Head-taker's dance. Konyak, Wakching village, 1936.

Pl. XII. Chapel with a picture of Jesus Christ on the crossbeam behind carved hornbills. Angami, Sangratsu village, 1986.

New brāhmaṇic rituals and special dates of the lunar calendar for particular observances were established over which only the brāhmaṇas could officiate. Appropriate myths were fabricated to introduce and legitimize new places of pilgrimage (situated on indigenous goddess cult spots), to integrate diverse groups by creating common origins (e.g., myths of descent), as well as to legitimize the changing social and political condition caused by brāhmaṇic hegemony. The *Mahābhārata* and the *Rāmāyaṇa,* which depict the social and military position of the ruling caste in ancient India, and especially the Purāṇas[37] are filled with such legitimizing mythology.

Both the *Mahābhārata* and Purāṇic texts borrow from the Ṛgvedic Puruṣa-sūkta and depict in myth a rationalization of the confiscation of tribal territory in the well-known story of Pṛthu.[38] The myth relates that various body parts of the wicked king Veṇa, who had to be murdered by the *ṛṣis* because of his unrighteous rule, were "churned" or dismembered (alluding to human sacrifice) to create his successors: from his left thigh was churned niṣāda, who, proving inadequate, was expelled to the forest to live as a hunter-gatherer. From Veṇa's right arm was churned the righteous Rājā Pṛthu, who introduced cattle-keeping and agriculture and bestowed so many benefits on the Earth, *pṛthivī,* that in gratitude, she gave him her name. Veṇa was deemed wicked and killed by the *ṛṣis* because he stopped performing the sacrificial ritual. The niṣādas are described in the Purāṇas[39] as black, low-statured, short-armed, with copper-colored hair, high cheekbones, low-tipped noses, and red eyes. They were known to live especially by hunting. Likewise, the Buddhist Jātakas describe them as foresters and hunters.[40] "The dark, short, ugly niṣāda became the prototype of all forest-dwelling people," writes Thapar. "The myth sought to legitimize the expulsion of such groups when land was cleared and settled by agriculturalists."[41] As the Rudrādhyāya of the *Yajurveda*[42] verifies, half of the eight tribes associated with the niṣādas were hunters (Vrāta, Puñjiṣṭha, Svanin, and Mṛgayu), and the other half was comprised of members of the lower castes with no steady occupation (Kakṣan, Rathakāra, Kulāla, and Karmāra). Significantly, *ni* means "down" and *sad* means "to settle."

Similarly, in the *Bhagavadgītā,* the king is equated with God, and complete submission of individual desire and tribal law to divine will is required of all people. Arjuna, the hero, was forced to break the most accursed tribal taboo of killing his kinsmen in order to metaphorically disintegrate indigenous tribal values and convert the values of subaltern people to new conceptions of social relations based on the monopoly of state power. The structures of tribes and castes were diametrically opposite, and "the gradual conversion began with the assimilation of ruling groups among tribal societies into Hindu society generally by their being given kṣatriya status."[43] Thus, the autochthonous religious beliefs were incrementally syncretized with those of the brāhmaṇic cults, and community-based tribal order was replaced by patriarchal class society.

Brāhmaṇas, like priest everywhere in all times, were regarded as "human gods," divine seers (*ṛṣis*) with a direct line of communication between the gods and humankind, and the only men capable of properly performing the fire sacrifices that held the universe together and guaranteed successful cattle raids and attacks on villages. The ancient Indo-European mythical sacrifice and dismemberment of the world-soul in the form of an astral man or bull is common to Orphism, the Iranian Magi, and the Indian brāhmaṇas. The slaying of the First Man and the mythic bull constitutes the masculine countertext to the Great Mother of the Animals as the Creatrix of the world, and is the male cosmogonic source-myth of the sacrifice of both the Iranian First Man, Gayomart, and the Primordial Bull and the Vedic Cosmic Man or *Puruṣa* (Varuṇa). The mythic blood sacrifice was mimed by priests performing Indo-Iranian fire sacrifices based on homeopathic magic.

In their hegemonic expansion eastward, Aryan warriors were resisted by guerilla groups of indigenes in organized warfare. The tribals were only equipped with elephants and weapons, while the Aryans had horse-drawn chariots, each flanked by a warrior on foot, hence the Aryan's rapid victories in the north. The Indian indigenes, unlike the ruling class elites, did not believe that the brāhmaṇas were superior to them because of their monopoly on Sanskrit or because of their pale skin (*ārya-varṇa*). The two races gradually comingled and class distinctions were institutionalized later into four main classes based on the anatomical structure of the Cosmic Man.

Bhattacharyya has pointed out that the roots of Indian demonology lie in the Vedas, and "Vedic demonology is basically anthropomorphic, its personae being recruited from the gods of alien countries, races and religions, indigenous hostile tribes, and natural phenomena."[44] Basically, Indian demons are derived from the spirits of enemies. Many characteristics of the demons and malevolent spirits of Hindu mythology—*nāgas, yakṣas, rākṣasas, ḍākiṇīs, yoginīs,* and so on—can be traced to the marginal ("untamed" or "wild") tribes, and the Śakti cult, "with all its heterogeneous and theological fabrications," according to Dasgupta, "may be regarded as a contribution to the complex texture of the Hindu religion and culture mainly if not solely, by . . . the non-Aryan aborigines."[45]

It is a common warrior strategy to demonize the enemy or opponent, and it is due to their requisite martial function that demons have a long history in world religions. Vedic men, like all warring men throughout prehistory and history, saw the world as a Manichean, black and white structural binary of cosmic war between the demons (*asuras*) and themselves, the gods (*devas*). The term *asura* is cognate with the Zoroastrian Ahura (anti-god), signifying a demon or enemy of the gods. The last book of the *Ṛgveda* and the *Atharvaveda* both depict *asura* in this original sense of grand polarity. The word *asura* is without doubt of Indo-Iranian origin,[46] derived from the root *as*, meaning at once "to be" (the forms of existence) and "to frighten away," hence signifying the fierce aspect of deities. "The term *asura* came to represent some of the gods of pre-Vedic India," writes Alain Daniélou.

> Like other socioreligious groups, the peoples who fought for the domination of the Indian continent tended to represent their ideal of life, of morality, of goodness, the divine powers who protected their homes, their cattle, their society, as the true gods and the divinities protecting the other side as antigods or demons. Thus the Vedic poet saw mankind divided into the noble Aryas, worshipers of the gods and doers of sacrifices, and the unholy Dasyus (barbarians), builders of sinful cities, expert in magic. The heavens were similarly divided between the gods and the antigods.[47]

Supremely dualistic (a hallmark of patriarchy), the cosmic war mythic structure has survived in India and the present Islamic world since prehistory. Writ supremely large in the Muslim notion of struggle, *jihād*, this cosmology "has been employed for centuries in Islamic theories of both personal salvation and political redemption."[48] It was a key principle in Indo-Iranian religion before the two theologies split about 2500 BCE, and has remained paramount in the religious, political, and cultural ideology of Islamic societies to the present time.

The Aryans attempted to preserve their ethnic characteristics, especially their light-colored skin (*ārya-varṇa*) from "pollution" by intermarriage with the dark-skinned (*dasyu-varṇa*) Dravidians, or with the black-skinned proto-Australoids. The great Indra himself gave "protection to the Aryan color."[49] The double paranoia generated by ideals of the *Übermensch*, racial purity, and the consequent fear of miscegenation is common to Hinduism, American Christianity in the southern states before and after the civil rights era, and Nazism. As Swami Vivekananda, one of Gandhi's closest advisors, analyzed caste and *varṇa* in 1900 to an audience in Pasadena, California:

> There is something in caste, so far as it means blood: such a thing as heredity there is, certainly. Now try to [understand]—why do you not mix your blood with the Negroes, the American Indians? Nature will not allow you. Nature does not allow you to mix your blood with them. There is the unconscious working that saves the race. That was the Aryan's caste. . . . [W]e know that if certain races mix up, they become degraded. With all the strict caste of the Aryan and non-Aryan, that wall was thrown down to a certain extent, and hordes of these outlandish races came in with all their queer superstitions and manners and customs. Think of this: not decency enough to wear clothes, eating carrion, etc. But behind him came his fetish, his human sacrifice, his superstition, his diabolism. He kept it behind, [he remained] decent for a few years. After that he brought all [these] things out in front. And that was degrading for the whole race. And then the blood mixed; [intermarriages] took place with all sorts of unmixable races. The race fell down. But, in the long run, it proved good. If you mix with Negroes and American Indians, surely this civilization will fall down. But hundreds and hundreds years after, out of this mixture will

come a gigantic race once more, stronger than ever; but, for the time being, you have to suffer. The Hindus believe—that is a peculiar belief, I think; and I do not know, I have nothing to say to the contrary, I have not found anything to the contrary—they believe there was only one civilized race; the Aryan. Until he gives his blood, no other race can be civilized. No teaching will do. The Aryan gives his blood to a race, and then it becomes civilized. Teaching alone will not do. He would be an example in your country: would you give your blood to the Negro race? Then he would get higher culture.[50]

It was necessary for the brāhmaṇas to destroy the *asuras* not for their sins, but for their power, knowledge, and skill, which signaled a dangerous threat to the hegemonic aspirations of the Aryans. Later myths attempted to rationalize the shift in meaning of *asura* by placing Śrī, the goddess of fortune and beauty, in the *asuras'* milieu, dwelling with them in the beginning, when they were good and respectful of divine law. The *asuras* became self-assertive and proud, did not properly attend sacrifices, did not purify themselves at holy places, and challenged the gods. "In the course of time," we read in the *Mahābhārata,* "I saw that the Divine Law had disappeared from them, who were animated by passion and rage."[51] Thus, after temporarily dethroning Indra, they were deserted by Śrī. The demons, tree spirits, ghosts, and geniis worshiped and appeased by the aboriginal tribals and Dravidians, failing the test of divinity, subsequently became *asuras.*

The Purāṇas and the giant epic of divine battle, the *Mahābhārata,* are laced with allusions to cosmic war between the *asuras* and the *suras* (gods), and myths of the *asuras* and the *rākṣasas* proliferate in the Sanskritic tradition. These myths are referring to the Dravidians and autochthons with whom the Aryans were in mortal conflict when they settled northern India; according to Alain Daniélou, they "seem to include many episodes of the struggle of the Aryan tribes against earlier inhabitants of India." The primary *asuras* listed in the *Mahābhārata* are the *daityas* (genii) and the *dānavas* (giants), who were known to the Vedas, the *dasyus* (barbarians), the *nāgas* (serpents), the *piśācas* (eaters of raw flesh), the *kālejas* (demons of Time), *nivāat-kavacas* (wearers of impenetrable armor), *paulomas* (sons of the sage Smooth-Hair [Pulastya]), *kālakaḍjas* (stellar spirits), *khalins* (threshers), and *rākṣasas* (night wanderers).

Vedic and Post-Vedic Sylvan Goddesses

As it travelled along the ancient primitive tracks, the prehistoric routes of migration, the thrusting powers of the goddesses met and mingled, and gained common identity. In their journey across the great land mass, as they absorbed into their identity the massive earth Mātṛkās, virgins yet mothers; the water and vegetal spirits, the *apsarās* and *yakṣiṇīs*; the serpent-headed *nāginīs*; the female ghosts, the *bhūtinīs*; the blood-thirsty *ḍākinīs*; the Yoginīs or the Jogans, the practicers of magic, the forms of the sacred one underwent continuous transformations. A composite form of the female energies emerged as Mātā or

Devī. Neither male nor female nor neuter, incandescent with power and mystery; intimately linked with earth, water, vegetation; she held within her sacred auspicious being the secrets of life and destruction, fertility and death.[52]

* * *

I will be born
again and again.
As a devil,
a ghost,
as Kali,
and Isaki.
As the vengeful furies
I will terrorize you and follow you—

— dalit poem

Organized religions are descended from folk religions, which in turn emerged from the human predisposition to attribute *agency* to all complex life forms that move. Folk goddesses and female spirits mentioned in the *Atharvaveda* were worshiped and propitiated by their devotees, including women, "the folk," and warriors. The female deities subsumed unmarried sylvan goddesses or sacred tree spirits such as *yakṣiṇīs* (*yakṣīs*) and *apsarās, mātṛkās,* fairies, genii, demonesses, goblins, *rākṣasas* (witches or "night wanderers" to Aryans, but they in fact were the aboriginal tribal guerrillas who disturbed Vedic sacrifices), *nāginīs, bhūtinīs* (female ghosts), and fierce tribal goddesses, the latter demonized to serve as models for many of the female deities with malignant powers. As we have seen, Aryans regarded the spirits of tribal enemies as evil foils to conquer. Moreover, tribals had their own pantheons and demons; "they are haunted by evil spirits of all kinds, some malignant fiends, some mischievous elves, to which agency are attributed all forms of sickness and misfortune,"[53] according to N.N. Bhattacharyya. Tribals and simple villagers particularly feared ghosts of human beings, the *bhūta,* "malignant spirits of men, who for various reasons are hostile to the human race."[54] Lurking everywhere in the aboriginal world were evil spirits, hidden in caves, rocks, chasms, ravines, in trees, or in the air, waiting to attack anyone who might pass. They were believed to shift-shape (especially into animals), to afflict disease, and to possess a corpse and speak through his mouth. They were capable of making themselves invisible, and their powers were at their height at midnight, waning during the day.

So villagers turn for protection to the guardian deities of the villages, whose function is to ward off these spirits and protect the villagers from epidemics, cattle-disease, failure of crops, childlessness, fire, and other disasters. The village deities or *grāma-devatās* are generally non-human spirits, mostly female, since women are generally supposed to be more susceptible than men to spirit influence.[55]

Major Vedic goddesses associated with fertility and vegetation included Sītā and Pṛthivī (Earth Mothers), Uṣas (dawn goddess), Sarasvatī (river goddess), Aditi (at once Mother of the Universe, Primordial Vastness, the First Goddess, and Death), and Lakṣmī (Fortune). Kālī does not appear in brāhmaṇic texts until she is mentioned in the *Mahābhārata*, but she was probably a tribal and village goddess at least as early as the Vedic age. Closely related to Kālī is Nirṛti.

Nirṛti

> Whenever yonder person in his thought, and in his speech, offers sacrifice accompanied by oblations and benedictions, may Nirṛti, the goddess of destruction, allying herself with death, smite his offering before it takes effect! May sorcerers, Nirṛti, as well as Rākṣasas, mar his true work with error! May the gods, dispatched by Indra, scatter (churn) his sacrificial butter; may that which yonder person offers not succeed! The two agile supreme rulers, like two eagles pouncing down, shall strike the sacrificial butter if the enemy, whosoever plans evil against us! Back do I tie both thy two arms, thy mouth I shut. With the fury of god Agni have I destroyed thy oblation. I tie thy two arms, I shut thy mouth. With the fury of terrible Agni have I destroyed thy oblation.[56]

The notion of dangerous female deities, "the female principle as the personification of formidable malignant forces,"[57] is deeply rooted in the *Atharvaveda*. This principle is evoked by Nirṛti, the Vedic proto-Kālī, goddess of death, destruction, disease, and misery. Nirṛti is a Vedic deity, "older than Lakṣmī," according to the *Mahābhārata*, known in the *Ṛgveda* as the goddess of destruction and death and in the *Atharvaveda* as the tree goddess propitiated by warriors to guarantee victory in battle. The picture of ambivalence and contradiction, with her long, golden hair, black complexion, and all-black clothing, she was ritually propitiated to avert misfortune. Nirṛti was the crystallization of "poignant forebodings of female forces that destroy embryos and cast magic spells,"[58] and offerings to her were always pushed towards her with the left foot, "indicating her association with the sinister or darker side of life."[59]

Kālī and Nirṛti are both goddesses of death and destruction, *mātṛkās* or *yakṣiṇīs* who live in trees, mountains and hills, crossroads, jungles, caves, and cremation grounds. According to Daniélou, Nirṛti is the guardian protectress of the golden-hearted, downtrodden, luckless majority: "In this world all those who are born under a handicap, in the families of thieves or evildoers, and yet are virtuous and kind are protected by Nirṛti."[60] Nirṛti is said to live in the south, which is regarded as the land of the dead. Her husband and masculine aspect is Nirṛta. In later Hinduism, Nirṛti herself becomes the terrifying the Nirṛta, male *dikpāla* of the Southwest. (The *aṣṭa-dikpālas* are the eight gods that rule the eight directions).

References to Nirṛti in a few hymns of the *Ṛgveda* seek protection from her or seek to drive her away, connoting her role as goddess of death, destruction, calamity, misfortune, and disease.

His life hath been renewed and carried forward as two men, car-borne, by the skilful driver. One falls, then seeks the goal with quickened vigour. Let Nirṛti depart to distant places. Here is the psalm for wealth, and food, in plenty: let us do many deeds to bring us glory. All these our doings shall delight the singer. Let Nirṛti depart to distant places. May we o'ercome our foes with acts of valour, as heaven is over earth, hills over lowlands. All these our deeds the singer hath considered. Let Nirṛti depart to distant places. Give us not up as prey to death, . . . still let us look upon the Sun arising.[61]

In the *Yajurveda*, the sacrificer performs a magic ritual to coax Nirṛti, "she who knoweth all that is born," to unbind and release the iron bonds (of death or at least misfortune) placed by witchcraft on a person to "bind" him:

Homage to thee, O Nirṛti of every form,
Loosen ye this bond made of iron;
Do thou in accord with Yama and Yami
Mount this highest vault.
The bond that Nirṛti, the goddess,
Bound on thy neck, not to be loosened,
This I loosen for thee as from the middle of life;
Then living, let loose, do thou eat the food.
Thee in whose cruel mouth here I make offering,
For the loosening of these bonds,
As "earth" men know thee,
As Nirṛti, I know thee on every side.
Seek the man who poureth not offering nor sacrifices;
The road of the thief and robber thou followest;
Seek another than us, that is thy road;
Homage be to thee, O Nirṛti, O goddess.
Praising Nirṛti, the goddess,
Like a father his son, I weary her with my words;
She who knoweth all that is born,
Discerneth, the lady, every head.
Abode and collector of riches,
Every form she discerneth with might,
Like the god Savitṛ of true laws,
Like Indra, she standeth at the meeting of the ways.[62]

Nirṛti appears to be the first institutionalized fierce goddess in Vedic India. She is specifically described in the *Mahābhārata* as a goddess of poverty and disease, hence we may assume that she is an aboriginal or Dravidian goddess, possibly proto-Ko<u>rr</u>avai, who has been co-opted and demonized by the Aryans. In *Indian Demonology*, N.N. Bhattacharyya categorizes Nirṛti as an "abstract" demon,[63] going on to suggest that Aryan demons originated as the protective deities of Indian indigenes and Dravidians. Thus it is reasonable to consider both Kālī and Nirṛti as derivative of the Dravidian goddess Ko<u>rr</u>avai, and thus anti-brāhmaṇic in inception.

The question is, who are these horrible beings? That they were originally human, neither evil spirits of the hostile dead, or products of pure imagination, is

> attested by sources of the later period. Even in Vedic texts we find they are mortal beings, with wives, and families under a state system headed by the king. The original term *rakṣa*, of which the later *rākṣasa* is a derivative, denotes "protector." Were they the protectors of indigenous beliefs, cults and rituals from the encroaching hands of an alien culture? Data on their material culture and social institutions, religious beliefs, practices, and moral values, and the favors and privileges they used to obtain from Śiva and Devī, obviously lead us to this conclusion. The most striking fact about their activities is that they were opposed to the sacrificial religion of the Vedas. In every case we find them destroying the Vedic sacrifice and creating havoc among its participants. They did not hesitate to kill sages.[64]

"The old witch that peeps from behind the tree trunk is an image charged with formidable potency;"[65] indeed, in the *Mahābhārata*, we are told that Nirṛti's haunt is the sacred fig tree, the *pīpal*, the so-called Tree of Life and of Knowledge inscribed on Indus seals. Nirṛti is described as the older binary opposite of Lakṣmī, the goddess of fortune, who mysteriously visits Nirṛti every Saturday night. Nirṛti was present during the original "churning of the ocean" before Lakṣmī and Vedic goddesses existed. Nirṛti is older than Lakṣmī because she is a primordial autochthonous tribal goddess. The *Mahābhārata* describes her:

> Embodiment of all sins, she appeared at the time of the churning of the ocean before the goddess of fortune, Lakṣmī. Hence she is older than Lakṣmī. Her abode is the sacred fig tree, the *pippala*, where, every Saturday, Lakṣmī comes to visit her. To her realm belong dice, women, sleep, poverty, disease, and all the forms of trouble. She is the wife of Sin (Adharma), the son of Varuṇa. Her sons are Death (Mṛtyu), Fear (Bhaya), and Terror (Mahābhaya).[66]

Lakṣmī

In the Vedic literature of the Aryan conquerors, Lakṣmī and Śrī are both found as goddesses of "fortune," placed in a binary relation with Nirṛti. Lakṣmī is usually represented with only two arms, although she sometimes has four. She holds a lotus. When the ocean was churned by the gods and antigods, she emerged from the waves with a lotus in her hand. She is also represented floating on the ocean of milk seated on a lotus. She is made the consort of Viṣṇu, and later the consort of Rāma. In order to marry her to Rāma, she is identified as Sītā, a furrow created by the plow in the Earth. Lakṣmī's indigenous form as the harvest goddess associated with Mother Earth has been worshiped since the Vedic age by the Indian nonelite. As we have seen, when indigenous tribes were displaced by kings and their armies, tribal goddesses were routinely robbed of their ancient astral and fertility functions and subordinated to the masculine in patriarchal art and literature. The fears and fantasies of the conquering males were reflected in the goddesses they custom-designed to suit their needs. Thus the male authors of the Purāṇas made tribal harvest goddess Śrī (Lakṣmī) subordinate to her overlord Viṣṇu by demoting her from Creatrix into one of Viṣṇu's *śaktis* (wives or powers); i.e., male property, both generic and symbolic. Corresponding sculptural depictions of Lord Viṣṇu in the Gupta period and shortly after place Viṣṇu as the dominant figure, flanked on either side by Śrī (Lakṣmī) and Bhū, or Śrī, and Nīlā. Viṣṇu was only worshiped by elites, and Lakṣmī and Sarasvatī (the latter transformed from a river goddess to the *Śakti* of Brahmā) became the brāhmaṇic models that high caste wives were expected to emulate. Because of her role as *Śakti* of Viṣṇu, Lakṣmī becomes the quintessential *saumya* (or beneficent) wife-goddess—domestic, dependent, disenfranchised, submissive, and servile—and the antithesis of *ugra* Śakti and Nirṛti. (The *Lakṣmī-stotras,* however, also depict Lakṣmī's *ghora* or "terrible" aspect.)

Aditi

Aditi was frequently implored in the *Ṛgveda* to bestow blessings on children and cattle and to provide protection and forgiveness. She was the sky (*dyaus*) and the Earth,[67] the great mother of all the gods (*deva-mātṛ*). Her sons, the Ādityas, the sovereign principles of the universe, included Mitra (solidarity), Aryaman (chivalry), Bhaga (the inherited share), Varuṇa (fate), Dakṣa (ritual skill), Aṁśa (the gods' given share), Tvaṣṭṛ (craftsmanship), Pūṣaṇ (prosperity), Savitṛ (the magic power of words), Viṣṇu (cosmic law), Śakra (courage), and Vivasvat (social laws). Their sovereign principles vary somewhat in the *Mahābhārata*[68] and the Viṣṇu[69] and *Bhāgavata* Purāṇas,[70] but the highest principles of Ṛgvedic society would appear to be Aryan masculinist values applicable to war and conquest, with a complete absence of the female voice.

Sītā

Sītā, one of the first fertility goddesses co-opted by the Vedic Aryans, is personified in *Ṛgveda,* IV.57 as the furrow, Earth's womb, and "spousified" as Indra's wife; the ploughshare (*siraṇi halāni*) was personified as Śunāsīra (Indra). It is probable that Indra morphed into Rāma in the *Rāmāyaṇa,* an epic with the mythic structure of the Demeter-Persephone myth: "The heroine of the epic is born of a field-furrow, abducted by a Pluto of the underworld, and after all her adventures she returns to the earth," asserts Bhattacharyya. "The story of the quest of Sītā by Rāma and his troops resembles that of Demeter's quest for Persephone or that of the quest of Isis for the body of Osiris."[71] A primary difference, of course, is that in the *Rāmāyaṇa* myth, male warriors hunt for the missing goddess, while in the Greek and Egyptian myths, goddesses are heroically and mournfully in quest of their lost loved ones.

In post-Ṛgvedic texts, powerful male gods such as Indra, Mitra, Varuṇa, Pūṣaṇ, and others lost their omnipotence and "were subordinated to the ritualistic principle of *yajña* and in the age of the Upaniṣads and Sūtras to the metaphysical principle known as Brahman."[72] Uṣas disappeared entirely, and Aditi was demoted to the wife of Viṣṇu in the *Vājasaneyi Saṁhitā*[73] and later in the Purāṇas, she was given the sage Kaśyapa as a spouse.

Pṛthivī

Pṛthivī, Earth Mother, became fettered to husband Viṣṇu in the *Mahābhārata.* Legend relates that Pṛthivī, burdened by population pressure, descended down a hundred *yojanas* and asked for Viṣṇu's protection, whereupon Viṣṇu morphed into a boar and saved the now weak and vulnerable goddess, bringing her back up to her proper place. Sītā then assimilated many of Pṛthivī's qualities and became the deity of agriculture, and Pṛthivī's name became fractured into such goddesses as Vaiṣṇavī, Bhū, Mādhavī, Medinī, Dhāraṇī, and others in later texts. A small plaque that is supposedly a representation of Pṛthivī was found in a burial, regarded as Vedic, at Lauṛiyā-Nandangaṛh.

Sarasvatī

Until the Brāhmaṇa literature, Sarasvatī remained a river goddess, but she morphed into Vāc or "creation by the Word" in the Brāhmaṇas, and in post-Vedic myths she is the goddess of wisdom and eloquence and the mother of poetry who revealed language and writing to humankind. Sarasvatī became the spouse of Brahmā. Depicted as a graceful, white woman with two or eight arms, seated on a lotus, with a slim crescent on her brow. The iconography of the eight-armed Sarasvatī includes a lute, a book, a rosary, and an elephant hook, or a mace, a spear, an arrow, a discus, a conch, a plow, a bell, and a bow. No worshiper may read a book or play musical instruments on her consecrated day; rather, books and instruments are cleaned, placed on an altar, and worshiped as the dwelling place of the goddess.

Durgā

Kanaka-Durgā-Amma̱n, originally a Dravidian protectress of animals, was worshiped during cattle epidemics. This goddess had no image or temple. In Bellary, Durgā-Amma̱n was worshiped in an anthill. When she became a higher goddess, she acquired images and temples. In post-Ṛgvedic literature, Durgā, Kālī, Umā, and other archaic tribal goddesses became wives of Śiva. In the *Taittirīya Āraṇyaka*, Durgā-Gāyatrī is also known as Kātyāyanī and Kanyākumārī.

Later goddesses on Mathura coins dated from the second century BCE to the first century AD may be depictions of Durgā or Pārvatī seated either on a full lotus or standing with a lotus in her hand, some with a stag to her right. Bhattacharyya claims that it is not improbable that Durgā is also represented in the coins of Maues (20 BCE–AD 22), Azes I (5 BCE–AD 30), and Azes II, which show a female figure standing between trees.[74] The later Yoginīs and Śākinīs are the attendants of Durgā, and the Bhairavīs are fierce female servants of Śiva and Durgā.

Kālī

Kālī was a tribal and village goddess in both south and north India,[75] a *yakṣiṇī* or *mātṛkā* of great antiquity, the extremely ambivalent Goddess of Life and Death, long before her name was first recorded in the *Mahābhārata*. She was not credited with great significance in elite literature until she exploded from Devī's forehead into the annals of the dominant dharma in the *Devī-māhātmya*.

One would be wrong, however, in interpreting (in the colonial manner) Kālī as the mere primitive vestigial remnant of an arcane tribal antiquity. She and her fierce village *avatāras* have always been powerful and independent transgressors of gender boundaries; brāhmaṇas could not tame her as they did Lakṣmī, Sarasvatī, and even, to an extent, Durgā. They were forced to come to terms with her, on her own terms, in another sterling example of the triumph of the conquered over the conqueror. Despite brāhmaṇic efforts to eliminate animal sacrifice, Kālī and her *avatāras* are the only major deities worshiped in the twenty-first century to whom daily offerings of blood are made. Her stringent demands are met with devotion and self-sacrifice, and she remains the most beloved of goddesses.

Dravidian religion was steeped in the cult of the female principle, and the supreme goddess was Ko<u>r</u><u>r</u>avai in religion and war. As brāhmaṇic hegemony expanded, Tamil "female deities eventually came to be identified with the Purāṇic Pārvatī, Durgā, or Kālī,"[76] writes Bhattacharyya. Since the amalgamation of the archaic Ko<u>r</u><u>r</u>avai with Kālī, the Tamil Dravidians have also worshiped Kālī or Kālī-Amma<u>n</u> as a protectress deity. In Trichinopally villages, Kālī is worshiped as Madurai-Kālī-Amma<u>n</u>, and in the Mahākalikudi village, Kālī is known as Ujiniham-Kālī, attended by Elli-Amma<u>n</u>, Pullathal-Amma<u>n</u>, Viśālākṣī-Amma<u>n</u>, and Angal-Amma<u>n</u>. Non-brāhmaṇas were the original priests of this goddess. In Kerala, Kālī was an aniconic stone worshiped in an open space. The word *kāli* in Malayalam translates as "terrible," and Chutal-Bhadra-Kālī dances with her associates at midnight in her inhospitable abode in the cremation ground. The cult of Kālī in Kerala was originally composed of the underclass, but it came to be adopted by the Nāyars and later by the brāhmaṇas. The Puram, Kālī's festival, lasts several days, when the ritual drama depicting the slaying of Daruka *asura* is performed.

In post-Ṛgvedic texts, Durgā, Umā, and others became wives of Śiva Paśupati. We do not see Kālī's name in Aryan texts until her prominent role in the *Māhābhārata.* Arjuna invokes the goddess in the epic thus:

> I bow to you, leader of the Realized, noble-goddess (Āryā) who dwells in heaven. O tenebrous maiden garlanded with skulls, tawny, bronze-dark, I bow to you who are the auspicious Power of Time, the Transcendent-power-of-Time (Mahā-Kālī).[77]

In the *Muṇḍaka Upaniṣad,*[78] Kālī is one of the seven tongues of *agni.* In Kālī's fierce aspect as the Power-of-Time, "the power of disintegration [is] closely connected to the power of liberation. . . ."[79] Kālī is the quintessential fierce goddess who adores intoxicants, gory blood sacrifices, and lust. The *ḍākiṇīs* (eaters of raw flesh), are Kālī's attendants. Tāntrikas perform violent and orgiastic rituals in her honor. Of her meaning, Daniélou provides a nuanced explication:

> Life and death are inseparable. There is no life without death, no death without life. Hence there must be a common support for life and death. She who supports the living as well as the dead is the supreme happiness. She is the only

help of the living and the only help of the dead. All life rests on her, and on her also depends whatever remains after life. Death is not immediate, total annihilation. The dead leave traces behind which also rest upon her; hence she is represented as wearing on her breast a garland of skulls, the skulls that once carried life and are left behind as the reminders of death.[80]

Rākṣasas

The *rākṣasas* in the myths are tribal guerrillas, to use Daniélou's description, who despise and disrupt the Vedic sacrifices. Bhṛgu's wife, who was originally betrothed to the Rākṣasa Puloman, is kidnapped by a *rākṣasa.* Many alliances were contracted between Aryas and *asuras.* Indra is an intimate friend of the Naga Takṣaka.[81] In the Mahābhārata war, the Kurus are supported on the battleground by *asuras.*[82] Arjuna married King Vāsuki's sister. Mātali's daughter married the Naga Sumukha.[83] The *rākṣasī* woman Hiḍimbā bears a son Ghaṭotkaca, fathered by Bhīma. "The *asuras* are often grouped with different Hindu tribes such as the Kaliṅga, the Magadha, the Nagas,"[84] according to Daniélou. As we have seen, Naga tribes still exist in Assam.

Apsarās

The *apsarās* are sometimes depicted as the antecedents of the *yoginīs* and *ḍākinīs,* "the beauteous deities of vegetation and destiny, of death and wealth that permeate popular lore and art."[85] Eternal virgins, they are dancers, singers, and musicians who live in the waters and trees. They have the power to destroy men's minds with their beauty, and are in a later text known as the wives of Kāma, the god of love. The *matṛ-nāmāni,* hymns in the *Atharvaveda* that are obeisance to the Mothers, include the *apsarās.*

Grāma-devatās

Many of the *grāma-devatās,* local village deities that are almost always goddesses, probably originated as forms of Mother Earth worshiped by the non-Aryan aborigines and Dravidians.[86] For example, Bhūmi or the Earth "has always a place in the village cults and to this divinity are offered cakes, sweetmeats and fruits."[87] The fifty-one *pīṭhas* created by Satī's limbs are honored as sacred parts of the goddess, thus, according to the myth, "the earth is the body of Satī," who is at once "woman, earth, and Goddess."[88] Māriyammaṉ and cognate south Indian goddesses are depicted as heads sitting upon the land. This genre of goddess has been worshiped mainly in connection with agricultural seasons and farmer's astronomy, and therefore would be known to marginalized tribals who practice subsistence shifting agriculture, as well as to the indentured śūdras, untouchables, and tribals working the heavy plows in the fields of the elites.

Birth Goddesses

The birth goddess, or protectress of children, is a descendant of Ice Age goddesses who promote pregnancy, deliver infants safely from their mothers' wombs, and protect them from enemies and danger. Her counterparts in the Mediterranean/Western Asia area were the Greek Artemis and her Roman sister, Diana; the Greek Hera and her Roman equivalent, Juno; and the great Sumerian Ishtar, who were all originally sidereal goddesses associated with the zodiac.[89]

Protectresses were conceived as evil spirits with greater frequency in tribal areas of high infant mortality; in these cases, the goddess must be appeased to prevent her from harming the children. Nirṛti was one of these goddesses. Rākṣasī Jarā, the protectress of children and the city goddess of Magadha in the *Mahābhārata*,[90] was worshiped both with offerings of flowers, food, and incense, and with paintings or carvings of her image, surrounded by her children, on the walls of houses. Rākṣasī Jarā's legend suggests the archaic matriarchal tradition of group motherhood:

> King Bṛhadratha of Magadha had two wives, but he failed to obtain a son, even by means of auspicious rites and sacrifices. At last a great sage called Caṇḍakauśika gave him a fruit. His queens, dividing that single fruit into two parts, ate it up, and sometimes after, when the season came, each of the queens brought forth a fragmentary body, each having one eye, one leg, one arm, half a stomach and half face. Both the halves were thrown away on the road and were accidentally seen by Rākṣasī Jarā, who took the halves and united them. As soon as it was done, the baby became alive. It is interesting to note in this connection that the Egyptian sisters Isis and Nepthys were both mothers of Osiris—"the progeny of the two cows." Two goddesses were also associated with the birth of the Sumerian god Tammuz. They were Ishtar and Belitsheri. These legends may have some bearing on the idea of "group motherhood. . . ." Seven mothers were also associated with the birth of Skanda-Viśākha-Kārttikeya.[91]

City Protectresses

Because ancient cities were sustained by agriculture, we find a close correlation, overlap, and absorption among Earth Mothers, fertility goddesses, protectresses of children, and city protectresses. These associations are all found in Ishtar, who was at once the protectress of children and the presiding goddess of the ancient Semitic cities, and who was worshiped as Inanna, Zarpaint, Nina, and Annuit in the cities of Erech, Babylon, Ninevah, and Akkad, respectively. Isis and Athena were city goddesses, as was the Virgin Mary—the *Theotokos*, or Mother of God—who, as the protectress of cities and localities, was known as Our Lady of Walsigham, of Mount Carmel, of Zaragoza, of Glastonbury, etc.[92]

The city goddesses (*nagara devatā*) of India were also usually goddesses of luck and prosperity (*naraga-lakṣmī*), and immediate danger was signaled by their departure from the city they protected. The most common Puṣkalāvatī coins are stamped with depictions of the familiar motif of "city goddess and Indian bull." The *Rāmāyaṇa* refers to city goddess Laṅkā; Jarā, as mentioned above, was the protectress of Magadha, according to the *Mahābhārata*; the famous northern cities of Kalka, Chandigarh, Simla, and Nainital bear the names of their protective goddesses; Tripurasundarī is the protectress of the Tripura state, and her *pīṭha* is old Raṅgamatī or Udaypur (Radhakishorepur). Bhattacharyya emphasizes that the presiding goddesses of the *pīṭhas* were "originally local goddesses, the protectresses of cities or localities, and the story of Satī's death, the falling of her limbs in different *pīṭhas*, etc., were obviously invented to bring all these goddesses in relation to the growing concept of an all pervading Female Principle."[93]

Disease Goddesses

Disease goddesses, who signify both disease and its cure, are found in tremendous numbers among *ādivāsīs*, whose marginalization and subalternity have made conditions ripe for the rapid spread of infectious and deadly diseases for which they have no immunity. Nirṛti also falls into this category. The smallpox goddess is a dreaded form of the Devī worshiped by all castes, from "the most backward tribes and castes to the educated classes,"[94] whose function is to cause or avert smallpox. If she is not appeased, she may strike a victim with smallpox; if propitiated, however, it is believed that she will prevent or abate the disease. In northern India, she is one of the seven sisters called Śītalā Devī—a name that denotes her function of cooling—who control pustular diseases. Her iconography, first described in the Kāśīkhaṇḍa of the *Skanda Purāṇa*, was mirrored in later medical treatises: she is nude, her body is white, and her vehicle is an ass; she is three-eyed and bedecked with pearls (symbolic of smallpox pustules) and golden ornaments; she carries a vessel filled with water in one hand and a broomstick in the other.[95]

Śītalā is also known as Vasantabuḍi or Vāsantī Caṇḍī, and is worshiped everywhere in Bengal, along with various other Bengali Caṇḍīs, such as Olāi, Dhelāi, Kalāi, Mehāi, Kulāi, Khaḍa, Vasana, Ghoḍā, Dharā, Abāka, Kakāi, and so on. These were tribal and village goddesses worshiped in connection with disease and other troubles that were later incorporated by the brāhmaṇas into the Great Caṇḍī of the *Mārkaṇḍeya Purāṇa*. The Bengalese, however, continued to propitiate the disease goddess Caṇḍī.[96] If not placated, the epidemic disease goddesses deal out death. Kosambi provides the following observations, derived from his field research in Maharashtra, about these goddesses:

> Devī (Goddess) is simply the name for small-pox. Mari-āï has to be worshiped to prevent death from cholera, Śītalādevī is the particular goddess that can protect little children from smallpox, Gaurābā from measles. The goddesses are all usually worshiped in the towns by women (though the priests may be men) during the nine days of the Nava-rātra, beginning with the month of Āśvin (October new-moon). It is difficult to connect these 'nine nights' with the harvest; the real harvest festivals are nearly a month later. Moreover, most of the goddesses are given special offerings. In the villages, there are obligatory blood sacrifices, unless the cult has been brāhmaṇized by identification with some Purāṇic goddess, in which case the sacrificial animal may be shown to be

substituted. Finally, the *ṣaṣṭhi* and no-moon nights are also special in the worship of the goddesses, as the latter with Vetāl; blood-sacrifices have clearly been demanded (in fact are still occasionally made) on such nights.[97]

In south India, the smallpox goddess is Māriyammaṉ, a mortal woman who suffers disrespect, assaults, and ultimately, murder by human, demonic, and divine malevolent males. She ultimately retaliates against injustices against women wrought by men and becomes a goddess of vengeance.

Mātṛkās

Although all Indian goddesses may be called Mātṛkās, the term is used to distinguish those virgin mothers with a fierce, victorious nature. In this context, the massive Earth Mātṛkās share form and function with tribal war goddesses and *yakṣiṇīs*. The Mātṛkās evolved into the medieval Yoginīs, and are related to the *ḍākinīs* of Tantric Buddhism. The Mātṛkās, or Divine Mothers, first appear as syncretic deities in the *Mahābhārata* [98] and in fragmentary icons of the second and third centuries AD from Mathura. Like Earth Mothers, they hold within themselves the mysteries of life and death.

Dark and earthy, they are virgins, yet mothers. Bhattacharyya maintains that several Mātṛkās mentioned in the epics "may be regarded as the prototypes of the Devī or the supreme goddess of the Śāktas."[99] This conception is validated by two hymns, believed to be later interpolations of the *Mahābhārata*,[100] in which the Devī is addressed as "destroyer of the demon Mahiṣa," "having perpetual abode in the Vindhyas," "fond of spirituous liquor, flesh, and sacrificial victims," Kālī (black, or time as destroyer), "destroyer of Kaiṭabha," Caṇḍā (angry), Tāriṇī (deliverer), Siddhasenānī (general of the Siddhas), Mandaravāsinī (dweller on the Mandara), Karālī (frightful), Vijayā (victory), as well as "younger sister of the chief of cowherds," "mother of Skanda," "divine Durgā," "dweller in wilderness," Kumārī (maiden), and so forth.

Originally fierce tribal goddesses and *grāma-devatās*, these Mothers are described in the *Mahābhārata* as beautiful, youthful goddesses with sharp nails and teeth and protruding lips (although some are skeletal hags with sagging breasts, some have long ears, and others have large bellies). They are the quintessential *ugra* goddesses, incorporating the essence of all the indigenous goddesses explored here. Displaying their multi-tribal origins, these goddesses wear garments and garlands of different colors and styles, and are able to shape-shift at will. Many tribal Mothers were gruesome and beautiful at the same time, and are the origin of the bipolar Śakti. As the protectresses of her devotees, they are mothers who are at once beautiful and beneficent, hideous and punishing, incorporating in their polyvalent natures the military accouterments and triumphant nuances of the warrior, the nurturing maternity of the mother, and the frightening, awesome, hideous façade of the emaciated old hag.

The brāhmaṇic myths stripped away the parthenogenesis of the Mātṛkās; they are rather said to originate from the gods Yama, Rudra, Soma (Candra), Kubera, Varuṇa, Indra, Agni, Vāyu, Kummara (Skanda), and Brahmā, and their characteristics become mirror reflections of the gods to whom they correspond. The Mātṛkās reside in trees, at the meetings of crossroads, in caves, open spaces, cemeteries, on mountains, and at waterfalls. They have melodious voices and speak different languages, "indicating their varied tribal origin and pointing to the possible derivation of groupings of goddesses such as the Yoginīs from a variety of tribal and village deities."[101]

The association of the Mātṛkās with the crossroads has been intricately researched by Kosambi,[102] who provides evidence that the crossroads were the original Stone Age sites of the Mother-goddess cults of India, junctions of primitive nomad tracts where the Mothers were normally worshiped. Kosambi points out that these roads were originally made by the seasonal transhumance (boolying) of humans and herds, but have been modified by extensive farming.[103] Some of the tracts developed into trade routes, and traders preparing for their journeys made animal sacrifices to some deity at the crossroads, pledging more if the traveling business reaped profit. Major crossroads were the most auspicious sites for meritorious public works. In a Jātaka story,[104] king Pasenadi of Kosala was advised by the brāhmaṇas to make extensive blood sacrifices at every crossways as a remedy for his having had sixteen ominous dreams in a single night. It was "the travelling merchant's custom to salute and, if possible, sacrifice, to the Mother-goddess encountered during a voyage."[105]

In Bengal, Kālī is generally worshiped as Rakṣākālī, a fierce protectress deity, on the crossroads.[106] The cult of the Ramoshis in the southwestern regions worships Mātṛkās or female spirits associated with the demon Vetāla.[107] In Śūdraka's *Mṛcchakaṭika*, Cārudatta makes sacrifices to the Mothers at the crossroads. The association of crossroads with the Mātṛkās and Śiva, as well as with particularly shamanic aspects of nonelite religion, is emphasized by Bāṇa in his *Kādambarī*. In a description of various religious and philanthropic acts performed by Queen Vilāsavatī of Ujjayinī in order to acquire a son, we are told:

> She slept within the temples of [Caṇḍikā], dark with the smoke of *bdellium* [*guggulu*] ceaselessly burnt, on a bed of clubs covered with green grass . . .; she stood in the midst of a circle drawn by [great magicians], in a place where four roads meet, on the fourteenth night of the dark fortnight . . .; she honoured the shrines of the siddhas and sought the houses of neighbouring Mātṛkās . . .; she carried about little caskets of mantras filled with birch-leaves written over in yellow letters; . . . she daily threw out lumps of flesh in the evening for the jackals; she told pandits the wonders of her dreams, and at the cross-roads she offered oblation to Śiva.[108]

Saptamātṛkās, the Divine Mothers, are a class of tutelary goddesses, usually seven, although sometimes eight or sixteen, in number: Brahmāṇī, Vaiṣṇavī,

Ambikā, Indrāṇī, Kaumārī, Vārāhī, and Cāmuṇḍā (who will tolerate no husband), or Nārasiṅghī. We have mentioned the view that the Saptamātṛkās were originally sidereal Mother-goddesses whose home is in the Pleiades, and whose images appear on Indus seals of the "seven sisters" in conjunction with the vernal equinox and human sacrifice to the goddess. Although they are, except for Cāmuṇḍā, fettered in brāhmaṇic texts to gods as their *śaktis* (energies), they are traditionally associated with still earlier autonomous fierce goddesses who reigned over folk religion. The *Devī Purāṇa*, for example, depicts Devī primarily as war-goddess Cāmuṇḍā, said to be the powerful Śakti who creates, protects, and destroys the universe. According to this *Upa-purāṇa*,[109] Cāmuṇḍā lives in cemetery grounds and specializes in the destruction of enemies and the fulfillment of all desires, religious merits, final salvation, and worldly enjoyments.

The Seven Mothers embody nature in both its fecund and destructive aspects, and are often depicted on the lintel slabs of the main door of classical temples, their respective mounts forming the pedestal. Harper emphasizes the ambivalent nature of the Saptamātṛkās—their embodiment of both destructive and benign qualities—and how their iconic depictions as sensual, beautiful, benign mothers belie their literary depictions as bloodthirsty Mātṛkās, ghoulish, oral-aggressive, wrathful, all-consuming goddesses summoned to aid in battles against demon hosts. As Harper observes,

> The ambivalent nature of the group of seven is not the only contradiction inherent in the Mātṛkās. Considering the huge corpus of myths associated with major deities of the Hindu pantheon, myths about the Saptamātṛkās are comparatively few and most of those relegate the goddesses to a subordinate position either to the god Śiva or Narasiṁha, an avatāra of Viṣṇu. On the other hand, icons of the seven abound on the subcontinent. Most Śaivite temples at one time included Mātṛkā icons as part of the overall iconographic program. Some images are monumental and have a primary location within the temple. There are, as well, temples of the Medieval period that were consecrated solely to the Mātṛkās. Hence the Saptamātṛkās evidently were deities of consequence despite the meager literary references to them.[110]

The original number of seven Mātṛkās was expanded to eight, sixteen, thirty-two, and eventually sixty-four—a goddess pantheon known as the Sixty-four Yoginīs. A special group of Eighty-one Yoginīs was worshiped only by royalty.

Yakṣiṇīs

The *yakṣas*[111] and the *yakṣiṇīs*, malevolent deities of primal tribal conception who were propitiated in every village, were absorbed by the brāhmaṇas in epico-Purāṇic literature, and played a significant role in Buddhist and Jaina myths and religions. The *yakṣiṇīs* are also related to the *yoginīs*, *ḍākinīs*, and other incarnations of the fierce goddess, and contain the important primitive conception of vegetal spirits, genii, and fairies of the forest, divine Mistresses of plants, destiny, death, wealth, protection, and destruction. Their images were representative of "a purely indigenous art"[112] sculpted with "heavy earthly character of form"[113] and bulky proportions around the beginning of the Christian era. Numerous terracotta figurines of *yakṣiṇīs* were sculpted in the Maurya and Śuṅga periods. These indigenous sculptures became the prototypes of later images of goddesses and gods.[114] One of them, originally found at Tamluk in West Bengal and now in the Kensington Museum, London, exudes subtle elements of the fierce Devī:

> It is burdened with ornaments and its coiffure contains the artistic use of some miniature weapons. The cult of such female deities having five or three *āyudhas* (weapons) in the elaborate head-dress was prevalent in various parts of India from Punjab to Bengal in the Śuṅga period. . . .[115]

In the Buddhist Jātakas, the *yakkhiṇīs* are depicted as forest goblins or fairies; the horse-headed *yakkhiṇī* Assa-mukhī of the Padakusalamāṇava Jātaka "dwelt in a rock cave in a vast forest at the foot of a mountain, and used to catch and devour the men that frequented the road."[116] Most of the *yakkhacetiya* that are frequently mentioned in Buddhist and Jaina literature as the *bhavana* or haunt of certain *yakṣas* probably referred to sacred trees.[117] The *yakṣī* or *vṛkṣakā* of Gandhāra art, the poignant "woman and tree" motif, is the most important characteristic of the Graeco-Buddhist art of Gandhāra.[118] By the beginning of the Christian era, Buddhism had destigmatized the *yakṣiṇīs* and incorporated some of them in temple sculptures as goddesses and protectors. Among early *yakṣiṇī* sculptures of the first century BCE that influenced the iconographic style of goddesses in both contemporary and later religious systems are the Buddhist Sirimā Devatā and Culakokā Devatā and their brāhmaṇic counterparts in Barhut, Alakanandā and Sudarśanā *yakṣiṇīs*. The most important examples of *yakṣiṇīs* and *yakṣas* are the colossal and realistic free-standing stone images from Besnagar and Pārkham, dated about 50 BCE, who are " informed by an astounding physical energy . . .; this is an art of mortal essence, almost brutal in its affirmation, not yet spiritualized."[119]

The Jainas incorporated the cult of the *yakṣiṇīs* as an important feature of their pantheon. In the Jaina texts, *yakṣiṇīs* have semi-divine attributes and are characterized as the leaders of the women converts or as female attendants (*śāsanadevatās*) of the Tīrthaṅkaras. Deciphered historically, the *yakṣiṇīs* are derivative of the autochthonous substratum of Devīs.[120] Their names reveal aboriginal and Vedic goddesses synthesized with unique Jaina goddesses, viz., Ajitabalā (Rohiṇī), Cakreśvarī, Kālīkā (Vajraśṛṅkhalā), Duritāri (Prajñapti), Śyāmā (Manovegā), Mahākālī (Puruṣadattā), Śāntā (Kālī), Bhṛkuṭi (Jvālāmālinī), Aśokā (Mānavī), Mānavī (Gaurī), Caṇḍā (Gāndhārī), Bālā (Acyutā, Vijayā), Dhāriṇī (Tārā), Gāndhārī Camuṇḍā, Ambikā (Kuṣmāṇḍī, Āmrā), Siddhāyikā, and Padmāvatī. Many of these goddesses also evolved to Buddhist and Śākta Tantric goddesses.[121] In his *Abhidhānacintāmaṇi*, Hemacandra lists a wide range of goddesses, including cults of sixteen *śruta* or *vidyā devīs*. A significant number of the *vidyādevīs* (Rohiṇī, Prajñapti, Gāndhārī, Mahājvālā or Jvālāmālinī, Vajra-śṛṅkhalā, Vajrāṅkuśā, Apraticakrā or Jambunandā, Kālī, Mahākālī, Puruṣadattā, Gaurī, Mānavī, Vairotī, Mānasī, Acyuptā, and Mahāmānasī) are derivative of the *yakṣiṇīs* and *sāsanadevatās*.[122] The extreme antiquity of these goddesses is proven by the fact that they originally had neither a male consort[123] nor images in iconic form; rather, many are still "represented by numerous shapeless little stones daubed with minium, or by red marks on the sides of a tank, or on a rock, or on a tree by the water. . . ."[124] All the goddesses were fused into the Purāṇic Durgā, but her names and forms are legion.

Mythic Assimilation and Dilution of Goddesses

> What seems to be beyond doubt is that roughly between the beginning of the Christian era and the tenth century AD, many local and indigenous goddesses pushed themselves from the social sub-strata to find a place in the Hindu pantheon, and by a process of generalization, both religious and philosophical, were fused together and treated as aspects of the one universal mother goddess. It is not, therefore, a fact, as is sometimes wrongly conceived, that the many mother goddesses are later emanations from the one mother goddess; on the contrary, the one mother goddess of the Purāṇic Age seems to be a consolidation of the many mother goddesses. . . .[125]

Literary imagery and metaphor can plant subtle ideological seeds for the devaluation of feminine and subaltern nature, amounting to subliminal social programing or propaganda disguised as myth. The brāhmaṇas, by design or resignation, succeeded in synthesizing tribal, ethnic, and village deities into a unified mythological pantheon. Ancient goddesses were brāhmaṇized as wives or other property of brāhmaṇic gods. The new customized myths married off the more benign goddesses without a problem. In some cases, Vedic and Dravidian goddesses were fused, such as Durgā and Ko<u>rr</u>avai. Because they were unmarried (uncontrolled by a male), virgin, and hot, and therefore threats to the patriarchal system, most fierce goddesses were marginalized, relegated to the fringes of orthodoxy, and utilized by male elites as a warrior to defend the male gods. The myths also contain a proprietary element, in which the Aryan gods "own" or "possess" the native and Dravidian deities, as a master possesses a servant. These mythic elements became a metaphor writ large that legitimated both the imposition of the caste system on the indigenes and Dravidians and the stringent marriage and inheritance constraints that would be placed on upper caste wives. The male principle, at first mythically depicted as the insignificant, subordinate lover of the dominant goddess (as in the Sāṅkhya conception of *Puruṣa* and *Prakṛti*), gradually entered into the goddess cult, first as the begetter, equal in stature to the goddess, and eventually became the dominant partner.[126] The brāhmaṇas turned the original Sāṅkhya system on its head, therefore, by weakening *prakṛti* and elevating *puruṣa*, leading to the male-dominant scheme of Śiva-Śakti and its orthodox evolute, Vedānta.

The techniques the brāhmaṇas used to bring high-caste women and tribals to submission were literary/ideological, with later marriage and inheritance laws reinforcing the subtle indoctrination of epico-Purāṇic mythology. The literary assimilation involved the mutation of tribal totemic deities, occult village protectors, and exclusive farmer's gods and goddesses into subordinate aspects or emanations of standard brāhmaṇic deities, their spouses, vehicles, children, ornaments, weapons, or other symbolic property. The complex divine household-pantheon was organized as a kind of imperial court in the feudal period, reflecting the reality below. Śiva, for example, was made lord of the goblins and demons, of whom many, such as the cacodemon Vetāla, are highly primitive gods that are still popular in village worship. Skanda and Gaṇeśa became sons of Śiva, and Nandi, Śiva's bull, was worshiped in ancient India with no master riding him or plow strapped to him, appearing independently on a majority of the seals of the Indus culture.

The objectives of the brāhmaṇic patriarchs, to replace tribal shifting cultivation with plough agriculture and matriarchal with patriarchal caste social structure in which brāhmaṇas were pre-eminent, and to control the lives and reproductive activity of high-caste wives, were symbolically depicted in specially crafted metaphorical rationalizations, binomial Madonna/whore constructions, and mythic images. This subliminal epico-Purāṇic ideology neutralized the powerful tribal goddesses and their aura of matriarchy; demonized the low-caste majority, dalits, and *ādivāsīs*; and glorified motherhood, self-sacrifice, subordination, and marital fidelity as the highest feminine virtues. While ostensibly a synthesis of tribal, Dravidian, and brāhmaṇic values, the unified pantheon actually set in motion what was to become a constant struggle between the dominant castes, straining to maintain their rule, and the nonelite domain, struggling for justice and freedom from caste and gender oppression.

The story of the sacrifice of Dakṣa, the death of Satī, the dismemberment of her limbs, and their falling at different sites that became the fifty-one holy resorts or *pīṭhas* of the goddess was one of the many literary means by which brāhmaṇas achieved consolidation. Similarly, in some Purāṇas, the Devī's 108 names are said to be worshiped in 108 sacred sites distributed overall of India, while other texts list one thousand names of the goddess. "Even a cursory glance at these lists," writes Dasgupta, "will convince one that some of these names represent the different attributes of the goddess, while others point to the fact that they are local goddesses later on generalized and merged in one great Mother-goddess."[127] The myth of the ten *mahāvidyās* into which the Mother-goddess Satī transformed herself in order to frighten Mahādeva, the great god, may likewise depict "ten different indigenous goddesses who have been later on associated with and assimilated to the great mother goddess with the help of both legend and theology."[128] In the same manner, the Skanda myth, in which the young god was born jointly (by intermediacy of the Ganges) of seven (later six) mothers-in-common (the Pleiades)[129] with a separate head to suckle six mothers, is a means of restraining the tribal goddesses, "who were easier to control through their child Skanda—invented for that special purpose—than by the imposition of violently hostile patriarchal cults."[130] Kosambi elaborates:

> Skanda (like his prototype Marduk[131] in Babylon) was assigned the function of killing a troublesome demon Tārakāsura, and recruited his army from goblins. He was also joined by the Mothers—not the ones who bore him, but thousands of others, of whom some 192 are named in the chapter 46 of the Śalyaparvan of the *Mahābhārata.* Three of the names are especially interesting. One companion-Mother is *Catuṣpathaniketanā,* "housed at the crossroads;" another is named *Catuṣpatharatā,* "enamoured of the crossways." Even more remarkable is Pūtanā. A demoness by this name was killed by the pastoral child-god Kṛṣṇa whom she tried to nurse with her poisonous milk. The name cannot be a mere coincidence,[132] for these Mothers-companion are described with horrifyingly sharp teeth and nails, protruding lips, etc., all standard terms for demonesses; and simultaneously as beautiful, eternally youthful women. THEY SPOKE DIFFERENT LANGUAGES—clear sign of varied tribal origin. The cults were therefore undoubtedly pre-Aryan, though in process of assimilation.[133]

Since the rural majority was illiterate, however, they were unconvinced by the new mythology, and continued to worship their aboriginal goddesses as autonomous and supreme while paying lip service to elite amalgamated divinities. Obligatory blood sacrifices are offered to these goddesses in the villages, unless the cult has been brāhmaṇized by identification with some Purāṇic goddess, in which case a sacrificial human or animal may be substituted. Particularly auspicious times to worship the fierce tribal goddesses are the *ṣaṣṭhī* (full moon) and new moon nights, when blood-sacrifices were clearly demanded and are still occasionally made. Kosambi points to the great Jogeśvarī of Poona as a typical reflection of this custom. Every early morning, this goddess, the most senior of the city, is dressed for the day, and a silver mask is placed on her face, with one exception: on the day of the new moon, her primitive, stone-relief image is left uncovered and visible, and a fresh coating of red pigment (minium in oil) is painted on her image, "clearly a derivative of a still earlier blood-rite."[134]

Furthermore, the brāhmaṇas disempowered the parthenogenetic and supreme tribal Mother-goddess by giving male gods credit for her derivation in all the Śākta Purāṇas: she became the united forces of the gods, and as such, the Mother of all became the creation or property of male elites, the overt product of their masculine power and ingenuity. In postulating that she was formed of the *tejas* (lustre or energy) of all the gods,[135] these texts tacitly negate and overturn the aboriginal belief that she is the self-originating Creatrix of the cosmos. This account with some variations is initially found in the *Devī-māhātmya* interpolation of the *Mārkaṇḍeya Purāṇa* (written between the third and sixth centuries AD), where it is said that Viṣṇu transmuted his lustre first, followed by the other gods' contribution, to form Caṇḍikā or Ambikā.[136] The unspoken rationale for her creation is the conception that only the combined superior energies of the males, densely packed into a war goddess, could eradicate the buffalo demon Mahiṣa and his troop of *asuras*. This highly effective literary device evokes and consolidates the fierce tribal Mātṛkās who were first acknowledged as a prominent subaltern force in the Śalyaparvan of the *Mahābhārata*, and then demotes the aboriginal goddesses into the property and soldiers of brāhmaṇic gods. Because the brāhmaṇic synthesis involved collapsing all the goddesses of the subaltern peoples into the amalgamated Purāṇic Durgā, the *ugra* goddesses lost their autonomy and original identity as tribal protectress and fertility/war goddess, often of the wild head-hunting tribes, and their essence was incorporated along with all the other goddesses as Durgā (or Caṇḍī, a form of Durgā), and given brāhmaṇic Śiva as her husband. Brāhmaṇas metaphorically instilled ideas about social structure, privilege/poverty, gender relations, relative power, and duty in all who heard them.

According to the *Devī Purāṇa*, when Śiva became worried about the demons, one *tejas* appeared before him and changed into a goddess called Śakti, Kālī, or Katyāyanī.[137] The text emphasizes that this *tejas* was the property of Śiva, who desired to kill the demons.[138] Likewise, the *Devī Bhāgavata Purāṇa* contains the same account, adding that the gods became frightened when they saw the lustre, but it suddenly turned into a very beautiful damsel, the brāhmaṇized and civilized Purāṇic Devī, standing before them. Significantly, the horrifying sight of the *ugra* Devī called Bhuvaneśvarī[139] was avoided in the same Purāṇa, while the goddess Umā-Haimavatī is said to emerge from the *tejas*.[140]

While fierce goddesses were worshiped at all times by low castes and tribals, they were not patronized in north India by the learned and influential elites between the days of the Indus culture and the Gupta period, a latent period that corresponds with the decline in woman's position and prestige due to changes in the mode of production and the step by step imposition of father-right social structure in law and mythology. However, in south India, Koṟṟavai was the fierce goddess *par excellence*, and in her mold followed Māriyammaṉ.

Śiva's Anti-Brāhmaṇic Origin

At the time the *asuras* were named in the epico-Purāṇic texts, the archaic Śiva cult presented the strongest opposition to the establishment of the Vedic religion in India,[141] hence all the demonized goddesses are referred to as worshipers of Śiva in Sanskritic literature. Śiva's vehicle is a white bull, and his servant is the lion Kumbhodara (pot-bellied), who represents greed for food which must be controlled. The Vedic counterpart of Śiva was Rudra, the Atharvavedic fierce protector of cattle, "the god that kills,"[142] with a hundred heads and a thousand eyes; the Ṛgvedic lord of songs, sacrifices,[143] the wielder of the thunderbolt,[144] as fierce and destructive as a wild animal; the Purāṇic god of destruction, one with the antigods; later depicted as the god of transcendent darkness, the embodiment of *tamas*, in the Upaniṣads. His most destructive aspect is Bhairava, later to become the consort of fierce Devīs.

Śaivism belongs to an ancient substratum that predates the Vedic religion and was slowly absorbed by the Aryan conquerors. The myths and rituals of the Śiva cult are elaborated in the Purāṇas and Āgamas, an immense literature of some of the oldest records of Indian religions extant. As Daniélou emphasizes (in an amazing single sentence),

> Śaivism had always been the religion of the common people, for whom there was little place in the aristocratic Aryan fold, but it had also remained the basis of secret doctrines, transmitted by the initiative orders, whose mission it was and still is to carry the higher forms of metaphysical speculation through the periods of conflict and decadence, such as that which followed the Aryan conquest of India, when conquerors proclaimed the superiority of comparatively crude religious forms and conception over the age-old wisdom of the land, gradually, however, to be themselves deeply affected by Indian religious philosophy.[145]

Śaivism and the fierce goddesses were persecuted and demonized, depicted in the epics as the cult of demons and *asuras.* Rāvaṇa, the demon king of Ceylon in the *Rāmāyaṇa,* worshiped Śiva. After the Aryans were sure of their hold on Indian property and minds, the Vedic religion gradually assimilated the religion of the underclass. At that point, they began to translate the ancient sacred writing of the non-Aryans into Sanskrit. Many Śiva myths are found in the early Tamil Caṅkam literature, which predated in many cases the Purāṇic texts. The Tamil Murukaṉ, who is merged with Śiva in brāhmaṇic myths, is known for his wild dances (as *Śiva Naṭarāja,* the "Lord of the Dance"), spirit possession séances, animal sacrifices, ritual shamanic ordeals of self-mortification, his passionate marriage to tribal girl Vaḷḷi and their *hieros gamos* symbolism, and in ancient times, for his fierceness on the battleground with mother Koṟṟavai and father Śiva by his side. Rarely called by the name Śiva in Tamil literature, he was the supreme being, known as "King of Kings" and "the Admirable." He lives under the giant banyan tree, carries a trident (a form of *vel* or spear) and cobras, rides a white bull, has a third eye on his forehead (a symbol of his omnipotence), and swallows poison that blackens his throat.

In north India, where he was also well-known, evidenced by his association with the Himalayas and the Ganges, Śiva is a more inactive god, disinclined to the frenzied possession dance, preferring to spend his time in meditation, and substituting the cremation grounds for the battleground, which he subjects to his powers of creation and destruction. When he abandons himself to wild dancing in the cemetery, he reverts to the early martial Dravidian model. Northern Śiva's austere asceticism probably reflects the influence of Buddhism, since the Tamil Śiva is almost never depicted as an ascetic.

Later Vedic texts and the Upaniṣads reflect the influence of the Śaiva cult and its cosmology. Śaivism's complexity and abstraction is infused with some of the oldest and most profound cosmological teachings in the world, as well as the yogic arts, the source of spiritual growth and realization in both later Hinduism and Tantrism.

THE ACCOUTERMENTS OF ARYAN WARRIORS

According to Heesterman, both brāhmaṇas and kṣatriyas were warriors in Vedic India.[146] All soldiers going to war, whether indigenous, Dravidian, or Aryan, used battle charms (*saṅgrāmikaṇi*) that mystically complemented their weapons. The charms empowered them and their weapons to either drive away the enemy or to confuse and disorient him by deception.[147] Special *mantras* called *rāṣṭrabhṛts* (from *rāṣṭra,* "kingdom," *bhṛt,* "bearing sway") were chanted at the commencement of battle by warriors to ensure victory and strength. Indra, the "son of strength," and Agni, the "god of fire" (who cuts off the enemy's retreat by setting the forest aflame), are the two deities most frequently invoked in battle charms. These *mantras* also were chanted to regain the lost kingdom of an exiled king. An offering of one's own blood was required in order to bring a king, country, or fortified town under Aryan domination.[148] The word for warfare in numerous passages of the *Ṛgveda* was *gaviṣṭi* ("desire for cows"), descriptive of the original incentive of war; viz., booty, most often in the form of cattle. Protecting the community was another incentive.

Musical instruments were ritually washed in herbal baths and anointed with ghee. The *purohita,* the brāhmaṇic advisor to the king, then sounded each instrument three times before returning them to the warriors. A war dance was performed before battle in the same mode as the pre-battle dances of ancient African, American Indian, and Egyptian tribes.[149] The south Indian Tamils performed war dances, but the primary deity dancing was performed not by a male god, but by the fertility and war goddess Koṟṟavai and her blood-lapping demons. Aside from Nirṛti, the dark goddess to whom brāhmaṇas prayed for victory in battle, the Aryans' premier war god was hypermasculinized Indra. The *Ṛgveda*[150] refers to Indra miming his battle victories in dance, suggesting that the battle itself was regarded as a dance, much as it was in Homer's epics and Old German poetry. Colorful banners, transported in the army's van, further rallied the warriors. Vedic warriors were not mounted and they had no cavalry, but chariot horses of Mongolian stock were of paramount value, and the war chariot was personified, consecrated, and worshiped to ensure victory. As Margaret Stutley explains, there were many weapons, war techniques, drums, and horns in those prehistoric battles between the indigenes and the Aryans:

> Traps, snares and nets were used in war; old ropes were burned to produce thick smoke and a nauseating smell; the thunderous sounds of the battle-drum (*dundubhi; ānaka*) both rallied the Aryan warriors and endowed them with vigour, but struck terror into the enemy. The *bakura,* a kind of horn or wind instrument, was also used to rally troops in battle.[151]

Warriors' weapons have been universally personified and instilled with magical powers, from the Indians, Sumerians, Babylonians, and Canaanites, to the Shoshone Indians, Europeans, English, Irish, and Celts.[152] Indra's favorite weapon was the *vajra,* or "thunderbolt," with a hundred or a thousand edges or joints[153] and the power to destroy both enemies and witchcraft.[154] The *cakra*, a sharp-edged discus, possibly used as a slingshot, later became personified as Sudarśana, Viṣṇu's weapon. The bow and arrow, the most important weapon of the Aryan warriors, is metaphorically romanticized in the *Ṛgveda* by homologizing the twang of the bow with the whisper of a lovely woman.[155] In the *Atharvaveda*, the inherently magical wooden war-drum is personified as a warrior assured of victory,[156] just as the "medicated" drum cures snakebite.[157] The drum, considered as efficacious as weapons in conquering *daityas*, *rākṣasas*, and *asuras*, also served as a sacred shamanic vehicle for spirit possession and soul journeys. The function of the drum as both a shamanic and a military tool points to the ancient magico-religious warrior-priest stressed by Heesterman, as well as to the perceived sacred spiritual grounds of both the shamanic trance and the battlefield.

The *soma*-swilling Indra was fearless as a bull in large part because of the effect of the sacred *soma* juice, cognate with the Iranian *haoma*, and believed by Wasson[158] and others to be the hallucinogen *Amanita muscaria*, the fly agaric mushroom. Both *soma* and *haoma* were deified and invoked for victory, ecstasy, strength, and health by Aryans and Zoroastrians; the latter still worship *haoma* to ensure victory over the enemy.[159] Used regularly by Siberian shamans and others, including the Chukchi, Koryak, Samoyed, and Yakut tribes, the fly agaric has a mind-expanding effect, producing ecstatic states, hallucinations, visions, and delirium. Indra's great destructive powers were made manifest under the influence of *soma*, which produced wild, aggressive excitement and exhilaration, ox-like strength, and a ferocious demeanor, all assisting in the decimation of the enemy.[160] "Soma emboldened the warrior and worked him up into a battle-fury thus making him a terrifying enemy, but to the sage and poet it brought an intensity of feeling, and complete possession by the godhead, as well as the acquisition of mantic powers."[161]

Vedic Women

During the period of Śruti, the Vedas (records of revealed truth), the oldest sacred texts of the Hindus, reveal a social order in which women were less controlled by men than they would come to be in the fifth or sixth century BCE. This was also a period in which goddesses were conspicuous by their sparse appearance in the Aryan masculinist pantheon. In early Vedic times, women's position was a legacy of pre-Vedic and indigenous societies, but certainly not an expression of Aryan values, since the "patrilineal, war-oriented pastoralists were not likely to have viewed women as the social equals of men."[162] During that time, their relative equality with men was determined primarily by their marital autonomy, which meant that women had the right to enter love marriages, to participate equally in ritual with their husbands, or to decide not to marry, and to make independent economic decisions. Child marriage did not become popular until around the third century BCE; Vedic girls did not marry until the age of sixteen.

This liberal approach to marriage was matched by women's rights to mingle in public, to engage in artistic endeavor, and to receive an education. Although it was rare to find women scholars, female sages like Maitreyī and Gārgī Vācaknavī "rejected material wealth and pleasures in favor of a contemplative life and pursued profound questions about the nature of existence, the cosmos, and Brahman," according to Mandakranta Bose. "Women's participation in esoteric discourse was evidently acceptable in ancient times. But these privileges proved to be short-lived."[163] The *upanayana*, or the ceremonial initiation into Vedic studies, was available equally to boys and girls until the beginning of the Christian era. According to the *Atharvaveda*,[164] only a maiden properly educated during her period of studentship (*brahmacarya*) can have a successful marriage. Women students were either lifelong students of theology and philosophy (*brahmavādinīs*) or studied until their marriage at the age of fifteen or sixteen (*sadyodvāhās*), giving them at least eight or nine years of education. They memorized not only the Vedic hymns prescribed for prayers, but also various rituals and sacraments that would require their participation after marriage. Women, like men, offered regular morning and evening daily prayers, a practice reflected in the *Rāmāyaṇa*[165] when Sītā offers daily Vedic prayers.

In early Vedic times, the fidelity and chastity of high-caste wives had not yet become critical to the maintenance of property and power in the hands of male elites. If wives were unfaithful to their husbands, they could be pardoned in the *Varuṇapraghasa*, a ritual performed routinely every four months. In the ceremony, the sacrificer's wife was asked by the priest to hold up as many stalks of grass as she had had lovers since the time of the last ritual; the action purified her sins.[166] Women's sexual freedom in ancient Indian society stemmed from the primacy of motherhood. As Ramdhony explicates:

> The chief object of her marriage being the propagation of race by procreating children, her motherhood was considered as the most distinguished trait in a woman. The begetting of children was considered so very important that the impotency, absence, or death of a husband was no bar to her giving birth to children. This makeshift was termed as "Niyoga" in later literature. Although niyoga could be practiced on a woman by any kinsman of her husband, her *devar* seems to have been the favorite and the first preference. In that society sexual relationship was determined by other factors than what later came to be termed morality. One has only to look at the genealogy of several of the *Mahābhārata*'s outstanding personalities who by later code would be termed illegitimate or extramarital progeny. They have sometimes been described as chivalrous but not less "virtuous" in terms of the later measuring codes.[167]

There are indications that the daughter enjoyed some portion of her father's property, since she was permitted to grow old in his family if she should choose not to marry. Education was conducted in the family, where both daughters and sons chanted the hymns by rote. The girl seeking a husband in

Ṛgvedic times knew that her intellectual attainment was an important incentive to would-be grooms, and female education was highly valued. Music, dancing, archery, and especially singing were favored feminine accomplishments. Moreover, widows were not bound to chastity and the prohibition against remarriage,[168] in contrast with later times. In fact, the lives of widows were quite similar to the lives of other women. To maintain the widow in the family, she was allowed to marry the younger brother of the deceased husband.[169] The extreme misogyny implicit in *satī* (widow sacrifice) and widow neglect, *pardah* (seclusion of women), deprivation of education, and child-marriage were not yet established in Ṛgvedic society.

However, Vedic men were ambivalent toward women. Women participated as equal partners in fire sacrifices with husbands, yet they were called undisciplined and stupid. Because a sacrificer's wife was considered impure below the navel, she was enjoined to wrap herself in a cloth or skirt of *kuśa* grass to be purified. Woman's subordination to the male in this patriarchal society was clear: sons were preferred over daughters; high-caste women, like male non-heads of household, had no property rights;[170] wives who bore sons and who had "sweetness of speech" were becoming the new favored models of high-caste wives; and illegitimacy in the Ṛgvedic era was censured. Women were supposed to follow men—*striyaḥ puṁso nuvartmāno bhāvukāḥ*—and family, husband, and children (primarily sons) were the foci of their lives. In general, the majority of Vedic literature treats women as inferior to men.[171] With the exception of the case of a women with no brothers, women in general were blocked from receiving inheritance (*daya*). There is also evidence of women accused of immoral conduct (*duśśīla*), and of women offered as gifts. The *Śatapatha Brāhmaṇa* records that, at the end of an Aśvamedha, scores of women, including an unmarried girl and hundreds of maids, were offered as gifts.[172] In theory, Vedic woman was a goddess; in reality, she was dependent, inferior chattel.

Proto-Śramaṇa: the Wandering Mendicant

> The non-Aryan Vrātya priests of non-Vedic fertility cults, mentioned in the Atharva Veda, were the forerunners of the jogī, the fakīr and the wandering mendicant. The image of the homeless, wandering, holy men dressed in earth colors of red and yellow ochre, with amulets and rudrākṣa beads around their necks, rhinoceros-horn ear-rings in their ears, ashes on their arms and foreheads, unkempt hair tied in a top knot, singing praises of god, behaving like madmen, dancing, roaring like a bull, making the noises called *huḍukkāra, huḍu huḍu* is to dwellers of village India an archetypal image of profound terror, potency and poesy.[173]

Vedic literature is permeated with references to ascetics variously called *muni, yati,* and *parivrāṭ* and to their asceticism, or the practice of *tapas.* These mendicants and their *tapas* are the prototypes of the *śramaṇas* and their salvation religions.[174] One of the principal Upaniṣads, the *Muṇḍaka,* warns that Vedic *yajñas* are "unsafe boats" that perpetuate the vicious cycle of births and deaths; the author instead favors the path of renunciation, since "by austerity (*tapas*) Brahmā becomes built up."[175] Nor is the ideology of renunciation foreign to orthodox brāhmaṇism. Twelve celibate years in the service of a guru in a remote brāhmaṇical grove were required for the acolyte to master Veda, grammar, and ritual. The mandatory celibacy that followed initiation in patriarchal class society was a reversal of the function of the initiation ceremony in tribal life, which "was invariably an introduction to maturity and participation in sex life."[176] The brāhmaṇas turned the matriarchal sexual content of initiation on its head; rather than being initiated into sexuality, the Vedic initiate was prohibited from sexual relations and was encouraged to avoid women altogether.

The brāhmaṇical credo of the four *āśramas* (stages of life) places supreme value on the final stage of asceticism in the life of a *dvija* (twice-born). In the *Vaikhānasasūtras,* a post-Upaniṣadic law-book for ascetics of the dominant dharma, various types of ascetics and their respective practices are listed. "It would thus appear that asceticism had become an acceptable way of life for the brāhmaṇas even before the rise of the *śramaṇas* in the sixth century BCE," writes Jaini. "It must however be remembered that it was never accepted by the brāhmaṇas as a norm but as a concession to certain elements of the Aryan community who did not recognize the Vedic tradition."[177]

The non-Vedic *muni* (silent one) is mentioned once in the *Ṛgveda,* where he is depicted as completely outside the Aryan traditions, "for his ecstasy is not connected either with the sacrifice or with any of the rites ancillary to it or the entry of the youth into the full life of the community."[178] He wears soiled yellow garments, his long hair streaming, he is one with the wind, "looking upon all varied forms flies through the region of the air, treading the path of sylvan beasts, Gandharvas and Apsarasas."[179] He drinks a draught from the same cup as Rudra, and the hymn points to the identification of these *munis* with Rudra-Śiva, the ascetic yogī god of the later Hindu pantheon. In the fifteenth book of the *Atharvaveda,* there is frequent mention of the class of holy man known as *vrātya,* a traveling priest-magician of a non-Vedic fertility cult which involved flagellation and ritual dancing, breath control and sexual union as imitative magic. The *vrātya* travelled in a cart with a prostitute and a *māgadha* (a bard from Magadha, "the cradle of *śramaṇa* culture")[180] who assisted him in his rituals. Jayakar posits that the *vrātya* was a wandering yogī-magician who worshiped Rudra-Śiva, or Mahādeva, the latter identified as the buffalo-headdressed yogī in the Indus seal:

> [A] profound symbol to emerge from the Atharvan songs is the wandering Yogi, the star-marked mendicant and magician, the Vrātya, with his Lord, Eka Vrātya, who is also Mahādeva. A hymn evokes the image of the Yogi who stands erect with the immobility of stone, with indrawn breath, with arms and hands

stretched to the sides and with eyes fixed in meditative trance. This is a posture that had already found expression and form in the seals of the Indus Valley, the living manifestation of which must have been familiar to ancient seers.[181]

In the hymn to which Jayakar alludes, the Atharvan bard describes the *vrātya,* "He stood a year erect," and when asked, "Vrātya, why standest thou?" the *vrātya* calls for an *āsana,* a sacral seat. He ascends to the seat and sits in the distinctive wide-lapped position of the yogī. The "thus knowing" *vrātya* rises, moves, and encompasses all directions.[182] Briggs points out that the *vrātya* "laid emphasis on the doctrine of the breaths, naming three, five, six, ten, and even more, assimilating them to functions of the cosmic process."[183] Furthermore, the *vrātya* was honored as a guest in the courts of kings, where he was known as a *vidvān* or learned one. His permission was asked to prepare fire-offerings, and if the *vrātya* did not permit it, the host could not make the oblation.[184] The *vrātya* was a peripatetic mendicant who

> travelled about the country in strange processions, using song and choral ceremonial, dealing out blessings and curses according as they were honored or offended. Their clothing and ornaments were fantastic; their turban was peculiar and their white garments were marked with black figures. The Vrātya stood upon a cart drawn by horses and mules and carried a magic bowl and a spear. Before him went swift runners. . . . He was accompanied by a prostitute. The Vrātya represented the god and the prostitute the goddess. Their practices and ceremonial suggest the later Tantric ritual in the use of intoxicating drink, flesh, and grain, and in the association of Rudra with the goddess. The Vrātya seems to have known the experiences of concentration, of soul expansion, of the enhancement of personality-consciousness similar to those described by Patañjali in connection with samādhi, experiences which occur when the man in trance is raised above his own narrow I, over time and space. He was the greatly honored holy man, possessed of supernatural power, approximating divine personality, wandering about the country.[185]

The *vrātya* represented an undercurrent of magic and sorcery in constant dialectical juxtaposition with the dominant dharma. The *vrātyas* were considered Aryans who had "fallen from pure Aryanhood"[186] and therefore lived outside the orthodox community; they apparently could be readmitted to the brāhmaṇical fold through special rituals called *vrātyastomas.*[187] Jaini makes the case that these *vrātyas,*

> the dissident or the renegade Aryans, with their non-Vedic practices and close connection with kṣatriyas and the people of Magadha, together with the *yatis* . . . appear to be the forerunners of the later *śramaṇa* saints who also called themselves Aryans but persistently refused to conform to the Vedic scriptures and the brāhmaṇical institutions of rank (*varṇa*) and *āśrama.*[188]

Vedic Metaphysics

The Earth-based Atharvaveda

The most ancient Indian literature of the Neolithic Age was the *Atharvaveda,* magical poetry of incantations and magic spells older than the *Ṛgveda.* Pupul

Jayakar has characterized the *Atharvaveda* as "possibly the earliest record of the beliefs, the imagery, the rituals and worships of the autochthonous peoples of India as they met and transformed the conquering Aryan consciousness."[189] Over time, it has been greatly brāhmaṇized, resulting in a Vedic priest overlay on the charms and spells of Indian indigenes. The *Kauśikasūtra* (information on indigenous folk customs, beliefs, and practices) was a companion text to the *Atharvaveda.*

The culture described in the *Atharvaveda* believed that the Earth was alive. A fundamental idea of the Atharvavedic cosmology is that people contain a life-force, energy, or essence within them that is shared by non-human animals, rocks, rivers, and a multitude of spirits. An individual whose life-force is malevolent, more powerful, or somehow out of control can capture or harm the life-force in others. While it is prudent to protect oneself from such forms of psychic attack, specialists are sometimes required to deflect the attack back to the aggressor and counteract the harm caused by psychic aggression.

In a hymn to Goddess Earth in the *Atharvaveda,* the brāhmaṇas begin with blandishments and terminate with requests that Pṛthivī grant them prosperity and boons:

> Truth, greatness, universal order (rta), strength, consecration, creative fervor (*tapas*), spiritual exaltation (brahma), the sacrifice, support the earth (Pṛthivī). May this earth, the mistress of that which was and shall be, prepare for us a broad domain! The earth that has heights, and slopes, and great plains, that supports the plants of manifold virtue, free from the pressure that comes from the midst of men, she shall spread out for us, and fit herself for us! The earth upon which the sea, and the rivers and the waters, upon which food and the tribes of men have arisen, upon which this breathing, moving life exists, shall afford us precedence in drinking! . . . The earth that holds treasures manifold in secret places, wealth, jewels, and gold shall she give to me; she that bestows wealth liberally, the kindly goddess, wealth shall she bestow upon us![190]

Atharvavedic magic was structured by incipient *mantras, maṇḍalas,* and *mudrās,* and especially *japa,* or the repetition of *mantras* to achieve material or spiritual benefits. *Maṇḍalas* or geometric figures used for witchcraft practices abound in the *Atharvaveda* as means of releasing or binding men and women. The magic uses analogical, as opposed to empirical-discursive, reasoning, and is structured by epic catalogues of sympathetic (or homeopathic) correspondences homologizing desired outcomes with ritual objects and actions. There are many spells for women to find husbands and lovers, to conceive a child, to protect the fetus, and to inspire passion.

Magic and Medicine

Ancient peoples in one sense regarded themselves as being in debt to the spirits and standing in need of redemption. The ancient Babylonians, Greeks, Egyptians, Hebrews, and Indians (Aryans, Dravidians, and *ādivāsīs*) believed that many diseases, misfortunes, and death were punishments of the gods.

Indic people believed that goddesses and gods, demons, and genii—particularly ambivalent, often malicious tree goddesses—could cause human disease, calamity, and death. Anything that was construed as dangerous was attributed to powerful supernatural forces that had to be brought under control. In their view, the spirits might have visited much more bad luck upon them. This concept also underlies the doctrine of sin and salvation in which the soul is looked upon as coming into the world under forfeit (original sin). The soul must be ransomed; a scapegoat or surrogate must be provided. Propitiating these spirits, demons, and deities and making amends for the wrongful deeds committed (which often were breaking social or religious codes) was the professional domain of Vedic and Babylonian priests.[191] Inauspicious omens, such as the birth of twins and frightening dreams and nightmares, were neutralized by rituals and *mantras*. Humans were surrounded by malevolent spirits and grasping gods. Pitted against such a host of creditor deities, believers required all the priests, rituals, and sacrifices throughout an entire lifetime to redeem them from spiritual debt.

The sacrificial system evolved as a means of performing propitiation ceremonies, which grew up around the ideas of giving gifts, blandishments, and even entertainment to ambivalent deities, both as bribes so they will not punish them further, and as peace offerings for human infringements that have enraged the deity, normally a goddess. They believed that they must do something special to win the favor of the goddesses or gods, who were not, like many elite deities, consistently even-tempered and benevolent. Propitiation was insurance against immediate ill luck rather than investment in future bliss or enlightenment. Hence conceptions of the sacrifice included the idea of the gift sacrifice, which connoted the attitude of thanksgiving, and the debt sacrifice, which embraced the idea of redemption. Rituals involving exorcism, coercion, and propitiation all merge into one another. A separate category of ritual was reserved for male warriors and their battle charms, which are discussed separately.

For Atharvavedic physician-magicians, magic, religion, and medicine were identical. The culture placed great reliance on amulets and charms, spells, and *mantras* to treat disease and suffering. Charms to increase trade reveal a high standard of living for Vedic elites. Formulas for spells for recovery of loss are prevalent in the *Atharvaveda*. If the loss is due to gambling, an *apsarā* (Lady Luck) is invoked to assist the gambler with her *māyā* (magic):

> The successful, victorious, skillfully gaming Apsarā, that Apsarā who makes the winnings in the game of dice, do I call hither. . . . May she, who dances about with the dice, when she takes the stakes from the game of dice, when she desires to win for us, obtain the advantage by (her) magic! May she come to us full of abundance! Let them not win this wealth of ours![192]

The *Atharvaveda* emphasized the supreme importance of herbs in healing and protection from curses, and equates medicinal plants with goddesses and gods. All herbs are seen as divine, although some can inflict suffering, even death. Herbal medicine has been an important part of midwifery since Vedic times; medicinal herbs are associated with shamanic birth goddesses such as Bemata.[193] Although Vedic medicine did not incorporate ideas of the mind and its relation to disease, this became an objective of yogic training and techniques, requiring some knowledge of physiology.

Expiatory Rites and Charms

Vedic peoples accepted on faith that the universe is constructed of corresponding symbols and prophetic signs that formed the basis of a systematic ritual world of magic. If an individual became demonically possessed, a priest would exorcize the demon and transfer it to a scapegoat in the form of another person, animal, bird, or object. This form of exorcism is derivative of the primal notion that a surrogate must be offered for the demon as an "atonement." The *Ṛgvidhāna*[194] asserts that anyone who kills a brāhmaṇa (*brāhmahan*) must "communicate [confess] his deed [and] wander about for twelve years, bearing a skull and a club shaped like the foot of a bedstead (*khaṭvāṅga*) and covered in a cloth of bark." This method of atonement boils down to offering confessions and austerities as a surrogate. Any conscious act carried out against the laws of the gods and the cosmos was regarded as a sin that required expiation and purification. The *Atharvaveda* provides over forty expiatory charms intended to reverse the negative effects of nightmares, disease, accidents, insanity, the Evil Eye, errors in performing sacrifices, failing to pay debts, and crimes against social and religious laws.[195]

Vedic priests practiced black magic and exorcism. The *n'est plus ultra* of sacred Indian *mantras*, the Sāvitrī or Gāyatrī *mantra*,[196] is a prayer to the Sun; however, when uttered backward, it infallibly destroys enemies.[197] As the Sāvitrī *mantra* is whispered, *vibhitaka (Terminalia bellerica)* wood is tossed on the fire, fueling the obstruction and negative influence of the *mantra*. Such charms belong to the *ghora* (terrific) side of Vedic rites termed *abhicāra* and *yātuvidyā*.[198]

Witches and Demons

> The talismanic power of plants and trees to protect and to destroy, their usage as energy-transmuting amulets in magical rites, are understood and established. Plants are recognized as having an independent sacred presence, shining like light and as being rescuers of the simple, slayers of the demoniac. Plants are widely used as weapons against witchcraft, and to destroy sorcerers and hags. The distinction between the functions of the magician spellbinder and the witch is also of much interest and percolates through the whole fabric of the rural tradition. The magician-priest is the channel of communication through which cosmic forces flow. It is only through the magician Bhopa or Gunia that man can contact the invisible. The witch frustrates the cosmic principles; her spells thwart the laws of nature.[199]

In Atharvavedic India, witchcraft could be practiced by humans as well as supernatural beings, making sorcery possible for anyone who received specialized training. Witches are endowed with "horrible hairs," a possible link to the frightening long-haired "evil-wailers" mentioned in other charms of the *Atharvaveda*. In the *Śatapatha Brāhmaṇa*,[200] a *rākṣasa* arose from the lead head of the demon Namuci that Indra decapitated, saying, "Where are you going? Where will you rid yourself of me?" This points to the ancient belief that "guilt itself was an entity that actually adhered to the perpetrator of a crime."[201, 202] "May I die this day," vows a man in the *Ṛgveda*, "if I be a demon," whereupon he lays a curse upon the person who falsely accused him.[203] In the final *sūkta*, we find a panoply of imprecations against *rākṣasas, yātudhānas, kimīdins*, and other demons, forces, and spirits that threatened human existence. The *rākṣasī* who wanders silent as an owl at night is commanded to fall into a dark cavern or be pulverized by the *adri* (press-stones) of the Soma sacrifice. Of particular efficacy against demons, lead amulets[204] were ritual tools used in Vedic witchcraft to murder enemies and the manifold demonic spirits that creep around on the night of the full moon. A witchcraft rite[205] to defeat witches, rivals, *piśācas*, and *sadānvās* employs a *mantra* from the *Atharvaveda*[206] that is recited while adding reeds to a fire. In an Atharvavedic charm used ritually as a remedy for the fear of witches,[207] Agni is invoked and invited to "burn away" deceivers, *kimīdins*, sorcerers, and to coerce the *yātudhānī* (witch) to eat her own children.

Effigies, Spells, and Curses

Wax and other forms of effigies have been made for hostile purposes in many ancient and modern societies, including, Africa, Europe, Persia, Egypt, and India. In Egypt, effigies took the form of the monster Apep, the frightful enemy of the Sun. The British Museum now exhibits the papyrus of Nesi-Amsu, a chain of spells intended to overthrow Apep. His name was written on his effigy in green ink, then wrapped in new papyrus, tossed on the sacrificial fire, and kicked four times with the left foot, in a ceremony similar to that of the Vedic goddess Nirṛti, in which offerings to her were always pushed toward her with the left, or sinister, foot.[208]

In Babylonia, medico-magicians exorcised malignant devils from patients by making an effigy of the patient and reciting charms to persuade the demon to leave the patient and enter the effigy. Disease demons were removed by Hebrew priests into a scapegoat, either into a slaughtered kid or a wax figure.[209] In Atharvavedic India, the *kṛtyā* (a doll-like effigy, an evil charm or spell, a malefic spirit, a magic rite) was the cornerstone of magico-religious tools and is probably represented by many of the Indus female figurines, if the culture was Vedic. Kṛtyā is also the personification of magic as a blue and red goddess who clings intimately to her victim.[210] Some Indian lexicons indicate that sacrifices are offered to Kṛtyā for magical purposes.

Wooden human figures were also used as effigies of enemies, with complementary rituals and mantras to insure his destruction, similar to the Naga wooden effigies that are ritually decapitated. Kuśika, the ancestor of Viśvāmitra, performs this rite in the *Ṛgveda*. To cause the death of an enemy, he must fast, spend time in a cremation ground (*śmaśāna*), and chant and throw salt and mustard oil on the fire as preliminaries to making the image of the enemy in *śamyāka* wood. Holding the image, he says, "this [person] is the oblation," and his enemy will die within a week.[211]

REFERENCES

1. dalit India.org, http://www.dalitindia.org/poems/poem139.htm (accessed May 21, 2004).
2. *MS*, 10.84.
3. Shashi Bhusan Dasgupta, "Evolution of Mother-worship in India," in *Aspects of Indian Religious Thought* (Calcutta, 1957), 44.
4. *ṚV*, 1.168.33; 5.84 ["Great is our Mother Earth"]. Pṛthivī almost always is fettered to Father Heaven (Dyaus) as the composite Sky-Earth, Dyāvāpṛthivī, the Universal Parents; the divine pair was invoked to bestow an endless flow of crops, foods, and riches, to redeem the people from sins, and to protect them in war in six hymns, viz., *ṚV*, 1.159,160, 185; 4.56; 6.70; 7.53. "The idea of the Sky-Father and the Earth-Mother may, however, be said to be a common feature of all the ancient religions. Fertilizing of the Earth Mother by the Sky Father through the rains is a common belief acquiring a religious significance almost from the dawn of human civilization." [Ibid., 49; cf. Eliade, *The Sacred and the Profane* (New York, 1961), 145 ff.]
5. Kosambi, *An Introduction to the Study of Indian History* (Bombay, 1956), 24ff.
6. Feuerstein et al., *In Search of the Cradle*, 38.
7. Kosambi, *Ancient India*, 51.
8. G.B. Singh, *Gandhi: Beyond the Mask of Divinity* (Amherst, NY, 2004), 237.
9. *ṚV*, 10.90.
10. G.B. Singh, *Gandhi*, 238.
11. Ibid.
12. Ibid.
13. Fazlul-Huq, *Gandhi: Saint or Sinner* (Bangalore, 1992), 67.
14. Thapar, *A History of India*, vol. 1 (Baltimore, 1966), 46.
15. Kosambi, *Ancient India*, 172.
16. Thapar, *Interpreting Early India* (Delhi, 1993), 65.
17. Thapar, *A History of India*, vol. 1, 46.
18. Bhattacharyya, *The Indian Mother Goddess*, 61–62.
19. Ibid., 103.
20. "Naga" became a generic term for any of the forest aborigines, not necessarily interrelated, who had a cobra (*nāga*) totem or worshiped the cobra. Many of these Nagas were in the adjacent jungle at the time Kuru-land was first settled by Aryans. Food-gathering was easiest in the Gangetic forest, where the dense forest made it impossible for outside forces to conquer the Nagas or reduce them to virtual slavery, which had been accomplished with the *dāsa* and śūdra to the west. These tribes knew, as they all did, that if they remained free food-

gatherers and escaped the brāhmaṇic plough, they would never be forced into the rank of a low caste. Unlike the Nagas of Assam, these generic Nagas were never fighters or food producers.

21. Kosambi, *Ancient India*, 86.
22. Mark Nathan Cohen, *The Food Crisis in Prehistory: Overpopulation and the Origins of Agriculture* (New Haven, 1977).
23. According to Kosambi, the śūdras carried the name of a former tribal group. [Kosambi, *Ancient India*, 85–86].
24. Romila Thapar, *Interpreting Early India*, 108.
25. Bandyopadhyaya, *Development of Hindu Polity and Political Theories*, 170.
26. Ibid., 171.
27. Ibid., 172–73.
28. Ibid.
29. Chapter 78.
30. Bandyopadhyaya, *Development of Hindu Polity*, 171–72.
31. Kosambi, *Ancient India*, 21.
32. Basham, *The Wonder that was India*, 197.
33. *Jāti* = later castes of tribal origin that retained the endogamy and commensality of their former tribal existence. Because their gods now received respect from society as a whole, their position was guaranteed; since the tribals now worshiped other gods along with their own transformed deities, they became an integral part of that society.
34. Kosambi, *Ancient India*, 15.
35. Sanskritization is the term coined by Srinivas to describe his perception of the continuous historical process by which the orthodox Sanskritic religious and social traditions of the elites are superimposed on indigenous customs. Srinivas' term *tribalization* refers to a complementary process by which tribal and non-Sanskritic traditions percolate upward into Sanskritic Hinduism. [M.N. Srinivas, *Religion and Society among the Coorgs of South India* (London, 1952).]
36. Kosambi, *Ancient India*, 15–16.
37. The Purāṇas claim immemorial antiquity but were written or rewritten to order as specially invented brāhmaṇizing myths generally between the sixth and the twelfth centuries AD.
38. *Mbh.*, Śāntiparvan 59; *Viṣṇu P.*, 1.13; *Matsya P.*, 10.14–10.
39. *Viṣṇu P.*, 1.13; *Bhāgavata P.*, 4.14.44.
40. *Jāt.*, 4.413; 5.110.333.
41. Thapar, *Interpreting Early India*, 142.
42. For Vedic references to the niṣādas, see *Taittirīya Saṁhitā*, 4.5.4.2; *Maitrāyaṇī Saṁhitā*, 16.27; *Aitareya Brāhmaṇa*, 8.11.
43. Thapar, *Interpreting Early India*, 48.
44. N.N. Bhattacharyya, *Indian Demonology*, 35.
45. Dasgupta, *Aspects of Indian Religious Thought*, 44.
46. Alain Daniélou, *The Gods of India: Hindu Polytheism* (New York, 1985), 140.
47. Ibid.
48. Juergensmeyer, *Terror in the Mind of God: The Global Rise of Religious Violence*, 147.
49. *ṚV*, 3. 34, 9.
50. Swami Vivekananda, *The Complete Works of Swami Vivekananda*, vol. 3 (Mayavati, 1954), 533–34, quoted in G.B. Singh, *Gandhi*, 239–40.

51. *Mbh.*, 13.8360.[210].
52. Jayakar, *The Earth Mother*, 156.
53. Bhattacharyya, *Indian Demonology*, 31.
54. Ibid.
55. Ibid., 32.
56. *AV*, VII.70.
57. Jayakar, *The Earth Mother*, 62.
58. Ibid.
59. Stutley, *Ancient Indian Magic and Folklore*, 98.
60. Daniélou, *The Gods of India*, 138.
61. *Ṛ̣V*, 10.59.1–7.
62. *YV*, IV.2.5.
63. Bhattacharyya, *Indian Demonology*, 35.
64. Ibid., 41–42.
65. Jayakar, *The Earth Mother*, 62.
66. *Mbh.*, 1.67.52.
67. *AV*, 1.72.9;13.1.38.
68. *Mbh.*, 1.650, 2523.
69. *Viṣṇu P.*, 180.
70. 6.7.40.
71. Bhattacharyya, *History of the Śākta Religion*, 48.
72. Ibid., 50.
73. XIX.60.
74. Bhattacharyya, *The Indian Mother Goddess*, 157.
75. The tribal origin of Kālī and her *avatāras* is intertwined with the history of four distinct linguistic families in India: the Austric, the Tibeto-Burman, the Dravidian, and the Indo-European (Aryan). Among the three groups comprising the Tibeto-Burmans, the Naga and Kuki speakers were pushed up into the hills, and the Bodo, including all the non-Aryan languages of the Garo Hills, the North Cachar Hills, and the plains, became the dominant language. Before the Mongoloid peoples entered the Northeast, the Aryans "took up their trek into the North-East along the Brahmaputra," according to Bhattacharyya, "in consequence of which a fusion took place of the Sanskritic and Mongoloid cultures. . . . In this process of Sanskritization or Hinduization the original tribal divinities of these peoples became identified with the Vedic and Purāṇic gods and goddesses." [Bhattacharyya, *History of the Śākta Religion*, 20.] Mainao of the Bodo-Kacharis came to signify Kālī, Durgā, and Pārvatī, known as Balkungri.
76. Ibid., 25.
77. *Mbh.*, 6.23.4–5.
78. 1.2.4.
79. Daniélou, *The Gods of India*, 142.
80. Ibid., 272–73.
81. *Mbh.*, 1.18089.
82. Ibid., 7.4412.
83. Ibid., 5.3627.
84. Daniélou, *The Gods of India*, 142.
85. Jayakar, *The Earth Mother*, 61.
86. Dasgupta, *Aspects of Indian Religious Thought*, 53.
87. Bhattacharyya, *The Indian Mother Goddess*, 37.

88. Kartikeya C. Patel, "Women, Earth, and the Goddess: A Shakta-Hindu Interpretation of Embodied Religion," *Hypatia* 9, no. 4 (Fall, 1994): 79.
89. See Richard Hinckley Allen, *Star-Names and Their Meanings* (New York, 1936).
90. 2.17–18.
91. Bhattacharyya, *The Indian Mother Goddess,* 43–44.
92. Ibid., 48.
93. Ibid., 50.
94. Ibid., 53.
95. Ibid.
96. Ibid., 56.
97. Kosambi, "At the Crossroads: A Study of Mother-Goddess Cult Sites," in *Myth and Reality* (Bombay, 1962), 91.
98. 45.1–40 (Śalyaparvan).
99. Bhattacharyya, *The Indian Mother Goddess,* 107.
100. 4.6; 6.23.
101. Vidya Dehejia, *Yoginī Cult and Temples: A Tantric Tradition* (New Delhi, 1986), 68.
102. Kosambi, "At the Crossroads," 82–109.
103. Contemporary herders are paid in grain by the peasants to fold the sheep for a few nights on particular areas of land, thereby fertilizing the poor soil. The pilgrimage road connecting Āḷandī and Paṇḍharpūr is still followed seasonally (beyond the pilgrimage time) by a large vagrant population; the many intermediate cult-spots linked by the route make begging easier. (Ibid., 92ff.)
104. No. 77.
105. Bhattacharyya, *The Indian Mother Goddess,* 67.
106. Ibid.
107. R.V. Russell, *Tribes and Castes of the Central Provinces of India,* vol. 4 (London, 1916), 506ff.
108. Bāṇa, *Kādambarī,* trans. C.M. Ridding (London, 1896), 55–56; ed. P.V. Kane, vol. 1, text, 42–43.
109. *Devī P,* 39.14; 42.9.
110. Katherine Anne Harper, *The Iconography of the Saptamatrikas: Seven Hindu Goddesses of Spiritual Transformation* (Lewiston, NY, 1989), v–vi.
111. For a comprehensive overview of the *yakṣas,* see Ananda K. Coomaraswamy's *The Yakṣas* (repr., New Delhi, 2001) and *Yakṣas: Essays in Water Cosmology* (New York, 1993).
112. Coomaraswamy, *History of Indian and Indonesian Art,* 16.
113. Bhattacharyya, *History of the Śākta Religion,* 46.
114. Ibid.
115. Bhattacharyya, *The Indian Mother Goddess,* 155.
116. No. 432.
117. Coomaraswamy, *History of Indian and Indonesian Art,* 47.
118. Ibid., 50.
119. Ibid., 16.
120. Bhattacharyya, *The Indian Mother Goddess,* 109.
121. Ibid., 110.
122. Ibid.
123. Ibid., 90.
124. Ibid., 86.
125. Dasgupta, *Aspects of Indian Religious Thought,* 72–73.

126. Bhattacharyya, *History of the Śākta Religion*, 2.
127. Ibid., 87.
128. Ibid., 90.
129. The Pleiades cluster is womb-shaped, according to early Mesopotamian records, an association which corresponds to the birth of the new year or cycle; it is comprised of seven (later appearing as six) stars, known to the Greeks as the Seven Sisters, and to the Indians as the Saptamātṛkās, representing the end of one cyclical year and the rebirth of both the celestial and terrestrial new year. They are also depicted in the Vedas as the Seven Rivers, and woven into mythology as the Seven Mothers of Agni, who was born in the waters of the sky; the seven mothers of Soma, being the same seven rivers that are considered the mothers of plant, animal, and human life; and the foster mothers or nurses of Skanda, the son of Śiva, though only six of the Goddesses nursed Skanda. Skanda, the infant god of war, was equated with the planet Mars. Literally motherless, who took to himself six heads for his better nourishment; his name was Kārttikeya, "Son of the Kṛttikās." [Allen, *Star-names and Their Meaning*, 392.] Rising in conjunction with the vernal equinox, the Kṛttikās were viewed mythopoetically as the great sky rivers of light from which the universe was churned; as the *Taittirīya Saṁhitā* invokes: "Kṛttikā, the Nakṣatra, Agni, the deity. You are the radiance of Agni, of Prajāpati, of the Creator, of Soma." (4.4.11.)
130. Kosambi, *Myth and Reality*, 85.
131. Both Skanda and Marduk originally were the god-names of the planet Mars. The sidereal religion of Babylon deified the five planets known in antiquity, placing their native divinities Ishtar, Nebo, Nergal, Marduk, and Ninib in the heavens as Venus, Mercury, Mars, Jupiter, and Saturn, respectively, and transferring the mythic traits of these divinities to the stars. The religious and philosophical triad of Sin (Sun), Shamash (Moon), and Ishtar (Venus, also the constellation Virgo) comprises the three great rulers of the zodiac, and their symbols—crescents, discs, containing a star of four or six points—appear on the top of the boundary pillars (*kudurru*) from the fourteenth century BCE. [Franz Cumont, *Astrology and Religion Among the Greeks and Romans* (New York, 1960), 27–28.]
132. "The gloss *pautana*: *Mathurā-pradeśa* proves that Pūtanā was the special goddess of the Mathurā region." [Kosambi, *Myth and Reality* (Bombay, 1962), 109, n. 5.]
133. Ibid., 85. [All caps in original.]
134. Kosambi, *Myth and Reality*, 91.
135. *Devī-māhātmya*, 2.9–19.
136. Ibid.
137. *Devī P.*, 127.47–60.
138. Ibid., 127.45–48.
139. *Devī Bhāgavata P.*, 7.31. 25–54.
140. Ibid., 12.8.51–57.
141. Daniélou, *The Gods of India*, 143.
142. *AV*, 1.19.3 [330].
143. *ṚV*, 1.114; 2.33.
144. Ibid., 2.33.3.
145. Daniélou, *The Gods of India*, 188.

146. Heesterman, *The Broken World of Sacrifice*, 2.
147. Stutley, *Ancient Indian Magic and Folklore*, 70.
148. *Ṛgvidhāna*, III.18.3f.
149. Stutley, *Ancient Indian Magic and Folklore*, 72.
150. V.33.6.
151. Stutley, *Ancient Indian Magic and Folklore*, 71.
152. Ibid.
153. *ṚV*, I.80.6; VIII.66.
154. *AV*, VIII.5, 15.
155. *ṚV*, X.18.
156. *AV*, V.20–21.
157. *Suśruta Saṁhitā*, 737f.
158. See R. Gordon Wasson, *Soma: Divine Mushroom of Immortality* (New York, 1968); "Soma of the Aryans: An Ancient Hallucinogen?" Wasson, *Bulletin on Narcotics* 22:3, 25–30; Wasson, "Soma Brought Up To Date," *Journal of the American Oriental Society* 99, 100–105.
159. Stutley, *Ancieant Indian Magic and Folklore*, 75.
160. *ṚV*, VIII.12.1.
161. Stutley, *Ancient Indian Magic and Folklore*, 75.
162. Gatwood, *Devī and the Spouse Goddess*, 32.
163. Mandakranta Bose, *Faces of the Feminine*, 5, n. 2.
164. *AV*, XI.5, 48.
165. V.15, 48.
166. George L. Hart, "Women and the Sacred in Ancient Tamilnad," *Journal of Asian Studies* 32, no. 2 (1973): 247.
167. Reshmi Ramdhony, "On Our Vedic Origin: Women Speaking for Themselves," in *Revisiting Indus-Sarasvati Age and Ancient India*, ed. Bhu Dev Sharma and Nabarun Ghose, 246–47.
168. In the *Śatapatha Brāhmaṇa*, Sukanya states that "I shall not [sexually] forsake my husband while he is alive, to whom my father gave me;" similarly, a passage in the *Ṛgveda* addresses the widow: "Rise up woman, thou art lying by one whose life is gone, come to the world of the living, away from the husband."
169. Ramdhony, "On Our Vedic Origins," 246.
170. Altekar, *Position of Women*, 98.
171. Rama Nath Sharma,"Women in Vedic Rituals," in *Revisiting Indus-Sarasvati Age and Ancient India*, 263.
172. Ibid.
173. Jayakar, *The Earth Mother*, 78.
174. Padmanabh S. Jaini, "*Śramaṇas*: Their Conflict with Brāhmaṇical Society," in *Chapters in Indian Civilization*, ed. Joseph W. Elder, vol. 1 (Dubuque, Iowa, 1970), 45ff.
175. Robert E. Hume, trans., *The Thirteen Principal Upaniṣads* (London, 1962), 367.
176. Bhattacharyya, *History of the Śākta Religion*, 36.
177. Jaini, "*Śramaṇas*: Their Conflict," 45.
178. A. Berriedale Keith, *Religion and Philosophy of the Veda and Upanishads* (Cambridge, MA, 1925), 402.
179. Ibid.
180. Jaini, "*Śramaṇas*: Their Conflict," 46.

181. Jayakar, *The Earth Mother*, 62.
182. *AV*,15.1–18.1.
183. Briggs, *Gorakhanātha and the Kānphaṭā Yogīs*, 212.
184. Jaini, "*Śramaṇas*: Their Conflict," 46.
185. Briggs, *Gorakhanātha and the Kānphaṭā Yogīs*, 212–13.
186. Jaini, "*Śramaṇas:* Their Conflict," 46.
187. Ibid.
188. Ibid., 46–47.
189. Jayakar, *The Earth Mother*, 57.
190. *AV*, XII.1.1–3, 44.
191. Margaret Stutley, *Ancient Indian Magic and Folklore* (Boulder, CO, 1980), 104.
192. *AV*, IV.38.1, 3.
193. See Janet Chawla, "Negotiating Narak," in *Invoking Goddesses*,165–202.
194. 3.4, 5.
195. *ṚV*, 10.88 is the most efficacious expiatory text, according to *Ṛgvidhāna*, 3.25. 2.
196. *ṚV*, 3.62.10.
197. *Ṛgvidhāna*, 1.15.4ff.
198. *Abhicāra* = "exorcizing, employing spells for malefic purposes, incantation;" *abhicāra mantra* = incantation or prayer for working a spell. Demonic beings (the majority malignant, but some benevolent) are termed *yātu* in Indo-Iranian traditions. The term *yātu* originally denoted "demons" only, but later was applied to sorcerers and magicians who were capable of controlling the *yātus*. For more on the Avestan and Indian *yātus*, see F. Spiegel, *Die arische Periode und ihre Zustande*, 218ff.; A. Christensen, *Essai sur la demonologie Iranienne*. Cf. *yātudhāna* = lit., "holding a demon," an evil spirit; *yātumat*, "practicing witchcraft or sorcery," "malignant." [Stutley, *Ancient Indian Magic and Folklore*, 166n6.]
199. Jayakar, *The Earth Mother*, 58.
200. 5.4.1,9.
201. Stutley, *Ancient Indian Magic and Folklore*, 92.
202. For example, when Śiva cut off one of Brahmā's heads, it adhered to his hand until he had done penance for the crime. Indra finally succeeded in beating off Namuci with a disk of lead, and ever since, lead has been soft. Elsewhere in the *Śatapatha Brāhmaṇa*, Indra's *prāṇa* (life-breath) flows from his navel and becomes lead. This alludes to the association of lead with the persona of Śani (Saturn), lord of death in Vedic and European astrology. "Lead, the darkest and heaviest of the metals," writes Richard Cavendish, "was naturally assigned to Saturn, the dimmest and slowest-moving planet, which trudges heavily through its slow path round the sun." [Cavendish, *The Black Arts* (New York, 1967), 27.] In ancient cosmologies Saturn is regarded as the Lord of Death because it is the farthest planet from the sun, the ruler of life.
203. *ṚV*, 7.104.15f.
204. *AV*, 1.16; *Kauṣ.*, 47, 23.
205. *Kauṣ.*, 48,1.
206. *AV*. 2.18.
207. *Kauṣ.*, 26.
208. Stutley, *Ancient Indian Magic and Folklore*, 98.
209. Ibid., 99.
210. *ṚV*, 10.85, 28f.
211. *Ṛgvidhāna*, 2.4.5; 4.1ff.

6

Asceticism, Śramaṇism, and the Great Goddess Revival: *c.* 600 BCE–AD 300

Historico-Ideological Context of Śramaṇism

The Hindu state developed from the swelling wave of Indian nationalism vis-à-vis the Persian and Greek occupations. Northern India was incorporated as part of the Persian empire in the latter part of the sixth century BCE, followed by Greek occupation under Alexander the Great in 327 BCE. The production of surplus had facilitated the growth of trade, urban settlements, and a non-productive privileged class. Ancient tribal settlements (*janapadas*) were swallowed up by larger confederacies (*mahājanapadas*)—the precursors of powerful organized *rāṣṭras* or states—which prepared the terrain for the subsequent Magadhan imperialism.[1]

Among the sixteen *mahājanapadas*, the kingdom of Magadha ascended to prominence under several dynasties that reached their peak in power under the reign of Aśoka Maurya, one of India's most legendary emperors. Following the subjugation of two neighboring kingdoms, the kingdom of Magadha emerged as a major power due to its unparalleled military. The original tribal religions of the dynasties that ruled the Magadhan empire (320–185 BCE) and adjacent kingdoms are unknown; however, both Buddhism and Jainism claimed that the Haryaṅka kings of Magadha, Bimbisāra, and Ajātaśatru were devotees of their religions.

Overthrowing the reigning king Dhana Nanda, exiled general Candragupta Maurya founded the Maurya dynasty in 321 BCE, establishing the Mauryan Empire. Megasthenes, who was serving as an ambassador from the Seleucid Empire, reported that Candragupta Maurya built an army of thirty thousand cavalry, six hundred thousand infantry, and nine thousand war elephants (many modern historians dismiss Megasthenes' account as hyperbole). Candragupta conquered all of northern India, establishing an empire from the Arabian Sea to the Bay of Bengal. After conquering the regions to the east of the Indus river, he moved southwards, taking over much of the land in present-day central India. Six chairs, one for each of the four arms of the army (infantry, cavalry, elephants, and chariots), one chair for the navy, and one for logistics and supply, were the administrators for the entire army.[2]

This marked the first time that most of the subcontinent was united under a single government. Capitalizing on the destabilization of northern India by the Persian and Greek invasions, the Mauryan empire under Candragupta conquered most of the indigenous people and rival kingdoms on the Indian subcontinent, pushed its boundaries into Persia and Central Asia, and conquered the Gandhara region. Candragupta was succeeded by his son Bindusāra, who expanded the kingdom over most of present day India, with the exception of the extreme south and east. The kingdom was inherited by his son Aśoka the Great.

Candragupta was a patron of Jainism, while his grandson Aśoka patronized Buddhism, and his grandson Daśaratha patronized Ājīvikism. In addition, the ancient kings customarily paid tribute to the gods and rituals of the lands they vanquished to gain the good will of the conquered peoples. The pre-class religion of the Maurya kings is believed to have been that of the Mother-goddess. According to the account of king Aśoka by Lāmā Tārānātha, the king worshiped the Mother-goddess Umādevī and approved of the sexual rites connected with her cult; thus the king came to be known as Kāmāśoka.[3] The ancient tribal religious beliefs and practices probably continued to be observed by kings and nobles in their personal lives while they simultaneously patronized *śramaṇic* religions of their choice.[4] This aristocratic adherence to tribal forms, coupled with the unwavering faith of the rural majority in the fierce goddess, led to their accommodation in the new religions. Archaeological evidence of the worship of fertility goddesses in the Maurya and Śuṅga periods exists in a large group of Mother-goddess terracottas (the "folk" art medium) that was unearthed in the lowest, or nearly the lowest, levels of several sites scattered from Pāṭaliputra to Taxila. Coomaraswamy describes the images:

> These moulded plaques and modelled heads and busts represent in most cases a standing female divinity, with very elaborate coiffure, dressed in a tunic or nude to the waist, and with a *dhotī* or skirt of diaphanous muslin. Despite the garment, especial care is taken to reveal the mount of Venus in apparent nudity, a tendency almost equally characteristic of the stone sculpture in the Śuṅga, Āndhra, and Kuṣāṇa periods. In some cases the figure stands on a lotus pedestal and in two examples from Basārh, there are shoulder wings; the arms are generally akimbo, and there are often symbols represented in the space at the sides of the plaque. These types may have behind them a long history; they may have been votive tablets or auspicious representations of mother-goddesses

and bestowers of fertility and prototypes of Māyā-devī and Lakṣmī. Other plaques, often in high relief, represent male and female couples like the *mithuna* and Umā-Maheśvara groups of later art.[5]

Aśoka, a kṣatriya, was a mighty warrior king and bloody conqueror who initially sought to expand his kingdom. In the aftermath of the carnage caused in the invasion of Kaliṅga, however, he converted to Buddhism, repented of his fratricidal wars and violence, renounced bloodshed, and pursued a policy of non-violence or *ahiṁsā,* with the single exception of annihilating indigenous peoples or driving them from their ancestral land. By the third century BCE, Aśoka had unified most of the Indian subcontinent in his empire, which included all of northern India, Afghanistan, Kashmir, and the Deccan; only the deep south remained independent of Maurya rule.

As a penitent convert, Aśoka believed Buddhism to be the panacea for the world's ills. Buddhism was transformed into an aggressively proselytized state religion,[6] funded by the "vast resources at the disposal of the most powerful autocrat of that age [that] came to be devoted to the cause of the moral regeneration of mankind."[7] Under Aśoka, the Mauryan dynasty was responsible for the spread of Buddhist ideas throughout all of East Asia and Southeast Asia, thus shaping the history and development of Asia as a whole. He sent Buddhist missionaries to many areas of India and to Ceylon, and west to Syria and Egypt.

The Edicts of Aśoka are the oldest preserved historical documents of India. These monolithic pillar and rock edicts promoted the practice of the Dhamma, or (Buddhist) Law of Piety, and Aśoka is said to have built 84,000 *stūpas,* innumerable monasteries, as well as his magnificent palace complex at Pāṭaliputra. Aśoka the Great is viewed by many historians as one of the greatest rulers in world history. Although Aśoka proclaimed that all men were his children and supported the doctrine of *ahiṁsā,* banned animal sacrifices, regulated animal slaughter for food, reduced meat consumption in the palace to "negligible proportions,"[8] and encouraged the growth of vegetarianism in India, his pacifism was selective. The wild hill and forest tribesmen were a constant source of terrorism to the more settled parts of the empire, and earlier kings had waged ruthless genocidal campaigns of extermination against the aborigines. Aśoka wanted to tame and civilize them, but his civilizing mission statement included his readiness to repress them by force if they continued their raids on settlements:

> When the King, of Gracious Mien and Beloved of the Gods, had been consecrated eight years Kaliṅga was conquered. 150,000 people were thence taken captive, 100,000 were killed, and many more died. Just after the taking of Kaliṅga the Beloved of the Gods began to follow Righteousness [*Dharma*], to love Righteousness, to give instruction in Righteousness. When an unconquered country is conquered, people are killed, they die or are made captive. That the Beloved of the Gods finds very pitiful and grievous. . . . Today, if a hundredth or a thousandth part

of those who suffered in Kaliṅga were to be killled, to die, or to be taken captive it would be very grievous to the Beloved of the Gods. If anyone does him wrong it will be forgiven as far as it can be forgiven. *The Beloved of the Gods even reasons with the forest tribes in his empire and seeks to reform them. But the Beloved of the Gods is not only compassionate, he is also powerful, and he tells them to repent, lest they be slain.* For the Beloved of the Gods desires safety, self-control, justice, and happiness for all beings. The Beloved of the Gods considers that the greatest of all victories is the victory of Righteousness and that [victory] the Beloved of the Gods has already won here and on all his borders, even 600 leagues away in the realm of the Greek king Antiyoka, and beyond Antiyoka among the four kings Turamaya, Antikini Maga, and Alikasudara, and in the South among the Cōlas and Pāṇḍyas and as far as Ceylon.[9]

In the abundant literature of the time, the Dharmasūtras emphasize the duties of kings and laymen in the class system, while the Buddhist Canon, especially the Jātakas, provides insight into the prevailing nonelite mentality. People of the lower strata became increasingly alienated from their disintegrating tribes and villages, but kept their reciprocal relation with the natural world alive in their religious practices. The sexual and marital freedom of high-caste women declined sharply. We learn from Megasthenes that Aśoka's palace was no less opulent than the palaces of Susa and Ecbatana, and from Fa Hsien that it was still standing at the beginning of the fifth century, when its construction was attributed to the magic of the genii. The palace had been burned to the ground and almost deserted by the time Hsüan-tsang made his pilgrimage there in the seventh century.

The *Arthaśāstra*[10] of Kauṭilya makes overt reference to the sale of former tribal land. Debt bondage (*āhitaka* and *ātmavikreta*) was listed as a regular if infrequent category of slavery,[11] and *viṣṭi* (forced labor or a labor tax), also existed.[12] Both brāhmaṇic and Buddhist literatures explicitly state that oppressive taxation existed and that it was recognized as evil.[13] While the laws and regulations for the bequest, sale, and inheritance of land and other property are listed and discussed in socio-legal texts such as the Dharmaśāstras and the *Arthaśāstra*, the mine of copperplate and stone inscriptions of the later period after AD 500 offers more precise information on land grants.[14]

Aśoka was succeeded by a number of princes of the Maurya line. The last Maurya was murdered by his general Puṣyamitra, who founded a new line, that of the Mitras or Śuṅgas.

The Dialectic of Śramaṇism and Brāhmaṇism

The modern description of Hinduism has been largely that of a *brāhmaṇa*-dominated religion which gathered to itself in a somewhat paternalistic pattern a variety of sects drawing on a range of Buddhists, Jainas, Vaiṣṇavas, Śaivas, and Śāktas. . . . The picture which emerges of the indigenous view of religion from historical sources of the early period is rather different. The prevalent religious groups referred to are two, Brāhmaṇism and Śramaṇism with a clear distinction between them. They are organizationally separate, had different sets of beliefs and rituals and often disagreed on social norms.[15]

Śramaṇism is a term subsuming a variety of Buddhist, Jaina, Ājīvika, and other deviant sects that were opposed to orthodox brāhmaṇic basics such as Vedic Śrutis and Smṛti, the sacrificial *yajña*, the belief in a Creator, the caste system, and the violence involved in the killing of animals. Asceticism was the paramount feature of the *śramaṇas*; the path of passivity and non-action of these religions at once created Saṅghas of renunciates and precluded the establishment of urban militias. The notion of *ahiṁsā* or non-violence was fundamentally foreign to the dominant dharma:

> The degree to which castes and sects functioned independently even in situations which would elsewhere have been regarded as fundamentally of theological importance, can perhaps be seen in attitudes to religious persecution and the manifestations of intolerance. Among the normative values which were highlighted in recent times, has been the concept of *ahiṁsā* or non-violence. It has been argued that non-violence and tolerance were special features of Hinduism which particularly demarcated its ethics from those of Islam and to a lesser extent Christianity. Yet *ahiṁsā* as an absolute value is characteristic of certain śramaṇic sects and less so of brāhmaṇism. The notion appears in the *Upaniṣads*, but it was the Buddhists and the Jainas who first made it foundational to their teaching, and their message was very different from that of the *Bhagavad-Gītā* on this matter. That brāhmaṇism and śramaṇism were recognized as distinct after the period of the *Upaniṣads* further underlines the significance of *ahiṁsā* to śramaṇic thinking. This is also borne out by the evidence of religious persecution.[16]

The *śramaṇa*[17] is identified in the *Bṛhadāraṇyaka Upaniṣad*[18] with the *tāpasa*,[19] denoting that both were regarded as a class of mendicants.[20] In Pāli scriptures of the Theravāda school, the *śramaṇa* is a member of any of the heterodox orders of monks, contrasted with the *tāpasa* (but never *śramaṇa*) brāhmaṇa mendicant. Pāli scriptures also refer to the compound *śramaṇa-brāhmaṇa* when describing the holy men of two distinct groups, the deviant and the dominant dharma. The Buddha is described as a *mahā* (great) *śramaṇa*, and non-Buddhists refer to members of the Buddhist Saṅgha as the *śramaṇas*, the son of Śākya. Mahāvīra is also titled a *śramaṇa* in the Jaina texts.

The *śramaṇas* became a dominant spiritual expression in Indian life with the flowering of the great sixth century BCE salvation religions, Jainism and Buddhism, at the beginning of the Upaniṣadic period. The hostility between śramaṇas and brāhmaṇas began when the Buddhists converted the great emperor Aśoka and won for their order the backing of wealthy merchants who traditionally patronized brāhmaṇism. In his *Mahābhāṣya*,[21] Patañjali (*c.* 150 BCE) links together the competitive power play of śramaṇa-brāhmaṇa with "cat and mouse," "dog and fox," and "snake and mongoose," indicating that their social relations were that of predator and prey.

New social theories and philosophical doctrines from non-brāhmaṇical sources,[22] clearly identifiable with those of the later śramaṇas, began to mingle with the brāhmaṇical ideals. While the Upaniṣadic doctrine of *brahman* and *ātman* clearly derives from the Vedas and the Brāhmaṇas, the doctrines of *punarjanma* (transmigration), *karma* (action), and *mokṣa* (emancipation)—essential to the śramaṇa religions and all later Indian religions—are not equally derivative of the Vedic tradition. The kṣatriyas, the new teachers of the Upaniṣadic period, are probably the authors of these pivotal conceptions.

Buddhist thought and existence, circumscribed by the theories of *saṁsāra* and *karma* (transmigration and rebirth), developed for the first time into a system. Although Buddhism denied the existence of the soul, asserting that consciousness continues through a cycle of rebirths, it nevertheless attributed caste to the ethics of rebirth, a notion that became fundamental to both Buddhist and Hindu social philosophy. Thapar analyzes this deterministic dogma:

> *Karma* transformed the world into a strictly rational, ethically determined cosmos representing the most consistent theodicy ever produced in history. But it also required the strict fulfilment of caste obligation. Ethnic and economic factors were no doubt significant to caste structure, but *karma* reinforced it at the ethical level. There was no universally valid ethic but a compartmentalization of private and social ethic with each caste having its own ethic and, therefore, men were forever unequal. The absence of ethical univeralism led to striving for individual salvation based on attempts to escape the wheel of rebirth. Even asceticism was a striving for personal, holy status where gnosis and ecstasy were sublimated to personal salvation as also were the natural sciences. [23]

Thapar's perception that yogic meditation practice among the deviant cults contains an insurrectionary potentiality, if only of the spirit, is shared by Chatterjee, who compares ascetic yogic practices of the heterodox cults with popular protest, insurgencies, and civil disobedience, asserting that these are the only means by which oppressed peoples can reclaim and repossess their bodies and minds while emprisoned in the rigid class/caste system:

> Caste attaches to the body, not to the soul. It is the biological reproduction of the human species through procreation within endogamous caste groups which ensures the permanence of ascribed marks of caste purity or pollution. It is also the physical contact of the body with defiling substances or defiled bodies that mark it with the temporary conditions of pollution which can be removed by observing the prescribed procedures of physical cleansing. Further, if we have grasped the essence of caste, it is the necessity to protect the purity of his body that forbids the brāhmaṇa from engaging in acts of labor which involve contact with polluting material, and which, reciprocally, requires the unclean castes to perform those services for the brāhmaṇa. The essence of caste, we may then say, requires that the laboring bodies of the impure castes be reproduced in order that they can be subordinated to the need to maintain the bodies of the pure castes in their state of purity. All the injunctions of dharma must work to this end. . . . When popular religious cults deviate from the dogma of the dominant religion, when they announce the rejection of the Vedas, the sastric rituals or caste, they declare a revolt of the spirit. But the conditions of power

> which make such revolts possible are not necessarily the same as those that would permit a practical insubordination of laboring bodies. To question the ideality of caste is not directly to defy its immediate reality.[24]

Śramaṇism was characterized by a universal doctrine of salvation open to all castes, and "although social hierarchy was accepted, it did not emphasize separate social observances but, rather, cut across caste."[25] Most śramaṇic sects were not radically opposed to the two-tiered social order. In Buddhism, for example, upper castes in great numbers were initially recruited to the Saṅgha and became supportive lay followers. However, there were no restrictions on recruiting low-caste people and dalits, who in later periods became strong members of the ecclesiastical Saṅgha, giving the religion its levelling, democratic façade. Śāktism, on the other hand, is a revolutionary religion grounded in material outcome.

Cattle came to be valued as a way to facilitate trade, which discouraged the extravagant waste of cattle wealth in Vedic sacrifices. The primary animal used in Vedic sacrifice had been the cow, natural in a predominantly pastoral society. Although Vedic brāhmaṇas had indulged in a steady diet of sacrificial beef, the sixth century reforms drove this out of fashion, resulting in the absolute Hindu taboo against cattle-killing and beef-eating. However, Kosambi points out that the brāhmaṇas maintained a double standard:

> Lip service to Vedic *yajña* blood sacrifices accompanied the *ahiṁsā* (non-killing) that the brahmin had necessarily to preach after Buddhism. At the same time as obligatory vegetarianism, the *smriti* scriptures also contain a table of various types of meat that was to be fed to brahmin guests at a feast for the souls of departed ancestors.[26]

The Aśokan reform represented the final blow to the older Aryan tribal priesthood, the brāhmaṇa caste. The pastoral life and innumerable *yajña* sacrifices of the Panjab tribes had been the monopolistic foundation of the older brāhmaṇism. "This was wrecked beyond any chance of revival, first by Alexander's devastating raid and then by the immediately following Magadhan conquest,"[27] writes Kosambi. Aside from "a few sacrifices by the more simple-minded of the sixth-century kings,"[28] expansion of Vedic ritual into the Gangetic basin had been halted by Magadhan agriculture, philosophy, and the śramaṇic sects. No emphasis on the traditional brāhmaṇic *yajña* is found in the *Arthaśāstra*, although its author was a brāhmaṇa. Rather, the nature of the *yajña* was drastically altered.

The Ideological Shift from Yajña to Asceticism

A major effect of the ascendency of the kṣatriyas and of the doctrines of *saṁsāra* (the transmigration cycle) and *karma* (action) was the decline in importance of sacrifice (*yajña*) and its replacement by asceticism (*tapas*) as a means of achieving the new aim of life, salvation (*mokṣa*) from *saṁsāra*. The ancient institution of *yajña*, the center of the Indo-Aryan culture, around which moved the entire social and religious life of the Aryans, and which promised them abundance on earth and the worlds of fathers and gods after death, was now looked upon as a snare binding its performer ever more to the ignoble desires of life and perpetuating the cycle of endless births and deaths here as well as in heaven.[29]

* * *

> The dominant refrain of the Indian religions was that the world was unreal or a place of suffering. Life was a bondage from which release had to be obtained by cutting oneself away, as far as possible, from the world of activity and resorting to meditational or ascetic practices. From the sociological point of view, this approach to life was pessimistic, individualistic, and anti-social. . . . In the case of the orthodox schools, this view of life was further compounded by the paramount consideration of preserving the caste order. . . . Similarly, although Mahayana Buddhists took a prominent part in alleviating human suffering, they were inhibited from tackling political problems by their adherence to the doctrine of ahimsa (non-violence) and by regarding the world as a place of suffering. . . . Buddhism eschewed the use of force for any purpose whatsoever, and gave the doctrine of ahimsa a prominent place in its scheme of religious propaganda. In Jainism the application of this principle covered even the smallest of living beings. Later on, Brahmanism also partly accepted this approach. The cumulative result . . . was to help maintain the social status quo and entrench social reaction in the form of the caste order. All purposeful revolutionary movement towards human liberty and equality was either discounted or barred.[30]

In the late Vedic age (900–500 BCE), the incipient brāhmaṇic mission to decrease the political and socioeconomic power of low-caste groups and high-caste women gained momentum. Women and goddesses were now increasingly viewed as hedonistic creatures in need of male restraint,[31] and their subordinate role caused their sexuality to morph into vehicles of male enlightenment. The pattern of objectification and marginalization of women was worked out in male-oriented texts such as the Upaniṣads, where remnants of sexo-religious agricultural magic, first assimilated as ornamental accretions in Vedic *yajñas*, were now revalorized into symbols of spiritual practice.

In pre-class society, sexual union was performed as imitative magic in communal sacrifices to promote agricultural and material prosperity. Upaniṣadic imagery of female genitalia and sexual intercourse, however, is bereft of fertility magic with its homologization of women and Earth; sexual union, separated from its cosmic communal context of imitative magic, becomes instead a vehicle used by the male to gain reward and *mokṣa*. The *yajña* began to change its character, metamorphosing into a visualization process involving the male manipulation of female sexual energy to attain spiritual enlightenment (androgynous nondualism) and androcentric power that would become the goal of Buddhist and Hindu Tantrism. In numerous passages of the Upaniṣads, the sacrificial fire is symbolized by woman, who becomes the female sacrificial victim; her lower portion is the wood, the *yoni* is the flames, the male penetration is the carbon, and the coitus is the spark.[32]

In the *Bṛhadāraṇyaka Upaniṣad,*[33] the lower portion (*upastha*) of a woman is to be regarded as the sacrificial altar (*vedī*), the pubic hairs (*lomāni*) are the sacrificial grass, the outer skin (*bahirścarman*) is the floor for pressing the *soma* plants (*adhiṣavaṇa*), and the two labia of the vulva (*muṣkau*) constitute the inner fire. The text promises that he who remembers these metaphors during sexual union will receive the reward of the Vājapeya sacrifice, and propounds that the woman who refuses to engage in coitus must be coerced to do so.[34] Later, as Bhattacharyya points out,

> ingenious explanations were devised to explain away the vestiges of such practices. Even then, the evidences relating to sexual rituals and their connection with agriculture and the cult of the Mother Goddess could not be completely hushed up, and it is interesting to note that, in almost every period, Vedic literature shows traces of agricultural sexual rituals and of a pattern of sexual behavior different from the officially accepted norm.[35]

By the time of the Sūtras, the collective character of the *yajña,* its Neolithic themes of birth, death, and regeneration enacted in rituals involving sexual union and human and animal sacrifice, and its astro-agricultural base "had degenerated into a private affair,"[36] replaced by a whole new set of sacrifices to be performed by the householder alone. The growing trend toward asceticism among the new śramaṇic cults began to challenge the archaic sexual rituals of ancient Vedic and tribal religions, expressing "people's increasing alienation from their dissolving communities, and from the natural world itself."[37] As Kosambi observes, "When the *Upaniṣads* were added to supplement the various *Brāhmaṇas,* no direct acknowledgement was made of any change; but the contents of Brāhmaṇa books became entirely different. The *yajña* was now cited primarily for some mystical philosophy with generally fantastic interpretation, not for its original blood-and-guts performance."[38] It was this shift in the nature of sacrifices that ushered in a new emphasis on celibacy as the handmaiden to high-caste property consolidation:

> The triumph of the householder and his property inevitably carried along with it . . . stress on the value of celibacy. In early Buddhism and Jainism, it should be remembered, celibacy is also stressed. The emphasis on celibacy should demonstrate finally that sexual restrictions were inherent to the patriarchal tradition, and not to mysticism. The severe prohibitions on sexual relations outside of marriage were due to the overwhelming demand of private property, to make sure of the ancestry of the child. With property is associated the question of inheritance and herein lies the economic significance of . . . female chastity which is the contribution of the patriarchal class society.[39]

The shift from sexual ritual to asceticism was one of the products of the power clash between brāhmaṇas and kṣatriyas. It was the kṣatriyas, not the brāhmaṇas, who sponsored the *brahmavidyā* (knowledge of *brahman*) of the Upaniṣads. An important theme of Upaniṣadic thought resides in a secret doctrine that was known to only a few kṣatriyas who taught it to an exclusive group of trusted brāhmaṇas. We learn in the *Chāndogya Upaniṣad* that even so eminent a group as the *mahāśāla mahāśrotrīya*, the most learned among the brāhmaṇas, went to the kṣatriyas for instruction.[40] The subjects of the doctrine included the ideology of the soul (the *ātman*), the transcendental merging of *ātman* with *brahman* in meditation, and the fundamental notion of metempsychosis or the transmigration of the soul. Why was the doctrine secret and originally associated with the kṣatriyas? Few scholars[41] have addressed these questions. Among the obvious explanations is the fact that brāhmaṇas and kṣatriyas were non-productive elites with the privilege of leisure time in which they could indulge in conversations about idealistic philosophies and grand schemes of life after death. However, this is only a partial answer. Embedded in the amusements of the leisure class are socioeconomic influences on the secret doctrine of the kṣatriyas, viz., competition between brāhmaṇas and kṣatriyas, the social transformation from clan to individual orientation, and the spiritual anarchy of low-caste meditation practices. Thapar addresses the first of these aspects of the shift from ritual sacrifice to meditation:

> The adoption of meditation and theories of transmigration had the advantage of releasing the kṣatriyas from the pressures of a prestation [feudal] economy and permitting them to accumulate wealth, power, and leisure. . . . This also places a different emphasis on the function of the kṣatriya who had now ceased to be primarily a cattle-raiding, warrior chief. . . . The competition for status between brāhmaṇas and kṣatriyas and the separation of their functions, as well as their mutual dependence, is symbolized in the sacrificial ritual which becomes a key articulation of the relationship. The new belief was the reversal of the sacrificial ritual in that it required neither priests nor deities but only self-discipline and meditation.[42]

Moreover, the new belief contains "the first element of a shift from the clan to the individual;"[43] while the sacrificial ritual is clan-oriented, meditation and self-discipline, perhaps in opposition to the clan, are highly individualistic endeavors, symbols of the breaking away of the individual from the clan. Finally, the supplanting of the *yajña* by meditation

> introduces an element of anomie which becomes more apparent in the later development of these beliefs by various sects. These reflections were seminal to what became a major direction in Indian thought and action, the opting out of the individual from society and where renunciation is a method of self-discovery but can also carry a message of dissent. . . . But its inclusion may also partially have been motivated by the fact that when the doctrine was appropriated by heterodox teachers such as the Buddha, it could be maintained that even the roots of heterodoxy stemmed from the Vedic tradition.[44]

During the Buddhist period, brāhmaṇic hegemony received social challenges from various ideologies, including radical atheists such as the Lokāyatas, Jaina agnostics, and heterodox Hindus and Buddhists, who were opposed to absolute monarchical rule and the immense power of the priestly class, and wanted to create humane alternatives to the discrimination and persecution inherent in the caste system. In the meantime, despite the brāhmaṇas' attempts to maintain their monopoly by revamping Vedic dogma to accord with the exigencies of the times, "the old pre-pastoral rituals did not sink into oblivion, and the priestly class [was] not mentally ready to give up their traditional rituals."[45] The religious practices of the brāhmaṇas and their attitude towards trade thus became anachronistic and counterproductive for a time. Because of the growth of trade and urban settlements, kṣatriya rulers began to amass more property from the wealth of the traders than from the ritual powers of the brāhmaṇa priests, and they deemed the brāhmaṇical sacrificial religion useless.[46] The economic interests of kṣatriyas then became intertwined with that of prosperous vaiśya traders, "whose power had been growing without a corresponding elevation in their social status."[47]

Competition escalated between the two highest castes, and groups of kṣatriya landowners, locked in socioeconomic and religious conflict with brāhmaṇas, challenged brāhmaṇic political and religious leadership by aligning themselves with the Buddhist and Jaina heterodox sects, which theoretically opposed the caste system.[48,49] In reality, however, the *Chāndogya Upaniṣad* sanctions the caste system, promising individuals of pleasant conduct the prospect of entering a pleasant womb, either the womb of a brāhmaṇa, kṣatriya, or vaiśya woman. But those who do not comport themselves properly and observe dharma will enter a stinking womb, either the womb of a dog, a swine, or an outcaste.[50]

Furthermore, the kṣatriya landowners denied the authority of the Vedas and challenged other brāmaṇic traditions, viz., the Buddhist and Jaina emphasis on non-injury to animals. The latter credo "assumes a new economic significance in this context. . . . It is perhaps at this stage of development that the cow became identified with the Mother Goddess and beef-eating became a taboo."[51] Cattle should be protected, according to the *Suttanipāta*, for they are the givers of food, beauty, and happiness. This teaching had its economic base in the growing demands of the traders, for whom cattle constituted the most desirable mode of exchange. Buddhism offered moral support to all the exegencies of the trading class, including moneylending, usury, and slave-keeping, which are not condemned in the Buddhist texts.[52] Buddhist monastic centers also served as hubs of trade. The śramaṇic religions were popular among throngs of wealthier vaiśyas, "whose power had been growing without a corresponding elevation in their social status."[53] The appeal of the śramaṇic religions to low-caste peoples resided in the beckoning of their goddesses from śramaṇic pantheons, and in the possibility of renunciation and meditation as spiritual anarchy.

The Buddha, Asceticism, and Class Society

[T]he extension of the agrarian economy was generally accompanied either by Buddhist missions or by nucleii of *brāhmaṇa* settlements, through which Sanskritic culture was introduced into the new areas and the local culture of these areas was assimilated into the Sanskritic tradition. The interplay of these two levels of belief systems was a necessary process in the delineation of Indian culture. The stress so far has been on the high culture of the Sanskritic tradition which is inadequate for understanding the historical role of cultural forms.[54]

It was into a profoundly patriarchal class society, built upon the desecration of tribal values and the denigration of women, that Siddhārtha Gautama (*c.* 560–480 BCE), the historical founder of Buddhism, was born as a member of the privileged kṣatriya class. According to legend, the Buddha's mother, Māyā, experienced an immaculate conception (the Buddha was conceived by a white elephant in a dream, twice removed from reality); he miraculously left his mother's womb through the side of her hip rather than the birth canal; and Māyā died a week after giving birth. In Buddhism, the female principle, manifested in feminine sexuality, menstrual blood, conception, pregnancy, childbirth, or even the sight of a woman, represents the source of the curse of human life, which ultimately exhausts itself in sickness, old age, and death. The Buddha experienced both marriage and its polar opposite, sexual dissolution, as twin obstacles in his spiritual development that he had to overcome. He abandoned his wife and children, became a homeless mendicant, and distanced himself as far as possible from both domestic life and warfare.

As the Buddha repeatedly reinforced, woman *per se* functions as the first and greatest cause of illusion (*māyā*), as well as the energy that generates the phenomenal world (*saṁsāra*). The fundamental objective of every Buddhist is to overcome this deceptive *saṁsāra.* Māyā is the name of both Buddha's mother and the most powerful Indian goddess Māyā or Prakṛti, the World-Woman in whom the entire material universe is concentrated. Ceaselessly moving, she is the basic substance that contains the seeds of all phenomena. The word *māyā* is derived from the Sanskrit root *ma-*, the root of *mother* and *material.* This is the Great Mother of life, death, and the natural world, which Buddhist cosmology pits against the world of the spirit. According to Buddhist metaphors, *māyā* has woven a veil of illusion (the Platonic world of appearances) and cast it over the transcendental reality behind all existence (the spiritual principle). In order to be enlightened, a Buddhist must overcome *māyā*'s illusions, which are intended to bind the autonomous ego, yearning for freedom and the light, to her and the wheel of rebirth, thus destroying the male's salvation in eternity. The individual who has seen through her deceptions can have eternal life, but the person who is deceived by the World-Woman's tricks will be destroyed and reborn, like all living things, into an unceasing round of suffering, old age, and death. Viewing nature and spirit as an incompatible dualism, the Buddha was convinced that this contradiction could only be reconciled through the triumph of the spirit over *saṁsāra.*

The Buddha cultivated the ideology of *karma* and *saṁsāra* in a nihilistic paradigm that absorbed and blunted social inequities.[55] His theme of the source of human misery should be understood in the context of the "stupendous social transformations and wholesale bloodshed of the times."[56] His point of view was that of a rational social critic, idealist epistemologist, and deconstructionist:

> I behold the rich in this world, of the goods which they have acquired, in their folly they give nothing to others; they eagerly heap riches together and further and still further they go in their pursuit of enjoyment. The king, although he may have conquered the kingdoms of the earth, although he may be ruler of all land this side of the sea, up to the ocean's shore, would still insatiably covet that which is beyond the sea. The princes, who rule kingdoms, rich in treasures and wealth, turn their greed against one another, pandering insatiably to their desires. If these acts thus restlessly swim in the stream of impermanence, carried along by greed and carnal desire, who then can walk on earth in peace?[57]

A Śākya prince, the Buddha was aware that the brāhmaṇic epics propounded the ideology that "the [high-caste] individual was an end in himself and his self-realization was the highest goal of social existence."[58] This lofty individualism could best be attained through the *rāṣṭra,* or the organized political state, according to the elitist philosophy. Later Buddhism, in fact, modeled its structure on the *rāṣṭra,* and its monasteries, as miniature states, became foci of state wealth and power. The Buddha also absorbed and transformed into ascetic spiritual principles the *caturvarga* of *dharma, artha, kāma,* and *mokṣa* that comprised the four interdependent purposes of life in brāhmaṇism. In Buddhist nomenclature, the *caturvarga* was translated into the Four Noble Truths: (1) all is suffering; (2) suffering arises from desire; (3) suffering is ceased when desire ceases; (4) the Eightfold Path of Buddhist Dharma (right views, right intentions, right speech, right conduct, right livelihood, right effort, right mindfulness, right concentration) leads to the cessation of suffering. The Buddha did not revolt against orthodox brāhmaṇism; on the contrary, Bandyopadhyaya writes that

> it would be a serious misconception to regard the teachings of Buddhism as something extraneous to the spirit of Indian culture and tradition. . . . Buddha was never a revolutionary or tried to brush away the past. He was merely a reformer who wished to widen the social outlook and protested against the monopolies then claimed by the Brāhmaṇas. In doing so, . . . his criticisms were directed more towards pointing out the discrepancies between abstract principles and the contemporary practices than to create a new state of affairs.[59]

Bhattacharyya[60] and Chattopadhyaya[61] make a case for the Buddha's brilliant perception that the lost tribal ways of communalism and democracy left a great nostalgic void in the lives of the people. To fulfill the yearnings of an increasingly alienated low-caste and dalit domain, therefore, the Buddha recreated the structural façade of tribal collectivity within his heterodox cult. Early Buddhism's Saṅgha organization was patterned after the democracies of the non-monarchical tribes of the Eastern borderland, and "their republicanism was but a heritage of the past,"[62] designed to be "the ideal substitutes for a vanished way of life."[63] Chattopadhyaya has demonstrated in intricate detail the Buddha's comprehensive imitation of the tribal model in (a) the Saṅgha entrance procedure; (b) the Saṅgha's internal administration; and (c) personal or private property within the Saṅgha, concluding that

> at a critical stage of Indian history, while the free tribes of the times were being ruthlessly exterminated and, within the orbits of the expanding state powers, people were experiencing the rise of new values on the ruins of tribal equality, the Buddha was modeling his *saṅghas* on the basic principles of tribal society and was advising the brethren of his order to mould their lives according to these principles. This point is crucial. In building up his own *saṅghas*, the Buddha could provide the people of his times with the illusion of a lost reality, of the dying tribal collective. And it was only the great genius of the Buddha which could have built this coherent and complete illusion. Not only did he successfully build up his *saṅghas* on the model of the pre-class society, but he took great care to see that the members therein—the *bhikkhus* within the *saṅghas*—lived a perfectly detached life, *i.e.*, detached from the great historic transformation going on in the society at large, whose course was obviously beyond his power to change.[64]

Moreover, Buddhist *caityas*[65] were hewn from the rock of ancient Mother-goddess *pīṭhas*. As Kosambi has deciphered through empirical evidence, the sites of the local *grāmadevatā*, the village mothers, and their cults in Maharashtra are identical to the sites on the Western Ghats where the Buddhist monks created their cave temples. The goddess Manmodi (jaw-breaker) presided over the Junnar caves before the Buddhist caves were carved, and she returned, a thousand years later, to be worshiped without so much as a change of her name.[66] By choosing sacred goddess sites along the major trade routes as locations for Buddhist shrines, the monks profited from tribal hallowed ground. Tribal and village goddesses—denatured and converted into symbols of Buddhist doctrine—were incorporated into the Buddhist pantheon, and low-caste people were given sermons by the monks on ceasing their bloody sacrifices to their fierce goddesses. As Kosambi elaborates,

> The great Buddhist cave monasteries (all near mountain passes) at Karsambḷe, Thāṇaḷā, Bhājā, Kārle, Beḍsā, and Junnar fix the main trade routes without any doubt, particularly when smaller intermediate caves are linked up. It is logical to expect merchants to go along the tracks most frequented by whatever people lived there before the country was settled by fixed, plough-using villages. The Buddhist monks, not mere almsmen but expert food-gatherers, who penetrated the wilderness to preach *ahiṁsā* and peaceful social behavior, would initially follow the same tracks, in order to reach the greatest number of savages. Their religion insisted upon the cessation of blood-sacrifices, and the cult-spots were the most likely places for their preaching.[67]

The power spots and folklore associated with tribal and village goddesses were also essential elements of the Buddha's enlightenment:

> The sacredness of sites survives the changing of gods. A primordial sense of the sanctity of places, of the *sthala*, and an ancient knowing of the living, pervading

presence of the divinity of the Earth Mother, establishes her worship at crossroads and in aniconic stones. It is this element that was invoked when at the instant of enlightenment, the Buddha touched the earth with his hand and called the primordial Earth Mother to witness; for the site of the Buddha's enlightenment, the earth and the *bodhi* tree, were already holy and ancient. The earth under the *bodhi* tree was the abode of a Nāga, a cobra, the sacred protector of the site, who appeared and placed his hood over the Buddha's head to shelter the Holy One. . . . The moment of revelation, that still second of the birth of the unmanifest, is the mystery that, with the holy site, has to be guarded and protected.[68]

The illusion of a lost tribal ethos was created by the Buddha not only for his low-caste followers, but also for the elite males who wished to detach themselves permanently from bourgeois values. The Buddha's recruitment of high-caste males enabled them to renounce the most highly valued social traditions of class society (the brāhmaṇic traditions of *varṇa* and *āśrama*, service to parents, and family stability) to become itinerant beggars. "The Buddha's path," writes Jaini, "was essentially for a recluse who had, like the Buddha, rid himself of all possessions and had voluntarily accepted a life free from all worldly responsibilities, a life of a 'homeless wanderer'."[69] Young men by the hundreds, emulating the Buddha, abandoned their professions and wives to don the monastic yellow robes. The women were left virtual widows, forever childless (high-caste widows were not permitted to remarry, and high-caste women were not permitted to divorce and remarry), forever impoverished (women were not permitted to inherit property), or struggling to care for their children alone. As the Pāli scriptures report:

> Now at that time very distinguished young men belonging to respectable families of Magadha were leading holy lives under the Lord. People looked down upon them, criticized and disparaged them, saying: "The recluse Gotama [Gautama] wants to make (us) childless, the recluse Gotama is bent on making (us) widows, the recluse Gotama gets along by breaking up families."[70]

The Buddha's reply, one of studied and abstract indifference, values truth-seeking and the *dhamma* above all, and counters that those who object to the mass exodus of young men are envious of their wisdom:

> Verily great heroes, Truthfinders,
> lead by what is true *dhamma*.
> Who would be jealous of the wise
> led by *dhamma*?[71]

However, out of compassion for the abandoned wives whose husbands had joined the Order of Monks, the Buddha reluctantly established an Order of Nuns:

> But Gautama was not seeking only his own emancipation: he was a "Buddha;" he was determined to show the Way to thousands of others and was not to be stopped by worldly considerations of a stable society or by the tears of the wailing wives who rightly accused him of driving them into a forced widowhood

> and involuntary childlessness. For them also the Buddha, after great hesitation, opened the gates of freedom by founding an Order of Nuns. This new Order was admittedly subordinated within the Order of Monks, but the sisters were declared to be equals in the spiritual progress towards *nirvāṇa*.[72]

Both the Buddha and Mahāvīra permitted women to become cloistered nuns at a time when elite women of the dominant dharma were no longer permitted to study the Vedas. This was one of the more liberal aspects of institutionalized celibacy in Buddhism and Jainism, consistent with their wide recruitment of low-caste and untouchable women. Because celibacy was highly valued, the nuns of the deviant dharmas did not pose a threat to the misogynistic marriage and inheritance laws of the brāhmaṇical lawmakers. According to A.S. Altekar,

> When discipline became slack and unworthy persons began to be admitted into monasteries and nunneries, the tone of moral life deteriorated. It hastened the process of the downfall of Buddhism. Later Hinduism took a lesson from what it saw in Buddhist monasteries and nunneries and declared women to be ineligible for renunciation (*saṁnyāsa*). It maintained that not renunciation but due discharge of family responsibilities was the most sacred duty of women. Nuns therefore have disappeared from Hinduism during the last 1500 years.[73]

The Buddha was not opposed to slavery, property holding, or the decline in elite women's social status and freedom. The Buddha associated with considerable numbers of the wealthy and well-to-do merchant class, "the mainstay of all ascetics,"[74] who were responsible for and profited from the desecration of the old ways, and the Buddha upheld the moral imperative of laws that benefited elites, slave-owners, property-owners, and traders, viz., the Buddha declared that slaves and debtors were forbidden to run away from their obligations; private property could not be appropriated; and animals could no longer be killed indiscriminately.[75] One of the five fruits of wealth, spoke the Buddha, was the ability to pay taxes. In the brāhmaṇical hierarchy, the vaiśya or trading class was the third-ranking caste in society, but in the Buddha's paradigm, the status of the trading class was elevated. Similarly, the Buddha's objection to the sterility of the brāhmaṇic sacrificial religion saved property owners needless expenses. Thus the Buddha engaged both high and low castes by understanding where their interests resided.

Furthermore, the misogyny of the time was an intrinsic element in Buddhism, since lay Buddhists were kṣatriyas, vaiśyas, and converted brāhmaṇas, obsessed with the patriarchal consolidation of wealth and the consequent bracketing of women and the low-caste majority with chattel. The bourgeois interests of the householder and his property were inevitably accompanied by an emphasis on the value of celibacy, since the demands of private property and inheritance necessitated severe prohibitions on sexual relations outside of marriage to ensure the ancestry of offspring. In harmony with the socioeconomic pressures of patriarchal class society, early Buddhism and

Jainism also stressed the importance of celibacy, which should demonstrate that sexual taboos were inherent to patriarchy rather than to mysticism. Unchastity among Buddhist monks was a grave offense that caused immediate expulsion from the order. Celibacy, called *brahmacarya*, or conduct worthy of a brāhmaṇa or a holy man, was one of the three essentials of monastic life, in addition to poverty and non-violence (*ahiṁsā*).[76] Sexual union was decried by orthodox Buddhists as the "bovine" or "bestial" habit, and they cultivated a misogynistic contempt for women. Monks were programed via meditation exercises to equate women's bodies with human excrement and putrefied corpses. As Conze rationalizes, offering a psychoanalytic-climatic explanation: "This contempt is, of course, easily understood as a defense mechanism, since women must be a source of perpetual danger to all celibate ascetics—especially in a hot climate."[77] Monks were obviously cautioned to be perpetually on their guard, as the following short dialogue illustrates:

> Ānanda: How should we behave to women?
> Lord: Not see them!
> Ānanda: And if we have to see them?
> Lord: Not speak to them!
> Ānanda: And if we have to speak to them?
> Lord: Keep your thoughts tightly controlled![78]

When *bhikkhus* joined the Saṅghas, they entered into an ahistorical existence of psychological detachment that was contingent on their ability to suppress carnal desires, the cause of suffering (second to the primary cause of suffering, their mothers). Much of the monks' training to this day involves a systematic deconstruction of the material body, which they are taught to view as repulsive, offensive, and disgusting. Daily and repetitively they visualize in clinical detail the thirty-two parts of the body, and when a monk sees an attractive woman, he is trained to protect himself by immediately superimposing the following "manifold impurities" on her image.

> And further the disciple contemplates this body, from the sole of the foot upwards, and from the top of the hair downwards, with a skin stretched over it, and filled with manifold impurities. There are in this body:
> hairs of the head, hairs of the body, nails, teeth, skin;
> muscles, sinews, bones, marrow, kidneys;
> heart, liver, serous membranes, spleen, lungs;
> intestines, mesentery, stomach, excrement, brain;
> bile, digestive juices, pus, blood, grease, fat;
> tears, sweat, spittle, snot, fluid of the joints, urine.[79]

Both Buddhism and Jainism became institutionally based early in their development, and the orders escalated fairly soon to join the brāhmaṇas as large-scale property holders. "As such," writes Thapar, "the records of their evolution did not merely narrate the life of the Buddha and the history of the

Saṅgha (with its various divergent sects, each claiming status and authenticity), but also described the building of monasteries, the amassing of property and the rights to controlling these—rights which became complex and competitive with the fissioning off of sects from the main stems."[80] When the Buddha died in *c.* 480 BCE, numerous Buddhist monastic communities had already been established in northeast India. For over four centuries the Buddha's doctrine, the Dhamma, did not exist in written form, but rather, was committed to memory by the monks to recite or chant communally. (Like the brāhmaṇas, Buddhists were opposed to writing down their religious dogma.)[81]

About two hundred years after the Buddha's death, Buddhism split into two branches: the Theravādins (Hīnayāna Buddhists, or Old Wisdom School) in eastern India, the school that still dominates Burma, Thailand, and Sri Lanka; and the Sarvāstivādins, who flourished for 1,500 years, centered in Mathura, Gandhara, and Kashmir. The Hīnayānists confined their religion exclusively to monks. Although low-caste people were allowed to take the *triśaraṇa,* offer gifts to the Saṅgha, and observe a moral creed, organized worship and ritual were not provided. In addition, a more liberal sect that dissented from the Old Wisdom School, the Mahāsaṅghikas—originating in Magadha and the South around 250 BCE—evolved into a new version of Buddhism, the Mahāyāna, in the Andhra country from about the first century AD. At the time of Kaniṣka it was recognized as a form of Buddhism, and it spread over northern India in the first and second centuries AD, when Mahāyāna Buddhism became influenced by the existing cults of the female principle. When Buddhism flourished as a great religious system,

> its system of organization came to be modelled more and more on the Empire which was growing so fast. The Saṅgha itself was conceived as a great Dharma Empire. The Buddha was its Cakravartin, the Agraśrāvakas Sāriputta and Moggalāyanna were turned into the Dharma-senāpati and Amātya, respectively. Ānanda was conceived as the Dharma-bhāṇḍagārika and so on. The Dharma idea, as enunciated by the Tathāgata, acted on the universal political idea of the Empire and the latter reacted to it. The offspring of these two agents was the Imperialistic Dharma ideal of the Emperor Aśoka.[82]

We have observed that by yielding surplus, the patriarchal mode of production facilitates the growth of a non-productive privileged class, and that legal, military, and police systems are put in place as state machinery to protect and perpetuate the property interests of the elites. As further adjuncts of the state, both Buddhist and Hindu sects practiced what Max Weber termed "monastic landlordism," a system parallel to that of church lands in Europe[83] in which the powerful, opulent monastic centers of the period were the foci of political and economic control of the state. From both Hindu and Buddhist monastic centers, there arose "the foci of sectarian and political orthodoxy as well as heterodoxy and opposition which led them into varying relationships vis-à-vis political authority."[84] Such religious centers frequently acted as trade networks, which placed them in close contact with guilds, merchants, and itinerant yoginis and yogis. Both Śaiva and Vaiṣṇava sects, like the Buddhists before them, eventually established themselves in *āśramas* and *maṭhas* and became enormously wealthy property holders. Thus "intensified competition for patronage [had] to be supported by claims to legitimacy—which require a substantial input of historically phrased argument."[85] Thapar explains the linkage between property ownership, agriculture, monasteries, and trade:

> The link between agriculture and commerce is important for understanding the changes in the subsequent period. The opulence of those involved in commerce was poured into the adornment of religious monuments, monasteries, and images, and in the conspicuous consumption which is associated with the wealthier towndwellers of these times. This tends to obscure the agrarian scene where one notices less of *mahāśāla* landowners and large estates and more of those with small holdings. Small plots of land could be purchased and donated to religious beneficiaries and it seems unlikely, as has been argued, that such sales were restricted to religious donations. Smallholding together with the alienation of land could point to some degree of impoverishment among peasants.[86]

Thapar maintains that the disappearance of Buddhism in India was due to the Buddhist community's abstraction from social life, which "prevented it from denting the caste system;" and to the fact that the monastery closed its doors to those who would change the system by civil disobedience. "Philosophies of detachment and inaction are not conducive to change," she reasons, "and the theory of transmigration encourages neither reform nor revolt nor change."[87] Buddhist nuns and monks eventually spread the teachings of Buddha to Central Asia, East Asia, Tibet, Sri Lanka, and Southeast Asia.

The Ājīvikas and the Jainas

The Buddha's contemporaries among the śramaṇic religions included Gośāla, the leader of the Ājīvikas, and Mahāvīra, the leader of the Jainas, both of whom attempted to return to tribal values through the renunciation of class society. Gośāla was a fatalist who believed that we live in the grip of destiny, and nothing humankind can do will change the predetermined course of events. When the Vajjians, one of the few surviving free tribes, were destroyed, Gośāla perceived the event as "a great storm cloud" that swept away all hope, and he renounced the world:

> He died of despair and madness, pining in his delirium for the last drink (*carime pāne*), the last song (*carime geye*), the last dance (*carime natte*), and the last greetings (*carime añjalikamme*)—characteristics of simple undifferentiated tribal life. Thus from his death-bed he could only advise to his follower to play on the lute—quite consistent for a man who saw the whole world he stood for falling to pieces before his very eyes.[88]

Like Gośāla, Mahāvīra was profoundly disillusioned with the disintegration of tribal values and the inequities of class society. He believed that action should be undertaken to eliminate all actions. *Karma* is produced by action, thus ensuring the continuation of material existence. Following his predecessor Pārśva, Mahāvīra taught the four *vratas* of right conduct—do not kill, do not lie, do not steal, and disregard worldly things such as property—to which he added a fifth injunction against sexual intercourse. As Bhattacharyya points out, "The four rules of right conduct, prescribed by Pārśva, were simply the moral values of tribal society which were ruthlessly undermined in the age of the Buddha and Mahāvīra."[89]

Jainism was one of the chief religions of India by the end of the third century AD. In *c.* AD 512, the Second Jain Council at Valabhī produced the Jaina canon in its present form. The *śāsanadevatās* or goddesses, classified in Jaina texts such as *Uttarādhyayana Sūtra* and *Ācāra Dinakara*, were adapted from contemporaneous low-caste cults "as a submission to the demands of the lay followers of the creed."[90] The *śāsanadevatās* were regarded as adherents of the Jinas who merited customized rituals, and are identified as Cakreśvarī, Ajitabālā, Duritāri, Kālikā, Mahākālī, Śyāmā, Śaṇṭā, Bhṛkuṭi, Sutārakā, Aśokā, Mānavī, Caṇḍā, Viditā, Aṅkuśā, Kandarpā, Nirvāṇī, Bālā, Dhāriṇī, Dharaṇapriyā, Naradattā, Gāndhārī, Ambikā, Padmāvatī, and Siddhāyikā. Other important Jaina goddesses include Śri-Lakṣmī, the Mātṛkās (proto-Yoginīs), and the Vidyādevīs, the latter comprised of sixteen goddesses, including Sarasvatī as the goddess of learning, Kālī, Rohiṇī, Mahākālī, Prajñapti, Gaurī, Vajraśṛṅkhalā, and others. The Jainas also adopted the cult of the Sixty-four Yoginīs.

BHAKTI CULTS

How can I reach him through love?
On him, a snake is dancing
Preventing anyone to approach him.
Moreover, he himself
puts on necklaces of old skulls
and whitened bones,
and, rejoicing, rides
a bull.[91]

Beginning from *c.* 400 BCE, the political and social absolutism underlying the development of state power slowly expanded into the arena of religion, where it assumed the form of monotheistic ideas. At the dawning of the Christian era in southern India, a variety of devotional cults—referred to generically as Bhakti or Bhāgavata (devotional religion)—introduced a major new religious expression that negated caste and professed that divinity was accessible to all people through devotion and love. The *sine qua non* of Bhakti was absolute devotion to adored deities, conceived in human form, and worshiped as images. As discussed earlier, Bhakti was a fusion between the functions of the *akam* and *puṟam* traditions of the Caṅkam bardic age and brāhmaṇic and Indo-Aryan religion. Like Tantra, Bhakti challenges the hierarchical patriarchalism of orthodox brāhmaṇism, whose classical scriptures ordain that only twice-born males qualify for salvation. Both Bhakti and Tantra are populist religious movements in which salvation is equally available to men and women.

For Tantrics, every woman is an embodiment of the great Śakti, whereas for Bhaktas women are seen as being naturally better suited to love God than men are. In that tradition men must strive to feel and think as women in order to experience the greatest possible closeness to God. In some forms of late medieval Bhakti cults, the female principle in the form of Rādhā emerges as the dominant one, the godhead becoming feminine.[92]

On the other hand, Bhattacharyya and Thapar look at Bhakti as a sect of social relations, construing the self-surrender and consummate faith intrinsic in Bhakti cults as the institutionalization of a didactic symbolic model of the blind loyalties expected of landless laborers to their feudal overlord or king.

The idea of a supreme god ruling over the universe was based solely upon the new-fangled principle of absolute monarchy. In pre-class societies men had control over the gods; they believed that they could bring the forces of nature under their control by collective rituals and other performances. In class societies, this belief was shattered to pieces; the gods represented the ruling class, to be pleased only by propitiation and devotion; and monotheism was the logical consequence of this process.[93]

The elitist political agenda of Bhakti was subliminally expressed in patriarchal myths that discredited tribal values in favor of the class system. Specifically, the *Mahābhārata* "upholds the idea of the political unification of India under a Cakravartin, the human prototype of the divine Viṣṇu, mastering over the universe."[94] In the *Bhagavadgītā* (a part of the *Mahābhārata* composed about the second century BCE), the king, identified with god and divine will, is poised against Arjuna, the hero, who is equated with pre-class tribal values. Reluctant to kill his kinsmen and thus commit the supreme tribal taboo, Arjuna was persuaded that "this taboo had to be broken for the interest of newly developed values supposed to integrate the monopoly of state power."[95] Thus the *Bhagavadgītā* is a parable of individual submission to the "divine will" of the lord or king. Monotheism, in supplanting tribal polytheism, became a metaphor and model of the absolute supremacy of the feudal monarch; the role of the low-caste majority was to surrender and dedicate their lives to his service, which necessitated breaking all ties with the pre-class system.

The Vedic god Viṣṇu was resurrected as the divine counterpart of an earthly king, but Vāsudeva is not identified with Viṣṇu even in the earlier sections of the *Mahābhārata.* Iconographic depictions of the god Viṣṇu-Vāsudeva did not appear until the beginning of the Christian era, about the same period that goddesses were embraced by Viṣṇu and Vaiṣṇavite deities. It was not until the end of the third century BCE that Vaiṣṇavism became popular as a distinctive religion "supporting the cause of absolute monarchy and encouraging the destruction of the old tribal values."[96]

The new social relations on the ground were echoed in human relations with divine forces: Bhakti cults and the sects that emerged from them were premised on the devotees' dependence on and salvation through the deity. This god-centered ideology contradicted the human-centered nature of earlier indigenous religion, in which humans held sway over the gods. The worship of an icon, substituted for the ritual of sacrifice, became *de rigueur* in Purāṇic religion.[97]

But while devotees looked up to their god as a king, the god, unlike the human ruler, viewed all his devotees as individuals of equal worth. This latent individualistic and egalitarian content of Bhakti, its element of symbolic dissent, was co-opted, diluted, and rechannelized into an notion of *inward* freedom, no threat to the monopoly of state power:

> The significance of these new cults and sects may lie in part in the focus on loyalty to a deity which has parallel to the loyalty of peasants and others to an overlord. . . . The egalitarian emphases of the devotees in the eyes of the deity has rightly been viewed as the assertion of those lower down the social scale in favor of a more egalitarian society. But its significance grows when the social background to this belief is one of increasing disparity. Movements of dissent which had religious forms were often gradually accommodated and their radical content slowly diluted. The move away from community participation in a ritual to a personalized and private worship encourages the notion of individual freedom, even if it is only at the ideological level.[98]

The pre-Vedic Rudra, later known as Śiva, was resuscitated about the time that Viṣṇu resurfaced, and for the same purpose: the consolidation of state power. Śaivism became popular as a distinct low-caste monotheistic religion from about the beginning of the Christian era. Because the Śramaṇic and Bhakti cults were not initially "religions of the masses," they lacked Śaivism's great capacity to embrace and enfold the Mother-goddess elements of folk religions. The Bhakti poets are a part of a radical religious group that was integrated into Hinduism and reinterpreted as self-suppression. "Allowed to advance in the bold spirit of freedom and reform that they represented, these fiery statements could have created revolutions toward justice and equity in brahminical Indian society," writes Chitnis. "But, quietly absorbed into a tradition in which the capacity to serve and suffer silently is considered a virtue, they have been converted into gentle, soothing, peaceful, relatively blunt devotional verse."[99]

Śramaṇic Absorption of Indigenous Goddesses

> Behind the pale of Aryan orthodoxy and its tendency to abstract symbolism there lay an extensive and deep-rooted system of popular beliefs and cults and a decided tendency to anthropomorphic presentation. These popular beliefs implied an iconography. . . of Yakṣas and Nāgas, Devatās and Vṛkṣakās, the Earth and Mother-goddesses and divinities of fertility, fairies and goblins and human heroes. Gradually all of these found their place in a theistic Hinduism and Buddhism which were not purely Āryan, but Indian; partly in *propria persona* as minor divinities acting on behalf of the higher gods as guardians or servants, but also, by a fusion of concepts, representing them.[100]

We have seen that the Vedas and other literature before the second century BCE present an exclusionary view of Indian religion that, in terms of total population, represented only a tiny minority of elites. As anthropologist Fiona Bowie observes, "The Vedic (scriptural and priestly) elements of Hinduism are indeed only one strand, and most 'village' Hinduism would more closely fit the description of a primal religion."[101] The great mass of the people did not worship the abstract deities of priestly theology, but rather, the primal personifications of forces of nature—Mother-goddesses, feminine divinities of increase, and local genii.[102] The rich vernacular religions were alive with indigenous Earth Mothers and fertility goddesses, their primeval forest dwellings animated by tree spirits, mysterious beings, and semi-demons. The *gandharvas, yakṣas, yakṣiṇīs, nāgas,* and *apsarās* of the *Atharvaveda* were the protectors of the tribal-cum-śūdra agriculturists whose labor and taxes supported the elites.

The Buddhist *Aṅguttara Nikāya,* compiled between the third and second centuries BCE, and the *Mahāniddesa* and *Cullaniddesa,* dated between the second and first centuries BCE, reveal the dazzling array of archaic religions and cults that existed contemporaneously with the Śramaṇic cults and the dominant dharma. Among the low-caste faiths of the time were the Nirgrantha, Traidaṇḍika, Devadhārmika, Muṇḍa-śrāvaka, Jaṭilaka, Aviruddhaka, Gautamakam Maṇḍika, and Parivrājaka; the devotees of Vāsudeva, Pūrṇabhadra, Baladeva, Maṇibhadra, the cow, horse, elephant, crow, and dog; and the worshipers of *dik, deva, brahman,* Indra, Sūrya, Candra, Agni, the *nāgas,* the *asuras,* the *gandharvas,* and the *yakṣas.*[103] In fact, the contemporary Indian rural scene maintains the eclectic, mythic flavor of the first century BCE:

> An enquiry into the structure of worship in interior rural societies reveals a fragile and at times non-existent line that divides the quick and the dead, the today and the yesterday, the historical, the mythological, and the dim past of prehistory. A recent Government of India census publication documenting village festivals, gods, and rituals of Andhra Pradesh illustrates the living reality in the making of myth, legend, and village deities in rural India. In the detailed maps of districts and villages, one sees that the worship of Siddhas, the ancient magician-alchemists, the deified Yogis with their supporting myths and enshrined images, coexists with the blood-thirsty rites to the Grāma Devatās, the village mothers. Bāsavannā, the historical founder of the Vīra Śaiva cult, fuses with the ancient Yakṣa cult of Nandikesvara and is enshrined and worshiped in the form of a stone bull.[104]

From the beginning of the Christian era, the tribal and village goddess cults began to ascend in strength and importance, becoming the most evocative element of the Śramaṇic religions, Vaiṣṇavism (Bhakti), and Śaivism, and exposing deities and rituals of the lower strata of society to Indian elites. Conceptions of *bhakti* and individual salvation through a deity were interwoven with the newly absorbed tribal goddesses, diluting their revolutionary potentiality. These tribal goddesses would later emerge as Tantric Buddhist and Hindu *devīs.* Theravādin or Hīnayāna Buddhists (the Old Wisdom School) eschewed *bhaktic* notions of faith; rather, theirs was a path of wisdom earned by the austerities and self-abnegation of cloistered monks. Mahāyānism, on the other hand, "was sufficiently elastic to absorb the trend toward *bhakti*, and to provide it with a philosophical foundation."[105]

Early Buddhism

> The Old Buddhism had been a severely masculine system, and only a few quite subordinate feminine deities were admitted. The higher gods are sexless, so are the inhabitants of the Buddha-fields. Femininity was on the whole a bar to the highest spiritual attainment, and on approaching Buddha-hood the Bodhisattva ceased to be reborn as a woman. A woman cannot possibly become a Buddha.[106]

Primordial unmarried fertility goddesses of increase, metamorphosed into didactic symbols linking spiritual wisdom and material prosperity with proto-bourgeois property holdings, misogyny, and repressive morality, were admitted to the Old Wisdom School. The most important of the early Buddhist goddesses are Pṛthivī (Pathavi) or Dharaṇī, the Earth Mother, and Lakṣmī (Lakkhī) or Śrī (Siri). Siri-Lakkhī, according to the *Abhidhānappadīpikā*, is the Buddhist goddess of beauty and prosperity. She represents the paragon of the dutiful vaiśya wife who is subjected to the repressive morality borne of elite property interests. She is described as the goddess of *parivārasampatti* (family property) and *pañña* (wisdom) in the commentary on the *Sumaṅgala Jātaka*, and as the goddess of fortune, wisdom, and virtue in the *Sāikedāsa*, *Dhajavihetha*, and *Siri-Kālakaṇṇi* Jātakas. Because the Buddhist Lakkhī is also the goddess of wisdom, she is an amalgamation of the brāhmaṇical Lakṣmī and Sarasvatī. (There is also a Buddhist Sarasvatī.) She floated down to Earth through the air with golden raiment, ointment, and ornament, diffusing an auspicious bright yellow light, according to the *Siri-Kālkaṇṇī Jātaka*. She loved a merchant for his righteousness, guilelessness, honesty, gentleness, friendliness, liberality, blandness, and meekness—qualities required of devotees to win her favor—and lived with him in his time of distress. Lakkhī dwells in four objects: a fowl, a gem, a club, and a wife. Her immoral antithesis is Alakkhī, identified with Kālakaṇṇī, who is portrayed in the *Siri-Kālkaṇṇī Jātaka* as the daughter of king Virupākkha who descended to Earth diffusing an inauspicious blue light, wearing blue raiment, ointment, and jewels. She is said to love those who are wanton, treacherous, greedy, envious, hypocritical, and morose.

Mahāyāna Buddhism

Buddhism morphed from a male-oriented moral code of renunciation and austerity into the artful complexity of Mahāyānism. Among the śramaṇic sects, it was the Mahāyāna that incorporated the greatest numbers of low-caste goddess cults into its pantheon. Emerging as a systematic doctrine in the Andhra country from about the first century AD, Mahāyānism represents the folk aspects of Buddhism, much as Śaivism connotes folk Hinduism. The tribal and village goddesses, therefore, became increasingly influential in Mahāyānism, and were fused with *bhaktic* notions of devotion to personal saviors.

The first autonomous Mahāyāna Buddhist goddess was Tārā, imported into the Buddhist pantheon *c.* AD 150 as Avalokiteśvara's consort. Tārā became the savioress who helps devotees "cross to the other shore," removes dread and fear, and grants all wishes. Of primitive conception, Tārā was "a creation of the popular mind"[107] who, in the course of her evolution, had assimilated within herself numerous goddesses that symbolized various forms of the female principle. Bhattacharyya traces her etymological history from the late Vedic age:

> The epithets Tārā Tāriṇī, attributed to the Devī in the *Mahābhārata* and the Purāṇas, may be traced to the *Yajurveda* in which the term Tārā, meaning 'saviour' is an appellation of the god Śiva. Then there is the Sanskrit word *Tārā* or *Tarakā* meaning a star (cf. Persian *Sitāra,* Greek *Aster,* Latin *Stella,* and English 'star' and also the names of such foreign goddesses as Ishtar, Astarte, Atargatis, Astaroth, etc.) and the word might easily represent the name of a goddess dwelling among the stars. Many such streams later culminated in the conception of Tārā whose cult was established in different parts of India by the sixth century AD. . . . [T]he development of the Śākta religion received a great momentum from the Tārā cult of the Buddhists. The Śākta Tārā, also called Ugratārā, Ekajaṭā, and Nīla-Sarasvatī is undoubtedly an adaptation of the Mahāyāna Buddhist goddess of the same name.[108]

Prajñāpāramitā, often identified with Tārā, was not a goddess of the lower strata, but rather an abstract symbol invented to apply to a virtue, a book, a *mantra,* and a female divinity. The personification of transcendental wisdom, Prajñāpāramitā's conception originated among small groups of Buddhist ascetics at the beginning of the Christian era. In the *Prajñāpāramitā Sūtras,* she is "the Mother of all the Buddhas and Bodhisattvas," symbolizing the origin of a Buddha's enlightenment from the perfection of wisdom. Thus, the female principle was depicted as equal, prior, and even superior to the Enlightened Male. The elevation of the female principle in Mahāyānism, however, was essentially rhetorical and symbolic, competing as it did with the ideology of celibacy and the all-pervading misogynistic morality of the patriarchal class system. In Mahāyāna, the "Great Vehicle," the female is still regarded as inferior, powerless, and contemptible, unworthy and incapable of being a savior or *bodhisattva,* the holder of androcentric power. Woman's primary objective in life should be her liberation from her physical body; selfless compassion motivates the Mahāyāna monk to assist her in preparing for her transformation that will enable her to become a man in her next reincarnation. The female principle—life, the body, nature, and the soul—in both Mādhyamika and Yogācāra (Mahāyāna's foundational schools) is sacrificed to *citta,* or purely masculine absolute spirit.

> While . . . Buddhism acknowledged the importance of feminine attitudes of the world, and personified them into a multitude of feminine deities, a sexual attitude to femininity was generally discouraged, and the sexual implications, both of femininity, and of the relation between the masculine and the feminine principle, were glossed over. [By contrast,] [i]n the Left-handed Tantra, concepts

> derived from sexual life were openly introduced into the explanation of spiritual phenomena. . . . [T]he authors of the Prajñāpāramitāsūtras were aware that the pursuit of perfect wisdom could easily assume the character of a love affair with the Absolute. We are . . . told explicitly that a Bodhisattva should think of perfect wisdom with the same intensity and exclusiveness with which a man thinks of a "handsome, attractive, and beautiful woman" with whom he has made a date, but who is prevented from seeing him.[109]

Although many Buddhist goddesses such as Parṇaśabarī and others were adopted from tribal religious systems by Mahāyānists, their nature and function are fundamentally different from those of the non-Buddhist goddesses. Whereas tribal goddesses represented potential aid for practical, earthly purposes, Buddhist goddesses are denatured abstractions of Buddhist ideology. As Bhattacharyya explicates:

> Goddesses of the Epics and Purāṇas are syncretistic products revealing in their conception a prolonged historical evolution. It is a fact that the existing cults of the Female Principle exerted a tremendous influence on Buddhism and practically saturated it. But the goddesses that were produced in Buddhism under such an influence lacked concreteness. The Buddhists started an unrelenting process of deification by turning all objects, cosmic and philosophical principles, literature, letters of the alphabet, the directions, and even the desires into gods and goddesses, with forms, colors, poses of sitting, and weapons.[110]

Vajrayāna Buddhism

According to Buddhist tradition, the *Vajrayāna* ("the Diamond Vehicle"), the name by which Buddhist Tantrism is conventionally known, was introduced by Asaṅga (*c.* AD 400), the famous Yogācāra master, and Nāgārjuna (second or third century AD), the eminent founder of Mādhyamika and among the most highly celebrated and elusive personalities in medieval Buddhism. Probably the most ancient and most important Vajrayānic text, often attributed to Asaṅga, is the *Guhyasamāja Tantra.*

The doctrine of Manicheism, founded by the Babylonian Mani in the third century, bears a definite resemblance to the most esoteric of the Vajrayānic sects, Atiyoga or Dzogchen. A syncretistic Gnostic religion, Manicheism spread from Iran and West and East Turkestan to China, and in the other direction, to North African. Eastern Manicheism penetrated into the Iranian-Indian frontier districts and the Punjab. Like most proselytizers, Mani "adopted . . . the religious and mythological language of whatever people he was trying to convert . . ., facilitated the penetration of Manicheanism everywhere, and favored the spread of syncretism. . . ."[111] The aspect of Mani's doctrine that is especially similar to Dzogchen is the Manichean Father of Light and its five light eons, which correspond, both philosophically and artistically in the *maṇḍalic* sacred art it generated, to the Vajrayāna teachings of Ādibuddha and the five Tathāgatas (the so-called Dhyāni-Buddhas) and to the Dzogchen conception of the five pure lights.

Tantrism developed in India's two border regions: in the east—Bengal, Bihar, parts of Orissa, and especially in Assam—and in the northwest, on the frontier of Afghanistan. In its flourishing years, Tantric Buddhism coincided with the rule of the Pāla kings who dominated the political and cultural scene of Bengal and Bihar for approximately four centuries, from the middle of the eighth to the middle of the twelfth centuries AD. Nāgārjuna was a native of southern India in the region of Andhra Pradesh, in the deep heartland of Dravidian India. From these facts we might conclude with Eliade that, "especially in the beginning, Tantrism developed in the moderately Hinduized provinces where the spiritual counteroffensive of the aboriginal stocks was at its height,"[112] and where fierce goddesses, *yakṣiṇīs,* and *ḍākinīs* were worshiped by rural peoples. "The confluence of Buddhism and Śāktism," writes Miranda Shaw, "is such that Tantric Buddhism could properly be called 'Śākta Buddhism'."[113]

Jainism

According to the *Ācāra Dinakara,* Jaina goddesses were classified into three genres: *prāsāda-devīs* or general goddesses worshiped as installed images; *sampradāya-devīs* or sectarian goddesses; and *kula-devīs,* Tantric goddesses worshiped with occult rituals and *mantras.* In the latter genre reside Kālī, Mahākālī, Kaṅkālī, Cāmuṇḍā, Kapālinī, Durgā, Bhadrakālī, Lalitā, Gaurī, Rohiṇī, etc. In his *Abhidhānacintāmaṇi,* Hemachandra lists a wide range of goddesses, including the eight Mothers such as Brahmāṇī, Māheśvarī, etc.; the mothers of Tīrthaṅkaras such as Vijayā, Marudevī, etc.; and the cults of sixteen Śruta or Vidyā *devīs,* discussed in the typology above, which were derivative of the *yakṣiṇīs.* In addition, Śrutadevī or Sarasvatī and Śrī or Lakṣmī, almost identical to the brāhmaṇic goddesses of the same names, were admitted into the Jaina pantheon. The cult of the Sixty-four Yoginīs was also incorporated into Jainism, but most of their names were changed from the brāhmaṇic names of Yoginīs to unique Jaina names. They include Mahā Yoginī, Siddha Yoginī, Yugeśvarī, Pretākṣī, Ḍākinī, Kālī, Kālarātrī, Niśācarī, Baṭṭālī, Klimkarī, Bhūtaḍāmarī, Kumārikā, Vārāhī, Caṇḍikā, Kaṅkālī, Bhuvaneśvarī, Lakṣmī, Kuṇḍalī, Divyayogī, Gaṇeśvarī, Hṛṅkarī, Siddhi, Vitālā, Vīrabhadrāṁśī, Phakarī, Dhumrākṣī, Rājasī, Kalahapriyā, Rājasī, Ghoraraktāsī, Bhayaṅkarī, Virupākṣī, Jālakī, Bairī, Dhurjatī, Kāmakī, Kapālā, Yantravāhinī, etc. Iconographical characteristics of these goddesses are described in the *Ācāra Dinakara,* Hemcandra's *Abhidhānacintāmaṇi* and *Triṣaṣṭiśalākāpuruṣacarita,* Vasunandi's *Pratiṣṭhāsārasaṅgraha,* Jinasena's *Uttarapurāṇa* and also such texts as *Nirvāṇākalikā, Pratiṣṭhā-sāroddhāra, Mandira-pratiṣṭhā-vidhāna, Deva-pūjā,* etc. The Jaina Yoginīs have multiple arms, each hand holding a symbolic weapon or ornament meaningful to the doctrine. Like brāhmaṇic and Buddhist images, the Jaina goddesses are depicted with their hands and feet in special *mudrās* (formulaic gestures or positions).

The rise of śramaṇism was linked to major technological changes, to mercantile patronage, and to urbanism, but above all, to the incorporation of tribal and village goddesses as the centerpiece of the sects. Through their universal ethic, the śramaṇic sects cast their nets across all castes to harvest a wider social range of devotees, readily receiving converts from all groups of people, and absorbing innumerable tribal and ethnic cults and deities. Like the Buddhists, the Jainas were influenced (but not transformed, as was Buddhism) by the indigenous goddesses of the lower castes, accepting them into their pantheon at the beginning of the Christian era. In this way, tribal practices percolated upwards in the caste system, although the original symbolism and meaning of aboriginal fertility rites were revalorized. This process of detribalization in the śramaṇic cults preceded and necessitated the development of the Śākta religion:

> Later religions like Buddhism and others, in order to get themselves popular among the masses, had to make compromise with . . . existing cults and beliefs, and it was one of the processes through which the Tantric deities and rituals of the lower strata of society could have access to the upper levels. This process began to work in full motion about the beginning of the Christian era, and the subsequent history of the Indian religions was the history of the conflict and fusion of the Tantric elements with the so-called higher religions. Tantric elements profoundly influenced Buddhism and transformed it beyond recognition. Śaivism, due to its popular character, was saturated with Tantric ideas, practically since its inception as an organized religion. Vaiṣṇavism too could not avoid this popular influence. Jainism alone withstood this current and could largely maintain its rigid orthodoxy. Still it had to make room for a good number of Tantric goddesses.[114]

Thus even fundamentally atheistic religions like Buddhism and Jainism were required to give the low-caste goddesses a very prominent position as the beckoning force in their pantheons guaranteed to recruit subaltern converts. Original Buddhism, Jainism, and Vaiṣṇavism all appropriated a large number of the tribal cults, cleverly superimposing upon their primitive traditions intellectual and logical doctrinal schemes. Consequently, the tribal religious systems were transformed into sophisticated metaphysical constructions. The śramaṇic sects dominated Indian society for a long while, in large part because they readily received converts from all groups of people, and absorbed innumerable tribal and ethnic cults and deities.

References

1. Bhattacharyya, *History of the Śākta Religion*, 38.
2. "Military History of India," *Wikipedia*, http://en.wikipedia.org/wiki/Military_history_of_India, accessed April 12, 2006.
3. *Tāranātha's History of Buddhism in India*, trans. Lama Chimpa and Alaka Chattopadhyaya, ed. Debiprasad Chattopadhyaya (Simla, 1970), 53.
4. Bhattacharyya, *History of the Śākta Religion*, 42.

5. Coomaraswamy, *History of Indian and Indonesian Art,* 20–21.
6. Ibid., 115.
7. Bandyopadhyaya, *Development of Hindu Polity,* 193.
8. Basham, *The Wonder that was India,* 54.
9. J. Bloch, *Les Inscriptions d'Asoka* (Paris, 1950), 125. [Italics added.]
10. viz., 2.1.7; 3.9.3,15–17; 10.9.
11. *Arthaśāstra,* 3.2.
12. Thapar, *Interpreting Early India,* 126.
13. *Viṣṇu P.*, 4.24; *Mahāsupina Jātaka,* no. 77; *Mahābhārata,* Āraṇyakaparvan, 188.18ff.; Śāntiparvan, 254.39ff.
14. Since they were the legal charters pertaining to the grants, these inscriptions have become the primary source for the study of land transfer and the agrarian structure of the first millennium AD. [Thapar, *Interpreting Early India,* 14.]
15. Ibid., 62–63.
16. Ibid., 72–73.
17. From Skt. *śram,* to exert: practitioner of religious exertions.
18. 4.3.22.
19. From Skt. *tap,* to warm: practitioner of religious austerities.
20. Jaini, "*Śramaṇas*: Their Conflict," 42.
21. Franz L. Kielhorn, *Vyākaraṇa Mahābhāṣya of Patañjali,* vol. 1 (Bombay, 1892), 476.
22. The new doctrines evolved from kṣatriyas like Aśvapati Kaikeya, Ajātaśatru of Kāśī, Janaka of Videha, Pravahaṇa Jaivāli, and Sanatkumāra, all of whom served not as disciples, but as authorities, and occasionally, as teachers of the brāhmaṇas.
23. Thapar, *Interpreting Early India,* 50.
24. Partha Chatterjee, "Claims on the Past: The Genealogy of Modern Historiography in Bengal," in *Subaltern Studies* 8: Essays in Honour of Ranajit Guha, ed. David Arnold and David Hardiman (Delhi, 1994), 203–4.
25. Thapar, *Interpreting Early India,* 64.
26. Kosambi, *Ancient India,* 174.
27. Ibid., 166.
28. Ibid.
29. Jaini, "*Śramaṇas*: Their Conflict," 44.
30. Jagat Singh, *The Sikh Revolution: A Perspective View* (New Delhi, 1981), 86–87.
31. Lynn E. Gatwood, *Devī and the Spouse Goddess* (Riverdale, MD, 1985), 37.
32. *Chāndogya Up.*, 5.18.1–12; *Bṛhad.*, 6.2.13.
33. 6.4.3.
34. 6.4.6–7.
35. Bhattacharyya, *History of the Śākta Religion,* 34.
36. Ibid., 36.
37. Gatwood, *Devī and the Spouse Goddess,* 37.
38. Kosambi, *Ancient India,* 103.
39. Bhattacharyya, *History of the Śākta Religion,* 36.
40. *Chāndogya Up.*, 5.11.11ff.
41. Paul Deussen, *The Philosophy of the Upaniṣads* (Delhi, 1979),17ff.; A.B. Keith, *Religion and Philosophy of the Vedas and Upanishads* (Cambridge, Mass., 1925), 495ff.; D.P. Chattopadhyaya, *Indian Philosophy* (New Delhi, 1964), 85ff.
42. Thapar, *Interpreting Early India,* 134.

43. Ibid., 135.
44. Ibid.
45. Bhattacharyya, *History of the Śākta Religion*, 38.
46. Ibid., 35.
47. Gatwood, *Devī and the Spouse Goddess*, 41.
48. Thapar, *A History of India*, vol. 1, 67–69.
49. The Buddhist Order included, from the very beginning, "brāhmins who might have renounced caste but retained their intellectual traditions." [Kosambi, *Ancient India*, 179.]
50. *Chāndogya Up.*, 5.10.7.
51. Bhattacharyya, *History of the Śākta Religion*, 35.
52. Ibid.
53. Gatwood, *Devī and the Spouse Goddess* 41–42.
54. Thapar, *Interpreting Early India*, 15.
55. Ibid., 135.
56. Bhattacharyya, *History of the Śākta Religion*, 38.
57. H. Oldenberg, *Buddha: His Life, His Teachings, His Order* (Calcutta, 1927), 64.
58. Bandyopadhyaya, *Development of Hindu Polity*, 169.
59. Ibid., 173.
60. Bhattacharyya, *History of the Śākta Religion*, 39ff.
61. Bandyopadhyaya, *Development of Hindu Polity*, 175ff.
62. Ibid., 175.
63. Bhattacharyya, *History of the Śākta Religion*, 39.
64. Chattopadhyaya, *Lokāyata*, 485.
65. Temples or shrines are known in the epics as *caitya, devatā-āyatana, deva-gṛha*, and *devagāra*. The word *caitya* (from *ci-*) means "something built or piled up;" the related derivative *citya* refers to fire-altar or altar. Thus the normal usage of the word applies to funeral mounds such as the Buddhist and Jaina *stūpa* erected to honor prophets, teachers, or heroes. However, *caitya* also denotes many other sacred sanctuaries: *caitya-vṛkṣa*, sacred trees, are probably the most often named in the epics. Not even a leaf of a *caitya* may be harmed, for *caityas* are the resort of *devas, yakṣas* and *yakṣiṇīs, nāgas, apsarās, bhūtas*, etc. [Coomaraswamy, *History of Indian and Indonesian Art*, 47.]
66. Kosambi, *Myth and Reality*, 96.
67. Ibid., 95–96.
68. Jayakar, *The Earth Mother*, 31.
69. Jaini, "*Śramaṇas*: Their Conflict," 67.
70. *Vinaya Piṭakaṃ* 1, 43.
71. *The Book of the Discipline*, vol. 4, 56.
72. Jaini, "*Śramaṇas*: Their Conflict," 69.
73. Altekar, *Position of Women*, 210.
74. Ibid., 67.
75. Bhattacharyya, *History of the Śākta Religion*, 39–40.
76. Edward Conze, *Buddhism: Its Essence and Development* (New York, 1951), 54.
77. Ibid., 58.
78. Quoted by Conze in ibid., 58.
79. Ibid., 97.
80. Thapar, *Interpreting Early India*, 162.

81. This reliance on memory was common to high religions in ancient times, and is found as far west as Gaul, where, according to Julius Caesar, the Druids were masters of memorization and staunchly against committing their philosophy to writing. [Julius Caesar, *De Bello Galico*, 6, 14.]
82. Bandyopadhyaya, *Development of Hindu Polity*, 175.
83. Thapar, *Interpreting Early India*, 110.
84. Ibid., 56.
85. Ibid., 162.
86. Ibid., 126.
87. Ibid., 40.
88. Bhattacharyya, *History of the Śākta Religion* (1974), 40.
89. Ibid., 41.
90. Ibid., 65–66.
91. Kârâvêlane, *Kâreikkâammeyigr* (Pondicherry, 1956), 33.
92. Frédérique Apffel Marglin, *Wives of the God-King: The Rituals of the Devadasis of Puri* (Delhi,1985), 302–3.
93. Ibid., 41.
94. Bhattacharyya, *The Indian Mother Goddess*, 44.
95. Ibid.
96. Ibid.
97. Thapar, *Interpreting Early India*, 66.
98. Ibid., 132.
99. Suma Chitnis, "Exploring Tradition and Change among Women in Marathi Culture," in *Faces of the Feminine in Ancient, Medieval, and Modern India*, ed. Mandakranta Bose (New York, 2000), 268.
100. Coomaraswamy, *History of Indian and Indonesian Art*, 46.
101. Bowie, *Anthropology of Religion*, 24.
102. Ibid., 42.
103. Bhattacharyya, *History of the Śākta Religion*, 46.
104. Jayakar, *The Earth Mother*, 28–29.
105. Conze, *Buddhism: Its Essence and Development*, 145.
106. Ibid., 192.
107. Ibid.
108. Bhattacharyya, *The Indian Mother Goddess*, 209.
109. Conze, *Buddhism: Its Essence and Development*, 193–94.
110. Bhattacharyya, *The Indian Mother Goddess*, 113.
111. Ibid., 51–52.
112. Eliade, *Patañjali and Yoga* (New York, 1975), 176.
113. Shaw, *Passionate Enlightenment: Women in Tantric Buddhism* (Princeton, NJ, 1994), 33.
114. Bhattacharyya, *History of Indian Erotic Literature*, 12–13.

7

Brāhmaṇic Devaluation of Women versus Liberation Symbology

The Vanishing Freedom of Women: Post-Vedic Period

The sharp class division and decline in women's status in the post-Vedic period was intimately related to "the increasing consolidation of property into brāhmaṇa and kṣatriya hands, which required the monitoring and control of the reproductive functions of high caste women."[1] Among the elite minority, the importance of male progeny in the family greatly increased,[2] and polygamy began to be widely sanctioned to increase the number of male heirs.[3] Even more important to male elites was the certainty of the paternity of their offspring; thus their wives' fidelity and chastity were strictly and constantly guarded from view by other men by some male member of the family—either father, husband, or son.[4,5] The *raison d'être* of elitist asceticism was a pragmatic strategy ultimately intended to consolidate property in the hands of the brāhmaṇa, kṣatriya, and wealthier vaiśya castes by undermining the sexo-social freedom of high-caste women:

> Celibacy and marital chastity began to replace the use of Soma and erotic ritual characteristic of the early Vedic age. Combined with the emerging requirement for the legitimization of sons among the brāhmaṇa, kṣatriya, and wealthier vaiśya castes, the new religious trend initiated a sharp decline in female marital and sexual autonomy. Thus, in contrast to the relative socio-sexual freedom of women in classical Vedic times, sexuality and women in general were increasingly viewed by men as distractions from the path of enlightenment by late Vedic times.[6]

The seclusion of high-caste women was rationalized by misogynistic ideas that had been introduced in the epics. Among a thousand women, according to the *Mahābhārata*, or even hundreds of thousands, only one woman who is devoted to her husband may be found, and she, once under the influence of her passions, will care for neither family, father, mother, brother, or husband;[7] naturally, therefore, the feminine fatal flaw—manifested by "their sex organs becoming slippery as soon as they come across any man"[8]—must be inhibited. Another way of ensuring the line of patrilineal elites was to marry girls off before puberty; if parents did not marry off their daughter while she was still a *nagnikā*, they were accused of moral lassitude.

In addition, growing urbanization during the post-Vedic period probably offered women greater scope of movement, provoking fear that girls might succumb to sexual transgression in the marketplace, for example, and providing another justification to marry girls off at an early age and increasingly restrict their freedom of movement.[9] Large-scale field agriculture affected women's position in society in several ways:

> Craft specialization, which followed the wake of agricultural expansion to some extent, must have led to the separation of home and the workplace. Such a development tended to heighten the role of the family as a unity for individual consumption and means of biological reproduction and regulation of sexuality. It also led to women being increasingly restricted economically, spatially, and ideologically to its domain.[10]

During the period of the later Vedas and Dharmasūtras, women gradually withdrew from public life and economic production, becoming increasingly dependent on male kinsmen. A girl's opportunities to pursue Vedic learning were automatically limited by early marriage, and her deficiency in education eventually led to her exclusion from religious sacrifices. "The withdrawal of her right to study the Vedas and participate in religious ceremonies," writes Nath, "lowered her ritual status and placed her at par with the *śūdras*."[11] By AD 200, marriage itself was regarded as a girl's initiation, and the *upādhyāya* had vanished. When girls lost their separate initiation at adolescence, there was no longer any impediment to lowering a girl's marriage age to nine or ten, or even younger. Another misogynistic trend that emerged with the increasing importance of patrilineal inheritance was the growing disapprobation of widow remarriage. Although some widows continued to remarry until the period of the Dharmasūtras,[12] the practice was greatly discredited and denigrated, particularly among the elites. A strict behavioral code centered in the observance of celibacy came to be prescribed for widows.[13] At the end of the Vedic era, the confluence of brāhmaṇized mythological imagery, war, increasing urbanization, and elite land consolidations had a devastating effect on the status of both low-caste peoples and high-caste women. During the rise of the Hindu state, the political, socioeconomic, and ritual status of elite women fell to the ideological level of chattel, a role that accords with the subservient, reflective role of wife-goddess found in brāhmaṇic literature.[14]

LEGAL TREATISES GOVERNING MARRIAGE AND INHERITANCE

The Arthaśāstra

After he converted to Buddhism, Aśoka "encouraged official tolerance toward the new heterodoxy, thereby staying the rising power of the brāhmaṇa caste for about a century,"[15] writes Gatwood. As a result of his patronage of Buddhism, brāhmaṇic restrictions on women were temporarily halted in their progress toward the repressive *Manusmṛti*. The *Arthaśāstra*, a product of Aśoka's "tolerance for diversity"[16] in matters pertaining to women's social status, was a secular law-book probably composed and written by the celebrated author Kauṭilya *c.* 320 BCE. Kauṭilya was a brāhmaṇa teacher of Candragupta, who was the founder of the Mauryan line and the grandfather of Aśoka. The *Arthaśāstra* teaches that tribal people were useful to elites in times of war, a teaching the Gupta kings put into practice.

The *Arthaśāstra* mentions both approved or "dharmic" and unapproved or "non-dharmic" marital practices, the latter referring to options available to low-caste women that harkened back to matrilineal tribal customs. The *Arthaśāstra* took into consideration the fact that low-caste and dalit landless laborers were stuck in a lifetime of economic quicksand. There was no threat to the class system in permitting people of low station to contract non-dharmic marriages, since the elite males would not lose property through śūdra marriage or inheritance. Therefore, woman who married non-dharmically could contract either a *gandharva* or love marriage after puberty, or an *asura* marriage, common among the matrilineal tribes, which included a *śulka* (bride-price) to be paid to the bride's family. These women were permitted to divorce and remarry, but they were not permitted to transmit property to their children. The rationale for this ban on their children's inheritance was their "late" (post-puberty) marriage, a clear indicator to males that they were promiscuous, rendering the parentage of their offspring uncertain. Furthermore, reference is made to *vidhavāṃ candavasinim*, "A widow living according to her will,"[17] an allusion to the acceptance of the subaltern matriarchal tradition supporting the widow's freedom to inherit and remarry.

At the opposite end of the social spectrum, elite women had to bear the moral, legal, and social burden of the class system by forfeiting their freedom. Although the marriage was not consummated until after puberty, brāhmaṇas required the bride's pre-pubescence, as well as the *strīdhana* or dowry.[18] The woman who entered into a dharmic marriage based on the brāhmaṇic conception of feminine duty was rewarded with economic security, but she was not permitted to choose her mate, to remarry if she became widowed, or to divorce. By her chastity and fidelity to her husband, she was guaranteed a comfortable life for herself and her children—unless, of course, he assumed the yellow robes of the Order of Monks. The wife also retained usufruct, or use rights, as well as exclusive rights to her *strīdhana*, in her husband's property after his death. As Gatwood points out,

> The acknowledgement in the *Arthaśāstra* of the existence of two distinct directives, one orthodox and the other not, indicates that Indian society at the time of Aśoka was divided principally between the brāhmaṇas (and brāhmaṇa-emulators) and everyone else. It implies that intercaste marriage among *dvija* castes for purposes of the consolidation of land and power was not so extensive as it was to become later, although the ascendency of the kṣatriya caste was already underway. This is evident both in Aśoka's policy of toleration and in the *Arthaśāstra*'s legal recognition of the existence of the *dvija* status of kṣatriyas. Finally, the *Arthaśāstra* demonstrates that there was as yet little concern for orthodox hegemony over the śūdra castes, who were free, and even encouraged, to practice "unapproved" forms of marriage.[19]

By 180 BCE, the vast Mauryan Empire suffered a collapse of its agricultural economy, and its overly-centralized political *rāṣṭra* degenerated into numerous warring states. The *Arthaśāstra* became the model of Vātsyāyana's *Kāmasūtra* and disappeared soon after the Mauryans. Between 200 BCE and AD 300, urbanization continued in the south and east, trade expanded, and the first written recensions of the epics were produced as didactic personifications and articulations of the oppressive religious and legal system inscribed in the *Manusmṛti* (*Laws of Manu*). Between the first and fifteenth centuries, India is estimated to have had the largest economy of the ancient world, controlling between one-third and one-quarter of the world's wealth up to the time of the Mughals, when it rapidly degenerated during European rule. India's classical civilization flourished for the next fifteen hundred years.

The Manusmṛti

> (Some declare that) the chief good consists in the acquisition of spiritual merit and wealth, (others place it) in (the gratification of) desire and (the acquisition of) wealth, (others) in (the acquisition of spiritual merit alone, and others say that the acquisition of) wealth alone is the chief good here (below); but the (correct) decision is that it consists of the aggregate of (those) three.[20]

The *Manusmṛti* was compiled and written around the second century AD, irrevocably fixing guidelines for the behavior and function of women, the regimentation and institutionalization of the caste system, and the supremacy of the brāhmaṇas. India may be the only country in the world in which an elite group that constitutes a tiny two per cent of the population made education their exclusive monopoly. Strict penalties were imposed on learning by the persecuted low castes. The penalty on learning included cutting the tongue and pouring molten lead into ears.

Before that time, no real code of laws existed in India. In the five hundred years that elapsed between the *Arthaśāstra* and the *Manusmṛti,* the further devaluation of high-caste women was legally implemented by the brāhmaṇas in order to consolidate property among the elites. "Our evidence also shows that whenever property and its inheritance was in question, everything else was sacrificed and significant changes made in favor of property and its inheritance."[21] The brāhmaṇas, threatened by vaiśya competition for property and power, were compelled to memorialize and codify their superior position, shared with kṣatriya kings and nobles. The mercantile vaiśya caste, although technically *dvija* (twice-born), were regarded as inferior to brāhmaṇa and kṣatriya castes.[22]

> He who carefully guards his wife, preserves (the purity of) his offspring, virtuous conduct, his family, himself, and his (means of acquiring) merit. The husband, after conception by his wife, becomes an embryo and is born again of her; for that is the wifehood of a wife (*gāyā*), that he is born (*gāyate*) again by her. As the male is to whom a wife cleaves, even so is the son whom she brings forth; let him therefore carefully guard his wife, in order to keep his offspring pure.[23]
>
> No man can completely guard women by force; but they can be guarded by the employment of the following expedients: Let the husband employ his wife in the collection and expenditure of his wealth, in keeping everything clean, in the fulfilment of religious duties, in the preparation of his food, and in looking after the household utensils. Women, confined in the house under trustworthy and obedient servants, are not well guarded; but those who of their own accord keep guard over themselves, are well guarded. Drinking spirituous liquor, associating with wicked people, separation from the husband, rambling abroad, sleeping at unseasonable hours, and dwelling in other men's houses, are the six causes of the ruin of women. Women do not care for beauty, nor is their attention fixed on age; thinking, "It is enought that he is a man," they give themselves to the handsome and to the ugly. Through their passion for men, through their mutable temper, through their natural heartlessness, they become disloyal towards their husbands, however carefully they may be guarded in this world. Knowing their disposition, which the Lord of creatures laid in them at the creation, to be such, every man should most strenuously exert himself to guard them. When creating them Manu allotted to women a love of their bed, of their seat and of ornament, impure desires, wrath, dishonesty, malice, and bad conduct. For women no sacramental rite is performed with sacred texts, thus the law is settled; women who are destitute of strength and destitute of the knowledge of Vedic texts, are as impure as falsehood itself, that is a fixed rule.[24]

Women had no legal or property rights, since both they and their children were regarded as chattel of the male who owned them. Since brāhmaṇas were obsessed with the purity of their persons as well as of the blood of their offspring, women were supervised by male kinsmen throughout their lives. "[S]ome women, unwilling to be completely circumscribed or subjugated, sought out Buddhism and its protected monasteries or other less restrictive religions to continue their higher studies and to maintain a semblance of personal liberty."[25]

In elite families, female slaves, concubines, and polygamy undermined the position of wives. Because they were a small minority of the population, brāhmaṇas needed to increase their number while maintaining their exalted status. They accomplished this by the approval of intercaste "hypergamous" marriages of upwardly mobile kṣatriya women and brāhmaṇa men, in which case the woman and her children would be promoted to brāhmaṇa status. While condoning and legitimizing polygamy, the *Manusmṛti* inveighed against the unmarried state, celibacy, and unfaithfulness in monogamous marriages. The brāhmaṇas' superiority of wealth and status was ensured by polygamy, stipulating that each wife was to be of a different caste, and that the wife of the husband's caste was to receive precedence. Under the Code's inheritance laws, little of the husband's estate is left to the widow. Instead, the primary beneficiary is the eldest son(s) of the eldest wives of the highest castes.[26] "Thus, polygamy subverted polyandry, and the Code subverted women's rights."[27] Later, when female infanticide greatly reduced the female population of an area, marriageable males were overly abundant, and polyandry, on occasion, was resurrected.

The *Manusmṛti* also increased the scope of dharmic marriages by including *gandharva* marriage within the kṣatriya and brāhmaṇa unions. This law not only increased the size of the brāhmaṇa caste, but also "sacralized intra-kṣatriya unions, resulting in the elevation of the ritual status of the kṣatriya caste."[28] The laws ensured patriarchal brāhmaṇical and kṣatriya control of property, eliminating *asura* marriages (bride-price) for all castes except untouchables. As Gatwood elaborates,

> In this manner, brāhmaṇic hegemony now included the śūdras, who, along with the kṣatriya and vaiśya castes, were expected to undertake *gandharva* marriages. An important effect of the prohibition on *asura* marriages was the weakening of the matrilineal kinship systems of the śūdras through loss of the brideprice that flows from the family of the groom to that of the bride in matrilineal societies.[29]

The law of transmigration was used by the brāhmaṇas to justify misogynistic laws that protected their property. A metaphysical conception of the eternal dharmic marriage bond was conveniently invented to rationalize the abuse of widows: remarriage in an individual lifetime was impossible, they decreed, since the souls of brāhmaṇa couples remained bonded as a pair across successive incarnations. Theoretically, this applied to both men and women of the brāhmaṇa caste; in practice, however, women were forbidden to remarry when widowed or divorced, while widowed men were permitted and often encouraged to remarry. Because a husband's death was believed to result from his wife's sin against him—usually adultery—in a past incarnation, even pre-pubescent girls who were widowed were prohibited from remarrying.

In early Vedic marriages, husband and wife were instructed to regard one another as god and goddess. In the *Manusmṛti*, on the other hand, only the husband is depicted as a deity to his spouse; a woman was instructed in dependence on and devotion to her husband in the same sense as one regards a guru or a god:

> In childhood a female must be subject to her father, in youth to her husband; when her lord is dead, to her sons; a woman must never be independent. . . . Though destitute of virtue, or seeking pleasure elsewhere, or devoid of good qualities, yet a husband must be constantly worshiped as a god by a faithful wife.[30]

A patriarchal society places the highest priority on a husband's proprietary right over his wife, which reinforces the family's patrilineal character, the aggressive nature of male authority, and the identity of the high-caste wife as property. While a husband's absolute power and control over his wife was formally sanctioned in the period of the Purāṇas, most references to actual instances of gift, sale, pledging, or staking of wives at the gambling matches occur either in Vedic literature or in the *Mahābhārata*, and are rarely mentioned in Purāṇic texts. The exercise of this male right to sell or give away their wives in Vedic literature, according to Nath, "indicates not just the assertion of male authority in the family, but also a strongly entrenched patriarchal system in which even the closest kith and kin, that is, wife and children, are treated as alienable items of property."[31] With the production of surplus, the emergence of class society, and the question of patrilineal inheritance, however, a man's wife and family could no longer be gifted, pledged, or sold.[32] Nath continues:

> Such strong patriarchal traditions can exist only as long as there are large landholdings held collectively by extended families and presided over by an autocratic patriarch. These large landholdings existed till the Vedic period, when limited use of iron had not yet made intensive field agriculture and craft specialization possible so that tribal traditions continued to be quite dominant. But once iron technology . . . gave rise to a surplus producing agrarian system, the tribal order was replaced by a stratified class society with individual households. In the emergent social order patrilineal inheritance became a recurrent problem. It not only undermined the authority of the patriarch, but also heightened the importance of individual members in the family. The patriarch was now no longer empowered to gift, pledge or sell any member of the family, be it son or wife.[33]

The *Manusmṛti* gives the husband ultimate control over all property owned by the wife,[34] while maintaining that neither by sale nor by repudiation is a wife released from her husband.[35] Elsewhere, the *Manusmṛti* declares magnanimously that because a wife "is obtained from the gods; she is not received like cattle and gold in the market;"[36] in other words, she cannot be purchased outright, since the gods freely provide her as chattel. Similarly, the Dharmaśāstras proclaim that if a father fails to get his daughter married before she reaches the age of puberty, the girl is free to find her own husband.[37] While the injunction clearly negates a father's unqualified proprietary hold over his daughter, the right of daughters of all castes to inherit paternal property in the absence of sons was denied by Manu; rather, the paternal property was awarded to the daughters" sons (*putrikaputra*). The wife's usufruct rights and her exclusive rights to her *strīdhana* after her husband's death directed by the *Arthaśāstra* were also eliminated in the *Manusmṛti*.

The archaic custom of child marriage, requiring all young girls to be married before puberty, was given religious legitimization by Manu. Intended originally to prevent intercaste liaisons, child marriage relegated wives to "a mentally incompetent, inferior, eternally childlike status"[38] and consigned the control of their own property, as well as all of their other affairs, to their husbands.[39] Women's childlike characters and dependency were further institutionalized by Manu's prohibition against women learning the Vedas, other sacred texts, or sacramental rites. This was accomplished by extending the property inheritance laws to include the acquisition and inheritance of knowledge, thus guaranteeing the brāhmaṇic monopoly on education.[40]

At the time of the Smṛtis and the Purāṇas, high-caste women were reduced to a role of total subservience and became bracketed with property and śūdras.[41,42] The entrenchment of the institutions of private property and the patrilineal family was directly responsible for women's subjection to their male kinsmen, and the protection of women and property became the key to the stability of the dominant class family. According to R.S. Sharma, the institutions of private property and the family centered around the wife were the "chief reasons of the origin of the state" and the "main motives for social action."[43]

Women could be cast aside by their husbands if they had a temper, traits their husbands disliked, or a fondness for alcohol.[44] If a woman was barren by the eighth year of marriage, if over eleven years of marriage she had borne only daughters, or if all her children died by the tenth year of marriage, the husband was free to replace her with another wife with seniority over her. Frequently, the new wife would be of a lower caste, creating painful domestic tension. The disgraced wife could be confined to closed quarters or evicted from her home if she dared to complain.[45]

The "base-born" of Aryans and those whose birth was a violation of caste laws were assigned by the *Manusmṛti* occupations considered reprehensible by the twice-born:

> Those who have been mentioned as the base-born (offspring, *apasada*) of Aryans, or as produced in consequence of a violation of the law (apadhvaṁsaga), shall subsist by occupations reprehended by the twice-born. To Sūtras belongs the management of horses and of chariots; to Ambashthas, the art of healing; to Vaidehakas, the service of women; to Māgadhas, trade; killing fish to Niṣādas; carpenter's work to the Āyogava; to Medas, Andhras, Kuñkus, and Madgus, the slaughter of wild animals; to Kshattris, Ugras, and Pukkasas, catching and killing animals living in holes; to Dhigvaṇas, working in leather; to Venas, playing drums. Near well-known trees and burial-grounds, on mountains and in groves, let these tribes dwell, known by certain marks, and subsisting by their peculiar occupations. But the dwellings of Kandālas and Svapakas shall be outside the

> village, they must be made Apapātras, and their wealth shall be dogs and donkeys. Their dress shall be the garments of the dead, they shall eat their food from broken dishes, black iron shall be their ornaments, and they must always wander from place to place. A man who fulfils a religious duty, shall not seek intercourse with them; their transactions shall be among themselves, and their marriages with their equals. Their food shall be given to them by others (than an Āryan giver) in a broken dish; at night they shall not walk about in villages and in towns. By day they may go about for the purpose of their work, distinguished by marks at the king's command,[46] and they shall carry out the corpses of persons who have no relatives; that is a settled rule. By the king's order they shall always execute the criminals, in accordance with the law, and they shall take for themselves the clothes, the beds, and the ornaments of such criminals.[47]

To further increase their population, brāhmaṇas recruited tribal chiefs and priests into the brāhmaṇa and kṣatriya castes through special initiation ceremonies, which served the dual purpose of creating more elites and keeping the tribals who had been converted to low-caste or untouchable status under the rule of their former chief, now freed from tribal laws and fortified with kṣatriya military strength. The conversion of *ādivāsī* chiefs to the status of kings necessitated that the tribals be spiritually "reborn." Thus the inventive brāhmaṇas created the Golden Womb (*hiraṇya-garbha*) ceremony, which is described in some Purāṇas, to memorialize the spiritual rebirth of otherwise highly polluting *ādivāsīs*. Several southern kings of tribal origin boast that they were reborn in this ritual of imitative magic, a patriarchal co-optation of the female gestation and birthing process. For the ritual, a large vessel of solid gold, representing the mother's womb, was prepared. The chieftain, inserted in the fetal position in the womb vessel, would lie immobile while hired priests chanted the brāhmaṇic ritual *mantras* for pregnancy and childbirth. When the man arose from the "womb of gold," he not only was reborn, but he also acquired a new caste, perhaps for the first time, usually kṣatriya with the *gotra* of the brāhmaṇa priest. "The brahmin priests," remarks Kosambi, "received the golden vessel as part of their fee, which made everyone happy."[48]

While favored tribals were reborn as kṣatriyas and brāhmaṇas in such ceremonies, those at the other end of the class spectrum, tribals who offended brāhmaṇic supremacy by neglecting sacred rites or failing to consult the elite priests, were demoted by Manu to the level of śūdras:

> But in consequence of the omission of the sacred rites, and of their not consulting Brāhmaṇas, the following tribes of kṣatriyas have gradually sunk in this world to the condition of śūdras, viz., the Pauṇḍrakas, the Koḍas, the Draviḍas, the Kāmbogas, the Yavannas, the Sakas, the Pāradas, the Pahalvas, the Kinas, the Kirātas, and the Daradas. All those tribes in this world, which are excluded from the community of those born from the mouth, the arms, the thighs, and the feet of Brahman are called Dasyus, whether they speak the language of the Mlekkhas (barbarians) or that of the Aryans.[49]

Literary Indoctrination of Male Dominance: An Overview

The wild-cat shall meet with the jackals,
and the satyr shall cry to his fellow, yea,
Lilith shall repose there,
and find her a place of rest.

—*Isaiah* 34: 14

We have observed that the patriarchal brāhmaṇas, like the Hebrew prophets—not to mention contemporary leaders, authors, and corporate advertising executives—use literature didactically, twisting words and images to program the values of the masses. A literature of propaganda, an explanatory religious narrative, was needed by the brāhmaṇas to validate and justify the social upheaval caused by their civilizing mission. Externally, the subjugation of tribals and the co-optation of their deities in literature was the extra-caste mission of the brāhmaṇas in securing property and power and converting indigenous peoples to indentured agricultural labor. Internally, within the high-caste milieu, dramatic structural upheavals were scripted into brāhmaṇic literature that would stimulate the subsequent reversal of the status of high-caste women in the late Vedic era. Like the brāhmaṇic conversion of tribals into producers of surplus, the suppression and disempowerment of high-caste women as a means of ensuring paternity of offspring and the consolidation of property was propagandized as myth.

Each of the Mother-goddesses, as Varāhamihira instructed in the *Bṛhatsaṁhitā*,[50] was to be given the attributes of that god whose name she translates into the feminine; "this is in the Vedic patriarchal tradition, where the Mother-goddess is but a shadowy consort for the male god."[51] Consequently, the pairing during the Vedic period of Indra-Indrāṇī, Śiva-Bhavānī, and Varuṇa-Varuṇī established "slots for the wifely, dependent goddesses . . ., paving the way for the spousification process in Hinduism."[52] The collapse of tribal institutions was thus synchronized with the rise of patriarchal bourgeois values as the complement to state power, which was sustained by "new forces of injustice and untruth."[53]

One of the most significant didactic messages of the epics and Purāṇas was contained in the sudden acquisition of husbands by formerly autonomous aboriginal fertility goddesses, followed by their transformation into passive, submissive wife-goddesses who were to function as models for high-caste women to emulate, divine prototypes of the dominant husband and his servile, marginalized, dependent wife, whose primary duties were to husband and sons. Matriarchal elements were thus subordinated to the brāhmaṇic system by affixing to the Mother-goddess some god-husband, e.g., Durgā-Pārvatī (who might herself bear many local names such as Tukāi or Kālubāi) was joined with the low-caste god Śiva, Sarasvatī was given the supreme Brahmā as husband, and Lakṣmī was wed to Viṣṇu. Durgā, Sarasvatī, and Lakṣmī, all unmarried, were stripped of their archaic functions as Earth Mother, river goddess, and harvest goddess, respectively, and the literary model for high-caste wives was enriched by the entrapment of the latter two into their role as repressed *saumya* wives of patriarchal Aryan gods.

Vedic corn mother Sītā [literally, "furrow"], whose name symbolizes "a ploughed field, or the parting of the hair on the head . . . [and] also implies the female vaginal furrow as the source of life,"[54] was an autonomous Earth Mother in the *Ṛgveda* who was propitiated to ensure the fertility of the fields and a bountiful harvest: "Auspicious Sītā, come thou near: / we venerate and worship thee / That though mayst bless and prosper us / and bring us fruits abundantly."[55] The *Harivaṁśa* also depicts Sītā as Earth Goddess and the deity of farmers: "O goddess, you are the altar's center in the sacrifice, / the priest's fee, Sītā to those who hold the plough, / And Earth to all living beings."[56] In the *Vālmīki Rāmāyaṇa*, however, Earth Goddess Sītā has been fettered to husband and master Rāma, whom she follows into exile, selflessly sharing his fate. Her words reveal the extreme authoritarianism of male domination, the subtle indoctrination of Sītā's devotion and dependence, and the consequent disenfranchisement of the Earth Goddess and high caste women:

> A wife wins the fate of her husband, and not her own, O bull of a man. Knowing this, I shall live in the forest from now on. Here and hereafter there is only a single goal for a woman: her lord, and not her father, her child, herself, her mother nor her friends. . . . O take me with you, noble husband! Do as I ask, for my heart is devoted only to you. If you leave without me, I shall die![57]

In the Araṇyakāṇḍa of the *Vālmīki Rāmāyaṇa*, King Rāvaṇa's sister Śūrpaṇakhā, a *rākṣasī*,[58] is cruelly maimed—her nose, ears, and in some versions, her nipples are cut off—by Rāma's brother Lakṣmaṇa, under the direction of Rāma, for her failed attempt to seduce Rāma and Lakṣmaṇa and her attempt to murder Sītā. Kathleen Erndl has analyzed the theme of Śūrpaṇakhā's mutilation in five different rescensions of the *Rāmāyaṇa* as the articulation and justification of a misogynistic moral code grounded in fear of women's sexual independence. The leitmotif of male supremacy and the subordination of women in all *Rāmāyaṇas* is a transparent means of propounding authoritarian patriarchal ideology. The characters of Śūrpaṇakhā and Sītā, according to Erndl, are didactic personifications of the twin poles of patriarchal conceptions of evil and good, immoral and moral women. There has been discussion among scholars about whether Sītā was a child bride, a consideration born of the fact that marrying girls off before puberty became one of the surest ways to ensure the consolidation of property and inheritance among the elites. Itinerant Śūrpaṇakhā—"evil, impure, dark, inauspicious, and insubordinate,"[59] is intended to represent the polar opposite of Sītā—"good, pure, light, auspicious, and subordinate."[60] Śūrpaṇakhā's chief sin, aside from being a *rākṣasī*, the dark "Other" with the ability to shape-shift at will, was her sublime independence from male domination, while Sītā's great virtue lay in her benign submission to her husband's absolute domination over her, coupled with unquestioned sexual fidelity and the selfless desire to serve her lord. That Śūrpaṇakhā is said to be a widow reinforces the cruel ostracization of widows, who were "considered dangerous and inauspicious circumstances having rendered them unable to bear children," writes Erndl. "Their chastity is also suspect, since they are no longer under the control of a husband, and women are believed to have in satiable sexual appetites."[61]

Rāma protests numerous times that Sītā "occupies an inferior place in his heart to that of his male relatives and his subjects,"[62] although his love for Sītā and his tortured grief over her abduction are depicted. Furthermore, he repudiates Sītā twice to protect his reputation, and banishes her, pregnant, to the wilderness, all but a death sentence. As Goldman offers, "It would appear that the poets wanted to rescue their hero from the censure that Indian tradition heaps upon those who place too high a value on sexuality and who indulge in expressions of it in violation of their duty to their elders."[63]

Like Euripedes' *The Bacchae* and the Tamil *Cilappatikāram,* the legend reveals the "deep suspicion of women's power and sexuality when unchecked by male control,"[64] and bears symbolic resemblance to the Hebrew legend of Lilith, a woman cast out of society because she refused to be subjugated by her husband:

> In the beginning "male and female created he them." God formed Lilith, the first woman, just as he had formed Adam, from pure dust. Adam and Lilith never found peace together because Lilith contested Adam's claim to be supreme. They were created simultaneously from the same dust, she reasoned, and were therefore equal. When he asserted he was to be her master, she insisted there was no justification for his supremacy. When he wished to lie with her, she took offense at having to lie beneath him. Adam tried to force her obedience. Rather than accept subjugation, Lilith chose to leave Adam and live alone by the Red Sea. She found peace there on the hard-rock-sand lining the deep blue Gulf of Aquaba, making love with satyrs, minotaurs, and centaurs.[65]

Part of the curse laid on Lilith by God was that a hundred of her demon children would die every day. She has dominion over all natural instinctual creatures in Zoharic texts. In the Akkadian *Epic of Gilgamesh,* Lilith "forms with the Anzu-bird and the snake a triad of sexual, lawless creatures who live outside the bounds of the Sumerian community and seek power only for themselves."[66] According to Samuel N. Kraemer, this demonic triad becomes

> Inanna's unexpressed fears and desires, which have now been "named". . . . Inanna had wanted a throne and bed. She had wanted the end result—her rule and womanhood. Yet the snake, the bird, and Lilith are essential to Inanna's achieving her wishes, for they give her fears an external form so that she can begin to *see* them. The three creatures embody the primitive, grasping, human aspects . . . [constituting] the creatures who will not be tamed.[67]

Gatwood provides evidence that changes in the literary symbolism of Indian goddesses preceded significant changes in the lives of women.[68] Because the literary model of goddess subjugation preceded the drop in the status of high-caste women, Gatwood logically concludes that "marginalization and incipient spousification in the realm of religious ideology . . . helped create similar changes in the lives of women during Vedic times."[69] The perception that high-caste women's status declined as a result of the disenfranchisement of goddesses by brāhmaṇas at a time in history when women were powerful

> contradicts the commonly held materialist view that ideology functions in a solely passive, or reflexive, role in relation to material and social conditions. Were this the case, a Devī-like goddess would have been worshiped by the focal and independent women (and men) of the early and middle Vedic period. Instead, the prevailing conceptualization of feminine deity was almost totally at odds with the lives of real women, even those of relatively high status.[70]

We have observed that the ideology of male dominance was symbolically introduced when the female principle in her many independent forms became fettered to some Vedic god as a shadowy expression of his qualities, or as tools of conflict in the pantheon.[71] Furthermore, the Epico-Purāṇic containment of tribal and Vedic goddesses by brāhmaṇic gods as their creations, emanations, or wives (i.e., the goddesses became the "property" of the gods) historically precedes the decline of secular female status around AD 200. It is in the *Mahābhārata*[72] that for the first time Mother Earth is linked to Viṣṇu, and in the course of time, she becomes his consort.[73] The incipient marriage of aboriginal Mother-goddesses like Aditi and Pṛthivī to Viṣṇu "provided the ideological ground for [high-caste] women's decline in status."[74] The mythology of Epico-Purāṇic literature was the dramatization of the ideology of male dominance, and the myths were intentionally written by brāhmaṇas to subliminally stimulate acceptance of the shift to father-kin bourgeois social relations. Bhattacharyya observes that the "misogynistic ideas were designed to serve as the theoretical basis for the establishment of patriarchy."[75] Thus the social relations of deities in mythology were altered by the brāhmaṇic authors of the epics and Purāṇas to accord with the changing modes of power and production in history:

> Even in the earlier stages of human history, the Mother Goddess was a composite deity. Basically, she was the symbol of generation, the Female Principle, conceived as the actual producer of life. In course of time, however, . . . a male principle was introduced, evidently as an insignificant lover of the goddess, to play his role as the begetter. With the establishment of husbandry and domestication of animals especially among the pastorals, as well as with the introduction of the cattle-drawn plough, the economic importance of the males increased further, as a result of which the insignificant male god became co-equal and eventually the predominant partner.[76]

In both the epics and the Purāṇas, women were bracketed along with property in essentially two contexts: where the need to protect property is emphasized, and where property is described as yielding prestige and status.[77]

As we have discussed, to ensure patrilineal inheritance of property, the protection and preservation of women's chastity assumed supreme importance. The very stability of the family now more or less depended upon the protection of its women and property. Just as property, both movable and immovable, had to be carefully guarded against encroachment, women, especially wives, had to be jealously shielded from approaches by other men in order to ensure the purity of the offspring.

In both the *Mahābhārata* and the *Rāmāyaṇa*, it is clear that Vaiṣṇavism and Śaivism become the leading cults of the time, but that Śiva is more closely associated with the female principle than Viṣṇu in the *Mahābhārata*. Only Pṛthivī, Mother Earth, is linked to Viṣṇu. In Śaivism, "the ideas centering round Śakti or the female principle have found a soil most favorable for their expansion," according to Bhattacharyya. "The history of Śaivism in many of its stages is not different from that of Śāktism. . . ."[78]

When Indian goddesses are decoded as ideological and religious symbols, they reflect the socioeconomic context of the times, and bring into high relief the position of women, polarized by caste, within the increasingly misogynistic system. "The status of a goddess," writes Gatwood, "thus corresponds to the dominant ideological status of women at a given time."[79] The fierce aspects of Śakti in all her incarnations were tribal goddesses linked with subsistence agriculture and hunting. The assimilation of Caṇḍī, Cāmuṇḍā, Kālikā, Bhuvaneśvarī, Kāmākhyā, and others along the fringes of orthodoxy, and their incorporation as local manifestations of the female principle, began around the first century AD.

The sharp decline in social status only befell women of the dominant class, the upper strata; it was the interests of elites that were served and safeguarded by the brāhmaṇical lawgivers, and had "nothing to do with the greater section of peoples, the lower castes and tribes, who still adhere to the surviving matriarchal values."[80] Interpreted as a reflection of the nonelite women who propitiated her, *Ugra* Śakti, with her great unbridled feminine power, depicts the relative autonomy and freedom of low-caste women and the values they embody. The relatively free social lives of subaltern women and the fierce, omnipotent tribal qualities of their goddess are the dialectical opposite of the oppressive, reclusive lives of elite wives and their mythological paragons, the subordinate, idealized *saumya* wife-goddesses.

The seclusion of women was a repressive custom of the dominant class spear-headed by the partiarchal Smārta tradition. Since the nonelite domain did not follow the injunctions of the Smṛtis,[81] lower-caste women worked and moved freely in the fields, markets, mines, and industries, as they do today. The condition of the lower social strata of post-Vedic India, comprised mainly of petty traders, artisans, agriculturists, and wage-earners belonging to the vaiśya and śūdra castes, is better articulated in Pāli literature and other texts such as the *Arthaśāstra*. Nonelite women were known to earn their livelihood independently by weaving, dyeing, basket-making, and selling flowers. Large numbers of women pursued higher learning, or renounced the world to become cloistered nuns, fulfilling their yearning for the authentic community of tribal order. Even those who became prostitutes—such as the *nṛtyas* or professional dancers whom Vātsyāyana, in his fourth century AD *Kāmasūtra*, referred to as *devadāsīs*, are described as being respectable women and repositories of art.[82] (However, despite their exalted origin, the institution of the *devadāsīs* became corrupted, and they began to lose their privileged status in the medieval period.) The self-reliance of low-caste women perhaps also accounts for the tradition of bride-price (*śulka*) that was paid to the bride's family as compensation for losing her services. Although generally denounced by the brāhmaṇical lawgivers, brideprice survived among the lower castes[83] and was even formally sanctioned for them by the earlier Dharmasūtra writers. The *ārṣa* form of marriage involving the gift of a cow and a bull,[84] which was differentiated from the *āsura* form involving the sale and purchase of the girl, appears to be a vestige of the earlier practice of paying bride-price.[85]

Ironically, because nonelite women were oppressed by their lowly castes, they were excluded from the patriarchal tradition of inheritance, the single obsession of which was the purity and fidelity of the high-caste wife; thus, their subordinate station enabled nonelite women to enjoy relative freedom in the socio-religious sphere. Kālī reflects this liberal subaltern model of society, based on female power and traditional tribal views against alienation of land; conversely, the *saumya* wife-goddess symbolizes the repressive elite model of femininity, based on male dominance and property ownership. Thus the fierce goddess is a symbol of the revolutionary sentiments in the minds of the Indian majority and their enmity for patriarchal bourgeois culture. This constant philosophical struggle between the misogynistic Indian patriarchy of the dominant class and the matriarchal leanings of the conquered peoples has been named the cause of the "ambivalent and paradoxical attitude of the high-caste Hindus towards sex."[86] Bhattacharyya elaborates:

> The root of this contradiction should be sought . . . in the conflicts of patriarchal and matriarchal values by which the Indian patriarchy is constantly tormented. . . . [Many] sophisticated scholars of India and outside have no idea of the less patriarchal societies of the simpler peoples. They are eighty percent of the total population of India, and yet they are excluded from the scene of Indian history. Among the simpler peoples of India there is no ambivalent and paradoxical attitude toward sex, because women in their societies enjoy considerable freedom. They work with men in the fields, in the mines and factories and in other spheres of worldly activities, and thus they have developed a more decent, healthy and human attitude toward sex. This reality of Indian social life with which the greater section of the people is concerned, is generally and most unfortunately overlooked by most of the scholars.[87]

Vijaya Nath also addresses the inverse freedom ratio of elite and subaltern women:

Pl. XIII. *Durgā*: The goddess Durgā, standing on the head of Mahiṣa. Sculpted on a *maṇḍapam* (pillar) in front of the Trimūrti Cave Temple, dedicated to Durgā. Trimūrti Cave Temple, Mahābalipuram, Chengalpattu. Pallava (sixth–ninth centuries AD), Granite.

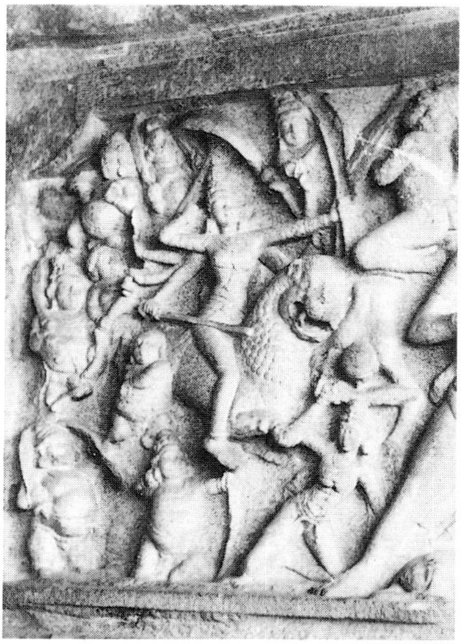

XIV **XV**

Pls. XIV–XV. *Mahiṣāsura-mardinī*: Riding astride a lion, Durgā slays the buffalo demon Mahiṣa on the quintessential cosmic war front. As his troupe of demons is defeated, Mahiṣa wields an impotent club against victorious Durgā. Mahiṣāsura-mardinī Cave Temple, Mahābalipuram, Chengalpattu. Pallava (sixth–ninth centuries AD), Granite.

Pl. XVI. *Yakṣī*: Flanked by lions, seated on a throne under the sacred pipal tree. The *yakṣī* is a female Earth spirit of fertility found in Hindu, Buddhist, and Jaina mythologies. Often referred to as Mother-goddess, she dwells in trees, lakes, and wells. She and her male counterpart, the *yakṣa*, are revered as protectors that must be propitiated to avert harm or induce fertility. A *yakṣī* is frequently depicted as a young, sensual woman often holding the branch of a tree while striking the well-known *tribhaṅga* (three-bend) pose (bending at neck, waist, and hip). Gurunātha Sastri Home, Pondicherry.

Pl. XVII. *Yakṣa*: Śrī Pārśvanātha, Jaina Temple, Hassan, Channarayapatna, Śravaṇabelgola (sixth–seventh centuries AD), Stone.

Pl. XVIII. *Yakṣa and Lion*: Śiva Temple, Śrī Mukteśvara, Bhuvaneśvara, *c.* AD 950 (fourth–fourteenth centuries AD), Gaṅga period.

Pl. XIX. *Amman̲*: Śrī Māriyamman̲ Temple, Tiruchirappalli. Early Coḷa (ninth–tenth centuries AD). Granite cave temple. One of the most popular shrines in Tamilnadu, the temple is dedicated to Māriyamman̲, a Tamil manifestation of the primeval energy Śakti, personified as the Mother-goddess. Māriyamman̲ is associated with prosperity and health; she is the cause and the cure of diseases such as smallpox and chickenpox. Every Sunday, Tuesday, and Friday, hundreds of devotees throng the temple and perform *pūjās*.

Pl. XX. *Kālī-Makālī*: Goddess Kālī Temple, Śrī Makālī Ammaṉ, Rayampuram, Tiruchirappalli, Ariyalur. Early Coḷa (ninth–tenth centuries AD), Stone.

Pl. XXI. *Saptamātṛkās—Maheśvarī and Cāmuṇḍī*: Śiva Temple, Śrī Tarukavaneśvara Tirupparaitturai. Coḷa (ninth–twelfth centuries AD), Stone.

Pl. XXII. *Saptamātṛkā—Cāmuṇḍā*: Śrī Kundattu Kaliyamman Temple, Pariyur, Coimbatore, Gopichettipalaiyam, Coḷa (ninth–tenth centuries AD), Stone.

Pl. XXIII. *Saptamātṛkā—Cāmuṇḍā*: Śrī Kundattu Kaliyamman, Pariyur, Coimbatore, Gopichettipalaiyam, Coḷa (ninth–twelfth centuries AD), Stone.

Pl. XXIV. *Saptamātṛkās—Kaumārī, Vaiṣṇavī, Indrāṇī, Varāhī, Cāmuṇḍā, and Gaṇapati*: Śiva Cave Temple, Śrī Kokarṇeśvara, Tirukokarṇam. Pallava (sixth–ninth centuries AD), Stone.

Economic dependence of women increasingly became synonymous with the curtailment of their freedom, whether it was of choosing a husband, remarriage, higher education, participating in religious ceremonies or social life. It is significant that women of lower social orders, who contributed equally to family earnings, are known to have enjoyed greater freedom than their counterparts in the upper strata.[88]

Before the medieval period, the cult of the Mother-goddess belonged exclusively to the low-caste majority, and it was originally regarded with elitist contempt by the upper strata of Indian society. When services were needed from subaltern peoples, however, the elites feigned cultural alliance of the two sections by adopting some of the tribal and folk cults and rituals, their original vernacular form embellished to reflect the grandeur of the deities of the elites.

Mahiṣāsura-mardinī

At this time, the Vedas, Brāhmaṇas, and Upaniṣads, theoretically the most sacred of the scriptures of the Vaidika culture, were unavailable to those seekers who had not become *dviya* (twice-born) in the brāhmaṇic ceremony of initiation. Thus these ancient holy texts became the privileged monopolistic religion of the brāhmaṇas, "who themselves often interpreted them figuratively in the light of the new doctrines."[89] The epics, the Purāṇas, the Books of Sacred Law, as well as hymns and religious poems were available to everyone, including low-caste groups and women, making this body of sacred literature the nonelite scriptures of India. The epico-Purāṇic texts, originally oral narratives of Indian history, were written by brāhmaṇas as social models, and served as the ideological rationale and justification of their misogynistic and inhumane laws.

Low-caste peoples, who regarded the brāhmaṇas as their oppressors, were familiar with the epico-Purāṇic myths of the marriages and other alliances of their archaic vegetation and fertility goddesses to Aryan gods. They no doubt perceived the implicit social programing of brāhmaṇic mythology. By what means could the illiterate subaltern population publicly decry their state? How could they liberate themselves from the cruel system that bound them in servitude? The only means available to them were folk tales and the medium of art, both of which were co-opted and twisted by brāhmaṇic interpretations. For tribal peoples, art is not so much ornamental and aesthetic as it is homeopathic magic. The ceremonious creation of religious images is believed to set in motion a series of events that will culminate in the actual materialization of the symbol. The triumphant feminine strength that magnetizes the image of Mahiṣāsura-mardinī stands in curious, stark contrast to the picture of the married and denatured Sītā, Sarasvatī, and Lakṣmī. Unlike the resigned submission of high-caste women to the brāhmaṇic paradigm, the low-caste reaction to the inherent master-slave dialectic of class society was the symbolic overthrow, in folk art and myth, of the male demon (and his ideology) by their protectress, whose aboriginal role was the destruction of the enemies of her people. As Bhattacharyya articulates,

> The wide distribution of the Mahiṣāmardinī sculptures, the popularity of the concept of the goddess slaying the demons, must have a clear social significance. . . . The class became more sharp and imposing . . ., as is proved by the evidence of the Smṛti literature. The priestly and ruling classes, the landlords and big traders enjoyed the surplus of social productions, and those who were responsible for this social production, on whose labor rested the class society in which the rich became richer, the powerful became more powerful, were mostly śūdras, divided into innumerable jātis following different lower occupations, for whom was reserved a miserable life of endless oppression, brutal physical torture and ever-agonizing humiliation. . . . But throughout the ages, the urge for freedom against oppression prevails which often finds expression in the forms of popular revolts. In any case, the oppressed peoples dream of their freedom and even resort to imagination, the imaginative victory of the goddess over the demons, when the reality goes against their hopes and aspirations. The Devī's fight with demons thus served as the best ideology that the ancient age could provide to the toiling masses struggling against the intolerable conditions of life, the social importance of which we ought not to minimize.[90]

We have discussed the archaic foundation of the buffalo-slaying goddess, a mythic leitmotif reflecting seasonal regicide that is explained by innumerable narratives throughout Near Eastern and South Asian history. According to one version, the Buffalo Demon (Mhasobā), a farmers' god common to whole regions, originally had no consort, and, for a time, he was in conflict with the earlier unwed Mother-goddess of the food-gathering tribes. When the two groups merged, their deities were accordingly married. Such divine marriages connote human marriage as a recognized institution, indicating social fusion of their formerly autonomous and even separatist worshipers.[91] The earliest representations of Mahiṣāsura-mardinī are certain terracotta plaques discovered at Nagar near Uniyara in the Tonk district, Rajasthan. One of these has been assigned to the first century BCE or the first century AD. Another Mahiṣāsura-mardinī plaque of white clay dated around the first century AD has been found in Sambhar.[92] Kosambi's exquisitely detailed field-work in Maharashtra has uncovered evidence of the evolution of the original crude tribal conception of Mahiṣāsura-mardinī. The intertwined symbology relates that the Mother-goddess is given the buffalo demon, a dire enemy of her people, as an intolerable husband, and she, true to her nature, destroys him:

> The goddesses are Mothers, but unmarried. No father seemed necessary to the society in which they originated. The next step is shown by marriage to some male god. Jogubāī has a 'husband' Mhātobā at Kothrūḍ and Vākaḍ. The extraordinary feature of this marriage is that Mhātobā is really Mhasobā = *mahiṣāsura*, while the wife Jogūbī is Yogeśvarī = Durgā, whose most famous act was killing the buffalo demon. This is by no means an isolated case, for Mhasobā is again married to Jogubāī at Vīr, under the name of Maskobā. In both cases the slight change of his name is made apparently to permit the nuptials. The

Vīr god was set up by immigrant shepherds, and still goes in procession once a year to a hillock adjoining the one on which his cult is located. The hillock is still called Tukāī's pasture and her little shrine there contains a crude red-daubed relief which shows the goddess crushing a tortured buffalo—*Mahiṣāsura-mardinī.*[93]

As told by the brāhmaṇas in their didactic Purāṇas, the Mahiṣāsura-mardinī allegory succeeded in consolidating the tribal goddesses, incorporating Ko<u>rr</u>avai into the orthodox pantheon, and marrying the Mātṛkā of the food-gathering tribes to the buffalo demon Mhasobā. Of the myriad incarnations of the Indian war/mother goddess, Durgā is the most popular. As Mahiṣāsura-mardinī ("slayer of Mahiṣāsura"), she is represented as a ten-armed woman warrior, astride a lion, brandishing her ten weapons, vanquishing the demon-buffalo *Mahiṣā,* the enemy of the elites. This image refers to the well-known mythical event related in the *Devī-māhātmya* ("Praise of the Goddess"), the essential text of Durgāpujā, as well as in Tamil Caṅkam myths of Ko<u>rr</u>avai slaying the buffalo demon/consort in south India. In the *Devī-māhātmya,* the elite brāhmaṇic gods are helpless before an intrepid enemy demon, Mahiṣāsura, who could be vanquished only by a woman. Thus the gods created the savior goddess Durgā, who indeed slayed the buffalo demon.[94]

References

1. Bhattacharyya, *History of Indian Erotic Literature,* 55.
2. Thapar, *Ancient Indian Social History: Some Interpretations* (Delhi, 1966), 3.
3. *Ś. Br.,* 9.4.1.6: "One man may have many wives."
4. *Gautama Dharmasūtra,* 17.1; *Vasiṣtha Dharmasūtra,* 5.1; *Baudhāyana Dharmasūtra,* 2.2.50–52; *MS,* 5.146; F. Engels, *The Origin of the Family, Private Property and the State* (Moscow, 1948), 58.
5. *MS,* 9.79; *Nāradasmṛti,* 8.30: "Through independence women go to ruin."
6. Gatwood, *Devī and the Spouse Goddess,* 37.
7. *Mbh.,* 8.19.92–94.
8. Ibid., 8.39.26.
9. Vijay Nath, "Women as Property and Their Right to Inherit Property up to the Gupta Period," in *The Indian Historical Review* 22, nos. 1–2 (July 1993 and January 1994): 6.
10. Ibid., 5.
11. Ibid., 6.
12. *Āpastamba Dharmasūtra,* 2.6.13.3–4.
13. P.V. Kane, *History of Dharmaśāstra,* vol. 2 (Poona, 1968), 583–86.
14. Gatwood, *Devī and the Spouse Goddess,* 40.
15. Ibid., 42.
16. Ibid.
17. 3.20.16.
18. Prabhati Mukherjee, *Hindu Women: Normative Models* (Calcutta, 1978), 96.
19. Gatwood, *Devī and the Spouse Goddess,* 44.

20. *MS*, 2.224.
21. Mukherjee, *Hindu Women: Normative Models*, 103.
22. However, vaiśyas were elevated in the Buddhist religion, and their prosperity expanded with the religion.
23. *MS*, 9.7–9.
24. 9.10–18.
25. Theodora Foster Carroll, *Women, Religion, and Development in the Third World* (New York, 1983), 17.
26. *MS*, 9.1–220.
27. Carroll, *Women, Religion, and Development*, 18.
28. Gatwood, *Devī and the Spouse Goddess*, 45.
29. Ibid.
30. *MS*, 5.147–68.
31. Nath, "Women as Property," 6–7.
32. *Āpastamba Dharmasūtra*, 2.6.13.11; *MS*, 9.2–11.
33. Nath, "Women as Property," 7.
34. *MS*, 8.416.
35. Ibid., 9.46.
36. Ibid., 4.32; 9.95.
37. *Gautama Dharmasūtra*, 18.20–23.
38. Carroll, *Women, Religion, and Development*, 23.
39. *MS*, 9.104–219.
40. Ibid., 9.3;18; 317.

41,42. *Agni P.*, 253.63–64; R.S. Sharma, *Indian Society, Historical Probings* (New Delhi, 1974), 39–40; Nath, "Women as Property," 1.

43. Sharma, *Perspectives in Social and Economic History of Early India* (New Delhi, 1983), 43.
44. *MS*, 9.12–16.
45. Ibid., 9.80–83.
46. i.e., Kandālas and Svapakas were made to identify their outcaste station by wearing distinguishing symbols such as thunderbolts, iron ornaments or peacock's feathers, or by sticks, axes, adzes, etc., used for executing criminals and carried on the shoulder.
47. *MS*, 10.46–56.
48. Kosambi, *Ancient India*, 171.
49. *MS*, 10.43–5.
50. 58.56.
51. Kosambi, *Myth and Reality*, 83.
52. Gatwood, *Devī and the Spouse Goddess*, 39.
53. Bhattacharyya, *History of the Śākta Religion*, 40.
54. Cornelia Dimmitt, "Sitā: Fertility Goddess and *Śakti*," in *The Divine Consort: Rādhā and the Goddesses of India*, ed. John Stratton Hawley and Donna Marie Wulff (Berkeley, 1982), 211.
55. *ṚV*, 4.57.6, 7.
56. 2.3.14.
57. *Rāmāyaṇa*, 2.24.3, 4, 18.
58. The *rākṣasas* are a class of fierce, bloodthirsty demons regarded as the implacable enemies of brāhmaṇic patriarchal ideology and culture. Their king and the

main antagonist of the *Rāmāyaṇa*, the ten-headed Rāvaṇa who rules from the marvelous island-fortress of Laṅkā, is the culprit who abducts Sītā.

59. Kathleen M. Erndl, "The Mutilation of Śūrpaṇakhā," in *Many Rāmāyaṇas: The Diversity of a Narrative Tradition in South Asia*, ed. Paula Richman (Berkeley, 1991), 83.
60. Ibid.
61. Ibid., 84.
62. Robert Goldman, trans., "Introduction," *The Rāmāyaṇa of Vālmīki: An Epic of Ancient India*, vol. 1 (Princeton, 1984), 56.
63. Ibid.
64. Ibid., 68.
65. Hebrew legend cited by Jennifer Stone, "Woman with an Iron Whim," *Commentaries*, Pacifica Public Radio, KPFA 94 FM, Berkeley, CA, 2 May 1999.
66. Wolkstein and Kraemer, *Inanna, Queen of Heaven and Earth*, 142.
67. Ibid.
68. Gatwood, *Devī and the Spouse Goddess*, 33.
69. Ibid., 39.
70. Ibid., 38–39.
71. Wendy Doniger O'Flaherty, *Hindu Myths* (Middlesex, UK, 1975), 238.
72. 3.141.
73. By contrast, among the vast masses of Indian subalterns, male deities are relegated to the inferior secondary position to which goddesses were demoted in the brāhmaṇical pantheon. [Bhattacharyya, *History of Indian Erotic Literature*, 8.]
74. Gatwood, *Devī and the Spouse Goddess*, 38.
75. Bhattacharyya, *History of Indian Erotic Literature*, 38.
76. Bhattacharyya, *The Indian Mother Goddess*, 5–6.
77. Sharma, *Perspectives in Social and Economic History of Early India* (New Delhi, 1983), 39–44.
78. Bhattacharyya, *History of the Śākta Religion*, 47.
79. Gatwood, *Devī and the Spouse Goddess*, 3.
80. Bhattacharyya, *History of Indian Erotic Literature*, 2.
81. Manu says, "Vedas are known by Śruti, and Dharmśāstra is known by Smṛti."
82. Nath, "Women as Property," 8.
83. Sharma, *Perspectives in Social and Economic History of Early India*, 49.
84. *MS*, 3.53. The *āsura* form of marriage was justified and upheld on the ground that the gift of a cow and a bull was only a token of respect and consideration for the bride.
85. Nath, "Women as Property," 9.
86. Bhattacharyya, *History of Indian Erotic Literature*, 3.
87. Ibid.
88. Nath, "Women as Property," 9.
89. Basham, *The Wonder That was India*, 299.
90. Bhattacharyya, *History of the Śākta Religion*, 83–84.
91. Kosambi, *Ancient India*, 170.
92. Bhattacharyya, *The Indian Mother Goddess*, 158.
93. Kosambi, *Myth and Reality*, 90–91.
94. The Mahiṣāsura-mardinī may also mark the conjunction of Taurus the Bull with the Sun at the vernal equinox, which marked the beginning of the year

during the Age of Taurus (*c.* 4,000–2,000 BCE). It was probably in connection with the New-Year festival or sacrifices at both equinoxes that the bull sacrifice, widely attested to in the ancient Near East and Eastern Mediterranean, was performed. Parpola believes that the sacrifices to the Bull of Heaven in Mesopotamia are historically related to the Vedic buffalo sacrifices, which, together with the *Aśvamedha* and *Puruṣamedha*, serve as the prototype for the medieval *vāmācāra* Śākta buffalo and human sacrifices to Durgā. In addition, *bali* in both Vedic and Śākta ritual is linked to ritual copulation and agricultural metaphors. [Parpola, "The sky Garment: A Study of the Harappan Religion and its Relation to the Mesopotamian and Later Indian Religions," *Studia Orientalia* 57 (1985): 150–51].

8

The Rise of the Śākta Counter Culture: The Classical Period (AD 300–700)

The Historico-Religious Preconditions

> The mass strength behind the Female Principle placed goddesses by the side of the gods of all religions, but by doing so, the entire emotion centering round the Female Principle could not be channelized. So a need was felt for a new religion, entirely female-dominated, a religion in which even the great gods like Viṣṇu or Śiva would remain subordinate to the Goddess. This new religion came to be known as Śāktism.[1]

The Gupta empire, which spanned from AD 320 until the mid-sixth century AD, brings into sharp relief the ever-widening chasm between elites and the rural majority in Indian society. For elites, it was a classical golden age of high culture and achievement in art, architecture, the sciences, and literature. The first Gupta king was Candragupta I (AD 320–35), the real founder of the line. His son Samudragupta (*c.* AD 335–75) boasts that he subjugated the entire Ganges valley. He apparently cleared out "new and petty or old and decaying kingdoms,"[2] which brought peace and prosperity to the country. In clearing the forests of the Ganges for large-scale agriculture, Samudragupta exterminated nine Naga kings in Āryāvarta proper and then reduced all kings of forest tribes to servitude:

> The innumerable forest chiefs were strengthened by the intrusion of small-scale agriculture to become raiders upon older settlements on a scale which might be petty in each case, but was a major nuisance in the aggregate, seeing the extent of the mischief. Samudragupta cleared the Gangetic heartland of this last obstacle to peaceful food production. Forest tribes of various kinds, more or less advanced towards food production and kinship, remained in marginal regions: Nepal, Assam, and the central Indian jungle.[3]

Candragupta II (AD 380–414), Samudragupta's son, conquered Malwa, Gujarat, and Kathiawar, and established a powerful, well-organized government for the wealthiest and most densely populated areas of India. In the early Gupta period, expanding village settlement produced unprecedented new wealth for the powerful, well-run central government. Trade was increasing again, and economic support was available to many sects in abundance. The *Kāmasūtra* and other literary records of the time reveal the leisure, opulence, and luxurious lifestyle enjoyed by the upper class.

At the opposite pole of society, however, the low castes, dalits, and *ādivāsīs*, whose labor supported the prosperity of the elites, were marginalized and pauperized, forced to live on the outskirts of the high caste localities with none of the privileges of the higher castes. The caṇḍālas were untouchables, forbidden to walk around at night, sequestered outside the boundaries of towns and market places; in the daytime, they were ordered to wear distinguishing marks when they traveled, lest they infect an unsuspecting elite with their genetic pollution. The labor laws inscribed in the Smṛtis only served the interests of owners and employers; low castes, dalits, and tribals were either forced labor (belonging exclusively to the state), or slave labor (belonging exclusively to individual entrepreneurs) in the field of production. Hired labor, albeit only temporary, was used for cattle-raising, agriculture, industry, and trade. Low-caste beggars and thieves roamed the cities, and subaltern girls and women were prey to wealthy men, who seduced them (the method is fully disclosed in the *Kāmasūtra*), exploited them as concubines for a while, and finally rejected them, forcing them to the degraded position of public women.

The decline and fall of the Gupta Empire in the second half of the sixth century divided India once again into numerous independent states. The Cālukya empire ruled parts of southern and central India from 550 to 750 (from Badami, Karnataka) and again from 970 to 1190 (from Kalyana, Karnataka). The Pallavas of Kanchi were their contemporaries to the south. For about a hundred years, the two kingdoms were engaged in frequent low-intensity wars to claim the other's capital. The kings of Sri Lanka and the Keralan Ceras rendered support to the Pallavas, while the Pāṇḍyas rendered support to the Cālukyas.

In the seventh century, Harṣavardhana consolidated his power on the ashes of the Gupta empire; however, the political situation had changed entirely. The locus of state power had shifted to the Deccan and south India, and when Harṣa was defeated by the Cālukya king Pulakeśin,

> It marked not only the end of Northern supremacy over the South but also the beginning of Southern supremacy over the North. . . . From the seventh century onwards, religious movements of the South began to exert tremendous influence on the North. The prosperity of the South, as is revealed by her architectural

greatness, was evidently due to the inter-oceanic trade, of which the North was deprived. The disintegration and fall of the Roman empire, caused mainly by the vandalism of the Teutons and the Huns, acted severely upon the overland trade-routes connecting north India with Rome. The natural flow of foreign trade was thus ceased abruptly, the North faced a grave economic crisis, ultimately leading to her political and cultural decline.[4]

At the end of Harṣa's empire, the northern ideal of a pan-Indian empire collapsed, but the concept migrated to the south. Some of the greatest examples of both rock-cut and freestanding temples are products of the two dynasties.

Although monasteries still received many generous donations, "[t]he villages had to be more or less self-contained and self-supporting. Tax-collection by a highly centralized but non-trading state was no longer a paying propositon, because commodity production per head and cash trade were low; this is fully attested by the miserable coinage."[5] There was an increase in the granting of land, further annihilation of tribal lands through the introduction of plough agriculture and the subjection of tribals to the caste system. Trade and commodity production declined, adversely affecting the growth of urban centers, the decentralization of the army, and a concentration of wealth at local courts. Accompanying this was the spread of Bhakti cults, whose signature loyalty and devotion to the tutelary deity model the elite's conception of the ideal feudal social relations, based on blind loyalty and devotion to the local king or landlord, and adherence to the Dharma's scheme of selective persecution.

Social Surplus and the Subaltern Temple Builders

By Gupta times, the temple, centered round the shrine to the primary deity, had reached its zenith. Ironically, the association of tribal and village cults with new social groups led to the blossoming of the popular and pervasive Purāṇic religion, in which icons of brāhmaṇical gods Viṣṇu and Śiva came to be worshiped as the pre-eminent deities. Normally the temple was situated adjacent to a river, with a "tank" or flight of stairs connecting them together. Ritual ablution was essential. The temples also frequently contained a meeting hall, where the epics, Purāṇas, and other sacred literature were recited for all who wished to listen. A rest house for pilgrims was also often provided, as well as many other offices and annexes, some of which served the social needs of the people.

The thrust of Purāṇic religion was the assimilation and accommodation of scores of new cults, sects, and castes into the social and religious hierarchy. Caste identities generally predetermined religious observance.[6] Vaiṣṇavism and Śaivism became more closely linked, evidenced by attempts to merge Viṣṇu and Śiva in a single icon combining the attributes of different Vaiṣṇavite and Śaivite deities.[7] Brahmā of the Vedic pantheon was added to Viṣṇu and Śiva, thus forming the official male trinity.

The Vedic religion was left untended, and Vedic deities were ousted or subordinated. This was due in large part to the social and economic prosperity of the Gupta empire, which forever transformed the nature of Indian religious expression. For economic reasons, the day of the monopolistic *yajña* officiated by affluent brāhmaṇa priests passed into foggy memory. The social surplus reaped from the bustling economy of the Gupta empire was poured into the erections of wealthy temples installed with elegant images of male gods Viṣṇu, Śiva, and the Buddhist and Jaina gods (accompanied by their subordinate consorts). In order to mystify and legitimate Śiva's rise to equal status with Great Goddess Kālī, she was given a husband by brāhmaṇic myth-makers. The original independence of Śakti fell in the medieval era, when orthodox texts and art emphasize the importance of Śiva over his wife in the figure of Pārvatī. Meanwhile, in low-caste and tribal worship, the unmarried Śakti remained the central deity worshiped throughout the Gupta period, while the "Brahmanic attempt to sanction Śāktism by means of Śaivite spousification contributed to the polarization of goddess worship along socioeconomic lines."[8]

Thus, a popular new religious ideology centered round the icon and the temple arose which assimilated the cults and rituals of Purāṇic Hinduism with the genesis of the Bhakti tradition.[9] Thapar emphasizes the need for such ideological assimilation "when there is an increase in the distancing between such groups as well as the power of some over others and the economic disparity between them."[10]

The hereditary craftsmen who were ordered by the royal courts to produce the temples and icons for the elites were, of course, low-caste, dalit, and tribal workers. The artisan community developed its *śreṇīs* or guilds during this period, and artisan guilds emerged as patrons of the arts. The importance and centrality of ritual worship in the Gupta Age, then, can be directly attributed to the social surplus and the spectacular temple art produced by the underclass. These craftsmen, who also produced icons and crafts for tribals, were, as Jayakar observes, receptacles of aboriginal culture who invigorated the artistic expression of elite Purāṇic gods with vernacular form:

> The craftsman was the link between the monumental forms of the great tradition, the rural gods and the tribal deities of the forests and the mountains. However, diverse the forms and distorted the images, the roots of the creative process lay in this artisan tradition. It was from this tradition that the great temples were built and the sculpture of the Purāṇic gods found expression; it was in the same tradition that the artefacts for the tribal peoples of this country, the grinding stone mills, the hero stones, the memorial tablets to the dead, were produced. It was the blacksmith, a lower caste craftsman, who cast in the lost-wax process . . . metal images of horses and riders and the icons of the goddess. A curious relationship developed between the tribals and the artisans who served them. The Rajasthan, the craftsmen who provided the icons and objects to the tribal Bhils were known as the *kamins* or servants of the Bhils. These included carpenters, blacksmiths, stone masons, bards, basket-workers, and *jogis* or mendicants.[11]

Śakti's Counter-Culture

The cult of the revolutionary Śakti arose amid the miserable, oppressive life of the lower castes, dalits, and *ādivāsīs* whose forced and slave labor in the field of production supported unprecedented wealth for the high castes and a luxurious standard of living in town life. The archaic Saptamātṛkās, Yoginīs, and Kāpālikas emerged as Śāktic cults comprised of subaltern believers who worshiped the fierce Devī (Cāmuṇḍā, Kālī, Kāmākhyā, Cāṇḍikā, and others). Although Śāktism was incorporated into Mahāyāna Buddhism, Jainism, and Vaiṣṇavism, its greatest influence was impressed upon the Śaiva religion. By the end of the third century AD, Jainism (now one of the principal religions of India) had accepted the demands of their lay followers and adopted the Saptamātṛkā (proto-Yoginī) cult. Jaina texts like *Uttarādhyayana Sūtra, Ācāra Dinakara,* etc., list many Jaina goddesses (*śāsanadevatās*) who were adapted from the existing cults, e.g., Kālikā, Mahākālī, Śāntā, Caṇḍā, Dhāriṇī, and Ambikā. The cult of the Sixty-four Yoginīs was also adopted by the Jainas.

The Mother-goddesses began to be worshiped in special temples in the Gupta period. In Gangadhar, which lies within the belt of existing Yoginī temples, an inscription dated to AD 423 has been found. This early fifth century inscription recounts a story about a certain official named Mayūrākṣaka,

> minister of the king, who established, to gain merit,
> this most awful temple,
> a temple filled with demonesses, . . .
> sacred to the Mothers, who shout
> most loudly in the thick darkness,
> where the lotuses are shaken
> by the fierce winds
> aroused by magic spells.[12]

The practice of worshiping the goddess was "initially new to upper caste religion,"[13] steeped in the worship of male gods. In numerous ways the dialectic of all the androcentric religions, the Śākta sects apparently inspired more enthusiastic popular support than Vaiṣṇavism and Śaivism in the Gupta period. Recognized sects gradually crystallized from the first century AD, to which the literature and epigraphy of the period bear witness. In the post-Gupta period, some high-castes and intellectuals broke with their brāhmaṇic tradition, joining Śākta sects:

> Some of these sects deliberately broke the essential taboos of brahmanism relating to separate caste functions, commensality, rules of food and drink and sexual taboos. That some of the beliefs of the Śākta sects were later accepted by some *brāhmaṇa* sects is an indication of a break with Vedic religion by these *brāhmaṇa* sects although the legitimacy of the Vedic religion was sometimes sought to be bestowed on the new sects by them. Such religious compromises were not unconnected with the brahmanical need to retain social ascendency. However, some brahmanical sects remained orthodox.[14]

BUDDHISM

When the Mahāyāna movement superseded the Old Wisdom School, Buddhism underwent rapid and dramatic transformations in dogma, ritual, and metaphysics. Buddhism made a turn from austerity, renunciation, and chastity to the highly complicated system of Mahāyāna, while Jainism made changes very slowly. For obvious reasons, Tantric metaphysics overwhelmed the gentility and simplicity of Bhakti, and propelled Mahāyānism back in time to reclaim original tribal goddesses as co-deities with the Buddhas. In the Vajrayāna, the Ādi Buddha acquired Prajñāpāramitā, known by a multitude of other names, as a consort. About AD 750, consorts or Śaktis—Vajrasattvātmikā, Locanā, Māmakā, Paṇḍarā, and Ārya-Tārā—were provided for each of the Ādi Buddha's emanations, known as the Dhyāni Buddhas,[15] but more accurately, their Sanskrit names were "the five Tathāgatas" or "the five Jinas." They were Vairocana, "the Illuminator or the Brilliant;" Akṣobhya, "the Imperturbable;" Ratna Sambhava, "the Jewel-born;" Amitābha, "the Infinite Light;" and Amoghasiddhi, "the Unfailing Success." These Buddhas revolutionized the conception of the Enlightened One. While previous pre-Tantra Buddhas, who began as animals or ordinary humans, had earned their Buddhahood by progressive purification through millions of reincarnations, the five Jinas had been Buddhas from beginningless time. They constituted the body of the Universe, each Jina bearing a mystical correspondence with the five elements, the five senses and sense objects, and the five cardinal points (the fifth being the center). An epic catalogue of correspondences was assigned to each Jina, including letters of the alphabet, parts of the body, colors, types of vital breath, sounds, celestial Bodhisattvas, and, of course, a *Śakti* accessorizing each Jina.

The cults of Avalokiteśvara and Mañjuśrī flourished in the Gupta age and for many centuries afterwards. The cult of Avalokiteśvara was associated with the goddess Tārā, the personification of knowledge (*prajñā*), and the cult of Mañjuśrī with Lakṣmī, Sarasvatī, or both. Subsequent Buddhism came under the complete grip of the Tārā cult, which was evidently a force from outside. According to the Mahāyāna conception, she is the primordial female energy, the consort of Avalokiteśvara, who enables her devotees to surmount all sorts of dangers and calamities. A mere prayer to this goddess is sure to remove the eight *mahābhayas* (great dangers). She is also known as the goddess Prajñāpāramitā, as it is by the fulfillment of the *pāramitā* that a Bodhisattva reaches the goal. Sometimes she is conceived as the supreme being, the mother of all the Buddhas and Bodhisattvas. She became a very popular deity in India during the early centuries after Christ when the Mahāyāna pantheon was developing rapidly, and passed out of India to Tibet and China. In Tibet, where her cult developed about the seventh century, she was known as Sgrol-ma (Dol-ma) and conceived under a large variety of subsidiary forms.

Before the Pālas, both Hīnayāna and Mahāyāna Buddhism existed in Bengal, but due to the esoteric inclinations of the Pāla kings, Vajrayāna became the evolute of the Pāla era:

> [I]n the historical evolution of Buddhism, Mahāyāna, with its more liberal policy and generous ideal of the final goal, could capture the mind of the public much more than Hīnayāna with its strict monasticism and ethical rigorism, and as a result Mahāyāna was fast gaining in popularity. During the time of the Pālas, however, a tendency towards esoterism was manifest and Buddhism very soon underwent another great change from Mahāyāna to Vajrayāna.[16]

TANTRISM AND ŚĀKTISM

Everything about Tantra originated as a challenge to the dominant dharma. The central Tantric tenet is the revolutionary ideology of the Motherhood of God. As manifestations of Prakṛti or Śakti, all women are objects of respect and devotion, and offending them incurs the wrath of the goddess. Each aspirant must realize the latent female principle in his or her heart, and it is solely by becoming female that he is entitled to worship the supreme being (*vāmā bhūtvā yajet parām*). In its social sphere, Tantrism is free of class and patriarchal bigotry. The populist nature of Tantrism is evidenced by the engagement of low-caste, dalit, and tribal people, otherwise excluded from Hindu ritual, in Tantric practice on at least a part-time basis.[17,18] In the *Devī Purāṇa*, for example, the Pukvasas, Caṇḍālas, and other outcaste tribes and groups are permitted to perform the rituals and sacrifices to the goddess, and preference for her worship is given to a virtuous śūdra over a worthless member of one of the higher castes.[19]

Beginning around the fifth century, the more moderate forms of Tantric practice were given brāhmaṇic approval, leading to a popular uprising of the Śākta counter-culture, in which all gods were subordinate to the Great Goddess. In its evolved form, the Śākta religion became almost indistinguishable from Tantrism, the religion of the Hindu majority which was "identical with Hinduism in medieval times," according to Sharma. "Its outlook was highly secular and materialistic, and no other sect was so close to the life of various classes of people as it was."[20] Śākta doctrine and symbology are contingent upon protection and empowerment by a female Godhead, freedom from oppression, insulation from the external world, and lack of bourgeois bigotry. These values, reminiscent of tribal forms, reinvigorated the great masses of subaltern groups. Intellectuals, some belonging to the high castes, were drawn to Śāktism's liberalizing aspects, its anti-caste stance, and its elevation of women, and orthodox religious trends moved toward the heightened accommodation of the deviant dharmas. Bengali literature in particular popularized the cults of the subaltern goddesses among the elites and identified them with different manifestations of the Śākta Devī.[21]

Kumar propounds that some scholars have mistakenly attributed the origin of Tantrism to Śaivism, while in actuality it is an independent cult of the female principle. There is a subtle difference between Śāktism and Tantrism. The motivation of a true Śākta is purely materialistic: to obtain *siddhis* (supernatural faculties) through Devī's help, or to destroy one's enemies through her cooperation.[22] The meaning of Śakti has come to connote in Tantrism, on the other hand, the hidden evolutionary potential we as humans possess within our minds, *cakras*, and *nāḍīs*; our highest activity, according to Tantric dogma, is to activate this Śakti. When viewed historically, Śāktism can be viewed as a synthesis of tribal religions and brāhmaṇical co-optation. It must be separated from Tantrism, which is

> a system of magical and sacramental ritual, taught in the sacred Hindu texts known as *tantras*. The *tantras* profess to teach the attainment of the highest aims of religion by such methods as spells, diagrams (*yantras*), gestures (*mudrās*) and other physical exercises (*yoga*), Tantrism is nothing but a simplification of religion on mechanical rather than on emotional lines.[23]

Philosophically grounded in Yoga and Sāṅkhya, often ascending into the abstractions of Vedānta, the Tantras all pertain to the mechanics of the mind, the science of mind training, and the magical outcome of Tantric ritual, discussing such subjects as the creation and destruction of the universe; the attainment of *siddhi*; worship of goddesses and gods; union with the Supreme Being; and the tools of *mantra, yantra, prāṇāyāma, āsana,* and meditation. In the end the yogī's soul become identified with Śiva through the Kuṇḍalinī, and the yogic psycho-physical disciplines help to awaken and raise the goddess Kuṇḍalinī up the *cakras* to unite with Śiva. In that union, the female principle dissolves into neutered nondual awareness. The polar opposite of androcentric Tantric Buddhism is Śāktism, in that the rituals of Kālī and her *avatāras* epitomize the Neolithic principle of male sacrifice for the benefit of the community, subsuming the Śākta and folkloric motifs of man-destroying sexuality, divine rage, death, and regeneration.

Although Śāktism interacted closely with Vaiṣṇavism and Śaivism, the Śāktic influence was met with greatest receptivity by the Śaivites, who introduced Tantrism to the Hindu great tradition. "In their pristine and more orthodox forms, however, both Vaiṣṇavism and Śaivism continued to be the religions of the State and of the elite."[24] Śāktism was ultimately influenced by Śaivite androcentric priorities, which centered around male dominance. Thus, while the fierce Śakti was worshiped in subaltern practices such as Left-hand Tantrism, she took on the secondary role of the dependent wife of Śiva in orthodox Śaivite sects. As Gatwood articulates, however,

> it was the god, and not the goddess, who was spousified in Śaivism: Devī was given a husband only in order to legitimize Śiva's claim to equality with the popular Śakti. In this case there was a gain rather than a loss in the spouse's (here Śiva's) status. Over time, the effect of Śiva's marriage in high caste Śaivite circles became virtually identical to that of Devī's spousification in Vaishnavism. The independent stature of Devī had become a tenuously shared status, paving the way for an orthodox medieval prioritization of Śiva over his wife in the figure of Pārvatī.[25]

Meanwhile, in nonelite worship, the fierce Śakti reigned throughout the Gupta period as the central object of devotion, and the image of Mahiṣāsura-mardinī—the fierce, unwed Devī's battles with the buffalo-demon—became the ideology of the oppressed masses.[26] Durgā was the archaic goddess into whom all fierce tribal goddesses and village *grāma-devatās* were incorporated; she, seated upon a totemic lion, her multiple arms and weapons representing the many tribal goddesses she had absorbed, became the symbol of victory over the enemies of the people. While the brāhmaṇas used Durgā as a literary vehicle to weaken the tribal goddesses and to express brāhmaṇic pre-eminence (Durgā was created by elites to slay their enemies), Mahiṣāsura-mardinī was regarded as an anti-brāhmaṇic symbol by subaltern groups. To repeat Bhattacharya's assertion,

> but throughout the ages, the urge for freedom against oppression prevails which often finds expression in the forms of popular revolts. In any case, the oppressed peoples dream of their freedom and even resort to imagination, the imaginative victory of the goddess over the demons, when the reality goes against their hopes and aspirations. The Devī's fight with demons thus served as the best ideology that the ancient age could provide to the toiling masses struggling against the intolerable conditions of life, the social importance of which we ought not to minimize.[27]

Śāktic beliefs began to be expressed in popular Tantric practice following brāhmaṇic approval of its more moderate forms around the fifth century. All gods now had subordinate wife-goddesses by their sides. Purāṇic mythology, written to order roughly between the sixth and twelfth centuries AD (but which claims immemorial antiquity), was tailored to weaken tribal goddesses' supreme autonomy by degrading them into brāmaṇic property, viz., the fierce goddesses became the collective emanations of the gods' lustre or, less frequently, the wives of brāhmaṇic animal-gods, for example, Vārāhā/Vārāhī, Nārasiṁha/Nārasiṅghī, and so forth. As we have observed, the goddess of the masses became the wife of Śiva, the high god of the nonelite, as well as the container of all the fierce tribal goddesses whose native forest and jungle habitats were devastated by high-caste socioeconomic interests. From this period until the wave of devotional Vaiṣṇavism swept northern India early in the Muslim period and halted the progress of her cult, the Great Goddess continued her reign and increased her influence. Śāktism is still a stronghold in Bengal and Assam, and is well known in other parts of India.

Purāṇic Literature, Brāhmaṇic Property, and Land-Grants

The assimilative nature of Purāṇic literature was an inevitability given the secular and religious grants of land to brāhmaṇas to settle in areas of tribal societies, where exposure to brāhmaṇic culture had been at best fleeting and certainly irrelevant to tribal peoples, who had no sense of bourgeois property ownership. This system of land-grants predominated in tribal areas to "facilitate their conversion to a peasant economy (where lineage could also be used for economic control) and to a *varṇa* and *jāti* network" in which the "identification with *varṇa* status would have acted as a bridge to a peasant economy and prevented a rupture with the lineage system."[28]

The Purāṇic texts with their numerous sub-categories were psychologically sophisticated, subtly didactic ideological tools of the brāhmaṇic mission to confiscate land and consolidate property.[29] As we have observed, brāhmaṇic ideology was injected into local folk cults by transforming tribal spirits and divinities into the property (weapons, ornaments, creations, or wives) of brāhmaṇic gods, inventing respectable stories and lineages about tribes, aboriginal cults, pilgrimage places, and deities to embroider into Sanskrit mythology, and incorporating officiating brāhmaṇa priests and rituals into aboriginal, female-dominated religious rites.[30] While the cultures of the dominant and the oppressed remained distinct in the Purāṇas, they were mythologically depicted as parts of a whole.

A central objective of the epics and Purāṇas, as discussed earlier, was to teach new codes of behavior based on brāhmaṇic and kṣatriya values, especially relating to high-caste women's reproductive behavior (allegorically depicted in the *Rāmāyaṇa* and *Mahābhārata*) and the subordination of tribals and the low caste majority (metaphorically depicted in *Mārkaṇḍeya Purāṇa* and in other) by containment of their fierce goddesses within the *tejas* of brāhmaṇic gods. Because women and property became the primary sources of social conflict, the Purāṇas contain special ethical exhortations and warnings that stress the taboo against using another's property or taking another's wife.[31] Even the son is viewed suspiciously because he could jeopardize his father's wife and property.[32] High-caste women in ancient India had limited opportunity to own property since they were regarded as chattel[33] who could be gifted, sold, pledged, or disposed of in any way by their male guardians. According to the *Agni Purāṇa*, "Women and animals can be kept as pledge and interest on them is the seventh part of their original value."[34]

Literary and Archaeological Evidence

There is a plethora of literary[35] and sculptural/archaeological evidence during the Gupta and post-Gupta age of fierce tribal goddesses adopted in the Śākta pantheon as *ugra* demon slayer (Caṇḍikā, Kauśikī, Durgā, and Kālī), savioress of the oppressed, or as Yoginīs. Among the earliest Purāṇas, the *Mārkaṇḍeya* and *Vāmana* depict the Mahiṣāsura-mardinī episode, a concept that had enormous popular appeal with a clear social intent. The Gupta age *Viṣṇu Purāṇa*[36] describes her fondness for wine and meat. In the *Devī Purāṇa*, used extensively as an authority on Śakti worship, the Devī appears mainly as war-goddess Cāmuṇḍā, described as the powerful Śakti, i.e., able to create, protect, and destroy the universe. The skeletal, emaciated Cāmuṇḍā is said to live in cemetery grounds, and destruction of the enemies is attributed to her, as well as fulfillment of all desires, religious merits, final salvation, and worldly enjoyments. Cāmuṇḍā was the principal deity of the Kāpālikas and the most awe-inspiring fierce goddess of the Yoginī cult. In the *Devī Bhāgavata Purāṇa*, the brāhmaṇic cosmology is turned on its head and undercut. In the Śākta scheme of cosmic evolution, the unmanifested Prakṛti alone existed before creation. She wished to create, and having assumed the form of the Great Mother, she created Brahmā, Viṣṇu, and Śiva out of her own body.[37] In her highest form, she is depicted as Mahādevī, at once the consort and creatrix of Śiva.[38] This is the antithesis of the brāhmaṇic fettering of fierce tribal goddesses, signifying the powerful influence of the Śākta cult.

In secular literature, Bāṇabhaṭṭa's *Kādambarī* (seventh century AD) mentions the Goddess cult of the untamed Śabaras and their dark rites, and his *Harṣacarita* describes the destructive nature of the goddess. Subandhu's *Vāsavadattā* reveals the bloodthirsty goddess Kātyāyanī or Bhagavatī of Kusumapura. Vākpati's *Gauḍavaha*[39] (AD 725) vividly depicts the frightening ambience of the temple of Vindhyavāsinī (goddess worshiped by the Śabaras with human sacrifice). The work also details the goddess slaying the buffalo-demon, and associates her with peacocks and bloodthirsty rites.

We have earlier observed the wide distribution of Mahiṣa-mardinī sculptures. Numerous sets of stone Saptamātṛkās, both rock-cut (Badoh-Pathari) and freestanding (Besnagar) images,[40] still stand. Sculptures of at least eight Mother-goddesses holding infants have been found in Thanesara-Mahādeva,[41] and a series of at least seventeen sculptures of Mother-goddesses at the site of Samalaji in Gujarat,[42] which Dehejia identifies as probably proto-Yoginī cult images.[43]

The Yoginī and Kāpālika Cults

We find both archaeological and literary evidence of the strong presence of the Yoginī and Kāpālika cults in the classical period. The famous Gangadhar stone inscription quoted above, which refers to the temple of Divine Mothers as the fierce dwelling of *ḍākinīs*, provides evidence that the fierce Śakti was worshiped in temples in the Gupta period. As the inscription tells us, the goddesses themselves are heard shouting *mantras* in outbursts of joy, stirring up the oceans with the winds that they cause to rise from their Tantra or magical rites. Although some of the most exquisite sculptures of the Gupta and later periods depict the goddesses of the Vaiṣṇava, Śaiva, Buddhist, and Jaina sects, the fierce Devī of the Mahiṣa-mardinī form surpassed all others in popularity.

In the *Mārkaṇḍeya Purāṇa*, one of the oldest Purāṇas, Śakti is depicted as a demon-slaying savior goddess, who, originating from the concentrated and cumulative energy of all the gods, is created to destroy the demon Mahiṣāsura and his fierce tribe. She is Omnipresent, Omniscient, and Omnipotent, the Creatrix, Preserver, and Destroyer of the universe. The *Mārkaṇḍeya Purāṇa* also records the origin of the Mātṛkās,[44] whom Das terms "basically the Yoginīs."[45] The counterpoints of the chief gods, the Mātṛkās helped Ambikā to kill the demon Raktabīja, the ally of demon Śumbha, who cloned himself by manufacturing demons in his blood. When drops of his blood oozed from his wounds and touched the ground, demons rose up like clones from the blood drops. The job of the Yoginīs was to drink his blood before it dropped to the ground. Unable to multiply himself, the demon was ultimately overcome and killed.

The *Mahābhāgavata Purāṇa* refers to Yoginīs and Bhairavas who were entrusted with and responsible for the protection of the residence of Kālī—a vast walled city with four gates in four directions. Kālī is seated in the middle on a lion-throne, surrounded by her attendants, sixty-four Yoginīs and sixty-four Bhairavas. The *Matsya Purāṇa* tells the story of the mighty demon Andhaka's oppression over and invulnerability to the gods and goddesses in heaven. When he tried to abduct Pārvatī, Śiva became furious and waged a violent war against the demon. When Śiva's Pāśupata weapon was discharged against the demon, innumerable Andhaka demons emerged from the blood drops gushing from the demon's wounds. When these demons were beheaded, multiple formidable demons sprang up from the blood. Lord Śiva created about Divine Mothers to eliminate the demons by drinking their blood, including Māheśvarī, Brāhmī, Cāmuṇḍā, Vārāhi, Kālī, Mahākālī, Kapālī, Aditi, Caṇḍā, Karālinī, Māyā, Kāmarūpā, Maṅgalā, Kumārī, Śivā, and many others.

Like Ko<u>rr</u>avai's demonesses, the Mātṛkās were greatly gratified by drinking the blood of the demons. After the demon Andhaka was killed, the Mothers began their campaign of terror and destruction of the universe, assuming horrific forms. Śiva, desperate to subdue the Mothers, prayed to Narasiṁha, who instantly appeared, his tongue darting like an electrical spark and his claws smeared with the gore of Hiraṇyakaśipu. Brimming with wrathful energy, Narasiṁha roared and thundered like oceans through his great teeth and fangs; with thunderbolt nails, red eyes burning furiously like the sun, clad in exquisite garments and ornaments, the lustre of his beautiful face illuminating the universe.

Because the Divine Mothers were poised to disregard Śiva's orders and devour the whole universe, Narasiṁha created thirty-two supremely powerful Divine Mothers to subdue the destructive mothers; viz., Ghaṇṭākarṇi, Trailokyamohinī, Sarvasattvasaṅkarī, Cakrahṛdayā, Vyomacāriṇī, Śaṅkhinī, Lekhanī, Kāmasaṅkāsinī, Saṅkarṣiṇī, Aśvatthāmā, Vijabhāva, Aparājitā, Kalyānī, Madhudantasrī, Kamolatpalohastikā, Ajitā, Sūkṣmahṛdayā, Vṛddhā, Vessamodanasanā, Nṛsiṅghabhīrabā, Vilvā, Garutmahṛdayā, Jayā, Ākarṣaṇī, Sabhatā, Uttaramālikā, Padmakarā, Jwālāmedhi, Bhīṣaṇikā, Kāmadhensā, and Balikā. The wrathful flash emanating from the eyes of these Divine Mothers subdued those created by Śiva, and all the Mātṛkās took refuge with Narasiṁha. He decreed that they should assist the highest Devī, fostering and guarding the universe as men and animals look after their children, and should obtain oblations made by the devotees.

Das points out that the Purāṇas also inform us of the dominance of the Yoginī cult in the seventh and eighth centuries:

The proposition in the Matsya Purāṇa regarding the origin of Mātṛkas, who are basically the Yoginīs, certainly deserves attention. Most of the names of Mātṛkas found mention in this Purāṇa have been accepted and described in the several other texts as Yoginīs. The date of composition of Matsya Purāṇa along with Skanda Purāṇa, Garuḍa Purāṇa and Devi Bhāgavata Purāṇa may be placed approximately in the 7th–8th centuries AD. Therefore, the account of this Mahāpurāṇa composed in the 7th–8th centuries AD prompts us to conclude that the cult of Yoginīs was widely prevalent during this period. But this does not prevent the origin of the Yoginīs from being yet earlier.[46]

Varāhamihira's *Bṛhatsaṁhitā*[47] (sixth century AD) states emphatically that only those trained in *maṇḍalakrama* (circle-worship mode) may worship the Mothers (*matṛgaṇa*). The *Guhyasiddhikrama*[48] refers to *aṣṭāṣṭakakrama* (mode of worship of sixty-four) associated with the circle of Yoginīs, specifically stipulating that the rites of the Yoginī cult were a specialized type of worship conducted by a select group of priests, identified by Das[49] as the Kāpālikas. Kalhaṇa's *Rājataraṅgiṇī*[50] recounts that King Baka was captured by a beautiful Yogeśvarī (a word used synonomously with Yoginī in the work) as an offering to a circle of goddesses (*devīcakra*). Bhavabhūti's *Mālatī-Mādhava*[51] describes a temple of the goddess Cāmuṇḍā near Padmāvatī where regular human sacrifices were offered by Kāpālikas. (Aghoraghaṇṭa, a Kāpālika, kidnaps the heroine to offer as a sacrifice.) "This eighth century authority," writes Bhattacharyya, "not only testifies to the prevalence of human sacrifice before the goddess, but also to the interesting fact that the Kāpālikas were followers of the Goddess cult."[52] The *Mattavilāsa-prahasana* (attributed to Pallava Mahendravarman I, *c.* AD 600–685) offers detailed descriptions of the Kāpālikas and their cults. The *Lalitavistara*, a Buddhist text of the early Christian era, speaks of the Kāpālikas besmearing their bodies with ashes, wearing red garments, and carrying a triple staff (*tridaṇḍa*), a pot, a skull, and a *khaṭvāṅga*. Several important Purāṇas describe the Kāpālikas in disparaging terms. The *Brahmāṇḍa*,[53] *Vāyu*, and *Matsya* Purāṇas (datable to the period between the third and seventh centuries AD) narrate stories of the Kāpālikas.

The journals kept by Chinese on holy pilgrimages are the only extant eyewitness accounts of the topography of Central Asia and India between the fifth and seventh centuries. Three Chinese monk-scholars kept particularly important records of their travels to India: Fa-hien spent fourteen years on pilgrimage through Central Asia, India, and Sri Lanka in the fifth century; Hsüan-tsang traveled in the seventh century for twenty-four years; and I-tsing was a pilgrim for sixteen years in the seventh century. The latter two studied at Nālandā, the great Buddhist university near Rājagṛha. "Many died on such a pilgrimage; a few chose to spend the rest of their lives in the heartland of the Dharma," writes Tarthang Tulku. "Of the Chinese pilgrims, it has been estimated that only two per cent of those who embarked for India ever returned to China. Those who did return brought with them teachings that profoundly influenced the course of Buddhism in China."[54]

ASCETICISM: THE REPOSSESSION OF THE BODY

Although asceticism was a socioeconomic imperative in both the dominant dharma and the new religions, it served contradictory purposes among elite and low-caste members. We have seen that prohibition against marital infidelity was a sure means of consolidating property through inheritance. The enforced chastity of high-caste females and brāhmaṇas following initiation were means of maintaining patrilineal inheritance and the consolidation of power and property among male elites.

At the low-caste socioeconomic pole, the grand indifference if not outright hostility of śramaṇic ascetics to the human body and the material universe appears to be in conflict with earthy subaltern sexo-religious and *bali* practices, so grounded in materialistic concerns and outcomes. Why did low-caste peoples turn to yogic practices that were hostile to material phenomena? First, as Chatterjee cogently suggests, inner practice amounts to a reclamation of the body: "Caste attaches to the body, not to the soul."[55] Although Chatterjee writes about contemporary Sahajiyā cults, his ideas apply to ascetics of all times. The revolutionary ideology underpinning asceticism among the deviant cults involves the reclamation and repossession of the worshiper's own body, the negation of "the daily submission of one's body and its labor to the demands made by the dominant dharma," and the assertion of "a domain of bodily activity where it can, with the full force of ethical conviction, disregard those demands."[56] The practical aspects of the religions of the deviant cults are all fundamentally concerned with the body.

In the sixth century AD, the Yogācārins constructed a dynamic dualistic metaphysics embraced by many deviant cults in which external reality was conceived as derivative of ignorance, and the universal reality of yogic potentiality was derivative of the cosmic mind or "store-consciousness." Among the rich texts of subaltern yogic poetry and scripture, the body is metaphorically depicted as an artifact, a physical construct, an instrument or product of labor—a boat, a cart, a house, a potter's wheel, or a weaver's loom—the property of elites who own the means of production. "But the very secretiveness of these cult practices," writes Chatterjee, "the fact that they can be engaged in only, as it were, outside the boundaries of the social structure, sets the limit to the practical effectiveness of the claim of possession; not surprisingly, it draws upon itself the charge of licentiousness."[57]

The practical religion of the low-caste groups involves physiological self-discipline in the course of daily social life. The metaphysics of these cults maintain that the body can be used by its owner with skill and wisdom, such as the Haṭhayoga practices of the Nātha cults, or spent and burned out by profligacy. The main principle of *sādhana* is expressed in yogico-Tantric exercises that produce a regressive or upward movement in the bodily processes. It is believed that normally, the force of *pravṛtti* (activity and change) moves in a downward direction, taking the body along the path of decay and destruction. The aim of yogic self-discipline is to reverse this process by moving the energy upward, in the direction of *nivṛtti* or rest. More specifically, for male practitioners, the bodily practices involve the retention of the *bindu* or *śukra* (semen), and preventing its waste. The full range of Haṭhayoga practices can be performed only in a strict state of celibacy, the objective being the attainment of the perfect *siddha* state of immortality. The deviant cults produced, therefore, a new *āśramadharma* for their adherents constituted by a graded series of bodily disciplines that can be integrated into religious and social life. For most lay followers, semen retention is as far as their *sādhana* is expected to go. However, for the fortunate few,

> a successful life . . . is followed by the state of *nityan* where there is complete unconcern for the world. This is a stage of life spent outside the bonds of family and kin. The final and most perfect state is . . . [one of] complete freedom and hence of unconditioned proprietorship over one's bodily existence. . . . There are unmistakable signs here of a consciousness alienated from the dominant dharma, but apparently bound to nothing else than its spirit of resolute negativity. Its practical defeat too is borne out by the facts of social history. Yet, is there not here an implicity, barely stated, search for a recognition whose signs lie not outside, but within one's own self? Can one see here the trace of an identity which is defined not by others, but by oneself? Perhaps we have allowed ourselves to be taken in too easily by the general presence of an abstract negativity in the autonomous domain of subaltern beliefs and practices and have missed those marks, faint as they are, of an immanent process of criticism and learning, of selective appropriation, of making sense of and using on one's own terms the elements of a more powerful cultural order. We must, after all, remind ourselves that subaltern consciousness is not merely structure, characterized solely by negativity; it is also history, shaped and developed through a changing process of interaction between the dominant and the subordinate.[58]

A second powerful reason that subaltern people turn to yogic practices lies in the promise of *siddhis* or magical power achieved through *sādhana*. As Basham bluntly puts it, "The original motive of Indian asceticism was the acquisition of magical power."[59] The yogic attainment of *siddhis*, the material manifestation of yogic practice, strengthens the subversive ideology of subaltern asceticism. The yogic practice of meditation during which time the yoginī unites with the divine bears the psychic imprint of the shamanic spirit possession trance that bestows magical abilities on the shaman. The doctrine and practices of yoga evolved into a systematic identification and cultivation of the priest-magician's magical powers. Patañjali's *Yogasūtra*, dated between 200 BCE and AD 300, states that the practice of *saṁyama*[60] produces a large number of magical powers, including the ability to know the present, past, and future; to become invisible; to become strong as an elephant; to enter another person's body; to walk on water or thorns; to hear the inaudible; and to fly. Patañjali writes elsewhere that the *siddhis* may be achieved by any of five methods: birth, drugs, *mantras*, penance, and *samādhi*. King Bhoja's

Rājamārtaṇḍa commentary on Patañjali in the early eleventh century contains a list of eight *mahāsiddhis* (great *siddhis*) that can be obtained by yoga, including *aṇiman*, the power of becoming small; *laghiman*, the power of levitation; *gariman*, the power of becoming heavy; *mahiman*, the power of becoming boundlessly large; *īśitva*, control over the five elements; and *kāmāvasāyitva*, fulfillment of desires.[61]

Many modern Western and Indian scholars have stated that practitioners should ignore *siddhis*, since they are byproducts of yogic practice that can be obstacles to final liberation. Such statements are backed up by a single *sūtra* of Patañjali (III.37), in which he refers back to powers mentioned in the previous one or two *sūtras*, but does not intend to include the many *siddhis* mentioned afterwards. As Lorenzen stresses, "This attitude [that siddhis should be ignored] may have been operative in Vedāntic and Buddhist circles and is now popular among practitioners imbued with the spirit of the Hindu Renaissance, but it was not the view of Patañjali and certainly not the view of medieval exponents of Haṭha Yoga."[62]

References

1. Bhattacharyya, *The Indian Mother Goddess*, 223.
2. Kosambi, *Ancient India*, 192.
3. Ibid., 193.
4. Ibid., 64–65.
5. Kosambi, *Myth and Reality*, 29.
6. Thapar, *Interpreting Early India*, 66.
7. Bhattacharyya, *History of the Śākta Religion*, 65.
8. Gatwood, *Devī and the Spouse Goddess*, 60.
9. Thapar, *Interpreting Early India*, 132.
10. Ibid.
11. Jayakar, *The Earth Mother*, 43.
12. J.F. Fleet, ed., *Corpus Inscriptionum Indicarum 3: Inscriptions of the Early Gupta Kings* (Calcutta, 1888), 79ff.
13. Thapar, *Interpreting Early India*, 64.
14. Ibid., 64–65.
15. Although Euro-American literature frequently name them the "Dhyāni Buddhas," this term is not found in the Tantric texts. Rather, the early texts refer to the "Five Tathāgatās" or the "Five Jinas." Jina, an old epithet of the Buddha, means victor or conqueror—specifically, victory over passion and desire. [Conze, *Buddhism: Its Essence and Development*, 89.]
16. Shashi Bhusan Dasgupta, *Obscure Religious Cults* (Calcutta, 1962), 11.

17,18. Sharma, *Perspectives in Social and Economic History of Early India*, 175; Ajit Mookerjee and Madhu Khanna, *The Tantric Way: Art, Science, Ritual* (Boston, 1977), 27.

19. *Devī P.*, 22.5–6; 23–24; 24.17; 51.4–5; 88.4; 89.19; 91.1.
20. Sharma, *Perspectives in Social and Economic History of Early India*, 176.
21. Bhattacharyya, *The Indian Mother Goddess*, 129–32ff.
22. Pushpendra Kumar, *Śakti Cult in Ancient India* (Varanasi, 1974), 1.

23. Ibid., 2.
24. Gatwood, *Devī and the Spouse Goddess*, 59.
25. Ibid., 60.
26. Bhattacharyya, *History of the Śākta Religion* (1974), 84.
27. Ibid.
28. Thapar, *Interpreting Early India*, 117.
29. Kosambi, *Ancient India*, 49ff.
30. See Milton Singer, *Traditional India: Structure and Change* (Philadelphia, 1959); D.D. Kosambi, *Ancient India: A History of Its Culture and Civilization* (New York, 1965); Kosambi, *Myth and Reality* (Bombay, 1962); M.N. Srinivas, "A Note on Sanskritization and Westernization," *Far Eastern Quarterly* 15 (August 1956).
31. *Garuḍa P.*, 108.13; *Harivaṁśa*, 3.80.79.
32. *Garuḍa P.*, 114.60.
33. Sharma, *Perspectives in Social and Economic History of Early India*, 43.
34. *Agni P.*, 253.63–64.
35. I am using Hazra's chronology of the Purāṇas, *Studies in the Upa-purāṇas*, according to which most portions of the *Mārkaṇḍeya, Brahmāṇḍa, Vāyu*, and *Viṣṇu* Purāṇas were written before the fifth century AD, those of the *Bhāgavata* in the sixth century, and of the *Matsya*, between the sixth and seventh centuries.
36. 5.2.84.
37. *Devī Bhāgavata P.*, 3.1–6.
38. We learn from Narendra Nath Bhattacharyya that '[i]n Punic Africa, she is Tamit with her son; in Egypt, Isis with Horus; in Phonecia, Ashtaroth with Tammuj; in Asia Minor, Cybele with Attis; in Greece (and especially in the Greek Crete itself), Rhea with young Zeus. Everywhere she is *unwed*, but made the mother first of her companion by Immaculate Conception, and that memory of these original facts her cult (especially the most esoteric mysteries of it) is marked by various practices and obliteration of sex. Such tales of virgin mothers are relics of an age when the father had no significance at all, and of a society in which a man's contribution to the matter of procreation was hardly recognized.' [Bhattacharyya, "Śāktism and Mother-Right," in *The Śakti Cult and Tārā*, ed. D.C. Sircar (Calcutta, 1967), 73.]
39. 285–347.
40. Vidya Dehejia, *Yoginī Cult and Temples: A Tantric Tradition* (New Delhi, 1986), 68.
41. R.C. Agrawala, "Some Unpublished Sculptures from Southwestern Rajasthan," *Lalit Kalā* 6 (1959): 63–71; Agrawala, "Some More Unpublished Sculptures from Rajasthan," in ibid., 10 (1961): 31–33.
42. U.P. Shah, *Sculptures from Samalaji and Roda* (Baroda, 1960).
43. Dehejia, *Yoginī Cult and Temples*, 70.
44. Chap. 88.
45. H.C. Das, *Tantricism: A Study of the Yogini Cult* (New Delhi, 1981), 4.
46. Ibid., 5.
47. *Bṛhatsaṁhitā*, 2.59; 19; 56.57.
48. *Guhyasiddhikrama*, in *Bṛhatsūcipatram*, ed. Buddhisagar Sharman, vol. 4 (Kathmandu, 1964), 109.
49. Das, 26.
50. *Rājataraṅgiṇī*, bk. 1, vv. 331–33.
51. Act 5.

52. Bhattacharyya, *History of the Śākta Religion*, 77.
53. According to the *Brahmāṇḍa Purāṇa*, Swayambhu (Śiva) created Paśupatayoga first and Kāpālikayoga last.
54. Tarthang Tulku, ed., *Holy Places of the Buddha* (Berkeley, 1994), 12.
55. Chatterjee, "Claims on the past: The Genealogy of Modern Historiography in Bengal," in *Subaltern Studies*, 8: *Essays in Honour of Ranajit Guha*, ed. David Arnold and David Hardiman (Delhi, 1994), 203.
56. Ibid.
57. Ibid.
58. Ibid., 206.
59. Basham, 244.
60. *Yogasūtra*, III.16–50. The term *saṁyama* signifies the final, and highest, three "limbs of Yoga": concentration (*dhāraṇā*), meditation (*dhyāna*), and *samādhi*.
61. Commentary on *Yogasūtra*, III.44, cited by Eliade, in *Yoga: Immortality and Freedom*, 88.
62. David N. Lorenzen, *The Kāpālikas and Kālāmukhas: Two Lost Śaivite Sects* (Berkeley, 1972), 94.

9

The Flowering of Esoteric Yogic Cults amid Islamic Invasions: The Early Medieval Period (AD 700–1300)

The Rise of Islam

The religion of Islam is central to contemporary political unrest in South Asia, and Islamists are today equated with the buffalo demon, the cultural *bête noir* of Mahiṣāsura-mardinī and the Indian subcontinent itself. As we should expect, Islam follows the universal blueprint of patriarchal religions: a group (often a trinity) of indigenous polytheistic goddesses is supplanted and suppressed by a male god. Ancient goddess-oriented religio-cultural systems are subsequently co-opted to serve the interests of elite males and the new patriarchal religion.

Pre-Islamic Semitic Polytheism in Arabia

Yahweh-worshiping Hebrews conquered Canaan (Palestine) in the second millennium BCE at a time when Egyptian, Hittite, and Sumerian empires were no longer powerful, and the potential great power, Assyria, had not yet organized its forces. Under Moses' successor, Joshua, the Yahweh tribes traversed the Jordan River, conquered the town of Jericho and the surrounding plain, and established themselves in western Palestine, more by intermarriage and alliance than by force. The Yahweh tribes, united by their religious covenant, their tradition of common descent, and their democratic ideal, secured their land and become known as the Israelites. They fought off invasions by the Moabites, the Midianities, and most, of all, the fierce Philistines, who migrated from the territory around the Aegean Sea. The Jewish state came to an end in AD 70, when the Romans begin actively to drive

Jews from the home they had lived in for over a millennium. From this point on, "Hebrew history would only be the history of the Diaspora as the Jews and their worldview spread over Africa, Asia, and Europe."[1]

Bedouin societies—some camel and goat herders, others agriculturalists in oasis towns—were the pre-Islamic inhabitants of the Arabian Peninsula. In southern coastal regions, flourishing commercial and agricultural town centers were reflections of Bedouin culture. Social organization was based on mobile kin-related clans, which mushroomed into larger tribal units that were activated during crises. Women had key economic roles in clan life, descent was traced through the female line, and males paid a bride-price to the wife's family. Women were neither veiled nor secluded, and both men and women had multiple marriage partners. However, male warriors occupied the pinnacle of the social hierarchy, and men's rights were privileged over women's in matters of property control, inheritance, and divorce. *Shaykhs*, or leaders, were usually wealthy males whose decisions were enforced by free warriors. Clan loyalty was paramount in the inhospitable desert environment. Slave families served leaders or the clan as a whole. Inter-clan rivalry and conflicts over water and pasture sparked centuries-long feuds, which weakened Bedouin societies' defenses against its rivals. The trading system linking the Mediterranean to East Asia was punctuated by cities that developed as entrepôts, Mecca (pilgrim and tourist center) and Medina (oasis farming center) being the two most important.

During Muhammad's time, Semitic animistic polytheism, not yet influenced by Judeo-Christian cultural forms, constituted the core religion of Central Arabia,[2] and can be compared in many respects to the earlier Semitic religions of ancient Mesopotamia and Palestine, since ancient Sumerian and West Semitic religion share numerous important motifs in common. Trees and vegetative life, stones, springs, wells, and animals were the natural abodes of goddesses, angels, jinns (genii), stars, gods, and spirits, and in the universal mode, Bedouins performed religious rituals to placate these spirits and implore them for aid. The Ugarit and Palestinian kingdoms were minor stratified aristocratic societies that flourished independently, yet they received many cultural elements from their neighbors to the east and south.

Yahweh, like Tammuz and Baal, was originally worshiped as a fertility deity,[3] linked with consort Asherah by the fifth century BCE.[4] In the time of Kings, queen mothers of Israel were overseers of the goddess cult in Asherah groves upon sacred hilltops. Solomon built a temple for both Yahweh and Ashtoreth,[5] daughter of Asherah and cognate of Anath. A carved image of Asherah was even placed within the Jerusalem Yahweh Temple itself.[6] During the times of Judges and Kings, unless, Baal Yahweh's outright rival, was worshiped, Yahwists did not interfere with Anath and Asherah worship, as long as she was only worshiped as Yahweh's bride. Eliade likens the pre-Islamic Arabian religion to the popular religion of Palestine in the sixth century BCE, citing their veneration of Yahweh and Anath, alongside Bethel and Harambethel, as reflected in papyri of the Jewish colony on the island of Elephantine on the Upper Nile.[7]

A prominent feature in both the biblical field and the epic literature of the Near East (Akkadian, Sumerian, Hittite, and Hurrian) is the cult of the dying and rising god and his wife, the goddess of war and love—Tammuz and Ishtar, Dumazi and Inanna, Baal and Asherah/Anath. Coupled with the rites of sacred marriage, this mytho-ritual meme is connected with the annual spring festival, when the return of Tammuz from the Netherworld was celebrated to symbolize the revival of life and the renewal of the state. The general structure of the Sumero–Akkadian, the Ugaritic, and the Hebrew myths is as follows:

> At the beginning we meet with the "steppe" flourishing with verdure beginning the pasturage of the herds. Then, the enemies from the desert enter the god's field, destroy it, and make it a desert, at this moment the god descends to the Nether World. Then, the change occurs, and finally, the god's triumph over his enemies and his return to life are celebrated, the field again becoming the flourishing dwelling-place of the cattle.[8]

Mythology and history overlap; the desert is equated with the Land of the Dead (or the parched field of battle in India) and both are bound up with the cult of fertility deities. Since very early periods (before 2,000 BCE), it seems that this cult played an important cultural role not only in the rather homogeneous civilization of the whole Near East,[9] but it also infused the Dravidian Tamil culture of ancient India and the Semitic polytheism of ancient Palestine and Arabia. As Alfred Haldar explains.

> The idea of the desert as the dwelling-place of demons and monsters—hence equivalent to the dwelling-place of the dead, or the Nether World—may easily be assumed to be a feature inherent in all of the various Near Eastern civilizations. At any rate, in the rituals where the idea of the parallelism between the "desert" and the Nether World occurs, there is evidence of processions to this place during the annual festival symbolizing the death of the fertility god. In the Sumerian religion this is particularly the case in the Tammuz cult.[10]

At some point, the ancient mother-son worship morphed into patriarchal father-daughter worship, represented by *Allāh* and goddess trinity Manāt, al-Lāt, and al-Uzzā. Called "Daughters of *Allāh*" in pre-Islamic Mecca (Makkah),[11] the three goddesses were the most popular supernatural beings of pre-Islamic Arabia, and each had a shrine not far from Mecca. *Allāh* was what Eliade terms a *deus otiosus,* a god sidelined by prominent local goddesses. Although regarded as a creator god, *Allāh* was not formally worshiped on a regular basis,[12] and his cult had been reduced to offerings of first fruits (grains and animals) that were given to him conjointly with other polytheistic fertility divinities.[13] Many scholars identify *Allāh* as Babylonian and Canaanite fertility god Baal (Arabian Hubal, or Hu-Baal, the high god of Mecca).[14] It appears that in pre-Islamic Arabia, *Allāh* was the name of Hubal, and Hubal was Arabic for Baal. The Arabian goddesses Manāt, al-Lāt, and al-Uzzā, according to this construction, are cognate forms of Baal's mythological wives Asherah and Anath. There are unconvincing claims that this connection is based on false or confusing etymology; the title Baal meant "lord" and was given to many local gods in Syria and Palestine, and Eliade points to "the confusion that existed during the Age of the Judges, between Yahweh and Baal. Names with *baal* as an element are found even in families known for their Yahwistic faith. In the beginning Baal must have been accepted as 'god of the land,' the supreme specialist in fecundity. It is only later that his cult was execrated and became the paradigmatic proof of apostasy."[15]

It seems clear from the evidence that Muhammad rebelled more against the triple goddesses—Manāt, al-Lāt, and al-Uzzā than against Baal, the patron god worshiped by his own Quraysh tribe, the leading Bedouin tribe of Mecca. When he conquered Mecca in AD 630, the Prophet destroyed the idol of Baal in the Ka'bah,[16] stripped Baal of his link with fertility and goddesses, and then promoted him, naming him the monotheistic Supreme Being of his unifying new world religion. The icons of the goddesses and their *ka'bahs* were similarly destroyed, their legitimacy was denied in the *Qur'ān,* and memory of them faded. Baal lived on as monotheistic *Allāh,* and some of the sacred pagan rituals were now carried out in his honor alone.

The magico-religious tradition of Manāt, al-Lāt, and al-Uzzā centered round the worship of the supreme cult object of Arab paganism, *al-hajaru'l-aswad,* the Black Stone. Fasting, making pilgrimage or *hajj,* circling the Ka'bah, and kissing the Black Stone were originally sacred communal pagan rites. Arabians, like ancient Egyptians, Mesopotamians, Canaanites, and Indians, worshiped engraved stone icons that they believed were containers of the life-force of their gods and goddesses. Like the Nagas and other people of megalithic cultures, they regarded stones as containers of supernatural power, and they worshiped both aniconic and iconic forms of stone deities (often termed "stone fetishism"). Because stones were regarded as residences of a goddess or god, Byzantine Christian writers of the fifth and sixth centuries named such sacred stones *baetyls,* from *bet'el,* or *bethel,* "house of the god."[17] The most famous of all *baetyls* is the Black Stone. Ancient Arabia was dotted with *ka'bahs* containing *baetyls* representing polytheistic deities, and pilgrims would seasonally migrate to these shrines to receive communal blessings.

Mecca was from its beginning a ceremonial center and pagan pilgrimage destination around which a city progressively grew.[18] Situated in the middle of the consecrated land, Hima, was the roofless sanctuary of the Ka'bah [lit., "cube"], the container of the Black Stone. Variously defined as an agate, basalt lava or a meteorite, the Black Stone is reddish black in color, believed by Muslims to have fallen from the sky in the time of Abraham and his son Ishmael (while pagans make the case that the Black Stone predates the Abrahamic patriarchs). The Ka'bah, which according to Islamic faith was rebuilt by Abraham, is today situated inside the great mosque in Mecca. During the *hajj* (pilgrimage) the pilgrims attempt to kiss or touch the Black Stone as they circumambulate the Ka'bah seven times. "In pre-Islamic times, just as it does today, the circumambulation of the Stone comprised an important ritual of the annual pilgrimage (*hajj*) to Arafāt, which is located several kilometers from Mecca."[19] During the yearly pagan *hajj*, an obligatory annual truce in inter-clan feuds was declared between warring Bedouin tribes so that pilgrims could safely migrate to the holy *baetyls*.

> Throughout pre-Islamic Arabia, "truces of God" allowed people to attend in security the yearly pilgrimage to important shrines. The rites included purification and the wearing of special clothing, sexual abstinence, abstention from shedding blood, and circuits performed around the sacred objects; they were concluded by the slaughter of animals, which were eaten in collective feasts. Today such practices still form the core of the Islamic pilgrimage to Mecca.[20]

In pre-Islamic Mecca, only members of influential Bedouin families and clans were entitled to participate in the service in the sanctuary. In addition to the northwestern *kāhin* (shaman or soothsayer), there were several kinds of priests and priestesses who interpreted divinations by the oracles. Most of their revelations were apparently cleromancy, in which answers to questions of the gods were obtained by drawing lots from a batch of marked arrows or sticks. Oneiromancy (dream divination) was also practiced and is well attested in Sabaean texts.[21] Ancient Arabian pagans worshiped 360 goddesses and gods, each represented by a stone idol housed in the Ka'bah and tended by priests and priestesses and oracles. (By contrast, eastern Christianity under Constantine V officially banned the cult of images in AD 726, and icons were declared anathema by the iconoclastic Synod of Constantinople on 754. Thus Muhammad was in harmony on this point with his Christian peers.) In the pagan sanctuaries, stone altars held the typical array of offerings:

> To the gods were offered, on appropriate altars, sacrifices of slaughtered animals, libations and fumigation of aromatics, votive objects, or persons dedicated to serve in the temple. A ritual slaughter of enemies in gratitude for a military victory is mentioned at the rock sanctuary of the Sun goddess Himyar.[22]

The main focus of creativity in Bedouin society was in orally transmitted poetry. Before Muhammad became the primary Arabian visionary, shamans or *kāhins* were the most influential religious personages of ancient Arabia; as spirit mediums or seers, they uttered sacred magic formulas in rhymed prose, entered a trance state in which visions would guide them to heal the sick or assist people in locating lost relatives, camels, or other valuables. Poets' inspiration was believed to be due to spirit possession by invisible supernatural beings, or *jinn* (Arabic: sing., *jinni;* English: "genie"). The shamans and poets of pre-Islamic Arabia were thus regarded as repositories of sacred power, and the fruits of their labor—healing, magic, and poetry—were construed by the medieval Arabian mind as expressions or manifestations of the divine or heavenly realm. "Poetic contests were held periodically and the greatest honor," according to Denny, "was to have one's verses engraved on sheets and hung in the Ka'bah sanctuary at Mecca."[23] Poetry was not only the major art form in early times, but it also functioned as a historical narrative of Arabia, a divinely inspired, imagistic expression of the collective memory of the pre-Islamic past.

The nature of pre-Islamic Arabian religion is cognate with Dravidian Indian, Babylonian, and Canaanite cultures; they all share common roots in their worship of a Kālī-like tree goddess of love and war. This goddess dramatized the overarching mytho-ritual motif of *hieros gamos* with her consort/brother/son, the dying and rising fertility god. Temples filled with incantations to deities and burning incense housed priests and priestesses, sacred dancer-prostitutes of the goddess, and oracles who became divinely possessed and uttered prophecies.

Muhammad and Islam

> In his "politics," Muhammad's mission reminds one of certain figure and concepts in the various books of the Old Testament. His "politics" is inspired, directly or indirectly, by Allāh. Universal history is the uninterrupted manifestation of God; even the infidels' victories fulfill God's will. Total and permanent war is thus indispensable in order to convert the entire world to monotheism. Whatever the case, war is preferable to apostasy and to anarchy.[24]

Muhammad was born into the powerful Quraysh tribe, orphaned at the age of six, and raised by male kinsmen, first by his grandfather and later by his influential maternal uncle, Abū-Tālib. As Eliade explains, the Prophet's birth and childhood soon morphed into the standard mythic template of "exemplary saviors."

> During her pregnancy, his mother heard a voice announcing that her son would be the lord and the prophet of his people. At the moment of his birth, a brilliant light illuminated the entire world (cf. The births of Zarathustra, Mahāvīra, and the Buddha. . .). He was born like a lamb, circumcised and with his umbilical cord already severed. As soon as he was born, he took a handful of earth and looked to the heavens. A Jew from Medina knew that the Paraclete had come into the world, and communicated this to his co-religionists. At the age of four years, two angels threw Muhammad to the earth, opened his chest, took out a drop of black blood from his heart and washed his viscera with the melting snow that they carried in a cup of gold (cf. *Qur'ān*, *sūrah* 94: lf., "Did We not expand thy breast for thee . . .," etc. This initiatory rite is characteristic of shamanic initiations). At the age of twelve, he accompanied Abū Tālib on a caravan trip into Syria. At Bostra, a Christian monk recognized on Muhammad's shoulder the mysterious signs of his prophetic vocation.[25]

At the age of twenty-five, he began to work for a wealthy older widow, Khadīja, who sent him on caravan journeys to Syria and Mesopotamia. Muhammad and Khadīja married when she was forty. Exhibiting great personal restraint, Muhammad waited until Khadīja died before marrying his next nine wives.[26] Seven children were born of their union—three sons who died at young ages, and four daughters, of whom Fātima, the youngest, married Alī, Muhammad's cousin and founder of the Shi'ite sect. Khadīja was a great source of encouragement to Muhammad as he struggled with his religious vocation, expressed as ecstatic visionary experiences during his annual cave retreat. It was not a Semitic polytheistic tradition to take long spiritual retreats (*tahannuth*) in caverns and other solitary places, thus Eliade assumes that "Muhammad was inspired by the night vigils, prayers, and meditations of certain Christian monks whom he had known or heard speak during his journeys."[27] The Abrahamic connection was only one part of Muhammad's broader objective, which was to unite pagan, Zoroastrian, Judeo-Christian, shamanic, and poet-seer traditions in a syncretistic world religion.

In the sixth century AD, Muhammad's work and travel with the trading caravans that moved between the Indian Ocean and the Mediterranean gave him the opportunity to have contact with Near Eastern and Central Asian religions and cultures. Muhammad met Christians, Jews, and perhaps even Zoroastrians as he covered the Arabian peninsula and traveled to Byzantine cities such as Damascus. These religions shared in common a belief in one God, a scripture believed to be the word of God, and an eschatology that taught that the world would come to a violent end and the righteons would go to heaven while the nonbelievers would be torured in hell. In addition to appropriating the Black Stone from goddess worshipers and giving Abraham credit for the construction of the Ka'bah, Muhammad—a gentile—claimed to be the last Prophet in the biblical tradition of prophets, following Abraham, Moses, Jesus, and other Judeo-Christian prophets. To this end, he employed numerous evocative Judeo-Christian and Gnostic metaphors and symbols (cosmic war, messianism, the ecstatic voyage to heaven, the Holy Book, the violent and punishing eschatological catastrophe, the archangel Gabriel, and the piligrimage) as a method of symbolic synthesis and psychological persuasion, much as Vedic brāhmaṇas co-opted the goddess cults of the Indian aboriginals they intended to conquer. Muhammad claims that God revealed to him that God is One; the implication is that the polytheists must change their religion and beliefs. In the Meccan *sūrahs* of the *Qur' ān*, the collection of recitations revealed to Muhammad, the Prophet claimed that his role was that of "warner" (or threatener) to polytheists, Jews, and Christians that they would burn in eternal hellfire if they did not convert.

During his private religious meditations in a mountain cave outside Mecca, Muhammad heard a voice declaring he was the messenger of God, which Muhammad interpreted as visitations from the archangel Gabriel. Just as much earlier Hebrew prophets heard the voice of Yahweh, Muhammad was convinced that he received his visions and auditory revelations directly from *Allāh*, mediated by Gabriel. His visions contained a major theme of Muhammad's preaching (found also in Zoroastrianism, Tantric Buddhism, Judaism, and Christianity)—revolutionary messianism—a romantic eschatological worldview that focuses on waiting for a world messiah, the apocalypse, an imminent Day of Judgment, and the resurrection of the dead. He has visions of a cosmic conflagration, an eschatological catastrophe that catapults the universe to a violent death in jets of flame. A Meccan passage of the *Qur'ān* explicates the dark characteristics of Judgment Day:

When the sun shall be covered up,
And when the stars swoop down,
And when the mountains are set moving,
And when the pregnant camel is abandoned,
And when the wild beasts are herded together,
And when the seas are made to overflow,
And when the souls shall be joined (to their bodies),
And when the buried-alive infant is asked
For what sin she was put to death,
And when the pages are spread out,
And when the firmament shall be pulled down,
And when Hell shall be set blazing,
And when the Garden is brought near,
Then shall a soul know what it has produced.[28]

God, flanked by eight angels and encircled by celestial troops, will appear to judge all people, condemning all miscreants to hell. This revelation describes the judgment as a state of consciousness experienced immediately after death. The warring martyrs of the faith are immediately transported into a sensual paradise and pleasure palace filled with delectable food and drink, houris (chaste virgins created by *Allāh*), and beautiful young boys serving ambrosial drinks. This heavenly reward reveals a Nestorian influence, as does Muhammad's belief that death renders the soul unconscious.[29] All pagan ancestors, according to the revelation, were irredeemably condemned to hell.

For Muhammad, his own visions echoed and reconstituted ancient narratives of the Abrahamic prophets receiving the word of God. In his "word"—visionary experiences, revelations, and prophecies—Muhammad was able to weave together and assimilate the ethereal qualities of the shamanic seer and the poet, the grand Manichean themes of the Zoroastrian and Judeo-Christian traditions, and the community rituals of Arabian paganism. At age 40, Muhammad began to proselytize his new Islamic religion.

Although his *modus operandi* would later reverse, Muhammad's initial method for spreading the religion of Islam was somewhat Christ-like: that is, non-coercive, gentle, and non-threatening. His first converts included his first wife, the loyal Khadīja, and his slave Zaid. After five years of hard work, under the patronage of his influential uncle, Abū-Tālib, Muhammad had succeeded in building the Muslim discipleship in Mecca, Islam's birthplace, to a modest group of about forty men and women. After thirteen years of being headquartered in Mecca, Muhammad had only a hundred converts: he was criticized not only because the apocalypse had not occurred as he, the "warner," had predicted, but also because he failed to produce any miracles and, since no angels wre seen visiting him, he could offer no proof that he was divinely inspired. The ridicule heaped on him by the people of Mecca led the Prophet to relocate his religious base from Mecca to Medina, an agricultural oasis and commercial center to the northeast.

While his mission was to destroy polytheistic deities, Muhammad cleverly incorporated the local idolatrous traditions in his new religion to lure converts. Muhammad co-opted pagan rituals focused on the Black Stone and declared them to be rituals of Islam, with a remnant of Abraham. According to early biographical and historical accounts of Muhammad written by respected Muslim scholars such as at-Tabarī and Ibn Sa'd, Muhammad yearned for close ties with his community. While meeting with the chiefs of his Quraysh tribe of Mecca, he pledged allegiance to the tribe's goddesses in order to guarantee the tribe's conversion to Islam. God revealed the following two verses to Muhammad:

Have ye thought upon al-Lāt and al-'Uzzā
And Manāt, the third, the other?[30]

In a version of *sūrah* 53:19, now deleted, known as the "satanic verses," Muhammad advocated the worship of the three pagan Arabian Daughters of *Allāh*, to whom he assigned the "exalted" status of cranes, intermediaries before *Allāh*:

These are the exalted cranes(intermediaries)
Whose intercession is to be hoped for.[31]

He soon recanted this position, and the account continues that Jibrīl (Gabriel), the angel of revelation, informed Muhammad that Satan deceived him and made him give the goddesses exalted status that they did not deserve. The verses that follow display Muhammad's conviction that God cannot possibly have daughters, since God is One with no second.

Are yours the males and his the females?
That indeed were an unfair division![32]

In other words, Muhammad chides them, "You Arabs can have sons (whom you greatly prefer to daughters), yet you claim that God has daughters! How unfair!" The Prophet himself may have felt it unfair that he had at the time four daughters and no living sons, His revised version of the function of al-Lāt, al-'Uzzā, and Manāt reads in the *Qur' ān,*

They are but names which ye have named, ye and your fathers, for Which *Allāh* hath revealed no warrant. They follow but a guess and that which (they) themselves desire. And now the guidance from their Lord hath come unto them.[33]

Muhammad, in an inspired state of possession by *Allāh*, thus describes the demeaning fall of the Arabian goddesses from a divine state to mere names or symbols that nevertheless were guided by *Allāh*. The technique of devaluing popular goddesses and replacing them with male gods is identical to that of Indian brāhmaṇic authors of sacred texts, the Hebrew authors of the *Old Testament* and *Talmud*, and the Babylonian authors of *Gilgamesh*.

Muhammad's former image as a peaceful, tolerant prophet was supplanted by a warrior persona who spread his message quite effectively by using numerous methods of coercion and persuasion: teaching, reciting the *Qur'ān*, warfare, money bribes and gifts, assassinations, compulsion, torture, destroying competing religious shrines, and retaining most of the animistic pre-Islamic practices, viz., the pagan time for fasting, the Ka'bah pilgrimage, the Black Stone, and ritual incantations. Muhammad proclaimed that *Allāh* instructed all Muslims to employ not only words, but also swords, to fight for the cause. They were to use *jihād*, missionary warfare, as the primary means of subduing populations to the will of *Allāh*. Muhammad's commands from that point, coupled with his Muslim band's actions, were red flags to non-Muslim Arabs that he nullified his old promises and treaties with them. Muhammad was soon joined by large bands of Arabs who at once feared his pitiless plundering and lusted after the booty from the Muslims' looting of caravans, temples, and villages. Muhammad's promise of paradise was equally persuasive, and offered to those who fought not only forgiveness for all sins, but the promise of an afterlife filled with high social status, virgins, expensive clothes, and beautiful houses tended by slave boys and surrounded by luscious irrigated gardens with abundant fruit and rivers of wine, milk, and honey. Such promises are found in *Qur'ān*, 4:95; 44:51–54; 47:15; 56:17, 34–35; 61:10–12; 76:19; and 78:31–33.

Before Muhammad's armies would attack a tribe they would invite them to accept Islam first.[34] The Muslims then raided tribes and caravans, destroyed their *ka'bahs* and inside placed idols, killed opponents, and captured goods, slaves, and territories. While Muhammad's peaceful persona had garnished only a few friends and family to the fold of Islam, his warrior persona organized an army of 10,000 to attack Mecca eight years after arriving in Medina. The first caliphs were in fact highly skilled warriors led, according to their beliefs, by *Allāh*, whose magnificent victories on the battlefield insured the perpetuity and triumph of Islam. "As with the Jews and the Romans, Islam—especially in its initial phase—saw in historic events the episodes of a sacred history," writes Eliade. "It is the spectacular military victories won by the first caliphs that assured first of all the survival, and then the triumph, of Islam."[35] In April 628, the Prophet received a revelation[36] from *Allāh* guaranteeing that the faithful could commence the pilgrimage to the Ka'bah. In January 630, Muhammad suspended the tribal truce, occupied the city of Mecca, destroyed the idols in the Ka'bah, purified the sanctuary, and abolished all the rights and privileges of the polytheists as he and his 10,000-men army faithful celebrated the ritual of the pilgrimage to the Black Stone as an Islamic tradition.

The Meccans surrendered to Islam after Muhammad's victory, inspired less by belief in *Allāh* and his Prophet than by fear of the sword of *jihād*. Arab armies began to use warrior strong-arm tactics, subjugating and heavily taxing polytheistic populations, who were treated as second-class citizens. In a poem composed before the Islamic conquest of al-Tā'if following the fall of Mecca in AD 630, the Islamic brand of missionary warfare is defined:

If you offer peace we will accept it
And make you partners (with us)in peace and war.
If you refuse we will fight you doggedly. . .
We shall fight as long as we live
Till you turn to Islam, humbly seeking refuge.
We will fight not caring whom we meet
Whether we destroy ancient holdings or newly gotten gains . . .
And we cut off their noses and ears
With our fine polished Indian swords,
Driving them violently before us to the command of God and Islam,
Until religion is established, just and straight.[37]

The Ka'bah at Mecca was replicated in many other *ka'bahs* that were pilgrimage destinations for the Arabs during the year. Muhammad decimated these rival *ka'bahs* and their polytheistic idols, thus giving the Arabs only one religious choice: the Islamic worship at Mecca.[38] "The conquest of Mecca and the foundation of a theocratic state," writes Eliade, "proved that his political genius was not inferior to his religious genius."[39] The warrior energy of the men, previously frittered away in intertribal wars, was channeled into fierce wars against the pagans fought in the name of *Allāh*. Muhammad subdued all of Arabia by coercive violence, and at the time of his death, he was sending an army to take Syria. Within twenty years of its founding in AD 622, Islam spread by the sword, and began to establish an empire beginning with the Arab-Islamic conquests in Palestine, Syria, Egypt, North Africa, Iraq, and the Iranian highlands and beyond. The Islamic empire gradually came to control a substantial portion of the known world, including the conquests in Spain, sub-Saharan Africa, the Indian subcontinent, Southeast Asia (Malaysia, Indonesia, and Brunei), the Philippines, and Thailand.

In the first dynasty of the caliphs, the Umayyads (AD 661–750), interaction (intermarriage and conversion) between Arabs and their subjects was not prohibited by Umayyad policy. *Malawi*, Muslim converts, were blocked from important positions in the army or bureaucracy and did not receive a share of booty, yet they still paid taxes. Most of the conquered peoples were *ẓimmīs*, or people of the book, which originally referred to Jews and Christians; later the term also included Zoroastrians and Hindus. The *ẓimmīs* had to pay taxes, but they were permitted to retain their own religious and social organization. However, they were treated as second-class citizens who were controlled by a mountain of prohibitions.

The Umayyad Dynasty was followed by continuous disunity within the *ummah* (the Muslim world community). After Muhammad's death, the various factions within Arabia, including Jews and Christians, revolted against Islam. The first of the caliphs, Abu Bakr, had to recall the Muslim army from the anticipated conquest of Syria to quell a revolt at home, which resulted in the Apostasy War, waged against the masses who were attempting to quit the bonds of Islam. The Muslims and their threats prevailed. Thirty years after the Prophet's death, Muslims were divided into the *Sunn'ite*, followers of the reigning caliph; the *Shi'ite*, faithful to the first "true" caliph, 'Alī; and the *Khārijites* ("Secessionists").

The first caliphs expanded their military enterprises until AD 715, when the Turks forced the Arab army to abandon the region of the Oxus, followed by their humiliating defeat by Charles Martel, King of France, in 733. At this point, the Arab empire ceased its hegemonic military ventures, and Muslims from non-Arab ethnic backgrounds, following the cosmic warfare dictum that Muhammad commands in the Holy Book, soon resumed the religious warrior mode. From AD 715 on, the converts supported all forms of rebellion against the *ummah*'s injustice and social inequities; they wanted equality with the Arabs. When Mu'āwiya shifted the capital of the Empire from Medina to Damascus, Persian, Hellenistic, and Christian influences began to emerge in Islam through the Umayyad dynasty, primarily manifested in religious and civic architecture. The Abbasids promoted the assimilation of Oriental and Mediterranean culture, and Islam developed an urban civilization model based on trade and bureaucracy. No longer religious leaders, the caliphs retreated to their palaces, where they sought advice from Islamic theologians and canon law specialists, the '*ulamā*', and dealt with ordinary problems of the faithful. In 762, Baghdad became the new capital, signifying the end of the Arab Islamic majority. The Arabic term *imām* originally signified the one who led public prayer—the caliph. "For the Shī'ites, the Imām has, in addition to his role as spiritual leader, the role of representing the highest politico-religious dignity."[40]

Islam in India

In the first century after the death of the Prophet Muhammad in AD 632, Islam entered into South Asia. An expedition sent by the Umayyad caliph in Damascus to Balochistan and Sindh in 711 went as far north as Multan. Unable to control that region and expand Islamic rule to other areas of India, Muslims established a colony in Sindh that became an important site of coastal trade and cultural exchange, including the introduction into the subcontinent of saintly teachers.

With the fall of the Gupta Empire, the political superiority of northern India practically ended. Harṣavardhana, Yaśovarman, and Lalitāditya founded brief kingdoms, but, due to the economic collapse of the Roman trade in northern India, none succeeded in constructing a stable empire. In the mid-eighth century, three great dynasties rose up in three corners of the subcontinent: in western India, the Gurajara Pratihāras; in eastern India, the

Pālas; and in the Deccan and south India, the Rāṣṭrakūṭas. In a colossal waste of power and resources, these three powers began to fight with one another for the possession of the city of Kanauj, which had been made an imperial capital by Harṣa and Yaśovarman. Furthermore, there were outside threats. Tibet exerted impressive military strength against India and China, and according to Tibetan chronicles, dominated parts of India during the period AD 750–850.

The Muslims, although checked temporarily in Sindh, could never relinquish their ambition to push their conquests to India. Because the south was partially protected by India's geography, its magnificent temples and sculptures largely escaped the brutal destruction and desecration inflicted by the Muslims in the north. After the Arab-Turkic invasion of India's northern neighbor, Persia, various short-lived Islamic empires invaded and spread across the subcontinent. Prior to Turkic invasions, Islamic trading communities flourished throughout coastal south India, particularly Kerala, where small numbers of trader arrived from the Arabian peninsula through trade routes via the Indian Ocean. Almost three hundred years later, the Turks, Persians, and Afghans launched the Islamic conquest in India via the traditional invasion routes of the northwest.

Pre-Islamic India was one of the world's great civilizations. In the domains of philosophy, mathematics, and natural science, tenth century India equaled or surpassed its contemporaries in the East and the West. Indian sculptural and architectural masterpieces were the purely indigenous achievements of an advanced culture. The true Islamic conquest of India dates from the beginning of the eleventh century, when Mahmoud Ghauri of Ghazni (979–1030), the head of a Turco-Afghan dynastic, first destroyed, pillaged, and massacred everything Hindu in his path. After a series of violent raids against Rajput kingdoms and wealthy Hindu temples, Mahmoud succeeded in establishing a base in Punjab for future incursions. The raiders demolished temples, defaced or fragmented sculptures, plundered palaces, killed vast numbers of men, and abducted their women and children to be sold as slaves, including sex slaves. Sultan Mahmoud invaded India seventeen times between AD1000 and 1027 in order to plunder Hindu temples for gold and art treasures. Mahmoud turned the former provincial city of Ghazni (in present-day Afghanistan) into the wealthy capital of an extensive empire that included present-day Afghanistan, most of modern Iran and Pakistan, and parts of northwest India.

Existing traditions were kept alive by the Hindu dynasties of India—the Cahamānas, the Paramāras, the Cālukyas, the Coḷas, the Gahaḍavālas, the Calacuris, the Hoysalas, and numerous others. The Karnataka Empire, also known as the Vijayanagara Empire, was founded. In 1336 by the brothers Harihara and Bukka. The Vijayanagara Empire under the reign of Kṛṣṇadevarāya thrived until it sufferd a major defeat in 1565, but the empire continued to rule in an attenuated form for another century. In south India, kingdoms extended their influence as far as Indonesia and controlled vast

Southeast Asia empires. India came to be subdivided into a large number of political areas that were each dominated by a strong sovereign power. Over the course of time, the number of such states multiplied, and on the eve of the Muslim conquest,"India lost her political unity and became a mere geographical expression."[41] Feudal organization dominated all the principalities, and the number of petty dynasties multiplied.

Eight centuries later, Indians and Muslims would temporarily unite under the banner of Bhārata Mātā and the ruling meme of fierce buffalo-slayer Mahiṣāsura-mardinī to successfully drive the British out of India. Why did Indians fail to organize around their goddess of victory and defend India against Islamic hegemony in the eleventh century? The first and most obvious reason is that Hindus were no match for the advanced martial skills of the Islamic invaders. Second, neither Mahiṣāsura-mardinī nor any other Indic war goddess or god morally obligates believers to engage in warfare against the rest of humankind until final world victory is achieved. The low-caste Indian majority not only had no standing order and divine inspiration from their goddess to engage in warfare, but they also had no loyalty to the brāhmaṇas, who were unable in any case to organize the underclass to resist the Muslims and protect them. The vulnerability of the Hindu states thus derived in part from the injustice of the caste system and the oppression, alienation, and inertia of the low-caste majority.

> [T]he people ceased to take an active part in politics and the history of the period was simply the history of short-lived dynasties fighting for supremacy. Everything was left to the kings and to the masses were relegated the duty of producing the necessaries of life, paying tribute to their masters and of obeying their commands implicitly. Whatever other activities they had were confined to their own cooperative undertaking in the village communities, the guild and the municipalities. These liberties in their turn undermined the power and authority of the kings and the idea of political solidarity practically disappeared from the country. The demoralization and apathy of the people in general is apparent from the narrative of the Muslim historians who describe how the cavalry raids of Mahmud was [*sic*] absolutely unopposed and mark the apathy of the people. The work of defense had been monopolized by kings and the people were not only apathetic but remained absolutely powerless to resist the march of an enemy either Indian or foreign. Indian princes, too, had become so devoid of moral and political sense that far from uniting against the common enemy, most of them thought it expedient to ensure their safety by forming alliances with extra-Indian powers whose main objective was to complete the subjugation of the country at the earliest opportunity.[42]

Intellectual decay and social and religious demoralization preceded the political downfall. "The vigour of the Indian intellect," writes Bandyopadhyaya, "had long been undermined. The ramification of caste, the multiplication of sub-castes and the growth of mutual jealousies among caste-people destroyed the idea of a social whole which had been built up out of diverse ethnic elements."[43] The instability of the political realm reflected an increasing decadence in elite social life and a decline in the literature and art of the period, which became stilted and artificial. At the opposite pole of the caste system, the social and religious oppression of śūdras, *ādivāsīs*, and dalits became intolerably harsh. The decadence, licentiousness, and blood sacrifice in Indian life and religion mirrored in a macabre sense the fanatical ritual violence of the Muslim *jihāds*, yet served to facilitate rather than prevent Islamic victory.

The disappearance of Buddhism from the subcontinet is attributed by most historians, in part at least, to the intolerance of the Muslim invaders of the twelfth and thirteenth centuries. These Muslim raids tolled the death knell for Buddhism in northern India. The monks who escaped massacre fled to Nepal, Tibet, and the south. Muslim invaders became the ruling groups in north India from 1100 to 1800. Between 1175–92, the Turkic Muslim Ghurids overran the Ghaznavids and extended the conquests in northern India. Shahabuddin Ghauri repeatedly raided Hindu cities and annexed Lahore to this kingdom in 1186. Qutb al-Dīn Aibek conquered Delhi and began a dynasty known as the Delhi sultanates (1206–1526). In the fourteenth century, Alauddīn Khiljī extended Muslim rule south to Gujarat, Rajasthan, and Deccan. Various other Muslim dynasties also formed and ruled across India from the thirteenth to the eighteenth centuries such as the Qutb Shahi and the Bahmani, but none rivaled the power and extensive reach of the Mughal Empire at its peak.

Since its founding in AD 622, Islam has destroyed Zoroastrianism in Iran-Persia; Buddhism, Hinduism, Sikhism, and possibly Zoroastrianism in Afghanistan; Hinduism, Sikhism, and Jainism in Pakistan; Buddhism in India; Hinduism and Buddhism in Bangladesh (East Pakistan); and Buddhism in the Central Asian Republics, Malaysia, and Indonesia.

Gender and Caste Oppression

While the status of the goddess reached its zenith from the eighth century throughout the medieval period in both north and south India, the socio-legal position of north Indian women among the higher caste elites continued to decline:

> The intense pressures on Hindus to accommodate Islam and to accept at least its external manifestations severely affected the women of northern India. Islam and the Code of Manu combined to further deny females a sense of self-worth or individualism. To this day a purdah mentality remains in much of the northern region, except where Sikhism prevails, in contrast with the south where women tend to participate more freely in community life, the pursuit of educational goals, and even politics.[44]

Echoing and strengthening Manu's "perpetual tutelage" dictum, medieval legal codes made existing restriction on women even more severe: the age of marriage for brāhmaṇa girls now averaged ten years, before the onset of pubescence and fertility. The idea was to wed her to a husband before her own blossoming desires could afflict her with prosmiscuity, which would jeopardize the patrilineal line. Daughters of kṣatriyas could marry at age fourteen or fifteen because their parents feared that their young daughter, if married to a soldier, could become a widow.

> It is not known whether or to what extent this rule applied to vaiśyas, śūdras, or untouchables; indeed, the omission of information on these castes is commonly not even acknowledged. It is known that the prohibition upon widow remarriage, which included child widows by about 1000 AD, was also gradually extended in some degree to widows of lower classes who wanted to appear respectable. The prohibition upon widow remarriage came to be regarded as the most important criterion for the respectability of a Sanskritizing caste. *Purdah*, the house-and-courtyard seclusion of high caste women, was common after about 1200 AD, its popularity reinforced by Moslem invasions during the 13th century. Finally, formal education for girls of all castes ceased after 1200 AD, due in part to Moslem influence.[45]

As Bose emphasizes, "Whether in the home, in the community, or in the temple, women were expected to follow and did follow the dictates of religion as laid out by a paternalistic establishment"[46] in the medieval period.

> Despite the influence of the *śakti* cults, women's lives were undoubtedly coming under increasingly greater constraints. In this era, the growth of women's self-expression became evident, as much in literature and art as in religious practice. . . . [W]omen of this era, whether Hindu, Buddhist, or Jain, were, indeed, denied key religious roles as defined in normative religious texts and in popular understanding and . . . they nevertheless occupied central positions in the actual practice and organization of worship.[47]

Thanks to the social engineering of the Purāṇas, brāhmaṇic ideology and secular power were once again in ascendency. In addition to the medieval misogyny that plagued high-caste women, numerous changes in the caste system occurred during the thousand years of the medieval period that resulted in a further decline in the status of subaltern groups. After the ninth century, because of increasing differences in custom between the high castes, intercaste marriages among high castes became illegal. Due to earlier social pressure from the Buddhists and Jainas, brāhmaṇas no longer permitted themselves to eat meat or to take part in either ancestral or Vedic animal sacrifices; thus successful intercaste marriages were made difficult, if not impossible.[48]

The overriding state power in both north and south created a deeper chasm between elite and low-caste social poles, which in turn sparked an unmistakable caste-bound religious differential in which the religions of the dalits were initially stigmatized along with those elites who participated in the heterodox dharmas. The tentacles of untouchability expanded, and now some deviant dharma sects, as well as individual members of heterodox groups from high caste backgrounds, were considered untouchables; the very sight of them was polluting to a brāhmaṇa. Śūdras were reminded that they, a relatively clean cultivator caste, were superior to the unclean artisan and menial untouchables.

The mercantile vaiśyas, however, gradually lost power in the early medieval period because land ownership, now the locus of feudal power, became increasingly limited to the brāhmaṇa caste.[49]

As Bandyopadhyaya points out, a more complex set of contradictions existed in the socio-religious fabric of the falling society:

> The Śūdra came to be denounced in opprobrious terms, women were socially and intellectually degraded while the lowest castes were relegated to a position worse than that of animals or beasts of burden. And this stands in strange contrast with the time-honored tradition of India. A people which worshiped the deity in the female form, denounced womanhood in opprobrious terms, and while pantheistic philosophy delighted in regarding everything animate as the incarnation and manifestation of the superb all-pervading Brahman, its votaries struggled hard to be conscious that men were degraded by their contact with their socially degraded fellowmen. Such being the prevailing mentality of the day, the priesthood also sank low in the intellectual scale. The Brahmin ceased to be the philosopher and became the slave of society, the guardian and protector of a code of life divorced from reason and morality.[50]

The exotic array of goddesses, Tantric cults, religious sexuality, and animal and human sacrifice that had risen to prominence at the end of the Gupta period became increasingly influential in the early medieval era. Despite initial elite disapproval, the ascent of these popular underclass cults impelled the brāhmaṇas to once again use literary means to place the deviant dharmas under the powerful brāhmaṇic umbrella. Indigenous cults were absorbed by the brāmaṇical tradition and woven into more Purāṇic myths centered on the supremacy of brāhmaṇic gods. Aboriginal Earth goddesses were described by the patriarchs as creations or property of the gods. Eventually, theistic yogic schools emerged such as orthodox Vedānta, a male-centered syncretistic sect that was strictly within the domain of the elite.

At the other end of the socioeconomic spectrum, the low-caste revolutionary ideology was propagated in the medieval period by wandering hymn-singers and teachers of the various deviant dharmas, most notably the Sahajiyās. Vāmācāra rites became the norm of religious expression among the underclass, the remnants of the tribal ways buried at the bottom of the caste system. As Bhattacharyya points out, the Sahajiyās were fiercely anti-brāhmaṇical:

> Of the leading features of Sahajayāna the following may be noted:
> (1) sharp criticism and rejection of all external formalities in regard to religious practices; (2) protest against and rejection of priestly and scriptural authority, celibacy, penances, austerities and the like; (3) recognition of the human body as the seat and habitat of all religious and spiritual experience; (4) recognition of the *guru* as essential for any spiritual quest; and (5) recognition of the experience of the ultimate reality as one of inexpressible happiness (*mahāsukha*). The Tantric Buddhist identification of Śūnyatā with the male and Karuṇā with the female principle occupied a significant place in Sahajayāna and with the consideration of the human body itself as the seat of all human experience including that of *sahaja-mahāsukha*, the image and practice of *mithuna* (sexual

commerce) became the most important element in the religious practice of Sahajiyā Buddhism in which women came to occupy the most important position.[51]

The only point of unity extant among the conflicting religious communities of India was the conception of *śakti*, "power" or the active, hot, and self-perpetuating female energy of the Hindu cosmos. Ultimate reality came to be seen as a balance of male and female principles in Buddhism (*upāya* and *prajñā*), Śaivism (Śiva and Śakti), and Vaiṣṇavism (Kṛṣṇa and Rādhā), creating a common philosophic ground among the orthodox brāhmaṇic and śramaṇic religions. The stark discrepancy between the glorification of goddesses as forms of Śakti and the misogynistic repression of mortal women became an even greater contradiction during this era.

Yogic Cults of the Kaula Mārga

The Yoginīs and Kāpālikas, along with the later Nātha yogīs, are overtly associated with the Kaula school. The place of Kaulācāra in the literary genre of Hindu Tantra is within the Śakti Kaula Tantras, comprising the texts of the Śāktas, which emphasize Kaulācāra and the left-hand worship of Śakti. The principal Tantric rituals open the door to potential sociopathic detachment and consequent loss of social conscience, since the practitioner indulges either symbolically or literally in "forbidden sensory experiences, both pleasurable and disgusting, in the pursuit of enlightenment."[52] Because of work in cemeteries or through intense yogic practice, the advanced *yogins* and *yoginīs* of the esoteric Kaula schools attained *sama-rasa*, the ability to regard *saṁsāra* as equivalent to *nirvāṇa*, pleasure as identical to pain. The idea of *sama-rasa* refers in its deepest sense to the oneness of the universe in the midst of diversity and pairs of opposites, "the realization of one truth as the flow of a unique emotion of all-pervading bliss."[53] In this highest attainment, the practitioner loses the emotions of hope, fear, disgust, and all sensual and moral differentiation, having trained himself to not feel human emotion. As Yeshe Tsogyal says,

> Saṁsāra is nothing to be rejected,
> And nirvāṇa is nothing to be accomplished.
> Saṁsāra and nirvāṇa are indivisibly *dharmakāya*.
> That is the realization of the Buddhas.
> Worthy people, realize this meaning![54]

The Sahaja, or the ultimate state, according to the *Hevajra Tantra*, is characterized by the absence of any sense of duality or difference anywhere, a state in which everything, from the euphoric to the disgusting, is realized as "the same taste." *Sama-rasa* is metaphorically depicted in Buddhist and Hindu Tantric texts as the union of Prajñā and Upāya, or Śakti and Śiva, or as "the intense bliss that is derived from the sexo-yogic practice, which, in its highest intensity, has got the capacity of producing an absolute homogeneity in the psychical states and processes."[55]

A Tantric Catalogue

A brief digression into the organization and content of Hindu Tantric scriptures will allow us to place the Kaula texts in their proper historical and existential context.[56] Tantra as a literary genre was unknown to *Amarakośa* (*c.* AD 500) and the system is not mentioned in the *Mahābhārata*. In the ninth century, Śaṅkara noted sixty-four Tantras, traditionally credited to Dattātreya, few of which can be identified today. They were written as early as the seventh century, and became well-known from at least the tenth century. These Hindu Tantras, as they engaged greater numbers of elite and intellectual followers, came to be regarded as the fifth Veda, which we are informed are the appropriate scripture for our degenerate age of Kaliyuga. They are of two types, the Niyamas, structured as instructions from the Devī to Sadāśiva, and the Āgamas, teachings from Lord Śiva to the Devī. The Āgamas, of particular interest in our inquiry, trace the yogic doctrine of the Gorakhanāthīs to Mīnanātha (Matsyendranātha), who learned it by taking the form of a fish and listening while Śiva explicated the doctrine to Pārvatī on the seashore. Another version describes a fish that lay immovable, mind concentrated, and heard all. Realizing this, Ādinātha (Śiva) sprinkled water upon him, making him a *siddha*, and called him Matsyendranātha. The cast of characters in the Āgamas is restricted almost without exception to these two divinities.[57] These are the Kaula texts of the Śāktas, based on the *Kaula Upaniṣad*, the most significant being the *Rudrayāmala Tantra* (*c.* tenth century AD) of which the *Jātimālā* is an important section. Other Śakti Kaula Tantras are the *Sādhanamālā*,[58] *Śakti-saṅgama, Viśva-sāra, Mahānirvāṇa, Vīra, Kulārṇava, Śyāma-rahasya, Śāradā-tilaka*,[59] *Uḍḍīśa, Kāmākhyā, Viṣṇu Yāmala, Kālīkā, Tantratattva,* and *Yoginī*.[60]

As we have emphasized, the Tantra does not make caste or gender distinctions in worship. As Woodroffe explains:

> All may read the Tantras, perform the Tantric worship, and recite the Tantrika mantra, such as the Tantrika Gāyatrī. All castes, even the lowest caṇḍāla, may be a member of a cakra, or Tantric circle of worship. In the cakra all its members partake of food and drink together and are deemed to be greater than Brāhmaṇas; though upon the break-up of the cakra the ordinary caste and social relations are re-established. All are competent for the special Tantrika worship, for in the words of the Gautamīya-Tantra, the Tantra-Śāstra is for all castes and for all women. The latter are . . . excluded under the present Vaidika system. . . . According to the Tantra, a woman may not only receive mantra, but may, as a Guru, initiate and give it. She is worshipful as Guru, and as wife of Guru. The Devī is Herself Guru of all Śāstras and women, as, indeed, all females who are Her embodiments are, in a peculiar sense, Her earthly representatives.[61]

Kaula is considered the *n'est plus ultra* of Tantrism, the pinnacle of knowledge gained only through practice and study in many lifetimes. As Avalon remarks:

> If [a *sādhaka*] is born into *Kaulācāra*, and so is a Kaula in its fullest sense, it is because in previous births he has by *sādhana*, in the preliminary stages, won his

entrance into it. Knowledge of Śakti is, as the Niruttara Tantra says, acquired after many births; and, according to the Mahānirvāṇa Tantra, it is by merit acquired in previous births that the mind is inclined to *Kaulācāra.*[62]

There are seven levels of worshipers in the Tantric evolutionary paradigm; ranging from the lowest to highest they are, according to the *Kulārṇava Tantra*: Vedācāra, Vaiṣṇavācāra, Śaivācāra, Dakṣiṇācārā, Vāmācāra, Siddhāntācāra,[63] and Kaulācāra, the highest of all. These are not spiritual choices that people make, but "stages through which the worshipper in this or other births has to pass before he reaches the supreme stage of the Kaula."[64]

According to Woodroffe, the Kaula division of worshipers is hierarchically organized into the *prakṛti*, or common Kaula following *vīrācāra*, habituated to ritual practice and *sādhana* with *pañca-tattva*; the *madhyama-kaulika*, or middle Kaula, accomplishes the same *sādhana*, but her mind is more tuned to meditation, knowledge, and *samādhi*; and the highest type of Kaula (*kaulikottama*) is the practitioner who, "having surpassed all ritualism, meditates upon the Universal Self."[65] Practitioners of this tradition no longer require elaborate ritual and use of *mūrtis* for union with the divine; as the *Bhāgavata* explains, "God should be worshiped in an Image, who abides in all creatures, until a devotee experiences Him in his heart."[66] The experience of feeling the divine presence in the heart *cakra* signifies that the *sādhaka* has progressed to a higher stage of union with the Divine.

Kaula Mārga as Anarchy

Through the gatherings of various Vāmācāra cults, doctrines and practices were shared and blended. Nālandā and other illustrious university-monasteries were, until destroyed by Islamic warriors, centers of higher learning of Tantric arts and science where Tantric physics and metaphysics were taught by learned yogī-scholars. When studied in depth, the metaphysics of Vajrayāna and Dzogchen reveal their origin in Kaula doctrine and practice synthesized with Mahāyāna Buddhism. This connection is illustrated by a story recounted in the *Brahmayāmala*, in the *Rudrayāmala*, and in the introduction to *Sādhanamālā* (all Hindu Tantric works), viz., Vaśiṣṭha, after years of performing austerities to gain *siddhi*, had failed at his effort, and cursed Tārā. She appeared before him and explained that perfection does not lie along that path; rather, she sent him to Buddhist Tibet (Mahācīna), country of Buddhists. When Vaśiṣṭha arrived there, he found the Buddha engaged in all sorts of carnal indulgences with naked Śaktis. Incredulous, Vaśiṣṭha requested guidance in attaining perfection, and asked the Buddha about the use of wine and meat and unclothed women who were drinking blood and wine and appeared inebriated. The Buddha answered with an explication of the Kaulas, including their mysteries, duties, uses, and secret rites. Ultimately, through the lavish practice of the *pañca makāras*, Vaśiṣṭha found the *siddhi* he sought.[67]

One of the best-known Tantras of the Kaula school, the *Kulārṇava*, points to the high status of the Yoginīs among followers of the Kaula path. The published

English readings are selected, unfortunately; Avalon uses the term "Yoginī" only one time. However, the original Sanskrit text of the *Kulārṇava Tantra* contains a multitude of clear references to the Yoginīs. A second Tantric text, the *Kaulajñānanirṇaya,* which resides in the "Yoginī Kaula" school, is also a helpful source. The *Kaula Upaniṣad* is very late, yet still regarded as the major scripture and highest authority of the Kaula sect of the Śāktas. Śaṅkara disapproved of the Kaulas, disparaging the methods of the Kaula circle in his *Saundarya-laharī.*

The *Mahānirvāṇa Tantra* (*Tantra of the Great Liberation*) is a later Kaula Tantra that sheds light on the medieval practices and beliefs of the Kaulas. Avalon describes the intrinsic antisocial nature of the Kaula, but, in true Orientalist tradition, he emphasizes that the "lower physical desires" of eating, drinking, and copulation must be suppressed. In fact, Avalon is indulging his Victorian consciousness in devalorized, brāhmaṇized abstractions of the material means and objectives of their practices:

> [T[he term *Vāmācāra* does not mean, as is vulgarly supposed, "left-hand worship," but the worship in which woman (*vāmā*) enters that is *latā-sādhana.* In this *ācāra* there is also worship of the Vāmā Devī. *Vāmā* is here "adverse," in that the stage is adverse to *pravritti.* . . . In *Vāmācāra* . . . the method . . . is to use the force of *pravritti* in such a way to render them self-destructive. The passions which bind may be so employed as to act as forces whereby the particular life of which they are the strongest manifestation is raised to the universal life. Passion, which has hitherto run downwards and outwards to waste, is directed inwards and upwards, and transformed to power. But it is not only the lower physical desires of eating, drinking, and sexual intercourse which must be subjugated. The *sādhaka* must at this stage commence to cut off all the eight bonds (*pāśa*), which mark the *paśu* which the Kulārṇava Tantra enumerated as pity (*dayā*), ignorance (*moha*), shame (*lajjā*), family (*kula*), custom (*śīla*), and caste (*varṇa*). . . . Freed of these, the *jīva* is liberated from all bonds arising from his desires, family, and society. He then reaches the stage of Śiva (*Śivatva*). It is the aim of the *Vāmācāra* to liberate from the bonds which bind men to the *sangsāra,* and to qualify the *sādhaka* for the highest grades of *sādhana* in which the *sāttvika guṇa* predominates. To the truly *sāttvika* there is neither attachment, fear, or disgust. That which has been commenced in these stages is by degrees completed in those which follow—viz., *Siddhāntācāra,* and according to some, *Aghorācārya* and *Yogācāra.* The *sādhaka* becomes more and more freed from the darkness of the *sangsāra,* and is attached to nothing, hates nothing, and is ashamed of nothing, having freed himself of the artificial bonds of family, caste, and society. The *sādhaka* becomes, like Śiva himself, a dweller in the cremation ground (*śmaśāna*). He learns to reach the upper heights of *sādhana* and the mysteries of yoga. He learns the movements of the different *vāyu* in the microcosm the *kṣudra-bramāṇḍa,* the regulation of which controls the inclinations and propensities (*vritti*). He learns also the truth which concerns the macrocosm (*brahmāṇḍa*). Here also the Guru teaches him the inner core of *Vedācārya.* Initiation by *yoga-diksha* fully qualifies him for *Yogācāra.* On attainment of perfection in *aṣṭāṅga-yoga,* he is fit to enter the highest stage of *Kaulācārya.*[68]

Avalon goes on to explain that Kaula-dharma is the heart of all sects, and a Kaula is one who, in previous lives, has passed through the Śaiva, Vaiṣṇava, and Śākta stages, "which have as their own inmost doctrine (whether these worshippers know it or not) that of Kaulācāra."[69] The outward form and appearance, the apparent sect of the Kaula is indifferent. As Woodroffe observes, "The form is nothing and everything. It is nothing in the sense that it has no power to narrow the Kaula's own inner life; it is everything in the sense that knowledge may infuse its apparent limitations with an universal meaning."[70] Understood in this way, form is never a prison for a Kaula. The *Viśva-sāra Tantra* says of the Kaula:

> For him there is neither rule of time nor place. His actions are unaffected either by the phases of the moon or the position of the stars. The Kaula roams the earth in differing forms. At times adhering to social rules (*śiṣṭa*), he at others appears, according to their standard, to be fallen (*bhraṣṭa*). At times, again, he seems to be as unearthly as a ghost (*bhūta* or *piśāca*). To him no difference is there between mud and sandal paste, his son and an enemy, home and the cremation ground.[71]

When the practitioner reaches this stage, she or he attains to *brahma-jñāna*, which Woodroffe describes as "the true gnosis in its perfect form."[72] After receiving *mahāpūrṇa-dīkṣā*, he performs his own funeral rites, symbolizing his death to *saṁsāra*. Seated alone in some quiet place, he remains in constant *samādhi*, attaining its *nirvikalpa* form. The Supreme Prakṛti Mahāśakti then swells in the *sādhaka*'s heart, the cremation ground of all passions. The *sādhaka* then becomes a *Paramahaṁsa*, totally liberated yet living.

Most of these Kaula texts are written in Sandhabhāṣā that embroiders and obfuscates secret teachings by encoding them in esoteric Tantric symbology understood only by the initiate. When read by the uninitiated, such texts seem incomprehensively steeped in ambiguity, polyvalency, and eroticism. In fact, the secrets of Tantric cults are never made explicit; obviously occult by nature, cults associated with Tantra are organized around a quintessential initiation by a guru, who introduces the initiate to the secrets of the cult.

Because of the dearth of research material on the Yoginī and Kāpālika cults, we must rely on the practices and doctrine of the more accessible deviant cults with whom the Yoginīs and Kāpālikas congregated in order to grasp the dynamics of their gatherings. The available literature describes the development of taboo rites, their origin in tribal religions and agricultural motifs, and their development from the seventh to twelfth centuries AD into a homogenous Vāmācāra Tantric form of worship, yoga, art, and magic.

"In the North-East, as in other parts of India, Śaivism is inextricably blended with Śāktism"[73] in the so-called Śākta-Tantric cults of the region. Flourishing Śākta-Tantric cults promised power, protection, and prosperity, the very benefits the elites were most in fear of losing, as the outer result of Śākta-Tantric practice. Somewhat ironically, then, and primarily stemming from economic power motives, the dominant dharma tended toward "the increasing accommodation of unorthodox systems of belief and worship,"[74] amid the greater milieu of the elite-subaltern social polarization in medieval India.

However, with the expansion of the Muslim invasions, the brāhmaṇas were brought to their knees: they needed both the low-caste groups and their fierce goddesses to defend them. They therefore instructed underclass artisans to erect magnificent temples to honor *Ugra* Śakti in her many images, forms, and names, in an attempt to buy her aid and that of her faithful devotees. Kings and high-caste ruling elites patronized and participated in the fierce Śakti's worship to save their lives and property from the onslaught of the Muslims. The upper class often depended upon the active aid of the lower castes, but neither the lower castes nor the Devī cooperated with them during the Muslim invasions.

The eastern coast of medieval India was dotted with sacred pilgrimage sites and meeting places of a variety of Tantric cults, composed of wandering subaltern yogins and yoginīs who ostensibly belonged to different sects, but who shared the common denominators of participation in left-hand Śākta rituals and worship of Bhairava and Cāmuṇḍā, the fierce, destructive aspect of Śiva and his wrathful consort, the *Ugra* Śakti. These cults gathered together at sacred power spots and temples, exchanging ideas, icons, and anti-brāhmaṇical traditions that had become the very heart of Indian medieval religion.

The state of Orissa, isolated from the rest of India by various mountain ranges, is open to the east, washed by the Bay of Bengal. Orissa today is a fertile, beautiful land of tall palms, green paddy fields, mud huts, and swaying casuirna trees, one of the least developed states in India. Between AD 600 and 1300, however, Orissa was one of the bustling hubs of Tantrism, the home of innumerable exquisite temples of a remarkable architectural sophistication and homogeneous style, today considered among the finest expressions of Indian temple architecture.[75] Esoteric yogic cults in Orissa established their meeting places in the cremation-grounds, where some of these cults' most transformational practices were enacted; the Vaitāl Temple, where human sacrifice was made to the presiding deity, Cāmuṇḍā; or at one of the Cauṁsaṭha Yoginī shrines where *cakrapūjās* involving the "five Ms" were performed. The latter Yoginī shrines were stark, enigmatic, roofless, circular temples, the inside walls installed with exquisitely sculpted images of the Sixty-four Yoginīs. Uḍḍiyāna, known as the birthplace of Tantric Buddhism, is one of the most important *pīṭhas* mentioned in both Buddhist and Hindu Tantras. It is not our purpose here to pursue the evidence that Orissa was Uḍḍiyāna; since the case cannot be proven, we need only point out that many indigenous scholars, including Sahu,[76] Panda,[77] B. Bhattacharya,[78] and M.H.P. Sastri,[79] propound that Orissa and Uḍḍiyāna were identical. They base this conclusion on archeological, textual, and epigraphic evidence that point to Orissa rather than the Swat Valley, where most Western scholars prefer to locate Uḍḍiyāna.

Orissa played a vital role in evolving a culture of Śākta-Tantric idealism expressed in the religion, art, architecture, literature, and social order of east India during the pre-Muslim period.[80] Along a broad alluvial belt stretching down the three hundred miles of the Orissa coastline lie most of the important towns of ancient and present times, as well as all the better-known temples of Orissa, including the many shrines of the temple town of Bhubanesvar, a Śakta *pīṭha* and sacred site for the heterodox cult meetings under scrutiny. The schools that participated in left-hand rituals—the Kaulas (subsuming the Yoginī cult, the Kāpālikas and their successors, the Kānphaṭa [or Nātha] yogīs), the Sahajiyās, and Vajrayāna Buddhists—have each contributed knowledge told in a different genre of literature or depicted in art, about the heterodox doctrine and rituals that so profoundly influenced India during the Middle Ages.

The Yoginī Cult

> If we are to look for the origins of the Yoginīs, it appears that we must turn to the simple village cults and to the *grāma devatās*, the local village goddesses. In the villages of India, these are the favored deities, the major Brahmanical gods being of lesser importance. Each *grāma devatā*, be she Manakkal Nangai or Chilka Kalijai, presides over the welfare of her village. Frequently she has a special boon to confer, for instance Kolaramma (Mother of Kolar) grants freedom from scorpion sting to those who propitiate her. These village goddesses seem to have been gradually transformed and consolidated into potent numerical groupings of sixty-four (sometimes of eighty-one, sometimes of forty-two), acquiring thereby a totally different character. It was Tantrism that elevated these local deities and gave them new form and vigour as a group of goddesses who could bestow magical powers on their worshippers. The philosophy, rituals and cultus of these deities along with others that were originally non-Brahmanical, were brought together under the rubric Tantra and thus given legitimacy in later Hinduism.[81]

In the centuries following AD 600, the Tantric worship of the Yoginīs, most frequently in a series of sixty-four, rose to prominence over large portions of India. The prescription of the number sixty-four corresponds to the sixty-four Bhairavas, sixty-four arts, and sixty-four *ratibandhas* (modes of sexual enjoyment).[82] The dominant orthodox religious cults of the sixth and seventh centuries were Śāktism, Tantrism, Śaivism, the Solar cult, and combinations of these, particularly the homogenous Śākta-Tantrism. The cult of the Yoginīs, an arcane, mysterious, and less familiar sect of the heterodox Kaula-mārga, attracted increasing numbers of devotees who were apparently drawn to the cult by promises of the supernatural abilities bestowed by the Yoginīs on their worshipers, as well as by the deep autochthonous essence of these goddesses and their particular brand of worship. To the nonelite masses, who were formerly free from the system of imposed labor in which they were now unwilling captives, the cult represented the lost world of the forest, their maternal home. "The Yoginī cult," writes Dehejia, "definitely tantric in nature

Pl. XXV. *Saptamātṛkā—Kaumārī*: Śrī Ponniyamman Temple, South Arcot, Ulundurpet, Iruveḷippaṭu. Coḷa (ninth–twelfth centuries AD), Stone.

Pl. XXVI. *Narthanā Kālī*: Śiva Temple, Śrī Mīnākṣī—Sundareśvara, Madurai. Pāṇḍya (twelfth century AD), Stone. The Śrī Mīnākṣī temple is dedicated to Lord Śiva and goddess Mīnākṣī, who were married in Madurai, according to legend. Between AD 600–1300, Madurai, the capital of the Pāṇḍya dynasty built on the banks of the Vaigai river, was the true center of Dravidian culture, and Pāṇḍya kings patronized not only literary *caṅkams*, or academies, but also the construction of great temples. Tamils in this era were prosperous maritime merchants who traded via the Arabian Sea with the Greeks and Romans. South India's oldest city, Madurai flourished under several dynasties until the early 1300s, when the Muslim rulers penetrated the barriers of the Vindhyas and Nilgiris to loot the prosperous towns in the south, including Madurai. Soon afterwards, Madurai was incorporated into the Delhi Sultanate.

Pl. XXVII. *Cāmuṇḍā*: Śrī Māriyamman̲ Temple, Madurai. Pāṇḍya (twelfth century AD), Stone.

Pl. XXVIII. *Devī Reṇukā*: Śiva Temple, Śrī Colīśvara, Kadakattur, Dharmapurī. Pallava (sixth–ninth centuries AD), Stone.

Pl. XXIX. *Durgā*: Śiva Cave Temple, Śrī Durgā Bhairava, Kottapalli, Prakasam, Kanigiri. Cola (ninth–twelfth centuries AD), Stone.

Pl. XXX. *Kālī and Musician*: Frenzied dance accompanied by drums and music is the prelude to spirit possession by Kālī. Śiva Temple, Śrī Mallikārjunasvāmī Temple West shrine. Basral, Māṇḍya, Karnataka (eighth–twelfth centuries AD), *c.* AD 1234, Soapstone.

Tanjavur (Tanjore): Under the reign of the great King Rājarāja, founder of the Coḷa empire which stretched overall of south India and its neighboring islands, the great Temple of Tanjavur, dedicated to Lord Śiva, was constructed between 1010 and 1003 BCE. Surrounded by two rectangular enclosures, the Bṛhadeśvara, built from blocks of granite and, in part, from bricks, is crowned with a pyramidal thirteen-storied tower, the *vimāna*, topped with a bulb-shaped monolith.

Pl. XXXI. *Amman̲—Māriyamman̲*: Cholampettai, Tanjavur, Mayuram, Śiva Temple, Śrī Tantonrīśvara. Coḷa (ninth–twelfth centuries AD).

Pl. XXXII. *Vadabhadra Kālī*: Tanjavur Temple, Tanjavur—Kilvasal. Coḷa (ninth–twelfth centuries AD), Granite.

Pl. XXXIII. *Ammaṉ*: Śrī Māriyammaṉ Temple, Tiruchirappalli. Early Coḷa (ninth–tenth centuries AD), Granite.

Pl. XXXIV. *Kāmākhyā*: Icon of the fierce form of the goddess as she is known at Kāmākhyā, Assam, the sacred spot where the *yoni* of the goddess mythically fell to Earth. Rajasthan, nineteenth century AD. Water-color on paper 13 x 10 (33 x 25). [Ajit Mookerjee Collection.]

and tantra itself, with primitive ideas on the efficacy of magical rituals and spells, sounds and gestures, is a movement that has deep connections with rural and tribal traditions."[83]

Furthermore, the imagery of the Yoginīs "may have in all likelihood sent out a positive image and may have been viewed by women not only as a powerful affirmation but as a sign of affirmative engenderment."[84] Nilima Chitgopekar emphasizes that the Yoginīs, while sensual, are not necessarily constructed to stimulate the male gaze, and "despite the erotic overtones of the Yoginī worship none of the Yoginī temples have erotic depictions on them;" rather, "they have simple exteriors unlike the richly adorned, almost excessively luxuriant temple carvings in contemporaneous temples."[85]

With its rise in popularity, the magnetic power of Yoginī worship could no longer be ignored by the dominant dharma, and in a later stage of syncretism, the Yoginī cult was assimilated and incorporated into Śāktism. The cult of the Yoginīs gained popular supremacy among Śākta-Tantric cults, particularly in the eastern zone of India, and was sponsored by royalty in the ninth and tenth centuries, when only royal families were permitted to worship the Eighty-one Yoginīs.

Most scholars believe that the participants of the Yoginī cult sought material gain rather than spiritual liberation, and that they particularly requested magical powers (*siddhis*) from the Yoginīs.

> Some of these *siddhis* include the ability to fly, to enter the bodies of beautiful women and animals, to revive the dead and foretell the future. They ensured the destruction of enemies, the success of an army, territorial gains, freedom from fear when attacked by enemy kings, and even gave succor to those who lost their kingdom. The belief that Yoginīs can attain such powers has contributed to their mystical awe. The goddess is addressed usually as *bhukti-mukti* (liberation in the hereafter). Yoginīs were worshiped solely for powers usually leading to worldly success and the word *mukti* is conspicuously absent from every textual source that deals with these deities.[86]

With their propensity to skew aboriginal ideas in popular stories for their own social programing purposes, the brāhmaṇas came to depict the Yoginīs as energetic goddesses emerging from the body of the Great Goddess of the brāhmaṇical tradition, interpreted as Durgā's fierce and peaceful aspects, emanations, and manifestations. Alternatively, they were given the lower rank of *gaṇas* or attendant deities to the Great Goddess, parallel to the troupe of semi-divine animal- and bird-headed *gaṇas* that attended dancing Śiva. Although their names were never standardized, the number of Yoginīs became conventionalized at some point in history to sixty-four.

Chitgopekar points to the underlying patriarchal gynophobia of brāhmaṇic literary depiction of Yoginīs:

> One thing will become clear after the depictions from the Purāṇas that it is men who impute supernatural power to the Yoginīs. In contrast to the sculptural

> images of the yoginīs, which tend to reflect a more positive dimension of the female, the literary expressions serve in many contexts, as projections of violent paranoiac fears of menace by the Indian male upon the Indian female. Yet this attitude may be contrasted with that found in Tantric literature which not only recognizes—indeed glorifies—the terrifying aspects of the feminine, but yet do not associate vindictiveness with it.[87]

Yoginīs are mentioned in Vedic and post-Vedic literature as manifestations of the female principle, identical in some accounts to the Mātṛkās. By invoking the aid of the Yoginīs, the members of the cult acquire magical and supernatural faculties, particularly the ability to subdue and destroy enemies, both spiritual and material. Like other Indic fierce goddesses linked with disease and its cure, the Yoginīs are associated with magico-religious medicine. Yoginī-worship is recommended by the *Kulārṇava Tantra* to cure diseases, and the *Agni Purāṇa* links the Yoginīs to protective medicinal plants.[88]

The Yoginī cult has been virtually ignored in books and publications in the fields of archaeology, Orientalist Indology, iconography, and the respective histories of religion, art,[89] and architecture. The omission of the Yoginīs is particularly difficult to understand in the study of Indian art, iconography, and sculpture, given the exquisite delicacy of detail and compelling iconography of the sculpted images in some of the temples, and in the history of religion, where one finds that the Yoginī cult and temples are bypassed and omitted not only in most works on Śāktism and Mother-goddess worship, but also in works focused specifically on obscure and heterodox medieval cults and sects,[90] as well as in studies on Tantra.[91] The cult's mysterious origin, the cloak of silence and secrecy guarding its rituals, and the absence of authentic texts all bespeak the Yoginīs' ability to instill fear and trembling in initiate and non-initiate alike. As Vidya Dehejia explains:

> One reason why the Yoginīs and their temples have been neglected may be due to the deep sense of fear and awe that they inspire in the average person. People generally refer to the Yoginīs in hushed tones, if at all they mention them. This secrecy is maintained to such an extent that the very existence of the Yoginī temple at Hirapur became public knowledge only as recently as the year 1953. It is quite amazing that this well-preserved shrine, barely ten miles from the major temple centre of Bhubanesvar, should have remained unknown all these years. There is a widespread apprehension that one may be cursed by the Yoginīs for a whole host of reasons and it is believed that even approaching too close to their temples may have disastrous consequences. This deepseated fear makes the average villager and even town dweller steer clear of the Yoginī temple. He would rather not talk to you about Yoginīs, much less lead you to one of their shrines.[92]

The dreaded curse of the Yoginīs, recorded in both Purāṇas and Tantras, then, appears to be the chief explanation for both scholarly and popular ignorance of the Yoginī cult. (Such defensive silence is also typical of scholarly reluctance to fully explicate the history and sacred texts of Islam, since Islamists warn that the penalty for criticizing Islam or Muhammad is death.) The familiar poem *Lalitā Sahasranāma* ("Thousand Names of Lalitā"), which is incorporated in the *Brahmāṇḍa Purāṇa*, concludes with a warning that any person who imparts the poem to a non-initiate will suffer the curse of the Yoginīs,[93] regarded as a most terrifying fate worse than death. Likewise does the *Jñānārṇava Tantra* warn that any person who imparts secret, sacred knowledge to the uninitiated will become food for the Yoginīs.[94]

Nilima Chitgopekar observes that the Yoginīs posed "a moral risk to patriarchal society" because "[t]hey are not portrayed in a domestic context and not only are they without a male counterpart but refreshingly their beauty is not ever exploited to win husbands."[95] The Yoginīs are part of the tradition of "antimodels" that "challenge comfortable and comforting fantasies about the way things are in the world," according to Chitgopekar. The antimodel is "not only part of Tantric spirituality but is a muted theme in much of non-Tantric Hindu tradition as well."[96]

Because they are never spousified in literature or art, the Yoginīs are distinctly different from the Indic fierce goddesses whose "dominant spouse-goddess" essence is dangerous to men and the patriarchal state when untamed by a husband. Chitgopekar cites the paradoxical behavior of Kālī as she dances on Śiva's corpse as a violation of "the basic Hindu categories of male-female relations."[97] On another level, the polyvalent image of Kālī standing on the corpse of Śiva is an evocation of the ancient idiom of the Great Goddess's *hieros gamos* with the dying and resurrected vegetation god, replete with the Neolithic undercurrent of ritual male sacrifice for the crops and the dramatization of the principle that life springs from death.

Frédérique Apffel Marglin asserts that this familiar motif in Indic art depicting Kālī performing "inverse sexual union" has a textual reference in a Sanskrit text on the funeral ceremony, the *Sūtras of Bharadvāja*, 1.5.14, which states that "[t]he uniting of the wife (with the deceased) and other rites should optionally be performed at this stage." The *sūtra* uses the Sanskrit word *samveśanādi*, composed of *samveśana*, "sexual union," "coitus," and *ādi*, "et cetera." This line is spoken just after the deceased husband has been laid on the cremation pyre, and reflects, like the use of the left-hand and reverse circumambulation, the pattern of "doing everything in reverse" at Indic funeral rites.[98]

Nothing is known about the construction, function, or character of the Yoginī temples. Almost all Yoginīs temples are located at remote sites that are difficult to access. With the exception of the temple at Khajurāho, which was erected on a narrow ridge that precluded circular architecture, all are hypaethral—open to the sky. These temples with neither roof nor secret *sanctum sanctorum* are an extreme departure from traditional Indian temple architecture. Known as Cauṁsaṭha (Sixty-four) Yoginī temples, each temple has sixty-four niches assigned to a series of Sixty-four Yoginīs, female images with remarkably beautiful bodies that are often topped with animal heads, reminiscent of Egyptian deities. "The animal head in sculpture makes its carrier, the human body, into a support of its inhuman, more than human power, that of the animal creation, which preceded human beings," according to Chitgopekar. "Recently these kind of deities are referred to as demi-animal instead of zoomorphic as it better describes those goddesses who are part human and part animal or who can transform themselves into animals."[99]

The remains of this intriguing variety of temple are scattered across northern India in a broad belt extending from the Orissa coast through central India up to the Rajasthan border; however, the cult was not restricted to this northern area. From the remains of Yoginī temples dating from the seventh to the twelfth centuries AD in various parts of India, it is clear that the cult flourished in all parts of the subcontinent for at least 500 years. In Uttar Pradesh, Madhya Pradesh, Orissa, and the Coimbatore district of Tamilnadu, nine Yoginīs temples have been discovered to date. Of these, five were discovered before 1875 by foreign archaeologists,[100] but few have been explored since. The Sixty-four Yoginīs are still paid "token homage" in the south Indian tradition of Devī worship.[101] The remains of five other Yoginī temples are found at Shahdol in Madhya Pradesh (images now preserved in the Dhubela Museum in Chatrapur district), at Mitauli and Dudahi in Lalitpur district of Uttar Pradesh, at Lokhari in the Banda district of Uttar Pradesh, and at Hirapur near Bhubaneswar in Orissa, discovered by Sri K.N. Mohapatra.

All the Devī *pīṭhas* were probably also significant centers of the Yoginī cult, even though there may be no surviving Yoginīs temples.[102] The Kāmākhyā temple in Assam, for example, even today includes an invocation of the sixty-four Yoginīs during the daily worship of Devī Kāmākhyā, but Assam has no remains of Yoginī temples. Likewise, Bengal has no surviving Yoginī temples, yet there is abundant evidence to suggest that it was a major Yoginī center. Major Tantric texts, including Krishnananda's *Tantrasāra*, were written in Bengal, and several texts on Kaula *cakrapūjā* refer to specific varieties of fish for the *matsya* offering[103] which were known only in Bengali waters.[104]

Before the era of royal patronage of magnificent temple art, Yoginī worship entailed concentration on the abstract symbology of *cakras* drawn on cloth or paper. Such single-pointed concentration based on symbolic homologization, probably the most ancient technique of invoking Yoginīs, lies at the abstract end of the spectrum of Yoginī worship. The other extreme, that of misplaced concreteness or overt consumption, was expressed in the stone temples built by medieval kings in which initiates practiced Kaula rituals that included drinking wine and blood, sacrificing animals, consuming the flesh of corpses, and ritual copulation—the cultural revalorization of aboriginal fertility rituals. There must also have existed a middle path between the symbolic and the literal extremes characterized by *bhakti* (worship) at the feet of the Yoginīs by groups of followers who prayed for their grace and mercy and who may have participated in some aspect of the rituals.[105]

The Yoginī doctrine and practices were systematized and explicated by Matsyendranātha in his famous work *Kaulajñānanirṇaya,* which has become the authoritative text of the cult.[106] The focus of Matsyendra's Yoginī Kaulamārga is the invocation of the Śaktis through yoga and external worship, associated with the worship of *yantras* composed of four, eight, twelve, sixty-four, and more angles. Centered among the angles is Śiva. The Sixty-four Yoginīs correspond to sixty-four angles of the *yantra,* symbolizing the sixty-four manifestations of Śakti embracing Śiva. This *yantra* forms a lotus reminiscent of the Śrī *cakra.*[107]

Dehejia has divided the lists of Yoginīs in literature into two categories, those that include and those that exclude the Mātṛkās. She has concluded that these categories "prove to be meaningful, and it appears that the Mātṛkā-inclusive lists assign a very high status to the Yoginīs, while lists excluding Mātṛkās relegate the Yoginīs to a somewhat lower position."[108] The Yoginīs are associated in an important way with the eight Mātṛkās in the *Agni Purāṇa.* There the Yoginīs are derived in groups from Brāhmaṇī, Māheśwarī, Kaumārī, Vaiṣṇavī, Varāhī, Aindrī, Cāmuṇḍā, and Mahālakṣmī; and the Purāṇas emphasize that they either were born (*sambhava*) from the Mātṛkā or belong to the same family (*kula*) as she. Dehejia found that the tradition that associates the Mātṛkās with the Yoginīs regards the latter "either as varying aspects of the Divine Female or as highly placed acolytes of the Goddess."[109]

According to Das,[110] the Yoginīs are classified into either three groups—Sahajā, Kulajā, Antyajā—or four groups —Kṣetrajā, Pīṭhajā, Yogajā, and Mantrajā. In the latter classification, the first two groups correspond to the sacred *pīṭhas,* the Yogajās are propitiated by yogic practices, and the Mantrajās by *mantra.* Brāhmaṇī, Māheśwarī, Kaumārī, Vaiṣṇavī, Varāhī, Aindrī, Cāmuṇḍā, (and Mahālakṣmī) constitute the seven (sometimes eight) Mother-goddesses, labeled Yoginīs,[111] who, according to the Purāṇas, were created to drink the oozing blood from the wounds of Raktabīja to prevent his cloning himself from the blood drops. The number sixty-four is at least in part derived from the eight Mother-goddesses from each of whom emanate seven Yoginīs.

The cult of the Yoginīs is linked to the cult of Śiva in his *ugra* form of Bhairava. Other *ugra* aspects of Śiva include Aghora, Vīrabhadra, and Birupākhya. According to Āgamic texts, there are Sixty-four Bhairavas divided into eight groups, corresponding to the Sixty-four Yoginīs. The origin of the mysterious Bhairavas is revealed in a story in the *Vāmana Purāṇa* that recounts that in ancient times, a bloody battle was waged between Mahādeva and Andhakāsura. When Andhaka hit Mahādeva's head with his mace, blood flowed down the four sides of his wound, and Mahādeva's gushing blood created the Bhairavas. Vidurāja Bhairava, extravagantly ornamented, resembling a blazing fire, was born from the blood flowing to the east. Rāmarāja Bhairava, deep black and associated with the *pretas,* was born from the blood flowing to the south. Nāgarāja Bhairava, Atasi Kusuma in color, dressed in leaves, was born from the blood flowing west. Svacchandarāja Bhairava, black in color, holding a *triśūla* (trident), was born from the blood flowing north. Finally, Lambitarāja Bhairava was born of the entire flow of Mahādeva's blood.[112]

In the literary texts, composed by brāhmaṇas, the *Skanda Purāṇa* (in which the Great Goddess herself has several names) lists the names of the Sixty-four Yoginīs, clearly collapsing them into the brāhmaṇical Devī's power. In this Purāṇa, only Brāhmī and Cāmuṇḍā are listed as Mātṛkās. Furthermore, in the list of Sixty-four Yoginīs in the *Skanda Purāṇa* and other texts, nearly half of the Yoginīs have bird and animal heads. The *Kālikā Purāṇa* lists of Sixty-four Yoginīs and also gives to the Supreme Goddess numerous additional names of Yoginīs. For instance, Caṇḍikā, included in the *Kālikā Purāṇa* as a Yoginī, is the principal name given to Devī in the *Devī-māhātmya.* Kālikā, Kauśikī, Ambikā, Śākambharī, Bhīmā, and Bhrāmarī, also Yoginīs, are additional names with which Caṇḍikā identifies herself in the well-known interpolation of the *Mārkaṇḍeya Purāṇa.* The list of Sixty-four Yoginīs in the *Kālikā Purāṇa* also includes several Mātṛkās. "The *Kālikā Purāṇa* clearly reflects a tradition in which the Yoginīs were not so much attendants of the Goddess as sixty-four varying aspects of Devī herself," writes Dehejia. "The chapter that contains this list tells us that the Sixty-four Yoginīs are to be worshiped individually (*yoginīstu catuṣaṣṭi pūjayet pṛthak pṛthak*), this statement reinforcing their elevated status."[113]

The *Matsya Purāṇa*[114] mentions Kālī in the Kālañjara mountain, Caṇḍikā in Makarandaka, and Vindhyavāsinī in the Vindhyas as different manifestations of the supreme goddess. The *Bṛhannandikeśvara Purāṇa* contains a complete set of Mātṛkās within its list of the Sixty-four Yoginīs, where Durgā and Pārvatī are regarded as Yoginīs. A manuscript entitled "Yoginī-mantra-yantrādi" in the Sarasvati Bhavan collection at Varanasi contains a third group of Sixty-four Yoginīs, who are depicted, as in the *Kālikā Purāṇa,* as aspects of the Divine Goddess. This list includes Bhadrakālī, Lalitā, Ambikā, Gaurī, Bhadrā, Tripurā, Sarasvatī, Nārāyaṇī, Kālarātri, Dhūmāvatī, Kātyāyanī, and Kuṇḍalinī. As Dehejia points out, a visual version of this list of names, with only minor variances of arrangement, is found on a paper *cakra* from Rajasthan.[115]

In the Tantric text *Kaulajñānanirṇaya,* Śiva, in answer to Devī's question as to how Yoginīs roam the earth, lists the forms they assume, including the bird forms of dove, vulture, swan, owl, crane, peacock, and cock, and the animal forms of jackal, goat, ox, cat, tiger, elephant, horse, snake, and frog.[116] The Yoginīs, however, have a divine status—evidenced by their haloes, multiple arms, and their possession of their own mounts—and are of inherently greater potency and elevation than Śiva's *gaṇas.*

The *Śrī Matottara Tantra,* which, previous to Vidya Dehejia's *Yoginī Cult and Temples* (New Delhi, 1986), was unknown outside India and never critically studied, provides us with many missing pieces in the puzzle of the Yoginī cult. Listed as one of the original sixty-four Tantras in some traditions, the *Matottarā*

Purāṇa ends each chapter with a reference to its doctrine as *Yoginīguhya*, meaning "Secret of the Yoginīs." Dehejia found this Tantra, composed in Sanskrit, in the Nepal National Archives, in over thirty manuscript copies in both the Newari and the Devanāgarī scripts, of which the earliest version dated in the text itself belongs to the Newari year 729 or AD 1609. Dehejia studied this Tantra in a complete version written in Devanāgarī (no. 4/2506), which she claims is at least four hundred years old.

The *Śrī Matottara Tantra* is written in the familiar Tantric paradigm of a dialogue between Śiva and Devī (in this Tantra, the Devī is Kubjikā). The structure of the text is based on the esoteric art of *cakras* (ritual circles): each chapter contains a description of the origin and significance of one *cakra*, coupled with instructions on diagraming the *cakra* for presentation. Four *cakras* detailed in this text are of particular importance: the Khecarī *cakra* and the Yoginī *cakra*, both *cakras* of sixty-four Yoginīs; and the Mālinī *cakra*, a *cakra* of fifty goddesses. The ultimate goal of Yoginī worship, the *Matottarā Purāṇa* suggests, is the acquisition of a variety of occult powers. This Tantra also points to the ritual practices associated with the cult.

The *Agni Purāṇa* (ninth century AD) is the earliest known brāhmaṇic text that contains lists and physical descriptions of the Sixty-four Yoginīs in its sixteen-line *Devīpratimālakṣaṇa* ("Attributes of Images of the Goddesses"), evidences that images of the Yoginīs were being made. "For this admittedly heterodox cult to have found acceptance in a Purāṇa by the ninth century must testify to the powerful hold it exerted over its increasing fold of followers," writes Dehejia. "One would imagine that the cult was fairly well-known for some time before that date and hence it is likely that, whatever its precise antiquity, sometime between AD 600 and 850, the cult of the Yoginīs had been accepted in the mainstream of Hinduism."[117] In addition, the *Kubjikāmata*[118] (seventh or eighth century) refers to the *Agnimata* or doctrine of the Yoginīs, and a chapter is written on the Yoginīs. The *Kaulajñānanirṇaya* (eleventh century) attributes to Matsyendranātha, the first Nātha guru, the introduction of the Yoginī cult to the Kaulas. Since Matsyendranātha lived well before AD 900, this text attests to the cult's popularity by the tenth century, as well as its association with the Kānphaṭa (or Nātha) yogīs, successors to the Kāpālikas. The infamous *Kālikā Purāṇa* contains much material on the Yoginī cult and Kāmarūpa, Assam.

The first Śākta Tantras date from the seventh century onward and constitute Śāktic scriptures that treat cosmology and cosmogony, science and medicine, and laws governing kings and societies. These works are difficult to date with any precision. The Saptamātṛkās, according to the Śākta doctrine, preside over impurities (*mala*) and over the fourteen vowels plus the *anusvāra* and *visarga* of the Sanskrit language. The symbology of Śāktism comprises a network of such esoteric correspondences connecting material and intuitive reality, which, through formulaic discipline of thought and meditation, lead the Śākta to various *siddhis*. The *Śākta Upaniṣads* (eleventh century) regard Śakti as identical to *brahman* or *īśvara*. The *Kaula Upaniṣad* is very late, yet still regarded as the major scripture and highest authority of the Kaula sect of the Śāktas, the Vāma-mārga of Śāktism. Śaṅkara disapproved of the Kaulas, discrediting the methods of the Kaula circle in his *Saundarya-laharī*.

Existing Yoginī temples radiate in a broad arc across northern India, from the Orissa coast through central India to the Rajasthan border, although the cult was not restricted to this area and once influenced large sections of India. All Devī *pīṭhas*, Dehejia hypothesizes, were important centers of the Yoginī cult, e.g., the Kāmākhyā temple in Assam is one of the few Devī shrines where the names of Cauṁsaṭha Yoginīs are still invoked in the daily worship of Kāmākhyā;[119] Bengal was a major Yoginī cult site, although no Yoginī shrines remain there; and Orissa is dotted with archaeological remains of Yoginī cult temples.

The Kāpālika Cult

> [The Kāpālikas] went about naked, wore a cap while travelling, smeared their bodies with funeral ashes, were armed with a trident or sword, carried a hollow skull for a cup or begging bowl, were half-intoxicated with spirits which they drank from the hollow skull, were known to commit acts of violence; their garments (when they wore them) were of patch-work, they slept on the ground, and wore a rosary of rudrākṣa seeds. They offered human sacrifices to Cāmuṇḍā in order to obtain magic powers, and often resorted to tricks to ensnare victims. Dust from their feet was supposed to cure disease and water from the washing of their feet drove away demons. The powers which they acquired included the ability to fly through the air. Their wits were sharpened by the use of wine, eating disgusting food, and the embrace of the Śakti of Bhairava. They were always lewd, and on occasion carried off maidens.[120]

Lorenzen points out that both the Kaula path and the Kāpālikas belonged to the Vāmācāra tradition, and had many similarities.[121] Rather than creating symbolic equivalents or sublimating the taboo practices into mental exercise, as in the Dakṣiṇācāra tradition, both paths use real women and real wine in the ritual of the *pañcatattva*. The Kāpālikas were low-caste wandering ascetics who spent much time in charnel grounds (*śmaśāna*), honing their art. That they worshiped and served the goddess Kālī as well as Cāmuṇḍā and other fierce manifestations of the *śmaśāna* goddess is revealed in the *Pārśvanātha-caritra*, an early medieval Jaina work, which describes a Kāpālika who collects skulls for Kālī. The goddess praises him, saying that when she collects her 108th skull, her purpose will be fulfilled.[122]

During his South Asian travels, the Chinese pilgrim Hsüan-tsang describes the different types of Buddhists and other sects in the areas he visited *c.* AD 630–44. In Kāpiśa (contemporary Nuristan) in eastern Afghanistan, Hsüan-tsang saw over a hundred Buddhist monasteries, as well as "some ten temples of the Devas, and 1000 or so of heretics (*different ways of religion*); there are naked ascetics, and others who cover themselves with ashes, and some who make chaplets of bones, which they wear as crowns on their heads."[123] Buddhist monasteries were obviously outnumbered ten to one by "heretical" temples, and the Kāpālikas and other anti-brāmaṇical cults probably wandered as far as the border of Zhang Zhung in eastern Afghanistan in the seventh century, just prior to the takeover of Zhang Zhung by the Tibetans in the eighth century.

Hsüan-tsang describes the rich Tantric culture in India proper, where we can identify the presence of the Kāpālikas by their skull bone necklaces, potent symbols also prevalent in Vajrayāna and Dzogchen iconography:

> The dress and ornaments worn by non-believers are varied and mixed. Some wear peacocks' feathers; some wear as ornaments necklaces made of skull bones . . .; some have no clothing, but go naked . . .; some wear leaf or bark garments; some pull out their hair and cut off their moustaches; others have bushy whiskers and their hair braided on the top of their heads.[124]

Epigraphical evidence that points to the activity of the Kāpālikas is slight; however, three inscriptions have been found from southern Mysore State which show that the Kāpālikas were present in southern Mysore during the ninth and tenth centuries. One of them, dated during the reign of the western Gaṅga king Mārasiṁha III (AD 960–74), reads:

> Famous was the glory of Maṇḍalika-Triṇetra (a Triṇetra or Śiva among the *maṇḍalikas* or chieftains) as if to make the . . . Kāpālikas arrange in a string all the newly cut off heads of the Pallavas and firmly proclaim to hostile chieftains—Aho! do not allow your newly cut off heads to be added to this string; have audience and live happily in the ranks of his servants.[125]

The intention of this inscription, according to Lorenzen, is to demonstrate the king's fierce strength against his traditional enemies, the Pallavas. The Kāpālikas appear to be "either religious mercenaries or simply battlefield scavengers," writes Lorenzen. He emphasizes:

> The possibility that they were militant religious mercenaries is strengthened by the description of a warlike Kāpālika band in Mādhavācārya's *Śaṅkara-digvijaya.* The strings on which the Kāpālikas of the inscription arrange the heads of the king's Pallava enemies are apparently the traditional skull garlands of these ascetics.[126]

The Kāpālikas were expert commissioners in human sacrifice.[127] There are numerous literary allusions to Kāpālikas making offerings of human flesh, performing rituals of human sacrifice, or performing *pūjā* with corpses in cemeteries and cremation grounds. For example, Śaṅkarācārya dramatizes a Kāpālika who describes Bhairava as blatantly bloodthirsty: "If he (Kāpālin-Śiva) does not receive Bhairava worship with liquor and blood-smeared lotuses which are human heads, how can he attain joy when his body is embraced by the lotus eyed Umā. . . ?"[128] In other literature of the time, a Kāpālika in Kṛṣṇamiśra's *Prabodhacandrodaya*[129] says that at the end of their fast, "Mahā Bhairava should be worshiped with offerings of awe-inspiring human sacrifices from whose severed throats blood flows in torrents." He adds that the worshipers offer this god oblations of "human flesh mixed with brains, entrails, and marrow."[130] In the same drama, a Kāpālika introduces himself in the following way: "My necklace and other ornaments are made of human bones; I break my ceremonial fast by drinking consecrated wine from the skull cup of a Brāhmaṇa corpse; our sacrificial fire is kept burning with the offering of human flesh, skull, lung, etc.; we propitiate our terrific and fierce god by offering him human blood and sacrifice."[131] According to Eliade, it is probable that "these simultaneously ascetic and orgiastic sects, which still practiced cannibalism at the end of the nineteenth century, had assimilated certain aberrant traditions connected with the cult of skulls (which also frequently implies ritual eating of relatives). . . ."[132]

On an internal plane, the counterpart of animal and human sacrifice is self-sacrifice, a conception that embraces a wide spectrum of Indian religious behaviors, "from self-immolation or suicide to self-mutilation and from physical penances to simple exercises of mental discipline."[133] There is evidence that the Kāpālikas sometimes practiced self-mutilation by cutting flesh from their own bodies to offer as sacrificial oblations.

The *Vāmana Purāṇa* was composed in the Kurukshetra region as a text for the glorification of the local centers of pilgrimage (*Sthala-māhātmya*). It was probably written around the first half of the seventh century AD, when Harṣavardhana ruled the north and Mahendravarman Pallava the south. The *Vāmana Purāṇa* is filled with literature about the Pāśupata-Śaiva religion, especially its cult-worship and popularity in Kurukṣetra and other principal centers of north India. Chapter six of this Purāṇa, which reconstructs the history of the Pāśupata Śaivas, also provides solid information about the different Śaiva sects—Śaiva, Pāśupata, Kāladamana, and Kāpālika. Although the stories of their origins and lineages are likely, Agrawala suggests that fictions may have been invented to establish Vedic origins or an early history for each sect.[134] The Kāpālikas are characterized as *Mahāvratins*, who descended from a teacher named Dhanada.

The Kāpālikas were well acquainted with the mystical physiology of Haṭha-yoga. The fifth act of Bhavabhūti's *Mālatī-Mādhava* begins with Kapālakuṇḍalā, the female disciple of the Kāpālika Aghoraghaṇṭa, entering the stage on an aerial path from the sky. In her initial invocation to Śiva, she asserts that the god's "*ātman* is situated in the midst of the ten *nāḍīs* and six *cakras*" and that he "gives *siddhis* to those who know (him)."[135] Kapālakuṇḍalā then describes, in a context evocative of Tibetan Ḍākinīs (*khandromās* or sky dancers), how she clears the clouds before her as she flies through the sky. "She claims to perceive the *ātman* manifested in the lotus of the heart as the form of Śiva through her power of yogic absorption (*laya-vaśāt*) and to fix it in the six *cakras* by the practice of *nyāsa*. Then she causes the drawing off of the five elements from the body by means of the swelling of the *nāḍīs* (with the breath restrained by *prāṇāyāma*) and flies up into the air."[136] Thus she has won the *siddhi* of flying by practicing Haṭhayoga.

According to Banerjea, the Kāpālikas were driven out of many countries and gradually concentrated in the countries of the Mālavas and the Ābhīras in western India:

> The reason for the unpopularity of these fierce sectaries is found in their unsocial and terrific religious practices. The Kālāmukha rites also consisted of such abhorrent actions as "eating food from a human skull," "rubbing ashes of a burnt human corpse all over his body," "eating those ashes," "always keeping with him wine inside a *kapāla* and invoking his god in it." Among these religious extremists, however, there was a lessening of the stringency of caste-rigour, for according to them there was no barrier to men of lower castes to be initiated in the *mahāvrata*, and any such properly initiated person was regarded as belonging to the highest caste.[137]

Like the Yoginī cult, the Kāpālikas have been largely ignored by modern scholars. No religious texts of this order survive; research material on the Kāpālikas consists of two Sanskrit dramas, Bhavabhūti's *Mālatī-Mādhava* and Kṛṣṇamiśra's *Prabodhacandrodaya*, as well as two legendary biographies of Śaṅkarācārya, Mādhavācārya's *Śaṅkara-digvijaya* and Ānandagiri's *Śaṅkara-vijaya*. Extremely hostile accounts of the Kāpālikas were written by two Vaiṣṇava sages, Yāmunācārya and his pupil Rāmānuja. Yāmunācārya (*c.* 1050) classifies together the Śaivas, Pāśupatas, Kāpālas [Kāpālikas], and Kālāmukhas in his *Āgama-prāmāṇya*, and his pupil Rāmānuja repeats his words, at times verbatim. Most later commentators follow the classification scheme of Yāmunā. Rāmānuja says of the four Pāśupati sects:

> All these make an analysis of reality and an hypothesis about the attainment of bliss in this world and the next which are opposed to the Vedas. They make a distinction between the instrumental and material cause (*nimittopadānāya* or *bhedam*) and designate Paśupati as the instrumental cause (but not the material cause of the Universe).[138]

Rāmānuja describes the major tools or symbols of Kāpālikas ritual, and in so doing, he reveals their extensive use of *sandhābhāṣa*:

> As the Kāpālas declare: "He who knows the essence of the six insignia (*mudrikā-ṣaṭka*), who is proficient in the highest *mudrā* (*para-mudrā-viśārada*)[139] and who meditates on the Self as seated in the vulva (*bhagāsanstha*), attains *nirvāṇa*." They define the six insignia (*mudrā*) as the *kaṇṭhikā* (necklace), the *rucaka* (another neck ornament), the *kuṇḍala* (earring), the *śikhāmaṇi* (crest-jewel), ashes, and the sacred thread. A person bearing these insignia is not born again in this world.[140]

This passage reveals one of the many commonalities between Vajrayāna symbolism and that of the Kāpālika cult: the Kāpālikas' meditation on the "Self as seated in the vulva" echoes the Tantric Buddhist metaphor of "the jewel in the lotus," a stereotypical Buddhist *sandhābhāṣa* term in which the word "lotus" (*padma*) is invested with the erotic meaning of "womb" (*bhaga*).[141]

The Kāpālika conception is also identical to a standard beginning of Buddhist Tantras, "Buddhahood resides in the woman's vulva,"[142] "Buddha (*vajra-sattva*) rests in the mysterious *bhaga* of the Bhagavatīs,"[143] or "Once upon a time the Lord of all Tathāgatas . . . was dwelling in the vulva of the *vajra*-woman," expressed as follows:

> Sanskrit: *ekasmin samaye bhagavān sarvatathāgatakāya-vāk-citta-hṛdaya-vajrayoṣit-bhageṣu vijāhāra.*
>
> Tibetan: *Bdom ldan 'das de bzin gśegs pa thams cad kyi sku dangsun dan thugs gyi sñin po rdo rje btsun mo'i bha ga la bzugso.*[144]

Like most Śaivite ascetics, the Kāpālikas smeared their bodies with ashes and wore sacred threads and *rudrākṣa* beads, but they have two secondary insignia (*upamudrā*) that are both peculiar to the Kāpālikas: the skull (*kapāla*) and the club (*khaṭvāṅga*, literally, "limb of a bedstead," so named because of its distinctive sillhouette). This Kāpālika *khaṭvāṅga*, well-known in the *Kāpālika Tantra*, is described as "a banner made of a skull mounted on a stick (*daṇḍa*)."[145] Both the Tibetan Siddha Padmasaṁbhava and Bhairava carry this staff as a central part of their iconography, and its history is intertwined with the Great Vow of the Kāpālikas—the "chief penance prescribed for the removal of the sin of killing a Brāhmaṇa."[146] Most of the major law-books list the rules for this penance, called the Mahāvrata in the *Viṣṇusmṛti*, which says that a man who has unintentionally killed a brāhmaṇa must perform the following acts for twelve years: (1) live in a hut of leaves in a forest; (2) bathe and perform prayers three times a day; (3) wander from village to village collecting alms and proclaiming his deed; (4) sleep on grass; (5) "he who is performing any of those penances must carry (on his stick) the skull of the person slain, like a flag."[147] Yājñavalkya suggests that the penitent must carry a skull (generally identified as that of the person he has killed) in his hand as well as on his staff. The commentators disagree about whether the penitent should use the skull as a begging bowl.[148]

Śiva in the form of Bhairava commits the sin of brāhmaṇicide: to punish Brahmā, the creator god, for his arrogance, Bhairava cut off one of his heads with his left thumb-nail. His penalty for being a *brahmahan* was to wander as a beggar for twelve years, carrying Brahmā's skull attached to his hand. When Bhairava entered the precincts of the sacred city of Benares, his sins were expiated and the skull dropped off his hand. As Muller-Ortega points out:

> Many powerful tantric themes are densely packed into the figure of Bhairava. The skull-bearing transgressor of *dharma* who is fearful and terrible resonates with the yogic and tantric cremation-ground culture of heterodox and transgressive groups who sought power through control of and possession by hordes of frightening goddesses.[149]

The Kāpālika's adoption of the *khaṭvāṅga*, then, contains the symbolism of penance for the most transgressive act of the *brahmahan*, symbolically containing the Tantric ironic reversal of all values: in the domain of illusion, the most heinous criminal (the *brahmahan*), like the lowest caste washerwoman (the ḍombī), becomes the most holy and accomplished ascetic in the domain of the spirit.

The iconography associated with the Indian Kāpālikas—particularly the skull bowl, the trident, and the *khaṭvāṅga*—all seem to be duplicated in the prolific symbology of both Bönpo and Buddhist Tantric art. Thus the two secondary insignia that differentiate the Kāpālikas from other Tantric cults are also characteristics of Padmasaṁbhava and Dzogchen. Lorenzen points to three elements of the Kāpālikas that link the cult contextually to Sahajiyā Buddhism and Vajrayāna: the Kāpālikas used the term *nirvāṇa* rather than its Hindu equivalent, *mokṣa* or *mukti*; the Sahajiyā Buddhist poet Kāṇhapāda "elevates the Kāpālika to the rank of perfected yogin;"[150] and Vajrayāna literature "refers to ritual paraphernalia typical of Kāpālika worship—such as bones, blood, flesh, and skulls—more often than Hindu Tantras do."[151] In addition, the high value placed on practice in cemeteries, as well as the prominence of the skull bowl and decapitated heads, are among the major features of Tibetan art, texts and *terma*s: "Even [the] mild form of the image of Ogyän Guru [Padmasaṁbhava]," writes Waddell, "has decapitated human heads strung on to his trident."[152]

Bhairava is the form of Śiva (as Destroyer) found in many of the revealed texts of the non-dual Śaivism of Kashmir, as well as being the deity worshiped by the Kāpālikas. The Vedic god Rudra, who is both terrible and beneficent, is considered by some scholars to be an early form of Bhairava-Śiva. The latter is "equally reminiscent of the pre-Aryan, yogic Lord of the beasts deity, while his consorts resemble the sacrifice-exacting Mother-goddesses of the same period"[153] (i.e., the Indus civilization, *c.* 2000 BCE). Images of this god depict a wrathful, fanged face wearing a headdress of snakes and a necklace of skulls, and whose weapons are his third eye, through which he destroys his enemies with fire; a trident (*pinaka*), a symbol of lightning that characterizes Śiva as the god of storms; a sword; a bow (*ajagava*); and a club with a skull at the end (*khaṭvāṅga*). He is a god of terror and death, transformation and release. The name Bhairava is derived from the Sanskrit root *bhī*, "to be afraid," and the adjective *bhīru*, "fearful, timid." The words are inverted in Bhairava, translated as that which is terrible, frightful, horrible.

Bhairava has his counterpart in the wrathful aspects of all Tibetan male deities, and may be related in hoary antiquity to the Bönpo tutelary deity Zhang Zhung Meri (dBal-chen Ge-khod) who, like Śiva, is a mountain god associated with Kailāsa. The latter is extremely fearsome, with three eyes, an open mouth from which issues a rain of thunderbolts and blood, with teeth clenched and tongue twisted; he wears necklaces and bracelets of blue snakes whose scarves are decorated with skulls. He is a wrathful deity in motion, carrying symbolic weapons (sword, axe, wheel, thunderbolt arrow, fire, sharp sword, stick and wheel, bow and arrow, lasso, hammer, chain, hook, antelope horn, and magic water) in each of his eighteen arms, wearing a lower garment of tiger skin decorated at the hem with leopard skins, and tied with a belt of red lightning; he dances on a corpse, which in Tantric Buddhist teachings symbolizes ignorance. Like Bhairava, his weapons carry an abstract purpose: to destroy the demons of negativities and ignorance. The initiation of Zhang Zhung Meri is necessary in order to study and practice the *Bönpo Zhang Zhung Nyan Gyud* teachings,[154] which Meri protects.

Vijñāna Bhairava, a Tantric text, is a manual of mystic practices that was well known in the eighth century AD, and may have been written during the seventh century.[155] Like *rigpa* in Dzogchen, *Bhairava* means "Supreme Consciousness," and true meditation is defined in *Vijñāna Bhairava* as "[u]nswerving *buddhi* without any image or support. . . . Concentration on an imaginative representation of the divine with a body, eyes, mouth, hands, etc., is not meditation.."[156] The following verse continues, "Worship does not mean offering of flowers, etc. It rather consists in setting one's heart on that highest ether of consciousness which is above all thought-constructs. It really means dissolution of self with perfect ardour (in the Supreme Consciousness known as *Bhairava*)."[157]

The symbology of the graveyard is ideal for Tantric purposes, since it enfolds the mirror image leitmotif of external and internal reality at the heart of Tantric metaphysics. As Rawson explicates:

> Cremation-grounds in India usually lie to the west of a town. In them corpses are laid out and cremated on carefully constructed piles of wood, so that the spirit may move on to a fresh birth. The burning is often far from complete. Dogs, jackals, crows and vultures live there, feeding on the remains and scattering the bones. Contact with the dead, from the point of view of caste, is deeply defiling, especially if the dead are themselves of lower castes. To handle corpses is the task of the lowest members in the whole caste hierarchy. The graveyard, nevertheless, is where high and low alike end up, and is a perpetual reminder of the death which consummates life.[158]

The symbolic significance of the cemetery (*śmaśāna*) in a number of Indian esoteric cults is well-known:

> [T]he cemetery represents the totality of psychomental life, fed by consciousness of the "I"; the corpses symbolize the various sensory and mental activities. Seated at the center of his profane experience, the yogin "burns" the activities that feed them, just as corpses are burned in the cemetery. By meditating in a *śmaśāna* he more directly achieves the combustion of egotistic experiences; at the same time, he frees himself from fear, he evokes the terrible demons and obtains mastery over them.[159]

Eliade regards a material interpretation of the *śmaśāna* metaphor "the degradation of an ideology through failure to comprehend the symbolism that forms its vehicle."[160] The graveyard imagery used extensively and seemingly literally in accounts of Padmasaṁbhava's life is ambiguous, ironic, and cryptic; the Tantric messages are deliberately cloaked in *sandhābhāṣa* in order to hide their esoteric meaning as well as to disengage the conceptual mind. Tantric practice in charnel grounds is traditionally associated with the

Indian Aghorīs or Aghorapanthīs,[161] descendants of the Kāpālikas. To this day, the Aghorīs are regarded as highly skilled Tantric masters who have spent many years perfecting the advanced system of Aghora, which emphasizes *mantra, yantra,* and *tantra.* (It should be remembered that Vajrayāna is also known as "Mantrayāna" because of its focus on the manipulation of sound, an art the Aghorī has developed to a high degree.)

From the seventh century to the present, Kāpālikas-*cum*-Aghorīs have resided in cemeteries, eaten from human skull-bowls, and, at the end of the nineteenth century, still practiced cannibalism. Crooke reports having seen an Aghorī from Ujjain eating a corpse from the burning ghat in 1887.[162] In an effort to destroy sensory disgust and delight, to fully realize *sama-rasa* in which no difference is sensed between pleasant and unpleasant experiences, these yogins eat refuse and all flesh except horse flesh. "Even as human excrement fertilizes a sterile soil, so assimilating every kind of filth makes the mind capable of any and every meditation."[163] They reject notions of superior castes and religions, and regard parents as accidents. Any Śaiva of any caste can become an Aghorī, including Jainas, but Vaiṣṇavas are not admitted. They do not worship images, and respect only God and their *guru.* They are vagabonds, and a disciple (*celā, śiṣya*) cannot become a *guru* until twelve years after his spiritual master's death. Because their path is "fast, terrible, and intense," they are said to have developed many *siddhis.* The *gurus* are always accompanied by a dog. When Aghorīs die, their bodies are buried in a seated position with legs crossed.

Like many of their practices, the Aghorīs' predilection for lying near burial sites has shamanic undertones. Eliade emphasizes the important role of the graves of ancestors to neophyte shamans, pointing to Eskimo and Australian apprentice shamans who, wishing to become medicine people, lie next to graves.[164] The belief is that the soul of the deceased shaman will participate in shamanic initiations.

Aghorīs worship the Divine Mother in her wrathful aspects as Śmaśāna Tārā, Kālī, Śītalā Devī, or Parṇagiri Devī.[165] This goddess, like that of the Kāpālikas, shares much iconography in common with both Bön and Tibetan Buddhist Tantric art. The Ḍākinī of Vajrayāna and Dzogchen is related thematically to Śmaśāna Tārā, Kālī, and the other fierce goddesses who are found in cemeteries and who initiate yogins by the red glow of cremation pyres. She is described in detail by a devotee who invoked her through *mantra-japa:*

> [A]ll of a sudden there was Smashan Tara standing before me, smiling, asking what I wanted from Her.
>
> Tears come to my eyes whenever I remember that scene. For years the scar remained on my hand as a reminder of the night when I was there in that cemetery sitting on that corpse, and I caught my first glimpse of Smashan Tārā.

> I don't know what your condition would be if you were to catch sight of Her. You might even die of shock. She is very tall, and Her skin is a beautiful deep midnight-blue color. Her eyes are beautiful; that's the only way I know to describe them. She has a long red tongue lolling from Her mouth. Blood, the blood She is eternally drinking, drips slowly from the tip. She is *ghatastani,* or pot-breasted, and *lambodari,* or full-bellied. Around Her neck there is a garland of freshly severed human heads which are freshly bleeding. She wears wristlets and armlets of bones, and anklets of snakes. Her four hands grasp a pair of scissors, a sword, a noose, and a skull. She wears a skirt of human arms, and to me She is one of the loveliest beings in the universe, because She is my Mother.[166]

The *sādhaka* may call her Durgā, Kālī, or Tārā, and all the accouterments of the cemetery—the corpses and the defiled corpse-handlers, the jackals and the crows, the social defilement and death—are her agents and agencies. Until the *sādhaka* can confront and assimilate his loving Mother in all her aspects as Creatrix, Preserver, and Destroyer of the world, he is not worshiping her completely. In the graveyard, she assumes a hideous form to facilitate the devotee's spiritual progress: "She is the girl with the axe or sword, the smallpox, cholera and famine-lady who grins as She drains his blood and cracks his spine."[167] Yet the Devī in this form is identical to the beautiful mother and lover; to succeed in uniting and superimposing her various personae is "perhaps the solidest beginning on the road of *sādhana.*"[168]

The funeral pyre is a potent vehicle of release from attachment:

> Ghora is darkness, the darkness of ignorance. Aghora means light, the absence of darkness. Under the Tree of Knowledge is an Aghorī, a follower of the path of Aghora. He has gone beyond ignorance thanks to the Flame of Knowledge which billows from the funeral pyre. The funeral pyre is the ultimate reality, a continual reminder that everyone has to die. Knowledge of the ultimate reality of Death has taken the Aghorī beyond the Eight Snares of Existence—lust, anger, greed, delusion, envy, shame, disgust, and fear—which bind all beings. The Aghorī plays with a human skull, astonished by the uselessness of limited existence, knowing the whole world to be within him though he is not in the world. His spiritual practices have awakened within him the power of Kundalini, which takes the form of the goddess dancing on the funeral pyre: Smashan Tārā. He is bewildered to think that all is within him, not external to him; that he sees it not with the physical eyes but with the sense of perception. The Flame of Knowledge is that which preserves life, the Eternal Flame, the Supreme Ego, the Motherhood of God which creates the whole Maya of the universe and thanks only to Whose grace the Aghorī has become immortal.[169]

Legendary Tantric Buddhist yogins are often initiated by a Ḍākinī by the dying red embers of graveyard pyres. The graveyard ultimately symbolizes the *sine qua non* of Tantrism: the absolute destruction of the limitations of ignorance, ego, the negative passions, disgust, and fear. A standard pattern is a meditation sequence performed by Tantric masters in "eight cremation grounds" located in the sacred geography of the Mount Kailāsa area. Padmasaṁbhava spent much of his time in charnel grounds (Tib.: *dur khrod*), sites where bodies were left to decompose or be eaten by wild animals. Frequented by ghosts and spirits, such grounds are considered suitable places for advanced practitioners to gain progress in their realization.[170] When Yeshe Tsogyal is initiated by Padmasaṁbhava, the great *guru* teaches her that the method of keeping her *samaya* (*dam tshig*), or sacred pledges of Vajrayāna practice, is through secrecy. Among the ritual accouterments of practice that she is instructed to keep secret are "the eight adornments of the charnel ground, bone ornaments, etc., and in particular, the *damaru* (small hand drum), the *kapāla* (*thod-źal*, skull bowl), and the *rkang-gling*"[171] (thigh-bone trumpet), all of which are Bönpo ritual articles used by hermit-sages.[172]

Buddhist and Bönpo deities frequently wear flayed-off skins of animals[173] or men and necklaces of human heads, and carry symbolic tools like skull bowls filled with blood, flaying knives (*gri-gug*), and bloody clubs, axes and swords. "The Tibetans used their fathers' skulls," according to Eliade, "but today the family cult has disappeared and . . . the magico-religious role of skulls appears to be a tantric (Śaivite) innovation." However, it is also possible that "Indian influences were superimposed on an ancient stratum of local beliefs."[174] Such symbolic garb and implements indicative of Kāpālika influence were abundant in ninth-century imagery of Buddhist of Bihar and Bengal.[175] The standard Tibetan cremation ground symbology repeatedly presents the image of meditation on corpses, one of the specialities of the Aghorī in which the corpse is sometimes revived by *mantra-japa*. In the *Phetkārinī Tantra*, it is stated that "He who does japa many times on a corpse in a cremation ground attains all kinds of success,"[176] and complete instructions are given in the *Kulajñānanirṇaya* for appropriate *mantras*, *yantras*, and meditation on corpses.[177] The graveyard imagery is also infused in Tibetan visualization practices: the famous *chöd* (*gchod*) ritual, for example, "which a solitary monk may perform far from human habitation to purge his consciousness, consists at bottom in an act of mystical self-butchery and self-feeding to all demons. Behind the Tibetan shamanized and internalized fantasy lie the extreme Indian facts."[178]

Shamanic aspects of Indian and Tibetan Tantrism, according to Eliade, include the significant roles played by human skulls and by women.[179] The use of skulls by the pre-Christian Nagas to channel fertility energy to their village and crops, and the function of warfare to fertilize Tamil villages and crops, illustrates this magico-religious complex. Shamanic notions about the sacredness of animal and human bones are revalorized in the so-called skeleton dance of Tibetan Buddhism and in the *chöd* initiatory meditation exercise of Tibet. Both the Eskimo shaman and the Mongolian Buddhist must contemplate his own skeleton for his initiation, which "furnishes certain revelations regarding experiences after death"[180] including, in the Buddhist cosmology, the appearance of wrathful tutelary deities whom one will meet in the *bardo*, the intermediate state between death and reincarnation. Eliade writes that "this type of meditation belongs to an archaic, pre-Buddhistic stratum of spirituality, which was based, in one way or another, on the ideology of the hunting peoples (the sacredness of bones) and whose object was to 'withdraw' the soul from the practitioner's own body for a mystical journey—that is, to achieve ecstasy."[181]

Tantric graveyard symbolism in Nepal is a conglomeration of Tantric Buddhism and Hinduism. When the Muslim invaders drove out the Tantric Buddhists from northeastern India in the twelfth century, the Buddhist monks and refugees from the plains were welcomed in Nepal, which was not conquered by the Muslims, as well as in Tibet, Bhutan, and Sikkim in the Himalayas. While Tibet, Bhutan, and Sikkim had completely converted to Buddhism (incorporating the indigenous Bönpo deities and teachings), Nepal remained Hindu. "So in Nepal Tantric Buddhism and Hinduism have flourished side by side, influencing each other, and combining their doctrines in a quite individual way."[182] Graveyard symbolism in Nepal was synthesized with that of the Vedic sacrifice in prescriptions for meditative practice: "The Hindu altar with its fire assimilates the symbolism of the pyre towards which the inner *pūjā* is directed; and all around the graveyard are placed mixed Buddhist and Hindu emblems, arranged in directional patterns."[183]

There is evidence that all Kāpālika cult members, as well as the "materialists" and the "cynics," the Lokāyatikas (those who rejected the Vedic tradition and Hindu values), participated in seasonal collective orgies in the spring (*vasantotsava*) and autumn (*kaumudīmahotsava*). Eliade points out that seasonal festivals and orgies were dominant features of the ancient, pre-Indo-European vegetation cult. Eliade points to the synthesis of Tantrism and indigenous practices that defines these festivals:

> It is interesting to note that some traditions make the Kāpālikas the originators of the seasonal orgies in which the Lokāyatikas also took part; here festivals of vegetation, tantric orgies, and the eccentric practices of the "materialists," cannibals, and wearers of skulls are merged in a single system. This detail shows us the direction of the future coalescence between tantric yoga and the aboriginal spiritual values.[184]

There is good reason to believe that many famous temples were once staffed by Kāpālika ascetics. The Kāpālikas were apparently given royal grants to worship the god Kapāleśvara. Nāgavardhana, the nephew of the Cālukya ruler Pulakeśin II, records in a copperplate inscription the grant of a village near Igātpurī "for the worship of the god Kapāleśvara, and for the maintenance of the *mahāvratins* residing in the temple."[185] The most prominent among the temples that housed Kāpālikas was the Vaitāla temple in Bhubaneshwar, Orissa, built in the eighth century, probably as a Kāpālika shrine, with the goddess Cāmuṇḍā as the presiding deity. The *Svaṇṇādri-mahodaya* refers to the Vaitāla temple and the presiding goddess: "the venerable goddess Cāmuṇḍā garlanded with skulls exists at a spot on the west not far from the tank. . . . [S]he is of terrific form and is known as Kāpālinī."[186] Kāpālinī is one of the 108 indigenous goddesses incorporated into the Great Goddess Durgā by the brāhmaṇic patriarchs. Bhavabhūti, in his *Mālatī-Mādhava*, describes the temple of Karālā-Cāmuṇḍā and her worshiper, the Kāpālika Aghoraghaṇṭa. The dramatist lists the name Manojavā, cognate with Manojavas, which is one of the names of Yama, the god of death, in the *Vājasaneyī Saṁhitā*.[187] The last in Bhavabhūti's list of the Saptamātṛkās is Cāmuṇḍā, who is characterized in some late texts as Yāmī or the consort of Yama.

In eastern India, especially in the Himalayan regions of Nepal, Tibet, and Assam, many traditions of the Kāpālika and Śākta cults were intermingled not only with those of the Siddhas and Siddhācāryas peculiar to Sahajīyā Buddhism,[188] but also with themes, traditions, and practices of the Nātha Siddhas. In fact, as Dasgupta emphasizes, a fundamental heterogeneity existed among the various Himalayan yogic cults.[189]

Inscriptional evidence indicates that the Kāpālikas were present in almost all parts of India in the medieval period and were associated with Śākta-Tantric temples. The Vaitāla temple at Bhubaneswar, originally a Kāpālika shrine, houses an image popularly known as Kāpālinī, representing Cāmuṇḍā in fierce form. Pāṇigrahī argues that the Kāpālikas were the followers of Śiva but that Cāmuṇḍā was the deity of their worship.[190] Das concludes that "the Kāpālikas were very likely associated with the cult of the Yoginīs along with other Śākta-Tantric cults and acted as the priest-magicians. The descriptions of the Kāpālikas in various texts, their *sādhana* and rituals connected with propitiation of Śiva and Śakti, prompt the scholars in the field to relate this mysterious sect with the mystic cults of Yoginīs."[191]

The Kaula cult was at the height of its popularity during the tenth century AD, when a group of thirty Kaula (Yoginī)-Kāpālika temples, secluded in fields and jungle at Khajurāho in Madhya Pradesh, were constructed. Built under the patronage of the Candela rulers from AD 950 to 1050, they were dedicated to Śiva, Viṣṇu, and the Jaina faith. The temples are known chiefly for their erotic wall carvings depicting group sex associated with the Kaula and Kāpālika cults. The Kāpālikas are recognizable by the clubs they carry over their shoulders. As Dehejia observes, "A number of scenes at Khajurāho actually depict the Kaula and Kāpālika ascetics partaking of sexual orgies."[192] Since Candela patronage, the temples have remained deserted.

In addition, the Vārāhi shrine at Caurāsī depicts a series of eight erotic scenes which have been identified as the eight stages of ritual love-making, or *aṣṭa-kāmakalā-prayoga*, detailed in the unpublished Oriya Tantric text, the *Kaula Cūḍāmaṇi*.[193] One of these eight erotic scenes depicts the Kāpālika and Kaula monks participating in a sexual initiation ceremony for newcomers; Dehejia purports that this particular Vārāhi temple was associated with sexual rituals (and other five Ms) known to be practiced by the Vāmācāra Kaula-Kāpālika sect.[194] One monk has a club over his shoulder, one of the signs of the Kāpālika sect. The Somavaṁśī rulers of Orissa appear from their copper-plate charters to have been followers of the Kaula cult, since all their charters begin with the following verses about their capital city Yayātinagara,

> where the enjoyment of love is being continually intensified and still more intensified by the close embraces (of lovers) by which fatigue is removed, in which the hissing sound often appears, and in which hairs stand on end, although such enjoyment suffers interruptions as the ardent young couple show their skill in the minds subdued and fascinated by amorous thoughts.[195]

The erotic stone reliefs of the temples of Khajurāho (AD 850–1050) and Koṇārka (thirteenth century AD) are well-known. More recently, Desai has discovered numerous temples in central and western India that contain erotic reliefs.[196] As Bhattacharyya states:

> Their very occurrence on the temples, the supposed holy places, has evoked explanations from many quarters. Spiritual and other traditional forms of explanations are practically of no worth because they are solely guided by the contemporary values of our society. . . . [I]t is tempting to connect these sexual depictions with primitive sex rites and Tantrism, but before that we must be sure about the real extent of the influence which has been supposed to be exerted by the latter on the former. There was obviously a link between the two, since some popular sexual themes actually switched over from terracotta to stone under certain historical conditions. Secondly, if we are to take the geographical distribution of such temples as characterized by sexual depictions into consideration, our emphasis will naturally be laid upon Orissa which was always a very strong seat of Tantric cults and rituals.[197]

Purī, the seat of Lord Jagannātha, is also mentioned in the Tantras as a place where Jagannātha is the subordinate male consort (Bhairava) of the goddess Vimalā. The consort-god Jagannātha was regarded as the king of the land, of whom the actual rulers were vassals. Similarly, Virbius, the consort of the Roman goddess Diana, was regarded as the king of Nemi who was impersonated by the priest. The daily worship of Jagannātha bears a strong Tantric imprint, and, during the feast of Jagannātha, a young woman was victoriously carried to the temple and solemnly wed to the god. The union, consummated during the night with a priest, ensured the people abundant harvest. It is difficult to miss the connection between tribal fertility magic and erotic carvings; however, as Bhattacharyya perceives,

> [T]here was obviously a link between the primitive fertility rites and sexual drawings and depictions, but when these came to reflect the art of the dominant class, they served a totally different purpose. From this point of view, the extravagance of Khajurāho and Konārak was mainly the reflection of the abnormal sexual desires of the dominant class of the men whose munificence was responsible for the construction of the temples.[198]

Sexual union in the temples was not a rare occurrence. *Devadāsīs* were employed at the temples as wives and servants to the gods; the great temple of Tanjore once had four hundred *devadāsīs* attached to it. The girls were formally married to the idol and regarded as wives of the gods. Impersonating the god, the priests would have intercourse with the *devadāsīs*, and their children by the priests often constituted a special caste. *Mithuna* is commonly depicted Indian art; the Khajurāho figures are "consciously and purposely sexual," as they are at Purī and Koṇārka, where "in the depiction of sexual acts one finds the widest possible varieties of copulative poses and techniques."[199] The copulative poses and techniques engraved on the temple walls are only described in the *Kāmaśāstras*, which were intended for the wealthy city dwellers, or *nāgarakas*. Thus the link with agricultural fertility magic seems weak when seen in the full light of the perversions of the licentious class. As Bhattacharyya emphasizes,

> Most of the copulative poses described in the Kāmaśāstras are absurd and it is impossible to follow them in practice. Their sole purpose was to excite perverse imagination relating to sexual acts. . . . In fact, what the licentious class wanted to have in their fantastic imagination was supplied on the one hand by the writers of the Kāmaśāstras and on the other by the designers of temple-reliefs.[200]

By the late medieval period (AD 1300–1700), many of the Kaula erotic carvings were dominated by the sexual fantasies of the licentious class. For example, a man is depicted standing on his head with legs folded, a woman is shown sitting in his lap, holding by their necks, two nude females who stand on each side, while the man titillates the sex organs of the standing nudes with his hands. In another carving,

> [a] standing woman is copulated by a man in the front face to face and at the same time she has anal intercourse with another man from behind. A woman is uplifted with bent knees and in that position locked in copulation. A woman's thighs are spread over the shoulder of a standing man who with bent head licks her cunnus, and she with her bent hanging head hold his erect penis with her hand and licks it with her mouth. These are clear reflections of the perversion of the aristocratic class and have no bearing on the primitive sex rites of fertility, so far as the purpose is concerned.[201]

Bhattacharyya concludes that

> [T]wo sets of beliefs and ideals simultaneously worked in the field of Indian history, one represented by the simpler peoples and another by the dominant class. Sometimes some of the beliefs and rituals of the former were adopted by the latter, but with a totally different purpose. Among the simpler peoples art is not a product of leisure. It is a guide to action, an illusory technique complementary to the deficiencies of the real techniques. By the symbolical representation of an event, primitive man thinks he can secure the actual occurrence of that event.[202]

Because of the connection between tribal fertility rites and sexual ritual, subaltern peoples tolerated and gave a kind of social sanction to "the sexual depictions on the temple walls revealing the lusty desires of the aristocratic class."[203] Bhattacharyya explains:

> This they did partly because they found in those depictions the illusion of a lost reality, the reality of their traditional beliefs and rituals, and partly because they were compelled to do so under the pressure of the dominant class. Artists and craftsmen had no freedom of their own. . . . They always came from the lower castes, and for their livelihood they had to meet up to the demands of their employers and customers, which had nothing to do with art or artistic inspiration. Although a few of them, evidently the earlier ones, were meant to serve ritualistic purposes, most of them, however, especially those with very pronounced sexual characteristics, were evidently intended for wealthy customers.[204]

The Nātha Cult: Gorakhanātha and the Eighty-four Siddhas

> [A]t a certain period (probably between the seventh and the eleventh century), a new "revelation" occurred, formulated by masters who no more claimed to be original than their predecessors had done (were they not "identified" with Śiva or with Vajrasattva?), but who had reinterpreted the timeless doctrines to conform to the needs of their day. One of the essential points of this new "revelation" was that it finally completed the synthesis among the elements of Vajrayāna and Śaivist tantrism, magic, alchemy, and Haṭha Yoga. In a way, it was a continuation of the tantric synthesis. But a number of the Nāthas and Siddhas put more emphasis than their predecessors had done upon the value of magic and Yoga as inestimable means for the conquest of freedom and immortality. It was especially this aspect of their message that struck the popular imagination; we still find it echoed today in folklore and the vernacular literatures.[205]

The Nātha cult (also called the Kānphaṭa[206] or Gorakhanātha [Gorakṣanātha] tradition), although enshrouded in mystery, was a Hindu Sahajiyā cult[207] that was "synchronous with the Buddhist Sahajiyā movement (though the origin of the cult may be much earlier)."[208] Many modern scholars believe that the Nātha school, founded by Gorakhanātha, was a later revision of the older Kāpālika Order, as many of the Tantric Practices of the Nātha Siddhas resemble those attributed to the Kāpālikas.[209] The Nātha Siddhas flourished in Bengal from the eighth century onward, and it is believed that Gorakṣa was from eastern India, probably Bengal.[210] Next to nothing is known about Gorakhanātha, the most prominent and deified of the Nāthas, and legends and myths about him abound in western and northern India, from Nepal to Rājputāna, from the Punjab to Bengal, from Sind to the Deccan. Scholars disagree about Gorakhanātha's date: Lorenzen writes that his "commonly accepted" date is *c.* AD 1200 while others date him in the tenth century, and Eliade maintains that he probably lived between the ninth and twelfth centuries. His great accomplishment was to forge a new synthesis among the Pāśupata traditions of Śaivism, Tantrism, and the little understood or studied Siddhas, or self-perfected yogins. "In some respects," writes Eliade, "the

Gorakhnāthīs continue such Śivaist sects as the Pāśupata, Lakulīśa, Kālāmukha, and Kāpālika. But they also practice the rites of 'left-hand' Tantrism, and, in addition to Gorakhnāth, whom they identify with Śiva, they venerate the nine Nāthas and the eighty-four Siddhas. It is in this milieu of the Siddhas and the Nāthas that we must place Gorakhnāth's message"[211] Bhattacharyya emphasizes the link between the Nāthas and archaic subaltern religions:

> Although on the basis of the Tibetan sources it is not difficult to show that the *historical* origin of Nāthism was somehow connected with the later phases of Buddhism, its *real* origin lay more outside Buddhism than inside it, which must be traced to the primitive cults, beliefs, and practices. The Buddhist tone and color were due to the fact that many of the primitive and proletarian elements which characterized Nāthism and other forms of contemporary religious systems were given for a time being shelter and nourishment by Mahāyāna Buddhism. . . .[212]

The doctrine of Nāthism, like Sahajiyā Buddhism and the Kāpālika cult, is constructed around an overarching theme of the bipolar nature of reality. Metaphorically expressed as the twin poles of the Sun and the Moon, the Nātha metaphysics depict the Sun as the symbol of the principle of destruction (*kālāgni*) through the processes of decay and transformation, and the Moon as the principle of immutability. "The final aim of the Nātha Siddhas," according to Dasgupta, "is the attainment of a non-dual state through the attainment of immortality in a perfect or divine body."[213] Haṭhayoga, a potent psycho-chemical yogic science, was the vehicle to an immutable and divine body for both the Nātha Siddhas and the Indian Rasāyana school.

In contrast with the solitary peripatetic asceticism and murderous missions of the Kāpālikas, Kānphaṭā yogins or "Gorakhanāthīs" organized themselves into monastic communities, and are famous for their treatises on Haṭhayoga, including the *Haṭhayoga-pradīpikā*, the *Gheraṇḍa Saṁhitā*, the *Śiva Saṁhitā*, the *Gorakṣa-śataka*, etc. The latter treatise, attributed to Gorakhanātha, has a commentary which explains the derivation of the word *haṭha* (lit., "violence," "violent effort") from *ha* = Sun and *ṭha* = Moon; Yoga is formed by the union of Sun and Moon. This conception is in perfect accord with the Sun-Moon symbolism applied to subtle channels and *nāḍīs* in Buddhist and Hindu Tantrism and Dzogchen. The Haṭhayoga texts contain "easily discernible"[214] Buddhist influences; for example, the *Haṭhayoga-pradīpikā* is articulated with Mādhyamika vocabulary (the term *śūnya*), and the *Śiva Saṁhitā* begins with a potent Buddhist verse (*ekamjñānam nityamādhyantaśūnyam . . .*). This ascetic order initiated "a movement of considerable importance that seems to have been highly popular after the twelfth century of our era and that formed the point of convergence for a large number of religious, magical, and alchemical traditions and practices, most of the Śivaistic, but some of them Buddhist."[215]

Originated by historical figures who later were mythicized as Gorakhanātha, Matsyendranātha (Avalokiteśvara), and other Siddhas, the relatively recent Nātha mythic and folk literature contains the emergence of "extremely archaic contents" of "spiritualities long unknown, and hence unrecorded, by the 'official' cultural circles—that is, by circles more or less dependent upon a *learned tradition,* whether Brāhmanic, Buddhist, Jaina, or 'sectarian'."[216] Their texts were inspired by Tantric and alchemistic saints and masters, but particularly by Siddhas who developed Haṭhayoga as an adjunct of their understanding of liberation as immortality. The folklore and literature of the Nāthas and the Gorakhanāthīs are brimming with the motif of immortality, which "continues and completes that of the *jīvana-mukta,* the 'liberated while living,' express[ing] the nostalgia of the whole Indian soul."[217] The term *siddha* could be applied to all yogins who attained "perfection," but the term derives from *siddhi,* "miraculous power," indicating that they had perfected magical accomplishments.[218]

The philosophical emphasis in both the Kāpālika and Kānphaṭa cults is on *akriyā* (inaction or non-performance of rites), since these teachings are said to be "beyond *dvaita* and *advaita.*" "In a sense," writes Lorenzen, "[such phrases] are rejections of all rational metaphysics. It is not knowledge, but ritual, devotion, and psycho-physical discipline (Yoga) which these schools emphasize."[219]

The literary and religious history of Nāthism, according to Dasgupta, is "intimately connected with that of many other provinces of India as also of the Himalayan regions like Nepal and Tibet."[220] Orissa, one of the great capitals of Vajrayāna previously discussed, was a site that brought together Nātha Siddhas and Tibetan masters:

> Tārānātha's *History,* Abhayadatta's *Lives of the Eight-four Great Siddhas,* and other sources mention Orissa as the home of many great siddhas, includidng Luyi-pa and Darika, who was once an Orissan king. From the tenth century onward, Orissa attracted masters from Tibet seeking to obtain the siddha's knowledge and lineages. Archaeological finds in the Asian Hill range indicate that the Mahāyāna flourished here between the eighth and twelfth centuries, when the intensive practice of Vajrayāna made this area an important place in the transmission of the Tantras.[221]

Assam was the home of two great Nātha Siddhas: the fisherman-poet Mīnanātha, both a Sahajiyā and a Nātha Siddha, who "heard the Dharma while living in the belly of a great fish who had swallowed him alive. After meditating in the fish's belly for twelve years, he attained realization;"[222] and Rāhula, who met his guru in a cemetery and learned "how to draw concepts into the orb of the Moon, then to eclipse them with the Rāhu of non-dual experience (Rāhu is the deity who devours the Moon during an eclipse). After practicing in this way for sixteen years, the old man obtained the *siddhi* of Mahāmudrā."[223] Assam (known as Kāmarūpa in medieval times) and Nepal were greatly influenced by the Tibetan empire-builder Srong-btsan-sgam-po, and may have formed part of the Tibetan empire during his reign. The few Buddhists who lived in Kāmarūpa practiced in secret, according to Tarthang Tulku,[224] yet

Kāmarūpa was recognized as a center of Śākta and Buddhist Tantrism by the brāhmaṇas at a very early time, sometime during the second-half of the first millennium AD.[225] The worship of the Mother-goddess in the form of Kāmākhyā, Kālī, and Durgā defeated Śaivism in Kāmarūpa, where matriarchy, bloody human sacrifice to the Divine Mother, and a cemetery culture related to ancestor worship[226] dominated the land. The Pālas are said to have been "austere followers of the Śakti-cult, and Durgā was one of their principal deities of worship. . . . The connection of the Pālas with places like Gaudha, Magadha, and Bengal proves political as well as cultural contact between [Assam] and those regions."[227]

There is an important link, according to Heine-Geldern, between the skull hunts and the human sacrifices that so dominate the archaic customs of Assam and Burma, and the matriarchal ideology still surviving in Tibet and the Himalayan regions.[228] In India, Śākta-Tantrism, which was centered in Assam—Kāmarūpa and Orissa, carried in its rituals and metaphysics the same archaic cultural elements, with emphasis on the Great Goddess as Creatrix of the universe, human sacrifice, and ritual sexuality. Eliade emphasizes the historico-religious aspect of the "spiritual revalorizaton of prehistoric customs entailing human sacrifices and the cult of skulls."[229] He speculates on this process as follows:

> [1] An archaic ideology, connected with a particular lunar symbolism, implied, among other things, human sacrifice and skull hunting; populations holding these ideas were, during the historical period, settled in zones bordering on Hinduism. [2] On the level of the highest Indian spirituality, the cemetery, corpses, and skeletons were revalorized and incorporated into an ascetico-mystical symbolism; to meditate seated on a corpse, to wear a skull, etc., now represented spiritual exercises that pursued a wholly different order of values from those, let us say, of the head-hunters. [3] When the two ideologies came into contact—whether in the frontier regions (Assam, Himalayas), or in the districts of inner India in which the elements of archaic culture had been best preserved—we witness phenomena of pseudomorphism and devalorization. In this light, we can understand how one or another tantric yoga becomes licentious on a certain cultural level imbued with matriarchal elements; we also understand why a particular Kāpālin forgets the yogic meaning of the "corpse" and the "skeleton" and becomes a head-hunter, thus reverting to cannibal behavior (minus the "philosophy" of cannibalism). . . . Above all, these reciprocal degradations and devalorizations are explained by "symbolic confusionism," by a symbolism being forgotten or inadequately comprehended. We [can] . . . observe the same phenomenon . . . in other cultural contexts and in connection with other symbolism, mythologies, or techniques incorporated into Yoga.[230]

Enshrouded in legend and myth, the origin and history of this yogic cult is open to speculation. Some scholars theorize that it is a crypto-Buddhist cult that later split off from Buddhism and fashioned itself into a Śaivite cult. Others insist that the Nātha cult is in essence Śaivite teachings that were assimilated into esoteric Buddhism, explaining how "we find in it a hotchpotch of esoteric Buddhism and yogic Śaivism."[231] Lorenzen emphasizes the similarity between the Tantric practices of the Kānphaṭa tradition and those of the Kāpālikas.[232]

Dasgupta points out that the Nātha cult is a specific phase of the Siddha cult of India, "a very old religious cult with its main emphasis on a psycho-chemical process of yoga, known as the Kāya-sādhana or the culture of body, with a view to making it perfect and immutable and thereby attaining an immortal spiritual life."[233] The Siddha cult's main objective was to escape death. As Śāstrī explains their doctrine,

> death may either be put off *ad libitum* by a special course of restrengthening and revitalizing the body so as to put it permanently *en rapport* with the world of sense, or be ended definitively by dematerializing and spiritualizing the body, according to prescription, so that it disappears in time in a celestial form from the world of sense, and finds its permanent abode in the transcendental glory of God.[234]

The Siddha school was doctrinally associated with the Indian school of Rasāyana or alchemy,[235] which held that through the use of *rasa* (some chemical substance), the body could be made immutable. The cult of the Nātha Siddhas replaced the *rasa* with "the nectar oozing from the moon situated in the Sahasrāra and the whole chemical process was changed into a psycho-chemical process of Haṭhayoga."[236] The extreme antiquity of the Rasāyana cult is attested to by Patañjali, who, sometime between the second and the sixth centuries AD, had knowledge of their attainment of *siddhi* by the application of herb or medicine (*auṣadhi*).[237] The Nātha Siddhas' theory of the Sun and the Moon, and their principle of gaining immortality by drinking nectar oozing from the Moon are explained in the *Bṛhad Jābālopaniṣad*, second Brāhmaṇa. As Dasgupta concludes:

> What we can be sure of . . . is that the science of Rasāyana was accepted much prior to the advent of Patañjali by a section of yogins for the attainment of the immutability of the body and for the attainment of many other supernatural powers and that escape from death through the perfection of body was regarded by these yogins as the highest achievement in religious life. As this is essentially the position held also by the Nāth Siddhas, the history of the Nāth yogins may be traced back to a period prior to Patañjali.[238]

The notion that the Nātha cult was originally an esoteric Buddhist cult reveals a basic misconception about the nature of the cult, and is disproven by the historicity outlined above. In eastern India, especially in the Himalayan regions of Nepal, Tibet, and Assam, many traditions of the Nātha Siddhas were intermingled not only with those of the Siddhas and Siddhācāryas peculiar to Sahajiyā Buddhism,[239] but also with themes, traditions, and practices of the Kāpālika and Śākta cults. In fact, as Dasgupta emphasizes, a fundamental heterogeneity existed among the various Himalayan yogic cults.[240]

Although the origin and history of the Nāthas and the Buddhist Siddhācāryas are steeped in mystery and confusion, there is a connection of some magnitude between the two cults. Mīnanātha, Matsyendranātha (Avalokiteśvara), Gorakhanātha, Jālandharī, and Cauraṅgīnātha, the most prominent Nāthas, were all listed as Buddhist Siddhācāryas (within the important tradition of the eighty-four Siddhas) who wrote works on esoteric Buddhism that were translated into Tibetan.[241] The name of Gorakhanātha (Gorakṣa) recurs in traditional Kānphaṭa lists of both the eighty-four Siddhas and nine Nāthas. The Nātha yogīs were also Vāmācāras,[242] for whom the Durgāpūjā and the Cakrapūjā were the highest forms of worship of *Ugra*Śakti. As Briggs points out, "Bloody, horrible, and erotic elements are to the front"[243] in these rites. Ward's moral outrage and Victorian self-censorship over the worship prevent him from providing a full description of the ceremony:

> The person who wishes to perform this ceremony must first, in the night, choose a woman as the object of worship. If the person be a *Dakṣiṇacārī* (right-hand practice), he must take his own wife; and if a *Vāmacārī*, the daughter of a dancer, a *kupalee*, a washerman, a barber, a chudalu or of a Musulman or a prostitute; and place her on a seat or mat; and then bring boiled fish, fried peas, rice, spirituous liquors, sweetmeats, flowers and other offerings; which, as well as the female, must be purified by the repeating of incantations. To this succeeds the worship of the guardian deity; and, after this, that of the female, who sits naked. . . . As the object of the worship is a living person, she partakes of the offerings, even of the spirituous liquors; and of the flesh, though it be that of the cow. The refuse is eaten by the persons present, however different their castes; nor must anyone refuse to partake of the offerings. The spirituous liquors must be drunk by measure; and the company while eating must put food into each others mouths. The priest then—in the presence of all—behaves toward the female in a manner which decency forbids to be mentioned; after which the persons present repeat many times the name of some god, performing actions utterly abominable; and here this most diabolical business closes.[244]

Buddhist Siddhācāryas of the Sahajiyā Cult

> But though an offshoot of popular Buddhism, the real origin of the Buddhist Sahajiyā cult is not to be traced exclusively or even mainly in any of the theories and practices of Buddhism proper, either in its Hīnayāna or Mahāyāna aspect. The real origin of the cult lies more outside Buddhism than inside it. The Buddhist Sahajiyā cult, notwithstanding the Buddhistic tone and color which it assumes, is essentially an esoteric yogic cult. Side by side with the commonly known theological speculations and religious practices there has been flowing in India an important religious undercurrent of esoteric yogic practices from a pretty old time; these esoteric practices, when associated with the theological speculations of the Śaivas and the Śāktas, have given rise to Śaiva and Śākta Tantricism; when associated with the Buddhistic speculations, have given rise to the composite religious system of Buddhist Tantricism. . . .[245]

Among the Tantric cults that congregated at Yoginī shrines and other sacred *pīṭhas* were the yogic bards of medieval Śāktism, the Sahajiyā[246] poets.

The songs and *dohās* of Bengali literature in the earliest period, as well as the form and language of the songs and *dohās* of many medieval saints, were inspired by the Buddhist Sahajiyā cult that developed during the reign of the Pāla dynasty when Vajrayāna Buddhism swept Bengal. The authors of the songs were freedom-seeking subalterns, wandering iconoclastic poet-yogins, perhaps descended from the *vrātyas*, who lived in or near Bengal; thus the religious practices and doctrines of the Sahajiyā Buddhists mark the beginning of Bengali language and literature. Their *dohās* also constitute a branch of ancient Assamese literature: "these compositions were done by popular preachers of the Buddhistic religion, the linguistic peculiarities of which connect them with old Assamese linguistic forms," according to Barua. "Certain morphological and phonological peculiarities connected with them . . . have come down in unbroken continuity from early to modern Assamese."[247] The Sahajiyās were famous yogins who were also members of the elite yogic society known as the eighty-four Mahāsiddhas ("Great Adepts"), some of whom first promulgated the Buddhist *Śrīcakrasaṁbara Tantra* and *Heruka Tantra*, while others wrote commentaries preserved in the Tibetan canon. With deft poetic skill, these poets transmitted in religious songs the paradoxical, transmutational, and taboo nature of their religion and practices.

That the Sahajiyās associated with the Kāpālikas and used their symbology in poetic form is clear: Kānhapāda proclaims in a song that he is a Kāpālī: "The yogin Kānha has become a Kāpālī, and has entered into the practices of yoga, and he is sporting in the city of his body in a non-dual form."[248] Two of Kāṇhapāda's poems are sung to the *ḍombī* (washerwoman), a woman of the Ḍoma-caste whom a brāhmaṇa cannot touch due to the defilement of her caste. In typical Sahajiyā paradox, the *ḍombī* reigns as the symbolic equivalent to the goddess Caṇḍālī or Nairātmyā (Emptiness or Essencelessness), the Buddhist counterpart to the Hindu Kula-kuṇḍalinī Śakti. Both Hindu and Buddhist goddesses symbolize an internal form of emptiness (*śūnyatā/ nairātma*) and great bliss residing in the different *cakras* in different stages of yogic practice.[249] Kānhapāda queries the washerwoman: "Of what nature is, O Ḍombī,[250] thy cleverness?—the aristocrats are outside thee and the Kāpālīs are within" (i.e., the arrogant pundits and the orthodox priests can never have any access to the Sahaja-Nairātma, but only the Kāpālī yogins can realize her).[251]

Both Kosambi[252] and Basham[253] have stated that the last tribes to submit to caste station became śūdras or untouchables. Because of her low station, one can assume that the ḍoma-caste was among the last tribal holdouts against the brāhmaṇic civilizing mission, eventually branded as highly polluting untouchables. The *ḍombī* was sought after in part because of her intimate and mysterious connection with the rhythms and fruits of the Earth or Māyā, the female principle that the yogī must conquer in a sacrificial offering in which the womb becomes the altar, in order to become liberated from matter and suffering. The very roots of desire are annihilated in the ecstasy (*samādhi*) of emptiness (*śūnyatā*). In another song, Kānhapāda embraces the life of a naked Kāpālī, wearing a garland of bones, and vows to kill the *ḍombī*, either literally or metaphorically, or perhaps both, in exchange for androcentric power.

> Outside the city, O Ḍombī, is thy cottage; thou goest just touching the Brahmins and the shaven-headed (and never reveal thyself to them). O Ḍombī, I shall keep company with thee and it is for this purpose that I have become a naked Kāpālī without aversions. There is one lotus and sixty-four are the petals,—the dear Ḍombī climbs on it and dances there. Honestly do I ask thee, on whose boat dost thou come and go? The Ḍombī sells the loom and also the flat basket (made of bamboo). For thee have I done away with this drama of life. Thou art the Ḍombī and I am the Kāpālī, for thee have I put on a garland of bones. The Ḍombī destroys the lake and eats up the lotus-stalk. I shall kill thee, Ḍombī, and take thy life.[254]

The Buddhist depiction of the final state of yoga as "the Sahaja state," "Sahaja-samādhi," or "Śūnya-samādhi" is the predominant subject of the idealist epistemology of the Buddhist Tantras and the Sahajiyā Buddhist *dohās* and songs. The yogin or yoginī becomes one with the universe, achieving a state of perfect equilibrium in which illusory, dualistic conceptual knowledge is transcended and the female principle is absorbed: "He himself is the goddess, himself the God, himself the disciple, himself the preceptor; he is at once the meditation, the meditator and the divinity (meditated upon)."[255]

"The invariable goal of these siddhas' *sādhanas* is *mahāmudrā-siddhi*," writes Dowman, which he defines as "the attainment of the ultimate mystical experience of the oneness of all things, the non-dual cognition of ultimate reality, clear light, gnostic awareness—the dissolution of the individuated personality in the universal mind."[256] The Mahāmudrā lineage is similar but not identical to the principle of *advaya* (non-duality), and flows out of a common esoteric Buddhist and Hindu view that absolute reality is composed of pairs of polar opposites—male and female, negative and positive, static and dynamic, rest (*nivṛtti*) and activity (*pravṛtti*), subjectivity and objectivity, the enjoyer and the enjoyed—which lie in union together in a state of absolute non-duality. The evolution of material reality is depicted in nihilistic Sāṅkhya cosmology—adopted by Hindu and Buddhist Tantrism—as a descent from undifferentiated light, the highest reality, through sound and the five elements to the gross physical plane, *māyā*, the great illusion. Dualism is the product of attachment to and desire for the material illusory world, mistakenly viewed as separate from one's own natural mind, which is often personified as the Great Goddess or one's tutelary deity. Inherent in dualism is suffering and bondage. The object of many esoteric Buddhist and Hindu *sādhanas* is final escape or liberation from the bonds of dualism, realized by returning to the primordial state of non-duality.

Tantric and alchemical art and literature are replete with imagery of sexual union that symbolically represents this conception of the reunion of the two polar principles in the aspirant's mind and body. In both Tantrism and alchemy, the nondual androgyne is the final product of the transmutation. As Dasgupta elaborates:

> The principle of conjugal union (*maithuna* or *kāma-kalā* as it is called in the *Kāma-kalā-vilāsa*) of the Śaiva and Śākta Tantras originally refers to the same principle. There also the designations of the male and the female or of the seed and the ovum were used originally to explain the two aspects of the absolute reality, static and dynamic, negative and positive; and their union refers to the unity in the ultimate truth. But though this analogy of the male and the female or of the seed and the ovum has often been declared to be merely a mode of expression, yet in practice it has, more often than not, been taken as real in both the Hindu and the Buddhist Tantras. We have seen that the two cardinal principles of Śūnyatā and Karuṇā or Prajñā and Upāya were transformed in Vajrayāna to the female and the male, and this will explain the representation of the Tantric Buddhist gods and goddesses in a state of union.[257]

The hallmark nihilistic metaphysics of the Buddhist Sahajiyā poets, then, is expressed in its philosophical idealism and the destruction of *māyā*, or illusion, common to Vedānta, Mādhyamika, Yogācāra, and Vijñānavāda Buddhism. Thus we find in the Caryā-songs an admixture of the philosophical views of these schools. Lui-pā, for example, asserts that the mind (*citta*) creates the illusory world: "In the unsteady mind enters Time,"[258] he writes. Dasgupta interprets the verse as a statement that "the disturbed mind is the cause of all our spatio-temporal experiences and the disturbance of the mind is due to the defiling principle of nature (*prakṛtyābhāsa-doṣavaśāt cāñcalyatayā*, etc.)"[259] This cardboard stage of existence is said to be only provisional (*svaṁvṛti-satya*), since its nature is change, impermanence, flux, and insubstantiality:

> [W]hatever came also went away; in this (rotation of) coming and going Kānhu has become convinced (of the unsubstantial nature of the fleeting world).[260]

But all things, in their true nature, are pure:

> Neither existence nor non-existence is impure in the least; all beings, produced in the six ways (*ṣaḍ-gatikā*), are pure by their ultimate nature.[261]

The phenomenal world is a mere artifice created by the mind; it is basket of fantasy costumes[262] to be worn on a theatrical stage, empty of anything real. The stage can be stripped of its power over the actors by the acquisition of "pure knowledge":

> By pure knowledge the mind must first be tranquilized, and when it becomes perfectly controlled, all the forces of the illusory world are subdued.[263]

This pacifying knowledge, the ultimate phase of yoga, causes the *sādhaka* to perceive empirical reality as a waking dream, "though we remain with our outward eyes open."[264] As Sarahapāda expresses this idealistic nihilism:

> O my mind, to drive away the impurities in the dream of ignorance the sayings of the preceptor are around you,—where shalt thou hide thyself and how? Curious indeed is the nature of illusion, through which the self and the not-self are seen; in this water-bubble of the world, the self is void itself in the Sahaja.[265]

The songs of the Sahajiyā poets survive in a Middle Indian dialect known variously as Old Bengali, Old Bihari, Old Mithili, and Old Oriya.[266] These are dated at the twelfth century, but no doubt many go back several centuries earlier; Naropa is one of the only Mahāsiddhas whose dates are known with certainty (AD 956–1040). These advanced yogins are associated with the Nātha and Kāpālika cults, which continued to practice as established religions in eastern India long after the rise and fall of Buddhism in that area.

Vajrayāna Buddhists

Of all the deviant anti-brāhmaṇical dharmas, the most systematized literature documenting the activities of these cults was produced by the Vajrayāna Buddhists, whose ideology is also infused with Kaula, alchemical, and Taoist doctrine. Their prolific translations of Indian Tantras, the unique Tibetan *termas* (hidden treasure texts) and other poetry, dense with enigmatic metaphors, *sandhābhāṣa* (twilight language), and erotic allusions, provide a rich tapestry of evidence of the common practices of all of these related "obscure religious cults." Since we know that these cults shared temples, fierce goddesses, Haṭhayoga, and metaphysics, the Buddhist translations of Indian Tantras can be extrapolated for clues to the elusive practices of the Yoginī and Kāpālika cults, about which there is, understandably, precious little documentation.

According to the Vajrayāna cosmological system, the world is composed of five elements that are deified in the forms of the Dhyāni Buddhas and the five Buddha families. Each Buddha is accompanied by a female consort, and both are ordinarily depicted in their "wrathful" aspects. Although Briggs frequently reveals his obtuse colonialism, shared with other Orientalists and early Buddhist scholars such as Conze, the facts are often delivered unembellished with disgust, to which the following description of the *pañca makāras* attests:

> While early Buddhism enforced unnatural and strict rules of behavior and forbade all kinds of worldly enjoyments, such as wine, women, fish, meat and all kinds of exciting food, the Tantrics embodied all these in their practice in the form of the five *makāras*. The *Srī-samāya* is the cause of all happinesss and divine perfection by *Mahāmudrā* and without her there is no emancipation. For them, . . . nirvāṇa is defined in terms of Śūnya, vijñāna and mahāsukha and the conditions of the Bodhi-mind in nirvāṇa is as in the embrace of a woman. Union with their śaktis is termed by Tantrics, "Yoga." The enjoyment of perfect truth, the *Prajña*, resides in all women, and they should be enjoyed without reservation. The highest class of Yoga-tantra cannot be practiced without the assistance of śaktis. In Vajrayāna art, the most complete form of a god is portrayed (and worshiped) in union with his Śakti.[267]

Briggs defines the teachings of the Buddhist Tantras as "a mixture of mysticism, sorcery, and erotics, accompanied by disgusting orgies" that historically "represent the later age of the degeneration of Buddhism in India. Their only connection with Buddhism," he claims, "is their claim that their tenets were delivered by the Buddha himself."[268] We have seen that *hieros gamos* and sacred regicide or bull sacrifice were offerings to the ancient Great Goddesses to promote the continuity of the female principle and insure the fertility of the crops, and that the beneficiary of the sacrifice was the whole community. As we earlier noted, some of the Upaniṣads contained conceptual antecedents to the Tantric Buddhist female sacrifice. The śramaṇic sacrifice was an androcentric inversion of the original Near Eastern and Dravidian rituals of *hieros gamos* and male sacrifice to the Great Goddess. The *Chāndogya Upaniṣad* describes woman as at once the *yajña* or sacrificial fire and the female sacrificial victim; viz., the wood is her lower portion, the flames are her *yoni*, the carbon is male penetration, and the spark is sexual union.[269] The symbolic correspondences between woman and sacrifice in the *Bṛhadāraṇyaka Upaniṣad*[270] are more intricate, but the pattern is the same: the sacrificial altar (*vedī*) and the woman's lower portion (*upastha*) are still homologized, her pubic hairs (*lomāni*) are the sacrificial grass, her outer skin (*bahirścarman*) is the floor for pressing the *soma* plants (*adhiṣavana*), and the two labia of the vulva (*muṣkau*) comprise the inner fire. The latter text instructs the yogī to rape the woman who refuses to engage in coitus.[271] The Buddhist method follows the Upaniṣadic model: in Vajrayāna texts, the yoginī's vulva (*bhaga*) becomes the altar, and the Tantric master or yogī transforms the woman into a goddess so that he can offer her as a real or symbolic sacrifice. By manipulating sexual relations and employing visualization techniques, the yogī robs the *śakti* of her female energy. The yogī himself, rather than a deity, is the beneficiary of this sacrifice; he becomes the "Grand Master" (*mahā siddha*), the winner of androcentric power via radical methods of sexual magic, culminating in the yogic process of burning away the five elements that define and delimit material existence. His partner's feminine essence, however, has not been lost in its yogic process of fiery dissolution; the Tantric master has co-opted, internalized, and absorbed the female energy through which he is able to restructure his internal *maṇḍala* and attain the glorified nondual state of a hermaphrodite or androgyne.

The Pāla rulers (eighth to twelfth centuries AD) were ardent Buddhists who patronized the Vajrayāna form, which constituted both a potent spiritual force and a vibrant aesthetic injection into the culture of the time. The period is lavishly expressed with Buddhist art and iconography that visually draws on the ancient Great Goddess, instrumentalized as a cipher of nihilistic Buddhist doctrine and androcentric asceticism and salvation. The goddess, Earth Mother Māyā or Prakṛti, became in one sense the object of Buddhist hostility; individual spiritual liberation from her delusory grip became the necessary antecedent to the idealized Tantric state of nondual awareness (the cession of thought) and permanent liberation from the wheel of rebirth. Vajrayāna eclipsed Mahāyāna Buddhism in the Pāla period, a golden age when Buddhist art and metaphysics reached a zenith.[272] The devotees and ritual practices of Vajrayāna Buddhism during Pāla rule were associated with Bhairava-worshiping yoginīs and yogins of Śākta and Śaiva cults (including the Yoginī cult) in the Cauṁsaṭha Yoginī temples, cremation grounds, and remote areas where heterodox exchange and ritual could proceed undisturbed. The commonly used terms in Buddhist Tantras, *ḍāka* (male) and *ḍākinī* (female), refer not only to the fierce entities who followed the spouse of Śiva—Durgā or the Devī—but also to the yogins and yoginīs who follow Śaivite and Śākta-Tantric rites. "To this day," emphasizes Miranda Shaw, "the Tantric Buddhists and Śaivite and Śākta movements share many sacred places in common and use the same term for them (*pīṭha* rather than *tīrtha*). Their meetings provided ample opportunity for mutual influence and borrowing."[273]

Snellgrove[274] deconstructs the various wrathful Tantric Buddhist deities such as Śambara Vajradāka, Heruka, Hevajra, Caṇḍamahāroṣana ("Fierce and Greatly Wrathful") and Cakrasaṁvara[275] as Buddhist adaptations of Bhairava ("The Terrible One"), or Śiva in his destructive aspect or fierce manifestation. As their names announce, the Tantras in which Bhairava or his Buddhist adaptation is Lord originated "amongst groups of yogins . . . whose practices brought them into close relationship with Śaivite communities."[276] According to Snellgrove, we can reasonably deduce that these Buddhist Tantras were composed as compendia of knowledge gained by Buddhists who gathered together with Bhairava- and Cāmuṇḍā-worshiping Śākta-Tantric Yoginīs and Yogins at their sacred retreat sites:

> Between the eighth and the twelfth centuries certain Buddhists began to take a special interest in forms of "violent yoga" (*haṭhayoga*) which were then in vogue in eastern India. Thus they frequented the places of retreat where such practices could be learned. Most of these yogins . . . lived deliberately as "outcastes" from society, rejecting its conventions and norms. However, while they were not "Hindu" in any strict Brahmanical sense, they were inevitably affected by the whole religious environment of their upbringing. . . .
>
> If we seek to know what kind of worship was practiced by these later yogins of eastern India or at least by their less advanced followers, the answer is clearly available in the relevant tantric texts at our disposal. They worshiped a divinity in terrible form, whether male or female, identifiable in Hindu tradition as a fierce form of Śiva or of his spouse the Great Goddess (Devī), using a variety of names, such as were adopted by the Buddhist practitioners who were associated with these groups.[277]

These numerous high-ranking wrathful deities are "essentially the same,"[278] according to Snellgrove, and the particular *cakras* where the cult was established determined the various traditions that developed concerning their names, attributes, feminine partners, and personal entourage. It is clear from the texts that these Tantric *cakras* drew upon and shared similar or identical source materials. As Rawson perceives:

> In one special "Spider's web" cakra the pairs might all be linked by tied lengths of cloth—an element of imagery taken over into art as radiating lines. Some of these cakras were performed for the magical benefit of third parties as for

kings before a battle. Despite the disclaimers of some scholars, such cakrapūjā customs must be the original Indian ritual facts which underlie the whole transformation system represented by the circular maṇḍalas of coupled devatās which appear in the Tantrik Buddhism of Tibet and Nepal. There can be little doubt that the cakrapūjā system is very ancient indeed.[279]

Snellgrove distinguishes between those Tantras composed within monastic compounds, which generally conform to Buddhist Mahāyāna teachings, and those written by the lay followers of Tantric yogins, which contain "many concepts for which there would appear to be no Buddhist sanction whatsoever."[280] He classifies the "Supreme Yoga Tantras" (Ati-Yoga-Tantra or Dzogchen) in the latter group, opining rather insidiously that the notion of "supreme" does not apply to their teachings, which he says are the same as the Yoga Tantras, but dressed in the garb of "the more outspoken and deliberately scandalous language and in the unorthodox terminology, which one might well expect of wandering yogins, who claim to have no allegiance anywhere except to their own revered teacher."[281] (It appears on the face of it that Snellgrove, like the medieval elites and the credo of his own heritage, endorses the brāhmaṇical caste system of India, and holds no quarter for the vagabond or the iconoclastic yogic hero.) These Tantras are set in a completely different milieu from that of the Mahāyāna Sūtras and those other Tantras (mainly *kriyā-caryā* and *yoga-*) that attributed their teachings to a peaceful Śākyamuni in a palace, park, or other pristine, idyllic place. The works are centered on the cult of Heruka and other similar fierce manifestations of Śiva, and the sites are even methodically listed. Although the Ati-Yoga-Tantras revealed the same teachings as the more orthodox Yoga Tantras, they were interpreted symbolically by commentators who propounded the theory of *sandhābhāṣa* or "enigmatic" meanings, thus mystifying the teachings by sublimating the taboo practices into civilized Buddhist symbols. Such abstractions of the material reality of the *cakras* created a respectable façade for the Buddhist Tantras, enabling them to be accepted into the mainstream of the Indian Buddhist tradition. Moreover, once they were accepted, much of their terminology might be used in Tantras composed in a monastic setting.

The *Guhyasamāja Tantra*, for example, first received in Tibet as one of a set of so-called Mahāyoga Tantras, was, when interpreted literally, a subversive tract that caused worry and consternation over two hundred years later. An ordinance of King Ye-shes-'od of Gu-ge (western Tibet), who flourished in the tenth to eleventh centuries (over two centuries after Tantra was introduced to Tibet), harshly castigates the taboo practices of free-roving Tantric yogins who gathered for their feasts and rituals at the sacred *pīṭhas*:

O village specialists, your tantric kind of practice,
If heard of in other lands would be a cause for shame.
You say you are Buddhists, but your conduct
Shows less compassion than an ogre.
You are more greedy for meat than a hawk or a wolf.

You are more subject to lust than a donkey or an ox [in] heat. You are more intent on rotten remains than ants in a tumbledown house.

* * *

To pure divinities you offer faeces and urine, semen and blood.
Alas! With worship such as this you will be reborn in a mire of rotting corpses.

* * *

If practices like yours result in Buddhahood,
Then hunters, fishermen, butchers and prostitutes
Would all surely have gained enlightenment by now.[282]

In medieval India, this extremely licentious ritual behavior of the Tantric yoginīs and yogins was regarded as a sign of their attainment of spiritual perfection. Liberated from all social conventions and taboos, they claimed to have conquered passion by means of the passions, and thus learned the secret of detachment. Eliade promotes the notion that *sandhābhāṣa* is merely a poetic, crypto-erotic technique of mind training, "a secret, dark, ambiguous language in which a state of consciousness is expressed by an erotic term and the vocabulary of mythology or cosmology is charged with Haṭhayogic or sexual meanings."[283] Eliade's definition exemplifies the approach among scholars and many Tantric *gurus* to textual descriptions of ritual indulgence in sociocultural taboos such as extra-caste, extra-marital group sex, Tantric activities involving corpses, murder, and human sacrifice, and the consumption of forbidden food and drink, including human flesh, semen, and blood. These archaic practices have been rationalized by scholars and *gurus* as Tantric ciphers symbolizing such general yogic motifs as the intuitive mind conquering the lower *paśu* emotions; the internal processes of Kuṇḍalinīyoga; Buddhist principles; or training in detachment. As Snellgrove and sweet logic insist, however, such purely symbolic readings of Tantric taboo practices hide the full truth:

> [W]hen modern apologists use the term "symbolic" as though to suggest that the external practices were never taken in any literal sense, they mislead us. Central to tantric practice is the refusal to distinguish between the everyday world (saṁsāra) and the experience of nirvāṇa. The outer practices were certainly performed in the centers where the materials of which such tantras consist were recited and eventually committed to writing. . . . Indeed many of them were so much part of the Indian scene, that their transference to Tibet was possible only in a partial form. . . .[284]

Vajrayāna Buddhism, as Briggs suggests, was less inspired by Buddhist doctrine than by the doctrines and practices of Indian esoteric yogic cults derivative of *vrātyas* and tribal religions. The Indian Sahajiyā Buddhists flourished in the period of the Pālas, their haunting, paradoxical songs functioning as poignant literary vehicles of the tradition. These poetic teachings, some of which glorified the Kāpālikas and cryptically explicated the principles of the Nātha Siddhas, became firmly established as part of Buddhism around the time it was being transmitted to Tibet, lending their idealistic character and lyrical expressions of yogic themes, as well as their dazzling metaphors (e.g., the natural or intuitive mind is "the reflection of the moon in water"), to Vajrayāna and Dzogchen. The interplay of the Sahajiyā Buddhists and the Kāpālika and Nātha cults in the creation of Vajrayāna and Dzogchen probably occurred along the border regions of Zhang Zhung before the eighth century, when the Tibetans assassinated King Ligmincha and took over the frontier land of Zhang Zhung.

During the eighth century, Tibetans began making pilgrimages to India to receive teachings and lineages and to meditate in sacred places known for their spiritual power. The arduous journey through the Himalayas to India, where Tibetan pilgrims were taught by the great Indian masters and received transmission of the Mahāyāna and Vajrayāna lineages, often took at least ten to twenty years to complete. A large percentage of devotees lost their lives, but some survived to record the histories of the lineages they brought back to Tibet, and many of their practices absorbed Kāpālika and Yoginī cult symbolism. The latter accounts are not yet translated, but offer valuable knowledge about the glories of eighth century India and Tibet.

Many important Buddhist establishments were founded during the period, in Bengal as well as in Bihar. Every monastic institution, including the Nālandā *mahāvihāra*, which flourished before the Pālas, became active centers of Tantric Buddhism. The famous *ācāryas* (teachers) of these monasteries are known to have systematized and perfected this complex and esoteric form of Buddhism, along with the rituals. The Vajrayāna became a potent and viable institution of aesthetics and mystery, of yogic literature and initiation, and was exported internationally—frequently at the invitation of kings—to Central, East, and Southeast Asia, by its illustrious missionaries Padmasaṁbhava, Śāntarakṣita, Amoghavajra, Śubhākarasiṁha, Vajrabodhi, and Atīśa.

Five hundred years later, the *Kālacakra Tantra* changed the nature of the Buddha completely. When King Sucandra asked the Buddha in the *Kālacakra Tantra* for the yoga that could liberate human beings from the bonds of Kali-yuga, the Buddha revealed that the human body contained the universe; he pointed to the importance of sexuality, and gave instructions in *prāṇāyāma* (breathing exercises) that would allow humans to control their own circadian rhythms and theoretically elude the physical and mental erosions caused by aging. Thus it was that the Vajrayāna signified for Buddhists "a new revelation of Buddha's doctrine adapted to the much diminished capacities of modern man."[285]

While original Mahāyāna depicted the true teachings of the cause of the universe as issuing from the Tathāgatas, the paradigm of the *Kālacakra Tantra* turns the Buddha into a kind of creator-god. In his simple form, Kālacakra is blue, with two arms; in his right hand is a *vajra* and in his left a bell. Kālacakra is in perpetual sexual union (*yap-yum*) with his consort, who holds in her right hand a cleaver and in her left a skull-cup. She is the fierce goddess of the conquered peoples. (The Kālacakrayāna incorporated scores of fierce goddesses, or *ḍākinīs*, who could be appeased with sacrifices, *mantras*, *maṇḍalas*, and other offerings.) In his fully elaborated forms, intended for the stage of "self-generation" (Skt.: *utpatti-krama*; Tib.: *bdag.bskyed*), or the practitioner's merging with the deity, Kālacakra has four faces (black, red, yellow, and white) with three eyes each and twenty-four arms, he is adorned with many jewel ornaments of symbolic significance, dressed in a tiger skin, and the first of his right black arms embraces his consort, a *vajra* in the hand. In the secret offering (Tib.: *gsang.ba'i.mchod.pa*), a mental offering of three types of *ḍākinīs* or consorts are made to the lāmā-yidam, who enters into sexual union with the *ḍākinīs* and experiences the wisdom of indivisible bliss and emptiness. In another great digression from early Buddhism that stands in sharp relief against the stern austerities of Hīnayāna monks, highly developed monks of Atiyoga schools are allowed by the Buddha to have sexual intercourse with women and to drink alcohol, practices which further their attainment of full enlightenment.

The Muslim warriors, who regarded idols as evil emblems of polytheism and followed the dictates of war given by *Allāh* in the *Qur'ān* by destroying idols, temples, monastic centers such as the Nālandā *mahāvihāra*, and infidels who were not converted or enslaved. After AD 1200, "the traces of Buddhism in upper India are faint and obscure."[286] Conze portrays the transformation of the Buddhas into Lords of the Yogīs or sexual magicians in the *Kālacakra Tantra* as the reason for the extinction of Buddhism:

> In the *Kālacakra Tantra*, and in some Chinese systems, the Buddha acts as a kind of creator. As Lords of the Yogīs, the Buddhas were transformed into magicians, who created the world by means of their creative meditation. All things are their magical creations. Everything that exists, they see in their creative meditation. . . . It had been usual for many centuries, in Yogācāra circles, to describe ultimate reality as the "Womb of the Tathāgatas." It is now from the Womb of the Tathāgatas that the world is said to issue. The elaboration of this cosmogony was the last creative act of Buddhist thought. Once it had reached this stage of development it could do no more than merge into the monotheistic religions around it.[287]

The *Kālacakra Tantra* belongs to the class of Atiyoga (Highest Yoga Tantra), and is said to have been taught originally by Śākyamuni Buddha to the Dharma King of Shambhala, Suchandra. It is based on an apocalyptic vision of the return of the Ati-Buddha, who will thereafter dominate human events, as do Semitic-Iranian messiahs in Abrahamic eschatologies. According to tradition, the lineage was maintained in Shambhala and later transmitted back to India and then to Tibet, where it has been preserved to the present day. Other Atiyoga Tantras are the *Hevajra* and *Vajrayoginī*. In the *Guhyasamāja Tantra* practice, the practitioner actualizes the illusory body apart from the gross body to attain full enlightenment. In the *Kālacakra Tantra*, the practitioners extinguishes the material body and actualizes the body of the deity and his consort. The visualization or actualization process of the generation stage involves moving the subtle energy into the central channel of yogic physiology, where the female principle is dissolved.

Androgeny is the inner goal of alchemy, Taoism, and Tantrism. In Taoism, the male and female can both use sexual intercourse to balance their energies and "immortalize" themselves. Aimed at developing the female spirit "of the valley" or "of the abyss," the Taoist practitioner visualizes his breath as being stored up in his belly and then condensed into a golden drop of concentrated light about three inches below his navel. The drop of light can also be seen as the circulation of light, Sun-and-Moon, or as an embryo that is progressively developed and nourished. The drop of light is made to ascend to the head through equalizing the male Sun-breath and the female Moon-breath, the two spiraling currents or serpents of energy (Skt.: Iḍā/Piṅgalā currents) which are driven by alternately rolling the closed eyes clockwise and then counter-clockwise like windmills.

> All the time the curled tongue is kept pressed up against the palate like an axle. It can also be employed to write the ideogram on the vault of the palate. When this practice is followed by a man during intercourse, the force of female erotic stimuation is brought to bear, as an additional spur to the process, on the drop of light in the abdomen, and it acts like water sprinkled on blazing oil or phosphorus. This peak of bliss and knowledge was attained by the Eight Taoist Immortals.[288]

In the *Vajra* games of love, sexual pleasure becomes a metaphor for emptiness (*śūnyatā*), and the female partner becomes the Yogī's vehicle to nondual androgeny.

> There is a minor void he reaches through self-effacing absorption in his partner, a major void attained by letting himself float upon the waves of pleasure, and finally, the "resonance of pleasure," in which the red and the white seeds of female and male—the subtle sensation or counterpart of the two reproductive fluids—coalesce, and the androgyne or embryo is born. Now the light of the higher world, of *dharmakāya*, appears. The art of prolonging this enlightenment leads to immortality. When the two serpents or contrary flows of energy—sun and moon, semen and blood, the symbols of masculine endeavor or compassion and female void—are balanced, compassion can no longer be a delusion, nor voidness mere apathy: they flow together.[289]

Kāya-sādhana, the specialty of the Nātha Siddhas, consists of processes of Haṭhayoga used to perfect the body, and is considered a necessary tool for the realization of the Sahaja-nature as supreme bliss.[290] The ontological and cosmological foundation of Gorakhanātha's Haṭhayoga is epitomized in the metaphorical content of the Śiva-Śakti union, which finds its counterpart in the ideology of *prajñā* and *upāya* of Tantric Buddhism, in the metaphors of the Sun and Moon in Nāthism and Taoism, in the idiom of "solar" and "lunar" channels in Nyingma Dzogchen, and in the channels known as *nirvāṇa* and *saṁsāra* in Bönpo Dzogchen. The esoteric cults all describe the human body as the microcosm and epitome of the universe, and subsumed within it is a bipolar system that mirrors the cosmic blueprint. The paradigm was probably derived from the bicameral human brain. They saw that, just as the material Yogī himself is created by the evolution of light through the five elements, and as the five elements combine to form his physical body around the central channel or axis mundi, his liberation from the physical and entry into the spiritual realm are accomplished by the devolution of his vital energy back up the axis mundi, purifying or burning through the five elements, finally to merge with the supreme cosmic source, non-dual light—the process of sacrificing and absorbing the female principle. This yogic process involves visualization and breathing techniques.

In the Tibetan Bönpo system, the inner *maṇḍala* is not identical in men and women; on the contrary, the male and female *maṇḍalas* are mirror images, and Bönpo teachings emphasize that females must not visualize the male subtle anatomy. In most Hindu and Buddhist systems, on the other hand, the subtle body is visualized identically by both sexes, and men and women perform the same yogic exercises. The consequences for Yoginīs of unisex visualization of the inner *maṇḍala*, as opposed to distinctly female visualization, has rarely been explored.

In Hindu Tantrism, Śiva and Śakti, or the primordial male and female, symbolize the poles of existence; Śiva, or pure consciousness, resides in the Sahasrāra (the crown *cakra*, or thousand-petalled lotus in the cerebrum region), and Kula-kuṇḍalinī Śakti, pure cosmic energy, rests coiled in the opposite pole, the Mūlādhāra *cakra*, an electric serpent of pure energy lying dormant. The objective of the *sādhana* is to rouse the sleeping Śakti, and cause her to ascend from her genital mire of origin through the *cakras* to the Sahasrāra, where she unites with Śiva in primordial non-dual reality. This union is considered perfection in Tantric yoga, exemplified by Śiva in his androgyne form as Ardhanārīśvara, vertically divided (yet often represented in his ithyphallic state) as half Umā and half Śiva. The female principle is said to exist in the left side of the body, and the male principle in the right, corresponding to the two important nerves in the left and right, the Iḍā and the Piṅgalā, and the two courses of the vital wind, *prāṇa* and *apāna*, which sustain and regulate the bipolarity of the body-mind. The courses of the vital wind in the two nerves are made to flow together through the middle nerve, the Suṣumnā. This schematic of the subtle anatomy constitutes the vital part of Haṭhayoga that can result in the experience of non-duality.

The corresponding Buddhist conception has the feminine fire energy, called Caṇḍālī, Ḍombī, Śavarī, Yoginī, or Sahaja-sundarī, residing in the *nirmāṇakāya*.[291] The Tantric Buddhist scheme, in an exact replica of the Hindu conception of subtle anatomy, refers to the left and right "veins" as *lalanā* and *rasanā*, respectively, corresponding to Wisdom and Means, Sun and Moon, in their separate states, delimiting the condition of *saṁsāra*. The breath or vital force passes up and down these channels with the nature of *rakta* to the left and *śukra* to the right. Thoughts dart about uncontrolled so long as breath is not harnessed to thought. The yogin might concentrate thought on the breathing process by visualizing the vowel series (*Āli*) passing in and out with the breathing to the left, and the consonant series (*Kālī*) passing in and out the right, thus bringing both thought and breath under control. A third vein, the Avadhūtī, runs up the center of the body, punctuated by four lotuses or *cakras* of varying numbers of petals. The objective of such yogic exercise is to bring the vital *prāṇa* to the Avadhūtī. As Kāṇhapāda's song expresses, "One is that lotus, sixty-four are the petals,—the *ḍombī* climbs upon it and dances."[292] Snellgrove explains the process as follows:

> Now the breath to which thought is harnessed is first made to pass regularly up and down the two outer channels, which thereby enact under strict control the process of *saṁsāra*. The breath becomes quiescent and the two psychic streams thus controlled are held and forced, as other escape is denied them, to enter the base of the central channel. At their meeting they arouse the *bodhicitta* which resides there. Their contact, which is the contact of Wisdom and Means, of Sun and Moon, is envisaged as Fire which is Caṇḍālī, and so Caṇḍālī burns. As seed-syllable she is the syllable A, and as a blazing A it may be imagined. She is therefore also Nairātmyā and may be known under any name that signifies the bliss of this union, as Avadhūtī, the name of the central vein itself, or as Ḍombī. She is now envisaged as moving upwards, consuming as she goes, from the navel to the heart and thence to the throat and the head. Then she reaches the *bodhicitta* in the head, the Moon, here envisaged as the syllable HAṀ. This melts at the contact and flows downward through the central vein, pervading the whole body through the various cakras as it goes. It reaches the lowest cakra and A and HAṀ become AHAṀ (= "I," the reintegrated self) in the Joy Innate.[293]

If we analyze the dynamics of this visualization, we may conclude that the practioner is creating a sexual orgasm in the brain. Caṇḍālī is the female fire, visualized as a dalit girl who burns out the five *cakras* through blind desire. When she reaches the brain *cakra*, she dies, and in so doing, she thaws the male sperm (*bodhicitta*, the "spirit of illumination") that rests like the ice cap of Mt. Meru on the Yogī's brain, dripping down into the lower regions burned out by the fire of Caṇḍālī. As the *bodhicitta* climbs the *cakras* (now purified, burned out, and liberated from the female principle), the body is hollowed out of ego and remade as a "diamond body" penetrated by wisdom. When the *bodhicitta* reaches the cranium and pours into the infinite emptiness, the Yogī experiences the extra-genital orgasm of *nirvāṇa*. The *bodhicitta* is said to actually push a hole through the scalp—an analogue of the male ejaculation.

Later Buddhism absorbed so many tribal goddesses and fertility rites that it has been called "nothing but a disguised Tantric cult of the Female Principle."[294] This connection with the supernatural was characterized by human-centered ritual in which deities, properly propitiated in Vāmācāra Tantric Buddhism with *pañca makāra* offerings, magic spells, mystic diagrams, and sexual intercourse, would fulfill the material and spiritual desires of the devotee. The goddess Kuṇḍalinī again appears as Caṇḍālī in the *Hevajra Tantra*:

> The Caṇḍālī burns in the navel and she burns the five Tathāgatas and the goddesses like Locanā and others, and when all is burnt, the moon pours down the syllable *huṁ.*[295]

This Kuṇḍalinī exercise rouses the goddess Caṇḍālī, or Prajñā, through yogic practice in the navel. The five *skandhas* or five elements, represented by the five Tathāgatas, and the goddesses such as Locanā who are paired with the Tathāgatas, are all sacrificed, burned away, purified, and "when all is burnt the moon, which represents the *Bodhicitta*, pours down *huṁ*, which again represents the ultimate knowledge (*vajra-jñāna*)."[296] The *Hevajra-pañjikā* contains as many as four interpretations of this verse. In the first interpretation, *Caṇḍā* (fierce, wrathful) symbolizes Prajñā, since she fiercefully vanquishes all the great and minor afflictions (*kleśopakleśa*), and *Āli* means Vajrasattva; thus *Caṇḍālī* means the union of Prajñā and Vajrasattva. Their union creates the fire of great emotion (*mahā-rāga*), which burns away the five *skandhas* or the five elements, and the *Śaśi* (*samādhi*) occurs as the Vajrasattva adopts the nature of *huṁ*, the Bīja *mantra* of Vajrasattva. Another interpretation depicts *Caṇḍā* as Prajñā, or the left nerve flowing from the left nostril, and *Āli* as Upāya or the right nerve; when they unite through the instruction of the preceptor, their union is called *Caṇḍālī*. All the five *skandhas* and the five elements are burned away through the fire of great emotion (*mahā-rāgāgni*) raging in the middle nerve, the Avadhūtikā. Yet another sectarian explication has *Caṇḍā* as Prajñā, meaning Śūnyatā-knowledge, and *Āli* as the mind full of universal compassion; *Caṇḍālī* is the union of Śūnyatā and Karuṇā, which causes *Śaśi*, an enlightened *samādhi* in which the worlds of the past, present and future are realized to be one.[297]

Wherever the yogic disciplines exist in Hindu and Buddhist Tantras, an internal-external cosmic mapping exists, usually told in the cipher of *sandhabhāṣa*: the human body is a mirror image of the universe. In the *Hevajra Tantra*, for example, the Lord (*Bhagavān*) is asked by a Bodhisattva whether there is any reason for the physical body and the physical world, given the emptiness of all material phenomena. The Lord replies that there is no chance for the realization of great bliss (*mahā-sukha*) without the body. Related to this micro-macrocosmic correspondence is the conception among the Sahajiyās, the Nāthas, and the Hindu and Buddhist Tantrics of sacred geography and sites of holy pilgrimage that exist both in the external world and within the human organism. All three cults categorize these as *pīṭha, upapīṭha, kṣetra, upakṣetra,* and *sandoha.* Such technical yogic terminology is shared by all the deviant yogic schools, Saraha's *dohā*-verses express this micro-macrocosmos equivalency:

> When the mind goes to rest,
> The bonds of the body are destroyed,
> And when the one flavor of the Innate pours forth,

There is neither outcast nor Brahmin.
Here is the sacred Jumna and here the River Ganges,
Here are Prayaga and Benares, here are Sun and Moon.
Here I have visited in my wanderings shrines and such places of pilgrimage,
For I have not seen another shrine blissful like my own body.[298]

In addition to the Vajrayāna sources, both sacred and popular Indian non-Buddhist texts contain limited knowledge of the profane activities of these heterodox cults, including the *Devī-māhātmya* interpolation of the *Mārkaṇḍeya Purāṇa*; the *Kālikā, Matsya,* and *Viṣṇu* Purāṇas; Bāṇabhaṭṭa's *Harṣacarita* and *Kādambarī*; and Bhavabhūti's *Mālatī-Mādhava*. The texts project a picture of the left-hand taboo practices of the deviant dharmas, and reveal a realistic social backdrop for the illicit theatre of medieval Tantrism and the two branches least removed from tribal fertility magic, the Yoginī and Kāpālika cults.

References

1. "The Hebrews," Washington State University, World Civilizations: An Internet Classroom and Anthology, http://www.wsu.edu/~edu/HEBREWS/HEBREWS.HTM (accessed May 12, 2007).
2. Eliade, *A History of Religious Ideas*, vol. 3, 63.
3. "It is an established fact that, when entering Palestine, the Hebrews adopted cult texts from the Canaanites," remarks Haldar. "Is it likely that they only took over the texts without assimilating the cult in general, or at least without being strongly influenced by it? It is true that in the OT there are many utterances opposing Canaanitic religious practices; but this does not exclude the fact that even their opponents were strongly influenced by them." [Alfred Haldar, *The Notion of the Desert in Sumero-Accadian and West-Semitic Religions* (Uppsala, 1950, 69].
4. See, for example, http://www.adath-shalom.ca/ugarit.htm, http://www.adath-shalom.ca/israelite_religion.htm#before (accessed February 8, 2008).
5. 1 Kings 11:33.
6. 2 Kings 21:4, 7.
7. Eliade, *A History of Religious Ideas*, vol. 3, 63. The Elephantine papyri dating from the late sixth century BCE indicate that Anath was one of the two goddesses worshiped at the Temple of Yahweh by the Jews on the island of Elephantine in the Nile. Located at the first Cataract of the Nile, the island provided a natural, easily defensible boundary between Egypt and Nubia, and served as a fortress through much of its history.
8. Alfred Haldar, *The Notion of the Desert*, 68.
9. Ibid., 6.
10. Ibid., 66.
11. *Qur'ān*, 53:19–22.
12. Fredrick M. Denny, *Islam and the Muslim Community* (Prospect Heights, III, 1987), 21.
13. Eliade, *A History of Religious Ideas*, vol. 3, 64.
14. See, for example, Samuel Noah Kramer, ed., *Mythologies of the Ancient World* (New York, 1961); "Hubal," *The Oxford Dictionary of Islam* (Oxford University

Press, 2003), 117; Sam Shamoun, "Did the Meccans Worship Yahweh God?" http://answering-islam.org.uk/Shamoun/ishmael-ball.htm (accessed March 25, 2008).

15. Eliade, *A History of Religious Ideas*, vol. 1, 184.
16. "Hubal," *The Oxford Dictionary of Islam* (Oxford University Press, 2003), 117.
17. See http:// www.livius.org/ba-bd/baetyl/baetyl.html: http://www.bible.ca/islam/islam-meteorite-worship.htm; and http://en.wikipedia.org/wiki/Baetylus (accessed October 12, 2007).
18. Eliade, *A History of Religious Ideas*, vol. 3, 64.
19. Ibid.
20. "Arabian Religions," *Merriam Webster Encyclopaedia of World Religions*, ed. Wendy Doniger (Springfield, 1999): 71.
21. Ibid.
22. Ibid.
23. Denny, *Islam and the Muslim Community*, 23.
24. Eliade, *A History of Religious Ideas*, vol. 3, 79.
25. Ibid., 62–63, n. 2.
26. Ibid., 63.
27. Ibid.
28. 81:1–14.
29. Eliade, *A History of Religious Ideas*, vol. 3, 77.
30. *Qur'ān*, 53:19, 20.
31. Deleted version of *Qur'ān*, 53:19. See Ibn Ishaq, *Sirat Rasul Allah*, trans. A. Guillaume, *The Life of Muhammad* (Karachi, 1998); William Montgomery Watt, *Muhammad at Mecca* (Oxford, 1953), 101–9.
32. *Qur'ān*, 53:21, 22.
33. Ibid., 53:24.
34. See Ibn Ishaq, *Sirat Rasul Allah*, trans. A. Guillaume, *The Life of Muhammad*; William Montgomery Watt, *Muhammad at Mecca*.
35. Eliade, *A History of Religious Ideas*, vol. 3, 80.
36. *Qur'ān*, 48:27.
37. Quoted in Ibn Ishaq, *Sirat Rasul Allah*, 287–88.
38. Ibn Ishaq, *Sirat Rasul Allah*, 565.
39. Eliade, *A History of Religious Ideas*, vol. 3, 77.
40. Ibid., 116, n. 11.
41. Narayan Chandra Bandyopadhyaya. *Development of Hindu Polity and Political Theories* (New Delhi, 1980), 399.
42. Ibid., 399–400.
43. Ibid., 400.
44. Carroll, *Women, Religion, and Development in the Third World* (1983), 32.
45. Ibid., 61–62.
46. Bose, ed., *Faces of the Feminine in Ancient Medieval, and Modern India* (2000), 107–8.
47. Ibid., 108.
48. Altekar, *The Position of Women*, 78.
49. Gatwood, *Devī and Spouse Goddess*, 62–63.
50. Bandyopadhyaya, 40–42.
51. Bhattacharyya, *Ancient Indian Rituals and Their Social Contents* (London, 1975), 135–36.

52. Gatwood, *Devī and the Spouse Goddess*, 59.
53. Dasgupta, *Obscure Religious Cults*, 31.
54. Yeshe Tsogyal, *The Lotus-Born: The Life Story of Padmasambhava* (Boston, 1993), 201.
55. Dasgupta, *Obscure Religious Cults*, 32.
56. For a comprehensive catalogue of Tantrism, see Sanjukta Gupta and Teun Goudriaan, *Hindu Tantric and Śākta Literature* (Wiesbaden, 1981); Sanjukta Gupta, Dirk Jan Hoens, and Teun Goudriaan, *Hindu Tantrism* (Leiden, 1979).
57. Briggs, *Gorakhnāth and Kānphaṭā Yogīs* (1973), 281.
58. This is known as the *Tārā Tantra*, "a secret Tantra belonging to the Yoga Tantra class which prescribes revolting practices. Bhairavī asks Bhairava the nature of the *mantra* by which the Buddha and Vaśiṣṭha obtained *siddhi*." [Ibid., 280.]
59. The *Śaradā-tilaka* is apparently "full of sorcery, both in its beneficent and in its horrible aspects and of the use of *yantra* and *mantra*, the latter in cases of black magic. It exhibits Kuṇḍalī and the *cakras*, and its doctrine, is of the Pāśupata type." [Ibid., 281.]
60. Lists are prepared by Sir John Woodroffe, *Principles of Tantra: The Tantra-tattva of Śrī Yukta Śiva Chandra* (Madras, 1978), lxv–lxvii.
61. John Woodroffe, *Introduction to Tantra Śāstra* (Madras, 1980), 75–76.
62. Arthur Avalon, "Introduction," *Mahānirvāṇa Tantra* (*Tantra of the Great Liberation*) (New York, 1972), lxxxiii. As one of the premiere Orientalists, Avalon (Woodroffe) propagated the common patriarchal elitist view that Tantrism is derivative of brāhmaṇism.
63. Siddhāntācāra is sometimes followed by two additional divisions of *ācāras*: Aghorācāra and Yogācāra. There is disagreement about whether Aghorācāra is a distinct sect. *Aghora* means "one who is liberated from the terrible (*ghora*) *saṁsāra*" and Woodroffe pronounces that "many worshippers for want of instruction by a diksha-guru have degenerated into mere eaters of corpses." [Woodroffe, *Introduction to Tantra Śāstra*, 76, n. 6.]
64. Ibid., 77.
65. Avalon, "Introduction," *Mahānirvāṇa Tantra*, lxxvi.
66. *Bhāgavata P.*, III. 29, 25.
67. Briggs, *Gorakhnāth and Kānphaṭā Yogīs*, 279–80.
68. Avalon, "Introduction," *Mahānirvāṇa Tantra*, lxxvi–lxxxii.
69. Ibid., lxxxii.
70. Ibid.
71. *Viśva-sāra Tantra*, chap. 24, cited by Woodroffe, in *Introduction to Tantra Śāstra*, 81.
72. Woodroffe, *Introduction to Tantra Śāstra*, 81.
73. Bhattacharyya, *Religious Culture of North-Eastern India*, 62.
74. Gatwood, *Devī and the Spouse Goddess*, 62.
75. Dehejia, *Early Stone Temples of Orissa* (New Delhi, 1979), 1.
76. N.K. Sahu, *Buddhism in Orissa* (Cuttack, 1958), 141–55. Sahu presents a comprehensive evaluation of the evidence that Orissa was Uḍḍiyāna.
77. Lakshman Kumar Panda, *Śaivism in Orissa* (Delhi, 1985), 58–59.
78. B. Bhattacharya, *Sādhana Mālā*, 2, Intro., 37, cited by Sahu, in *Buddhism in Orissa*, 143.

79. M.H.P. Sastri, "The Northern Buddhism," *Indian Historical Quarterly* 1[n.d.]: 469, cited by Sahu, in *Buddhism in Orissa,* 143.
80. Sahu, *Buddhism in Orissa* (1958), 141.
81. Dehejia, *Yoginī Cult and Temples,* 1–2.
82. Das, *Tantricism: A Study of the Yoginī Cult* (New Delhi, 1981), 3.
83. Ibid., 1.
84. Nilima Chitgopekar, "The Unfettered Yoginīs," in *Invoking Goddesses: Gender Politics in Indian Religion,* ed. Nilima Chitgopekar (New Delhi, 2002), 97.
85. Ibid., 98.
86. Ibid., 107.
87. Ibid., 101–2.
88. *Agni P.*, II.125.43–45.
89. Ananda K. Coomaraswamy in his *History of Indian and Indonesian Art* (New York, 1985), devotes one paragraph to the Yoginī temples [110].
90. The Yoginī cult and temples are entirely excluded by two specialists in esoteric medieval cults. Shashi Bhusan Dasgupta, *Obscure Religious Cults* (Calcutta, 1962); David N. Lorenzen, *The Kāpālikas and Kālāmukhas: Two Lost Śaivite Sects* (Berkeley, 1972).
91. Arthur Avalon, in his translation of *Kulārṇava Tantra* (Madras, 1965), fails to transliterate or comment on the Yoginīs described in the original Sanskrit.
92. Dehejia, *Yoginī Cult and Temples,* ix.
93. *Lalitā Sahasranāma* (Adyar, 1951), chap. 3, V. 83.
94. *Jñānārṇava* (1912), *paṭala* 13, v. 4: *Yoginīnām bhavedbhakṣya.*
95. Chitgopekar, "The Unfettered Yoginīs," 84.
96. Ibid., 111.
97. Ibid., 84.
98. Frédérique Apffel Marglin, *Wives of the God-King: The Rituals of the Devadasis of Puri* (Delhi, 1985), 237.
99. Chitgopekar, "The Unfettered Yoginīs," 99.
100. Cunningham, Beglar, and Col. Macferson: Bherāghāṭ and Khajurāho in Madhya Pradesh, Ranipur Jharia in Orissa, and Coimbatore in south India.
101. Chitgopekar, "The Unfettered Yoginīs," 111.
102. Dehejia, *Yoginī Cult and Temples,* 78.
103. The first of the Five Ms.
104. Dehejia, *Yoginī Cult and Temples,* 79.
105. Ibid., 186.
106. Das, *Tantricism: A Study,* 3.
107. Ibid.
108. Dehejia, *Yoginī Cult and Temples,* 187.
109. Ibid.
110. Das, *Tantricism: A Study* 27.
111. V. W. Karambelkar, "Matsyendranath and his Yoginī Cult," *IHQ* 31, no. 4 (1955): 366.
112. *Viśvakośa* (Bengali), ed. Nagendranath Basu (Calcutta, 13: 548), cited by Das, in *Tantricism: A Study* 28.
113. Dehejia, *Yoginī Cult and Temples,* 188.
114. 8.32ff.

115. Dehejia, *Yoginī Cult and Temples,* 191.
116. *Kaulajñānanirṇaya and Some Minor Texts of the School of Matsyendranāth* (Calcutta, 1934), *paṭala* 23.
117. Dehejia, *Yoginī Cult and Temples,* 72.
118. Buddhisagara Sharman, ed., *Bṛhatsūcipatram,* vol. 4 (Kathmandu, 1964), 58ff.
119. The Devī temple of Kāmākhyā, built on a hill overlooking the Brahmaputra river, is one of the most significant of the Śākta *pīṭhas,* being the spot where Satī's *yoni* fell according to the familiar myth of Śiva's destruction of Dakṣa's sacrifice.
120. Briggs, *Gorakhnāth and Kānphaṭā Yogīs,* 224–25.
121. Lorenzen, *The Kāpālikas and Kālāmukhas: Two Last Śaivite Sects* (1972), 49.
122. Ibid., 65.
123. S. Beal, trans., *Chinese Accounts of India,* vol. 1 (Calcutta, 1957), 117–18.
124. Ibid.
125. Cited by Lorenzen, in *Kāpālikas and Kālāmukhas,* 24.
126. Ibid.
127. Ibid., 85.
128. Ibid., 85–86.
129. Act 3, v. 13.
130. Ibid.
131. Act 3, v. 12.
132. Eliade, *Shamanism,* 434, n. 29.
133. J.N. Banerjea, *Paurāṇic and Tāntric Religion (Early Phase)* (Calcutta, 1966), 97.
134. Vasudeva S. Agrawala, *Vāmana Purāṇa: A Study* (Varanasi, 1964), ii.
135. Quoted by Lorenzen, in *Kāpālikas and Kālāmukhas,* 95.
136. Ibid.
137. Banerjea, *Paurāṇic or Tāntric Religion,* 97.
138. *Śrībhāṣya,* II.2.35–37, cited by Lorenzen, in *Kāpālikas and Kālāmukhas,* 2.
139. Lorenzen puzzles over whether the phrase *para-mudrā-viśārada*—translated as "proficient in the highest *mudrā*" or "the greatest skill in the use of *mudrās*" refers to the Kāpālikas, use of ritual hand gestures, or to the four stages in the creation of *bodhi-citta* in Buddhist Tantrism (*karma-mudrā, dharma-mudrā, mahā-mudrā,* and *samaya-mudrā*), or to the female partner in Buddhist Tantric ritual, known as a *mudrā.* The *mudrā* is also one of the Five Ms.
140. *Śrībhāṣya,* II.2.35–37, cited by Lorenzen, in *Kāpālikas and Kālāmukhas,* 2.
141. Eliade, *Yoga,* 252.
142. First found in the *Guhyasamāja Tantra,* the passage also occurs in the *Hevajra Tantra,* and is translated by Snellgrove in modest understatement and abstraction as ". . . the Lord dwelt in bliss with the Vajra Yoginī. . . ." [David L. Snellgrove, *The Hevajra Tantra: A Critical Study,* vol. 1 (London, 1959), 47.]
143. L. de la Vallée Poussin, *Bouddhisme Études et matériaux,* 134, cited by Eliade, in *Yoga,* 252.
144. Agehananda Bharati, *The Tantric Tradition* (Garden City, NY, 1970), 182.
145. Lorenzen, in *Kāpālikas and Kālāmukhas,* 75.
146. Ibid., 74.
147. *Viṣṇusmṛti,* trans. J. Jolly, 1.1–6, 15, cited by Lorenzen, in *Kāpālikas and Kālāmukhas,* 74.
148. Lorenzen, in *Kāpālikas and Kālāmukhas,* 75.

149. Paul Muller-Ortega, "Foreword," *The Yoga of Delight, Wonder, and Astonishment: A Translation of the Vijñāna-bhairava*, trans. Jaideva Singh (Albany, NY, 1991), xviii.
150. Lorenzen, in *Kāpālikas and Kālāmukhas*, 4.
151. Ibid.
152. Waddell, *Tibetan Buddhism* (1972), 314. Waddell is referring to the *khaṭvāṅga*, one of the six Kāpālika *upamudrā*.
153. Veronica Ions, *Indian Mythology* (London, 1967), 39.
154. Tenzin Wangyal, *Wonders of the Natural Mind: The Essence of Dzogchen in the Native Bön Tradition of Tibet* (Barrytown, NY, 1993), 8–9.
155. Singh, "Introduction," *The Yoga of Delight, Wonder, and Astonishment*, xxvi.
156. *Vijñāna-bhairava*, V.146; in Singh, "Introduction," 134–35.
157. Ibid., V.147; in ibid., 135.
158. Philip Rawson, *The Art of Tantra* (London, 1978), 112.
159. Eliade, *Yoga*, 296.
160. Ibid.
161. *A-ghora* = "not terrific;" *Aghorapanthī* = "one who follows the cult of Śiva in this form."
162. Eliade, *Yoga*, 296.
163. Ibid.
164. Mircea Eliade, *Shamanism*, 82.
165. Parṇagirī Devī is a goddess worshiped at Pāli, near Ajmer, who is viewed as the tutelary goddess of ascetics. [Eliade, *Yoga*, 297, n. 5].
166. Svoboda, *Aghora: At the Left Hand of God*, 50.
167. Rawson, *The Art of Tantra*, 112.
168. Ibid., 113.
169. Svoboda, text with cover art.
170. Tsogyal, *The Lotus-Born: The Life Story of Padmasambhava* (1993), 240.
171. Dowman, *Sky Dancer*, 30.
172. David L. Snellgrove, ed. and trans., *The Nine Ways of Bon: Excerpts from gZi-brjid* (London, 1967), 267.
173. Lorenzen points out that animal skins are a prescription for the penitent *brāhmahan*: "A few of the law-books specify the clothes the penitent must wear. Āpastamba says that a Bhrūṇahan [a learned Brāhmaṇa] 'shall put on the skin of a dog or of an ass, with the hair turned outside.' Baudhāyana prescribes the hide of an ass alone. For an ordinary *brāhmahan*, Āpastamba requires a plain hempen loincloth reaching from the navel to the knees." (*The Kāpālikas and Kālāmukhas*, 75.)
174. Eliade, *Shamanism*, 434–35; n. 30.
175. Rawson, *The Art of Tantra*, 116.
176. Cited in ibid., 117.
177. Ibid.
178. Ibid.
179. Eliade, *Shamanism*, 434.
180. Ibid., 435.
181. Ibid.
182. Ibid., 131.
183. Ibid.

184. Eliade, *Yoga,* 300.
185. J.N. Banerjea, *Paurāṇic and Tāntric Religion* (*Early Phase*), 97.
186. Krishna Chandra Pāṇigrahi, *Archaeological Remains at Bhubaneswar* (Bombay, 1961), 61, 233–34.
187. 5.2.
188. Eliade, *Yoga,* 252.
189. Dasgupta, *Obscure Religious Cults,* 194–95.
190. Pāṇigrahi, *Archaeological Remains,* 233–34.
191. Das, *Tantricism: A History,* 26.
192. Dehejia, *Looking Again at Indian Art* (New Delhi, 1978), 70.
193. J.N. Banerjea, "The Varahi Temple at Chaurasi," in *Felicitation Volume Presented to Mahamahopadhyaya Dr. V.V. Mirashi* (Nagpur, 1965). Bannerjea points out that six of the eight scenes carved at Chaurasi correspond precisely to six of the stages of the Kaula Chudamani manuscript, which he translates as: [1] *vasikarana* or bringing the Kumari under control; [2] *sanmoha,* enchanting her; [3] *akarsana* and *uccatana,* or attracting and preparing her for the sex act; [4] *yoni-abhiseka,* or consecration of the female organ; [5] *purascarana,* the preliminary stage of the act; [6] *rajpana* or drinking the *raja;* [7] *prastaya* or entering; [8] *nivriti* or return to the normal state. [Cited by Dehejia, *Early Stone Temples of Orissa,* 203n3.]
194. Dehejia, *Early Stone Temples of Orissa,* 71.
195. Cited in ibid., 203n4.
196. Bhattacharyya, *History of Indian Erotic Literature,* 27.
197. Ibid.
198. Ibid., 28.
199. Ibid.
200. Ibid.
201. Ibid., 28–29.
202. Ibid., 24.
203. Ibid., 30.
204. Ibid.
205. Eliade, *Yoga,* 305.
206. The term *kānphaṭa* derives from the cult's initiation ritual practice of splitting the disciples' earlobes to permit the insertion of enormous earrings (*kān* = ear, *phaṭa* = split).
207. Dasgupta, *Obscure Religious Cults,* xxiii.
208. Ibid., xxxvii.
209. Lorenzen, *Kāpālikas and Kālāmukhas,* 35.
210. Tulku, ed., *Holy Places of Buddha,* 402.
211. Eliade, *Yoga,* 303.
212. Bhattacharyya, *Ancient Indian Rituals and Their Social Contents,* 138.
213. Dasgupta, *Obscure Religious Cults,* xxxviii.
214. Eliade, *Yoga,* 229.
215. Ibid., 302.
216. Ibid.
217. Ibid., 303.
218. Ibid.
219. Lorenzen, *Kāpālikas and Kālāmukhas,* 36.

220. Dasgupta, *Obscure Religious Cults,* 191.
221. Tulku, ed., *Holy Places of Buddha,* 407.
222. Ibid., 434.
223. Ibid.
224. Ibid., 433.
225. Hem Barua, *The Red River and the Blue Hill* (Gauhati, Assam, 1962), 47.
226. "Ancestor-worship means that a spirit rules the graveyard of the dead, and this is often manifested into a deity. Kamakhya is a graveyard temple; since it is so, it might be a manifestation of this primitive ritual of ancestor-worship." [Ibid., 191.]
227. Ibid., 195.
228. Robert Heine-Geldern, "Ein Beitrag zur Chronologie des Neolithikums in Sśdostasien," in *Festschrift Publication d'hommage offerte au P.W. Schmidt,* ed. W. Koppers (Vienna, 1928), 809–43.
229. Eliade, *Yoga,* 300.
230. Ibid., 301.
231. Dasgupta, *Obscure Religious Cults,* 192.
232. Lorenzen, *Kāpālikas and Kālāmukhas,* 35.
233. Dasgupta, *Obscure Religious Cults,* 192.
234. V.V. Raman Śāstrī, "The Doctrinal Culture and Tradition of the Siddhas," in *The Cultural Heritage of India* 2: 303–19, cited by Dasgupta, in *Obscure Religious Cults,* 192.
235. For a comprehensive analysis of the alchemical traditions of the Siddhas, see David Gordon White, *The Alchemical Body: Siddha Traditions in Medieval India* (Chicago, 1996).
236. Dasgupta, *Obscure Religious Cults,* 194.
237. *Janmauṣadhi-mantra-tapaḥ-samādhijāḥ siddhayaḥ,* cited by Dasgupta, in *Obscure Religious Cults,* 193.
238. Dasgupta, in ibid., 194.
239. Eliade, *Yoga,* 252.
240. Dasgupta, *Obscure Religious Cults,* 194–95.
241. Ibid., 200.
242. Sir John Woodroffe, *Shakti and Shākta* (New York, 1978), 89.
243. Briggs, *Gorakhnāth and the Kānphaṭa Yogīs,* 171.
244. W. Ward, *View of the History, Literature and Religion of the Hindus,* vol. 1 (1817), 247–48, cited by Briggs, in *Gorakhnāth and the Kānphaṭa Yogīs,* 173.
245. Dasgupta, *Obscure Religious Cults,* xxxiii–xxxiv.
246. *Sahaja,* Skt., lit.: "natural;" according to the wise, truth is what is natural and original, whereas ignorance is what has been constructed by the mind. *Sahaja-avasthā* is the "natural state" or the "natural mind," the state of consciousness that all *sādhanās* are meant to lead to; the intuitive mind in the state of *samādhi.* Also translated as "emptiness," "the innate," "the unconditioned," or "alpha brain waves."
247. Barua, *Red River,* 47.
248. Cited by Dasgupta, in *Obscure Religious Cults,* 90.
249. Ibid.
250. The *ḍombī* is a woman of the ḍoma-caste whom a brāhmaṇa cannot touch due to the defilement of her caste.

251. Song no. 18, cited by Dasgupta, in *Obscure Religious Cults*, 104. Dasgupta interprets the symbology of the lines as follows: "Here, the Ḍombī is the Nairātmā [goddess] and we have already seen that as a Ḍombī . . . [she] cannot be touched by a Brahmin because of her low caste, so also the Nairātmā cannot be realized by the orthodox Brahmin, as she transcends all sense-perception. She, therefore, lives outside the city, i.e., outside the world of senses. In the metaphor of selling the loom and the basket of bamboo there seems to be a pun on some of the words; *tanti* in the vernacular means a loom, but it may also be associated with the Sanskrit word *tantrī* or *tantra*, the thread of mental constructions; the word *cāṁgeḍā* means a basket (made of bamboo), but the commentary explains it as *viṣayābhāsam*, i.e., the defiling principle of objectivity. The lake mentioned . . . is the body and the lotus-stalk is the Bodhicitta; and the Ḍombī, unless she is perfectly purified, spoils both of them. It is for this reason that the Ḍombī should be purified and made steady in order to attain the Bodhicitta." [*Obscure Religious Cults*, 104.] The Ḍombī's creative essence was coveted by male spiritual aspirants, who believed that sexual union with her would transmit knowledge and power to them. This notion that spiritual knowledge is transmitted through various forms of union—e.g., through sexual union, consumption of special human flesh, identification with sacrificial victims—is a common primitive motif.
252. Kosambi, *Ancient India*, 15.
253. Basham, *The Wonder That was India*, 197.
254. Song no. 10, cited by Dasgupta, in *Obscure Religious Cults*, 104.
255. *Akula*, B, 116–18, cited by Dasgupta, in ibid., 196.
256. Keith Dowman, *Masters of Mahamudra* (Albany, 1985), 5–6.
257. Dasgupta, *Obscure Religious Cults*, 30–31.
258. Song no. 1, *Journal of the Department of Letters (JDL)*, Calcutta University, cited by Dasgupta, in *Obscure Religious Cults*, 36.
259. Ibid., 36.
260. Song no. 7, *JDL*, cited by Dasgupta, in *Obscure Religious Cults*, 37.
261. Song no. 9, trans. Dasgupta, in ibid.
262. *Naḍapeḍā*, Skt., *naṭa-peṭikā* = basket for holding costumes for a dramatic performance.
263. Song no. 12, trans. Dasgupta, in *Obscure Religious Cults*, 37.
264. Song no. 13, trans. Dasgupta, in ibid.
265. Song no. 39, *JDL*, vol. 30, cited by Dasgupta, in ibid., 41.
266. See Per Kvaerne, *An Anthology of Buddhist Tantric Songs* (Oslo, 1977), for a more recent comprehensive edition of the songs.
267. Briggs, *Gorakhnāth and the Kānphaṭa Yogīs*, 278–79.
268. Ibid., 279.
269. *Chāndogya Up.*, 5.18.1–12.
270. *Bṛhadāraṇyaka Up.*, 6.4.3.
271. Ibid., 6.4.6–7.
272. Shaw, *Passionate Enlightement*, 33.
273. Ibid., 32.
274. David L. Snellgrove, *Indo-Tibetan Buddhism*, vol. 1 (Boston, 1987), 153.
275. Bhairava, Śambara, and Heruka were names of the fierce aspects of male divinity. The iconography of Cakrasaṁbara, however, includes his left foot treading on the figure of Bhairava, who symbolizes the extremity of *saṁsāra*.

"[T]he origin of [Cakrasaṁbara] must surely be clear. The naked ascetic smeared in ashes with piled-up matted hair, adorned with a lunar crescent, wearing skins of elephant and tiger, garlanded with skulls, holding trident, drum and *khaṭvāṅga*, all these attributes indicate Śiva as lord of yogins. . . ." [Ibid., 154–56.]

276. Ibid., 153.
277. Ibid., 157. [Emphasis added.]
278. Ibid.
279. Rawson, *The Art of Tantra,* 100.
280. Snellgrove, *Indo-Tibetan Buddhism,* vol. 1, 158.
281. Ibid.
282. Samten G. Karmay, "The ordinance of lHaBla-ma Ye-shes-'od," *Tibetan Studies in Honour of Hugh Richardson,* 156–57, re-translated by Snellgrove, *Indo-Tibetan Buddhism,* vol. 1 (Boston, 1987), 187.
283. Eliade, *Yoga,* 249.
284. Snellgrove, *Indo-Tibetan Buddhism,* vol. 1, 160.
285. Eliade, *Patañjali and Yoga,* 179.
286. Vincent A. Smith, *Oxford History of India* (Oxford, 1923), 221.
287. Conze, *Buddhism:, Its Essence and Development,* 191.
288. Elémire Zolla, *The Androgyne: Reconciliation of Male and Female* (New York, 1981), 15.
289. Ibid., 16.
290. Dasgupta, *Obscure Religious Cults,* 197.
291. The Buddhist equivalent of the image of Kuṇḍalinī rising, when not expressed as one of the goddesses (Caṇḍālī, Ḍombī, etc.), is depicted by the conception of *bodhicitta,* which resides in its relative, quiescent condition at the base of the genitals, the nexus of all three channels, known as Sun, and in its absolute, quiescent condition at the top of the head (*brahmarandhra*), where it is known as Moon.
292. Cited by Dasgupta, in *Obscure Religious Cults,* 99.
293. Snellgrove, trans., *The Hevajra Tantra,* vol. 1, 36–37.
294. Bhattacharyya, *History of Indian Erotic Literature,* 8.
295. *Hevajra Tantra,* 4 (B).
296. Dasgupta, *Obscure Religious Cults,* 100.
297. *Hevajra-pañjikā,* MS, 9 (B)-10(B), cited by Dasgupta, in ibid., 100.
298. Saraha's *Dohakośa,* cited by Snellgrove, in *The Hevajra Tantra,* vol. 1, 37.

10

The Medieval Cakrapūjā

THE ELEMENTS OF CAKRAPŪJĀ

The Yogin is from Kollagiri, the Yoginī from Munmuni.
Loudly the drum resounds; love is our business and not dissention.
Meat is eaten there zestfully and liquor is drunk.
Hey there! Worthy are we who are present; the unworthy are kept away.
Fragrant ointment and musk, frankincense and camphor are taken.
Spiced food and special rice are eaten with relish.
We come and go (in the dance) with no thought of pure or impure.
Limbs adorned with bone ornaments and the corpse duly present,
Intercourse occurs at the meeting, where the untouchable is not kept away.[1]

We have observed that the deviant Vāmācāra cults of the medieval period propitiated the fierce goddess by ritual indulgence in socio-cultural taboos such as extra-caste, extra-marital group sex, sociopathic Tantric activities involving corpses, murder, and human sacrifice, and the consumption of forbidden food and drink, including human flesh, semen, blood, and liquor. The secretive, antisocial nature of their doctrine and practices, their elevation of womanhood, and their propitiation of the fierce unmarried Śakti emphasize the insurrectionary, anti-brāhmaṇical content of medieval Vāmācāra Śākta-Tantrism. In the literature of the time, the bloody taboo rites and sexual intercourse of the *cakrapūjās* were depicted in Tantric texts, but interpreted as Tantric ciphers that symbolized basic androcentric Buddhist dogma. In medieval India, the taboo ritual behavior of the Kaula yoginīs and yogins was regarded as a sign of their attainment of spiritual perfection. Liberated from all social conventions, as well as from hope, doubt, and fear, they claimed to have conquered passion by means of the passions, and thus learned the secret of detachment. As Eliade expresses it:

> [F]reedom manifest itself in countless forms, some of them antisocial—a free man no longer takes his stand outside of all ethics and all social forms. The excesses and aberrations echoed in the legends of the Vāmācārīs, the cruelties and crimes of the Kāpālikas and the Aghorīs, are, for Indian feeling, so many proofs of a total freedom conquered from the human condition and outside of society. We must not forget that, for Indian thought, the "normal" human condition is equivalent to bondage, ignorance, and suffering; freedom, knowledge, and bliss are inaccessible so long as this "normality" is not destroyed. And the same premise is the metaphysical justification for all excesses and all aberrations, which are also effective methods of abolishing the human condition.[2]

Sexual intercourse was important in both proto-Tantric ritual as ancient fertility magic and in Tantric worship as a spiritual methodology. The heterodox Śākta cults all agreed that ritual intercourse was "a potent aid to salvation."[3] The Vāmācāra system, as we have earlier recognized, contains many elements of sympathetic magic that correspond with ancient fertility rites. The Tantric ritual of partaking of the *pañca makāras* (the Five Ms) or forbidden elements (meat, fish, wine, parched grain, and sexual intercourse)—the symbols of the fecundity of the Mother-goddess as Earth itself—is carried out literally by the Vāmācāras, while right-hand practice permits mainly symbolic usage of these elements, and allows only spouses to participate. Thus it is clear that a "more central and openly erotic female principle"[4] is involved in the Vāmācāra form. The sacred ritual coitus in Vāmācāra rituals is preferably performed by non-spouses; in many temples, sacred prostitutes were available. The male devotee or yogī sought to merge with Śakti in the form of a low-caste partner or yoginī who was, in early times at least, a resident *devadāsī* of the local Mahādevī temple. As Rawson explains:

> The basic sexual rites are these. For the householding Tantrika the Cakrapūjā served. Cakra means "circle." At this ceremony, drugs derived from hemp were sometimes taken as a sweet, as drink or smoked. Then the five powerful but usually forbidden enjoyments (fish, cooked hog-flesh, wine, cereals, and intercourse interpreted transformationally as the elements of the world) were ritually taken by a circle of couples as a kind of Eucharist presided over by the guru. In Cakrapūjā the participants forget all distinctions of caste and custom. All have to remember constantly that everything is a show of the One Brahman. The great Kaula text, the Kaulāvalīnirṇaya, points out that "all the men become Śivas, all the women Devīs, the hog-flesh becomes Śiva, the wine, Śakti. They take the fivefold Eucharist consecrating the twelve cups of wine with evocations, and unite in sexual intercourse." The bliss they experience is a manifestation in the body of the cosmic Bliss of the Brahman, purifying all those components of the body in which the divine energies dwell.[5]

Medieval *cakrapūjās* occurred within a *maṇḍala* or *yantra* inscribed on the temple floor or ground, and were organized around taboo offerings (the Five Ms) to an incarnation of the fierce Śakti with a great fondness for wine and strong spirits, meat, and human sacrifice. When the Śrīcakra *yantra* is used, male and female worshipers are placed in a circle around the officiating priest as representatives of the Bhairavas and Bhairavīs. The practice known as *coli-mārga* (coli = breast cloth) is the method of pairing the couples by drawing the breast cloths of the women as lots. When the ceremony is performed privately, "the worshipper may take a dancing girl, a prostitute, a female devotee, a washerwoman, or a barber's wife, and seating her before him, go through the various rites and partake with her of the fivefold *makāras.*"[6] They performed the rituals to advance their spiritual training, to gain *siddhis,* to comply with specific requests of royal patrons—boons, battles won, sons conceived for kings—and to thwart obstructions, viz., black magic rites were practiced in which *Ugra* Śakti accepted taboo offerings as her price to destroy enemies. The performers of the ritual were accomplished yogīs and yoginīs who, we might speculate, had many motivations, from self-protection to self-perfection, from gaining *siddhis* to black magic. The sites of Tantric feasts were individual's own houses or in secret spots or pleasant remote places, in mountain-caves, thickets, on seashores, in Mother-goddess temples, in cemeteries, or between the confluence of two rivers. "The remarkable 'black mass' of the tantric sects," writes Basham, "whether in Buddhism or Hinduism, became very popular in Eastern India in the late Medieval period. It is still sometimes practiced, but quite without publicity. . . ."[7]

When gaining control of impure spirits is the object of the ceremony, a corpse is required. "The adept, . . . alone, at midnight, in a cemetery, or a place where bodies are burnt or buried, seats himself upon a corpse, makes the usual offerings, without fear, makes the Bhūtas, the Yoginīs, and other male and female goblins his slaves. This is the *śava-sādhana.*"[8] Meditating while sitting on a corpse is one of the specialities of the Aghorī; the corpse is sometimes revived by *mantra-japa.* In the *Phetkārinī Tantra,* it is stated that "He who does japa many times on a corpse in a cremation ground attains all kinds of success,"[9] and complete instructions are given in the *Kaulāvalinirṇaya* for appropriate *mantras, yantras,* and meditation on corpses.[10] Kālī is intimately related to this practice, and can be seen in innumerable artistic depictions of her oversight of the *śmaśāna.* According to Snellgrove:

> The "spiced food" of the sacrament referred to in the Hevajra Tantra was a concoction of human, cow, elephant, horse, and dog flesh. The "kingly rice" refers to specially selected human flesh, that of a man who has been hanged, a warrior killed in battle or a man of irreproachable conduct who has returned seven times to a good human state.[11]

It is indisputable that these items were sought after and used according to their availability during the age of the *Hevajra Tantra,* which was composed about the middle of the eighth century AD. We are also informed by Kāṇha's commentary that the "special skull" means one of a brāhmaṇa, implying an obvious relation to the Kāpālika cult. The Tantra itself does not mince words:

One should mark out a "seven-timer" with the characteristics recounted in *Hevajra*. In the seventh birth there comes about that perfection which is typical of the "Joy of Cessation." He has a fair-sounding voice, beautiful eyes and a sweet-smelling body of great splendor and he possesses seven shadows. When he sees such a one the yogin should mark him out. By the mere act of eating him, one will gain at that moment the power of an aerial being.[12]

Snellgrove[13] goes on to state emphatically that these words should be taken as literal descriptions of such ritualized gatherings and confirmation of other accounts of their taboo practices. He explains that the code words "Fragrant ointment and musk, frankincense and camphor, spiced food and special rice" mean faeces and urine, blood and semen, a concoction containing five kinds of flesh (spiced food) and finally the special human flesh, as explained above. As Snellgrove perceives it:

Places such as these, whether listed as twenty-four or thirty-two represented in a real sense the whole world for these wandering yogins, and thus they could be arranged symbolically around a maṇḍala in order to express its universality in all directions. Furthermore, since the external world (macrocosm) comes to be identified in Tantric theory with the body of the practicing yogin (microcosm), all these places are identified with "veins" related to the various "lotus-centers" up and down the spinal cord. Despite these "symbolic" interpretations, the actuality of these "sacred sites and places" and other rites performed there links this class of Tantric literature, at least in their origins, with fraternities of yogins who were very well acquainted with them. Moreover, similar fraternities of yogins have continued to exist in India and their practices, found as abhorrent by modern observers, correspond in very many details with those referred to in Buddhist Tantras.[14]

The fierce Tantras indicate that human victims were hunted—"indeed there can be no doubt that the followers of the Great Goddess (Devī or Durgā as she may be known) sought out suitable sacrificial victims, a practice still attested in British days."[15] The Buddhist Chinese pilgrim-scholar Hsüan-tsang barely escaped with his life after being singled out as an acceptable victim for sacrifice to Devī. As he recounts in his travelogue:

The Master of Dharma left the kingdom of Ayodhyā having paid reverence to the sacred traces, and following the course of the River Ganges, proceeded eastward, being on board a vessel with about eighty other fellow passengers. He wished to reach the kingdom of O-ye-mu-khi (Hayamukha). After going about a hundred *li*, both banks of the river were shrouded by the thick foliage of an *aśoka* forest, and amidst these trees on either bank were concealed some ten pirate boats. Then these boats, propelled by oars, all at once burst forth into the midstream. Some of those in the ship, terrified at the sight, cast themselves into the river, whilst the pirates, taking the ship in tow, forced it to the bank. They then ordered the men to take off their clothes, and searched them in quest of jewels and precious stones. *Now these pirates pay worship to the Goddess Durgā and every year during the autumn, they look out for a man of good form and comely features, whom they kill, and offer his flesh and blood in sacrifice to their divinity, to procure good fortune. Seeing that the Master of Dharma was suitable for their purpose, both in respect of his distinguished bearing and his bodily strength and appearance, they exchanged joyful glances and said: "We were letting the season for sacrificing to our goddess pass by, because we could not find a suitable person for it, but now this monk is of noble form and pleasing features—let us kill him as a sacrifice and we shall gain good fortune."*

The Master of Dharma replied, "If this poor and defiled body of mine is indeed suitable for the purpose of the sacrifice you propose, I, in truth, dare not grudge (the offering), but as my intention in coming from a distance was to pay reverence to the image of Bodhi (= Bodhgayā) and the Gṛdhrakūṭa (the Vulture Peak), and to enquire as to the character of the Sacred Books and the Law, and as this purpose has not yet been accomplished, if you, my noble benefactors, kill this body of mine, I fear it will bring you misfortune."[16]

The "pirates," who may have included Kāpālikas, had no interest in his Buddhist logic and began to prepare the sacrificial altar. Hsüan-tsang began meditating upon Maitreya, and became so enraptured by the idyllic Maitreyan paradise that he was unconscious of his surroundings. Suddenly, a violent storm rose up from the four quarters, crashing down trees, whipping up great waves in the river, and creating sand storms. The "pirates" were terrified at such an omen, and so renounced their intention. Awakening from his trance, Hsüan-tsang "accepted their change of heart with compassion and preached to them on the evils of their way of living."[17] Snellgrove reasons that

> we have here a valid account of how a suitable victim might be found. If we are indeed dealing with "pirates," then they might well pass on a portion of such valuable flesh to related groups of yogins, who could use it for their own special purposes. Flesh was certainly required at these festivals, and one reason is given implicitly in the short passage [in the Hevajra Tantra] concerning the "seven-timer." By eating his flesh, one appropriates to oneself his exalted nature.[18]

When yogins and yoginīs assembled for their Tantric feasts, spirituous liquor was as important as flesh in their rituals. The *Saṁvarodaya Tantra* contains recipes for appropriate liquors and explains the regional distinctions among liquors. "Without the drinking of liquor," the Tantra emphasizes, "there can be no worship, just as there can be no burnt offering (*homa*) without butter, no religion without a good *guru*, and no salvation without religion. Without the production of liquor there can be no sacrament, and such is obtained by force of one's own merit thanks to a satisfied guru."[19]

"Union of the Assemblage (lit., web or net) of ḍākinīs of the Glorious Hevajra" (*Śrī-Hevajra-ḍākinī-jāla-saṁvara*) is the complete title of the *Hevajra Tantra*, and its meaning is equivalent to that of the *Cakrasaṁvara*, which can be interpreted as "Union of the Wheel or Circle" of divinities (or ḍākinīs) in the central divinity Heruka/Hevajra. Snellgrove explains the marriage of yogic arts and tribal fertility rites as primarily processes of internal yoga in which the various *cakras* are identified with numerous sets of deities, and for which the sexual union of Ḍaka and Ḍākinī symbolizes the highest integration of the self-perfected yogin. Specific divinities were believed to preside over various sacred *pīṭhas*, where the Five Ms would be performed as the externalization of stages of internal yoga. The importance of the sacred spots, particularly the Yoginī temples, to all the deviant dharmas is emphasized by Snellgrove:

> [A]lthough there is a certain vagueness concerning some of them, such places clearly existed. They are listed with their actual geographical names in Part I, Chapter Seven of the *Hevajra Tantra*, being quite widely dispersed over the Indian subcontinent, although the actual sites may be no longer identifiable. In this respect one may note the existence of certain Yoginī-shrines, the most impressive of which, precisely in the form of a circle, can still be visited near Hirapur, some twelve miles from the town of Bhubaneswar in Orissa. . . . This particular shrine is datable to about the tenth century. . . . Places such as these with their cults of presiding divinities provide the cultural background to much of the teaching in these tantras. In these resorts female partners were available to wandering yogins, who might use secret signs in order to identify suitable Yoginīs.[20]

References

1. *Hevajra Tantra*, vol. 2, IV.6–8.
2. Eliade, *Yoga*, 294–95.
3. Basham, *The Wonder That was India*, 171.
4. Gatwood, *Devī and the Spouse Goddess*, 65.
5. Rawson, *The Art of Tantra*, 98–99.
6. Briggs, *Gorakhnāth and the Kānphaṭa Yogīs*, 174.
7. Basham, *The Wonder That was India*, 336.
8. Briggs, *Gorakhnāth and the Kānphaṭa Yogīs*, 175.
9. Cited by Rawson, in *The Art of Tantra*, 117.
10. Ibid.
11. Snellgrove, *Indo-Tibetan Buddhism*, vol. 1, 161. These terms are Snellgrove's interpretations, which accord with commentaries on fixed meanings assigned to the code of Tantric *sandhābhāṣa*. For the interpretation, see *Hevajra Tantra*, 1.XI.5–9. For further details on the one who returns seven times, see *Hevajra Tantra*, 1.VII.21; XI.9–11.
12. *Hevajra Tantra*, 1.XI.9–11.
13. Snellgrove, *Indo-Tibetan Buddhism*, vol. 1, 169.
14. Ibid., 170.
15. Ibid., 161.
16. Li and Tsung, 86–90. (Emphasis added.)
17. Snellgrove, *Indo-Tibetan Buddhism*, vol. 1, 162.
18. Ibid., 162–63.
19. Shinichi Tsuda, trans., *Saṁvarodaya Tantra* (Tokyo, 1974), 26, 50–52, cited by Snellgrove, in *Indo-Tibetan Buddhism*, vol. 1, 164.
20. Snellgrove, in ibid., vol. 1, 167–68.

11
The Late Medieval Period (AD 1300–1700)

Babur, a descendant of Timur, swept across the Khyber Pass in 1526 and established the Mughal Empire, which flourished for over 200 years and at its peak occupied an area slightly larger than the ancient Maurya Empire. By 1600, most of the Indian subcontinent was ruled by the Mughal dynasty, marking the culmination of three hundred years of gradual encroachment of Turco-Islamic domination. After 1707, the Mughal Empire slumped into a slow decline and was ultimately defeated during the Indian rebellion of 1857.

Nomadic warrior clans from the grasslands and deserts of Central Asia, the Mughals, like the caliphs before them, had no agricultural fields to provide wealth, hence their only sources of income were raiding, conquering, and taxing settled agricultural civilizations (the fertile crescents of the Middle East, India, China, and eastern Europe), looting or taxing trade caravans, and slave-trading. The Mughals were experienced terrorists, masters in the art of warfare, whose favored technique was the army ambush. Like their predecessors, Mughal warriors asserted the primacy of Islam by looting and demolishing the temples and idols of its rival religions, thus eliminating the competition while confiscating their gold. Mughal emperors routinely demolished historical temples, idols, and monasteries that had stood as symbols of Hinduism since the Gupta age. The disjoined Indian states were no match for them; through the process of coercive Islamization, the Muslims consolidated an Islamic political authority and religio-cultural system that imposed severe taxes (*jizya*) on non-Muslims. Because the local populaces despised them, the victorious Islamic conquerors all failed to establish stable dynastic reigns. Rulers were regularly defeated by new invaders, none of whom established kingdoms of any size. Only brāhmaṇas, kāyasthas, the mercantile castes, moneylenders, and shopkeepers, by offering their services and allegiance, prospered in Mughal towns.

For *dalits* and the low-caste majority, persuasive arguments for conversion to Islam would seem to lie in the relative equality of Muslim males and the absence of the enforced poverty of the caste system, However, the Muslims were slave merchants whose social organization was not egalitarian, but hierarchical and clerical-authoritarian. Bhattacharyya emphasizes that the same "inequalities arising out of the hierarchical caste system, class division and social stratification among the Hindus also prevailed among the Muslims."[1] The rate of conversion was very low in both the south and in northern Indian strongholds of Muslim power, while in Bengal, particularly in the inaccessible eastern area, the conversion rate wase very high. It cannot be proven, therefore, the low-caste and outcaste people converted to Islam for the sake of social justice.

Enormous social change occurred in the subcontinent during the Mughal domination over the Hindu majority. With the arrival of Islam, the power in India shifted in favor of the mercantile class at the expense of agriculturists, due not only to the Muslim concessions to traders and their heavy taxation of farmers, but also to the enormous profits of the Muslim slave trade. The high taxes on the peasantry, however, were unsustainable, and caused Mughal power to unravel. Furthermore, the Mughals refused to expend any of their vast treasury reserves on modern education, while in Europe, universities and printed books were advancing science and technology. Although they were partially responsible for India's failure to fend back the rise of European military and cultural power, the Mughals resisted the British during the rebellion of 1857.

Hinduism was able to survive during the Islamic takeover in large part due to the internal conflict among the Muslim rulers themselves. As Bhattacharyya points out:

> Very few of the Muslim rulers could reign in peace, and challenge to their authority came, not from the conquered Hindus, but from men of their own religion, even from their kinsmen. The Muslim powers in India did not belong to the same level of material culture. Alauddin Khalji fought against the Mongols who were also Muslims and did not hesitate to put countless Muslim prisoners to death. The relation between the Muslims who had already settled in India and those who were still outsiders was bitter. The Hindus who were converted into Islam were also looked down upon by other groups. This inner conflict of the Muslim interest in India was one of the causes for the survival of Hinduism under the Muslim rule.[2]

Resistance to Islam was fiercest among the Rajput clans, who had adapted the Turkish method of warfare and now maintained compact units of cavalry sheltered in strong forts to oppose the invaders. The brāhmaṇas adopted *kūrmavṛtti,* the "habit of the tortoise," and withdrew into their shells as their culture deteriorated, the result of the unchallenged Muslim onslaught. Because they lacked power, the brāhmaṇas could not longer prevent the deviant cults and sects centered on Śākta-Tantric ideas from coming to centerstage from the fourteenth century onwards. Bhattacharyya explains:

> Śiva and Śakti formed the basis of the later Yogic schools, the Nātha cult, the Siddhas and other kindred sects. Side by side developed a saint tradition which insisted on the idea of direct communion with a personal God through love (*prema*) and devotion (*bhakti*). The medieval saints like Rāmānanda, Kabīra, Nānak, Nāmadeva, Caitanya, and others believed that the establishment of complete identity with God was possible only through complete surrender of one's own self to the beloved deity of one's heart. They did not believe in a caste system in the existing brāhmaṇical sense. A parallel movement is found in Islam; also in the development of Sufism. Arabic and Persian classical Sufism had already been known in India from about the tenth and eleventh centuries, but by almost the fourteenth, it had been fully absorbed in India and had taken a somewhat different form with a great deal of such local color and meaning as one finds in many a medieval mystic and devotional cult of India.[3]

The ferocity of the Muslim invaders was mirrored in the religious violence of late medieval Śāktism and related yogic cults. In addition to the *Kālikā Purāṇa*, which intricately details the performance of the head-offering to the Goddess Caṇḍikā, described below, two other Śākta Purāṇas were composed in this late period: the *Devī Purāṇa*, which lists the fierce goddesses worshiped at numerous Śākta *pīṭhas* and *tīrthas*, and the *Devī Bhāgavata*, which emphasizes that the Śākta Goddess is Ādyā Śakti, that primordial energy that "resides in Brahmā as the creating principle, in Viṣṇu as the sustaining principle and in Śiva as the destructive principle."[4]

Male Sacrifice to the Fierce Śakti

Śāktas do not sacrifice females either literally or via Tantric cipher, and their sacrifices are intended neither as proving grounds for hermaphrodite divine bodies nor as vehicles of spiritual enlightenment and secular power for male aspirants. As we have earlier observed, male sacrifice, or sacrifice of the male principle, was the basis of the seasonal regicide accompanying archaic *hieros gamos* rituals from Mesopotamia to south India, offered to the Great Goddess of Life and Death for the benefit of the agricultural fields and the entire community. Even vegetarian agriculturalists believe that the soil needs blood, and if it is not given, human lives will be taken. Although human sacrifice or the offering of human flesh is mentioned in the *Ṛgveda*,[5] the *Vājasaneyi Saṁhitā*,[6] the *Śatapatha Brāhmaṇa*[7] (at the time of the Aśvamedha sacrifice), and in the *Mahābhārata*,[8] it is the Purāṇic literature that mirrors historical events in medieval India and contains the greatest number of references to and descriptions of ritual male sacrifices to the fierce Śakti. The *Kālikā Purāṇa*, one of the most significant late medieval Śākta works, intricately details the performance of the male head-offering to the Goddess Caṇḍikā:

> Having placed the victim before the Goddess, the worshipper should adore her by offering flowers, sandal paste, and bark, frequently repeating the Mantra appropriate for sacrifice. Then, facing the North and placing the victim to face the East, he should look backward and repeat this Mantra: "O man, through my good fortune thou hast appeared as a victim; therefore, I salute thee; thou uniform and of the form of a victim. Thou, by gratifying Caṇḍikā, destroyst all evil incidents to the giver. Thou, a victim, who appearest as a sacrifice . . ., best to the giver. Thou hast my salutations. Victims were created by the self-born himself for sacrificial rites. I shall slaughter you today, and slaughter as a sacrifice is no murder." Thus meditating on that human-formed victim, a flower should be thrown on the top of his head with the Mantra: "O sword, thou art the tongue of Caṇḍikā and bestower of the region of the gods. Black and holding the trident, thou art like the last dreadful night of creation; born fierce, of bloody eyes and mouth, wearing a blood-red garland, salutations be to thee." The sword, having thus been consecrated, should be taken up while repeating the Mantra: "Om hum phat," and the excellent victim slaughtered with it. Thereafter, carefully sprinking the blood of the victim, water, rock-salt, honey, aromatics, and flowers, it should be placed before the Goddess, and the skull also, with a lamp burning over it, with this Mantra: "Om, Aim, Hrim, Śrim, Kausiki, thou art gratified with the blood."[9]

The *Kālikā Purāṇa* explains and justifies animal and human male sacrifice as the traditional archaic offering to the goddess:

> By a human sacrifice attended by the rites laid down, Devī . . . remains gratified for a thousand years; and by the sacrifice of three men, one hundred thousand years. By human flesh the goddess Kāmākhyā's consort Bhairava . . . remains pleased three thousand years. Blood consecrated immediately becomes ambrosia and since the head and flesh are gratifying, therefore should the head and flesh be offered at the worship of the goddess. The wise should add the flesh free from hair, among food offerings.[10]

In the realm of animal sacrifices to the Devī, proper oblations include "Birds, tortoises, alligators, fish, nine species of wild animals, buffaloes, bulls, he-goats, icheamoas, wild bears, rhinoceros, antelopes, iguanas, reindeer, lions, tigers, and men, as well blood drawn from the offerer's own body.[11] The sacrificial victim in the external propitiation of the Devī takes on the aspects of at once a savior and a scapegoat, as evidenced by the words of the sacrificer to his victim before execution: "Thou, by gratifying Caṇḍikā, destroyest all evil incidents to the giver. Thou, a victim, who appearest as a sacrifice . . ., hast my salutations."[12] Basham decries this "new type of bloody sacrifice almost certainly adopted from the non-Aryan aboriginals," which became popular in medieval India when the Śākta-Tantric cults were no longer inhibited by brāhmaṇic taboos. While most Vaiṣṇavite sects refrained from blood sacrifice, the ritual practice was adopted by some Śaivites and many devotees of Durgā. As Basham describes it:

> The animals were no longer killed with complicated ritual, but decapitated before the sacred icon, in such a way that some of the blood fell on it. The

> ritual slaughter of animals was justified by the doctrine that the soul of the victim went straight to heaven, but it was not approved by the best minds of the times, and its survivals in Bengal and elsewhere is a matter of shame to most modern Hindus.[13]

Human flesh was a medieval commodity that was purchased for, among other uses, Vāmācāra rites, both Buddhist and Hindu; offerings to the *pretas*, ḍākinīs, vampires, and ghouls that inhabited cremation grounds; and offerings to the *ugra* forms of the Devī. In the *Kathāsaritasāgara*, several tales relate that offering and consuming human flesh confer certain powers on the yoginī or yogī. In one story, witches flying in the air reveal that their magic powers are due to witches' spells made while eating human flesh. In another tale, a woman trades her anklet for some human flesh. The famous Sanskrit poet Bāṇa refers to the sale of human flesh.[14] In popular literature, Bhavabhūti's *Mālatī-Mādhava* depicts Mādhava, the hero, attempting to win the favor of the ghouls of the cemetery by making offerings of human flesh; he comes upon a Cāmuṇḍā temple just as the priest, Aghoraghaṇṭa, and his acolyte, Kapālakuṇḍalā, are about to sacrifice his beloved Mālatī to the Goddess. (Since Śāktas did not sacrifice females to the Goddess, Bhavabhūti's intent was not journalistic, but dramatic and literary). In melodramatic timing, he portrays a heroic rescue by Mādhava. In Kṛṣṇamiśra's *Prabodhacandrodaya*, a Kāpālika says that at the end of their fast, "Mahābhairava should be worshiped with offerings of awe-inspiring human sacrifices from whose severed throats blood flows in torrents."[15] He adds that the worshipers offer Mahābhairava oblations of "human flesh mixed with brains, entrails, and marrow."[16] During Hsüan-tsang's pilgrimage to India during the reign of Harṣavardhana of Sthāṇvīśvara (AD 606–47), he witnessed the aboriginal worship of the wild Śabara tribe of the Vindhya forest whose "one religion is offering human flesh"[17] to Caṇḍikā. Their chief's shoulders were "rough with scars from keen weapons often used to make an offering of blood."[18]

In the past, the Khodas offered victims to Tari Penu, the Earth Mother, to ensure prosperity and good crops, to avert disease and calamity, and to obtain success in war.[19] As we have seen, the Nagas also specialized in human sacrifices. The Bhuyuyas offered sacrifices to Ṭhakurānī Māī, and the Bhumij kidnapped and sacrificed children at the shrine of their goddess Raṅkinī. In the seventeenth century, the great reformer Guru Gobind Singh initiated his mission by sacrificing one of his disciples to Durgā.[20] According to Basham,

> The victims of human sacrifice were . . . often criminals provided by the secular arm, but victims were also obtained by more dubious means. We read of girls being kidnapped to serve as human sacrifices in secret rites, and of a temple of Durgā at which a daily human sacrifice was offered. Voluntary human sacrifice, or religious suicide in various forms, became quite common in the Middle Ages, especially in the Deccan, where numerous inscriptions commemorate the many pious souls who, in fulfillment of vows, or to ensure the success of their king, leapt from pillars and broke their necks, cut their own throats, or drowned themselves in a sacred river.[21]

About 150 persons were immolated by the Koch Bihar King Nara Nārāyaṇa in the sixteenth century. The *Haft Iqlim* states that in Koch Bihar persons called Bhojgis sometimes offered themselves as victims.[22] The same custom was followed in the Jaintai Parganas. Here, the decapitated head was placed before the goddess on a golden plate, the lungs were cooked and eaten by the participating yoginīs and yogīs, and the royal family sampled a bit of rice cooked in the blood. When voluntary victims were unavailable, as Basham has pointed out, people were actually kidnapped.

The cult of self-immolation was popular in south India, where the Chuityas and their successors, the Ahoms, decapitated themselves to make the ultimate head-offering to Devī. Vogel has noted that the sculptural forms of south India reflect the prevalence of this practice.[23] Frazer narrates many tales about the archaic practice of regicide. This custom once existed in Calicut, where the king was obligated by law to cut his throat in public at the end of a twelve-year reign. The rule was modified by the seventeenth century.[24] We find references to this rite in Sanskrit secular literature. Ghoshal cites a number of stories about king Vikramāditya, who strikes through his own neck with his sword to propitiate the fierce Goddess for granting him the desired boon.[25] Kumar mentions a story of Rājputra Vīravara, who cut off his own head as "an offering to the goddess Caṇḍikā for the purpose of saving his royal master from his impending doom."[26] As Kumar concludes:

> We may draw a conclusion . . . that the rite of head-offering was performed mostly for propitiation of the Goddess Durgā, to win some favor for the devotee himself or for others, and in some cases purely in a spirit of supreme sacrifice, but this practice was never given a social sanction.[27]

The practice of offering one's own blood to Kālī has been popular in India since ancient times, and is recommended in the *Kālikā Purāṇa*. As Payne emphasizes, "there is scarcely a respectable house in Bengal, the mistress of which has not at one time or other shed her own blood under the notion of satisfying the Goddess by the operation."[28] The hibiscus flowers offered to Kālī may symbolize this custom.[29] As Kumar details the practice:

> When a husband or son is dangerously ill, a vow is made that on the recovery of the patient the goddess will be propitiated with human blood. The vow is fulfilled either at the next Durgā Pūjā, or at once in some temple of Kālī. The wife or mother, after performing certain ceremonies, draws a few drops of blood from her breast with a nail-cutter, and offers them to the goddess.[30]

Certain forms of this rite are associated with ancient primal beliefs of the mystic power intrinsic in human flesh and blood, the conception at work in the pre-Christian Nagas. As Crooke notes, these beliefs are the base of various charms and black magic.[31] In the *Mārkaṇḍeya Purāṇa*, King Suratha and a merchant Samādhi erected the image of the goddess and propitiated her with various offerings, including those soaked with blood from their own bodies.[32] Being thus propitiated, the goddess appeared before them and granted all their desires.[33] On the other hand, the *Devī Bhāgavata Purāṇa*, although a Śākta work, criticizes and condemns the offering of one's own blood to the goddess.[34] "It is interesting to note," writes Kumar, "that the ritual works of the Śākta sect seek to impose a ban upon observance of the above rite by the brāhmaṇas."[35] (The *Kālikā Purāṇa, Tantrasāra,* and *Gāyatrī Tantra Haratattva Didhiti* forbid a brāhmaṇa to offer blood from his own body to the goddess.)

References

1. Bhattacharyya, *History of the Śākta Religion,* 158.
2. Ibid., 156–57.
3. Ibid., 127.
4. Ibid., 130.
5. *ṚV,* 124.
6. *Vājasaneyi Saṁhitā,* 30.
7. *Ś. Br.,* 13.III.6.5.
8. *Mbh.,* 3.81.33; 13.49.42.
9. *Kālikā P.,* 71.20–38.
10. Ibid., 71.39–46.
11. Ibid., 71.7.48.
12. Ibid.
13. Basham, *The Wonder That was India,* 336.
14. *Harṣacarita,* 92.
15. Act 3, v. 13.
16. Cited by Lorenzen, in *Kāpālikas and Kālāmukhas,* 85.
17. Bāṇabhaṭṭa, *Kādambarī,* trans. C.M. Ridding, 31.
18. Ibid., 28.
19. Kumar, *The Principle of Śakti* (Delhi, 1986), 90.
20. Ibid.
21. Basham, *The Wonder That was India,* 336–37.
22. *ERE,* 6:850.
23. J.P. Vogel, "The Head-offering to the Goddess in Pallava Sculpture," *Bulletin of the School of Oriental and African Studies* 6 (1932): 539–43.
24. Kumar, *The Principle of Śakti,* 91.
25. U.N. Ghoshal, *Studies in Indian History and Culture* (Calcutta, 1955), 483, n. 484.
26. Kumar, *The Principle of Śakti,* 93.
27. Ibid.
28. Ernest A Payne, *The Śaktas: An Introductory and Comparative Study* (New York, 1979), 13.
29. Woodroffe, *Shakti and Shākta,* 115.
30. Kumar, *The Principle of Śakti,* 90–91.
31. William Crooke, *An Introduction to the Popular Religion and Folklore of Northern India,* vol. 2 (Westminster, 1896), 171.
32. *Devī-māhātmya,* 13.9–12.
33. Ibid., 13.14–18.
34. *Devī Bhāgavata P.,* 5.35.28–29; 8.23.10.
35. Kumar, *The Principle of Śakti,* 93.

12

Fierce Goddesses in Modernity

The Birth of Modern Hinduism, the Thrust of European Empire

Official imperial history, both Western and Muslim, as well as song, story, myth, and memory, depict empire as the last frontier of male aggression, a landscape in which women are absent. Generating the quest for empire is "the spoor of the great imperial male, gun in hand, stalking across the sands of time,"[1] a macho archetype that, coupled with warfare, has dominated patriarchal states since the first epics were given written form.

India's civilization has been slowly shaped over the centuries by the Aryan migration, the Muslim conquests, and British colonialism. The era of Muslim invasions that began in the seventh century was temporarily halted by the European invasion of India, which commenced in the late fifteenth century when traders from Europe began to make inroads on the subcontinent. Muslim and British histories chronicle and valorize the predatory actions of the invading elite against the Indian peoples and their land, amounting to epic catalogues of military conquests and hegemony led by warriors, emperors, caliphs, and kings. The thrust of European Empire stimulated the growth of the Industrial Revolution and the dominion of humankind over nature, sanctified by Judeo-Christian scripture proclaiming "Man" to be the pinnacle of creation rather than a strand on the web of life. The imperial project, for both the West and Islam, was to conquer the Earth and the world. The rationale of Western imperialism is the idea of progress. The rationale for Islamic imperialism is the religious obligation of *jihād*, which is demanded of all Muslims by *Allāh*.

Between 1796 and 1818, the British seized Ceylon, South Africa, India, Burma, and Assam, and by the Opium War of 1842, they had colonized Hong Kong, Punjab, Kashmir, Afghanistan, and Singapore. Dutch, Spanish, French, and Portuguese colonies also sprouted in the male endeavor of carving up the Earth into Western empires, while settlers from Europe expanded westward into aboriginal American India territory, destroying or displacing the Native American tribals to create an American Empire that would come to outstrip the British model in size, economic might, and power. Islamic imperialism, by contrast, preceded British hegemony by a millennium and conquered more territory. In the years after Muhammad's death in 632, Islam expanded from Arabia northward to Palestine, Mesopotamia, Syria, Anatolia, Elam, and further west to Egypt, Armenia, and North Africa.[2] After invading Persia, Muslims conquered Sind in AD 712 and Mahmoud Ghauri of Ghazni invaded India in a series of seventeen *jihāds* between AD 1000 and 1027, when India's rich temples and irreplaceable art were plundered and sacked in Taliban-style cultural nullification. (By the mid-nineteenth century, the British supplanted the Muslim rulers in India and the Muslim's temple destruction ceased until after the British departed in 1947.) In AD 710 Islamic forces crossed the Straits of Gibraltar and swept through most of Spain and Portugal. France was invaded and one-third of it was captured. During the seconds wave of *jihāds* in the seventeenth century, the Ottoman Empire's Muslim Turks captured Greece, Yugoslavia, Bulgaria, and parts of Romania and Hungary. By 1683, they had reached the gates of Vienna. However, once again, and against all odds, Western forces were able to repel them. In the mid-nineteenth century, Western countries pressured the Ottoman Empire to stop collecting the *jizyah* tax from Christians and Jews living in the Islamic world.

In India, from the end of the seventeenth century, the British used the East India Company to spur commercial development. Increasingly, however, the government sought to influence the Company's actions, and imposed taxes that contributed substantially to the Exchequer. By the 1850s, indirect rule through the Company was failing. The Rebellion of 1857 led to the direct takeover of Indian rule by the British government. Clearly, the East India Company had been a major stimulus to the Industrial Revolution and the concomitant sociopolitical rise of bourgeois capitalism. As Arundhati Roy stresses, the free market (and "we know how free the free market is")[3] of capitalism was introduced through British colonialism in the late nineteenth century in India. European colonialism superimposed upon the caste system the bourgeois capitalist model. Human exploitation became endemic to the colonial system, in which the inborn characteristics of race, national origin, and gender serve as criteria for discrimination. In Africa, India, and other colonized continents, the exploitive relations and economic devastation of the marginalized landless workers have been recapitulated in contemporary globalism.

For the British and Indian elite women who enjoyed high rank, social position, and the freedom of the empire, life in the jewel in England's imperial crown was picturesque and luxurious. At its pinnacle, elite existence in the empire, as Kipling phrased it, was an enchanted experience "under the shadow of a dream." In the evenings, there were "moonlight revels" under trees festooned with red, white, and blue lights, parties of 500 or 1,000 formally attired people who danced all night on white carpets surrounded by walls of hydrangeas in full bloom. As the Vicereine of India describes the guest quarters on a visit to a maharajah's palace:

> pale blue silk hangings with lovely dressings and bathrooms with every known bath salt and perfume from the Rue de Paix. Next day we visited the fort, carried up in red velvet and gold chairs. . . . I wish you could have seen the Purdah Courtyard, all carved in white marble, like alabaster.[4]

When the British first consolidated their rule over India, they were confronted with the regime of the Muslim elite class, upon which the superstructure of British imperialism would be built. By the middle of the nineteenth century (1858), the British Crown had supplanted the Mughal Empire and achieved political control over virtually all of India. When the British overthrew the Muslim rulers, the Muslims became members of the oppressed majority and joined with other sections of the non-Muslim population in the common cause of fighting for the liberation of their adopted motherland. "It is a well-known sociological fact that in face of outside threat, people forget their internal differences and put up a common front to save the integrity of the larger entity," writes Harish Sharma. "It is this sociology of group dynamics that shaped the politics of the Indian freedom struggle, thus bringing the people of different religions and races under one banner to put up a united front against the colonialists."[5] This principal of the freedom struggle is exemplified in the famous couplet, *Hindu, Muslim, Sikh, 'Īsāī; Bhārata Mātā Sabkī Māī* ("Hindu, Muslim, Sikh, and Christians; all are children of Mother India").

The British promoted the spread of elite education among high-caste Hindus; Hindu elites were receptive to such changes, while the defeated Muslim elites resisted modernization, denying the faithful a British education. Between the Ṛgvedic Age and the Muslim invasions, the secular status of Indian women was depressed, and the Islamic influence was even more repressive. In the latter half of the nineteenth century, however, the dissemination of Western ideas, including practical knowledge of the dynamics of the colonial state, Enlightenment concepts of democracy, equality, freedom, justice, rule of law, and private property rights, as well as the institutionalization of the British education system, opened up new avenues of self-expression for Indian women, and contained the seeds of Indian resistance to colonial rule. British cultural imperialism gave rise to fears among Indian traditionalists of cultural deracination, often justified by the frequent devaluations of cultural modes and practices that seemed improper to British cultural values. Not only were many religious practices and social customs deemed barbaric and immoral but also whole domains of the arts and literature of India shared the blame as enervating if not outright corrupting influences. An example is the proscription against dancing, which was seen entirely as sexual commerce and elicited strong official disapproval. So deep was the impact of Britain's cultural domination that educated Indians felt nothing but embarrassment about the complement of erotic love in the legends of gods and goddesses and the explicit sexuality of temple sculptures. But in the usual irony of history, the cultural domination of the West contained the seeds of resistance to its political domination because Western ideals of democracy and liberty supplanted traditional Indian ideas of social organization and fostered the demand for self-determination that led to the collapse of British power in India in the twentieth century.[6]

Because the Indian indigenous population was so enormous and diverse, the colonial rule through a trading company could not simply dispossess the aboriginals as European settlers had done in North America and the West Indies. Subsequent British rule created an artificially divided India that simply did not incorporate the *ādivāsīs*. The communalist identities established by the colonialists belie the fact that India was comprised of thousands of cultures rather than just two,[7] and they were dynamically tied to the land and Earth Mother rather than to ancient texts and laws. As Vandana Shiva observes:

> The colonial powers . . . reduced India's diversity of cultures and her multiplicity of identities—those that tied together through a primary sense of culture and belonging that stemmed from the common land. . . . Specifically, [Warren] Hastings reduced the India of many cultures to a divided India of only two artificially drafted cultures. He created a legal framework for an apartheid based on false religious identity, one with which India is still burdened.
>
> For laws regarding marriage and inheritance, Hastings wrote, "The laws of the Koran with respect to Mohammedans, and those of the Shaster with respect to the Gentoos [Hindus] shall be invariably adhered to."
>
> These laws helped mutate an Arab geographical term "Hindu" into a fictional religious category "Gentoo." With these identities, the tribals—the Kols, the Bhils, the Hos, the Nagas, the Mizos—had all disappeared. The Sikhs, the Buddhists, the Jains, and the Zoroastrians also disappeared. The British had fought against and displaced the Muslim rulers—and by doing so had recognized the Muslim category—but the rest of Indian diversity was lumped into one unreliable category called Gentoo. . . .[8]

Women, "viewed as both the victims of an ignorant and oppressive society and the perpetuators of ignorance and superstition,"[9] became a primary focus of Indian and British reformers, since female status in Indian society was viewed as pathetically backward. Women's emancipation thus became part of the British civilizing mission.

> Indian social reformers made strenuous efforts throughout the nineteenth century to educate women and bring about legislation to benefit them, while

> the later period of nationalist struggle saw women's co-option into that struggle, though rarely on equal terms with men. Subjected to a multitude of forces, often contradictory, the women of India—not unlike women elsewhere—began to move toward self-perception, self-expression, and self-determination, slowly, indeed, and against tradition. The two world wars, especially the second, not only thrust India into the vortex of global political and economic forces but also brought far-reaching changes to women's lives.[10]

In Bengal, Tamilnadu, and Maharashtra, the nineteenth century was the era of social reform on behalf of women, particularly on issues such as abolition of child marriage, the right of upper-caste widows to remarry, women's education, purdah, the dedication of girls to temples, prostitution, the dowry system, economic bondage, and material slavery of women. This reform movement produced the Indian National Congress. When India gained independence, middle-class women in vast numbers were educated and had professional careers, some in politics: "even at lower levels of privilege, some sense of personal right was percolating into women's consciousness," writes Bose. "In the stereotype of the Indian woman as a submissive, homebound, mindless object of pity, women of midtwentieth century India could see no reflection of themselves."[11]

Although Mohandas Gandhi, Vallabhbhai Patel, and Jawaharlal Nehru led nonviolent resistance against British colonialism, the independence awarded to India in 1947 was not caused so much by the freedom movement as it was by the devastating effects of World War II, which forced the British government to dismantle its colonial empire, return home, and rebuild. In both World Wars, Indian armed forces in the British army played an essential and vital role. The Indian subcontinent was partitioned in 1947 into the Secular Democratic Republic of India and the smaller Islamic Republic of Pakistan.

Independent India's constitution provides for gender equality, gender justice, and the empowerment of women, but when British forces departed, Islamist organizations grew, ideologically pitted against the pagan Hindus. The consequential political use of religion in post-independence India has resulted in factionalism and religious fundamentalism that have overshadowed social reform on behalf of women. Archaic religious laws governing the delineation of women's lives—marriage, divorce, adoption, and inheritance—have been reasserted in the name of religion.[12] Hence movements for social change on behalf of women that might have become protest movements promoting change have been repeatedly nullified by their absorption into Hinduism, functioning as sects rather than as breakaway movements.

Ādivāsīs under British Colonialism

> You want us to preserve what we want them to forget. To you these may be just art forms, to us they are a symbol of their orgies and bouts of animals sacrifices and drinking.[13]

When the East India Company came to India, the physical isolation of tribals ended; railways, roads, and communication facilities were constructed through the hills and forests to facilitate imperial designs on Indian natural resources. "Law and order" was extended to the forest abodes of the *ādivāsīs*, opening the floodgates to dishonest traders and moneylenders intent upon exploiting and profiting from the tribal people. As a result, tribals lost their land and their economic independence to high-caste Indians, who invaded the sparsely populated aboriginal regions of central and south India and claimed tribal land. Indian settlers followed a common human pattern of tribal land confiscation by the powerful, backed up by military force. In order to survive without their land, some tribals worked as bonded laborers, but most became unskilled labor in mines and factories, or domestic servants. The erstwhile tribals had no recourse but to take out loans, which contractually bound them to exploitive moneylenders in a system of perpetual debt. During the British occupation, the tribals were controlled by the colonial system, supported by its own laws of armed force, in collaboration with the local elites. The guiding principle was profit; increasing colonial revenue was the justification for economic exploitation of India's natural resources and the consolidation of British political power over the *ādivāsī* population. All the insults to tribal peoples—dispossession of ancestral land, deforestation, socioeconomic oppression, tax and rent increases, violation of forest rights, forced labor and labor in payments of debts, and the establishment of outsiders in tribal land—resulted in tribal revolts, armed struggles, insurgencies, and guerilla warfare against local exploiters, the colonial administration, and, in recent decades, against the forces of globalism.

When Euro-North American ethnographers arrived in India, very few were interested in tribal culture,[14] and their work was culture-bound, reflecting their bourgeois colonial Christian point of view, their urge to proselytize and reform, and their dark fears of tribal religions. The anthropological pattern was established when Western ethnographers descended on the Native American populations. The white colonial gaze of European scholars, a biased and culture-bound pattern of studying, interpreting, and passing judgment on native peoples from the perspective of European norms, was initiated in America and replicated in South Asia, where it was brought to bear on fierce Indic goddesses. The story of the tragic survival of American Indians, their marginalization and pauperization, and the endurance for thousands of years of their goddess, Mother Earth,[15] is a historical pattern that shares many common threads with the aboriginal tribals and dalits of India. In both America and India, ethnographers and Christian missionaries flocked to the field, uninvited, following European colonization. Ironically, Native Americans, Dravidians, and autochthonous Indians possessed rich cultures that were in many aspects more advanced than those of the conquering Aryans and Europeans. As Jerry Mander articulates,

> There are still over one and a half million Indians in the US today. Significant numbers of these live in the wilderness and desert regions and the far north in Alaska, often practicing the same subsistence practices on the same lands where their ancestors lived for millennia. Contrary to popular assumptions, most of these Indians are not eager to become Americans, despite the economic, cultural, and legal pressures to do so.[16]

Europeans who first translated and interpreted indigenous texts composed by male brāhmaṇic elites, as well as nineteenth century Euro-North American male anthropologists, produced distorted picture of the religions of the Indian dispossessed majority. Just as the stereotypical ethnographic portrait of Plains Indian women was that of an impoverished European domestic servant ("an Irish housemaid of the late Victorian era clothed in a buckskin dress"),[17] the ethnographic essence of Indic aboriginal religion was tribal blood sacrifices to black, naked, leaf-clad Kālī, who kidnapped children, demanded liquor, orgies, bull sacrifice, and human heads, and sent her Thugs on murderous decapitation missions among British colonials. In recordings and hermeneutics, male indigenous elites and Indologists have attempted to enhance their own power and orthodoxy by emphasizing the primarily destructive elements of fierce goddesses and their low-caste worshipers. We must therefore question the truth-value of some of the claims of nineteenth and early twentieth century ethnographers, while recognizing that we encounter the fierce goddess complex in a wide variety of sources.

Although indigenous shamans were the traditional health care providers for Indian *ādivāsīs*, the British occupation was responsible for the infiltration of Christian missionaries, and later Indian nationalists, into tribal healing rituals. The *ādivāsīs*, the most impoverished people in India, were systematically repressed not only by the British, who sought revenue from the forests, the defied center of the tribal non-monetary economy, but also by landlords, usurers, and liquor dealers. David Hardiman studied a movement of self-assertion by tribal people against Parsi[18] liquor dealers who, empowered by a monopoly right of supply granted by the British, enriched themselves at the *ādivāsīs*' expense. This movement began in November 1922, when a new local goddess, Salabai, appeared before about 2,000 *ādivāsīs* in a field near Khanpur, on the eastern borders of the Surat district of Bombay. Gandhian social reformers, intent on establishing puritanical taboos against liquor and promoting spinning as a spiritual practice, influenced Salabai's message, communicated through the favored tribal mode of spirit mediums who sat under a *mandva* (a wooden frame covered with leaves), facing the crowd. Once possessed by the Devī, the spirit-mediums commanded the people to give up liquor and boycott the dealers:

> Stop drinking liquor and toddy,
> Stop eating meat and fish,
> Live a clean and simple life.
> Men should take a bath thrice a day,
> Have nothing to do with Parsis.[19]

Salabai, who acted as a Gandhian agent of reform, preached against alcohol and meat, told villagers to follow Gandhi, to spin on the *charkha*, to send their children to Hindu nationalist schools, and to continue to work the fields for their exploitative landlords. The spirit possession séances and commands of the Devī became popular cult happenings attended by vast crowds of *ādivāsīs*. In some areas, Salabai actively campaigned for Gandhi, instructing her devotees to stop practicing witchcraft and to give their allegiance to Gandhi. "It was believed that those who failed to obey her would suffer misfortune at the least and perhaps become mad or die."[20] By December of that year, the movement had spread into Surat district, all of Valod taluka, Bardoli, and Mandvi talukas. No tribal village escaped Salabai's influence; she commanded the *ādivāsīs* to take vows in the name of Gandhi, to wear *khadi* [hand-spun and hand-woven] clothing, and to send their children to nationalist schools. "Rumors were heard that spiders were writing Gandhi's name in cobwebs," writes Hardiman. "It was said that Gandhi had fled from jail and could be seen sitting in a well side-by-side with Salabai, spinning his *charkha*."[21]

Periods of nationalist hypermilitancy were linked with powerful peasant self-assertion movements during 1905–7 and 1921–23. When the Gandhi forces assaulted the state's authority, "the peasantry came to believe that the world was about to change in radical ways and that the moment had arrived to throw off their shackles."[22] The spirit of the Non-Cooperation movement of 1920–22 was replicated by the peasants' own challenge to the status quo. Their grievance was against the Parsi landlords and liquor vendors to whom (as we have seen) the British had granted a monopolistic right of supply, resulting in an accumulation of wealth by the Parsis—a clear exploitation of the tribals' vulnerabilities.

The *ādivāsīs* believed that Gandhi had generated the goddess Salabai as a vehicle for his message to be carried to remote villages. When the Devī was properly propitiated, Gandhi became the savior of the *ādivāsīs* who would somehow intervene and liberate the tribal groups, insuring their future prosperity. "At that stage of the movement the *ādivāsīs* were content to reform their lives in a merely passive manner and hope that the better life would follow automatically."[23] In tribal religion,

> grievances can be redressed only through the intervention of a benevolent superior power. The belief is not of course unrealistic, and it can cut both ways, for while in some cases it may dampen subaltern initiatives in other cases it may encourage protests: once it is perceived that there is a champion the oppressed may find the strength to rebel. This they may do even when the supposed champion is no more than a figment of the imagination.[24]

Possession cults are usually regarded by elites as vehicles for the underclass to blow off steam, "a safety valve through which the subversive emotions of the lower classes can be worked off with least disruption to society," but the rulers watch over the possession activities nervously, lest they "show any tendency to drift into politics."[25] When large crowds of peasants began to gather in the Mandvas, the subordinate officials become wary and suspicious of potential revolutionary activity. Officials had always looked upon the *ādivāsīs* as "a debased and docile people whom they could exploit with little trouble and no qualms,"[26] but when the self-assertion of the Devī movement foreclosed on the officials' income of bribes, free labor, services, and goods, the subordinate officials attempted to thwart the movement.

In 1922, higher officials were concerned primarily that the Devī movement was a nationalist invention, but on a visit to investigate the *ādivāsī* areas, the Collector, Macmillan, concluded that the Devī movement was religious rather than political, and spontaneous rather than Gandhi-instigated, and therefore benign. The local officials were instructed to allow the movement to progress and grow from village to village unhindered. The Gandhians attempted to transform the Devī movement by assuming roles of prominence at *ādivāsī* meetings and then by promoting *ātmaśuddhi* (self-purification) of the *ādivāsīs* so that they could rise to the high standard of "citizens" of post-British liberated India. There was an implicit guarantee that by assuming puritan values alone they would begin to ascend socially. When the *ādivāsīs* boycotted the Parsis, the Gandhians, bent on reinforcing a work ethic, told them they were wrong to refuse to work the fields, but they should not have to serve in liquor shops or tap toddy trees. Gandhi's wife Kasturba told them to go back to work in the fields, but the complete boycott continued, humiliating and nearly ruining the Parsis.

By mid-1923, the *ādivāsī* meetings were medleys of the voices of the Devī via her mediums, the Gandhians, and the social reformers. *Ādivāsīs* were warned that if they did not keep their vows of abstinence from meat and alcohol, they were disloyal to both Gandhi and the Devī. They were instructed that it was their duty to learn to spin and weave, which they believed to be a mystical kind of ritual that "would hasten both national independence and their own emanicipation."[27] The *charkhā* took an a numinous symbolic presence; not only had people earlier had visions of Gandhi in a well, spinning on a *charkhā*, but the *charkhā* was also a fabulous mystical weapon (*sudarśana-cakra*) used by Kṛṣṇa to destory enemies in the Mahābhārata war. The symbolic value of the *charkhā*, therefore, "far outstripped the rather limited material gains villagers could be expected to derive from a revival of archaic crafts."[28]

By mid-1924, a counter-movement to the puritanical Devī movement sprang up as *ādivāsīs* began to eat meat and drink alcohol again. When it was clear that reversion to their traditional cultural expressions of feasting and drinking was not immediately punished by Devī or Gandhi, within a year the whole population of many areas was once again eating meat and drinking alcohol. The Parsis encouraged them, of course, giving away free toddy and proclaiming the Devī a false and unreasonable goddess. During a few meetings, Devī mediums would become possessed by the Devī, "the command this time being that they could once more eat more and fish and drink *dārū* [distilled country liquor] and toddy."[29] The counter-movement was named Sarjela, from *sarjan*, "primordial creation," signifying that Sarjelas consumed what the gods created in nature, including goats, chickens, fish, toddy, and *dārū*. The puritanical reformers, called Varjelas (from *varjan*, "giving up"), were boycotted by the Sarjelas, and the fierce rivalry between the groups ended more than once in violence.

The paternalistic and condescending attitude of the Gandhians is reflected in the remarks of the leading Gandhian of the Vedchhi ashram, Jugatram Dave, when someone suggested that "tribal artifacts" should be preserved: "you want us to preserve what we want them to forget. To you these may be just art forms, to us they are a symbol of their orgies and bouts of animal sacrifices and drinking."[30] The Gandhians seemed bent on destroying native culture and replacing it with puritanical notions of self-purification and self-denial. Like Christian missionaries, the Gandhians disapproved of *ādivāsī* dances because males and females had excessively close physical contact, particularly when their arms encircled their partner's waist, and alcohol was consumed at dances. The payscales of Gandhian ashram workers also reflected a caste-based power disparity: "In 1924 the Brahman Chunnilal Mehta was paid Rs 50 a month out of Gandhian funds for his *khādī* activities, whereas the three *ādivāsīs* who worked with him were given only Rs 5 per month," according to Hardiman. "When pay-scales were revised in later years these differences were maintained."[31] By the mid-1930s, most tribals returned to their old values and the restrictions of the Gandhians were ignored. However, the Devī movement spawned a new confidence in the *ādivāsīs*, and they no longer feared and retreated from the British or the Parsis.

The tribal population has remained indifferent to the patriotic spirit of Mother India. Due to socioeconomic exigencies, certain castes, communities, or tribal groups in India slowly drifted into illegal activities, and the British Government labeled them as "criminals" as early as 1871, when they passed the criminal tribes act, which severely restricted the activities of some *ādivāsīs*, castes, and even a section of the Muslim population. While Gandhi theoretically opposed untouchability and allowed dalits to become educated in areas outside their scavenger vocation, they were forbidden to use their education as a means of social advance, and Gandhi required them to continue scavenging for a living. As G.B. Singh observes,

> It is true that Gandhism is prepared to remove the old ban placed by the Hindu *Shastras* on the right of the Untouchables to education and permit them to acquire knowledge and learning. Under Gandhism, the Untouchables may study law, they may study medicine, and they may study engineering or anything else they may fancy. So far so good. But will the Untouchables be free to make use of their knowledge and learning? Will they have the right to choose their profession? Can they adopt the career of lawyer, doctor or engineer? To these question the answer . . . Gandhism gives is an emphatic "no." The

> Untouchables must follow their hereditary profession. That those occupations are unclean is no excuse. That before the occupation became hereditary it was the result of force . . . does not matter. The argument of Gandhism is that what is once settled is settled forever even if it was wrongly settled. Under Gandhism, the Untouchables are to be eternal scavengers. There is no doubt that the Untouchables would much prefer the orthodox system of Untouchability. A compulsory state of ignorance imposed upon the Untouchability by the Hindu *Shastras* made scavenging bearable. But Gandhism, which compels an educated Untouchable to do scavenging, is noting short of cruelty. The grace in Gandhism is a curse in its worst form. The virtue of the anti-Untouchability plank in Gandhism is quite illusory. There is no substance in it.[32]

Bhārata Mātā and the Freedom Movement

Since the earliest phases of human existence, Earth Mother among hunting and agricultural peoples has represented a universal equation of the land and local goddesses of particular tribes, clans, and place. In her role as fierce and often bloodthirsty warrior, the Great Goddess recycles life by doling out death and rebirth. In the middle of the nineteenth century, the Mahiṣāsura-mardinī template, promoted as Bhārata Mātā ("Mother India"), became a symbol and an instrument of the Hindu resistance to British rule, and sparked the political overthrow of colonial power. During the revolution against the British rulers, the mythic demon-slaying goddess became a metaphor for India in the writing of eminent thinkers who were not all Śāktas, since "Śāktism had by this time ceased to be a sectarian religion, and there was no difficulty for anyone to accept its essence."[33] As Mahiṣāsura-mardinī, Bhārata Mātā evokes at least three classic portraits of the fierce Indian goddess: first, the *Devī-māhātmya*'s account of a ten-armed woman warrior, brandishing weapons, riding a lion, and vanquishing the buffalo demon; second, Caṅkam accounts of *Koṟṟavai*, accompanied by her demonesses, leading warriors to the battlefield and later cannibalizing the fallen enemies; and third, woman-based folk material based on the enraged, vengeful, conquering Devī.

The male commanders of the freedom movement understood the value of appropriating and instrumentalizing the whole feminine ethic of motherhood, conflated with specific Indian fierce goddesses as personifications of India, in order to mobilize women in the movement. As Dietrich emphasizes,

> Motherhood was . . . used by some nationalists to establish ideological control over women, to keep them out of education and professions, to reduce them to their reproductive roles. At the same time they were glorified for their ability to sacrifice, and conceptualized as mothers of the nation; as such, the benevolent powers of the goddess were ascribed to them.[34]

The character of Bhārata Mātā was created by the nationalist Bengali writer Bankim Chandra Chatterjee in a novel published in 1882, *Ānandamaṭha*. In the novel, a band of revolutionaries, the *santānas* (children who dedicate their lives to their country's cause) worshiped the goddess Kālī as the divine embodiment of Indian land in the Earth Mother tradition. In their temple, three images of Kālī are installed, representing the "Mother that was," the "Mother that is," and the "Mother that will be." "The imagery of the goddess Kālī in the *Ānandamaṭha* leaves no doubt that Bankim Chandra owed his inspiration to the Śākta tradition,"[35] according to Bhattacharyya.

Mahatma Gandhi's political strategies of non-violence and highly symbolic and mythically evocative activities such as spinning were intended to involve women fully in the nationalist struggle. Convinced that women's participation in the Indian freedom movement was necessary for India to gain independence, Gandhi created mobilization strategies targeting women. As Tripti Chaudhuri explains,

> Mass mobilization under Gandhian leadership brought more women to the national movement and forged a lasting connection between the Congress and women. Though Gandhi made women believe that they were integral to the national movement, women's participation was supported only within the strict framework of Gandhi's program. Women were mobilized for the nationalist movement, but they were assigned supporting roles. Gandhi had a genuine respect for women and sincere desire for their rise, but at the same time he limited women's sphere of action and did not encourage them to question their traditional roles. Admiring women's capacity for self-sacrifice and tolerant disposition, he considered them to be particularly adept at the technique of *satyāgraha* and nonviolent struggle for freedom.[36]

Understanding that the struggle must be framed in mythically evocative terms familiar to the masses, Gandhi chose as the model of the anti-colonial struggle the heroine goddess Sītā, the brāhmaṇic paragon of wifely (i.e., self-sacrificing) virtue and the martyred spouse of the god Rāma in the *Rāmāyaṇa* who engaged in a ferocious battle against Rāvaṇa, her husband's demon enemy. Her primary function in myths, of course, is her modeling of suffering and martyrdom to protect her husband/India. "By popularizing the myth of ideal, Indian womanhood as symbolized by Sītā, the obedient follower of her husband, he also retarded the growth of radical and independent ideas among his women followers."[37] In his addresses to women, Gandhi frequently alluded to Sītā's legendary fight against the demon Rāvaṇa, thus recasting Indian women's fight against the British as a modern iteration of the mythic episode of Sītā's violence. Because the intertwining of the political and the religious is a powerful means of persuasion (Muhammad's key to success), Gandhi's allusions to sacred myths were certain to evoke highly charged emotions without challenging the Indian patriarchy's repression of women.

Subhas Chandra Bose, a prominent Bengali leader of the Indian National Congress, chose Durgā as the mobilizing model, explicitly inciting women to emulate the goddess in her battle against the buffalo demon (the latter homologized with the British). Appealing to women's emotional sense of motherhood, and their dual duty to family and India, Bose fired women up with nationalistic zeal by alluding to the Mahiṣāsura-mardinī episode. Bhārata Mātā's iconography identifies her with Durgā, the most popular Indian war and Mother-goddess. She rides astride a big cat, either lion or tiger, and she has Durgā's round, benevolent, matronly face. Just as the gods called on Durgā for help against the *asuras*, and she slayed the demon, so Indian men were calling on their women for help against the British. Even when she was a warrior, the goddess was above all a supreme mother, thus her instrumentality in the freedom struggle probably strengthened women's social legitimization through the single avenue of motherhood.

Bhārata Mātā enabled women to emerge from their cloistered domestic responsibilities to find important public work in the anti-colonial movement. When the British ordered the partition of Bengal in 1940, the *Swadeshi* ("one's own country") emerged as the first mass movement of Indian nationalism (1904–7), advocating national schools liberated from British control and the promotion of indigenous products. For the first time, women participated in anti-colonial political agitations, street demonstrations, and boycotts for imported textiles. From 1930 onward, Bhārata Mātā's image adorned banners and flags. Artists like Abanindranath Tagore and Amrita Sher-Gill immortalized the image of the suffering, martyred mother, cognate with the glorification of the Virgin Mary by Mexican nationalists during various wars and revolutions. On her body are inscribed the frontiers of the subcontinent, and rousing hymns homologize the goddess and India. *Vande Mātaram* ("Hail, O Mother"), a patriotic hymn also found in *Ānandamaṭha*, became the anthem of the nationalist movement.

By invoking the goddess, a political endeavor becomes a religious mission. The ongoing struggle is then projected into a sacred dimension, the cosmic war between good and evil commences, and women's participation is thus legitimized. Indian women, like ancient warrior goddesses, can play a traditionally masculine role without disturbing the patriarchal social order. The icon of the goddess translates as women's religious duty to protect and defend the Motherland, and prevents any conflict with women's ordinarily restrictive domestic roles. The public domain, normally the exclusive sphere of men, opens to women, who are free to walk in the streets, mix with strangers, even with men who are not family members, without losing their respectability or threatening the social structure.

References

1. Rosalind Miles, *Who cooked the Last Supper? The Women's History of the World* (New York, 1988), 195.
2. See Bernard Lewis, *Islam and the West* (New York, 1993), 10–15, 74ff.
3. Arundhati Roy, "Arundhati Roy on India, Iraq, U.S. Empire and Dissent," in *Democracy Now* (May 23, 2006), http://www.democracynow.org/article.pl?sid=06/05/23/1358250, accessed May 24, 2006.
4. Iris Butler, *The Viceroy's Wife* (London, 1969), 101, cited in Miles, *Who Cooked the Last Supper*, 203.

5. Harish Sharma, *Communal Angle in Indian Politics* (Jaipur, 2000), 38.
6. Mandakranta Bose, ed., *Faces of the Feminine in Ancient, Medieval, and Modern India* (New York, 2000), 214.
7. Vandana Shiva, *India Divided: Diversity and Democracy Under Attack* (New York, 2005), 26.
8. Ibid., 25.
9. Bose, ed., *Faces of Feminine*, 215.
10. Ibid.
11. Ibid., 215–16.
12. Chitnis, "Exploring Tradition and Change among Women in Marathi, Culture," in *Faces of the Feminine in Ancient, Medieval, and Modern India*, ed. Mandakranta Bose (New York and Oxford: Oxford University Press, 2000), 251–69, 262.
13. Gandhian worker's response when questioned about preserving tribal artifacts. [Sandho Chaudhuri, "Cultural Policy for Folk and Tribal Art," in Satish Saberwal, ed., *Towards a Cultural Policy* (New Delhi, 1975), 152, quoted in Hardiman, *The Coming of the Devī: Adivasi Assertion in Western India* (Delhi: Oxford University Press, 1987), 207.]
14. The Indian government now prohibits fieldwork among South Asian aboriginal groups by foreign scholars.
15. See, for example, Åke Hultkrantz, "The Religion of the Goddess in North America," in *The Book of the Goddess Past and Present: An Introduction to Her Religion*, ed. Carl Olson (New York: Crossroads Publishing Company, 1983).
16. Jerry Mander, *In the Absence of the Sacred: The Failure of Technology and the Survival of the Indian Nations* (San Francisco, 1991), 5.
17. Perdue, *Cherokee Women*, 5.
18. The Parsis are a close-knit Zoroastrian community based in the Indian subcontinent. Descended from Persian Zoroastrians, Parsis emigrated to the Indian subcontinent over 1000 years ago to escape religious persecution after the Islamic conquest. In Iran, Parsis and their language are Fars and Farsi. During British colonial rule, Parsi youth took full advantage of the British schools, which provided them with not only literacy, but also an initiation into the mindset and behavior patterns of the British elite. More than any other South Asian community, the Parsis were able to mimic the British. Regarding their own racial and intellectual superiority as a given, the British consequently accepted the Parsis as mirror images of their own traits—conscientious, hard working, and intelligent—and utilized the Parsis as conduits to the other native communities, the latter stigmatized by the British as passive-aggressive and ignorant. ["Parsi," Wikipedia, http://en.wikipedia.org/wiki/Parsi (accessed August 4, 2006).]
19. David Hardiman, *Coming of the Devī*, 1.
20. Ibid., 4.
21. Ibid.
22. Ibid., 174.
23. Ibid., 175.
24. Ibid.
25. Ibid., 178.
26. Ibid., 177.
27. Ibid., 198.
28. Ibid., 198n25.

29. Ibid., 201.
30. Sankho Chaudhuri, "Cultural Policy for Folk and Tribal Art," in Satish Saberwal, ed., *Towards a Cultural Policy* (New Delhi, 1975), 152, quoted in Hardiman, *Coming of the Devī*, 207.
31. Hardiman, *Coming of the Devī*, 207–8.
32. G.B. Singh, *Gandhi: Beyond the Mask of Divinity*, 258–59.
33. Bhattacharyya, *History of the Śākta Religion*, 203–4.
34. Dietrich, "Women and Religious Identities in India after Ayodhya," *Against All Odds: Essays on Women, Religion and Development from India and Pakistan*, ed. Kamia Bhasin, Ritu Menon, and Nighat Sa'id Khan (New Delhi: Kali for Women, 1994), 35–50.
35. Bhattacharyya, *History of the Śākta Religion*, 205.
36. Tripti Chaudhuri, "Women in Radical Movements in Bengal in the 1940s," in *Faces of the Feminine in Ancient, Medieval, and Modern India*, ed. Mandakranta Bose (New York, 2000), 306.
37. Ibid.

13

Śakti in the Global Village

> With India's growing middle class buying homes, cars and cell-phones like never before, developers need space for malls, apartments and parking lots. Developers are hungrily eyeing big tracts of slum land and are willing to put up millions of rupees to resettle inhabitants.[1]

Forty years after the departure of Europeans, global capital and modern technology invaded India, commencing with what some would call a Faustian bargain between India and the West, the Green Revolution. In a span of less than fifteen years, capitalism and globalization have catapulted India into the Western corporate mode, and modern Hinduism has emerged as a dominant hegemonic ideology of the post-independence era. India's markets were opened to neoliberalism in the late 1980s and 1990s, during a time when, following the dictates of the World Bank policies of structural adjustment, the Indian state de-funded agriculture, rural development, transport, energy, and public health. The number of Indian millionaires grew an estimated sevenfold during the 1990s and the number of hungry children also increased, according to the United Nations' Food and Agriculture Organization. The rush of migrants from rural to urban areas has bloated India's cities. Since 1991, the number of cities with more than a million people has grown from twenty-three to at least thirty-five.[2]

In the twenty-first century, India has made impressive gains in economic investment and overall output. It stands as the world's largest democracy with a population exceeding one billion, an overall self-sufficient food supply, and the fourth largest economy in the world. At the same time, India is home to more than half of the world's malnourished children. India is the nation with the largest number of poor people in the world. Half of all Indian children remain malnourished, half of Indian women remain illiterate, and more than eighty percent of the Indian countryside has no access to telephones or toilets.[3] Although absolute poverty has been reduced substantially (in 2006, twenty-two percent of Indians lived below the poverty line), the already vast economic gap between the rich and the poor has increased dramatically,[4] and expanding social inequities have reinforced India's feudalism.

The Power of Collective Women

After independence, particularly since the 1960s, the Indian government instituted a policy to integrate the landless agricultural laborers whom Gandhi called *harijans* ("hill people"), including non-hinduized *ādivāsīs* and members of other low castes, into the Indian "mainstream." Enforced mainly by the Tribal Welfare Department, the policy of integration has disenfranchised *ādivāsīs* by weaning them from traditional slash-and-burn cultivation, controlled aboriginal land, resettled *ādivāsīs* outside their forests, and established a cash economy with private property ownership within a capitalist market system. Tribal children undergo Hindu reprograming ("hinduization") at boarding schools (ashram schools) by non-tribal teachers and are "taught to give up their 'bad' tribal habits,"[5] much as Native American children were removed from their matriarchal communities and sent to Christian mission schools, where they learned to be domestic servants in Christian nuclear families.

This policy has contributed to the increasing pauperization and marginalization of women in the subsistence sector, viz., women are being stripped of their former control of the land as the means of production. Throughout prehistory and history, the major source of Indians' livelihood has been land (traditionally deified as Devī), yet large areas of land have been co-opted from the Indian people primarily for the corporatization of agriculture and mega-projects such as the development of large hydroelectric dams. National and multinational corporations reap vast profits from their land acquisition and development schemes, and tribals and *dalits*, already without resources and powerless, are the groups most injured by such projects.

Down to the twenty-first century, the *ādivāsīs* have been victimized by an assortment of predatory elites, including Hindu and Muslim feudal landlords and moneylenders, British colonials, and contemporary empire-building globalists, whose mega-projects are responsible for the displacement of millions of indigenous peoples. Much of tribal land has been lost, and tribal peoples are destined to live lives of extreme hardship. Although *ādivāsīs* have had a cultural understanding and appreciation of equality between women and men since prehistory, capitalist penetration causes social asymmetry and polarization berween the sexes, reinforcing patriarchalism and sexism that enhances male power by giving men control over profits while destroying the aboriginal sexual division of labor.[6] Dispossession, illiteracy, and loss of identity have taken their toll on tribals throughout the world. Alcoholism, migration to cities in search of a livelihood, premature death, and unemployment are the primary realities of their lives.

In *India Divided,*Vandana Shiva posits that the organizational principle of *araṇya saṁskṛti,* or the culture of the forest, "the highest form of cultural evolution," has channeled Indian civilization and molded a distinctly Indian cultural identity. The harmony, diversity, and self-sustaining nature of India's forests and rievers, the primeval abode of goddesses, are being systematically destroyed by development and consumerism. "There is a war against tribals who try to defend their right to land and forests, rights guaranteed under Schedule V of the Constitution," writes Shiva. "In Nagarnar, in Wynad, and throughout tribal areas, the last remnants of our *aranya sanskriti* are being wiped out."[7]

It is important to perceive that the restoration of ecological integrity and the liberation of forests and rivers from the designs of the corporate monetized mind are not separate from women's liberation and the restoration of gender parity, as they are two faces of the same life-force. Martial power and the overt use of force are not Devī's only alternatives when facing an enemy. *Strī-śakti,* woman power, is an awesome weapon. Nowhere is this more evident that in late twentieth century struggles against violence and in the interest of ecology, women's collective power, food security, shelter, and legal aid. Gail Omvedt[8] describes the struggles of the hill women in the Chipko movement in Uttar Pradesh for forestry rights and preservation of natural resources, and the movement of rural women in the Shetkari Sangathana in Maharashtra for property rights and political representation. In Vandana Shiva's important work[9] on movements such as the Chipko struggle against corporate degradation of the environment, she emphasizes that the women regard nature as *Prakṛti,* Mother Earth, and they as her representatives are united in their collective struggle through the goddess-given cosmic energy of *strī-śakti.*

The movement was based on an eighteenth century legend from the Bishnoi community of Rajasthan about Amrita Devī, a local girl who died trying to protect the trees that surrounded her village. In the story, the tree cutters of a local maharajah arrive to cut the villagers' trees for wood for his new fortress. Amrita, with others, jumped in front of the trees and hugged them. In some versions, Amrita dies in her valiant attempt to save the trees; in others, the women's heroism prevented the forest's destruction. After this incident, the maharajah proclaimed a stringent royal decree against the cutting of trees in all Bishnoi villages.

Although India's deforestation policies began with the massive British appropriation of India's natural wealth, national economic development commenced in earnest in the 1960s, when more trees were cleared so that the wood could be exported to earn foreign exchange. As a result, hill soil washed away, causing landslides, floods, and silting in the rivers below the hills. Homes and crops were destroyed, and women's burdens increased as they were forced to trudge longer and longer distances for their fuel, water, and fodder. *Chipko* in Hindi means "to cling or embrace," reflecting the protesters' signature *modus operandi* of throwing their arms around the tree trunks designated to be cut and refusing to move. Even when confronted by guns, the women would threaten to hug the trees and die with them. The women pleaded with the woodcutters on behalf of their "maternal home," the forest, and the woodcutters were unable to harm the trees. The Chipko women coined the slogans "What do the forests bear? Soil, water, and pure air," and "ecology is permanent economy." Thousands of trees were spared because of the Chipko movement in the hills.

The rural hill women demonstrated that "only women themselves can determine how the record of the past can contribute to the present struggle."[10] They transcend religious differences by focusing on the wisdom traditions of ordinary women, their life practices and survival systems, based on the interdependence of the web of life and the primacy of the forest culture, Earth Mother herself. Women's movements allow women to identify and know their own power, as opposed to the powers bestowed on the goddess in male-authored myths. In one sense, such women's movements are the antidote to male myths in the violence-of-God tradition. It must ever be kept in mind that fierce Indic goddesses were originally tribal tree goddesses, rooted in the Earth of their Villages, To *ādivāsīs*, unscrupulous exploitation of land leads to malevolence; the spirit of Mother Earth is not happy. The perspective that divine benevolence and malevolence are related to their respect for and compact with the Earth has sustained tribals over the ages, keeping their small-scale societies in reciprocal balance with the endowments of their environment. They have lost their rights regarding land and are being driven out of their villages. When they leave, their culture dies, and with it, their deification of the land.

All Our Goddesses are Armed

> While patriarchal violence persists as crippling and, at times, life-threatening in daily life, the "external" threat of communal violence becomes overwhelming in times of conflict. Thus, the present climate of heightened communal tension unavoidably strengthens patriarchal controls within the community. At the same time, the process of women embodying the vestiges of culture has its own internal logic of women's empowerment with patriarchal approval.[11]

In the 1990s, Hindu-Muslim rioting and killing reached peaks of violence not seen since Partition in 1947, after two of the organizations of the RSS family, the VHP and the BJP, mobilized the Hindu community behind the removal of the Babri Mosque from its site in Ayodhyā,[12] a holy pilgrimage site where the Buddha once taught the Dharma. Hindus venerate Ayodhyā as the legendary birthplace of Rāma, and regarded the mosque built on a sacred Hindu spot as a deliberate affront to Lord Rāma. After the mosque was destroyed in 1993 (to be supplanted by a temple for Rāma), more than 250 people died in a string of bomb explosions in Mumbai, for which authorities blamed the city's underworld criminal gangs. Following the last wave of riots in 1993 in the aftermath of the demolition of the mosque, there was a marked decline in the incidence of communal (Hindu–Muslim) riots for nearly a decade. After many years of hearings, a special court convicted 100 people for their involvement in the 1993 serial bomb attacks in Mumbai.

As part of the late twentieth century RSS strategy, Mahiṣāsura-mardinī provided nationalist inspiration to elite secularist Hindutva women militants in Rashtra Sevika Samiti,[13] a nationalist paramilitary organization. Paola Bacchetta's study of the life of Kamlabehn ("All Our Goddesses are Armed"),[14] a young upper caste Indian woman in the RSS, reveals that the buffalo-slaying goddess was a focal point of the organization.Kamla was interviewed over a period of four years during the late 1980s. Her political work included recruiting more Sangh members (*swayamsevaks*; lit., "self-workers" or "volunteers")—the Samiti carries out humanitarian projects in urban slums and organizes free *pūjā* and Sanskrit classes in villages—and teaching paramilitary skills such as riflery, karate, and *lāṭhī*-wielding to other members while she worked on her degree in engineering. "She is physically tough and highly confident of herself," writes Bacchetta. "She is an atheist, and she believes that women are as able as men, including as warriors."[15]

Bacchetta argues that "Kamlabehn's notion of the feminine self and the space of relative freedom that she carves out for herself absolutely depend upon constructing 'the muslims'[16] as demonic, threatening to Hindu women."[17] Her skills in weaponry can only be justified "in the name of self-defense (of her own chaste Hindu femininity) and self-sacrifice (for the Hindu Nation where ultimately men rule) against the projected threat constituted by 'the muslims'."[18] Because Muslim males, in her construction, are the illegitimate offspring of Bhārata Mātā and sexually aggressive to women, anti-Muslim violence by Hindu women is the fulfillment of one's archetypal duty as a militant Hindu woman, the divine and just direct revenge "provoked by Muslim male sexual violation of Hindu femininity and womanhood."[19] Kamla has never met a Muslim male; thus her ideology is based on highly charged abstractions,historical memories, and possibly knowledge of Islamic texts.

Kamla defines belief in goddesses and gods as "superstition," and her mother is the only family member who "believes in all that and does *pūjā* every day."[20] However, she accepts three particular goddesses—Bhārata Mātā, Aṣṭa Bhuja (a unique eight-armed goddess invented by the Samiti to unify members), and Kālī (in her role in the *Devī-māhātmya*). "[I]n order to understand her mode of relating to the goddesses, one must separate the question of faith from the social and individual functions of the deities as symbolic references."[21] The Samiti inherited Bhārata Mātā from the Sangh, and for both groups the goddess represents the land of the Hindu Nation.Bacchetta emphasizes that "the Sangh has historically attempted to curb powerful symbolic femininity by depicting her as benevolent, violated by the enemies of the Hindu Nation, raped and vivisected by 'the muslims'."[22] Bhārata Mātā is a martyr who represents the feminine memory of kidnapped medieval Hindu women, abused, raped, and sold by Muslim slavetraders. Rather than dwelling on her victimization, however, the Samiti glorifies her fierce qualities. Since hoary antiquity, Indian consciousness has well understood that in battles against formidable enemies, only Śakti can save them.

Islamists and Maoists

"The modern nation-state came into being," writes Barbara Ehrenreich, "as a support system for the mass army."[23] Small arms trade now dominates the international marketplace, and anyone can now acquire the armaments and training of war. The contemporary nation-state is being challenged as the international unit of militarism by warlords with cash and followers. [24] The growth of not only Islamist, or *jihādī*, organizations, but also Marxist fundamentalist revolutionaries such as the Communist Party of India (Maoist), is testimony to the spread of militarism and terrorism in India since Independence and Partition.

In recent years, terrorist bombing incidents have occurred in public places as well as on public transportation, such as trains and buses, in markets and in other public areas, resulting in deaths or injuries. According to Indian officials, large-scale terrorist attacks in India, such as the horrific "26/11" Mumbai attacks in 2008, the deadly explosion on an India–Pakistan train line in February 2007, and the bombings of a Mumbai commuter railway in July 2006, are the work of Islamists fueled by the territorial dispute over India-controlled Kashmir.[25] A bomb blast at the revered Sufi shrine in Ajmer in October 2007 and other attacks on mosques did not result in communal riots, but officials have failed to prosecute most of the instigators of and participants in religious mob violence.[26] In Assam, over 200 civilians were killed as of late November 2007 by alleged members of the United Liberation Front of Asom (ULFA). One of the most violent states in the northeast in Manipur, where targeted killings and extortion are widespread. In August 2007, at least 42 people in Hyderabad were killed in twin bombings carried out, according to the Indian government, by Islamic militants based in Pakistan and Bangladesh.[27]

There were several significant terrorist incidents in India in the second-half of 2005 and the first-half of 2006 in New Delhi, Varanasi, and Mumbai. In March 2006, two near simultaneous explosions occurred in Varanasi, one in the main railway station and another in a popular Hindu temple, leaving more than twenty dead and over 100 injured.[28] In July 2006, seven bombs made of high-powered plastic explosives exploded on crowded commuter trains and at stations in Mumbai, India's financial hub, killing more than 160 people and wounding hundreds more. Suspicion centered on Islamists fighting New Delhi's rule in disputed Kashmir, who have been blamed for several bomb attacks in India in the past. A similar series of coordinated explosions occurred in New Delhi in October 2005, hitting crowded market areas, leaving more than 60 persons killed and more than 180 wounded.

The Communist Party of India (Maoist), an underground armed movement of Marxist fundamentalism, is active in thirteen of twenty-eight Indian states. It stretches from the tip of india to the northern border with Nepal, where the Maoists have set off full-scale civil war in their struggle to overthrow a popular monarchy. The radical Maoist movement began with a 1968 agrarian peasant uprising in West Bengal. In the years since, Naxalites,[29] as the rebels are known, have flourished by penetrating into the impoverished tribal and dalit corners, offering arms, ideology, and a war against the Indian state. Naxalites aim to return ancestral land to those dispossessed by globalism. The Naxalite insurgency is strongest in the areas with the most abundant natural resources, particularly the coal that powers the Indian economy. Naxalism represents a serious political risk to almost half of India's total energy supply. Coal constitutes about fifty-five percent of India's current primary energy sypply and some seventy-five percent of its electricity generation. The Naxalites are a major political force in some of the poorest and most densely tribal states—particularly Andhra Pradesh, Chhattisgarh, Orissa, Jharkhand, and West Bengal—that contain about eighty-five percent of India's coal resources.[30]

Destabilizing and terrorizing much of the countryside, the insurgents blow up railway tracks, seize land, and chase away forest guards, The Maoists extort taxes from anyone doing business in the forest. Since their ultimate goal is to overthrow the state, police posts, industrial plants, and government offices are preferred targets. Ironically, the Great Goddess who waged holy war, vanquished the enemy, and saved humanity causes even atheistic Maoist rebels in Nepal to suspend their armed activities for her annual festival each October. Appeals from the public have forced the Maoists to announce a nine-day unilateral ceasefire[31] for Nepal's most extravagant and beloved Hindu festival, Dashain, which celebrates Durgā in her buffalo-demon slaying mode. Many thousands of Nepalese refugees have fled from the Maoist violence to India.

As Jeremy Carl observes:

> [I]n essence, the core of the Naxalite rebellion can be seen as a response by many of India's poor against a perceived expropriation of their natural resources by the state. India's "coal mafias" largely control the industry, notorious for its poor infrastructure and corruption, while union leaders, mine managers and politicians routinely skim substantial profits from the state-owned coal companies. Meanwhile, the poor, largely tribal communities that make up much of the heart of India's coal country, see precious little of the profits while suffering substantial environmental destruction and feeling the effects of public corruption.[32]

Both Islamic and Maoist militant groups spin off from mainstream religious traditions in an attempt to establish and defend a righteous order in the midst of the decadent, seductive influence of Western consumerism:

> All male radical religious groups ... attempt to create and defend a righteous order in the face of massive social disorder. These forms of marginal, male-bonding, anti-institutional, semipolitical movements are not idiosyncratic to the contemporay era. There have been occasions in past centuries when noninstitutional men's associations have spun off from mainstream religious traditions, often with violence on their agenda. The *assassini* of medieval Islam are one example. The murderous, goddess-worshiping *thugs* of India—from which we get the English word *thug*—are another.[33]

Muslims make up India's largest minority group, constituting the world's second largest Muslim population after Indonesia. The contemporary Muslim community in India is mired in poverty and illiteracy, conditions that are often blamed on various Western imperial and moral sins. The lens through which Islamists view their oppression is the hyper-macho narrative of cosmic war against the generic infidel, who is conflated with the spectre of Western globalist hegemony. In the name of *Allāh,* Muslim warriors wage war against the god of free market globalism. Therefore, the aggressions of the West (specifically, British colonialism and US foreign policy), the specious argument contends, are responsible for Islamist *jihāds.* Such a viewpoint is based on ignorance of Islamic history, texts, and obligations. As a matter of historical fact, during the centuries of British rule preceding India's independence, and possibly in the period prior to the British conquest of India, the socioeconomic status of the Muslim masses was as distressed as it is today. Moreover, Indian Muslims share abject pauperization with their Hindu counterparts, the śūdras, *dalits,* and tribals, who suffer from caste-driven discrimination and repression, a condition that is not improved by conversion to Islam. In fact, a controversial report released by New Delhi's Sachar Committee in November 2006 found that India's Muslims lag behind the rest of Indians in terms of literacy, employment rates, and income.[34]

The Martyr

While Western hegemony is not blameless, the deepest motives of Islamists who feel compelled to make war more likely reside in earlier, post-seventh century Islamic history and, ultimately, in Muslim scriptures. Of far greater relevance to Islamist terrorism than Westen activities is the *Qur'ānic* conception of martyrdom, which is fundamentally different from the martyrdom of other religious persuasions. Mark Juergensmeyer emphasizes the centrality of martyrdom in the history of many religions, including early Christianity. Both Christ and Husain, the founder of the Shi'ite Muslim tradition, were religious martyrs. The word *martyr* stems from a Greek term for "witness," as in a witness to one's faith. "In most cases matyrdom is regarded not only as a testimony to the degree of one's commitment, but also as a performance of a religious act, specifically an act of self-sacrifice."[35]

The primal perception of sacrifice as an essential rite of destruction is a core teaching in all world religions, hinged to the notion of spiritual salvation. From the perspective of human sacrifice, Islam lacks the surrogate martyred god of Christianity and the shamanic ordeals of Hinduism; thus individual Muslim believers cannot be absolved by profession of faith or courageous acts from the necessity of martyrdom, since they are taught that they cannot have eternal life unless they give up the present life in the sacrament of *jihād*. As Spengler articuates,

> There is no Grace in Islam, no miracle, no expiatory sarifice, no expression of live for mankind such that each Muslim need not be a scrifice. On the contrary, the concept of jihād, in which the congregation of Islam is also the army, states thkat every single Muslim must sacrifice himself personally. Jihād is the precise equivalent of the Lord's Supper in Christianity and the Jewish Sabbath, the defining expression of sacrifice that opens the prospect of eternity to the mortal believer.[36]

Spengler begs several additional questions regarding the nature and the venue of the sacrament. First, it is important to see the whole evolutionary spectrum of religious sacraments, and hence distinguish between an actual blood sacrifice, a sublimated or symbolic blood sacrifice (the Christian Eucharist), and a supernaturally empowered food offering to a goddess or god (the Hindu *prasāda*). Second, in what context or venue does the sacrament occur? Both the Hindu *prasāda* and the Christian Eucharist are rites cofined to a temple, and altar, or a sanctified space. Islamist ideology, however, sees no separation vetween the religious and the social, and holds that the venue of their sacrament must be where all non-Muslims dwell: in the *dār al-harb*, or the "house of war," the Muslim terms for all that lies outside the "house of submission," or *dār al-Islām*. Thus the Muslim fundamentalist notion of martyrdom equates personal salvation with performance of sacred rites of human sacrifice , and the non-Muslim world is the site of both their sacrament and their salvation. Because it promotes open-ended war, this Islamic Weltanschaung would seem to represent the most archaic and primitive form of sacrament, the harsh father metaphor run amok. As Juergensmeyer points out,

> The term [*sacrifice*] suggests that the very process of destroying is spiritual since the word comes from the Latin, *sacrificium*, "to make holy." What makes sacrifice so riveting is not just that it involves killing, but also that it is, in an ironic way, ennobling, The destruction is performed within a religious context that transfroms the killing into something positive. Thus, like all religious images of sacrifice, martyrdom provides symbols of a violence conquered—or at least put in its place—by the larger framework of order that religious language provides. . . . There is some evidence that ancient religious rites of sacrifice, like the destruction involved in modern-day terrorism, were performances involving the murder of living beings. The later domestication of sacrifice in evolved forms of religious practice, such as the Christian ritual of the Eucharist, masked the fact that in

most early forms of sacrifice a real animal — in some cases a human—offered its life on a sacred chopping block, an altar.[37]

Linguist and metaphor analyst Geroge Lakoff[38] has neatly defined political types by their ruling meatphors, which he strings together to form a narrative of the progerssive and the conservative worldview. In terms of overarching metaphor, Lakoff's "harsh father" model defines the Islamist worldview, while Hindu goddesses flow more from Lakoff's "nurturant parent" metaphor (goddesses are "nurturing mothers"). Differences between martyred fierce savior goddesses and their Islamist counterparts can be analyzed as differences in their metaphors—the harsh, authoritarian father versus the loving, nurturing mother. Islamist martyrs are ruled by sacred texts that promote warfare against the non-Muslim world in the larger context of monotheism, eschatology, messianism, the Last Judgment, and assignment to eternal hell or heaven. Indian goddesses, by contrast, have remained polytheistic deities for over five thusand years, which accounts in part for India's reputation for religious tolerance, a moral precept based on empathy. Tamil goddesses such as Kaṇṇaki and Māriyammaṉ were ordinary housewives whose suffering and victimization under an unjust patriarchal system caused them to morph into revolutionary holy martyrs, insurrectionists sacrificed on the altar of Indian misogynistic law codes. Women's folklore communicates the sacrifice of women's lives to male authority figures—king, father, husband, sons—and the female fantasy of cathartic retribution. For low-caste and *dalit* women, goddess martyrs like Kaṇṇaki and Māriyammaṉ function as effective tools of folk medicine that remove any sense of blame (i.e., *karma*) for being abused from female victims while transmuting their suffering into a catalyst for potential rebirth as an immortal goddess. The goddesses offer love, empathy, and psychological nurturance to victims of injustice and abuse that is absent in the harsh father model.

Indic fierce goddesses are responsible warriors with heart, savior figures that are in metaphorically and ideologically pitted against both warriors—Prophet Muhammad and the Muslim messiah, the Mahdī.[39] They do not command their belivevers to kill or convert nonbelivevers throughout the world, nor assign all people to eternal damnation or reward based on their submission to a religious creed. In their broadest sense, fierce goddesses can be viewed as the first historical ancestresses of human females who produced the human race. Their origin and purpose, their messages of reciprocity, compassion, and transcendence, are cloaked in metaphors embedded in ancient texts, which warrior-priests with an agenda have distorted. As destroyers of negative emotions, Kālī and her *avatāras* embody the absence of the fear of evil. As spirits of the natural world, fierce goddesses demand reciprocity from humankind. Śakti's true revolution represents the cosmological shift from the misogyny, violence, and greed of the Kaliyuga into a new golden age.

Kāḷī in Wartime

> An "irrational" view of the world as peopled by spirits may be more adaptive and sustainable than a "scientific" view that sees the world in mechanistic terms.[40]

Around the world, civil war is the main cause of conflict, usually triggered by a dispute over scarce resources or territory that has changed hands in the past. Some of the conflicts involve the use of irregular troops to "invade" and attempt to conquer disputed territory; when Islamists are involved, they are fired by a divinely ordained obligation. This is the case in Kashmir, where for over a decade, Islamists have been trying to force all non-Muslims out of Kashmir in attempts to take it from India, and Pakistani Islamist groups continue to support terrorism in India and Afghanistan. In Sri Lanka, Tamil Tigers are attempting to partiton the island. Kashmir and Sri Lanka are only two of many rebellions that now beset South Asia. Because India and Pakistan have nuclear weapons, any escalation in the Kashmir conflict becomes a potential catastrophe. Recent peace talks have lowered the possibility of war, but both sides continue their arms race.

Patricia Lawrence's field study[41] of Kālī oracles in Batticaloa, on the war-torn east coast of Sri Lanka, illustrates the complex role of fierce goddesses in a milieu of extreme political violence. Unlike Muslims, Tamil Tigers deliberately keep religion out of the war, thus they neither believe that Kāḷī demands perennial war against the rest of the world nor support global terrorism. More than any other deity, Kālī is the protectress who, through *śakti* possession, provides healing and spiritual strength to traumatized Tamil families. Just as ancient Caṅkam literature describes grieving widows in wartime seeking solace in the ancient Dravidian temples of goddess Ko<u>rr</u>avai, Tamils trapped in contemporary Sri Lanka seek the aid of Kālī, the protectress of powerless people. Sri Lankan Tamils endured two decades of civil war that killed some 65,000 people before the 2002 ceasefire, which left parts of the north and east under rebel control. At this writing, military action has resumed as the Tamil minority battles to partition the island. Tamil rebels have advanced, while government jets bomb rebel positions and saffron-robed, hardline Buddhist monks support the state military and resort to physical violence against Tamils in street demonstrations.

The majority of the island's people (74 per cent) are Sinhalese, and Buddhism is the majority religion. Tamils, the largest minority (18 per cent), are predominantly Hindu. Descendants of nineteenth century economic migrants from south India, Tamils have been marginalized since Sri Lanka became a sovereign state in 1948. The struggle between the Liberation Tigers of Tamil Eelam (LTTE), the Tamil warriors fighting for the establishment of a separate state, and Sinhalese government security forces is based on political, socioeconomic, and educational discrimination against the Tamil minority by successive post-independence Sri Lankan governments.

Unchanged in structure since the Caṅkam age, Tamil rituals to Kālī in eastern Sri Lanka are underpinned by the primal Dravidian religious elements of healing and *śakti* possession, which are adapted to the horrors of kidnapping, "disappearances," torture, and constant warfare. "Some devotees say that only Kāḷī has the power to 'change the position' (*nilamai maṟṟutal*) of those experiencing immediate vulnerability to annihilation," writes Lawrence. "In today's desperate circumstances, she is considered one of the most responsive and powerful local goddesses in Batticaloa District."[42]

When the health care infrastructure and the judiciary collapsed in the 1980s and early 90s during the civil war, the oracles, known as deity-dancers (*tevyam āṭumākkaḷ*), became more prominent. Through her oracle, Kāḷī provides counseling and medical remedies for torture survivors, advises parents desperate to send their children out of the war zone and into the growing Tamil diaspora, informs suffering mothers that their missing sons are dead, and directs devotees to dispensaries of rice rations. The oracles most frequently become possessed by and speak through Kāḷī in the forms of Pattira-kāḷiyammaṉ, Vīrakāḷiyammaṉ, and Vīramahākāḷī; the other local goddesses Māriyammaṉ, Pecciyammaṉ Tiropataiyammaṉ, Nagakaṇṇiyammaṉ, Katalacciyammaṉ; the god Murugaṉ; and various guardian deities. While Lawrence was in Batticaloa, possession by Kāḷī was most common.[43] People fleeing from Sri Lankan Army ground operations and Air Force bombings in vulnerable interior Tamil villages periodically seek refuge at east coast Kāḷī temples, contributing to growing cross-caste participation in propitiatory ritual and shamanic ordeals. These small goddess temples are the destination of thousands of devotees (rather than hundreds, as in earlier years) who come to fulfill vows to Kāḷī in acts of intense devotion involving initiatory ordeals (walking on hot coals or skin piercing). Rituals may incorporate practices of blood sacrifice of goats and chickens or, alternatively, ash pumpkins.

When oracles unite with *śakti*, the active female energy of the Hindu cosmos, they describe the process of possession as a painful sacrifice of the body that causes unbearable heat and a feverish trembling. Śakti energy enters through the tops of the toes, up to the throat; Śakti speaks through the oracle's navel or throat region, and through dance.[44] Especially in Kāḷī mediums, an overwhelming feeling of *āvecam* ("uncontrollable emotion, fury, wrath") can be experienced. "Oracles' speech and body language are considered divine, not their own, and they are therefore not held responsible for their words and actions."[45] Oracles in Batticaloa have come in close proximity to death in some way: they have received the goddess's grace in surviving near-death illness, or they have lost children, husbands, wives, or parents. Oracles are both male and female, from both high and low castes, and are often related to living or deceased oracles. "The oracles themselves, ordinary people living in extraordinary historical circumstances of violence, experienced the additional trauma of bearing witness and affirming the terror of annihilation."[46]

Although Kāḷī has been appropriated in modern India for political purposes, the Tamil Tigers have not instrumentalized Kāḷī as a victory symbol for the Tamil warriors because "religion is not part of the consciousness of the struggle."[47] They keep religion out of the political life of LTTE because there are Tamil Christians, both Catholic and Protestant, in addition to the majority of Hindu Tamils, and they do not want to risk internal dissention. The goddess temples and Christian churches, rather than LTTE, are the sacred spaces set aside for the outpouring of emotion and "unconstrained expression of horror" endemic to war zones.

Under emergency regulations in Sri Lanka, which"dispense with the normal safeguards against arbitrary detention, disappearance and torture that are found in the ordinary law, and thus facilitate abuse,"[48] civilian Tamils have sometimes been detained for over five years without charges filed against them or a court order.[49] When young men are arrested and detained, they usually vow to Kāḷī and other *Ammaṉs* that if she releases them from detention, they will walk on hot coals and pierce themselves. Many young Tamils who are arrested and detained report that their mothers go many times to the Kāḷī temple to pray for their release; when they are being tortured by Sinhalese, they cry out Kāḷī's name; and often one of their first requests upon being released is to go to a Kāḷī temple. Cittiravel, a Tamil porter, crippled by torture, who was imprisoned for twenty-six months in four Sri Lankan detention centers, speaks of the Ammaṉ's "grace" in removing suffering from devotees who keep their firewalking ordeal vows to her. He was tortured because Sinhalese soldiers thought he was LTTE. Kāḷī bestows courage and defiant survival upon those who fulfill their ordeal vows to her. As Lawrence emphasizes,

> Torture is used to control "punishable" people, to force them into submissiveness and obedience, but through ritual ceremonies that dignify the violated body-self, Cittiravel's body is resignified. Before the gathered collectivity at the temple, during his enactment of the vow of crossing a scorching trench of glowing embers, his body symbolizes the capacity to persevere. He has improvised a "pivoting" manner of walking with his body bent at the waist, swinging one foot at a time as far as he is able. In his slow sideways manner of mobility, he continues to keep his promise to the goddess Kāḷī to cross the hot coals of the fire pit during her annual propitiation at the local temple. Within the reality of the local context, this is an act of defiant survival. Large numbers of local observers collectively voice the religiously validating mantra, *Haro harā*! in unison as he slowly crosses the deep firepit for Kāḷī–Viramākāḷī—the goddess of courage. At this moment, multiple and contradictory meanings are written onto this body.[50]

Lawrence describes a typical interaction between a devotee and an oracle concerning a disappearance. A women who has lost eight members of her family, including her husband, has come to ask the oracle if her missing son is alive. Her daughter and grandchildren are living with her in an abandoned house, since the army is occupying her home. The son's death is confirmed by the female oracle as she looks into the mother's eyes and sings a verse of a

Tamil song from a popular film [*Pālum Paḻamum*]:

> Let things gone be gone
> Who in this world is living eternally?[51]

The oracle advises the mother to devote herself now to her remaining family, and places the offering of betel leaves, areca nut, flower, and a ten-rupee note back in the mother's hands. She returns the offering if the person asked about is dead—sometimes ten offerings a day are returned. Frequently, the oracle closes the séance by instructing the devotee to perform a propitiatory ritual or to make a vow to Kāḷī to perform an ordeal such as firewalking, or she gives the devotee something from the Ammaṉ shrine. Kāḷī oracles enable crippled and suffering devotees, by enacting vows to Kāḷī of fire walking and piercing the body (in which physical wounds vanish and no pain is experienced), to undermine the power of the state and to liberate the tortured body from suffering through a shamanic ordeal.

Spirt or *śakti* possession is a vehicle of power for victims of gender or class oppression, a means of transforming and transcending their powerlessness and embodying divine authority. Devotees at the Sri Lankan possession séances, immobilized by military occupation, government checkpoints, detention camps, bunkers, and thousands of disappearances, find in the Kāḷī oracle a deep spiritual reservoir, a safe witness, for lives and bodies shattered by warfare, torture, and dislocation.

> Voicing the incoherent sounds of the tortured, representing injury on behalf of those silenced, oracles tansform absesnce into presence, giving pain a place in the world. It often seems that oracles are not attempting to make sense of unacceptable social suffering—but rather are trying to find a voice to express unresolved grief in an altered world where the rule is to "keep quiet" about broken connections in the closest circle of human relationships. . . . The oracle creates an opening for trauma to make its way into collective experience and memory. Moreover, she does not diffrentiate herself from the suffering of others. . . . The oracles' religious imagination incorporates and reflects the world of chaos in which both they and those who seek their help live—a world in which people do not enjoy a sense of control over events.[52]

The Progressive Potential of Goddesses

From ancient Arabia and Mesopotamia to contemporary Mexico and India, the presence of goddesses has never been an *a priori* signifier of mortal women's empowerment in historical times; on the contrary, there often seems to be an inverse relation between female status indices and the presence of goddesses. Although feminist thinkers have appropriated the attributes of fierce, independent goddesses such as Kālī, Durgā, and their numerous *avatāras* because these deities are infused with *strī-śakti*, Rajeswari Sunder Rajan believes that such goddesses are "feminist" only when viewed through the prism of the Western academy and Kālī studies, or as a byproduct of their political instrumentality in modern India:

> The "feminist" Hindu goddess, or more accurately the claim of the progressive potential of the goddess for women's liberation, is to be found chiefly in the following sites of discourse: South Asian studies scholarship in the Western academy, which is largely reflected in this volume [*Is the Goddess a Feminist*?]; Hindu "nationalism"; radical Indian feminism of a certain kind, and allied with it, Gandhian secularism.[53]

Ultimately, Indic fierce goddesses paraded out during times of emergency—war, revolution, political change, electoral campaigns, civil disobedience—are either warriors against the other (Muslims, British, Sinhalese)or authoritarian voices of puritan reform. As valiantly as they conquer the destroying demons that threaten androcentric order, they fail to challenge discrimination against and abuse of women; the inequities of casteism; the patriarchal family structure; the barring of women, low castes, dalits, and tribals from access to education, goods, and services available only to elite males; and discrimination on the basis of race and national origin. According to the 2008 Human Rights Watch World Report:

> India has a mixed record on women's rights: despite recent improvements in legal protections, gender-based discrimination and violence remain deeply entrenched. The low status of women and girls is revealed by the skewed sex ratio of 933 females of every 1,000 males and the high rate of preventable maternal deaths, with one woman dying in childbirth every five minutes.[54]

Mexico and India are among the very few extant cultures that have retained into modernity an institutionalized worship of female deities;[55] at the same time, both cultures have maintained stringent patriarchal-authoritarian states characterized by the glorification of female self-sacrifice and the oppression of indigenous peoples and lower classes/castes by a tiny male elite. While goddesses may function as a form of cultural compensation and solace for the subordinant status of Mexican and South Asian women, the idealized goddess stands in stark contrast to women's day-to-day secular status.

Indic goddesses, arising from the Indian landmass, their personas forged by the folk imagination of India, predate the Virgin Mary by at least four thousand years. Like the Indian Śakti, the Virgin Mother has had a long and intimate history with women and the agricultural workers of her land, and both female deites share in common their usefulness to the dominant culture. The Holy Virgin was imported from Spain to Mexico, where she supplanted the aboriginal Mexican goddesses and, as the mother of Christianity, she marginalized indigenous cultures. Since the eighteenth century, North American Indian inferiority has been judged not on the issue of souls, but because Indian belief systems, including their worship of a living Earth Mother, threatened European notions of private property and were "held to be prima facie evidence that Indians were less evolved than Europeans and that they stood against the tide of history."[56] During Hernando Cortez's murderous explorations of the mid-1500s, Europeans had doubts as to whether the autochthonous Indians of Central America and Mexico were really human, resulting in fierce disagreement within the Catholic Church about the fate of the Indians.

> The argument became focused in the historic sixteenth-century debates between Spanish scholar Juan Ginés de Sepúlveda and Domincan friar Bartolomé de as Casas, as to whether Indians had souls and ought to be saved for the Church, or whether they should be slaughtered or made into slaves. Sepúlveda argued the Aristotelian viewpoint that some people are born to slavery. De las Casa, who had traveled in Mexico with Cortez, and had been impressed with the Indians, was horrified at the invaders' brutality. He argued that murder and slavery contradicted the Gospels. Pope Pius V finally sided with de las Casas in 1566, ruling that Indians should be converted rather than killed. Apparently no consideration was given to permitting Indians to live as they had before the Spanish invasion.[57]

To further their decision to save Indian souls for the Church, the Spanish first introduced the Virgin Mary in the sixteenth and seventeenth centuries during their military campaign to colonize Mexico. A vision of the Virgin Mary appeared before a poor Indian, Juan Diego, who claimed the goddess gave him Castelian roses to take to the Bishop who was tutoring him in Christianity. The Virgin wanted a church to be built in the spot where the temple for the Aztec goddess Tonantsi once stood, in essence using the Virgin to supplant the indigenous religion with Christianity. (It will be recalled that the Buddha and his missionaries, blazing an earlier patriarchal trail, constructed Buddhist shrines and monasteries over Indian Mother-goddess shrines.) When Juan handed the roses to the Bishop, the image of the Virgin of Guadalupe appeared miraculously in his cape. This news was accepted by the Indian population as the miraculous incarnation of Tonantsi the Aztec Earth and fertility goddess associated, like Guadalupe, with the Moon.[58] The archives of the era reveal that "Guadalupism" became so widespread and ardent that many priests urged the destruction of the shrine and cult on the basis that they were "a satanic device to mask idolatry."[59] Nevertheless, her popularity grew, and the Virgin is credited with abating epidemics, causing floods to subside, and performing many miracles for individuals and families.

The Spanish conquerors were the first in a string of warriors and revolutionaries who held aloft images of the Virgin army general—the Mexican analogue of Bhārata Mātā—to lead them to victory. Since independence from Spain, the Virgin Mary has been appropriated as a military symbol by both Mexican ruling elites and peasant revolutionaries. Male soldiers identified the Virgin with victory, yet when her aid was invoked in the war with the United States, Mexico lost the war, along with a large tract of Mexican land. Despite the Virgin's failure to secure victory, the treaty ending the war was signed in the city of Guadalupe Hidalgo, the home of Guadalupe's shrine.The Virgin's allegiance shifted to the indigenous people she had earlier helped to conquer when her image was allied with the nationalist forces in the Civil War of 1911, "which effectively curtailed the influence of the hereditary elite and made full citizens of peasants and the urban poor"[60] until contemporary forces of globalism reversed the populist trend.

Two ideals deeply ingrained in the Mexican consciousness are feminine purity and the sacredness of motherhood, which flow out of the dual themes of honor and shame common to Latin America, Spain, and the entire Mediterranean world. These ideas forge an ideal female image—the Virgin Mary—consisting of a virginal, sexually modest, childlike woman, yet at the same time, a married, self-sacrificing mother. "The unmarried woman who is not preoccupied with protecting her virginity is a shame to family honor, a 'bad girl' who is fair game to all. Nevertheless, the society provides all females with an alternative: they may choose to be pure, virgin, submissive, and honored by all as wife and mother."[61] (They may also choose the convent.) This schizoid element in female role-playing may contribute to psychological problems among women. Campbell sees a causal relationship between the icon of the Virgin of Guadalupe, central to both folk and orthodox Mexican Roman Catholic religion, and the high levels of neurosis among Mexican women.

The inequities of the Mexican two-tiered social system (the elite parasitic class and the impoverished worker class) are supported and perpetuated by the gender role polarity of that culture. The gap between real Mexican women and the Virgin of Guadalupe symbol, like the gap between upper class and lower class women, is thought by some theorists to dichotomize women's roles and psyches. "The working mother in a quasi-feudal society can be self-actualized only if she can rely on servants, and the servant must neglect her own children. There are 'good girls' because there are 'bad girls'."[62] Further, Campbell perceives an inverse relation between goddess-worshiping societies in Hindu, Buddhist, and Roman Catholic countries and a high secular status among women.

> Thus, in the West, the worship of the Virgin stands alongside the self-abnegation of women and the patriarchal, authoritarian attitudes of males. In the East, the *Code of Manu*, India's book of religious laws, suggests that a husband should be worshiped by his wife even though he be unfaithful or totally devoid of good qualities.[63]

In the same vein, Rajeswari Sunder Rajan asserts that there is a correlation between a society that worships goddesses and low secular status of women, noting that "the symbolic valution of froms is not a reflection of the actual material and historical conditions in which they take shape."[64] Rajan identifies the true indices of the status of women—*equality of opportunity, female sex ratios, literacy, life expectancy, income, legal equality, and subjection to violence*—and points to the evidence that "societies that 'have' goddesses—and women leaders—score poorly on these counts. That the ideological promotion of powerful female models does not contribute to ordinary women's well-being may be contrary to certain feminist expectations, but it appears to be an empirically valid finding."[65] Patriarchy is therefore able to maintian the divide between goddesses and mortal women without and sense of contradiction.[66]

Nilima Chitgopekar asserts that Indian feminist discourse has been "slow and cautious and at times tinged with suspicion" about using Indian goddesses "as enabling models or as a symbolic resource for Indian women"[67] for a number of reasons. Along with Rajan and Campbell, Chitgopekar observes that "there is a great divide between the exalted image of the divine feminine and her inferior status on the social plane."[68] Rajan, although skeptical of the Western feminist appropriation of Indian goddesses, believes that goddesses can be recovered as feminist icons or resources as long as women appropriate the attributes of the fierce unmarried Kālī-like goddesses, since they are representative of *strī-śakti* (women-power).[69] *Strī-śakti* liberally infuses the women and goddesses of woman-centered folk materials, in which female personas are critical of the males and the authoritarian caste system that have abused and enslaved them, and frequently lash back, incandescent with rage, at the male establishment. In the other hand, Nilima Chitgopekar remarks that "we are told that the concept of *strī-śakti* with its reference to bloody Mother-goddess traditions imply too much endorsement of violence."[70]

Aside from the issue of female violence, Lindsey Harlan[71] has indirectly pointed to the possible speciousness of equating fierce goddesses with women power by illustrating that Rajput women who worship fierce goddesses, far from declaring their power, autonomy, and independence, are reinforcing and perpetuating their own cloistered lives and the patriarchal caste system as undying institutions. Similarly, Gabriele Dietrich has stressed that "western paradigms of feminist theology are not always easily applicable (e.g., the whole debate on goddess religion makes little sense in a country teeming with goddesses and yet as bloomingly patriarchal as India)."[72]

The warrior aspect of the goddess, then, serves elite male interests and their idea of cosmic order, which is crystallized in the caste system. As we have seen, while the Rajput *kuladevīs* are ostensibly warriors, "the female conception of the *kuladevī* entails a predominant notion of the goddess as wife and mother."[73] In his study of *Pāṇḍava-līlā*, a traditional ritual dramatization of the *Mahābhārata*, Sax found that women enacted violent scenarios "not as women *per se*, but as Rajputs supporting their warrior husbands,"[74] and concluded that episodes of violence are as much a function of *varṇa* or class and caste as of gender. In other words, the women's participation in violent enactments reinforces the caste duty of the kṣatriyas and the caste system as an institution.

The Feminist Dimension of Folklore

If the creation of a warrior goddess who demands gory blood rites and self-sacrifice on the battlefield is attributed to males who eventually wrote legitimating myths of cosmic war and gender and caste oppression, it is reasonable to assume that an underclass female counterpart, representing a strictly women's mythology, should exist that would present nonelite women's interests. Until the end of the twentieth century, the focus on elites perpetuated androcentric methodologies in which the machinations of brāhmaṇic males, their gods and subordinate wife-goddesses, and ruling class institutions predominated in academic studies of Indic religions in the West. The neglect of vernacular religious traditions, particularly the fierce goddess traditon among nonelite women, has caused significant biases in studies of Indian history that have "contributed greatly to the distortion of Indian views of the feminine."[75] When they are translated and studied, the hidden or suppressed accounts of these subordinate groups, found primarily in woman-based folk material, reveal a self-assertive, feminist worldview that symbolically decries social injustice and caste and gender oppression. The vernacular languages of Indian indigenous peoples contain a vast resource of mythology, folk songs, folklore, oral and documented history, and other forms of literature relating to women's attitudes and values. As Suman Chitnis emphasizes,

> To an extent, this is the feminist dimension of the postcolonial explosion of interest in recovering connection with indigenous life and culture. It is an aspect of the attempts made by independent India's Western-educated, English-speaking elite to return to the traditional culture from which they have been distanced through a century and a half of colonial rule and European education. The same impulse has generated the country's spectacular renaissance of indigenous art, craft, music, dace, and theater. The same quest has brought about the renewal and reinstatement of indigenous systems of medicine such as yoga, *āyurveda*, and *unānī* and indigenous sciences such as *Vāstu Śāstra*—that is, the science of architecture.[76]

In the mid-twentieth century, independent (non-academic) folklorist N. Vanamamalai[77] (1917–80) focused on the sociological meaning of historical folk ballads, the oral tradition of the unlettered Tamil masses that presents the view of history of the common people. These ballads are not chronicles of history, but folk interpretations of events in the memory of rural people (feudal serfs in the kingdom). Some ballads are still extant because they are sung at rural festivals, and heroes are often deified in their birthplace and festivals are held in their honor.[78] Usually performed through the folk preformance genre, *Villupattu* (Bow Song), these ballads involve a group of performers who chant, speak, sing, and play musical instruments in or beside temples that are dedicated to the spirits of the ballad heroes and heroines. The climax of the performance is a spirit possession séance in which the spirit of the slain hero enters both dancers in costume and audience members. In the tradition of reigious rituals for Murukaṉ and Māriyammaṉ, the possessed individuals perform a spirit possession dance and the hero speaks through them, giving prophecies and answering questions from the audience.

Tamil social ballads address the problems of caste oppression, a woman's misery in patrilineal joint family systems, intercaste marriage and its effects, the effects on women of patrilineal inheritance, and revenge against the caste system, the latter portrayed as the source of armed robbery, unemployment and its consequences, economic necessity, and frustration.[79] Scenarios involve local lower-caste men who were killed for breaking caste rules, either by marrying an upper-caste woman or defending lower-caste women or land from appropriation by upper-caste men, or lower-caste women who kill themselves because of their despair over inheritance or caste laws. "Nallathangal" is the story of a woman who drowns her children in a well before committing suicide because of her sister-in-law's abusive treatment, representative of the injustice of the system of patrilineal inheritance that bars daughters from the property of their natal family.

> Nallannan and his sister Nallathangal worked together while they were young and unmarried. They raised crops and planted trees. The family lived in prosperous circumstances. Then Nallathangal was given in marriage to a wealthy farmer living in a far off village. She bore seven children. Then there was drought for many years and her family began to be in want. Nallathangal's husband left the family in search of work. Nallathangal went to her parental home just to spend a few days and obtain from her brother a few bags of corn to tide over critical days. When she arrived in her brother's home, she found that her brother had gone to the fields. Her sister-in-law treated her as an unwanted guest. Disappointed in her expectations and broken hearted at the cruel taunts of her sister-in-law she left after a few hours. She then realized that though she had contributed her labor for many years to increase the wealth of her parental home, she had no right to even a moiety of that property because after marriage she had become an utter stranger to her own paternal family. The strange woman who had become the wife of her brother had all rights since her children would be heirs to that property. She throws her children into a well and threw herself down into it after them. The brother returned home and learned about her visit from the neighbor. Going in search of her he found her and the children dead. Having learned of his wife's behavior he took revenge on her and her parents by means of a stratagem and finally kills himself.[80]

In another ballad, "Kouthalamada kathai," a low-cast chakkli girl, Poovayi, goes to town everyday to sell curds and ghee. A high-caste man attempts to seduce her each day, and one day she asks a young Muslim man to accompany and protect her. The rogue approaches them and the two men fight and kill one another. "Poovayi was distressed to see that the man who had offered to save her from insult, was killed. She cursed the gods and killed herself."[81]

While husking or grinding in the courtyard, weeding or sowing in the field, or preparing for religious ceremonies, Indian women sing work and ritual songs associated with specific times of a woman's life. Although all the songs protest their neglect and denial of rights, the women never complain about their lot of heavy labor and poverty. As Vanamamalai emphasizes,

> The bulk of Tamil folk songs especially the lullaby, the dirge and love songs are the creations of women. Hence the picture of women in Tamil folk songs is largely autobiographical. . . . The worship of goddess of fertility Parvai, and goddesses of courage Mutharamman, Muthumari, Mariamman and exclusive rituals of women suggest a prehistoric matriarchal state of society in which women had predominance.[82]

In the late twentieth century, folklorists Stuart H. Blackburn, who followed up on Vanamamalai's Villupattu research, and A.K. Ramanujan[83] began collecting folklore and women's literature that represent cosmologies of the powerless, repositories of women's knowledge often structured as sardonic inversions of the elite brāhmaṇic model. Low-caste and dalit women compose songs, myths, and stories that do not blame the victim. In the worldview of the underclass, the "capriciousness of the gods, and the sheer contingency of events responsible for the disorder of their lives," as sociologist Veena Das has pointed out, "free those who suffer from having to take personal responsibility for their fate."[84] It is useful to juxtapose the elite mythic pattern of cosmic war mixed with perennial karmic debt and suffering with its counterpoint in women-centered folk material collected by folklorists such as Vanamamali, Blackburn, and Ramanujan.

Folk materials and folk Purāṇas are an important genre of women's mythologies, told in "the substandard, not necessarily rural, nonliterate dialects, those motherliest of mother tongue dialects."[85] Ramanujan provides cogent analytical evidence that these Indian women's tales, which often function as " 'counter-texts' to their better-known 'classical' analogues,"[86] essentially invert the orthodox social and moral order while ridiculing the elites and their male gods. Women's counter-texts are a statement about their experience of caste- and gender-based injustice, as we have seen in myths of south Indian village goddesses Māriyammaṉ and Ellaiyammaṉ.

The opening creation myth of *Mādeśvara,* for example, which might be construed as a female fantasy, involves parodied, sardonic inversion of many expressions of brāhmaṇical power, including sex, gender, and familial roles and cultural taboos set out in the Vedas, epico-Purāṇic texts, and Sanskrit classics. This creation myth takes the Vedic mythic scenario of Brahmā the Creator lusting after his daughter and turns it on its head: here Ādiśakti is the Creatrix who lusts after her sons. The goddess is hoodwinked by her own sons, who reveal great personal duplicity, greed for power, and, in the end, hypocrisy. In all of the brāhmaṇic Purāṇas, including the *Devī-māhātmyam* interpolation of the *Mārkaṇḍeya,* the gods bestow on the goddess their powers and mystical weapons; here Ādiśakti reverses the male pattern and bestows on Śiva her powers and her "eye of fire."[87] Ramanujan summarizes this woman's myth as follows:

> The myth here, like other women-centered folk materials, also suggests a very feminine (even a feminist) view of the Hindu pantheon: the source of all creation was a woman, who is tricked out of her power by her son, destroyed, divided, and domesticated into three lesser, docile, consort goddesses for the three gods, Viṣṇu, Śiva, and Brahmā. Though they refuse to sleep with their mother, refusing to break the incest taboo when she asks them to, they marry fragments of her once her powers are transferred to Śiva and she herself is reduced to ashes. Out of her ashes, they remake three manageable wives. They marry their mother, but only after fragmenting her.[88]

Whitehead[89] relates a slightly different version of the same myth about the supreme goddess Ammavaru or Aṅkamma, who hatches Brahmā, Viṣṇu, and Śiva out of a giant egg and punishes them when they refuse to worship her. At the end of this version, the goddess "took away all the wealth of the town while the nine kings were doing pūjā to Śiva."[90] When the nine kings come to her garden to steal her flowers, the goddess gets her revenge:

> As they were plucking the flowers, Ammavaru seized them, took them off to an open space, where she had erected stables of gold, silver, and diamonds, and impaled them in such a way that their blood could not curdle and no flies could touch them. She then placed her steed, the jackal, to guard the corpses, and then vanquished her enemies.[91]

Whitehead interprets the "weird rambling" myth as a metaphorical depiction of brāhmaṇic ascendancy in the south,

> the rise of a new form of religion side by side with the older cults of the village deities, the dislike that was felt by the upper classes for the worship of female deities, the struggle that took place between the old religion and the new, the varying phases of the conflict, the way in which disease and famine drove the masses back to the worship of their older deities, and then the drawn battle, as Śiva asserted his power and Ammavaru vanquished her enemies, and both continued to receive the worship of the people.[92]

In folk myth, Anataragaṭṭamma is a Kannada village disease goddess who is, like the folk goddesses Ādiśakti and Ammavaru, self-creating (unlike Purāṇic Mahiṣāsura-mardinī, who is created by male gods). Due to her subjugation by cruel social codes and her prescribed domestic duties, she was so enraged that she became a *Māri* (terrifying goddess), or Māriyammaṉ. Myths of Māriyammaṉ proliferate in the Kannada, Tamil, Telugu, and Malayalam areas in south India and among Kerala *ādivāsīs*, and her worship is accompanied by spirit possession rituals and animal sacrifice. A.K. Ramanujan reports that the village goddesses are seen as *avatāras* of Kālī or Śiva's relative.[93]

The village women who sing of hero-goddesses are not revolutionaries; rather, the women have used the classic patriarchal myths to give themselves a voice. We see from the songs the contingency of women's lives, their absence of identity unto themselves; their lives are defined by their husbands' lives. The myths of Ādiśakti and Māriyammaṉ are masks or personas through which women can express themselves and criticize the dominator hierarchy that abuses them as women and members of the underclass.

REFERENCES

1. John Larkin and Eric Bellman, "In India, the Path to Growth hits Roadblock: Slums," *The Wall Street Journal* (March 17, 2006).
2. Mike McPhate, "The India Bush Didn't See," *San Francisco Chronicle* (March 5, 2006).
3. Ibid.

4. Bill Hayton, "Asia faces 'growing poverty gap'," BBC News (February 8, 2007), http://news. bbc.co.uk/2hi/asia-pacific/6342599.stm (accessed March 14, 2007).
5. Mies et al., *Women: The Last Colony* (London, 1988): 38.
6. Ibid., 40 [italics in original].
7. Shiva, *India Divided,* 158.
8. Gail Omvedt, *Reinventing Revolution: New Social Movement and the Socialist Tradition in India* (New York, 1993).
9. Vandana Shiva, *Staying Alive: Women, Ecology and Development* (New Delhi, 1989).
10. Chaudhuri, "Women in Radical Movement," 307.
11. Dietrich, "Women and Religious Identities in India after Ayodhya," in Against *all Odds: Essays on Women, Religion and Development from India and Pakistan,* ed. Kamla Bhasin, Ritu Menon, and Nighat Sa'id Khan (New Delhi: Kali for Women, 1994): 35–50.
12. Paul R. Brass, *The Production of Hindu-Muslim Violence in Contemporary India* (Seattle, 2003), 61.
13. The Samiti is the women's wing of the paramilitary, non-party Hindu nationalist organization, the Rashtriya Swayamsevak Sangh. The social organization of both male and female groups is based on paramilitary hierarchy.
14. Paola Bacchetta, "All Our Goddesses are Armed," in *Against All Odds:* 133–56.
15. Ibid., 134.
16. Bacchetta explains that she uses the term "the muslims" in lower case, in quotes, and in the plural "to designate a non-entity, a projection, in the sense of Hitler's 'the jews,' as understood by Jean-Francois Lyotard in his *Heidegger and 'the jews'* (Minneapolis: University of Minnesota Press, 1990) in ibid., 154n8.
17. Ibid., 134.
18. Ibid., 148.
19. Ibid., 153.
20. Ibid., 143.
21. Ibid., 144.
22. Ibid., 137.
23. Ehrenreich, *Blood Rites,* 227.
24. Ibid.
25. "Networking in South Asia," Council on Foreign Relations (April 30, 2007), http://www.cfr.org/publicatilon/12773/ (accessed June 15, 2007).
26. Human Rights Watch World Report 2008, Country Summary: India (January 2008), http://hrw.org/englishwr2k8/docs/2008/01/31/india 17605.htm (accessed February 4, 2008).
27. "India Blames Islamic Militants for Blasts," *The New York Times* (August 27, 2007), http://www.nytimes.com/2007/08/27/world/asia/27india.html?_r=1&oref=slogin (accessed October 8, 2007).
28. US Department of State, Bureau of Consular Affairs, http://travel.state. gov/travel/cis_pa_tw/cis/cis_1139.html (accessed August 9, 2006).
29. The Maoist insurgents are also known in India as Naxalites, after Naxalbari, the town north of Kolkata (Calcutta) where an armed communist rebellion first erupted 38 years ago. After quickly being extinguished, the insurgency quietly reappeared.

30. Jeremy Carl, "Hindden Civil War Drains India's Energy," *Asia Times Online* (August 9, 2006), http://www.atimes.com/atimes/South_Asia/HH09Df01.html (accessed August 9, 2006).
31. "Nepal's Maoists Announce 9-Day Ceasefire" Radio Australia (October 15, 2004), http://www.abc.net.au/ra/news/stories/s1221315.htm (accessed August 11, 2006).
32. Carl, "Hidden Civil War" (accessed August 9, 2006).
33. Juergensmeyer, *Terror in the Mind of God*, 201.
34. "Networking in South Asia," Council on Foreign Relations (April 30, 2007), http://www.cfr.org/publication/12773/ (accessed June 15, 2007).
35. Juergensmeyer, *Terror in the Mind of God*, 167.
36. Spengler, "Jihād, the Lord's Supper, and Eternal Life," *Asia Times Online* (September 19, 2009), http://www.atimes.com/atimes/Front_Page//HI19Aa02.html (accessed September 19, 2006).
37. Juergensmeyer, *Terror in the Mind of God*, 167–68.
38. See George Lakoff, *Don't Think of an Elephant! Know Your Values and Frame the Debate* (White River Junction, VT, 2004).
39. Both Sunnī and Shī'ite sects are waiting for the Mahdī, who will emerge before the Day of Judgment, institute a kingdom of justice, and fight in the last days alongside the returned Jesus against the Dajjāl (Antichrist or false Messiah). Savior figures—the Zoroastrian, Saoshyant, the Christian, Jesus Christ, the Jewish messiah, and the Muslim, Mahdī—are central to the romantic Gnostic-Semitic eschatology shared by Zoroastrianism and the three Abrahamic religions. In the Shī'ite faith, the *marja'a*, the savior that the faithful await, represents the Twelfth Imām, Imām al-Mahdī, the Hidden Imām who will reappear one day to save humankind, while for Sunnīs, the Mahdī has yet to reveal himself. The conception of the Mahdī is primarily articulated in the earliest collections of Muhammad's sayings—the *hadīth* collection. According to Islamic doctrine, the Mahdī will end wars and corruption and place the world under the rule of a global Islamic caliphate. Thus there is an emphasis among Islamists on preparing for the Imām and being ready for his return. [See "Mahdī," *Wikipedia*, http://en.wikipedia. org/wiki/Mahdi (accessed August 4, 2006); Eliade, *A History of Religious Ideas*, vol. 3, 121–22; Pepe Escobar, "Waiting for the Mahdi, pt. 1: Sistani. Qim: In the Weird Heart of Shi'ism," *Asia Times Online*, http://www.atimes.com/atimes/Middle_East/GH31Ak03.html (accessed July 28, 2006); Escobar, "Waiting for the Mahdi, pt. 2: A Vision or a Waking Dream?" *Asia Times Online*, http//www.atimes.com/atimes/Middle_East/GI01Ak02.html (accessed July 28, 2006)].
40. Bowie, *Anthropology of Religion*, 110.
41. Patricia Lawrence, "Kāḷī in a Context of Terror: The Tasks of a Goddess in Sri Lanka's Civil War," in *Encountering Kālī: In the Margins, at the Center, in the West*, ed. Rachel Fell McDermott and Jeffrey J. Kripal (Berkeley, 2003).
42. Ibid., 107.
43. Ibid., 102.
44. Ibid., 115.
45. Ibid.
46. Ibid., 116.

47. Ibid., 106.
48. Elizabeth Nissan, *Sri Lanka: A Bitter Harvest* (London: Minority Rights Group, 1996), 30, cited by Lawrence, in "Kālī in a Context of Terror," 121n13.
49. Cited by Lawrence, in "Kālī in a Context of Terror," 121n13.
50. Ibid., 114.
51. Ibid.
52. Ibid., 118.
53. Rajeswari Sunder Rajan, "Real and Imagined Goddesses: A Debate," in *Is Goddess a Feminist? The Politics of South Asian Goddesses,* ed. Alf Hitlebeitel and Kathleen M. Erndl (Washington Square, NY, 2000), 272.
54. Human Rights Watch World Report 2008, Country Summary: India (January 2008), http://hrw.org/englishwr2k8/docs2008/01/31india17605.htm (accessed February 4, 2008).
55. Buddhist and Hindu goddesses are currently worshiped in Sri Lanka, Malaysia, Tibet, Bhutan, Nepal, Thailand, as well as in sects located in Europe, Trinidad, and North America.
56. Mander, *In the Absense of the Sacred: The Failure of Technology and the Survival of the Indian Nations* (San Francisco: Sierra Club Books, 1991), 200.
57. Ibid., 199–200.
58. Eva Campbell, "The Virgin of Guadalupe and the Female Self-image: A Mexican Case History," in *Mother Worship: Theme and Variations,* ed. J. Preston (Raleigh,1982), 7.
59. Ibid., 8.
60. Ibid., 9.
61. Ibid., 17.
62. Ibid.
63. Ibid.
64. Rajan, "Real and Imagined Goddesses," 272.
65. Ibid.
66. Ibid., 272–73.
67. Chitgopekar, "Indian Goddesses," 34.
68. Ibid., 32.
69. Rajan, "Real and Imagined Goddesses," 270.
70. Chitgopekar, "Indian Goddesses," 34.
71. Lindsey Harlan, *Religion and Rajput Women: The Ethics of Protection in Contemporary Narratives* (Berkeley, 1992).
72. Dietrich, "Women and Religious Identities," 37.
73. Harlan, *Religion and Rajput Women,* 71.
74. William S. Sax, "Gender and the Representation of Violence in Pāṇḍava Līlā," in *Inverted Identities: The Interplay of Gender, Religion and Politics in India,* ed. Julia Leslie and Mary McGee (New Delhi: Oxford University Press, 2000), 261.
75. Gatwood, *Devī and the Spouse Goddess,* 6–10.
76. Chitnis, "Exploring Tradition and Change among Women," 251.
77. N. Vanamamalai, *Studies in Tamil Folk Literature* (Madras, 1969).
78. Ibid., 51.
79. Ibid., 110–11.
80. Ibid., 119–20.
81. Ibid., 121.

82. Ibid., 124.
83. See A.K. Ramanujan, "Toward a Counter-System: Women's Tales," in *Gender, Genre, and Power in South Asian Expressive Traditions*, ed. Arjunn Appadurai, Frank J. Korom, and Margaret A. Mills (Philadelphia: University of Pennsylvania Press, 1991), 33–77; A.K. Ramanujan, ed., *Folktales from India* (New York, 1993); Ramanujan, *When God is a Coustomer: Telugu Courtesan Song* (Delhi and New York, 1995); Stuart H. Blackburn and A.K. Ramanujan, eds., *Another Harmony: New Essays on the Folklore of India* (Berkeley, 1986).
84. Veena Das, personal communication with Janet Chawla (August 1983), cited by Chawla, in "Negotiating Narak and Writing Destiny," 180n22.
85. A.K. Ramanujan, "On Mythologies and Folk Purāṇas," in *Purāṇa Perennis: Reciprocity and Transformation in Hindu and Jaina Texts*, ed. Wendy Doniger (Albany, SUNY Press, 1993), 102.
86. Ibid., 106.
87. Ibid., 113.
88. Ibid., 120.
89. Whitehead, *The Village Gods of South India*, 126–38.
90. Ibid., 137.
91. Ibid.
92. Ibid., 138.
93. A.K. Ramanujan, "Two Realms of Kannada Folklore" in Stuart Blackburn and A.K. Ramanujan, eds., *Another Harmony: New Essays on the Folklore of India* (Berkeley, 1986), 61.

Epilogue

> The gods and goddesses of these vanishing communities, silently and invisibly facing threats of extinction, are the ones who have made me aware of a divine species who . . . require something in addition to devotion. There are also the gods and goddesses of communities that, after centuries of oppression, the communities themselves have begun to undervalue or forget (so that they can redefine themselves as only a culture-less group of oppressed poor operating on a clean cultural slate). I believe that these gods and goddesses—as biographies of threatened cultures, as symbols of their resilience and resistance against the juggernaut of mega-development—deserve something more than standard, rationalist, dismissive ethnographies or archeologies. . . . We owe something not only to them and their humble devotees, but also to our own moral selves.[1]

Because they are endemic to the land of the subcontinent, Kālī-like goddesses as cultural symbols have been instrumental in furthering diverse and contradictory political causes in modern India relating to ecology, terrorism, and nuclear arms.[2] Violence and revolution are glorified as reifications of the mythological prototype of the demon-slaying goddess leading victorious warriors in cosmic sacred war, bringing forth order out of chaos. The shamanic Indian cure for illness, war, violence, and grief—chanted incantations, and initiatory ordeals, magic dance rituals and prophecies of Devī-inspired oracles—heals both individual and collective wounds through efficacious psychobiological energy transformation. Calling up the spirits of archaic tree goddesses of tribal forests, who speak through potent women's groups like Chipko of the need for reciprocity with the natural world, is a means of reversing the ecological degradation caused by development and consumerism.

While elite males have "spousified," militarized, demonized exploited, and "disappeared" these goddesses to gain political power, they have never, up until this point in history, managed to completely eliminate them in India. For vast stretches of time, fierce goddesses and the primal religions they symbolize have co-existed with the dominant dharma and exploitive social system because they have the power to psychologically nourish, spiritually strengthen, and emotionally unite the Indian people against internal and external enemies. Paradoxically, the success of indigenous people has made their land the site of most of the world's last remaining natural resources. The destruction of indigenous life and religion by global economic forces, including warfare, points to the fact that shamanic, Kālī-oriented spiritual traditions are as vulnerable as their Arabian, Near Eastern, and Sumerian counterparts to extinction by human predators.

Kālī, Ko<u>rr</u>avai, Durgā, Cāmuṇḍā, and Māriyammaṉ are powerful, autonomous life forces that are neither contingent on historical or social events nor controlled by human reason or personal elements. Rather, they are immanent as potentialities in individuals, nature, and societies. For their worshipers, fierce goddesses are tutelary powers that mold intellectual, social, and personal actions. Standing at the root of the human genetic tree, they are personifications of the fundamental structure of reality in vanishing vernacular cultures, and the last historical and sybmolic remnants of the Great Goddess lineage that once dominatd the world's first civilizations.

REFERENCES

1. Ashis Nandy, "Facing Extermination: Gods and Goddesses in South Asia," *Manushi* 99 (March–April 1997), http://www.indiatogether.org/manushi/issue 99/gods.htm(accessed April 14, 2003).
2. In keeping with the traditon of Mahiṣamardinī and Bahārata Mātā, Śakti and Pṛthivī were the Earth Mothers whose names were given to nuclear arms in the late twentieth century. In 1998,"Operation Shakti" was the epithet chosen for a series of underground nuclear explosins set off when India resumed nuclear testing. (The first Indian nuclear explosion, code named "Smiling Buddha," was conducted in 1974.) [Federation of American Scientists, htt://www.fas.org/ nuke/guide/india/nuke/ (accessed June 10, 2006).] India is believed to have between seventy-five and a hundred nuclear warheads; one of the dilvery systems (under the doctrine "No First Use") is named Agni, Prithvi, invoking the Vedic god of fire, Agni and the Earth-goddess Pṛthivī, or the elements of Fire and Earth. The Earth (Pṛthivī), abode of Agni (the earthly fire), is a multivalent Vedic, Upaniṣadic, and Tantric image. Pakistan, however, misinterpreted the warhead named Agni and Prithivi as a reference to Prithvi Raj Chauhan, the Indian king defeated in 1192 by Afghan king Shahabuddin Gahuri, who captured Northwestern India in the twelfth century. Although this missile was first named Hataf-V, the name was later changed to the highly symbolic Ghauri, whith the approval of the prime minister.

Bibliography

Primary Sources

The Agni Purāṇa, trans. N. Gangadharan, Ancient Indian Tradition and Mythology Series, vols. 27–30. Delhi: Motilal Banarsidass, 1984–87.

Aitareya and Kauṣītaki Brāhmaṇas of the Ṛgveda, trans. Arthur Berriedale Keith, HOS, vol. 25, 1920, 2nd Indian repr. Delhi: Motilal Banarsidass, 1981.

Āpastamba Śrautasūtra, trans. Herman Oldenberg and F. Max Müḷller, SBE, vol. 30, 1892, repr. Delhi: Motilal Banarsidass, 1964.

Atharvaveda Saṁhitā, trans. William Dwight Whitney, HOS, vols. 7–8, 1905, 2nd Indian repr. Delhi: Motilal Banarsidass, 1971.

Atharvaveda, ed. Rudolph von Roth and W.D. Whitney, 1856, 3rd edn. Bonn: Ferd. Dummlers Verlag, 1966.

The Baudhāyana-Dharmasūtra, ed. A. Cinnaswāmī Śāstrī and Umeśa Candra Pāṇḍeya, with the *Vivaraṇa* commentary by Śrī Govinda Svāmī. Varanasi: Chaukhamba Sanskrit Sansthan, 1991.

The Bhagavadgītā in the Mahābhārata, trans. J.A.B. van Buitenen. Chicago and London: Universtiy of Chicago Press, 1981.

The Bhagavad-Gītā, trans. and interpreted by Franklin Edgerton, 2 vols. Cambridge: Harvard University Press, 1944.

Bhāgavata Purāṇa of Kṛṣṇa Dvaipāyana Vyāsa, with Sanskrit Commentary Bhāvārthabodhinī of Śrīdharasvāmin, ed. J.L. Shastri. Delhi: Motilal Banarsidass, 1983.

The Book of the Discipline (Mahāvagga), trans. Isaline Blew Horner, ed. C.A.F. Rhys Davids, vol. 4. Oxford: H. Milford, Oxford University Press, 1951.

The Bṛhadāraṇyaka Upaniṣad: An Interpretive Exposition, ed. Swami Krishnananda. Shivanandanagar: Divine Life Society, 1984.

The Bṛhadāraṇyaka Upaniṣad, with the Commentary of Śaṅkarācārya, trans. Swāmī Mādhavānanda, 3rd edn. Almora: Advaita Ashrama, 1950.

Brahma Purāṇa, trans. Board of Scholars, AITMS, vols. 33–36. Delhi: Motilal Banarsidass, 1985–86.

Brahmāṇḍa Purāṇa., trans. G.V. Tagare, AITMS, vols. 22–26. Delhi: Motilal Banarsidass, 1983–84.

Bṛhatsūcipatram, ed. Buddhisāgara Śarma, vol. 1. Kathmandu: Vīrapustakālaya, 1964.

Buddha's Teaching: Being the Suttanipāta or Discourse-collection, HOS, vol. 37. Cambridge, Mass.: Harvard University Press, 1933.

Buddhism in Translations, trans. H.C. Warren, HOS, vol. 3. Cambridge, Mass.: Harvard University Press, 1915.

Buddhist Birth Stories; or Jātaka Tales, being the Jātaka-atthavaṇṇanā, T.W. Rhys Davids, 8 vols. London, 1880.

Caṇḍī-pāṭha (She Who Tears Apart Thought), also Known as the Durgā-saptaśatī (The Seven Hundred Verses in Praise of She Who Removes all Difficulties), and The Devī-māhātmyam (The Glory of the Goddess), trans. Swami Satyānanda Saraswatī. Napa, CA: Devi Mandir Publications, 1990.

The Chāndogya Upaniṣad, trans. Swami Swahananda, 1956, 2nd edn. Madras: Sri Ramakrishna Math, 1965.

The Cilappatikāram of Iḷanko Aṭikal: An Epic of South India, trans. R. Parthasarathy. New York: Columbia University Press, 1993.

Coburn, Thomas B. *Encountering the Goddess: A Translation of the Devī-māhātmya and a Study of Its Interpretation.* Albany, NY: SUNY Press, 1991.

The Devī-māhātmya or Śrī Durgā-saptaśatī, 4th edn., text and trans. Swami Jagadīśvarānanda. Madras: Sri Ramakrishna Math, 1972.

Devī Purāṇa, ed. Maṇḍanamiśra and D. Puṣpendrakumāraśarmā. Śāntiniketan and New Delhi: Śrī Lālabahādura Śāstrī Kendrīya Vidyāpīṭha, 1976.

Devī Upaniṣad, trans. Alain Daniélou, *Adyar Library Bulletin* 19, pts. 1–2 (1955): 77–84.

The Dhammapada, trans. S. Radhakrishnan, 2nd imprint. London, New York, Toronto: Oxford University Press, 1954; trans. Eknath Easwaran. Vineburg, CA: Engdahl Typography, 1990.

The Dharmasūtras, trans. Manmatha Nath Dutt. Calcutta: Society for the Resuscitation of Indian Literature, 1908.

Garuḍa Purāṇa, trans. A Board of Scholars, AITMS, vols. 12–14. Delhi: Motilal Banarsidass, 1978–80.

The Gauḍavaho: A Historical Poem in Prākrit by Vākpati, ed. Shankar Pandurange Pandit, BSS, no. 34. Bombay: Government Central Book Depot, 1887.

Gauḍavaho of Vākpati, ed. Narahara Govinda, PTSS, no. 18. Varanasi: Motilal Banarsidass, 1975.

Ghosha, P. *Durgā-pūjā.* Calcutta: Hindu Patriot Press, 1871.

The Glorification of the Great Goddess, ed. and trans. Vasudeva S. Agrawala. Varanasi: All-India Kashiraj Trust, 1963.

The Harivaṁśa, Being the Khila or Supplement to the Mahābhārata, ed. Parashuram Lakshman Vaidya, Critical edn., 2 vols. Poona: Bhandarkar Oriental Research Institute, 1969–71.

Harivaṁśa Purāṇa, trans. Ludwig Alsdorf. Hamburg: Friederichsen, DeGruyter & Co., 1936.

Harivaṁśa, translated into English Prose from the Original Sanskrit Text, ed. and trans. D.N. Bose. Calcutta: Elysium Press, 1897.

Harṣacarita of Bāṇabhaṭṭa, trans. E.B. Cowell and F.W. Thomas, 1897; repr. Delhi: Motilal Banarsidass, 1961; ed. P.V. Kane, 2nd edn. Delhi: Motilal Banarsidass, 1965.

The Hevajra Tantra: A Critical Study, trans. David L. Snellgrove, 2 vols. London: Oxford University Press, 1959.

Holy Bible, The New King James Version. Nashville: Thomas Nelson Publishers, 1979.

Hymns from the Rig Veda, trans. A.A. Macdonell. London: Oxford University Press, 1922.

Hymns of the Atharvaveda, trans. Ralph T.H. Griffiths, 2 vols., Chaukhamba Sanskrit Series, no. 66. Varanasi: Chaukhamba Sanskrit Series Office, 1968.

The Hymns of the Ṛgveda, trans. Ralph T.H. Griffith, 4th edn. Varanasi, Chaukhamba Sanskrit Series Office, 1963; repr. with a popular commentary, 2 vols. New Delhi: Munshiram Manoharlal Publishers, 1999.

The Jātaka Stories or the Buddha's Former Births, trans. from the Pali by various hands, ed. E.B. Cowell, Cambridge: Oxford, 1894; repr. [6 vols. (bd. in 3)]. New Delhi: Munshiram Manoharlal Publishers, 2002.

Kādambarī of Bāṇabhaṭṭa, trans. C.M. Ridding, 1896, repr. London: Royal Asiatic Society, 1974; ed. and trans. M.R. Kale, 4th edn. Bombay: Nirṇaya Sāgara Press, 1913.

Kālikā Purāṇa. Bombay: Śrī Veṅkaṭeśvara Press, 1964.

Kāma-kalā-vilāsa, trans. with commentary by Arthur Avalon. Madras: Ganesh & Co., 1961.

The Kathāsaritsāgara of Somadevabhaṭṭa, ed. Pandit Durgaprasad and Kasinath Pandurang Parab, 1889, 2nd edn. Bombay: The Nirṇayasāgara Press, 1903.

The Kathā Sarit Sāgara or Ocean of the Streams of Story, trans. C.H. Tawney, vol. 1. London, 1880; repr., 2 vols. New Delhi: Munshiram Manoharlal Publishers, 2010.

Karpūrādi-stotra (Hymn to Kālī), trans. Arthur Avalon. Madras: Ganesh & Co., 1965.

Kaulajñānanirṇaya and Some Minor Texts of the School of Matsyendranātha, ed. P.C. Bagchi, CSS, no. 3. Calcutta: Metropolitan Printing and Publishing House, 1934.

Kauṣītaki Brāhmaṇa, ed. E.R. Sreekrishna Sarma. Wiesbaden: Franz Steiner Verlag, 1968.

Kauṭilya's Arthaśāstra, trans. R. Shamasastry, 2nd edn. Mysore: Wesleyan Mission Press, 1923.

Kulārṇava Tantra, trans. with an Intro. Arthur Avalon (Sir John Woodroffe). Madras: Ganesh & Co., 1965.

Kūrma Purāṇa, trans. Ahibhushan Bhattacharya, Satkari Mukherji, Virendra Kumar Varma, and Ganga Sagar Rai, ed. Anand Swarup Gupta. Varanasi: All India Kashi Raj Trust, 1972.

Lakṣmī Tantra: A Pāñcarātra Text, trans. with notes by Sanjukta Gupta. Leiden: E.J. Brill, 1972.

Lalitā-Sahasranāman with Bhāskararāya's Commentary, trans. R. Ananthakrishna Sastry, 1951, repr. Adyar: The Theosophical Publishing House, 1976.

The Mahābhārata, bks. 1–3, 1973; trans. J.A.B. van Buitenen, 2 vols. Chicago: University of Chicago Press, 1975.

Mahābhārata, trans. C. Rajagopalachari, 9th edn. Bombay: Bharatiya Vidya Bhavan, 1968; trans. N.V.R. Krishnamacharya. Tirupati: Tirumala Tirupati Devasthanam, 1983.

Mahānirvāṇa Tantra (Tantra of the Great Liberation), 1913; trans. with Intro. and Commentary by Arthur Avalon. New York: Dover Publications, Inc., 1972.

The Mahāvastu, trans. J.J. Jones, 1949, vol. 1. London: Pāli Text Society, 1976.

Maitrāyaṇī Saṁhitā: Die Saṁhitā der Maitrāyaṇīya-Śākhā, ed. Leopold von Shroeder. Wiesbaden: Franz Steiner Verlag GmbH, 1972.

Maitrāyaṇīya Upaniṣad, ed. and trans. J.A.B. van Buitenen. The Hague: Mouton & Co., 1962.

Mālatī-Mādhava of Bhavabhūti, with Jagaddhara's commentary, ed. R.G. Bhandarkar. Bombay: Government Central Book Depot, 1905; ed. and trans. C.R. Devadhar and N.G. Sūrī. Poona: By the Editors, 1935.

Mānavaśrautasūtra, Belonging to the Maitrāyaṇīya Saṁhitā, ed. and trans. Jeannette M. van Gelder, *Vedapiṭaka*, vol. 1. New Delhi: International Academy of Indian Culture, 1961–63.

Manusmṛti (*The Laws of Manu*), 1886; trans. with extracts from seven commentaries by G. Bühler, SBE, vol. 25. Delhi, Varanasi, and Patna: Motilal Banarsidass, 1964.

The Mārkaṇḍeya Purāṇa, 1904, trans. with notes by F. Eden Pargiter. Varanasi: Indological Book House, 1981.

Matsya Purāṇa, ASS, no. 54. Poona: Ānandāśrama Press, 1907.

The Matsya Purāṇam, trans. B.C. Majumdar, S.C. Vasu, and Jamna Das Akhtar, ed. Jamna Das Akhtar. Delhi: Oriental Publishers, 1972.

The Minor Anthologies of the Pāli Canon, trans. F.L. Woodward, pt. 2, SBB, vol. 8. London: Oxford University Press, Humphrey Milford, 1935.

Mother of Knowledge: The Enlightenment of Ye-shes mTsho-rgyal, trans. Tarthang Tulku and revealed by Nam-mkha'i snying-po. Berkeley: Dharma Publishing, 1983.

Nārada Purāṇa, trans. G.V. Tagare, AITMS, vols. 15–19. Delhi: Motilal Banarsidass, 1980–82.

Nāradasmṛti, ed. Heramba Chatterjee Sastri, 2 vols. Calcutta: Institute of Nārada, Calcutta Sanskrit College, 1988–89.

Nāradīya Dharmaśāstra, or the Institutes of Nārada. London: Trübner &Co., 1876.

The Nine Ways of Bon: Excerpts from gZi-brjid, ed. and trans. David L. Snellgrove. London: Oxford University Press, 1967.

The Nyāyasūtras of Gotama, trans. M.M. Satisa Chandra Vidyābhūṣaṇa, rev. and ed. Nandalal Sinha, 1930, Sanskrit text with English translation, SBH, vol. 8. Delhi: Motilal Banarsidass, 1981.

Original Sanskrit Texts, translated and Illustrated by John Muir (1858); 3rd edn., 5 vols. Amsterdam: Oriental Press, 1967.

Padma Purāṇa, trans. N.A. Deshpande, AITMS, vols. 39–48. Delhi: Motilal Banarsidass, 1988–92.

Pañcatantra, ed. Nārāyaṇa Rāma Ācārya. Bombay: Nirṇayasāgara Press, 1959.

Prabodhacandrodaya of Kṛṣṇamiśra. Bombay: Nirṇayasāgara Press, 1916.

The Rājadharma, trans. Rangaswami Aiyangar, ALS, vol. 27. Madras: Adyar Library, 1941.

Rājataraṅgiṇī of Kalhaṇa (A Chronicle of the Kings of Kashmir), trans. with Intro., commentary, and Appendices by M.A. Stein, 2 vols., repr. Delhi: Motilal Banarsidass, 1979.

Rāma Prasāda's Devotional Songs: The Cult of Shakti, trans. Jadunath Sinha. Calcutta: Sinha Publishing House, 1966.

Rāma Prasāda's Grace and Mercy in Her Wild Hair: Selected Poems to the Mother Goddess, trans. Leonard Nathan and Clinton Seely. Boulder, CO: Great Eastern, 1982.

The Rāmāyaṇa of Vālmīki: An Epic of Ancient India, vol. 1, trans. with an Intro. Robert Goldman. Princeton: Princeton University Press, 1984.

The Rāmāyaṇa, trans. Manmatha Nath Dutt. Calcutta: Wealth of India, 1892–94.

Rig-Veda Saṁhitā: The Sacred Hymns of the Brahmans, ed. F. Max Müller, 6 vols. London: Trubner, 1849–74.

The Sacred Laws of the Āryas as Taught in the Schools of the Āpastamba, Gautama, Vasiṣṭha, and Baudhāyana, trans. Georg Bühler, SBE, vols. 2 and 14. Oxford: The Clarendon Press, 1879–82.

Śaiva Upaniṣads, trans. T.R. Srinivasa Aiyangar. Madras: The Adyar Library, 1953.

Śākta Upaniṣads, ed. A.M. Sastri. New Delhi: The Adyar Library, 1950; trans. A.G. Krishan Warrier. Madras: ALRC, 1967.

Sāmānya Vedānta Upaniṣads, trans. T.R. Srinivasa Aiyangar. Madras: The Adyar Library, 1941.

The Śatapatha Brāhmaṇa, trans. Julius Eggeling, 1900; SBE, vols. 12, 26, 41, 43, and 44. Delhi, Patna, Varanasi: Motilal Banarsidass, 1963.

The Saundaryalaharī or Flood of Beauty, ed. and trans. W. Norman Brown, HOS, vol. 43. Cambridge: Harvard University Press, 1958.

Siddha-Siddhānta-paddhati and Other Works of the Nātha Yogīs, trans. Kalyani Mallik. Poona: Poona Oriental Book House, 1954.

The Śiva Mahāpurāṇa, ed. Pushpendra Kumar. Delhi: Nag Publishers, 1981.

The Śiva Purāṇa, trans. A Board of Scholars, AITMS, vols. 1–4. Delhi, Varanasi, Patna: Motilal Banarsidass, 1969–70.

Śiva Saṁhitā, trans. Rai Bahadur Srisa Chandra Vasu, repr. New Delhi: Munshiram Manoharlal Publishers, 2004.

Śivasūtra (*The Aphorisms of Śiva with a Commentary by Bhāskarācārya*), translated with Exposition and Notes by Mark S.G. Dyczkowski. Varanasi: Dilip Kumar Publishers, 1991.

Skanda Purāṇa Sūtrasaṁhitā with Mādhavācārya's commentary, ed. V.S. Paṇaśīkara, 3 vols. Poona: M.C. Apte, 1893.

Sky Dancer: The Secret Life and Songs of the Lady Yeshe Tsogyel, trans. Keith Dowman and revealed by Taksham Nuden Dorje. London: Arkana, 1984.

The Śrīmad Devī Bhāgavatam, trans. Swāmī Vijñānānanda [Hari Prasanna Chatterji, pseud.], SBH, vol. 26, pts. 1–4, 1921–23, repr. New York: AMS Press, 1974.

Śrīmanmārkaṇḍeyapurāṇam. Bombay: Veṅkaṭeśvara Press, 1910.

Suttanipāta, trans. H. Saddhatissa. London: Curzon Press, 1985.

Tantravārttika: A Commentary on Śabara's Bhāṣya on the Pūrvamīmāṁsā Sūtras of Jaimini, trans. Kumarila Bhaṭṭa, SGDOS, nos. 9–10. Delhi: Śrī Satguru, 1983.

Tārānātha's Bka' Babs Bdun Ldan: The Seven Instruction Lineages, trans. and ed. David Templeman. Dharamsala: Library of Tibetan Works & Archives, 1983.

Tārānātha's History of Buddhism in India, trans. Lama Chimpa and Alaka Chattopadhyaya, ed. Debiprasad Chattopadhyaya. Simla: Indian Institute of Advanced Study, 1970.

The Teachings of Tibetan Yoga, trans. Garma C.C. Chang. New York: Citadel Press, 1993.

The Texts of the White Yajurveda or Vājasaneya-Saṁhitā, with the popular Commentary, trans. Ralph T.H. Griffith. Varanasi: E.J. Lazurus & Co., 1899; repr. New Delhi: Munshiram Manoharlal Publishers, 1987.

The Thirteen Principal Upaniṣads, trans. Robert E. Hume, 1921; rev. edn. London: Oxford University Press, 1962.

The Treasury of Good Sayings: A Tibetan History of Bön, ed. and trans. Samten G. Karmay. London: Oxford University Press, 1972.

Trivikrama-bhaṭṭa's Nalacampū, with Caṇḍapāla's Viṣamapadaprakāśa, ed. Durgāprasād and Śivadatta, 3rd edn. Bombay: Nirṇayasāgara Press, 1931.

Tsogyal, Yeshe. *Dakini Teachings: Padmasambhava's Oral Instructions to Lady Tsogyal*, revealed by Nyang Ral Nyima Oser and Sangye Lingpa, trans. Erick Pema Kunsang. Boston: Shambhala, 1990.

The Upaniṣads, trans. Patrick Olivelle. Oxford, NY: Oxford University Press, 1966; trans. Eknath Easwaran. Petaluma, CA: Nilgiri Press, 1987.

Vaiṣṇava Upaniṣads, trans. T.R. Srinivasa Aiyangar. Madras: The Adyar Library, 1945.

The Vājasaneyi Saṁhitā in the Mādhyandina and the Kāṇva Śākhā with the Commentary of Mahīdhara, Albrecht Weber, 2nd edn., CSS, no. 103. Varanasi: The Chaukhamba Sanskrit Series Office, 1972.

Vāmana Purāṇa, with English translation, ed. Anand Swarup Gupta, trans. S.M. Mukhopadhyaya, A. Bhattacharya, N. C. Nath, and V.K. Varma. Critical edn. Varanasi: All India Kashiraj Trust, 1968.

Varāha Purāṇa, trans. S. Venkatasubramonia Iyer, AITMS, vols. 31–32. Delhi: Motilal Banarsidass, 1985.

Varāhamihirācāryaviracita, Bṛhatsaṁhitā Śrīvara, ed. Avadhavihari Tripathi, 1890, repr. Varanasi: Tame Śakābde, 1968; with English translation, exhaustive notes, and literary comments, repr. Delhi: Motilal Banarsidass, 1981–82.

Vāyu Purāṇa, trans. G.V. Tagare, AITMS, vols. 37–38. Delhi: Motilal Banarsidass, 1987–88.

The Veda of the Black Yajus School entitled Taittirīya Saṁhitā, trans. Arthur Berriedale Keith, HOS, vol. 32, repr., 2 vols. Cambridge: Harvard University Press, 1914.

Vedic Hymns, trans. Edward J. Thomas. New York: E.P. Dutton & Co., 1923.

The Vinaya Piṭakam, One of the Principle Buddhist Holy Scriptures in the Pāli Language, ed. Hermann Oldenberg. London: Williams & Norgate, 1879–83.

Vinaya Texts, translated from the Pālī by T.W. Rhys Davids and Hermann Oldenberg, 8 vols. Oxford: Clarendon Press, 1881.

Viṣṇu Purāṇa, A System of Hindu Mythology and Tradition, trans. Horace Hayman Wilson, 1840, 3rd edn. Calcutta: Punthi Pustak, 1961.

Vividha-tantra-saṅgraha, ed. R.M. Chatterji. Calcutta: Bangabasi Press, 1881–86.

Woodward, F.L., trans. *The Minor Anthologies of the Pāli Canon*, pt. 2, SBB, vol. 8. London: Oxford University Press, 1935.

Worship of the Goddess According to the Kālikāpurāṇa, pt.1, trans. with intro. and notes of chaps. 54–69 by K.R. Van Kooij. Leiden: E.J. Brill, 1972.

Yājñavalkyasmṛti, with Vijñāneśvara's Mitākṣara Commentary, ed. N.R. Ācārya, 5th edn. Bombay: Nirṇayasāgara Press, 1949.

The Yajurveda, with Sanskrit text, ed. and trans. Devī Chand. New Delhi: S. Paul & Co., 1965; repr. New Delhi: Munshiram Manoharlal Publishers, 2009.

The Yoga of Delight, Wonder, and Astonishment: A Translation of the Vijñāna-bhairava, trans. Jaideva Singh. Albany, NY: State University of New York Press, 1991.

The Yogasūtras of Patañjali, SBH, vol. 4, 3rd edn. Allahabad: The Pāṇini Office, 1924; ed. and trans. J. Ballantyne, 4th repr. Calcutta: Susil Gupta (India) Private Ltd., 1963.

Yoga Upaniṣads, trans. T.R. Srinivasa Aiyangar. Madras: The Adyar Library, 1952.

Yoginītantra, edited with a Hindi translation by Paṇḍit Kanhaiyalal Mishra. Bombay: Gaṅgāviṣṇu Śrīkṛṣṇadāsa, 1957.

INSCRIPTIONAL, SCULPTURAL, AND ARCHAEOLOGICAL SOURCES

Agrawala, R.C. "Some Unpublished Sculptures from Southwestern Rajasthan," *Lalit Kala* 6 (1959): 63–71.

—. "Some More Unpublished Sculptures from Rajasthan." *Lalit Kala* 10 (1961): 31–33.

—. "More Sculptures from Amjhara, Rajasthan." *Arts Asiatiques* 12 (1965): 175–84.

—. "Some Interesting Sculptures of Varahi from North India." *Bhāratī* 12/14 (1968–71): 134–36.

Archaeological Survey of India, *Annual Report.* Calcutta: Superintendent of Government Printing, 1903–4.

Bloch, Jules, trans. *Les Inscriptions d'Aśoka,* 13th rev. edn., Collection Émile Senart, 8. Paris: Les Belles Lettres, 1950.

Boyer, A.M., E.J. Rapson, and E. Senart. *Kharoṣṭhī Inscriptions Discovered by Sir Aurel Stein in Chinese Turkestan, CII,* vol. 2. Oxford: Clarendon Press, 1920–29.

Fleet, John Faithful. "Inscriptions of the Early Gupta Kings and Their Successors." *CII,* vol. 3. Calcutta: Archaeological Survey of India, 1888.

—. *The Dynasties of the Kanarese Districts of the Bombay Presidency from Earliest Historical Times to the Musalman Conquest of* AD *1318.* New Delhi: Asian Educational Services, 1988.

—. "Sanskrit and Old Canarese Inscriptions Relating to Yādava Kings of Devagiri." *JBBRAS* 12 (1876): 1–50.

—, ed. and trans. "A Series of Sanskrit and Old Canarese Inscriptions Relating to the Raṭṭa Chieftains of Saundatti and Belgaum." *JBBRAS* 10 (1871–74): 167–298.

Hodder, Ian. "Contextual Archaeology: An Interpretation of Catal Hüyük and a Discussion of the Origins of Agriculture." *London University Institute of Archaeology Bulletin* 24 (1987): 43–56.

—. *Reading the Past: Current Approaches to Interpretation in Archaeology,* 3rd edn. Cambridge, UK and New York: Cambridge University Press, 2003.

—, ed. *On the Surface: Catalhöyük 1993–95.* Cambridge: McDonald Institute for Archaeological Research and British Institute of Archaeology at Ankara, 1996.

—. "Women and Men at Catalhöyük Mellaart." *Scientific American* (January 2004): 76–81.

Hultzsch, E. *Inscriptions of Aśoka,* vol. 1, new edn. Oxford: Clarendon Press, 1925.

Joshi, Jagat Pati, and Asko Parpola, eds. *Corpus of Indus Seals and Inscriptions,* vol. 1, *Collections in India.* Helsinki: Suomalainen Tiedeakatemia, 1987.

Mellaart, J. "Excavations at Catal Hüyük: First Preliminary Report." *Anatolian Studies* 12(1962): 41–65.

—. "Excavations at Catal Hüyük 1962: Second Preliminary Report." *Anatolian Studies* 13 (1963): 43–103.

—. "Excavations at Catal Hüyük: Third Preliminary Report." *Anatolian Studies* 14 (1964): 39–119.

—. "Excavations at Catal Hüyük 1965: Fourth Preliminary Report." *Anatolian Studies* 16(1965): 165–91.

—. *Catal Hüyük, A Neolithic Town in Anatolia.* London, 1967.

—. *The Neolithic of the Near East,* London, 1975.

Narasimhaiah, B. *Neolithic and Megalithic Cultures in Tamil Nadu.* Delhi: Sundeep Prakashan, 1980.

Noy, T., A.J. Legge, and E.S. Higgs. "Excavations at Nahal Oren, Israel." *Proceedings of the Prehistoric Society* 39 (1973): 75–99.

Panchamukhi, R.S., ed. *Karnatak Inscriptions,* vol. 1. Dharwar: Kannada Research Office, 1941.

Rajguru, S.N., "The Gangam Copperplate of Śatrubhañja Deva of Samvat 198," *OHRJ* 4, 67–78.

Ramachandran, K.S. *Archaeology of South India—Tamil Nadu.* Delhi: Sundeep Prakashan, 1980.

Rangacharya, V. *Inscriptions of the Madras Presidency,* 3 vols. Madras: Government Press, 1919.

Shah, Sayyid Ghulam Mustafa, and Asko Parpola, eds. *Corpus of Indus Seals and Inscription,* vol. 2, *Collections in Pakistan.* Helsinki: Suomalainen Tiedeakatemia, 1991.

Secondary Sources

Aghor Seva Mandal. *Two Worlds of Human Life: An Aghor Perspective.* Ghazipur, U.P.: Girnar Ashram, 1991.

Agrawala, Vasudeva S. *Vāmana Purāṇa—A Study (An Exposition of the Ancient Purāṇa–vidyā),* Varanasi: Prithvi Prakashan, 1964.

—. *Śiva Mahādeva: The Great God (An Exposition of the Symbolism of Śiva).* Varanasi: Veda Academy, 1966.

Aiyar, Indira S. *Durgā as Mahiṣāsuramardinī: A Dynamic Myth of Goddess.* New Delhi: Gyan Publishing House, 1997.

Allen, Richard Hinckley. *Star-Names and Their Meanings,* 1899; 2nd repr. New York: G.E. Stechert & Co., 1936.

Altekar, A.S. *The Position of Women in Hindu Civilization: From Prehistoric Times to the Present Day,* 1938; repr. Delhi: Motilal Banarsidass, 1956.

"Arabian Religions." *Merriam Webster Encyclopaedia of World Religions,* ed. Wendy Doniger (Springfield, Mass., 1999): 70–71.

Arberry, A.J. *The Koran Interpreted.* New York: Macmillan, 1964.
http://www.oneummah.net/quran/quran.html
http://www.usc.edu/dept/MSA/quran/
http://www.geocities.com/masad02/

Arnold, David, and David Hardiman, eds. *Subaltern Studies 8: Essays in Honour of Ranajit Guha.* Delhi, Bombay, Calcutta, and Madras: Oxford University Press, 1994.

Arokiaswami, M. "The Cult of Mariamman or the Goddess of Rain." *Tamil Culture* II, 2 (April, 1953): 153–57.

Atkinson, Edwin T. *Religion in the Himalayas.* Delhi: Cosmo Publications, 1974.

Aziz, Barbara. "Reincarnation Reconsidered: or the Reincarnate Lama as Shaman." *Spirit Possession in the Nepal Himalayas,* edited by John T. Hitchcock and Rex L. Jones. Warminster, England: Aris and Phillips Ltd., 1976, 343–60.

Babb, Lawrence A. "Marriage and Malevolence: The Uses of Sexual Opposition in a Hindu Pantheon." *Ethnology* 9, no. 2 (1970).

—. *The Divine Hierarchy.* New York: Columbia University Press, 1975.

Bacchetta, Paola. "All Our Goddesses are Armed." *Against All Odds: Essays on Women, Religion and Development from India and Pakistan,* edited by Kamia Bhasin, Ritu Menon, and Nighat Sa'id Khan. New Delhi: Kali for Women, 1994, 133–56.

Bachofen, J.J. *Das Mutterrecht* (1861), abridged and translated by Ralph Mannheim. In *Myth, Religion, and Mother Right: Selected Writings of J.J. Bachofen.* Princeton: Princeton University Press, 1967.

Bahn, P.G. "The 'Unacceptable Face' of the West European Upper Paleolithic." *Antiquity* 52 (1978): 183–92.

Bakunin, Mikhail. *God and the State.* New York: Dover, 1970.

Balter, Michael. *The Goddess and the Bull: Catalhoyuk, An Archaeological Journey to the Dawn of Civilization.* New York: Free Press, 2005.

—. "The Seeds of Civilization." *Smithsonian* 36, 2 (May 2005): 68–74.

Bamberger, J. "The Myth of Matriarchy: Why Men Rule in Primitive Society." *Women, Culture and Society,* edited by M. Rosaldo and L. Lamphere. Cambridge: Stamford University Press, 1974.

Bandyopadhyay, Pranab. *Mother Goddess Durgā.* Calcutta: United Writers, 1993.

—. *Nātha Cult and Mahānād: A Study in Syncretism.* Delhi: B.R. Publishing Corp., 1992.

Bandyopadhyaya, Narayan Chandra. *Development of Hindu Polity and Political Theories.* Edited with an Intro. Narendra Nath Bhattacharyya. New Delhi: Munshiram Manoharlal Publishers, 1980.

Banerjea, Jitendra N. *The Development of Hindu Iconography.* Calcutta: University of Calcutta, 1956; 5th edn. New Delhi: Munshiram Manoharlal Publishers, 2002.

—. *Religion in Art and Archaeology (Vaishnavism and Śaivism).* Lucknow: University of Lucknow, 1968.

—. *Paurāṇic and Tāntric Religion (Early Phase).* Calcutta: University of Calcutta, 1966.

—. "Some Folk Goddesses of Ancient and Mediaeval India." *IHQ* 14, no. 1 (1938): 101–9.

Banerji, Suresh Chandra, and Chanda Chakraborty. *Folklore in Ancient and Medieval India.* Calcutta: Punthi Pustak, 1991.

Baring, Anne, and Jules Cashford. *The Myth of the Goddess: Evolution of an Image.* London: Arkana/Penguin, 1991.

Barkataki, S. *Assam.* New Delhi: National Book Trust, 1969.

—. *Tribal Folk-Tales of Assam (Hills),* edited by C.P. Saikia. Gauhati, Assam: Publication Board, 1970.

—. *Tribes of Assam.* New Delhi: National Book Trust, 1969.

Barnett, Steve. "Identity Choice and Caste Ideology in Contemporary South India." *Symbolic Anthropology: A Reader in the Study of Symbols and Meanings,* edited by Janet Dolgin, David Kemnitzer, and David Schneider. New York: Columbia University Press, 1977.

Barua, Hem. *The Red River and the Blue Hill.* Gauhati, Assam: Lawyer's Book Stall, 1962.

Basham, A.L. *History and Doctrines of the Ājīvikas: A Vanished Indian Religion.* London: Luzac & Co., 1951.

—. *The Wonder That was India: A Survey of the Culture of the Indian Sub-continent Before the Coming of the Muslims.* New York: Grove Press, 1959.

Basu, Kaushik. "India's Economic Report Card." *Asia Times Online* (July 3, 2006), http://forum.atimes.com/topic.asp?TOPIC_ID=8155&whichpage=2 (accessed July 3, 2006).

Basu, Manoranjan. *Fundamentals of the Philosophy of Tantras.* Calcutta: Mira Basu Publishers, 1986.

Bazou, Leopold. "Kulatur, an Experience in Village Antiquity." *Tamil Culture* III, 2 (April 1954): 121–29.

Beal, Samuel, trans. *Chinese Accounts of India,* 1883, 4 vols. rev. edn. Calcutta: Susil Gupta (India) Ltd., 1957–58.

—, trans. *The Life of Hiuen-Tsiang* by the Shamans Hwui Li and Yen Tsung, 1911; 2nd edn. Delhi: Academica Asiatica, 1973.

Beane, W.C. *Myth, Cult and Symbols in Śākta Hinduism: A Study of the Indian Mother Goddess.* Leiden: E.J. Brill, 1977.

Beck, Brenda E.F. "A Praise-Poem for Murugan." *Journal of South Asian Literature* 11 (1–2).

—. "Color and Heat in South Indian Ritual." *Man* 4 (1969): 553–72.

—. *Peasant Society in Koṅku: A Study of Right and Left Subcastes in South India.* Vancouver: University of British Columbia Press, 1972.

—. "The Goddess and the Demon: A Local South Indian Festival and Its Wider Context." *Puruṣārtha* 3 (1981): 83–136.

—. *The Three Twins: The Telling of a South Indian Folk Epic.* Bloomington: Indiana University Press, 1982.

Beck, Peggy V., Anna Lee Walters, and Nia Francisco. *The Sacred: Ways of Knowledge, Sources of Life.* Tsaile, Arizona: Navajo Community College Press, 1990.

Behara, K.S. "The Evolution of Śakti Cult at Jajpur, Bhubaneswar and Puri." *The Śakti Cult and Tārā,* ed. D.C. Sircar. Calcutta: University of Calcutta, 1967, 74–86.

Benedict, Ruth. *Patterns of Culture.* New York: Mentor, 1934.
Bennett, Lynn. *Dangerous Wives and Sacred Sisters: Social and Symbolic Roles of High-Caste Women in Nepal.* New York: Columbia University Press, 1983.
Berkson, Carmel. *The Amazon and the Goddess: Cognates of Artistic Form.* Bombay: Somaiya Publications, 1987.
—. *The Divine and the Demoniac: Mahiṣa's Heroic Struggles with Durgā.* Delhi: Oxford University Press, 1995.
Bernal, J.D. *Science in History,* 1954; 3rd edn. New York: Hawthorn Books, 1965.
Berreman, Gerald D. "Himalayan Rope Sliding and Village Hinduism: An Analysis." *Southwestern Journal of Anthropology* 17, no. 4 (Winter 1961): 326–42.
—. *Hindus of the Himalayas: Ethnography and Change.* Berkeley: University of California Press, 1972.
Beyer, Stephan. *The Cult of Tārā: Magic and Ritual in Tibet.* Berkeley and Los Angeles: University of California Press, 1973.
Bhadrakumar, M.K. "Be skeptical . . . be very skeptical." *Asian Times Online* (August 18, 2006), http://atimes.com/atimes/South_Asia/HH18Df03.html (accessed August 18, 2006).
Bharati, Agehananda. *Great Tradition and Little Traditions: Indological Investigations in Cultural Anthropology.* Varanasi: Chaukhamba Sanskrit Series Office, 1978.
—. *The Tantric Tradition.* Garden City, NY: Anchor Books, 1970.
Bhattacharya, A.K. "A Nonaryan Aspect of the Devī." *The Śakti Cult and Tārā,* ed. D.C. Sircar. Calcutta: University of Calcutta, 1967, 56–60.
Bhattacharya, Bhabani Prasad. *Studies in the Śrautasūtras of Āśvalāyana and Āpastamba.* Calcutta: Sanskrit Pustak Bhandar, 1978.
Bhattacharyya, Haridas, ed. *The Cultural Heritage of India,* vol. 4, *The Religions.* Calcutta: The Ramakrishna Mission Institute of Culture, 1956.
Bhattacharyya, N.N. "Earth and Woman." *Ancient Indian Rituals and Their Social Contents.* Delhi: Manohar Book Service, 1975.
—. *The Geographical Dictionary: Ancient and Early Medieval India.* New Delhi: Munshiram Manoharlal Publishers, 1999.
—. *History of the Śākta Religion,* 2nd rev. edn. New Delhi: Munshiram Manoharlal Publishers, 1996.
—. *History of the Tantric Religion (A Historical, Ritualistic and Philosophical Study).* New Delhi: Manohar, 1982.
—. *History of Indian Erotic Literature.* New Delhi: Munshiram Manoharlal Publishers, 1975.
—. *Indian Demonology: The Inverted Pantheon.* Delhi: Manohar Publishers, 2000.
—. *Indian Religious Historiography,* vol. 1. Munshiram Manoharlal Publishers, 1996.
—. *The Indian Mother Goddess,* 2nd edn. New Delhi: Manohar, 1977.
—. *Religious Culture of North-Eastern India.* New Delhi: Ajay Kumar Jain, 1995.
—. "Śāktism and Mother-Right." *The Śakti Cult and Tārā,* edited by D.C. Sircar. Calcutta: University of Calcutta, 1967.

Blackburn, Stuart H. "The Folk Hero and Class Interests in Tamil Heroic Ballads." *Asian Folklore Studies* 37(1), 1978: 131–49.
—, and A.K. Ramanujan, eds. *Another Harmony: New Essays on the Folklore of India.* Berkeley, Los Angeles, London: University of California Press, 1986.
—. "Oral Performance: Narrative and Ritual in a Tamil Tradition." *Journal of American Folklore* 94 (372), 1981: 207–27.
—. "Death and Deification: Folk Cults in Hinduism." *History of Religions* 24 (3) 1985: 255–74.
—. *Singing of Birth and Death: Texts in Performance.* Philadelphia: University of Pennsylvania Press, 1988.
—, and A.K. Ramanujan, eds. *Another Harmony: New Essays on the Folklore of India.* Berkeley: University of California Press, 1986.
—, Peter J. Claus, Joyce B. Flueckiger, and Susan J. Wadley, eds. *Oral Epics in India.* Berkeley: University of California Press, 1989.
Bleeker, C.J. "Isis and Hathor: Two Ancient Egyptian Goddesses." *The Book of the Goddess Past and Present,* edited by Carl Olson. New York: Crossroad Publishing Company, 1983, 29–48.
Bloch, Maurice, and Jonathan Parry, eds. *Death and the Regeneration of Life.* Cambridge and New York: Cambridge University Press, 1982.
Bloch, Maurice. *From Blessing to Violence. History and Ideology in the Circumcision Ritual of the Merina of Madagascar.* Cambridge and New York: Cambridge University Press, 1986.
—. *Prey into Hunter. The Politics of Religious Experience.* Cambridge and New York: Cambridge University Press, 1992.
Bolon, Carol Radcliffe. *Forms of the Goddess Lajjā Gaurī in Indian Art.* University Park, PA: Pennsylvania State University Press, 1992.
Bose, D.N., and Hiralal Haldar. *Tantras: Their Philosophy and Occult Secrets.* Calcutta: Firma KLM, 1981.
Bose, Mandakranta, ed. *Faces of the Feminine in Ancient, Medieval, and Modern India.* New York and Oxford: Oxford University Press, 2000.
Bowie, Fiona. *The Anthropology of Religion: An Introduction,* 2nd edn. Malden, MA: Blackwell Publishing, 2006.
Brass, Paul R. *The Production of Hindu-Muslim Violence in Contemporary India.* Seattle: University of Washington Press, 2003.
Braverman, Amy M. "The Interpretation of gods." *University of Chicago Magazine* (February 2005), http://magazine.uchicago.edu/0412/features/index-print.shtml (accessed March 8, 2005).
Briffault, Robert. *The Mothers: The Matriarchal Theory of Social Origins,* 3 vols., 1927; repr. London: George Allen & Unwin Ltd., 1959.
Briggs, George Weston. *Gorakhnāth and the Kānphaṭa Yogīs.* Delhi, Varanasi, Patna, Bangalore, and Madras: Motilal Banarsidass, 1973.
Brighenti, Francesco. "Shamanistic Echoes in Rituals of Hindu Devotional Ordeals." http://www.svabhinava.org/friends/FrancescoBrighenti/ShamanisticEchos.htm (accessed June 25, 2005).

Brooks, Douglas Renfrew. *Auspicious Wisdom: The Texts and Traditions of Śrīvidyā Śākta Tantrism in South India.* Albany, NY: SUNY Press, 1992.

—. *The Secret of the Three Cities: An Introduction to Śākta Tantrism.* Chicago: University of Chicago Press, 1990.

Brown, C. Mackenzie. *God as Mother, A Feminine Theology in India: An Historical and Theological Study of the Brahmavaivarta Purāṇa.* Hartford: Claude Stark & Co., 1974.

—. "Kālī, the Mad Mother." *The Book of the Goddess Past and Present,* edited by Carl Olson. New York: Crossroad, 1983, 110–23.

—. *The Triumph of the Goddess: The Canonical Models and Theological Visions of the Devī-Bhāgavata Purāṇa.* Albany, NY: SUNY Press, 1990.

Brown, Donald E. *Human Universals.* New York: McGraw Hill, 1991.

Brubaker, Richard L. "The Ambivalent Mistress: A Study of South Indian Village Goddesses and Their Religious Meaning." University of Chicago, PhD dissertation, September 1978.

—. "The Untamed Goddess of Village India." *The Book of the Goddess Past and Present,* edited by Carl Olson. New York: Crossroad, 1983, 145–60.

Bryant, Edwin. *The Quest for the Origins of Vedic Culture: The Indo-Aryan Migration Debate.* New York: Oxford University Press, 2001.

Burkert, Walter. *Structure and History in Greek Mythology and Ritual.* Berkeley: University of California Press, 1979.

Butterworth, E.A.S. *The Tree at the Navel of the Earth.* Berlin: Walter De Gruyter & Co., 1970.

Caesar, Julius. *De Bello Gallico,* with Introduction, Notes, and Vocabulary by E.C. Kennedy. Cambridge Elementary Classics, vols. 1, 3, and 7. Cambridge: Cambridge University Press, 1959–60.

Cairns, Grace E. *Man as Microcosm in Tantric Hinduism.* New Delhi: Manohar Publications, 1992.

Caldwell, Sarah. "Bhagavati: Ball of Fire." *Devī: Goddesses of India,* edited by John S. Hawley and Donna M. Wulff. Berkeley, Los Angeles, London: University of California Press, 1996, 195–226.

—. "Margins at the Center: Tracing Kālī through Time, Space, and Culture." *Encountering Kālī: In the Margins, at the Center, in the West,* edited by RachelFell McDermott and Jeffrey J. Kripal. Berkeley, Los Angeles, London: University of California Press, 2003, 249–72.

—. *Oh Terrifying Mother: Sexuality, Violence and Worship of the Mother Kali.* New Delhi and New York: Oxford University Press, 1999.

—. "Waves of Beauty, Rivers of Blood: Constructing the Goddess in Kerala." *Seeking Mahādevī: Constructing the Identities of the Hindu Great Goddess,* ed. Tracy Pintchman. Albany: SUNY Press, 2001, 93–114.

Campbell, Eva. "The Virgin of Guadalupe and the Female Self-image: A Mexican Case History." *Mother Worship: Theme and Variations,* edited by J. Preston. Raleigh: University of North Carolina Press, 1982, 5–24.

Campbell, June. *Traveller in Space: In Search of Female Identity in Tibetan Buddhism.* New York: George Braziller, 1996.

Carl, Jeremy. "Hidden Civil War Drains India's Energy." *Asia Times Online* (August 9, 2006), http://www.atimes.com/atimes/South_Asia/HH09Df01.html (accessed August 9, 2006).

Carroll, Theodora Foster. *Women, Religion, and Development in the Third World.* New York, Philadelphia, Eastbourne, UK, Toronto, Hong Kong, Tokyo, and Sydney: Praeger, 1983.

Cavalli-Sforza, Luigi Lucas, and Francesco Cavalli-Sforza. *The Great Human Diasporas: The History of Diversity and Evolution.* Reading, MA: Addison-Wesley, 1995.

Cavanaugh, John, and Jerry Mander, eds. *Alternatives to Economic Globalization: A Better World is Possible,* 2nd edn. San Francisco: Berrett-Koehler Publishers, 2004.

Cavendish, Richard. *The Black Arts.* New York: G.P. Putnam's Sons, 1967.

Chakravarti, Chintaharan. "The Mārkaṇḍeya Purāṇa: Editions and Translations." *Purāṇa* 3, no. 1 (Jan 1961): 38–45.

Chakravarti, Pulinbihari. *Origin and Development of the Sāṁkhya System of Thought.* New Delhi: Munshiram Manoharlal Publishers, 1975.

Chalier-Visuvalingam, Elizabeth. "Bhairava and the Goddess." *Wild Goddesses in India and Nepal,* edited by Axel Michaels, Cornelia Vogelsanger, and Annette Wilke. Berne, Berlin, Frankfurt, New York, Paris, and Wien: Peter Lang, 1996, 253–301.

Chanda, Ramaprasad. *The Indo-Aryan Races: A Study of the Origin of Indo-Aryan People and Institutions,* 1916, with an Introduction by N.N. Bhattacharyya. Calcutta: Indian Studies Publications, 1969.

Charak, Sukhdev Singh. *History and Culture of the Himalayan States,* vol. 1. New Delhi: Light and Life, 1978.

Chatterjee, Partha. "Caste and Subaltern Consciousness." *Subaltern Studies 6: Writings on South Asian History and Society,* edited by Ranajit Guha. Delhi, Oxford, and New York: Oxford University Press, 1989, 169–209.

—. "Claims on the Past: The Genealogy of Modern Historiography in Bengal." *Subaltern Studies 8: Essays in Honour of Ranajit Guha,* ed. David Arnold and David Hardiman. Delhi, Bombay, Calcutta, and Madras: Oxford University Press, 1994, 1–49.

Chattopadhyaya, Debiprasad. *Lokāyata: A Stusdy in Ancient Indian Materialism.* 1959, 6th edn. Delhi: People's Publishing House, 1985.

—, ed. *Studies in the History of Indian Philosophy: An Anthology of Articles by Scholars, Eastern and Western.* Calcutta: K.P. Bagchi, 1978–79.

Chattopadhyaya, Sudhakar. *The Periplus of the Erythraean Sea and Ptolemy on Ancient Geography of India.* Calcutta: Asoke Ray, 1980.

Chaube, S.K. "Nation Building and ethno-Cultural Tensions in South Asia." *Ethnicity and Polity in South Asia,* edited by Girin Phukon. New Delhi: South Asian Publishers, 2002, 12–19.

Chaudhuri, Tripti. "Women in Radical Movements in Bengal in the 1940s." *Faces of the Feminine in Ancient, Medieval, and Modern India*, edited by Mandakranta Bose. New York and Oxford: Oxford University Press, 2000, 304–21.

Chawla, Janet. "Negotiating Narak and Writing Destiny: The Theology of Bemata in Dais' Handling of Birth." *Invoking Goddesses: Gender Politics in Indian Religion*, edited by Nilima Chitgopekar. New Delhi: Shakti Books, 2002, 165–202.

Chettiar, A. Chidambaranatha. "Ancient Tamil Kings—Their High Ideals." *Tamil Culture* III, 2 (April 1954): 103–9.

Chhachhi, Amrita. "Identity Politics." *Against All Odds: Essays on Women, Religion and Development from India and Pakistan*, edited by Kamia Bhasin, Ritu Menon, and Nighat Sa'id Khan. New Delhi: Kali for Women, 1994, 1–15.

Childe, V.G. *Prehistoric Communities of the British Isles*. London: Routledge, 1940.

Chinnappa, Nadikerianda. *Pattolé Palamé: Kodave Culture Folksongs and Traditions*. New Delhi: Rupa & Co., 2003.

Chitgopekar, Nilima. "Indian Goddesses: Persevering and Antinomian Presences." *Invoking Goddesses: Gender Politics in Indian Religion*, edited by Nilima Chitgopekar. New Delhi: Shakti Books, 2002, 11–42.

—. "The Unfettered Yoginīs." *Invoking Goddesses: Gender Politics in Indian Religion*, edited by Nilima Chitgopekar. New Delhi: Shakti Books, 2002, 82–111.

Chitnis, Suma. "Exploring Tradition and Change among Women in Marathi Culture." *Faces of the Feminine in Ancient, Medieval, and Modern India*, edited by Mandakranta Bose. New York and Oxford: Oxford University Press, 2000, 251–69.

Choudhury, Pratap Chandra. *History of Civilization of the People of Assam to the Twelfth Century*. Gauhati, Assam: Dept. of Historical and Antiquarian Studies in Assam, 1959.

Clarke, Sathianathan. "Reviewing the Religion of the Paraiyars: Ellaiyamman as an Iconic Symbol of Collective Resistance and Emancipatory Mythography." *Religions of the Marginalised: Towards a Phenomenology and the Methodology of Study*, edited by Gnana Robinson. Delhi: UTC, 1998, 35–53.

Coburn, Thomas B. "Consort of None, *Śakti* of All: The Vision of the *Devī Māhātmya*." *The Divine Consort: Rādhā and the Goddesses of India*, edited by John Stratton Hawley and Donna Marie Wulff. Berkeley: Religious Studies Series, 1982, 153–65.

—. *Devī-māhātmya: The Crystallization of the Goddess Tradition*, 1984, repr. Delhi: Motilal Banarsidass and South Asia Books, 1988.

—. "Devī: The Great Goddess." *Devī: Goddesses of India*, edited by John Stratton Hawley and Donna Marie Wulff. Berkeley, Los Angeles, London: University of California Press, 1996.

—. "The Devī-māhātmya as a Feminist Document." *Journal of Religious Studies* 8, no. 2 (1980): 1–11.

—. "The Study of the Purāṇas and the Study of Religion." *Religious Studies* 16, no. 3 (1980): 341–52.

Cohen, Mark Nathan. *The Food Crisis in Prehistory: Overpopulation and the Origins of Agriculture.* New Haven and London: Yale University Press, 1977.

Conze, Edward. *Buddhism: Its Essence and Development.* New York: Harper & Row, 1959.

—. *Thirty Years of Buddhist Studies.* Columbia, SC: University of South Carolina Press, 1968.

Coogan, Michael D., trans. *Stories from Ancient Canaan.* Louisville, KY: Westminster, 1978.

Coole, Diana. *Women in Political Theory: From Ancient Misogyny to Contemporary Feminism,* 2nd edn. Boulder, CO: Lynne Rienner Publishers, 1993.

Coomaraswamy, Ananda K. *The Dance of Shiva,* rev. edn. New York: The Noonday Press, 1972.

—. *Deciphering the Indus Script.* Cambridge: Cambridge University Press, 1994.

—. *History of Indian and Indonesian Art.* New York: Dover Publications, Inc., 1985.

—. *The Yakṣas.* New Delhi: Munshiram Manoharlal Publishers, 2001.

—. *Yakṣas: Essays in Water Cosmology,* edited by Paul Schroeder. New York: Oxford University Press, 1993.

—. *The Yakṣas.* The City of Washington: Smithsonian Institution, 80, no. 6, Publication 3926 (1928–31).

Cornelius, J.T. "The Dravidian Question." *Tamil Culture* III, 2 (April 1954): 92–102.

Cornford, Francis MacDonald. *Plato's Cosmology.* New York: Humanities, 1937.

Courtright, Paul B. "*Satī,* Sacrifice, and Marriage: The Modernity of Tradition." *From the Margins of Hindu Marriage: Essays on Gender, Religion, and Culture,* edited by Lindsey Harlan and Paul B. Courtright. New York: Oxford University Press, 1995, 184–203.

Cozort, Daniel. *Highest Yoga Tantra.* Ithaca, NY: Snow Lion Press, 1986.

Craddock, Elaine. "Reconstructing the Split Goddess as Śakti in a Tamil Village." *Seeking Mahādevī: Constructing the Identities of he Hindu Great Goddess,* edited by Tracy Pintchman. Albany, New York: SUNY Press, 2001, 145–70.

Crooke, William. "Aghorī." *ERE* 1 (1928): 210–13.

—. *The Popular Religion and Folklore of Northern India,* 2 vols. Westminster: Archibald Constable & Co., 1896.

Cumont, Franz, *Astrology and Religion Among the Greeks and Romans.* New York: Dover Publications, Inc., 1960.

Dange, S.A. *Sexual Symbolism from the Vedic Ritual.* Jawaharnagar: Ajanta Publications, 1979.

Daniélou, Alain. *The Gods of India: Hindu Polytheism.* New York: Inner Traditions International Ltd., 1985. (Originally published as *Hindu Polytheism,* New York: Bollingen Foundation, 1964.)

—. *Shiva and Dionysos,* translated by K.F. Hurry. London: East-West Publications, 1982.

Dasgupta, Shashi Bhusan. *Aspects of Indian Religious Thought.* Calcutta: A. Mukherjee & Co., 1957.

—. *An Introduction to Tantric Buddhism.* Berkeley and London, 1974.

—. *Obscure Religious Cults.* Calcutta: Firma K.L. Mukhopadhyay, 1962.

Das, H.C. *Tāntricism: A Study of the Yoginī Cult.* New Delhi, Bangalore, and Jullundur: Sterling Publishers, 1981.

Das, Paritosh. *Sahajiyā Cult of Bengal and Pancha Sakha Cult of Orissa.* Calcutta: Firma KLM, 1988.

Das, Veena. "The Goddess and the Demon—An Analysis of the Devī Māhātmya." *Manushi,* no. 30 (September–October 1985): 28–32.

—. "Subaltern as Perspective." *Subaltern Studies 6: Writings on South Asian History and Society,* edited by Ranajit Guha. New Delhi: Oxford, and New York: Oxford University Press, 1989, 310–24.

David, H.S. "The Original Home of the Dravidians: Their Wanderings in Prehistoric Times, B.C. 4,500 to 1,500." *Tamil Culture,* III, 2 (April 1954): 77–81.

Davies, Steve. "The Canaanite-Hebrew Goddess." *The Book of the Goddess Past and Present,* edited by Carl Olson. New York: Crossroad Publishing Company, 1983, 68–79.

Davis-Kimball, Jeannine. *Warrior Women: An Archaeologists Search for History's Hidden Heroines.* New York: Warner Books, 2002.

—. "Warrior Women of Eurasia." *Archaeology* 50, no. 1 (January/February 1997), http://www.archaeology.org/9701/abstracts/sarmatians.html (abstract), (accessed October 30, 2005).

Dawkins, Richard. *The Selfish Gene.* Oxford: Oxford University Press, 1976; rev. edn., 1989.

Dayal, Raghubir. *An Outline of Indian History and Culture,* vol. 1. New Delhi: Orient Longman, 1986.

Dean, John W. *Conservatives Without Conscience.* New York: Viking/Penguin, 2006.

Dehejia, Vidya. *Looking Again at Indian Art.* New Delhi: Ministry of Information and Broadcasting, Government of India, 1978.

—. *Early Stone Temples of Orissa.* New Delhi, Bombay, Bangalore, Calcutta, and Kanpur: Vikas Publishing House, 1979.

—, ed. *Royal Patrons and Great Temple Art.* Bombay: Marg Publications, 1988.

—. *Yoginī Cult and Temples: A Tantric Tradition.* New Delhi: National Museum, 1986.

De Nebesky-Wojkowitz, Réne. *Oracles and Demons of Tibet: The Cult and Iconography of the Tibetan Protective Deities.* The Hague, The Netherlands: Mouton & Co., 1956.

Dennett, Daniel C. *Breaking the Spell: Religion as a Natural Phenomenon.* New York: Penguin, 2006.

Denny, Frederick M. *Islam and the Muslim Community.* Prospect Heights, Ill.: Waveland Press, Inc., 1987.

De Riencourt, Amaury. *Sex and Power in History*. New York: David McKay Company, Inc., 1974.

Desai, Tripta. *Women in India: A Brief Historical Survey*. New Delhi: Munshiram Manoharlal Publishers, 1992.

Deussen, Paul. *The Philosophy of the Upanishads*. Translated by A.G. Geden, 1906; repr. New Delhi: Munshiram Manoharlal Publishers, 2002.

Dev, Usha. *The Concept of Śakti in the Puranas*. Delhi: Nag Publishers, 1987.

Dhargyey, Geshe Ngawang. *A Commentary on the Kālacakra Tantra*, translated by Gelong Jhampa Kelsang. New Delhi: Library of Tibetan Works & Archives, 1985.

Dhavalikar, M.K. "The Origins of the Saptamātṛkās." *Bulletin of the Deccan College Research Institute*. Poona 21 (1960–61): 19–25.

—, and S. Atre. "The Fire Cult and Virgin Sacrifice: Some Harappan Rituals." *Old Problems and New Perspectives in the Archaeology of South Asia*, edited by J.M. Kenoyer. Wisconsin: Archaeological Reports, vol. 2. Madison, WI: University of Wisconsin Press, 1989.

Dietrich, Gabriele. "Women and Religious Identities in India after Ayodhya." *Against All Odds: Essays on Women, Religion and Development from India and Pakistan*, edited by Kamla Bhasin, Ritu Menon, and Nighat Sa'id Khan. New Delhi: Kali for Women, 1994, 35–50.

—. "Digging Dholavira." *Hinduism Today*, January–February 2001: 44–46.

Dikshit, S.K. *Mother Goddess (A Study Regarding the Origin of Hinduism)*. Poona: International Book Service, 1943.

Dimmitt, Cornelia, and J.A.B. van Buitenen, "Sītā: Fertility Goddess and *Śakti*." *The Divine Consort: Rādhā and the Goddesses of India*, edited by John Stratton Hawley and Donna Marie Wulff. Berkeley: Graduate Theological Union, 1982, 210–23.

—, eds. *Classical Hindu Mythology: A Reader in the Sanskrit Purāṇas*. Philadelphia: Temple University Press, 1978.

Dimock, Edward C. "A Theology of the Repulsive: The Myth of the Goddess Śītalā." Unpublished essay, University of Chicago, 1982.

Diner, Helen. *Mothers and Amazons: The First Feminine History of Culture*. 1929. New York: Anchor Press/Doubleday & Co., 1973.

Divakaran, Odile. "Durgā the Great Goddess: Meanings and Forms in the Early Period." *Discourses on Śiva: Proceedings of a Symposium on the Nature of Religious Imagery*, edited by Michael W. Meister. Philadelphia: University of Pennsylvania Press, 1984, 271–88.

Doniger, Wendy. *Asceticism and Eroticism in the Mythology of Śiva*. London: Oxford University Press, 1973.

—. "Begetting on Margin: Adultery and Surrogate Pseudomarriage in Hinduism." *From the Margins of Hindu Marriage: Essays on Gender, Religion, and Culture*, edited by Lindsey Harlan and Paul B. Courtright. New York: Oxford University Press, 1995, 160–83.

—. *The Critical Study of Sacred Texts.* Berkeley: Berkeley Religious Studies Series, 1979.

—, trans. *Hindu Myths: A Sourcebook.* Harmondsworth: Penguin Books, 1975.

—. *The Origins of Evil in Hindu Mythology.* Berkeley: University of California Press, 1976.

—. *The Rig Veda: An Anthology.* Harmondsworth: Penguin Books, 1981.

—. *Śiva: The Erotic Ascetic.* Oxford: Oxford University Press, 1981. (Originally published as *Asceticism and Eroticism in the Mythology of Śiva.* London: Oxford University Press, 1973.)

—. *Tales of Sex and Violence: Folklore, Sacrifice, and Danger in the Jaiminīya Brāhmaṇa.* Chicago: University of Chicago Press, 1985.

—. *Women, Androgynes, and Other Mythical Beasts.* Chicago: University of Chicago Press, 1980.

Douglas, Mary. *Purity and Danger.* London: Routledge & Kegan Paul, 1966.

—. *Natural Symbols.* New York: Vintage/Random House, 1970.

—. *Implicit Meanings.* London: Routledge & Kegan Paul, 1975.

Douglas, Nik. *Tantra Yoga.* New Delhi: Munshiram Manoharlal Publishers, 1971.

Dowman, Keith. *Masters of Mahāmudrā.* Albany: SUNY Press, 1985.

—. *Sky Dancer: The Secret Life and Songs of the Lady Yeshe Tsogyel.* London: Arkana, 1984.

Drekmeier, Charles. *Kingship and Community in Early India.* Stanford: Stanford University Press, 1962.

Dubianski, Alexander. *Ritual and Mythological Sources of the Early Tamil Poetry.* Groninger, the Netherlands: Egbert Forsten, 2000.

Dumont, Louis. *Religion, Politics and History in India.* Paris: Mouton, 1970.

Dundes, Alan. "Projective Inversion in the Ancient Egyptian 'Tale of Two Brothers'." *Journal of American Folklore* 115(457/458) (2002): 378–94.

—. "The Ritual Murder or Blood Libel Legend: A Study of Anti-Semitic Victimization through Projective Inversion." *Temenos* 25 (1989): 7–32.

Durkheim, Émile. *Suicide: A Study in Sociology,* translated by John A. Spaulding and George Simpson. Glencoe, NY: Free Press, 1951.

Dyczkowski, Mark S.G. *The Canon of the Śaivāgama and the Kubjikā Tantras of the Western Kaula Tradition.* New York: SUNY Press, 1988.

Ehrenfels, Baron Omar Rolf. "Mother-Right in India." PhD dissertation. London: H. Milford, Oxford University Press, 1941.

—. "Traces of a Patriarchal Civilization Among the Kolli Mailayālis." *JRASB* 9 (1943): 29–82.

Ehrenreich, Barbara. *Blood Rites: Origins and History of the Passions of War.* New York: Henry Holt & Co., 1997.

Eisler, Riane. *The Chalice and the Blade: Our History, Our Future.* San Francisco: Harper & Row, 1987.

Elawar, May. "Mahisasuramardini: Early Mythology of the Goddess and the Buffalo." Unpublished paper. San Francisco, May 8, 2003.

Elder, Joseph W., ed. *Chapters in Indian Civilization*, vol. 1, *Classical and Medieval India*. Dubuque, Iowa: Kendall/Hunt Publishing Co., 1970.

Eliade, Mircea, and Ioan P. Couliano, eds. *The Eliade Guide to World Religions*. New York: HarperSanFrancisco, 1991.

—. *A History of Religious Ideas*, 3 vols. Translated by Willard R. Trask. Chicago: University of Chicago, 1978–85.

—. *Occultism, Witchcraft, and Cultural Fashions: Essays in Comparative Religions*. Chicago: University of Chicago Press, 1976.

—. *Patañjali and Yoga*. Translated by Charles Lam Markmann. New York: Schocken Books, 1975.

—. *The Sacred and the Profane: The Nature of Religion*. Translated by Willard R. Trask. New York: Harcourt, Brace & World, Inc., 1959.

—. *Shamanism: Archaic Techniques of Ecstasy*. Translated by Willard R. Trask. Princeton: Princeton University Press, 1964.

—. *Yoga: Immortality and Freedom*. Translated by Willard R. Trask. New York: Pantheon Books, Inc., 1958.

Eller, Cynthia. *The Myth of Matriarchal Prehistory: Why an Invented Past Won't Give Women a Future*. Boston: Beacon Press, 2000.

Elmore, Wilber Theodore. *Dravidian Gods in Modern Hinduism: A Study of the Local and Village Deities of Southern India*. Madras: Christian Literature Society, 1925.

—. *Lectures in Indian Civilization*. Dubuque, Iowa: Kendall/Hunt Publishing Co., 1970.

Ember, Carol. "Myths about Hunter-Gatherers." *Ethnology* 17 (1978): 438–48.

—. "A Cross-Cultural Perspective on Sex Differences." *Handbook of Cross-Cultural Human Development*, ed. Monroe and Whiting. New York: Garland Press, 1981, 531–80.

Engels, Friedrich. *The Origin of the Family, Private Property and the State in the Light of the Researches of Lewis H. Morgan* [*c.* 1942]. New York: International Publishers, 1972.

Enheduanna. *The Exaltation of Inanna*. Translated by William W. Hallo and J.J.A. VanDijk. New Haven: Yale University Press, 1968.

Erndl, Kathleen M. "The Mutilation of Śūrpaṇakhā." *Many Rāmāyaṇas: The Diversity of a Narrative Tradition in South Asia*, edited by Paula Richman. Berkeley, Los Angeles, Oxford: University of California Press, 1991, 67–88.

—. "Śerāṇvālī: The Mother Who Possesses." *Devī: Goddesses of India*, edited by John S. Hawley and Donna M. Wulff. Berkeley, Los Angeles, London: University of California Press, 1996, 173–94.

—. *Victory to the Mother: The Hindu Goddess of Northwest India in Myth, Ritual, and Symbol*. New York and Oxford: Oxford University Press, 1993.

Escobar, Pepe. "Waiting for the Mahdi, Part 1: Sistani Qom: In the Weird Heart of Shi'ism." *Asia Times Online*, http://www.atimes.com/atimes/Middle_East/GH31Ak03.html (accessed July 28, 2006).

—. "Waiting for the Mahdi, Part 2: A Vision or a Waking Dream?" *Asia Times Online,* http://www.atimes.com/atimes/Middle_East/GI01Ak02.html (accessed July 28, 2006).

Evans, A.E. "The Tomb of the Double Axis and Associated Group of Titual Vessels at the Little Palace at Knossos." *Archaeologia* 65 (1914): 1–94.

Evans, Arthur. *The God of Ecstasy: Sex Roles and the Madness of Dionysos.* New York: St. Martin's Press, 1988.

Evola, Julius. *The Yoga of Power: Tantra, Shakti, and the Secret Way.* Translated by Guido Stucco. Rochester, VT: Inner Traditions International, 1992.

Fabri, Charles. *History of the Art of Orissa.* Calcutta: Orient Longman Ltd., 1974.

Fairservis, Walter A., Jr. *The Roots of Ancient India,* 1971, repr. Chicago and London: University of Chicago Press, 1975.

Falk, Nancy Auer. "Mata, Land, and Line: Female Divinity and the Forging of Community in India." *Invoking Goddesses: Gender Politics in Indian Religion,* edited by Nilima Chitgopekar. New Delhi: Shakti Books, 2002, 140–64.

Fanon, Frantz. *The Wretched of the Earth.* Translated by Constance Farrington. New York: Grove Press, 1963.

Farquhar, J.N. *An Outline of the Religious Literature of India.* London: Oxford University Press, 1920.

Fazlul-Huq, *Gandhi: Saint or Sinner.* Bangalore: Dalit Sahitya Akademy, 1992.

Ferrill, Arthur. "Neolithic Warfare," http://www.witiger.com/centennialcollege/GNED117/neolithicwar.htm (accessed July 21, 2005).

—. *The Origins of War: From the Stone Age to Alexander the Great.* London and New York: Thames and Hudson, 1985.

Ferry, David. *Gilgamesh: A New Rendering in English Verse.* New York: Farrar, Straus and Giroux, 1997.

Feuerstein, Georg, Subhash Kak, and David Frawley. In *Search of the Cradle of Civilization: New Light on Ancient India.* Wheaton, IL: Quest Books, 1995.

Fielder, Christine, and Chris King, *Sexual Paradox: Complementarity, Reproductive Conflict and Human Emergence.* http://www.dhushara.com/paradoxhtm/3bl.jpg (accessed February 8, 2006).

Fields, Rick. *The Code of the Warrior.* New York: HarperPerennial, 1991.

Finley, M.I., ed. *The Greek Historians: The Essence of Herodotus, Thucydides, Xenophon, Polibus.* New York: Viking Press, 1959.

Fischer-Schreiber, Ingrid; Franz-Karl Ehrhard; Kurt Friedrichs; and Michael S. Diener, eds. *The Encyclopedia of Eastern Philosophy and Religion.* Boston: Shambhala, 1994.

Fisher, Elizabeth A. "Theodora and Antonina in the Historia Arcana: History and/or Fiction?" *Women in the Ancient World: The Arethusa Papers,* edited by John Peradotta and J.P. Sullivan. Albany, NY: State University of New York Press, 1984, 287–313.

Fisher, Mary Pat. *Living Religions.* Upper Saddle River, NJ: Prentice Hall, 2002.

Fluehr-Lobban, C. "A Marxist Re-appraisal of the Matriarchate." *Current Anthropology* 20 (1979): 341–60.

Foulston, Lynn. *At the Feet of the Goddess: The Divine Feminine in Local Hindu Religion.* Brighton and Portland: Sussex Academic Press, 2002.

Frazer, Sir James. *The New Golden Bough* (abridged), edited by Theodor H. Gaster. New York: Mentor, 1959.

Frymer-Kensky, Tikva. *In the Wake of the Goddesses: Women, Culture, and the Biblical Transformation of Pagan Myth.* New York: The Free Press, 1992.

Fürer-Haimendorf, Christoph von. "New Aspects of the Dravidian Problem." *Tamil Culture* II, 2 (April 1953): 127–35.

—. "The Problem of Megalithic Cultures in Middle India." *Man in India* 25 (1945).

—. *Return to the Naked Nagas: An Anthropologist's View of Nagaland 1936-1970,* 2nd edn. London: J. Murray, 1976.

—. *Tribal Populations and Cultures of the Indian Subcontinent.* Leiden: E.J. Brill, 1985.

Gait, Edward. *A History of Assam.* Calcutta: Thacker Spink & Co., 1963.

—. "Human Sacrifices in Ancient Assam." *JRASB,* 67(1903): 56–65.

Gastor, Theodore. *Myth, Legend, and Custom in the Old Testament.* New York: Harper & Row, 1969.

Gatwood, Lynn E. *Devī and the Spouse Goddess.* Riverdale, MD: The Riverdale Company Inc., 1985.

Geertz, Clifford. *The Interpretation of Cultures.* New York: Basic Books, 1973.

"Ghauri [Hatf-5]." http://www.globalsecurity.org/wmd/world/pakistan/hatf-5.htm (accessed June 1, 2006).

Ghoshal, U.N. *Studies in Indian History and Culture.* Calcutta: University Press, 1955.

Giles, H.A., trans. *The Travels of Fa-Hsien (399-414 AD), or Records of the Buddhistic Kingdoms.* Cambridge: Cambridge University Press, 1923.

Gilmore, David D. *Misogyny: The Male Malady.* Philadelphia: University of Pennsylvania Press, 2001.

Gimbutas, Marija. *The Civilization of the Goddess.* San Francisco: HarperSan-Francisco, 1991.

—. *Goddesses and Gods of Old Europe.* Los Angeles: Univerisity of California Press, 1982.

Girard, René. *The Scapegoat.* Translated by Yvonne Freccero. Baltimore: Johns Hopkins University Press, 1986.

—. *Violence and the Sacred.* Translated by Patrick Gregory. Baltimore: Johns Hopkins Press, 1992.

Glasenapp, Helmut von. "Tantrismus und Shaktismus." *Ostasiatische Zeitschrift,* N.F. 12, issue 3/4, Berlin, 1936.

—. *Buddhistische Mysterien. Die geheimen Riten und Lehren des Diamantfahrzeuges.* Stuttgart, 1940.

Gold, Ann Grodzins. "The 'Jungli Rani' and Other Troubled Wives in Rajasthani Oral Traditions." *From the Margins of Hindu Marriage: Essays on*

Gender, Religion, and Culture, edited by Lindsey Harlan and Paul B. Courtright. New York: Oxford University Press, 1995, 119–36.

Gonda, Jan. *Medieval Religious Literature in Sanskrit*. Wiesbaden: Otto Harrassowitz, 1977.

Goudriaan, Teun, and J.A. Schoterman. *The Kubjikamatatantra: The Kulalikamnaya Version*. Leiden, E.J. Brill, 1988.

—. *Māyā Divine and Human*. Delhi, Varanasi, Patna: Motilal Banarsidass, 1978.

—, eds. *Ritual and Speculation in Early Tantrism: Studies in Honor of André Padoux*, edited by Paul E. Muller-Ortega. SUNY Series in Tantric Studies. Albany, NY: SUNY Press, 1992.

Grahn, Judy. *Blood, Bread, and Roses: How Menstruation Created the World*. Boston: Beacon Press, 1993.

Gramsci, Antonio. *Selections from the Prison Notebooks*. Translated by Quintin Hoare and Geoffrey Nowell Smith. London: Lawrence & Wishart, 1971.

Graves, Robert. *The Greek Myths: I*. New York: Penguin, 1977. (Originally published 1955.)

Gray, John. *Near Eastern Mythology*. London: Hamlyn Publishing Group, 1963.

Grene, David, and Richard Lattimore, eds. *Euripedes V*. Chicago and London: University of Chicago Press, 1959.

Gross, Rita M. "Androcentrism and Androgyny in the Methodology of the History of Religions." *Beyond Androcentrism: New Essays on Women and Religion*, edited by Rita Gross, Missoula, Montana: Scholar Press for the American Academy of Religion, 1977.

—. *Buddhism After Patriarchy*. Albany, NY: SUNY Press, 1993.

"The Gulf of Khambat Debate." Interview with Asko Parpola and Iravatham Mahadevan. *Frontline* 18, issue 7 (March 30–April 12, 2002), http://www.frontlineonnet.com/fl1907/19070940.htm (accessed October 26, 2006).

Gupta, Lina. "Kali, the Savior." *After Patriarch: Feminist Transformations of the World Religions*, edited by Paula M. Cooey, William R. Eakin, and Jay B. McDaniel. Maryknoll, NY: Orbis Books, 1991, 15–38..

Gupta, Sanjukta, and Teun Goudriaan. *A History of Indian Literature*, vol. 2, facs. 2: *Hindu Tantric and Śākta Literature*. Wiesbaden: Herrossowitz, 1981.

—. "The Pañcarātra Attitude to Mantra." *Understanding Mantras*, edited by Harvey Alper, 244–48. SUNY Series in Religious Studies. Albany: State University of New York Press, 1989.

Gupta, Sanjukta, Dirk Jan Hoens, and Teun Goudriaan. *Hindu Tantrism*. Leiden: E.J. Brill, 1979.

—. "Women in the Śaiva/Śākta Ethos." *Roles and Rituals for Hindu Women*, edited by Julia Leslie. Rutherford, NJ: Fairleigh Dickinson University Press, 1991, 193–209.

Gurdon, P.R.T. *The Khasis*. 1907, repr. London: Macmillan & Co., 1914.

Haldar, Alfred. *The Notion of the Desert in Sumero-Accadian and West-Semitic Religions*. Uppsala and Leipzig: A.B. Lundequistska Bokhandeln, 1950.

Hardiman, David. *The Coming of the Devī: Adivasi Assertion in Western India.* New Delhi: Oxford University Press, 1987.

Hardy, F. *Viraha-bhakti: The Early History of Kṛṣṇa Devotion in South India.* Oxford: Oxford University Press, 1983.

Harlan, Lindsey. *Religion and Rajput Women: The Ethics of Protection in Contemporary Narratives.* Berkeley: University of California Press, 1992.

—, and Paul B. Courtright. "Introduction: On Hindu Marriage and Its Margins." *From the Margins of Hindu Marriage: Essays on Gender, Religion, and Culture,* edited by Lindsey Harlan and Paul B. Courtright. New York: Oxford University Press, 1995, 3–18.

Harper, Katherine Anne. *The Iconography of the Saptamātrikās: Seven Hindu Goddesses of Spiritual Transformation.* Studies in Women and Religion 28. Lewiston, NY, Queenston, Ontario, Canada, and Lampeter, Wales, UK: Edwin Mellen Press, 1989.

Harris, Marvin. *Cannibals and Kings.* New York: Vintage Books/Random House, 1977.

Harris, Stan. *The End of Faith: Religion, Terror, and the Future of Reason.* New York, London: W.W. Norton & Co., 2004.

Hart, George L. *The Poems of Ancient Tamil: Their Milieu and Their Sanskrit Counterparts.* Berkeley, Los Angeles, London: University of California Press, 1975.

—. "Women and the Sacred in Ancient Tamilnad." *Journal of Asian Studies* 32, no. 2 (1973).

—, trans. *Poets of the Tamil Anthologies.* Princeton: Princeton University Press, 1979.

Hasan-Rokem, Galit, and David Shulman. "Introduction." *Untying the Knot: On Riddles and Other Enigmatic Modes,* edited by Galit Hasan-Rokem and David Shulman. New York: Oxford University Press, 1996.

Hastings, James, ed. *Encyclopaedia of Religion and Ethics,* 13 vols. New York, 1928.

Hatt, G. "The Corn Mother in American and in Indonesia." *Anthropos* 46 (1951): 853–914.

Hawley, John Stratton, and Donna Marie Wulff, eds. *Devī: Goddesses of India.* Berkeley, Los Angeles, London: University of California Press, 1996.

—. *Sati, the Blessing and the Curse: The Burning of Wives in India.* New York: Oxford University Press, 1994.

Hays, H.R. *The Dangerous Sex: The Myths of Feminine Evil.* New York: Putnam, 1964.

Hayton, Bill. "Asia faces 'growing poverty gap'." BBC News (February 8, 2007), http:/news.bbc.co.uk/2/hi/asia-pacific/6342599.stm

Hayward Gallery. *Tantra.* London: Arts Council of Great Britain, 1971.

Hazra, R.C. "The Devī-Purāṇa." *New Indian Antiquary* 5 (April 1942): 2–20.

—. *Studies in the Purāṇic Records on Hindu Rites and Customs,* 2nd edn. Delhi: Motilal Banarsidass, 1975.

—. *Studies in the Upapurāṇas,* 2 vols.; vol. 1: *Śaiva and Vaiṣṇava Upapurāṇas,* vol. 2: *Śākta and Non-Sectarian Upapurāṇas,* Calcutta Sanskrit College Research, Series, nos. 2 and 22. Calcutta: Sanskrit College, 1958, 1963.

"The Hebrews." Washington State University, World Civilizations: An Internet Classroom and Anthology, http://www.wsu.edu/~dee/HEBREWS/HEBREWS.HTM (accessed May 12, 2007).

Heesterman, J.C. *The Broken World of Sacrifice: An Essay in Ancient Indian Ritual.* Chicago and London: University of Chicago Press, 1993.

—. "The Case of the Severed Head." *Wiener Zeitschrift zur Kunde des Sud-und Ostasiens* 11: 22–43.

Heine-Geldern, Robert. "Ancient Homeland and Early Wanderings of the Austronesians" [partial translation of "Urheimat und Früheste Wanderungen der Austronesier." *Anthropos* 27 (1932)], in *Prehistoric Indonesia: A Reader,* edited by Pieter van de Velde. Dordrecht, Holland: Foris Publications, 1984.

—. "Ein Beitrag zur Chronologie des Neolithikums in Südostasien." *Festschrift Publication d'hommage offerte au P. W. Schmidt,* edited by W. Koppers (Vienna: Mechitharisten-Congregations-Buchdr, 1928), 809–43.

Heras, H. "The Problem of Ganapati." *Tamil Culture* III, 2 (April 1954): 151–213.

Highwater, Jamake. *The Primal Mind: Vision and Reality in Indian America.* New York: Meridian, 1981.

Hill, Sarah H. *Weaving New Worlds: Southeastern Cherokee Women and Their Basketry.* Chapel Hill and London: University of North Carolina Press, 1997.

Hiltebeitel, Alf. *Rethinking India's Oral and Classical Epics: Draupadi among Rajputs, Muslims, and Dalits.* Chicago: University of Chicago Press, 1999.

—. *The Cult of Draupadi,* vol. 1: *Mythologies: From Gingee to Kurukṣetra.* Chicago: University of Chicago Press, 1988.

—. *The Cult of Draupadi,* vol. 2: *On Hindu Ritual and the Goddess.* Chicago: University of Chicago Press, 1991.

Hinz, Walter. "Elam." *Cambridge Ancient History* 1, 2 (1971): 662–64.

Hitchcock, John T., and Rex L. Jones, eds. *Spirit Possession in the Nepal Himalayas.* Warminster, England: Aris and Phillips Ltd., 1976.

Holy Places of the Buddha, Crystal Mirror Series, vol. 9. Berkeley: Dharma Publishing, 1994.

Hooke, S.H. *Middle Eastern Mythology.* Harmondsworth, England: Penguin Books Ltd.,1963.

Hopfe, Lewis M. *Religions of the World.* 5th edn. New York: MacMillan, 1991.

Hughes, Lotte. *The No-Nonsense Guide to Indigenous Peoples.* Oxford: New Internationalist Publications, Inc., 2003.

Hughes, Thomas Patrick. *A Dictionary of Islam.* London: W.H. Allen & Co., 1895; New Delhi, Madras: Asian Educational Services, 2001. http://answering-islam.org.uk/Books/Hughes/index.htm (accessed February 24, 2008).

Hultkrantz, Åke, *Shamanic Healing and Ritual Drama: Health and Medicine in Native North American Religious Traditions*. New York: Crossroad, 1992.

—. "The Religion of the Goddess in North America." *The Book of the Goddess Past and Present: An Introduction to Her Religion*, edited by Carl Olson. New York: Crossroads Publishing Company, 1983, 202–16.

Human Rights Watch World Report, 2008, Country Summary: India (January 2008), http://hrw.org/englishwer2k8/docs/2008/01/31/india 17605.htm (accessed February 4, 2008).

Humes, Cynthia Ann. "Is the *Devī-māhātmya* a Feminist Scripture?" *Is the Goddess a Feminist? The Politics of South Asian Goddesses*, edited by Alf Hitlebeitel and Kathleen M. Erndl, Washington Square, NY: 2000, 123–50.

Hurtado, Larry, ed. *Goddesses in Religions and Modern Debate*. Atlanta, GA: Scholars Press, 1990.

Hutton, J.H. *The Angami Nagas: With Some Notes on Neighboring Tribes*. London: Macmillan & Co., Ltd., 1921.

—. "The Meaning and Method of the Erection of Monoliths by the Naga Tribes." *Journal of the Royal Anthropological Institute* 52 (1922).

—. "The Significance of Head-Hunting in Assam." *Journal of the Royal Anthropological Institute* 57 (1928).

—. "Diaries of Two Tours in the Unadministered Area East of the Naga Hills." *Memoirs of the Asiatic Society of Bengal* 12 (1929).

Hutton, Ronald. *The Pagan Religions of the Ancient British Isles: Their Nature and Legacy*. Oxford, UK; Cambridge, Mass.: Blackwell, 1993.

Ibn Ishaq, *Sīrat Rasūl Allāh* (*The Life of Muhammad*). Translated by A. Guillaume. Karachi: Oxford University Press, 1998.

Imsong, Rev. Mar. "God's Community: Communion in the Suffering and Rejoicing." *Minister*: A Journal of the American Baptist Ministers Council Speaking to the Practice of Ministry, vol. XXVIII, no. 1 (Summer 2005), Valley Forge, PA, http://www.ministerscouncil.com/Periodicals/documents/Summer 05.pdf. (accessed August 12, 2006). "Indigenous Women." Shannonthunderbird.com http://www.shannonthunderbird.com/indigenous_women_rights.htm (accessed March 12, 2005).

"India Blames Islamic Militants for Blasts." *The New York Times* (August 27, 2007), http://www.nytimes.com/2007/08/27/world/asia/27 india.html?_r=1&oref=slogin (accessed October 8, 2007).

"Indus: Clues to an Ancient Civilization." *National Geographic* 197, 6 (June 2000): 114–29.

Ions, Veronica. *Indian Mythology*. London: Paul Hamlyn, 1967.

"Iran's Massive War Games Called 'Holy Prophet'." http://www.globalsecurity.org/wmd/library/news/iran/2006/iran-060329-irna03.htm (accessed March 30, 2006).

Iyer, L.K. Ananthakrishna. *The Cochin Tribes and Castes*, vol. 1. London: Luzac & Co., 1909.

Jacobs, Julian. *The Nagas: Society, Culture and the Colonial Encounter.* London: Thames and Hudson Ltd., 1990.

Jacobson, Doranne. "The Women of North and Central India: Goddesses and Wives." *Women in India: Two Perspectives,* edited by Doranne Jacobson and Susan Wadley. New Delhi: Manohar, 1977.

Jain, Madhu. *The Abode of Mahashiva: Cults and Symbology in Jaunsar-Bawar in the Mid-Himalayas.* New Delhi: Indus Publishing Company, 1995.

Jaini, Padmanabh S. "*Śramaṇas*: Their Conflict with Brāhmaṇical Society." *Chapters in Indian Civilization,* edited by Joseph W. Elder, vol. 1: Classical and Medieval India. Dubuque, Iowa: Kendall/Hunt Publishing Co., 1970, 39–81.

James, E.O. *The Cult of the Mother-Goddess: An Archaeological and Documentary Study.* New York: Frederick A. Praeger, Inc., 1959.

Jash, Pranabananda. *History of Śaivism.* Calcutta: Roy and Chaudhury, 1974.

Jayakar, Pupul. *The Earth Mother.* New Delhi: Penguin Books (India) Ltd., 1989.

Jay, Nancy. *Throughout Your Generation Forever: Sacrifice, Religion, and Paternity.* Chicago: University of Chicago Press, 1992.

Jones, Bill. "Did American Aborigines have Culture?" *Explore North* (2000), http://www.explorenorth.com/library/history/bl-billjones1.htm (accessed March 12, 2005).

Jones, Rex L. "Limbu Spirit Possession and Shamanism." *Spirit Possession in the Nepal Himalayas,* edited by John T. Hitchcock and Rex L. Jones. Warminster, England: Aris and Phillips Ltd., 1976, 29–55.

—. "Spirit Possession in Society in Nepal." *Spirit Possession in the Nepal Himalayas,* edited by John T. Hitchcock and Rex L. Jones. Warminster, England: Aris and Phillips Ltd., 1976, 1–11.

Juergensmeyer, Mark. *Terror in the Mind of God: The Global Rise of Religious Violence.* Berkeley, Los Angeles, London: University of California Press, 2001.

Kakati, Banikanta. *The Mother Goddess Kāmākhyā, or Studies in the Fusion of Āryan and Primitive Beliefs of Assam.* Gauhati, Assam: Assam Pub. Corp., 1948.

Kane, Pandurang Vaman. *History of Dharmaśāstra (Ancient and Medieval Religious and Civil Law),* 5 vols. (1930); 2nd edn. Poona: Bhandarkar Oriental Research Institute, 1968.

Kapadia, K.M. *Marriage and Family in India,* 3rd edn. London: Oxford University Press, 1966.

Karambelkar, V.W. "Matsyendranath and his Yogini Cult." *IHQ* 31, no. 4 (1955).

Kârâvêlane, *Kâreikkâammeyiâr.* Pondicherry: Institut Français d'Indologie, 1956.

Kashyap, P.C. *Surviving Harappan Civilization.* New Delhi: Abhinav Publications, 1984.

Keeley, Lawrence H. *War Before Civilization: The Myth of the Peaceful Savage.* New York: Oxford University Press, 1996.

Keith, A. Berriedale. *Religion and Philosophy of the Veda and Upanishads,* HOS, vol. 32. Cambridge, MA: Harvard University Press, 1925.

Kelly, Joan. *Women in History and Theory: Essays of Joan Kelly.* Chicago: University of Chicago Press, 1985.

Kenoyer, J.M., *Ancient Cities of the Indus Valley Civilization.* Oxford: Oxford University Press, 1998.

—. "Urban Process in the Indus Tradition: A Preliminary Model from Harappa." *Harappa Excavations* 1986–90, 29–60.

Kersenboom-Story, S.C. "Viṟali." *Journal of Tamil Studies* 19 (June 1981): 19–41.

Keuls, Eva C. *The Reign of the Phallus: Sexual Politics in Ancient Athens.* New York: Harper & Row, 1985.

Khanna, Madhu. "The Goddess-Woman Equation in Śākta Tantras." *Faces of the Feminine in Ancient, Medieval, and Modern India,* edited by Mandakranta Bose 109–23. New York and Oxford: Oxford University Press, 2000.

—. *Yantra: The Tantric Symbol of Cosmic Unity.* London: Thames and Hudson, 1994.

Khurshid Hasan, Shaikh. "Ethnoarchaeology as an Aid to Interpret Indus Civilization." *Pakistan Archaeology,* XXVI (1991): 108–14.

Kielhorn, Franz L. *Vyākaraṇa Mahābhāṣya of Patañjali,* vol. 1. Bombay: Government Central Book Depot, 1892.

Kinsley, David. "Freedom from Death in the Worship of Kali." *Numen* 22, no. 3 (1975).

—. *The Goddesses' Mirror: Visions of the Divine from East and West.* Albany: State University of New York Press, 1989.

—. *Hindu Goddesses: Visions of the Divine Feminine in the Hindu Religious Tradition.* Berkeley: University of California Press, 1986.

—. "The Portrait of the Goddess in the *Devī-māhātmya.*" *Journal of the American Academy of Religion* 46, no. 4 (December 1978): 489–506.

—. *The Sword and the Flute: Kālī and Kṛṣṇa; Dark Visions of the Terrible and the Sublime in Hindu Mythology.* Berkeley: University of California Press, 1975.

Kishwar, Madhu. *Gandhi and Women.* Delhi: Manushi Prakashan, 1986.

Kondos, Vivienne. "Images of the Fierce Goddess and Portrayals of Hindu Women." *Contributions to Indian Sociology,* n.s., 20, no. 2 (1986): 173–97.

The Koran. Translated by J.M. Rodwell. New York: Bantam Dell, 2004.

Kosambi, D.D. *Ancient India: A History of Its Culture and Civilization.* New York: Pantheon Books, 1965.

—. *The Culture and Civilization of Ancient India in Historical Outline.* London: Routledge & Kegan Paul, 1965.

—. *An Introduction to the Study of Indian History.* Bombay: Popular Book Depot, 1956.

—. *Myth and Reality.* Bombay: Popular Prakashan, 1962.

Kramer, Samuel Noah, ed. *Mythologies of the Ancient World.* New York: Anchor Doubleday, 1961.

—. *Sumerian Mythology: A Study of Spiritual and Literary Achievement in the Third Millennium B.C.,* rev. edn. New York: Harper, 1961.

—. *The Sumerians: Their History, Culture, and Character.* Chicago: University of Chicago Press, 1963.

Kramrisch, Stella. "The Indian Great Goddess." *History of Religions* 14, no. 4 (May 1975): 235–65.

—. *The Presence of Śiva.* Princeton, NJ: Princeton University Press, 1981.

Kroeber, Clifton B., and Bernard L. Fontana. *Massacre on the Gila: An Account of the Last Major Battle Between American Indians, with Reflections on the Origin of War.* Tucson: University of Arizona Press, 1986.

Kulkarni, S.D., ed. *The Purāṇas: The Encyclopedia of Indian History and Culture,* vol. 2. Bombay: Shri Bhagavan Vedavyasa Itihasa Samshodhana Mandira [Bhishmo], 1993.

Kumar, Pramod. *Folk Icons and Rituals in Tribal Life.* Atlantic Highlands, NJ: Humanities Press, Inc., 1984.

Kumar, Pushpendra. *The Principle of Śakti.* Delhi: Eastern Book Linkers, 1986.

—. *Śakti and Her Episodes.* Delhi: Eastern Book Linkers, 1981.

—. *Śakti Cult in Ancient India (with Special Reference to the Puranic Literature).* Varanasi: Bharatiya Publishing House, 1974.

La Barre, Weston. *The Ghost Dance: Origins of Religion.* Garden City, NY: Doubleday & Co., 1970.

Lakoff, George. *Don't Think of an Elephant, Know Your Values and Frame the Debate.* White River Junction, VT: Chelsea Green Publishing Co., 2004.

Lal, B.B. "The Direction of the Writing on the Indus Script." *Antiquity* 50 (1966): 52–55.

—. "India adds New Dimensions to the Indus Civilization." *Revisiting Indus-Sarasvati Age and Ancient India,* edited by Bhu Dev Sharma and Nabarun Ghose. Atlanta: World Association for Vedic Studies, 1998, 1–21.

—. "India: New Dimensions of Indus Civilization." *Keynote Address* at International Conference on Indus-Sarasvati Age and Ancient India, 5 October 1996, Atlanta, GA.

—. "Some Reflections on the Structural Remains at Kalibangan." *Frontiers of the Indus Civilization,* edited by B.B. Lal and S.P. Gupta. New Delhi: Books and Books, 1984, 55–65.

Lalye, P.G. *Studies in Devī Bhāgavata.* Bombay: Popular Prakashan, 1973.

Larkin, John, and Eric Bellman. "In India, the Path to Growth hits Roadblock: Slums." *The Wall Street Journal,* March 17, 2006.

Lawrence, Patricia. "Kāḷī in a Context of Terror: The Tasks of a Goddess in Sri Lanka's Civil War." *Encountering Kālī: In the Margins, at the Center, in the West,* edited by Rachel Fell McDermott and Jeffrey J. Kripal. Berkeley, Los Angeles, London: University of California Press, 2003, 101–23.

Leeming, David, and Jake Page. *Goddess: Myths of the Female Divine.* New York and Oxford: Oxford University Press, 1994.

Lefkowitz, Mary R., and Maureen B. Fant. *Women in Greece and Rome.* Toronto and Sarasota: Samuel-Stevens, 1977.

Lerner, Gerda. *The Creation of Patriarchy*. New York, Oxford: Oxford University Press, 1986.

—. *The Creation of Feminist Consciousness*. New York, Oxford: Oxford University Press, 1993.

Leslie, Julia. *The Perfect Wife, The Orthodox Hindu Woman According to the Strīdharmapaddhati of Tryambakayajvan*. Delhi: Oxford University Press, 1989.

Lévi-Strauss, Claude. *The Origin of Table Manners*. Translated by John and Doreen Lévi-Weightman. Chicago: University of Chicago Press, 1990.

Lewis, Bernard. *Islam and the West*. New York: Oxford University Press, 1993.

Lewis, I.M. *Ecstatic Religion: An Anthropological Study of Spirit Possession and Shamanism*. Harmondsworth: Penguin Books, 1971.

Lloyd, J.B. "Anat and the 'Double' Massacre of KTU 1.3 ii." *Ugarit, Religion and Culture: Essays Presented in Honour of Professor John C.L. Gibson*, edited by N. Wyatt, W.G.E. Watson, and J.B. Lloyd. Münster [Germany]: Ugarit Verlag, 1996.

Lorenzen, David N. *The Kāpālikas and Kālāmukhas: Two Lost Śaivite Sects*. Berkeley and Los Angeles: University of California Press, 1972.

Luiz, A.A.D. *Tribes of Kerala*. New Delhi: Bharatiya Adimjati Sevak Sangh, 1962.

Macdonell, Arthur Anthony. *A Practical Sanskrit Dictionary*. Oxford: Oxford University Press, 1954; repr. New Delhi: Munshiram Manoharlal Publishers, 2010.

Mahapatra, Sitakant. "The Meria Sloka: Songs of the Kondh Accompanying the Rite of Ritual Sacrifice." *Man in India* 54 (1974): 73–82.

"Mahdi." Wikipedia, http://en.wikipedia.org/wiki/Mahdi (accessed August 4, 2006).

Majumdar, R.C. *Classical Accounts of India: Being a Compilation of the English Translations of the Accounts Left by Herodotus*. Calcutta: Firma KLM, 1960.

Malalasekera, G.P. *Dictionary of Pāli Proper Names*, 2 vols. London: J. Murray, 1937–38; repr. New Delhi: Munshiram Manoharlal Publishers, 2002.

Mander, Jerry. *In the Absence of the Sacred: The Failure of Technology and the Survival of the Indian Nations*. San Francisco: Sierra Club Books, 1991.

Mankad, D.R. *Purāṇic Chronology*. Gujarat: Gangajala Prakashan, 1951.

Marglin, Frédérique Apffel. "Female Sexuality in the Hindu World." *Immaculate and Powerful: The Female in Sacred Image and Social Reality*, edited by Clarissa W. Atkinson, Constance H. Buchanan, and Margaret R. Miles. Boston: Beacon Press, 1985, 39–59.

—. "Types of Sexual Union and Their Implicit Meanings." *The Divine Consort: Rādhā and the Goddesses of India*," edited by John Stratton Hawley and Donna Marie Wulff. Berkeley: Berkeley Religious Studies Series, 1982, 298–315.

—. *Wives of the God-King: The Rituals of the Devadasis of Puri*. Delhi: Oxford University Press, 1985.

—. "Woman's Blood: Challenging the Discourse of Development." *Ecologist* 22, no. 1 (Jan–Feb 1992): 22–32.

Marshall, Sir John, ed. *Mohenjo-Daro and the Indus Civilization,* 3 vols. London: Arthur Probshain, 1931.

Mathur, P.R.G. *The Khasi of Meghalaya (Study in Tribalism and Religion).* New Delhi: Cosmo Publications, 1979.

McDaniel, June. *The Madness of the Saints: Ecstatic Religion in Bengal.* Chicago: University of Chicago Press, 1989.

McDermott, Rachel Fell. "The Western Kālī." *Devī: Goddesses of India,* edited by John Stratton Hawley, and Donna Marie Wulff. Berkeley, Los Angeles, London: University of California Press, 1996, 281–313.

—, and Jeffrey J. Kripal, eds. *Encountering Kālī: In the Margins, at the Center, in the West.* Berkeley, Los Angeles, London: University of California Press, 2003.

McKean, Lise. "Bhārata Mātā: Mother India and Her Militant Matriots." *Devī: Goddesses of India,* edited by John S. Hawley and Dona M. Wulff. Berkeley, Los Angeles, London: University of California Press, 1996, 250–80.

McNeill, William H. *A World History.* New York: Oxford University Press, 1967.

McPhate, Mike. "The India Bush Didn't See." *San Francisco Chronicle* (March 5, 2006).

Meek, C.K.A. *Sudanese Kingdom.* London: K. Paul, Trench, Trubner & Co., 1932.

Mehta, R.N. "Origins of the Śakti Cult." *The Śakti Cult and Tārā,* edited by D.C. Sircar. Calcutta: University of Calcutta, 1967, 61–64.

Mellaart, J. "Excavations at Çatal Hüyük: First Preliminary Report." *Anatolian Studies* 12 (1962): 41–65.

Merz, Brigitte. "Wild Goddess and Mother of Us All." *Wild Goddesses in India and Nepal,* edited by Axel Michaels, Cornelia Vogelsanger, and Annette Wilke. Berne, Berlin, Frankfurt, New York, Paris,Wien: Peter Lang, 1996, 343–54.

Meyer, Marvin W., ed. *The Ancient Mysteries: A Sourcebook.* New York: HarperSanFrancisco, 1987.

Mies, Maria, Veronika Bennholdt-Thomsen, and Claudia von Werlhof. *Women: The Last Colony.* London and New Jersey: Zed Books Ltd., 1988.

Miles, Rosalind. *Who Cooked the Last Supper? The Women's History of the World.* New York: Three Rivers Press, 1988.

"Military History of India." *Wikipedia,* http://en.wikipedia.org/wiki/Military_history_of_India (accessed April 12, 2006).

Millett, Kate. *Sexual Politics.* Garden City, NY: Doubleday & Co., Inc., 1970.

Mills, J.P. *The Ao Nagas.* London: Macmillan & Co., Ltd., 1926.

—. "Certain Aspects of Naga Culture." *Journal of the Royal Anthropological Institute,* 56 (1926).

Misra, Om Prakash. *Mother Goddess in Central India.* Delhi: Agam Kala Prakashan, 1985.

Mitra, R.L. *Indo-Aryans: Contributions Towards the Elucidation of Their Ancient and Medieval History,* 2 vols. (1881); repr. Delhi: Indological Book House, 1969.

"Mob Stones India Police After Rites for Muslims Killed in Mosque Blast." *The New York Times* (May 20, 2007), http://www.nytimes.com/2007/05/20/world/asia/20india.html?pagewanted=print (accessed May 31, 2007).

Moffatt, Michael. *An Untouchable Community in South India.* Princeton: Princeton University Press, 1979.

Mookerjee, Ajit. *Kālī: The Feminine Force.* Rochester, VT: Destiny Books, 1988.

—. *Kundalini: The Arousal of the Inner Energy.* Rochester, NY: Destiny Books, 1991.

—. *Tantra Asana: A Way to Self-Realization.* Basel, Switzerland: Ravi Kumar, 1971.

—, and Madhu Khanna. *The Tantric Way: Art, Science, Ritual.* London: Thames and Hudson, 1977.

Mooney, James. "The Ghost-Dance Religion and the Sioux Outbreak of 1890." *14th Reports of the Bureau of American Ethnology* (Washington), pt. II (1892–93; pub. 1896): 641–1136.

—. *Historical Sketch of the Cherokee.* Chicago: Aldine Publishing Co., 1975.

—. *Myths of the Cherokee: Sacred Formulas of the Cherokee, from 19th and 7th Annual Reports B.A.E., 1900 and 1891.* Nashville: Charles and Randy Elder Booksellers, 1982.

Morgan, Lewis Henry. *Ancient Society, or, Researches in the Lines of Human Progress from Savagery through Barbarism to Civilization* [1877], edited by Eleanor Burke Leacock. Cleveland: World Publishing Co., 1963.

—. *Houses and House-life of the American Aborigines.* Salt Lake City: University of Utah Press, 2003.

—. *League of the Iroquois.* Secaucus, NJ: Citadel Press ,1972.

Mudaliyar, S. Arumugha. "The Antiquity of Tamil and Tolkappiyam." *Tamil Culture* II, 3 & 4 (Sep 1953): 340–61.

Mukherjee, Prabhati. *Hindu Women: Normative Models.* Calcutta: Orient Longman, 1978.

Muthuswami, E.S. *Tamil Culture as Revealed in Tirukkural.* Madras: Makkal Ilakkia Publications, 1994.

Nagar, Shanti Lal. *The Jātakas in Indian Art.* Delhi: Parimal Publications, 1993.

Nagaraju, S. "Prehistory of South India." *South Indian Studies,* edited by H.M. Nayak and B.R. Gopal. Mysore: Geetha Book House, 1990, 35–52.

Namkhai Norbu. *The Crystal and the Way of Light.* Edited by John Shane. New York: Routledge & Kegan Paul, 1986.

—. *DzogChen: The Self-Perfected State.* Translated by John Shane and edited by Adriano Clemente. London: Arkana, 1989.

Nandy, Ashis. "Facing Extermination: Gods and Goddesses in South Asia." *Manushi* 99 (March–April 1997), http://www.indiatogether.org/manushi/issue 99/gods.htm (accessed April 14, 2003).

—. "Sati As Profit versus Sati as a Spectacle: The Public Debate on Roop Kanwar's Death." *Sati: The Blessing and the Curse,* edited by J.S. Hawley. New York: Oxford University Press, 1994.

Narayan, Kiran, and Urmila Devī Sood. *Mondays on the Dark Side of the Moon: Himalayan Foothill Folktales.* New York: Oxford University Press, 1997.

Nath, Vijay. "Women as Property and Their Right to Inherit Property up to the Gupta Period." *The Indian Historical Review* 20, nos. 1–2 (July 1993 and Jan 1994): 1–15.

Nayak, H.M., and B.R. Gopal, eds. *South Indian Studies.* Mysore: Geetha Book House, 1990.

Nelson-Pallmeyer, Jack. *Is Religion Killing Us? Violence in the Bible and the Quran.* Harrisburg, PA: Trinity Press International, 2003.

"Nepal's Maoists Announce 9-Day Ceasefire." Radio Australia (Oct 15, 2004), http://www.abc.net.au/ra/news/stories/s1221315.htm (accessed August 11, 2006).

"Networking in South Asia." Council on Foreign Relations (April 30, 2007), http://www.cfr.org/publication/12773/ (accessed June 15, 2007).

Neumann, Erich. *The Great Mother: An Analysis of the Archetype.* Bollingen Series. Princeton, NJ: Princeton University Press, 1963.

Nicholson, Linda J. *Gender and History.* New York: Columbia University Press, 1986.

Ochshorn, Judith. "Ishtar and Her Cult." *The Book of the Goddess Past and Present,* edited by Carl Olson, 16–28. New York: Crossroad Publishing Company, 1983.

Okin, Susan Moller. *Justice, Gender, and the Family.* New York: Basic Books, Inc., Publishers, 1989.

Oldenberg, H. *Buddha: His Life, His Doctrine, His Order.* London and Edinburgh: Williams and Northgate, 1882.

Olson, Carl. "Introduction." *The Book of the Goddess Past and Present: An Introduction to Her Religion,* ed. Carl Olson. New York: Crossroad, 1983.

Omvedt, Gail. *Reinventing Revolution: New Social Movements and the Socialist Tradition in India.* New York: M.E. Sharpe, 1993.

The Oxford Dictionary of Islam. Oxford: Oxford University Press, 2003.

Padoux, André. "Hindu Tantrism." *The Encyclopedia of Religion* 14, edited by Mircea Eliade. New York: Macmillan, 1986.

Pal, Pratapaditya. *Hindu Religion and Iconology According to the Tantrasāra.* Los Angeles: Vichitra Press, 1981.

Panda, Lakshman Kumar. *Śaivism in Orissa.* Delhi: Sundeep Prakashan, 1985.

Panigrahi, Krishna Chandra. *Archaeological Remains at Bhubaneswar.* Bombay: Orient Longmans, 1961.

Panther-Yates, Donald. "Remarks on Native American Tribal Religions." Lecture at Georgia Southern University, Statesboro, Georgia (March 5, 2001), http://216.239.57.104/search?q=cache:4jidKAks7LAJ:www.wintercount.org/remark. doc+native+americans,+matriarchy&hl=en&ie=UTF-8 (accessed May 17, 2004).

Parpola, Asko. *Deciphering the Indus Script,* 2nd edn. Cambridge: Cambridge University Press, 2003.

—. "Of Rajaram's 'Horses', 'decipherment', and Civilisational Issues." *Frontline* 17, Issue 23 (Nov. 11–24, 2000), http://www.dalitstan.org/holocaust/negation/twohorse.html (accessed Oct 18, 2005).
—. "The Pre-Vedic Background of the Śrauta Rituals." *Agni: The Vedic Ritual of the Fire Altar*, edited by Frits Staal, Berkeley: Asian Humanities Press, 1983, vol. 2, 41–74.
—. "The Sky Garment: A Study of the Harappan Religion and its Relation to the Mesopotamian and Later Indian Religions." *Studia Orientalia* 57 (1985): 8–210.
"Parsi." *Wikipedia*, http://en.wikipedia.org/wiki/Parsi (accessed Aug. 4, 2006).
Patel, Kartikeya C. "Women, Earth, and the Goddess: A Shākta-Hindu Interpretation of Embodied Religion." *Hypatia* 9, no. 4 (Fall, 1994): 69–87.
Pathak, V.S. *Śaiva Cults in Northern India.* Varanasi: Indological Book House, 1960.
Paul, Diana Y. *Women in Buddhism: Images of the Feminine in the Mahāyāna Tradition.* Berkeley, Los Angeles. London: University of California Press, 1985.
Paul, Robert. "Some Observations on Sherpa Shamanism." *Spirit Possession in the Nepal Himalayas*, edited by John T. Hitchcock and Rex L. Jones. Warminster, England: Aris and Phillips Ltd., 1976, 141–52.
Payne, Ernest A. *The Śāktas: An Introductory and Comparative Study.* New York and London: Garland Publishing, Inc., 1979.
Peradotta, John, and J.P. Sullivan, eds. *Women in the Ancient World: The Arethusa Papers.* Albany, NY: State University of New York Press, 1984.
Perdue, Theda. *Cherokee Women.* Lincoln & London: University of Nebraska Press, 1998.
Perkins, John. *Confessions of an Economic Hit Man.* San Francisco: Berrett-Koehler, 2004.
Phallic Tree Worship: Cultus Arborum (n.a.) 1890; repr. Varanasi: Bharat-Bharati, 1971.
Phukon, Girin, ed. *Ethnicity and Polity in South Asia.* New Delhi: South Asian Publishers, 2002.
Piggott, Stuart. *Prehistoric India to 1000 B.C.* Harmondsworth & Middlesex: Penguin Books, 1950.
Pillai, J.M. Somasundaram. *A History of Tamil Literature.* Annamalainagar: J.M. Somasundaram Pillai, 1968.
Pillai, M.S. Purnalingam. *A Primer of Tamil Literature.* Madras: Ananda Press, 1904.
Pillai, S. Vaiyapuri. "History of Tamil Language and Literature." *Tamil Culture* III, 3 & 4 (Oct 1954): 331–58.
Pintchman, Tracy, ed. "The Ambiguous Female: The Conception of Female Gender in the Brahmanical Tradition and the Roles of Women in India."

Ethical and Political Dilemmas of Modern India, edited by Ninlan Smart and Shivesh Thakur, London: Macmillan, 1993, 144–59.

—. *Seeking Mahādevī: Constructing the Identities of the Hindu Great Goddess.* Albany: SUNY Press, 2001.

—. *The Rise of the Goddess in the Hindu Tradition.* Albany, NY: SUNY Press, 1994.

Playfair, A. *The Garos.* London: D. Nutt, 1909.

Pomeroy, Sarah B. *Goddesses, Whores, Wives, and Slaves: Women in Classical Antiquity.* New York: Schocken Books, 1975.

Power, Carla. "Caste Struggle." *Newsweek* (July 3, 2000): 30–37.

Preston, James J. *Cult of the Goddess: Social and Religious Change in a Hindu Temple.* Prospect heights, Ill.: Waveland Press, 1980.

—, ed. *Mother Worship: Theme and Variations.* Chapel Hill: University of North Carolina Press, 1982.

Pritchard, James B., ed. *Ancient Near Easter Texts Relating to the Old Testament,* 3rd edn. Princeton: Princeton University Press, 1969.

Przyluski, Jean. "The Great Goddess in India and Iran." *The Indian Historical Quarterly* 14 (1934): 405–30.

Radhakrishnan, Sarvepalli, and Charles A. Moore, eds. *A Sourcebook in Indian Philosophy.* Princeton, NJ: Princeton University Press, 1957.

Rafy, Mrs. *Folk-Tales of the Khasis.* London: Macmillan & Co., Ltd., 1920.

Rajan, Rajeswari Sunder. "Real and Imagined Goddesses: A Debate." *Is the Goddess a Feminist? The Politics of South Asian Goddesses,* edited by Alf Hitlebeitel and Kathleen M. Erndl, Washington Square, NY: NYU Press, 2000, 269–84.

Rajaram, Navaratna S., and David Frawley. *Vedic "Āryans" and the Origins of Civilization: A Literary and Scientific Perspective.* Quebec: WH Press, 1995.

—. *Āryan Invasion of India: The Myth and the Truth.* New Delhi: Voice of India, 1993.

Ramanujan, A.K. *A Flowering Tree and Other Oral Tales from India.* Edited by Stuart Blackburn and Alan Dundes. Berkeley, Los Angeles, and London: University of California Press, 1997.

—, and Stuart H. Blackburn, eds. *Another Harmony: New Essays on the Folklore of India.* Berkeley: University of California Press, 1986.

—, ed. *Folktales from India.* New York: Pantheon Books, 1993.

—. "On Folk Mythologies and Folk Purāṇas." *Purāṇa Perennis: Reciprocity and Transformation in Hindu and Jaina Texts,* edited by Wendy Doniger. Albany: SUNY Press, 1993, 101–20.

—. "Two Realms of Kannada Folklore." *Another Harmony: New Essays on the Folklore of India,* edited by Stuart H. Blackburn and A.K. Ramanujan. Berkeley: University of California Press, 1986, 41–75.

—, ed. and trans. *When God is a Customer: Telugu Courtesan Songs.* Delhi and New York: Oxford University Press, 1995.

—. "Who Needs Folklore?" *The Collected Essays of A.K. Ramanujan.* New Delhi: Oxford University Press, 1999, 532–52.

Ramdhony, Reshmi. "On Our Vedic Origin: Women Speaking for Themselves." *Revisiting Indus-Sarasvati Age and Ancient India*, edited by Bhu Dev Sharma and Nabarun Ghose. Atlanta: World Association for Vedic Studies, 1998, 242–52.

Rao, B.K. Gururaja. "Racial background of South Indian History." *South Asian Studies*, edited by H.M. Nayak and B.R. Gopal. Mysore: Geetha Book House, 1990, 23–34.

Rao, S.R. "Further Excavations of the Submerged City of Dwaraka." *Proceedings of Second Indian Conference of Marine Archaeology of Indian Ocean Countries*, Jan 1990. Published for the Society for Marine Archaeology National Institute of Oceanography India, 1991. http://www.attributetohinduism.com/Dwaraka.htm#1.Further%20Excavations%20of%20the%20Submerged%20City%20of% 20Dwarka (accessed October 30, 2005).

Rao, T.A.G. *Elements of Hindu Iconography*, vol. 2. Varanasi: Indological Book House, 1971.

Rawson, Philip S. *The Art of Tantra.* London: Thames and Hudson Ltd., 1978.

—. *Tantra.* Catalogue of the Hayward Gallery. London: Arts Council of Great Britain, 1971.

Ray, Niharranjan. *The Sikh Gurus and the Sikh Society.* Patiala, Punjabi University, 1970.

Renfrew, Colin. *Archaeology and Language: The Puzzle of Indo-European Origins.* Cambridge: Cambridge University Press, 1987.

Richman, Paula. *Many Rāmāyaṇas: The Diversity of a Narrative Tradition in South Asia.* Berkeley, Los Angeles, Oxford: University of California Press, 1991.

Robinson, Gnana, ed. *Religions of the Marginalized: Towards a Phenomenology and the Methodology of Study.* Bangalore and Delhi: UTC, 1998.

Rocher, Ludo. *The Purāṇas.* Wiesbaden: Otto Harrassowitz, 1986.

Roy, Arundhati. "Arundhati Roy on India, Iraq, U.S. Empire and Dissent." *Democracy Now* (May 23, 2006), http://www.democracynow.org/article.pl?sid=06/05/23/1358250 (accessed May 24, 2006).

—. "Public Power in the Age of Empire." Open Media Pamphlet Series. New York: Seven Stories Press, 2004.

"Ruins in the Gulf of Cambay." *Wikipedia*, http://en.wikipedia.org/wiki/Ruins_in_the_Gulf_of_Cambay (accessed October 24, 2005).

Russell, R.V., and Rai Bahdur Hira Lal. *Tribes and Castes of the Central Provinces of India*, 4 vols. London: Macmillan & Co., 1916.

Sachau, E.A. *Alberuni's India, an Account of the Religions, Philosophy, Literature, Geography, Chronology, Astronomy, Customs, Laws, and Astrology of India about A.D. 1030, 1888*, vol. 1, Abridged edn. New York: Norton, 1971.

Sacks, Karen. "State Bias and Women's Status." *American Anthropologist* 78:565–69.

"Sacred Spaces: Traditions that Care for the Environment." Government of India Ministry of Environment and Forests Annual Report 2004–5, www.envfor.nic.in/divisions/ic/wssd/doc3/chapter10/css/chapter 10.htm (accessed December 5, 2002).

Sahlins, Marshall. *Stone Age Economics.* Chicago and New York: Aldine Atherton, Inc., 1972.

Sahu, N.K. *Buddhism in Orissa.* Cuttack: Utkal University, 1958.

Sakthivel, S. *Folklore Literature in India: A Review.* Madurai: Meena Pathippaka, 1976.

Sandars, N.K., trans. *The Epic of Gilgamesh,* rev. edn. Harmondsworth, Middlesex, England: Penguin Books, 1960.

Sanday, Peggy Reeves. *Female Power and Male Dominance: On the Origins of Sexual Inequality.* Cambridge: Cambridge University Press, 1981.

Sanderson, Alexis. "Purity and Power among the Brahmans of Kashmir." *The Category of the Person: Anthropology, Philosophy, and History,* edited by Michael Carrithers, Steven Collins and Steven Lukes. New York: Cambridge University Press, 1985, 190–216.

—. "Śaivism and the Tantric Traditions." *The World's Religions,* edited by Stewart Sutherland, L. Houlden, P. Clorke, and F. Hardy. London: Routledge and Kegan Paul, 1988, 660–704.

Saraswati, S.K. *Tantrayāna Art: An Album.* Calcutta: Asiatic Society, 1977.

Sastri, K.N. *New Light on the Indus Civilization,* vol. 1, *Religion and Chronology.* Delhi: Atma Ram & Sons, 1957.

—. *New Light on the Indus Civilization,* vol. 2, *Disposal of the Dead, the Aryan Problem and the Atharva Veda.* Delhi: Atma Ram & Sons, 1965.

Sax, William S. "Gender and the Representation of Violence in Pāṇḍava Līlā." *Inverted Identities: The Interplay of Gender, Religion and Politics in India,* edited by Julia Leslie and Mary McGee. New Delhi: Oxford University Press, 2000, 252–64.

Schopenhauer, Arthur. *Parerga and Paralipomena,* vol. 2. New York: Oxford University Press, 2001.

Segal, Charles. "The Menace of Dionysus: Sex Roles and Reversals in Euripides' Bacchae." *Women in the Ancient World: The Arethusa Papers,* edited by John Peradotta and J.P. Sullivan. Albany, NY: State University of New York Press, 1984, 195–212.

Seielsted, M., E. Minch, and L. Cavalli Sforza, "Genetic Evidence for a Higher Female Migration Rate in Humans." *Nature Genetics* 20/3 (1998): 278–80.

Sen Gupta, Sankar. *A Study of Women of Bengal.* Calcutta: Indian Publications, 1970.

Seng, Khasi. *Essays on Khasi Heritage* (A Collection). Umsohsun, Shillong: Ri Khasi Press, 1969.

Sen, Sukumar. *The Great Goddesses in Indic Tradition.* Calcutta: Papyrus, 1983.

Settegast, Mary. *Plato, Prehistorian: 10,000 to 5000 B.C. Myth, Religion, Archaeology.* Hudson, NY: Lindisfarne Press, 1990.

Shaffer, Jim. "The Indo-Aryan Invasions: Cultural Myth and Archaeological Reality." *The People of South Asia: The Biological Anthropology of India, Pakistan and Nepal*, edited by John R. Lukacs. New York: Plenum Press, 1984, 77–88.

Shah, A.M., B.S. Baviskar, and E.A. Ramaswamy, eds. *Social Structure and Change: Women in Indian Society*, vol. 2. New Delhi: Sage Publications, India, 1996.

Shah, U.D. *Sculptures from Samalaji and Roda.* Calcutta: Indian Society of Oriental Art, 1966.

"Shakti Nuclear Weapons Tests, May 11–13, 1998." http://www.globalsecurity.org/wmd/world/india/shakti-pix.htm (accessed May 6, 2006).

Shamoun, Sam, "Did the Meccans Worship Yahweh God?" http://answering-islam.org.uk/Shamoun/ishmael-baal.htm (accessed March 25, 2008).

Shankaranarayanan, S. *Glory of the Divine Mother (Devīmāhātmyam)*. Madras: Ganesh & Co., 1968.

Sharma, B.N. *Social Life in Northern India.* New Delhi: Munshiram Manoharlal Publishers, 1966.

Sharma, Harish. *Communal Angle in Indian Politics.* Jaipur and New Delhi: Rawat Publications, 2000.

Sharma, Rama Nath. "Women in Vedic Rituals." *Revisiting Indus-Sarasvati Age and Ancient India*, edited by Bhu Dev Sharma and Nabarun Ghose. Atlanta: World Association for Vedic Studies, 1998, 259–68.

Sharma, R.S. "Material Milieu of Tantrism." *Indian Society, Historical Probings*, edited by R.S. Sharma. New Delhi: Peoples' Publishing House, 1974.

—. *Perspectives in Social and Economic History of Early India.* New Delhi: Munshiram Manoharlal Publishers, 2003.

Shastri, A.M. *India as Seen in the Bṛhatsaṁhitā of Varāhamihira.* Delhi, 1978.

Shastri, Pushpendra. *Introduction to Purāṇas (The Light House of Indian Culture).* New Delhi: Rashtriya Sanskrit Sansthan, 1995.

Shaw, Miranda. "Is Vajrayogini a Feminist? A Tantric Buddhist Case Study." *Is the Goddess a Feminist? The Politics of South Asian Goddesses*, edited by Alf Hitlebeitel and Kathleen M. Erndl. Washington Square, NY: NYU Press, 2000, 166–80.

—. *Passionate Enlightenment: Women in Tantric Buddhism.* Princeton, NJ: Princeton University Press, 1994.

Shlain, Leonard. *The Alphabet Versus the Goddess: The Conflict Between Word and Image.* New York: Penguin/Arkana, 1998.

Shiva, Vandana. *India Divided: Diversity and Democracy Under Attack.* New York: Seven Stories Press, 2005.

—. *Staying Alive: Women, Ecology and Development.* New Delhi: Kali for Women, 1989.

—. *Stolen Harvest: The Hijacking of the Global Food Supply.* Cambridge, Mass.: South End Press, 2000.

—. *Biopiracy: The Plunder of Nature and Knowledge.* Boston: Smith End Press, 1997.

Shulman, David Dean. "Battle as Metaphor in Tamil Folk and Classical Traditions." *Another Harmony: New Essays on the Folklore of India*, edited by Stuart H. Blackburn and A.K. Ramanujan. Berkeley, Los Angeles, London: University of California Press, 1986, 105–30.
—. "The Murderous Bride: Tamil Versions of the Myth of Devī and the Buffalo Demon." *History of Religions* 16, no. 2 (Nov 1976): 120–47.
—. *Tamil Temple Myths: Sacrifice and Divine Marriage in the South Indian Śaiva Tradition*. Princeton: Princeton University Press, 1980.
Singer, Milton, ed. *Traditional India: Structure and Change*. Philadelphia: The American Folklore Society, 1959.
Singh, Andrea Menefee. "The Study of Women in India: Some Problems in Methodology." *Women in Contemporary India*, edited by E. de Souza. New Delhi: Manohar, 1975.
Singh, Bhupinder, and J.S. Bhandari, eds. *The Tribal World and Its Transformation*. New Delhi: Concept Publishing Company, 1980.
Singh, G.B. *Gandhi: Beyond the Mask of Divinity*. Amherst, NY: Prometheus Books, 2004.
Singh, Jagat. *The Sikh Revolution: A Perspective View*. New Delhi and Chandigarh: Bahri Publications 1981.
Singh, Mahatam. "Immigration of Aryans' to India: A Fact or a Fiction!" *Revisiting Indus-Sarasvati Age and Ancient India*, edited by Bhu Dev Sharma and Nabarun Ghose. Atlanta: World Association for Vedic Studies, 1998, 130–33.
Singh, Raghunath, ed. *Rājataraṅgiṇī*. Varanasi: Orient, 1969.
Sinha, Jadunath, *Shakta Monism: The Cult of Shakti*. Calcutta: Sinha Publishing House Pvt. Ltd., 1966.
Sircar, D.C. *The Śākta Pīṭhas*. Delhi: Motilal Banarsidass, 1973.
—. "Śakti Cult in Western India." *The Śakti Cult and Tārā*, edited by D.C. Sircar. Calcutta: University of Calcutta, 1967, 87–91.
—, ed. *The Śakti Cult and Tārā*. Calcutta: University of Calcutta, 1967.
—. *Studies in the Religious Life of Ancient and Medieval India*. Delhi: Motilal Banarsidass, 1971.
Sivathamby, K. "The Ritualistic Origins of Tamil Drama." Paper presented at First International Tamil Conference-Seminar, Kuala Lumpur, Malaysia, April 1966. http://www.tamilnation.org/ culture/drama/sivathamby.htm (accessed April 12, 2005).
Sjöö, Monica, and Barbara Mor. *The Great Cosmic Mother: Rediscovering the Religion of the Earth* (1987); edited by Wendy Doniger, 2nd edn. San Francisco: HarperSanFrancisco, 1991.
Smart, Ninian. *Dimensions of the Sacred: An Anatomy of the World's Beliefs*. London: HarperCollins, 1996.
—, and Shivesh Thakur, eds. *Ethical and Political Dilemmas of Modern India*. London: Macmillan, 1993.
Smith, Vincent A. *The Oxford History of India* (1923); repr. London: Clarendon Press, 1963.

Snellgrove, David L., and Hugh Richardson. *A Cultural History of Tibet.* Boulder, CO: Prajna Press, 1980.

—. *Indo-Tibetan Buddhism,* 2 vols. Boston: Shambhala, 1987.

Spengler. "Jihad, the Lord's Supper, and Eternal Life." *Asia Times Online* (Sep 19, 2006), http://www.atimes.com/atimes/Front_Page/HI19Aa02.html (accessed Sep 19, 2006).

Spivak, Gayatri Chakravorty. "Can the Subaltern Speak? Speculations on Widow-Sacrifice." Wedge nos. 7/8 (Winter / Spring 1985): 120–30.

—. "Subaltern Studies: Deconstructing Historiography." *Selected Subaltern Studies,* ed. Ranajit Guha and Gayatri Chakravorty Spivak, New York and Oxford: Oxford University Press, 1988, 3–32.

Srikanth, H. "Understanding Ethnic Conflicts in Northeast India." *Ethnicity and Polity in South Asia,* edited by Girin Phukon. New Delhi: South Asian Publishers, 2002, 195–207.

Srinivas, M.N. *Religion and Society among the Coorgs of South India.* London: Clarendon Press, 1952.

—. "A Note on Sanskritization and Westernization." *Far Eastern Quarterly* 15 (1956).

—. *Social Changes in Modern India.* Berkeley: University of California Press, 1966.

Srivastava, M.C.P. *Mother Goddess in Indian Art, Archaeology, and Literature.* Delhi: Agam Kala Prakashan, 1979.

Stablein, William. "Mahākāla the Neo-Shaman: Master of the Ritual." *Spirit Possession in the Nepal Himalayas,* edited by John T. Hitchcock and Rex L. Jones. Warminster, England: Aris and Phillips Ltd., 1976, 343–60.

Stone, Merlin. *When God was A Woman.* New York: The Dial Press, 1976.

Stutley, Margaret. *Ancient Indian Magic and Folklore.* Boulder, CO: Great Eastern, 1980.

Svoboda, Robert E. *Aghora: At the Left Hand of God.* Albuquerque, NM: Brotherhood of Life, Inc., 1986.

Swaminathan, A. "Temple Lands and Society." *Journal of Tamil Studies* 20 (December 1981): 18–26.

Swarup, G.A.K. Bag, and K.S. Shukla. *History of Oriental Astronomy.* Cambridge: Cambridge University Press, 1987.

Tagore, Rabindranath. *Collected Poems and Plays.* New York: Macmillan, 1967.

Tambs-Lyche, Harald, ed. *The Feminine Sacred in South Asia.* New Delhi: Manohar, 1999.

—. "The Great Goddess: Past or Myth?" *The Feminine Sacred in South Asia,* edited by Herald Tambs-Lyche. New Delhi: Manohar Publishers, 1999, 9–35.

Tantrayāna Art: An Album, with Introduction and Notes by S.K. Saraswati. Calcutta: The Asiatic Society, 1977.

Tarthang Tulku (Kun-dga' dge-legs Ye-shes-rdo-rje), gen. ed. *Holy Places of the Buddha.* Crystal Mirror Series 9. Research, compiling, and manuscript preparation by Elizabeth Cook. Berkeley: Dharma Press, 1994.

Tenzin Wangyal Rinpoche, Geshe. *Wonders of the Natural Mind: The Essence of Dzogchen in the Native Bön Tradition of Tibet.* Barrytown, NY: Station Hill Press, 1993.

Thapar, Romila. *Ancient Indian Social History: Some Interpretations.* New Delhi: Orient Longman, 1978.

—. *Aśoka and the Decline of the Mauryas.* London: Oxford University Press, 1961.

—. *A History of India,* vol. 1. Baltimore: Penguin Books, 1966.

—. *Interpreting Early India.* New Delhi, Oxford, and New York: Oxford University Press, 1993.

Thomas, Edward J. *The Life of Buddha as Legend and History.* New York: Alfred A. Knopf, 1927.

Thomas, P.J. "When the Dravidian South Led India." *Tamil Culture* II, 3 & 4 (Sept 1953): 245–54.

Thompson, James C. "Women in the Ancient World" (June 2005), http://www.womenintheancientworld.com/hammurabilawcode.htm (accessed Aug 1, 2005).

Thomas, Patricia. *Women and Marriage in India.* London: George Allen and Unwin Ltd., 1964.

Thomson, G. *Aeschylus and Athens.* London: Lawrence & Wishart, 1951.

Thurston, E., and K. Rangachari. *Castes and Tribes of Southern India,* 1909, vol. 6, repr. Delhi: Cosmo, 1975.

Thurston, Edgar. *Castes and Tribes of Southern India.* Delhi: Cosmo Publications, 1975.

Tinker, Irene. "The Adverse Impact of Development on Women." *Women and World Development,* edited by Irene Tinker and Michele Bo Bramsen. Washington, DC: Overseas Development Council, 1976.

Tiwari, J.N. *Goddess Cults in Ancient India (with Special Reference to the First Seven Centuries AD).* Delhi: Sundeep Prakashan, 1985.

Trial by Fire: A Report on Roop Kanwar's Death. Bombay: Women and Media Committee, Bombay Union of Journalists, 1987.

Tsogyal, Yeshe. *The Lotus-Born: The Life Story of Padmasambhava,* revealed by Nyang Ral Nyima Öer. Boston and London: Shambhala, 1993.

Udayakumar, S.P. "Local Histories and Global Futures." *Gandhi Marg* 19, no. 2 (July–Sept 1997): 223–28.

Ulansey, David. *The Origins of the Mithraic Mysteries: Cosmology and Salvation in the Ancient World.* New York and Oxford: Oxford University Press, 1989.

Vanamamalai, N. *Studies in Tamil Folk Literature.* Madras: New Century Book House, 1969.

Van der Veer, Peter. *Imperial Encounters: Religion and Modernity in India and Britain.* Princeton and Oxford: Princeton University Press, 2001.

Verma, K. Krishna, ed. *Aghor Tradition and an Aughar in India.* Freehold, NJ: Krishna Verma, 1987.

Victus, Solomon. "Dalits, Development, and Ecology." *Gandhi Marg* 19, no. 2 (July–Sept 1997): 228–35.

Visuvalingam, Elizabeth-Chalier. "Bhairava's Royal Brahmanicide: The Problem of the Mahābrāhmaṇa." *Criminal Gods and Demon Devotees: Essays on the Guardians of Popular Hinduism*, edited by Alf Hiltebeitel. Albany: SUNY Press, 1989, 157–230.

Vogel, J.P. "The Head-offering to the Goddess in Pallava Sculpture." *Bulletin of the School of Oriental and African Studies* 6 (1932): 539–43.

—. *Indian Serpent-lore or the Nāgas in Hindu Legend and Art*. Varanasi and Delhi: Indological Book House, 1972.

Vyas, R.T. *The Bṛhadāraṇyaka Upaniṣad: A Critical Study*. Vadodara: Oriental Institute, 1987.

Waddell, L. Austine. *Tibetan Buddhism, with its Mystic Cults, Symbolism and Mythology, and in its Relation to Indian Buddhism*. New York: Dover Publications, 1972. (Reprint of the 1895 edn., which was published under title: *The Buddhism of Tibet*.)

Wadley, Susan S. "No Longer a Wife: Widows in Rural North India." *From the Margins of Hindu Marriage: Essays on Gender, Religion, and Culture*, edited by Lindsey Harlan and Paul B. Courtright. New York: Oxford University Press, 1995, 92–118.

—, ed. *The Powers of Tamil Women*. Syracuse: Syracuse University Press, 1980.

Warner, M. *Alone of All Her Sex: The Myth and the Cult of the Virgin Mary*. New York: Alfred Knopf, 1976.

Watters, Thomas. *On Yuan Chwang's Travels in India*, 2 vols. London: Royal Asiatic Society, 1904–5.

Wayman, Alex. *Yoga of the Guhyasamājatantra*. Delhi: Motilal Banarsidass, 1991.

Weinberger-Thomas, Catherine. *Ashes of Immortality: Widow-Burning in India*, translated by Jeffrey Mehlman and David Gordon White. Chicago: University of Chicago Press, 1999.

Wendorf, F. "Site 117: A Nubian Final Paleolithic Graveyard Near Djebel Sahaba, Sudan." *The Prehistory of Nubia* II, edited by F. Wendorf. Dallas, 1968, 954–95.

Wheeler, Mortimer. *Civilizations of the Indus Valley and Beyond*. London: Thames and Hudson, 1966.

White, David Gordon. *The Alchemical Body: Siddha Traditions in Medieval India*. Chicago: University of Chicago Press, 1996.

Whitehead, Henry. *The Village Gods of South India*. London: Oxford University Press, 1921.

Wittfogal, Karl A. *Oriental Despotism*. New Haven, CO: Yale University Press, 1957.

Wolkstein, Diane, and Samuel N. Kraemer. *Inanna, Queen of Heaven and Earth: Her Stories and Hymns from Sumer*. New York: Harper & Row, 1983.

Woodroffe, Sir John [Arthur Avalon, pseud.]. *Introduction to Tantra Śāstra.* 1956. Madras: Ganesh & Co. 1980.
—. *Shakti and Shākta.* New York: Dover Publications, Inc., 1978.
Woolley, Sir Leonard. *Excavations at Ur.* London: Ernest Benn Ltd., 1954.
—. *Ur of the Chaldees.* London: Pelican Books, 1938.
Zolla, Elémire. *The Androgyne: Reconciliation of Male and Female.* New York: Crossroad, 1981.

Index